WORLD RELIGIONS TODAY

John L. Esposito

Georgetown University

Darrell J. Fasching

University of South Florida

Todd Lewis

College of the Holy Cross

WORLD RELIGIONS TODAY

SECOND EDITION

NEW YORK ♦ OXFORD

OXFORD UNIVERSITY PRESS

2006

Oxford University Press, Inc., publishes works that further Oxford University's
objective of excellence in research, scholarship, and education.

Oxford New York
Auckland Cape Town Dar es Salaam Hong Kong Karachi
Kuala Lumpur Madrid Melbourne Mexico City Nairobi
New Delhi Shanghai Taipei Toronto

With offices in
Argentina Austria Brazil Chile Czech Republic France Greece
Guatemala Hungary Italy Japan Poland Portugal Singapore
South Korea Switzerland Thailand Turkey Ukraine Vietnam

Published by Oxford University Press, Inc.
198 Madison Avenue, New York, New York 10016
http://www.oup.com

Library of Congress Cataloging-in-Publication Data
Esposito, John L.
    World religions today/John L. Esposito, Darrell J. Fasching, Todd Lewis.—2nd ed.
        p. cm.
    ISBN–13: 978–0–19–517699–5

    1. Religions. I. Fasching, Darrell J., 1944-II. Lewis, Todd Thornton, 1952-III. Title.
BL80.2.E76 2005
200—dc22

Printing number: 9 8 7 6 5 4

Printed in the United States of America
on acid-free paper

*For
Jean Esposito
Melissa and Nathan Lewis
and in memory of Harold Gushin*

Contents

Preface   xii

1 Introduction
2

Globalization: World Religions in Everyone's Hometown
3

Understanding Religious Experience and Its Expressions   5
The Great Transition   14
The Great Religious Stories of the World   16
Modernization in Global Perspective   25
Modern Colonialism, the Socialist Challenge,
    and the End of Modernity   28
Postmodern Trends in a Postcolonial World   31
Discussion Questions   33
Key Terms   33
Notes   33

2 Primal Religions
34

Overview
35

The Modern Human as *Homo Religiosus*   37
Hunter-Gatherers and the Prehistoric Origins of Religion   39
Animism and Afterlife   42
The Shaman   46
Primal Religions and the Cataclysms of Colonialism   55
Primal Religions Today   56
Conclusion   60
Discussion Questions   61
Key Terms   62
Suggested Readings   62
Notes   62

3 The Many Stories of Judaism:
Sacred and Secular   64

Overview   65

Encounter with Modernity: Modern Judaisms and
   the Challenge of Ultra-Orthodoxy   68
Premodern Judaism: The Formative Era   74
Premodern Judaism: The Classical Era   89
Judaism and Modernity   102
Judaism and Postmodern Trends in a Postcolonial World   116
Conclusion   125
Discussion Questions   128
Key Terms   128
Suggested Readings   129
Notes   129

4 Christian Diversity and
the Road to Modernity   130

Overview   131

Encounter with Modernity: The Fundamentalist–
   Modernist Controversy   136
Premodern Christianity: The Formative Era   140
Premodern Christianity: The Classical Era   155
Christianity and Modernity   164
Christianity and Postmodern Trends in a Postcolonial World   182
Conclusion   192
Discussion Questions   192
Key Terms   193
Suggested Readings   193

5 Islam: The Many Faces of the Muslim Experience — 194

Overview — 195

Encounter with Modernity: The Challenge of
 Western Colonialism — 201
Premodern Islam: The Formative Era — 204
Premodern Islam: The Classical Era — 217
Islam and Modernity — 235
Islam and Postmodern Trends in a Postcolonial World — 241
Islam: Postmodern Challenges — 260
Conclusion — 267
Discussion Questions — 267
Key Terms — 268
Suggested Readings — 268
Notes — 269

6 Hinduism: Myriad Paths to Salvation — 270

Overview — 271

A Far-Ranging Spiritual Tradition — 272
Encountering Modernity: Hindu Challenges to
 India as a Secular State — 276
Premodern Hinduism: The Formative Era — 279
Premodern Hinduism: The Classical Era (180 BCE–900 CE) — 284
Premodern Hinduism: The Postclassical Era (1500 BCE–900 CE) — 294
Hinduism and Modernity — 301
Hinduism and Postmodern Trends in a Postcolonial World — 308
Hinduism in Practice — 317
Conclusion — 334
Discussion Questions — 338
Key Terms — 338
Suggested Readings — 339
Notes — 339

7 Buddhism: Ways to Nirvana 340

Overview 341

Encounter with Modernity: Socially Engaged Buddhism 346
Premodern Buddhism: The Formative Era 349
Premodern Buddhism: The Classical Era 361
Premodern Buddhism: Buddhist Expansion 373
Buddhism and Modernity 380
Buddhism and Postmodern Trends in a Postcolonial World 392
Conclusion 410
Discussion Questions 414
Key Terms 414
Suggested Readings 415
Notes 415

8 East Asian Religions: Traditions of Human
Cultivation and Natural Harmony 416

Overview 417

Encounter with Modernity: Postcolonial Confucian Economics 424
East Asian Religions in the Premodern Era 425
East Asian Religions in the Early Modern Era 453
East Asian Religions and Postmodern Trends in
    a Postcolonial World 463
Conclusion 489
Discussion Questions 492
Key Terms 493
Suggested Readings 494
Notes 494

9 Globalization: From New to
New Age Religions 496

Overview 497

New Religions 499
New Age Religions 504
Religious Postmodernism and Global Ethics 519
Discussion Questions 530
Suggested Readings 530
Notes 531

Glossary   532
Art Credits   547
Index   549

PREFACE

Around the world, religion has become an increasingly important and pervasive force in personal and public life, and faith and politics now play a powerful role in international affairs. *World Religions Today* addresses this reality within the context of an introductory volume for college and university students of world religions.

World Religions Today grew out of several decades of experience in teaching world religions and the conviction that there was a more effective way to both attract and hold student interest from the very beginning of the course and to demonstrate the dynamism and relevance of the major world religious traditions not only in the past but also today. Textbooks on world religions, like those on individual traditions, too often tended to emphasize the historical origins and development of religions, focusing on the past and giving short shrift to the modern or contemporary period. Many stressed a textual, theological/philosophical, and legal approach with insufficient attention to the importance of social contexts. As a result, students came away with a maximum appreciation for the origins and development of the classical traditions and a minimal awareness of the continued dynamism and relevance today of so-called non-Western traditions in particular. However, despite the change in recent years with the growing visibility and impact of a global religious resurgence and of the globalization of religion, most world religion textbooks did not quite catch up.

This second edition of *World Religions Today* has been substantially revised in light of comments from colleagues across the country who have used it and in light of our own subsequent experiences and reflections. Oxford has also solicited comments from reviewers with regard to the overall plan, approach, breadth of coverage, and level of sophistication. Chapters were revised to make the amount of historical data more manageable and to make the writing style more accessible as an introductory volume for undergraduate students. The book's major theme and its chapters on Judaism, Christianity, Islam, Hinduism, Buddhism, and East Asian Religions have been retained (though revised), and two new chapters on Primal and New Religions have been added. All the chapters have been updated in light of recent events, especially the Islam chapter that addresses the impact of Osama bin Laden, global terrorism, and the Iraq War on the contemporary Muslim experience. Furthermore, as should be obvious to anyone holding this book, the second edition features a dynamic new two-color design, twice as many photographs and illustrations as the first edition, and two sections of full-color photographs. It is our hope that this new treatment reflects and enhances the colorful and lively discussion of the text.

Moving beyond the almost exclusive emphasis on premodern history in many books in the field, *World Religions Today*, Second Edition, continues to take the fresh approach of the first edition, using historical coverage of religious traditions as a framework to help students understand how faiths have evolved to the present day. To help students grasp what might be "new" about the emerging era of religious life in the twenty-first century, we open each discussion with a contemporary scenario of religious experience, "Encounter With Modernity," that illustrates the tension between premodern views and modernity. Each chapter not only connects today's religions to their classical beliefs and practices but also shows how they have responded to and been transformed by the modern world. Thus, the interconnectedness of faith, culture, politics, and society provide insights into the diverse ways in which contemporary human beings are religious.

Although this is a multiauthored text with each of us taking primary authorship of different chapters (John Esposito: Islam; Darrell Fasching: Judaism, Christianity, and New Religions; and Todd Lewis: Asian traditions and Primal Religions), it has truly been a collaborative project from start to finish. We have worked out our overall vision, which is articulated in the first chapter, and implemented it in the chapters on the religious traditions. Throughout the entire process we shared and commented on each other's material. Oxford colleagues and outside reviewers provided feedback at every stage.

We have been fortunate to work with an excellent team at Oxford, led by Robert Miller, Executive Editor in Oxford's Higher Education Group. Karen Shapiro, Emily Voigt, and Sarah Calabi have been extraordinarily supportive throughout a long and sometimes difficult production process.

John L. Esposito
Darrell J. Fasching
Todd Lewis

GREENLAND

Arctic Circle

ICELAND

UNITED KINGDOM

IRELAND

FRA

PORTUGAL   SPA

MOROCCO

CANADA

NORTH
ATLANTIC
OCEAN

NORTH
PACIFIC
OCEAN

WESTERN SAHARA

UNITED STATES

Tropic of Cancer

HAITI

CUBA

DOMINICAN REPUBLIC
PUERTO RICO

CAPE VERDE IS.

MAURITANIA

MEXICO

BELIZE

TRINIDAD-TOBAGO

SENEGAL
GAMBIA
GUINEA BISSAU
GUINEA
SIERRA LEONE
LIBERIA
BURKINA FASO   GHA
IVORY COAST
SÃO TOMÉ AND PRÍNC
EQUATORIAL GUIN

JAMAICA

GUYANA

GUATEMALA
EL-SALVADOR
NICARAGUA
COSTA RICA
PANAMA

VENEZUELA

SURINAM

FRENCH GUIANA

COLOMBIA

ECUADOR

Equator

PERU

BRAZIL

WESTERN
SAMOA

TONGA

Tropic of Capricorn

BOLIVIA

PARAGUAY

SOUTH
PACIFIC
OCEAN

CHILI

ARGENTINA

URUGUAY

SOUTH
ATLANTIC
OCEAN

World population by Religion	
Christian	1,965,993,000
Muslim	1,179,326,000
Hindu	767,424,000
Non-religious	766,672,000
Buddhist	356,875,000
Tribal Religion	244,164,000
Atheist	146,406,000
New Religions	99,191,000
Sikh	22,874,000
Daoist	20,050,000
Jewish	15,050,000
Baha'i	6,251,000
Confucian	5,067,000
Jain	4,152,000
Shinto	3,571,000
Parsi (Zoroastrian)	479,000

Antarctic Circle

ARCTIC
OCEAN

RUSSIA

SWEDEN
FINLAND
RWAY
27
26
25 24
16 18
9 8
10 8 23
12 7 22
3 4 21
11 2 20
(9) 1
2

KAZAKHSTAN
UZBEKISTAN
TURKMENISTAN
28
KYRGYZSTAN
TAJIKISTAN
TURKEY 29
CYPRUS 30
LEBANON SYRIA
IRAQ IRAN
ISRAEL
JORDAN
EGYPT KUWAIT
BAHRAIN
SAUDI ARABIA
YEMEN
DJIBOUTI

MONGOLIA

NORTH
KOREA

JAPAN

SOUTH
KOREA

CHINA

AFGHANISTAN
QATAR
PAKISTAN
UNITED
ARAB
EMIRATES
OMAN

NEPAL
BHUTAN
BANGLADESH
MYANMAR
(BURMA)

INDIA

TAIWAN

PACIFIC
OCEAN
Tropic of Cancer

ERIA TUNISIA
LIBYA
GO
NIGER CHAD
NIGERIA CENT. AFR.
CAMEROON REP.
NIN
RWANDA
PUBLIC BURUNDI
OF
ONGO
ANGOLA
ZAMBIA

ERITREA
SUDAN

LAOS

ETHIOPIA

SOMALIA
UGANDA
KENYA
TANZANIA
MALAWI
COMOROS

THAILAND
SRI LANKA
MALDIVES CAMBODIA
(KAMPUCHEA)
SINGAPORE
Equator SEYCHELLES

DEMOCRATIC
REPUBLIC
OF CONGO

VIETNAM
BRUNEI
MALAYSIA

PHILIPPINES

MICRONESIA

MARSHALL
ISLANDS

NAURU

INDONESIA

PAPUA
NEW GUINEA
SOLOMON
ISLANDS

KIRIBATI

TUVALU

NAMIBIA

MADAGASCAR
MAURITIUS

INDIAN
OCEAN
Tropic of Capricorn

VANUATU FIJI

AUSTRALIA

BOTSWANA

SOUTH
AFRICA
SWAZILAND
LESOTHO

NEW
ZEALAND

1. MACEDONIA	16. GERMANY
2. ALBANIA	17. DENMARK
3. BOSNIA	18. POLAND
4. SERBIA	19. GREECE
5. CROATIA	20. BULGARIA
6. SLOVENIA	21. ROMANIA
7. HUNGARY	22. MOLDOVA
8. SLOVAK REPUBLIC	23. UKRAINE
9. CZECH REPUBLIC	24. BELARUS
10. AUSTRIA	25. LITHUANIA
11. SWITZERLAND	26. LATVIA
12. ITALY	27. ESTONIA
13. LUXEMBOURG	28. GEORGIA
14. BELGIUM	29. ARMENIA
15. NETHERLANDS	30. AZERBAIJAN

Antarctic Circle

WORLD RELIGIONS TODAY

CHAPTER ONE

Introduction

Globalization: World Religions in Everyone's Hometown

In the 1950s, if you walked down the streets of almost any city in the United States, you would have expected to find churches, both Catholic and Protestant, and Jewish synagogues. When people thought about religious diversity, it was limited largely to Protestants, Catholics, and Jews. In the twenty-first century, a new millennium, the situation is dramatically different. Almost daily the newspapers take note of new religious members of the community—announcing a retreat at a Korean Zen center in the suburbs of Providence, Rhode Island; the opening of an Islamic mosque in St. Louis, Missouri; or the dedication of a Hindu temple in Tampa, Florida.

The beliefs and practices of world religions have become part of the mosaic of American society. "Karma" has become part of the American vocabulary, Hindu visualization practices are used in sports training, and Buddhist meditation techniques have been adopted in programs of stress management. No matter where we live today, it is more and more likely that our next-door neighbors are ethnically, politically, and yes even religiously diverse—coming from many parts of the globe (see Map 1.1). In an emerging global economy, most neighborhoods, workplaces, and schools reflect this diversity as well.

In this book we focus on the diverse ways in which we humans have been religious in the past and are religious today. Indeed, the last decades of the twentieth century brought a global religious resurgence, a development that defies countless theorists who predicted that the irresistible secularization of civilization would lead to the disappearance of religion. Religions, it was thought, are tied to ancient premodern worldviews that have been replaced by a modern scientific worldview. Indeed, the clash of traditional religions with modern scientific and secular society is a major concern of this textbook. Awareness of this is essential if we are to understand the interactions between religions and cultures in the world today. Starting with Chapter Three, then, we will begin each chapter not with a discussion of the origins and early history of religious communities but with examples of the encounter of each religion with the "modern" world that illustrate the tension between religion and modern states and societies.

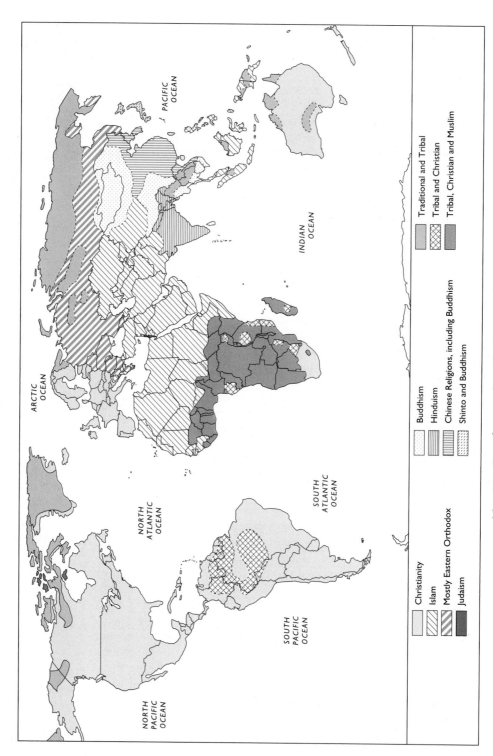

Map 1.1   *Distribution of world religions today.*

Legend:

- Christianity
- Islam
- Mostly Eastern Orthodox
- Judaism
- Buddhism
- Hinduism
- Chinese Religions, including Buddhism
- Shinto and Buddhism
- Traditional and Tribal
- Tribal and Christian
- Tribal, Christian and Muslim

ARCTIC OCEAN

PACIFIC OCEAN

INDIAN OCEAN

NORTH ATLANTIC OCEAN

SOUTH ATLANTIC OCEAN

SOUTH PACIFIC OCEAN

NORTH PACIFIC OCEAN

We describe our present time as one in transition between "modernity" and a new, or "postmodern," era that seems to be emerging. To understand what is "new" about our situation, we will have to understand the premodern period of the different religious traditions and how the premodern worldview of each relates to and contrasts with the modern period. In particular we will have to compare the premodern period in each tradition with the changes brought about by an era that began with the rise of science after 1500 and declined after World War II. In surveying the great world religions, we shall not be able to cover everything that could be said about them. Our selection will be governed primarily by the following question: What do we need to know about the past to understand the role of religion in the world we live in today? To begin, we must introduce some core concepts.

With the Space Age, awareness that all humans share life in a global village has come to the religions and cultures of the earth.

UNDERSTANDING RELIGIOUS EXPERIENCE AND ITS EXPRESSIONS

The first thing we need is a working definition of the term "religion." To help explain how we are using the term, let's suppose we have a time machine and can transport ourselves back to the city of Rome in the first century. Why are we interested in that time and place? Because the word "religion" has its roots in Latin, the language of the Romans, understanding how the Romans defined the concept should help us understand our topic.

Imagine yourself now walking down a street in Rome in the first century. When you approach a small group of people on a street corner and ask them: "What religion are you?" they look at you strangely. They understand the individual words you have spoken, but they don't normally put those words together as you have done. Some give you blank stares, while others just look puzzled. Frustrated, you try rephrasing your question: "Are you religious?" Suddenly their faces light up and they smile and say, "Of course, isn't everyone?"

By its wording, the original question assumes that religion is a noun applied to distinct social bodies in the world, such that you can be a member of one only if you are not a member of another. So the question seeks to find out the distinct religious group to which you belong. This way of understanding religion naturally arises among monotheists, who by definition have chosen one god and excluded all others. However, such an exclusiveness was foreign to antiquity, and it also is not appropriate today for studying religious traditions among many African and Asian peoples.

In rephrasing the original question as "Are you religious?" you are no longer treating "religion" as a noun, describing something you join. Instead, you are treating it as an adjective, describing an attitude toward the human condition—a way of seeing, acting, and experiencing all things. In most times and places throughout history, religion and culture were like two sides of the same coin. Therefore people did not think of their practices as "a religion"

—a separate reality they had to choose over and against another. Today, in Japan for instance, it is possible to follow Buddhism, Daoism, Confucianism, and Shintoism at the same time. This seems odd from the monotheistic perspective of Western religion, where one can be, for instance, either a Muslim or a Jew but not both at the same time. And yet, paradoxically, Jews and Muslims claim to worship the same God.

In first-century Rome, with very few exceptions, people didn't belong to a religion in any exclusive sense. They were, however, religious. Our first-century respondents would probably continue the discussion you had started something like this: "Am I religious? Of course I am. Isn't everyone? It's simply a matter of common sense. I respect all those powers of nature that govern my destiny. Therefore I worship all the gods and goddesses. It would be stupid not to. If I am going to war I want the god of war on my side. So I perform the correct ritual sacrifices before going into battle. And when I am looking for a mate, I petition the goddess of love to help me. And needless to say, if I am planting my crops I will try very hard to ensure that the goddess of fertility and the gods of the wind and rain are on my side. I am not a complete idiot. To ignore or antagonize the gods would be stupid."

What does this tell us? For the ancient Romans, and nearly all other human beings in all places and all times throughout history, religion has been about power and meaning in relation to human destiny. Although its exact root is uncertain, the word "religion" is probably derived from the Latin *religare,* which literally means "to tie or bind" and the root *ligere* which has the connotation of "acting with care." It expresses our sense of being "tied and bound" by relations of obligation to whatever powers we believe govern our destiny—whether these powers be natural or supernatural, personal or impersonal, one or many. Ancient peoples everywhere believed that the powers governing their destiny were the forces of nature. Why? Because nature was experienced as that awesome collection of powers that surround and, at times, overwhelm human beings. On the one hand, nature provides life and all its necessities (food, clothing, shelter, etc.); but on the other hand, nature may turn on people, destroying them quite capriciously through earthquakes, storms, floods, and so on. Therefore the forces of nature evoke in human beings the ambivalent feelings of fascination and dread. Rudolf Otto, the great twentieth-century pioneer of the study of comparative religions, argued that the presence of these two ambivalent emotions is a sure sign that one is in the presence of the sacred. They are a defining mark of religious experience across cultures. They are the emotions that are elicited by the uncanny experience of being in the presence of that power or powers one believes have the ability to determine whether one lives or dies, and, beyond that, how well one lives and dies.

Religion as a form of human experience and behavior, therefore, is not just about purely "spiritual" things. Religion is not just about gods or God. People's religiousness is as diverse as the forms of power they believe govern their destiny, whether it be the gods as forces of nature, or wealth, or political power, or the forces of history. Religious attitudes in the modern world can be discerned in what many people would consider to be purely secular and very "unspiritual" attitudes and behaviors in relation to power. Hence, whatever powers we believe govern our destiny will elicit a religious response from us and inspire us to wish "to tie or bind" ourselves to these powers in relations of ritual obligation. Thus tied or bound, we will act respectfully and carefully in relation to the powers, to ensure that they will be on our side. How do we know what our obligations to these powers are? Throughout history this knowledge has been communicated through myth and ritual.

Myth and Ritual

Our word "myth" comes from the Greek *mythos,* which means "story." Myth, we could say, is a symbolic story about the origins and destiny of human beings and their world; myth relates human beings to whatever powers they believe ultimately govern their destiny and explains to them what the powers expect of them. Unlike the contemporary English use of "myth" to indicate an untrue story or a misunderstanding based on ignorance, in every religious tradition "myth" conveys the essential truths of life. These truths, in turn, are embedded in grand stories of origin and destiny rather than in abstract theoretical and scientific theories. The world's major religions have preserved their mythic accounts in the most durable material available in each age: first on stone, parchment, and tree bark, later on paper, and today in CD-ROM format.

A Shinto priest and believers purify their bodies in icy water for the New Year's ceremony at the Teppozu Shrine in Tokyo.

Passover Myth and Ritual

Passover is one of the most important holy days in Judaism. At Passover, Jewish families gather for a meal, called a seder, at which they hear the story of the Exodus, the liberation of the Jews from slavery in Egypt. As the story is retold, participants eat certain foods as reminders of what was important in the past. The Passover seder is a symbolic occasion, not a literal reenactment of the Exodus. Nevertheless, this symbolic reenactment is experienced as having the power to make each seder guest an actual participant in the original event. The distance between past and present is felt to dissolve, and the events of the Exodus are "happening now."

Through participation in the Passover seder, Jews experience who they are—a chosen people, called by the God of all creation to live justly and be an example to all nations. This celebration reminds Jews that God acts in history and will one day overcome suffering and death. Thus each Jew knows that no life is trivial. On the contrary, each life has cosmic significance, helping to bring about the fulfillment of all things. Myth and ritual thus perform a religious function—that is, they "tie or bind" the life of the individual into a great cosmic drama, serving the highest power, the source of the meaning and purpose of life. This description of the function of Passover myth and ritual in Judaism applies to the myths and rituals of all religions.

Ritual actions connect the individual and the community to the sacred. Such actions often involve the symbolic reenactment of the stories that are passed on from one generation to the next. Myth and ritual are closely tied to the major festivals or holy days of a religious tradition and illuminate the meaning of human destiny in relation to sacred powers. By celebrating a cycle of festivals spread throughout the year, people come to dwell in the stories that tell them who they are, where they came from, and where they are going.

Naturally the leaders of religious communities over many generations have sought to make myth and ritual, worldview and ethos, belief and practice, idea and emotion, mutually reinforcing. Yet some of the great schisms within the faiths of the world have been based more on practice than on belief.

To live well, have many descendants, and live a long life—these are three great treasures in Chinese culture. A Chinese woman prays for prosperity, posterity, and longevity at a Buddhist temple on the island of Lantau.

Rituals often precede the myths used to explain them, with the result that over centuries a ritual may continue, but the mythic explanation may change. In many cases it is difficult to discern which came first—the myth or the ritual.

We should not assume that rituals communicate only ideas or beliefs. Religions are not confined to doctrines regarding the sacred. Rather, they include many *careful acts* that, in their own right, *tie and bind* people to each other and to cosmic meaning. Being religious thus entails taking decisive action at times, abstaining from certain acts at others—offering, for instance, precious gifts to supernatural beings, making pilgrimages to sacred places, or engaging in meditation or other disciplines of spiritual practice.

For devout persons of many faiths, acting in the prescribed manner, called *orthopraxy*, is more important than *orthodoxy*—acceptance of the often intricate doctrines set forth in texts and formulated by scholars. Performing the five daily Muslim prayers, visiting a Buddhist or Hindu temple to offer flowers on the full moon day, cleaning a Chinese family's ancestral grave during the spring festival, or being baptized as a Christian—all these acts are as central to "being religious" as is adopting the beliefs defined as orthodox.

Carefully choreographed religious rituals recall important events in the history of each faith: the "Night Journey" of the Prophet, Muhammad, the enlightenment of the Buddha, the birthday of Krishna. In other rituals, the faithful donate gifts to the supernatural beings to whom they ascribe power to profoundly affect their lives. Still other rituals require circumcision, tattoos, or burn marks to set the believers off from nonbelievers, fostering group solidarity. The consumption of certain foods as part of some rituals suggests that

Hindu women pay homage to the god of the sun during the Chat Puja festival on the banks of the Hooghly River in the eastern Indian city of Calcutta. Thousands of Hindu devotees reached the riverside at sunset and will spend the night praying.

the believer can acquire the "same essence" as the divine through ingestion, as in the Christian communion, Hindu puja, or tribal eating of a totemic animal to affirm common identity.

The great annual festivals in the world's religions give devotees a break from the profane time of normal working life, times for special rituals, for fasts or feasting, and periods of rest and reflection on the fundamental truths. These events also reinforce life's most important ties with family and fellow devotees. The need to orchestrate such crucial religious actions also leads followers to create institutions that occupy central places in their societies.

Pivotal figures of each world religion are the priests or ministers who mediate between the deity and the community. The world's oldest religious specialist is the shaman, a man or woman who goes into a trance to be able to leave his or her body to go to the spirit realm and communicate with sacred ancestors and supernatural beings (spirits, gods, demons, ghosts). Practitioners of this art (also called "mediums" or "oracles") are depicted on cave walls across Eurasia from the Neolithic period 25,000 years ago. Shamans still exist in many parts of the world, not only among the remaining tribal peoples but also within the great world religions.

Since all the modern world religions have relied on written materials, there have always been scholars who have learned to write and read and thereby interpret the sacred texts, translating them for the great majority of rank-and-file followers, most of whom, until the modern era, were illiterate. Among this group are those who specialize in being spiritual teachers (e.g., the Hindu guru, the Jewish rabbi, the Sufi Muslim shaykh). Although we can point to interesting comparative patterns among religious rituals and between religious teachers, it is also true to say that each tradition can be known by its own unique set of religious practitioners and institutions. To understand the great world religions thus entails not only knowing what believers believe but also how they are expected to act, what rituals are essential, what distinctive institutions have supported the community and in what unique architectural settings (mosque, church, synagogue) individuals practice meditation, pray, venerate their ancestors, and praise or please their gods (or God).

A healer from Nepal seeks to enter a trance by donning the mask of the goddess Durga.

Morality

In most religious traditions, ritual and morality have been closely intertwined. "Right" is often defined by "rite"—the ritual patterns of behavior that keep life sacred. Morality is an inherent dimension of religious experience, for religion is not only about sacred powers, it also describes the way of life the powers require and make possible.

The religious experience of sacredness—what matters most to a given community—provides the ground for the moral experience of the virtuous life. Whatever is sacred provides a yardstick for measuring rightness of human actions. The blueprint for right action is expressed in myth and ritual. For Muslims, the teachings of the Quran (Islam's sacred book) and *hadith* (stories or traditions about the Prophet, Muhammad) exemplify the moral way of life that God expects of human beings. These ideals and requirements will be communicated from one generation to the next through the ritual reenactment and recitation of Islam's sacred stories of origin and destiny.

A 2-year-old Muslim boy, living in predominantly Catholic East Timor, prays alongside his father at a mosque in Dili.

This is just one example of how a religious tradition shapes morality. It is important to recognize that even the most secular and seemingly nonreligious morality, insofar as it treats anything as sacred, can be understood as having a religious dimension. In the former Soviet Union, May Day was a great national festival celebrating the Russian revolution of 1917 and the founding of an atheistic state. At this celebration, the values of the way of life in the U.S.S.R. were held up as sacred—worth living for and worth dying for. Although not connected in any way to one of the world's religions, this festival served a profound religious purpose: it told Soviet citizens that their individual lives were important, a part of the great historical drama that would inevitably lead to a pure and egalitarian communist society.

Once we realize that religion is about what people hold sacred and the way of life that is called for by such beliefs, then it makes sense to say that all religion requires morality. We can also say that every morality (no matter how nonreligious it appears) is grounded in religious experience, namely in the experience of what is held sacred (i.e., matters most) in a given community. Such an observation leaves open the philosophical question of the degree to which sacred morality of a tradition is truly ethical. For ethics is the questioning of our sacred moralities, asking whether what people customarily say is good or virtuous really is good or virtuous.

Thus, we can see that myth and ritual tie and bind individuals in three ways: to whatever power(s) they believe govern their destiny, also to each other in a community of identity, and also to the cosmos in which they live. This is accomplished through a complex of stories and ritual obligations that express a morality or sacred way of life.

Religious Language

One of the most challenging tasks facing anyone trying to understand the diversity of religious experience is to grasp the nature of religious language. To interpret religious language literally will cause you to misunderstand it. This is because religious language is primarily symbolic. For example, in Western religious experience, especially in the biblical tradition of the psalms, people often say things such as "God is my shepherd" or "God is my rock." We know such statements are not meant literally. God is literally neither a rock nor a shepherd. To speak like this is to speak metaphorically, that is, to use things that are more familiar to help explain what is less familiar, even mysterious. Shepherds and rocks we can see and know something about, God is a little more mysterious. A person who says "God is our shepherd" has expressed the thought that God is like a shepherd, in the sense that God watches over and cares for persons in the same way a shepherd tends his sheep. Similarly, "God is our rock" simply means that God is real, firm, and solid as a rock—a reality that can always be relied upon.

Not all religious experiences, however, are theistic, reflecting belief in one or more gods. Theravada Buddhists in ancient India refused to use the Hindu words roughly equivalent to the English word "God" to describe their religious experiences. Instead they spoke of "emptiness" and "the void" and the inadequacy of all spoken metaphors to explain their goal, the blissful state of *nirvana* (see Chapter Seven). And yet they too used metaphors to try to help people understand what they had experienced as "the blissful," as "having suchness," or as "true awakening." In fact, the word "God," which is so central to Western religious experience, is just one of a class of diverse terms used in different religions and cultures across the world to designate the reality that expresses the ultimate in value and meaning for the group. This class of terms includes not only the God of Western theism but also the impersonal Brahman of Hinduism, the transpersonal nirvana of Buddhism, and the impersonal power of the *Dao* at work in all things that is central to Chinese religions. At the same time one can find some parallels to Western theism in Asia, too: T'ien, the Lord of Heaven, in China; incarnations of Brahman or Purusha in gods such as Shiva or Krishna in devotional schools of Hinduism; and the cosmic Buddhas and bodhisattvas to whom Mahayana Buddhists pray.

All these expressions for what is truly ultimate and meaningful may in fact refer to different forms of religious experience—or perhaps different people use language unique to their own cultures and times to point to what may ultimately be the same reality. Here lies the challenge, mystery, and fascination of studying the religions of the world: Do differences in religious terminology reflect experiences of different realities? Or are they different expressions of or ways of describing the same reality? Because religious metaphors come out of particular historical and cultural times and places and because they are symbolic forms of expression, to understand the religious languages and messages of different religious traditions, to put ourselves in the time and place of their origins we must use imagination.

Metaphor and Symbol in Religious Language

If religious language is primarily symbolic, where do these metaphors and symbolic expressions come from? To answer this question requires a little sympathetic imagination. Think of a beautiful warm summer evening: the sky is clear, and millions of stars are shining brightly. The evening is so breathtaking that you decide to go for a walk in the rolling hills just outside the city. As you walk, you are suddenly in the grip of an experience so overwhelming that it cannot be expressed in words. After a short time, which seems like an eternity, you return to your normal consciousness and wander back to the city, where you run into some friends at the local cafe. You order a cola and then you say to them: "You'll never guess what happened to me tonight. I had the most incredible experience, so incredible it defies description." Yet paradoxically, your friends immediately ask, "What was it like?" With that question, we have entered the realm of metaphor and symbolic language.

Your friends are asking you to describe what you have just said is indescribable. To answer at all, you must draw analogies to things they already know about. So you might say that the experience was like being in the presence of a shepherd who really cares for his flock. At least you might say that if you and your friends were nomads familiar with the raising of sheep, like the people of ancient Israel. Roughly a thousand years before the start of the Common Era, however, the people stopped being nomads and settled into a fixed territory under the rule of a king. Although many continued to raise sheep, they started speaking of God as a king who protects his subjects. Today some people seem unsure of how to speak of God. Women often point out that most images of God have been male. Some seek to shock their hearers into an awareness of the metaphorical nature of religious language by referring to God as "our Mother."

Religious language, as symbolic language, can take one of two forms: analogy or negation. The metaphors just quoted ("God is my shepherd" and "God is my rock") are examples of the way of analogy (*via analogia*). In these metaphors, we used familiar words to create an analogy that describes something less familiar. However, there is another form of religious language, the way of negation (*via negativa*). This way of speaking religiously proceeds not by asserting what God or ultimate reality is (or, is like) but by saying what it is not. This approach is very typical of mystical traditions. The mystic declares that God is "nothing," stating that God is beyond (i.e., transcends) or is different from anything in our material universe and experience. God is not this thing and not that thing. God is in fact no "thing" at all. Being beyond all finite things, God must be said to be no-thing.

In general, Western monotheism has emphasized the way of analogy by saying that there is one God who is like humans, able to "know" and to "love," but in a superior fashion. Thus, God is described as all-knowing, all-loving, or all-powerful. By contrast, Buddhism, of all the religions, has emphasized most strongly the way of negation, insisting that what is most valuable cannot be either named or imaged. Yet both ways are found in all traditions. Some Jewish, Christian, and Muslim mystics have referred to God as a "Nothingness," even as some Hindus have referred to the ultimate reality as a cosmic person (*purusha*) rather than an impersonal power (Brahman). Moreover, we should note that these two ways are not really in conflict, for the way of analogy itself implies the way of negation. That is, every time we say God is *like* some thing, we are at the same time saying God is *not* literally that thing. Every analogy implies a negation.

Our discussion of religious language should help us to appreciate just how challenging and at times confusing it can be to study and compare various religious traditions. Just as religious communities and religious traditions from different parts of the world use different metaphors and symbols, they also mix the way of analogy and the way of negation in varying degrees. Therefore, two different traditions sometimes talk about the same human experience in ways that seem to be totally contradictory. For example, it may seem that a Jewish theist and a Theravada Buddhist hold diametrically opposed religious beliefs. For Jews believe in a personal God and Theravada Buddhists do not. Yet, when we look more closely at Jewish beliefs we discover that Jews believe that God can neither be named nor imaged, even as Theravada Buddhists believe that ultimate truth is beyond all names and images. And yet, in both traditions, experiencing the nameless is said to make one more human or compassionate, not less.

Perhaps theistic and nontheistic experiences are really not far apart. However, it is also possible that they are truly different. To pursue this great human question, we must begin by withholding judgment and simply try to understand how stories and rituals shape people's lives—their views, values, and behavior. Perhaps the real measure of comparison should be how people live their lives rather than the apparently diverse images and concepts they hold. If both Jews and Buddhists, for example, are led by their religious experiences and beliefs to express compassion for those who suffer or are in need, then clearly the two faiths are similar in that important respect.

THE GREAT TRANSITION: FROM TRIBAL LIFE TO URBAN LIFE AND THE EMERGENCE OF WORLD RELIGIONS

From about 8000 BCE the domestication of plants and animals made village life possible. Acquisition of agricultural skill then allowed the development of cities, from approximately 3000 BCE, bringing about a great transformation in human experience. Urban life drew people together out of different tribal cultures. In a tribe, everyone lived in close harmony with the rhythms of nature, in extended families or clans that shared a common set of stories and rituals. Now in the cities people came together from different tribes, bringing with them different stories, different rituals, and different family identities.

The complexities of urban life led to the specialization of labor. Whereas in tribal societies everyone shared the tasks of hunting and gathering, in the cities the agricultural surplus created by the peasant farmers made it possible for some to engage in diverse occupations such as carpentry, blacksmithing, and record keeping. Society became more complex and differentiated into classes (peasants, craftsmen, noblemen, priests, etc.). In a parallel fashion, elaborate and detailed mythologies emerged in the cities, assigning special powers and tasks to each of the many gods and spirits of the different tribes now embraced as the gods of the city.

These changes, and others, fundamentally transformed human identity. In the tribe, identity was collective because everybody shared the same stories and actions. The cities, by contrast, were communities of strangers. People did not automatically share a collective consciousness. Tribal persons were confronted with differences that forced them to individuate their identities. Urban life enhanced awareness of how one person differs from another.

The loss of tribal collective life and the emergence of large, impersonal, and often brutal urban city-states in Egypt, India, China, and Mesopotamia was in effect a change from paradise to a world of suffering and cruelty. These new city-states, populated by strangers and ruled by absolute monarchs who were considered to be gods or representatives of the gods, were soon enmeshed in a threefold crisis of mortality, morality, and meaning. In the tribe identity was collective. The tribe was experienced as eternal; it never dies. When an individual died, the disappearance of his or her physical remains was seen as less important than the person's new position in the community. The dead took their place among the sacred ancestors, who were believed to continue to dwell with the living in a single community. Under the impact of urban individuation, however, humans began to think of themselves as individuals, and death suddenly loomed as a personal problem even as life seemed more cruel and uncertain. With the development of individual self-awareness, death presented people with a new and unsettling problem—the loss of self. Having achieved individual identity they now asked, "What happens to my (individual) "self" when I die?

Urban individuation also created the new problems of law and morality. In the tribe the right thing to do was prescribed by ritual, and the same rites were known and respected by all. In the cities people from a variety of mythic and ritual traditions lived together, yet as individuals, each looking out for his or her own good, if necessary at the expense of others. Thus in the cities law emerged to set the minimum order necessary to sustain human life, and it became necessary to develop a system of ethics to persuade people to live up to even higher ideals. Too often city dwellers experienced themselves as living in a world without morality, the pawns of rulers who governed arbitrarily and waged wars of conquest at their expense. The situation evoked a crisis of meaning. Can life really have any meaning if it is filled with injustice and ends in death? The first written expression of this great question appeared in the ancient Near East at the beginning of the urban period (c. 3000–1500 BCE). This metaphorical tale, known as the Epic of Gilgamesh, expresses the anguish of the new urban individual.

It is to answer the questions raised by the crises of morality, mortality, and meaning that the great world religions emerged. Once city dwellers were individuated in their identities, the old tribal answers no longer worked. Once people became individuals, they could not deliberately return to the old collective sense of identity. The only possible response to the kind of loss of innocence represented by individuation was to move forward and discover deeper wells of religious experience. Only from these sources could people achieve a new sense of human identity—of being unique parts of one cosmic body. To resolve the urban problems of mortality, morality, and meaning, the new identity would have to account for the common humanity of diverse peoples by transcending local tribal and city identity. That is the challenge the great world religions faced as they emerged in the three great centers of civilization in the ancient world—China, India, and the Middle East. Between 1000 BCE and 1000 CE all the great world religions developed their classical expressions, dividing much of the world among them (see Map 1.2).

The world religions emerged in conjunction with the formation of great empires that united peoples of various tribes and city-states into larger political entities. These new political orders created a need for a new sense of what it means to be human. They redefined the meaning of being human in terms beyond the boundaries of the tribe and the city-state, seeing a higher unity to reality beyond the many local gods and spirits. In China, all humans were said to share in common the *Dao* (the hidden power of harmony that governs the universe); in India, for Hindus, it was the reality of *Brahman* (the universal, impersonal, eternal spirit that is the source of all things), and for Buddhists, the *Buddha nature* (understood as the interdependent becoming of all things); in the Middle East it was that all were children of the *one God* (the source and creator of all things).

Yet the earliest ideas about the meaning of being human remain central to an understanding of the world's great religions. And to grasp this mind-set, we must return to the great religious stories.

THE GREAT RELIGIOUS STORIES OF THE WORLD

Since the beginning of historical time people have told stories. We human beings are not just storytellers, we are "storydwellers." We live in our stories and see and understand the world through them. Even our understanding of what is good and evil, right and wrong, is shaped by the kind of story we see ourselves in and the role we see ourselves playing in that story. Although

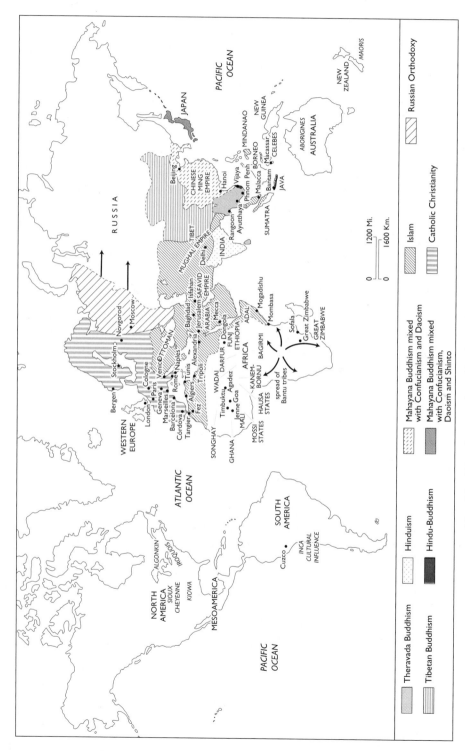

Map 1.2 Distribution of world religions circa 1500 CE.

religious stories need not only be about gods and other spiritual beings, most of the earliest stories that have shaped human religious life have been.

While specific religious stories are indeed unique and diverse, we can group religious stories into four main types, each of which presents a symbolic story of the origins and destiny of human beings and the challenges they face in striving to realize their sacred destiny. These four main types of sacred story are the myths of nature, the myths of harmony, the myths of liberation, and the myths of history (see Chart 1.1).

The Myths of Nature

If one goes back far enough into the history of any society, the earliest religious stories, found everywhere, are versions of the myths of nature. These are stories about the forces of nature that govern human destiny, which portray them as either personal forces (gods, spirits, and sacred ancestors) or impersonal magical forces. Such religions tend to see time as cyclical, always returning to the moment just before creation. Just as winter and death are followed by spring and new life, starting the earthly cycles all over again, time is an endless loop. Myth and ritual are the means to erase the distance between "now" and the time of origins, "in the beginning," when the gods and ancestral spirits first created the world fresh and new. In such stories the problem of life is time. Time is the enemy. Time brings decay. It brings old age, sickness, and death. The ideal of life is to return to the newness of life at the beginning of creation before time began.

The means for bringing about this return is the recitation of myths and the performance of ritual reenactments of the stories of creation. Hunter-gatherer stories emphasize the fertility of the earth, the need for the ritual renewal of life in harmony with the seasons, and the eternal place of the tribe in the cosmic order. In these societies, it is the shaman who is the spiritual leader, making trance journeys to the spirit world to bargain with ancestral spirits and restore harmony between human community and the forces of nature.

Few groups that survive in the contemporary world have maintained such primal traditions, which we shall explore in Chapter Two. Nevertheless, belief in the spirit world and the shaman's ability to communicate with it did not vanish with the coming of the city. Instead, it was embraced in the new world religions (in prayers to the saints and angels in Catholic Christianity and to the Boddhisattvas of Buddhism, for example). More recently New Age religions have embraced many shamanistic practices, as we shall see in the final chapter. Hence these beliefs and practices continued through the ages and are very much alive today.

The primacy of shamanistic and polytheistic forms of religion yielded to the development of the great world religions during the cultural and societal transition discussed earlier—the transition from tribal hunting and gathering cultures to complex urban life sustained by agriculture. Out of this transition emerged the great world religions, communicated through three new types of story.

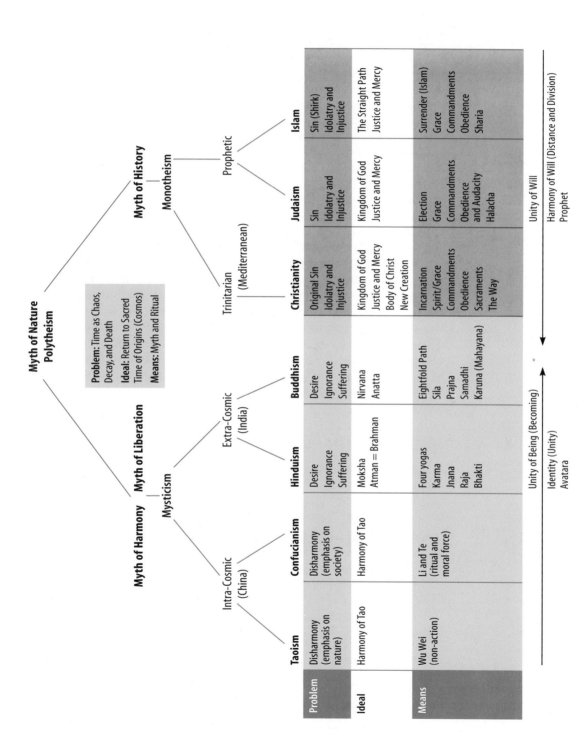

Chart 1.1   The world's religions in perspective.

China and the Myths of Harmony

In China the great cosmic story that emerged was that of the Dao (sometimes rendered Tao). The universal Dao, which all beings share, is the hidden harmony of the universe at work in all the forces of nature. One's true self is knowable only in relation to the Dao. All of creation works via the opposites of *yin* and *yang*, of dark and light, of earth and heaven, of female and male. Yin and yang are never polar opposites, but rather each flows into the other with no absolute division, the way day flows into night and night into day, so that nothing is ever the total opposite of anything else. There is a little day in every night, a little male in every female (and vice versa). The ideal of life then is balance and harmony. The great problem of existence is the disharmony that occurs when the elements of society and/or the universe are out of balance.

To restore balance, two different religions emerged in China: both Daoism and Confucianism sought to bring harmony between heaven and earth, self and society. These two traditions offered different means to overcome the problem and realize the ideal. Daoist sages urged humans to start by seeking harmony with the rhythms of nature through cultivating simplicity through *wu-wei*, the art of "not doing," or not interfering with the natural flow of life. Out of that harmony, the harmony of society would flow spontaneously. Confucian sages urged humans to seek to establish harmony in society through the practice of *li*, the ritual observance of obligations attached to one's station in society. They taught that people can spontaneously be in harmony with the rhythms of the universe only when social harmony has been achieved.

India and the Myths of Liberation

In India, as in China, life was seen through the metaphors of the natural cycles and rhythms of nature, but in India the rhythms were to be escaped from rather than affirmed. Life was seen as suffering, not because there is nothing good about life but because no matter how good it is, it is transient, it always ends in old age, sickness, and death. The problem of life is human entrapment in an endless cycle of suffering, death, and rebirth because of ignorance of one's true identity.

The goal of religion is to destroy the illusions fostered by our selfish desires, for only when these are mastered can humans be freed from the wheel of death and rebirth (*samsara*). In that moment of liberation or enlightenment, one will come to realize the ultimate reality and find union with it.

For Hindus, the true self (*atman*) is merged with the eternal Brahman in either the personal or impersonal form. Buddhism offers the possibility of removing selfish attachments and realizing enlightenment (*sambodhi*) within the suffering and impermanence of life, achieving the indescribable and transpersonal reality called nirvana.

Hinduism and Buddhism, as two embodiments of the myth of liberation, developed a variety of means for achieving enlightenment. These include meditation, the selfless performance of one's duties, spiritual knowledge and insight, and selfless love or devotion toward a divine incarnation of the ultimate truth or reality.

The Middle East and the Myths of History

The myths of nature, of harmony, and of liberation use the human experience of the rhythms and cycles of nature as the basis for religious metaphors and symbolic language expressed in sacred stories. In the myths of history, by contrast, it is not nature but history that comprises the realm of human experience from which the metaphors for religious experience are primarily drawn. While all religions communicate their traditions by telling stories, only the religions of the Middle East, beginning with Judaism, make "story" itself the central metaphor of religious expression. Unlike the eternally cyclical rhythms of nature, stories have a beginning and an end. Ancient Judaism conceived of the cosmos as a great unfolding story told by a great divine storyteller (God): in the beginning God spoke, the world was created, and the story began. The story is the story of the God who acts in time and leads his people through time toward a final fulfillment. The story begins with an initial harmony between God and humans, proceeds through a long period in which that harmony is disrupted by human idolatry and selfishness or sin, and looks with hope toward an end of time when all injustice, suffering, and death will be

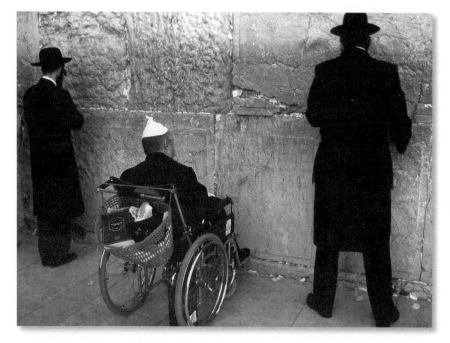

All that remains of the great temple in Jerusalem, destroyed by the Romans in 70 CE, is the Western Wall. It is considered to be the holiest of sites where observant Jews come to pray.

overcome and the wronged will be compensated—a time when the dead shall be raised and the whole of creation transformed.

Three versions of this story arose in the Middle East—first the Judaic, then the Christian, and finally the Islamic. For each of these, human beings are human by virtue of being children of the one God who created all things. All three traditions trace themselves back to the patriarch Abraham, whom each considers to be the true model of faith, and to Adam and Eve as the first human beings. In all three, the problem of life is viewed as "sin"—failing to follow God's will, a combination of idolatry and human selfishness that leads to injustice. The ideal goal of life is the restoration of human wills to harmony with the will of God, whereupon peace and justice will reign and death will be overcome. The means for bringing this about include but are not limited to obedience to the will of God, dialog and debate with God (Judaism), acceptance of divine grace or aid through the incarnation of God (Christianity), and submission to the will of God (Islam). Thus, although the story of the cosmos has many ups and downs, many trials and tragedies, it is seen as the story of a journey that is headed for a happy ending for faithful believers. In contrast to the myths of nature, harmony, and liberation, in the myths of history time is not the enemy but rather the vehicle for encountering the ultimate reality, which is God. The goal is not to escape time by returning to the beginning through myth and ritual, nor rising above time in mystical ecstasy, but of meeting God in time and making a journey with God through time. Time is promising, and the future ultimately hopeful.

Religious Diversity and Historical Change: The Structure of This Book

Each of the great narrative traditions sought to address the problem of mortality by going beyond collective eternal identity to the route of the primal religions. In India and China the answer was essentially mystical: all selves find their true identity through inner transformation, achieving union or harmony with the same ultimate reality (whether Brahman or the Dao) or in the case of Buddhism, experiencing the same ultimate destiny of nirvana. In the Middle East, the answer was not primarily mystical but apocalyptic— the end of time, which leads to the resurrection of the dead.

Each of these traditions speaks to the problem of morality as well, by helping the individual get beyond the self-centeredness that came with urban individualism and grasp the essential unity and interdependence of all human beings. And each sought to provide life with meaning by depicting individuals and communities as participating in a great cosmic story that gives drama and purpose to human life. These were stories that were not interrupted and made absurd by death. Rather, their purpose was to show individuals a way to transcend death.

Finally, it is necessary to qualify our statement about the unity and diversity of religions. When we stand back at a great distance we can use the four types of myth or story—those of nature, harmony, liberation, and history—to classify the various religions. As we get closer, we discover that each of these stories has diverse versions that express the differences in doctrines and in practices. And as we draw even closer to any one of these religions, we will discover even more diversity. Those familiar with Christianity need only recall how many different kinds of Christianity there are. There is such a great difference between a simple Quaker service, an enthusiastic Southern Baptist service, and a formal Anglican service that it is hard to believe they are all examples of the same religion. This range of diversity is true of every religious tradition. So the discovery of some forms of unity in the diversity of religions must not fool us into thinking that we have gotten rid of the diversity. The diversity is as important as the unity, and no form of human religiousness can be understood without taking both into account. As we will see, part of the challenge today for every religious tradition is to make sense of the seemingly irreducible multiplicity of paths by which humanity seeks ultimate meaning, value, and salvation.

In the chapters to come we will be examining how human beings struggle to continue the religiousness of their ancestors in a new and radically different world. We will see how Western civilization gave birth to modernity and, through its colonial expansion, spread its religious and cultural influence around the world, disrupting premodern religious cultures everywhere. By "colonialism" we mean the political, social, cultural, and economic domination of one society by another. Colonialism is as old as civilization and is part of the story of virtually all religions and civilizations, East and West. But modern Western colonialism came closest to achieving global domination. Propelled by European colonialism, Christianity became the first faith to spread globally, forcing every religion to reckon with its beliefs, its practices, and its critiques of non-Christians.

In the chapters ahead we will see how colonialism, in turn, provoked a postcolonial reaction that has tended to divide those in each religious and cultural tradition into three groups. The fundamentalists reject important aspects of modernity and want to go back to what they perceive as the purity of an "authentic" social/political order manifested in the sacred way of life of their ancestors. The modernists adapt their religious tradition to modernity. The postmodernists, while rejecting the dominance of Western modernity, seek to go forward into a new situation that affirms both diversity and change in their religious tradition.

Among fundamentalists, a few purist religious movements reject everything modern, but most accept aspects they do not interpret as threatening the essential beliefs and purity of their religious tradition. Thus many embrace modern technology while rejecting changes suggested by the sciences that would call into question the fundamentalists religious worldview. Among modernists and postmodernists, a few movements reject everything in their religious tradition that is not consistent with their understanding of the "modern worldview." Most pick and choose, however, arguing that some parts of the religious tradition must change while some must not. What is distinctive about the modernist end of the spectrum is the view that the human understanding of religious truth and practice is subject to historical change and development, a notion that the fundamentalist end of the spectrum finds abhorrent, even blasphemous.

Beginning with Chapter Three, our treatment of these issues will be organized as follows:

- Overview
- Encounter with modernity
- Premodern
- Modern
- Postmodern
- Conclusion

The overview at the start of each chapter introduces the basic worldview of the religious tradition under discussion. The following section, *Encounter with Modernity*, describes a particular moment in which premodern religious traditions clashed with the modern worldview and explains the diverse responses that emerged from that encounter. Next, each chapter will leap back to the *premodern* period and begin to trace the origins and development of the tradition, to better understand why modernity represents a challenge to it. This history is accounted for in two phases—a "formative period," which traces the origins of the traditions, and a "classical period," which explains its fully developed premodern worldview (both beliefs and rituals).

The section on *modernity* traces the diverse fundamentalist and modernist responses that developed in each tradition as it was challenged and threatened by Western colonialism and its modern scientific/technological worldview. This material is followed by a *postmodern* section in which we survey the most recent reactions to the adaptations each tradition has made to the modern world. These reactions tend to be postcolonial attempts (in most regions, after 1945) to reclaim religious and cultural identities that existed before the advent of modern Western colonialism. In this way we hope to promote understanding of why the world, with all its possibilities for coexistence and conflict, is the way it is today. The *conclusion* to each chapter addresses the implications of this history for the future of each tradition.

MODERNIZATION IN
GLOBAL PERSPECTIVE

Before we can move on to explore the struggle of peoples everywhere to continue the religiousness of their ancestors in a new and radically different world, we need to be clear about the terms "premodern," "modern," and "postmodern." In general, *premodern* history around the globe describes a wide range of cultures in which religion played the decisive role in explaining and ordering life. In premodern societies religion provided the most certain knowledge one could have of the world, and consequently religious authority played a central role in each culture's social, political, and economic ordering of public life. In this respect, all premodern cultures have more in common with each other than with modern "secular" (i.e., nonreligious) culture.

With the advances in science that began to gather steam in the eighteenth century, science itself came to replace religion as the most certain form of knowledge. The *modern* period is marked by a tendency to view religion as a matter of personal faith or opinion rather than objective knowledge. Gradually every area of public life was secularized. That is, religion no longer played a governing role in politics, economics, or public education. The most dramatic institutional expression of this change in the West was the emergence of the separation of church and state. The secular state was the expression of "modern" reality—politics governed a society's public life and religion was a private matter for individuals and their family.

Every premodern culture saw its universe through explicitly religious eyes and pronounced its vision of life sacred. Since all premodern societies were dominated by the influence of religious authority, they all understood and ordered their worlds through myths and rituals that had been passed down for many generations. Modern culture, by contrast, understands its world through the myths and rituals of rational and empirical science. And, as we shall see in Chapter Four, the scientific worldview brought with it certain distinctive features, especially the tendency to reject the premodern past, and to regard its beliefs and traditions as irrational and superstitious. In addition, history was understood as representing inevitable progress toward an ideal future, and the knowledge that could bring about this glorious future could be had only through science, with its "objective view" of the world, finally ending the centuries of human hatred and bloodshed caused by religions.

While much more can and will be said in the remaining chapters about the premodern/modern contrast, we have at least suggested that the contrast between premodern and modern is dramatic and clear. But a word needs to be said about our use of the third term in this sequence. Our *postmodern* situation, according to the postmodernist thinker Jean-François Lyotard, is characterized by the collapse of all *metanarratives*, those grand allencompassing sacred stories through which human beings interpreted life in their respective cultures.[1] In ancient cultures, metanarratives were typically religious myths of the four types we have described, and the notion that they were true for all times and places went unquestioned. This is no longer the case. In modern culture the primary metanarrative has been the story of history as progress driven by science and technology. However, the globalization of religious and cultural interaction that began in the twentieth century has tended to relativize all such stories, including the modern one.

In the premodern world a single grand narrative or religious worldview was typically experienced as true, valuable, and meaningful by the overwhelming majority of people in a given culture. It is that kind of metanarrative that has collapsed in our day. However, our postmodern world of religious and cultural diversity is explained by a new metanarrative of religious and cultural pluralism. In this metanarrative, postmodernists believe, no single story can possibly be all encompassing for all people in a given culture—especially as a global culture emerges and practitioners of the world's religions are found in everyone's home town. Diversity relativizes all stories. The grand stories of the world religions have thereby become miniaturized. Everyone is left with his or her own stories, knowing full well that other people live by other stories.

The very creation of textbooks on world religions encourages just such a postmodern awareness of the diversity of all our stories. In this situation the adherents of each religious tradition have to deal with conflicting and often bewildering diversity within their own traditions, as well as the total diversity of the many other religious traditions. All, but especially those who follow the great missionary faiths—Christianity, Islam, Buddhism—are challenged to explain how it is that the world continues in this ever-multiplying religious pluralism and why their own ultimate reality (God, Allah, Brahman, Buddha nature, Dao) has not led all the world into their own path.

We suggest that there is a strong correlation between the postmodern challenge to modernity and the postcolonial challenge to colonialism. A postcolonial era typically begins with a rejection of the modern Western historical metanarrative of scientific–technological progress and in this way opens the door to postmodern awareness and critiques. However, that door swings two ways, with some arguing for a return to premodern fundamental notions of religious truth and practice, insisting that there is only one true religious story and way of life, and others embracing the postmodern situation by welcoming diversity. What fundamentalisms and postmodern pluralisms have in common is a rejection of the earlier (i.e., modern) strategy of privatizing religion. Both insist that religion ought to play a role in influencing not only private but also public life. But fundamentalists advocate accomplishing this by returning to an absolute religious metanarrative that should shape public life for everyone, whereas postmodernists, at least as we will use the term, reject such "totalism" in favor of the acceptance of a plurality of narratives, recognizing the public benefits of pluralism in contemporary society.

We do not use the contrast between "modern" and "postmodern" to describe either a philosophy or an existing historical period but rather a newly emerging historical trend. A postmodern trend deserves to be called "new" because it challenges the assumptions of modernity without simply reverting to premodern views of reality. In particular, postmodern pluralism challenges modern "science" as the single form of objective knowledge about the world and also the modern practice of privatizing religion. Today, virtually all the world's religions are caught up in the struggle between their premodern, modern, and possible postmodern interpretations.

Because Christianity is the dominant religion of the civilization that produced modernization, it went through the trauma of accommodation to modernity first, and in slower stages than those religions that did not encounter modernization until it had attained a more developed form. Chapter Four on Christianity, will therefore also trace the history of the emergence of modernity in relation to Christianity and the West.

Some have charged that modernization is a form of Western cultural and perhaps even religious imperialism that has been forced on other cultures. However, modernization and secularization challenge all sacred traditions and identities, including those of Western religions. As we shall see in the remaining chapters of this book, the patterns of modernization's impact on diverse religions and cultures are quite variable, as are the responses elicited. Modernization did not have an impact on all religions simultaneously, nor did all react in exactly the same way, although there are striking similarities. Therefore, we should not expect all religions and cultures to exhibit exactly the same patterns and responses.

A Christian army chaplain administers Holy Communion to a member of the 173rd Airborne Brigade prior to an assault during the Vietnam War.

MODERN COLONIALISM, THE SOCIALIST CHALLENGE, AND THE END OF MODERNITY

In the nineteenth century the synergy of Western science, economics (capitalism), and technology fostered among the dominant European nations, especially England and France, a thirst for building colonial empires. These colonial ambitions were paralleled in the modern period by those of only one Asian nation—Japan. By 1914 most of the world was under the domination of Western European culture. Geographically the Russians and the British controlled about a third of the globe. In terms of population, the British Empire controlled about a fifth of the human race—nearly 400 million people, while France controlled over 50 million colonial subjects. (See Map 1.3.)

The spread of science, technology, and capitalism along with colonial politics was accompanied by a strong sense of paternalism that was traumatic to indigenous cultures and their religious traditions. The impressive achievements of Western civilization often prompted an initial phase of emulation of Western ways, leading many to embrace such manifestations of modernization, as the privatization of religion. Almost inevitably, however, there would be a religious and political backlash, seen in struggles for national liberation as indigenous peoples sought to reclaim their independence and autonomy and to reaffirm the value of their original ways of life. This backlash often included a resurgence of religious influence as a force in anticolonial struggles. Most independence movements readily adopted a key element of Western civilization—nationalism—in their attempts to resist foreign occupation and to protect their religious and cultural identities by resisting exploitation.

Many of these movements paradoxically struck an alliance with socialism, the philosophical and political movement that arose in the nineteenth century in Europe among the new urban working class as a protest against the poverty and social dislocation created by early capitalism and the Industrial Revolution. Socialism was itself a modernist movement, sustained by a vision of scientific progress, and yet it also championed premodern values of community against the rampant individualism of modern capitalism. In Karl Marx's formulation of "scientific socialism," it became an international movement that had an impact on world history as profound as that of any world religion. Indeed, as religious societies around the globe revolted against European imperialism, most experimented with some form of socialism as a modern way of protesting and of dialing back modernity itself. The twentieth century produced examples around the world of Jewish, Christian, Islamic, Hindu, Buddhist, and neo-Confucian forms of socialism. In its secular form socialism or communism became the dominant element in Russian culture, spreading throughout Eastern Europe and across China, the largest country of Asia, as well.

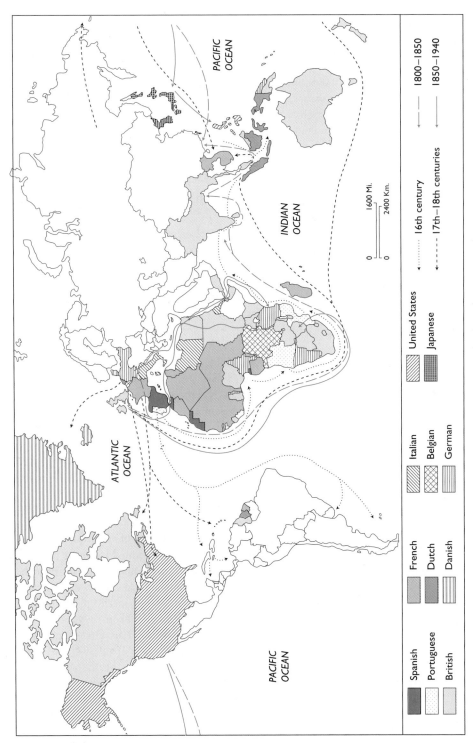

Map 1.3 *Missions and colonialism.*

Spanish	French	Italian
Portugese	Dutch	Belgian
British	Danish	German

	United States		16th century	1800–1850
	Japanese		17th–18th centuries	1850–1940

PACIFIC OCEAN

ATLANTIC OCEAN

PACIFIC OCEAN

INDIAN OCEAN

0   1600 Mi.
0   2400 Km.

The Power of Modern Myth: Karl Marx's View of History

Consistent with the myth of modernity, the German socialist Karl Marx saw history as progressively unfolding in three stages. He defined these stages in terms of a class theory of society that went from primitive communism (tribal societies) in which all were equal, through the rise of complex urban civilizations, which gave birth to societies ruled by bureaucracies, pitting privileged classes against the masses, to a final stage of history in which society would once more be communistic. In this last age all were again to be equal—for all complex, class-defined institutions would wither away, and people would live together in spontaneous harmony. As many who have studied Marx and his followers have suggested, this vision takes the biblical myth of history, culminating in the appearance of the messianic age, and recasts it in secular form as the coming to earth of a classless society in an earthly community.

Marx secularized the biblical myth of history by replacing the will of God as the directing force of history with what he maintained were "scientific" laws of social development that guide the progressive unfolding of history. Marx believed that capitalism depended on a large class of urban workers, who, once they were gathered together in the industrial cities of the modern world, would organize, creating an international workers union that would lead a worldwide revolution. This revolution would result in the replacement of capitalist societies based on hereditary wealth and privileges with a new classless society of freedom, equality, and social justice for all.

Socialism represents as an ambivalent rejection of a modern scientific world dominated by an economic system, capitalism, that seemed to make the rich richer and the poor poorer. Yet it claimed to be "modern," "secular," and "scientific." However, unlike capitalism, Marxism retained much of the religious and ethical power of biblical tradition with its emphasis on justice for the poor, the widow, the orphan, and the stranger as the final outcome of history.

While socialism provided a vehicle to protest the impact of modernity on human life, two world wars decisively undermined belief in inevitable progress toward greater scientific understanding, prosperity, and benevolent coexistence. World War I (1914–1918) and World War II (1939–1945) were the great wars of modern technology that shattered this myth. Science and technology, which had been viewed as the engines of progress, had become, as well, the means of unprecedented destruction. The utopian dream of technological progress ended as a nightmare in August 1945, when newly invented atomic bombs were dropped on Japan.

The use of atomic bombs brought World War II to an end, only to usher in a "cold war" between the Soviet Union and the United States. Throughout the second half of the twentieth century, an armed standoff between these two superpowers threatened to plunge the whole human race into a third and final war of thermonuclear annihilation. The makers of the modern myth of progress had failed to foresee that a technology that increases efficiency can be applied not only to the production of less expensive consumer goods but also to the invention and manufacture of weapons of mass destruction. Indeed, since World War II, progress in the means of destroying large numbers of humans has been staggering. It took the Nazis six years to kill 6 million Jews and others in their death camps. Today, the nuclear powers could destroy virtually the whole human race in a few days.

Finally, it is important to note that World War I and especially World War II not only called into question the "scientific age of progress" but also brought an end to the modern age of empires. The twentieth century saw the withdrawal of European powers from the Middle East, South Asia, Southeast Asia, East Asia, and Africa. European colonial powers left behind independent nation-states whose rulers were unelected. Many of these new political entities had arbitrarily drawn boundaries. Often, moreover, people were divided without regard to ethnic identity or religious communities, and the legacy of exploitative colonial practices was a series of underdeveloped local economies.

POSTMODERN TRENDS IN A POSTCOLONIAL WORLD

In the modern period the social authority of religion was undermined by the new scientific rationalists whose descriptions of reality, they believed, explained how the world "really is," in contrast to the fanciful myths of religions. The postmodern world begins with the further loss of innocence as many argued that not only religious knowledge but also scientific knowledge is relative in important ways. That is, science too is an imaginative interpretation of the world based on faith (faith in the intelligibility of the world) and does not offer the final truth about reality, either. Of course, many today dispute this understanding of science. Nevertheless, these arguments are similar to the arguments between premodern religious philosophers (defending religion) and the new secular scientists (challenging religion) at the beginning of the modern period. No matter who is right, the very existence of such disputes suggests that the postmodern situation is one in which unquestioning faith in science, which characterized the modern era, no longer exists.

From the perspective of postmodernists, all knowledge is relative, including religious and scientific knowledge. Postmodern trends seem to promote a radical cultural and ethical relativism. Some rejoice in this, arguing that it means the end of all the absolutes that have been used to justify violence by some against other people. Others are afraid that total relativism will lead to the end of civilization and the beginning of a new barbarism—that once we have relativized the absolute distinction between good and evil, we will plunge into an ethical void in which any atrocity can be justified.

Thus in the postmodern period scientific knowledge is on equal intellectual footing with religious knowledge: they are equally relative and equally subject to criticism by those who reject their main precepts. Therefore the position that scientific secularism is a source of public and certain knowledge while religious knowledge is mere private opinion no longer seems as valid as it once did. Consequently, the appearance of postmodern trends has been accompanied by a resurgence of religion in the public realm—a resurgence whose diverse forms are responses to both the threat and the promise of postmodernity.

In the new postmodern world and civilization, another stage in the history of religions has emerged, one in which the world religions encounter each other and undergo globalization. Until the modern period the great world religions had largely divided the globe between them with some modest overlap. But in the postmodern world, more and more, all the world's religions have members in every country or society. For example, we find Hindus, Buddhists, and Muslims in significant numbers in virtually all large American and European cities and increasingly in smaller ones. Anyone using the Internet can view the major temples, shrines, churches, mosques, or monasteries from around the world, and offer ritual prayers or make monetary offerings to them. This is globalization.

The Postmodern Situation: We Are All Heretics

In the premodern period, people, for the most part, acquired their religious identities because of where they were born. In the postmodern world, however, every individual is faced with what sociologist Peter Berger, calls "the heretical imperative."[2] Berger notes that *heretic* comes from an ancient Greek word that means "to choose." In our postmodern world every religious person becomes a heretic, that is, one who is not simply born into a given religion or identity but must choose it, even if it is only to choose to retain the identity offered by the circumstances of his or her birth.

In this world of "heretics," all the world's religions, each of which originated to provide a universal answer to the question of human identity, have been forced to take account of the others. They have come face to face with their own particularism in a world of diverse faiths. Until postmodern trends set in, other people's religions could be readily dismissed in a series of negative stereotypes. When people of diverse religions are neighbors, this option is both more difficult and more dangerous. To the degree that stereotyping and discrimination persist, they promote prejudice, conflict, and violence. The alternative is to develop a new understanding of the relation between world religions and global cultures—one that allows the peoples of the earth to follow their respective faith traditions yet also share their wisdom with each other in an atmosphere of mutual respect and understanding.

This alternative—to appreciate what we have in common as well as to acknowledge our distinctive differences—has been explored brilliantly by two of the great religious figures of the twentieth century, Mohandas K. Gandhi and Martin Luther King Jr. Each spiritual leader "passed over" from his native religion and culture to the religious world of the other and came back enriched by that second tradition without having abandoned his own. You are invited to embark on a similar journey through the world's religions today.

Discussion Questions

1 Define religion, myth, and ritual and explain the possible relations among them.

2 How do the authors understand the relationship between religion and morality?

3 In what way does religious language complicate the question of whether there is agreement or disagreement between religions on various issues? Describe in terms of the via analogia and the via negativa, giving examples of each.

4 Explain the four types of religious story and give an historical example of each.

5 Why did urbanization lead to the emergence of the great world religions? That is, what new urban problems did these religions address?

6 What is colonialism, and what is its significance for the religions and cultures in the modern period?

7 How are the terms "premodern," "modern," and "postmodern" being used in this text and how are they related to modern colonialism?

8 According to the authors, modernization privatizes religion, whereas in premodern and postmodern religious movements religion plays a public role in society but in different ways. Explain.

9 Explain Marxist socialism and tell why it was an attractive option to religious movements protesting modernity.

10 How might you justify the statement that both postmodernist and fundamentalist religious movements are examples of Peter Berger's "heretical imperative?"

Key Terms

metanarrative	postmodern	ritual
modern	premodern	via analogia
myth	religion	via negativa

Notes

1. Jean-François Lyotard, *The Postmodern Condition: A Report on Knowledge* (Minneapolis: University of Minnesota Press, 1984).

2. Peter Berger, *The Heretical Imperative* (New York: Doubleday, 1979), p. 60.

CHAPTER TWO

Primal Religions

Overview

At some point in the misty recesses of time, perhaps a hundred thousand years ago, *Homo sapiens* emerged from a 4-million-year process of hominid evolution to become the animal who speaks, makes tools, buries its dead, and thinks symbolically. Long before agriculture and urbanization, the first humans lived in hunter-gatherer societies. By studying their artifacts, as well as the small-scale societies that still subsist in this mode of life, we can imagine what their existence was like. We know they lived and ate well, yet without the material possessions we now consider to be essential. We know they made efforts to communicate with the spirits of their ancestors and with animals. We also think that they regularly sought assistance from these spirits through trance and altered states of consciousness, which may have been the origins of religion.

Just as the core meanings of modern words can be discovered by uncovering their root derivations, so can our appreciation of world religions today be enriched by understanding religion's origins in prehistory, the characteristics of "primal religions," and their existence in the world today.

Although the earliest humans used language, writing had not yet been invented. Consequently these societies had oral cultures in which everything that was known was known only because someone remembered it. And memories were made readily accessible because they were expressed in stories—stories of sacred ancestors, spirit beings, and heroes. These stories were not expressed in written texts but rather coursed through their veins and sinews, kept alive in song and dance.

Moreover, time and space were not cold abstractions but were reckoned according to ancestral myths and sacred experiences. Religion has its origins at sites at which people believe the powers that govern the universe first manifested themselves. Whether sacred groves, the banks of a river, or a mountain top, human beings experienced each such place of revelation as the "center of the world" (*axis mundi*). Indeed, in the primal religions, most everything is alive—the world itself is a collective of living entities. The trees, the mountains, the rivers, special stones, animals, and of course humans are said to have souls or spirits that give them life or "animate" them. Anthropologists use the term *animism* to describe a worldview in which conscious life is attributed to all entities, including those that lack the power of speech.

In simple subsistence societies, where human life is bound up with the recurring rhythms of nature, people live by the rising and the setting of the sun and moon, and by the seasons of the year. Time is circular, following the pattern of the celestial and natural world. The sun rises, climbs in an arc to its height at noon, then sets in the evening only to rise again the next morning. The moon also follows a regular pattern of waxing and waning. So, too, revolve the seasons from life to death, as from spring to summer, fall to winter and then spring and returning to new life again. In myth and ritual, through song and dance, and in contact with their sacred centers of revelation, primal peoples feel themselves to be part of the large rhythms of life. There is flow and equilibrium in the environment, and finding the good life has meant learning to live with the spirits that share their world, discerning the spirits' motivations and intentions, their love and anger. Primal religions convey the truth that people, like the land, the sea, and the forests, undergo an eternal process of birth, death, and rebirth.

Each of the thousands of primal peoples have (or had) a unique *cosmogony*, or account of the world's origins and its essential powers. Because in most hunter-gatherer cosmogonies the group was a part of the everlasting cycle of nature's rhythms, it never died. Like nature, the group was eternal. Everything in primal group life reinforced a collective sense of common identity: all shared the same occupations (hunting and gathering, simple agriculture), the same myths and rituals; and all without exception were part of the group itself. As a result, a person's identity was not tied primarily to unique and

Issues of Terminology and Imagination: "Primitive," "Tribal," "Primal"

Writers who wish to refer to the peoples living in simple subsistence societies, both modern and prehistoric—face a problem of nomenclature. The term "primitive" was once popular, but it falsely suggests a lack of cultural development or factual understanding, since in fact many native peoples have complex languages and mythologies. In choosing the term "primal religions," we are implying that the social and religious lives of a given people are primary. This, in turn, implies that the first mode of religious life known in the record of human history is inextricably bound to social life. In making this choice, we are not equating modern hunter-gatherers with humans living in this mode of life 50,000 years ago or suggesting that these contemporary groups are "living fossils," since none today live isolated from the developed world and all have distinct histories. Our term "simple subsistence peoples" designates small-scale societies that survive by hunting-gathering or simple agricultural methods. The oft-used terms "tribe" and "tribal" refer to a specific type of social organization in which social relations are ordered by kinship. Such kinship relationships are found both in hunter-gatherer and agricultural-urban societies.

transitory individual experiences but deeply embedded in the collective, eternal identity of the group. One lives in the group, to be sure. More importantly, however, the group lives in the individual, even after his or her own death.

This collective worldview is radically different from the individualism that dominates Euro-American cultures today. In the following chapters on the world's great religions, we will show how each in its own way pushed humanity out of the collective community mind-set and toward greater individualism. An understanding the world religions will be deepened by comprehending the "otherness" of the primal religions. An understanding of this "otherness" will also make clear how the world religions have drawn upon some of the basic features of the primal religions, simultaneously reinterpreting and transposing them as the details of human existence have changed.

THE MODERN HUMAN AS *HOMO RELIGIOSUS*

Although animals do not possess religion, our human nature endows us with certain qualities that underlie the most basic expressions of religion. These include a propensity for repetitive behaviors (ritual), a virtually unique cognitive ability to create meaning, the enhancement of survival by identification with land or territory (sacred space), and a strong mother–offspring bond (devotion).

Archaeologists have ascertained that about 30,000 years ago humans just as intelligent as we now are established themselves across Eurasia. They wove cloth for clothes, used finely wrought fish hooks, constructed boats that crossed large bodies of water, and were experts in subsistence wherever they lived, from the tropics up to the edge of the Ice Age glaciers. The record of human life indicates that in every society over the last 100,000 years, a progressive complexity in the mastery of tools was accompanied by the development of language ability and the unmistakable presence of religion.

The universality of religion in human societies even led Mircea Eliade, the well-known scholar of comparative religions, to call our species *Homo religiosus*, or "religious humanity." In fact, now as well as from the earliest days of the modern species, religion has been at the very center of human culture. Thus, we can say that religion was an integral, even essential part of humanity's recent evolutionary path, from supporting the success of small hunter-gatherer groups to the domestication of plants and animals, and on to the rise of cities, empires, and superpowers. We now turn to the beginning of this extraordinary story.

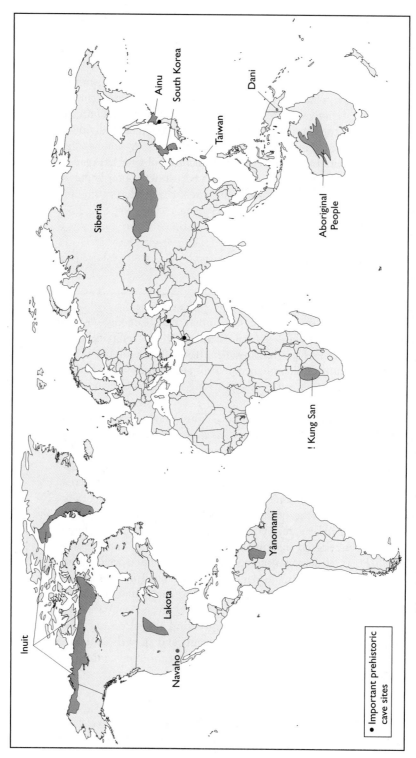

Map 2.1 Locations of some of the prehistoric and ethnographic cultural groups discussed in this book.

HUNTER-GATHERERS AND THE PREHISTORIC ORIGINS OF RELIGION

For 99 percent of human history, our bodies and brains developed when our species lived as nomadic hunter-gatherers. Although our world has been transformed in so thoroughgoing a manner that few people anywhere on the planet live in this mode now, our basic physiology, biology, and cognitive capacity remain the same as they were 30,000 years ago.

The earliest *Homo sapiens* were much like the people we refer to today as belonging to primal or "simple subsistence" societies. Small (usually fewer than fifty) groups of related individuals "lived off the land and ocean," moving with the seasons to find wild fruits and vegetables and to be close to the animals or fish they hunted. Close-knit bonds within these living groups were essential to everyone's survival, with all individuals sharing the food and relying on the others for protection. Also typical was a division of labor, with men predominantly the hunters and women the gatherers. Scholars have used data from anthropological studies of modern hunter-gatherer groups to reconstruct the usually good lives of early *Homo sapiens* as follows:

> Life lived by our prehistoric ancestors was not characterized by constant deprivation . . . with both men and women contributing substantially to the family, the economy, and the social world. . . . Life was rich in human warmth and aesthetic experience and offered an enviable balance of work and love, ritual and play.[1]

The !Kung San of southern Africa, one of the most studied, late-surviving hunter-gatherer groups, are typical. A short, lean, muscular nomadic people, the !Kung utilize simple tools and build temporary houses. An intricate knowledge of their environment is expressed in a language that recognizes 500 species of plants and animals, yielding a diet that consists of 105 different foods. Utter mastery of an environment shared with large predators is typical of such groups. Once scholars gained firsthand knowledge of hunter-gatherers like the !Kung, they began to appreciate the highly skilled nature of primal cultural life, the clear rationality of the people, and the very sophisticated languages and cultures that had evolved among them. This new understanding disproved the theories of leading nineteenth-century social scientists, who had speculated that religion had its origins in the fear and ignorance of humans facing a threatening and incomprehensible world.

The human capacity for language to create and build culture was almost certainly present by 100,000 BCE among the Neanderthals and those who succeeded them, the *Homo sapiens*. By 30,000 BCE, humans were performing ceremonial burials, painting and carving art, keeping rudimentary records on bone and stone plaques, and crafting elaborate personal adornments.

From this time onward, the record shows humans constantly adapting and refining their material world, and it is by this time that humans acquired the capacity to think symbolically, almost certainly as a result of their development of more complex languages. We who cannot conceive of complex thought without the medium of language can easily imagine the advantages (in hunting, warfare, etc.) that a leap ahead in linguistic capacity must have given to those early humans. Since as we saw in the first chapter, religion is so much centered on humans establishing and expressing life's ultimate truths, scientists have posited a breakthrough in cognitive ability that changed the destiny of our species forever: "categorizing and naming objects and sensations in the outer and inner worlds, and making associations between resulting mental symbols . . . for only once we create such symbols can we recombine them and ask such questions as 'What if . . .?'."[2] The simultaneous emergence of modern humans and religion indicates that many "what if" questions were aimed at explaining the unseen powers of life, the inner world of personhood, and the ultimate mystery, that of death. Artifacts of prehistoric religion have been found that reflect consideration of each of these realms.

"Venus figure" from northern Europe, one of many similar icons found that indicate early human concerns with fertility.

Fertility

One striking kind of object found across Eurasia in late prehistory is what scientists have called "Venus figurines," small stone sculptures of females with large breasts and hips, often with their genitalia emphasized. To understand these objects, we must enter into the reality of prehistoric human life. Small tribes were doubtless greatly concerned with ensuring the regular birth of healthy children to keep their own group numerous enough for success in subsistence, hunting, and warfare. Further, since at that time all pregnancies and all childbirths were high-risk events, and since it was realized that mothers' bountiful lactation helped ensure the survival of children, it is likely that the figurines are related to concerns about birth and the survival of children in small community groups. Some scholars therefore interpret the Venus figurines as icons representing a protecting, nurturing "mother goddess." They have speculated that the makers of these objects recognized and revered a special female power that lay behind the mystery of conception and birth; they focused on the miracle of females producing beings from their own bodies and celebrated the ability of women to perpetuate human life.

Added to this evidence of veneration of a mother goddess is another strong archaeological find: after 15,000 BCE the dead were uniformly buried in mounds or graves in the fetal position, suggesting that people now perceived the earth as a womb from which some sort of resurrection was expected. Some have gone further, to conclude that the so-called Venus icons indicate the predominance of hunter-gatherer groups that were dominated by women, who alone could bring new life and hence were expected to lead a society in harmony with nature. This presumed matriarchal period, in which women had superior status, is said to have ended with the expansion of groups dominated by aggressive warrior males (such as the

Indo-Europeans), who adopted settled agriculture and ruled the new, patriarchal, societies. With little more than figurines and burial practices as evidence, it is difficult to prove or confirm these speculations, or to declare their universality.

Prehistoric Hunters and the Secret of the Cave Ritual

In the famous cave paintings of Eurasia, hunted animals such as bison, bear, and deer are rendered with grace and subtlety in a variety of styles. Humans are also shown, some in poses that are still puzzling, challenging us to understand who created the images and the meaning of their context.

Again, we must use our imagination to understand the context and to surmise the place of religion. Caves could be dangerous places, and groups of individuals taking the trouble to go several hundred yards under the earth, traversing narrow, damp passageways, seem to engage in no ordinary task. Archaeologists surmise that these sites were related to the hunts undertaken by bands of able-bodied men. Hunter-gatherers needed animals for their survival. They hunted to secure the meat essential for their diet, the skins for clothing, and the bones and sinew used for tools and adornment. Some painted cave scenes also indicate that the prehistoric hunt was often dangerous: wild bison, cave bears, and large cats are shown inflicting lethal injuries on humans.

The hunt required group coordination for success, since tracking, stalking, encircling, and using spears or stones to kill at close range could not be achieved without coordinated action, individual bravery, and strong group loyalty. A hunting expedition could fail if a single member broke ranks and failed at his station, endangering not only himself and others in the group, but the entire tribe, which was depending on the hunters. Having documented similar rites among modern hunting tribes, scholars view the prehistoric caves as ritual theaters for initiating adolescent boys into the ranks of hunters, sites of instruction in hunting lore, killing practices, and ritual. Perhaps it was to these remote sites that elders brought frightened initiates and dramatically staged rituals that revealed the prey the men pursued and established the youths' new identity as adult hunters. Through hunting ritual, young men bonded with the other adult males with whom they would risk their lives.

Such practices in the service of human survival formed the basis of the first religions according to the definitions set forth in Chapter One: they helped *bind* a group critical to the society's success, and they reinforced the human need to *be careful* with regard to the unseen powers surrounding them. The second point is especially important if we assume that the elders taught that each animal, like every human being, has an inner spirit or soul, one that must be respected in death and returned to the world, or sent on its way to the afterlife. We now turn to this topic.

Prehistoric cave art: the first shaman. Over fifty examples of animal–human figures like this one suggest that shamanism had its origins in the prehistoric era.

ANIMISM AND AFTERLIFE

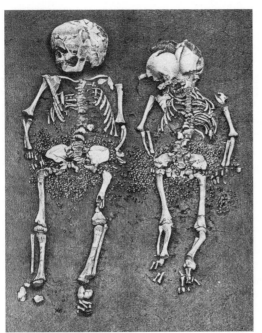

Burial of children from 20,000 BCE: with the remains are perforated shells and remnants of decorated clothing.

The presence of a human belief in some sort of afterlife emerges from the earliest archaeological records of ceremonial burials. In hundreds of excavations, burial clearly was done to preserve the body and provide it with decoration (colors, jewelry, flowers, animal skulls or antlers), foods (meat, grain), and tools (spears, sticks). These arrangements suggest that early humans felt that there was a nonmaterial component, an essence that "lived on" after the physical body had perished and decayed. Thus the disposal of human corpses is clearly more than merely functional. In the primal staging of which we have evidence, death seems to be likened to sleep, not mere dissolution, and the function of burial seems to be to open a gateway to an afterlife.

We have noted that the belief that not only living beings but inanimate objects possess a special life force is called *animism*. An early and still widely popular articulation of animism was made in 1871 by E.B. Tylor [1831–1917], who argued that religion originated in the universal human perception that there is an invisible and intangible soul or spirit inside our visible, tangible bodies. He argued that in all "primitive societies," this animism shaped similar belief systems that imagined humans sharing a spiritual bond with each other, and with animals, plants, and the dead.

More recent studies of primal religions focus less on belief in vaguely defined "spirits" and more on the phenomenon of how primal peoples perceive and establish relations with a range of others, human and nonhuman, through bodily experience. For primal societies, being religious is not about credal texts that need interpreting; instead, people experience an embodied engagement with the world, one in which stones, animals, trees, and the dead may "speak" through cultivated human mediation and in which emotions, memory, direct experiences, and altered states of consciousness play a part.

In primal religions, people establish a very physical human relationship with the world, one in which the ecosystem is deeply sensed as alive, as fertile, and in the flow of a larger ordered cosmos. This human assertion of practical and integral relatedness to the natural world of hunted animals, landforms, and plants of the home environment, is realized through the engagement of all the bodily senses and emotions. Similarly, the senses have a role in assuring the passage of time through the seasons and (as we shall see) keeping order through the ecstatic supernatural journeys of the shaman. We might say that primal religions are sung, danced, fasted, and tranced by the collective group experience.

All known primal societies have imagined a universe populated by a multitude of spirits that interact with the people in life and in the afterlife. In the primal religions, accordingly, these spirit beings (or souls) are the ultimate reality and thus a central object of concern. In most known animist belief systems, ancestors are in some way still connected with the living. Tylor argued that it would have been natural for this belief to have arisen independently among human groups because the need for sleep is universal. Thus the dreams or visions of people everywhere would have supported the idea that the dead "return" in nonmaterial form. As we will see, this belief also could be supported by spirit mediums who served as communicators with the dead, supposedly empowered to enable the departed soul to speak to the living "from the other side." Although many today do not take the content of dreams or trance state pronouncements as seriously as facts derived from "normal waking reality," for most humans before the modern era, dreams and visions were accepted as representing reality.

In many primal societies, death is not an ultimate, irrevocable end, nor does it imply a disconnection between the living and the dead. On the contrary, death is an elevation of one's status to that of sacred ancestor. Ancestors, in turn, are venerated as spirits who can help the living by guiding them to the hunting grounds and bringing prey animals their way, or by invigorating the wild foods or cultivated crops. By the same token, misfortune in a community may be the fault of the living, who have incited the ancestors' anger and punishment by breaking a moral law or neglecting a ritual. In such situations, harmony between the living, the dead, and all of nature needs to be restored.

Most primal peoples view ancestral spirits as ambivalent forces and as custodians of the traditions. Thus the spirits may harm those who flout custom and bless those who are faithful to it. Some scholars following Tylor believe that earliest religion may have evolved from the animist view of the world, and efforts to manage the activities of supernatural spirit-beings. Recent archaeological evidence suggests that the most elaborate burials in late prehistory were conducted to protect the living from the power of malevolent souls. And perhaps powerful ancestral spirits became the world's first gods.

Among the Dani, a simple agricultural group in highland New Guinea, belief in the soul surviving into an afterlife profoundly shapes the ways of the living. In their death rituals, the Dani try to direct the soul of a person who has just died to a distant ghost hamlet. Yet many ghosts are thought to return to cause problems, especially if their last rites were not done properly or their death is not avenged in timely fashion. Thus Dani elders take great care performing funerals, and they erect small guest houses in each hamlet to accommodate, and pacify, ghost visitors.

Further, rival Dani villages engage continuously in lethal warfare, whose main purpose is for the men to satisfy a newly departed kinsman's spirit by killing someone on the enemy's side. The Dani moral code includes the precept of "a life for a life." Since, moreover, losing a kinsman inevitably weakens the collective community, avenging the loss of the deceased is the only means to restore the vitality of the survivors' souls. In fact, Dani kinship and food production is organized around supplying the feasts that must be held to mark deaths and celebrate revenge killings. Appeasing ancestral ghosts is always in mind.

Some primal peoples, in prehistory and in a few surviving modern groups, have believed that they needed to eat the flesh of the dead to effectively control the threat and power of their disembodied souls. Some held that the spirit of the dead could be freed and "recycled" back into life only if the corpse was consumed by the living; others feasted on slain enemy warriors to capture for themselves the powers of the souls of the departed. It is an uncomfortable but certain fact that *cannibalism* is a part of the human inheritance from our hominid ancestors. Religious beliefs have sustained what was a widespread primordial practice.

In primal societies, people use a group symbol, or *totem*, to establish primal identities, promote collective solidarity, and regulate their relations with outsiders. A totem is an animal, reptile, insect, or plant that is emblematic of the community and is treated as sacred. The relationship between totems and humans reveals a special circle of kinship and connection between humans and the rest of nature.

Totemism is still found among Native Americans and the various Aboriginal groups of Australia. To understand this belief system, we can take an example from the latter: members of the Aboriginal kangaroo clan believe that their origins occurred in the "Dreamtime," when the world as we know it was being created. Their myths inform them that their clan consists of the descendants of their totemic progenitor, the first kangaroo, who created them from her own body and essence, established their existence as humans, then led them to their current home territory. Accordingly, the group members decorate their bodies with kangaroo drawings, and before children are considered to be adults, they must learn the distinctive dances and songs recounting the group's totemic story. Elder men pass down these secrets to the young men and are most protective of the sacred symbols, the polished wood or stone *churinga* that symbolize the totem and are inscribed with the most sacred maps or tales of the founder and other heroes. The group is also protective of its own "songlines," the myths that are sung to trace in detail the progenitor's trail of creation over the land, an oral record giving the group claims to shared identity and territory.

Harming or eating a kangaroo is almost always forbidden, or *taboo*, to members of the kangaroo clan. The totemic kangaroo spirit that dwells in the home territory is thought to be alive and protective of the group. Elders pray to and invoke it for healing and guidance. Women of the kangaroo clan who want to become pregnant visit the places where the totemic spirit resides, for they believe that conception cannot occur without exposure to the totem's life force.

There is also a unique and regularly performed ritual that unifies the totemic group. But in addition to singing and acting out their myth of origins, all

Aboriginal men from Arnhemland, Australia, painting their bodies to show their identification with a totemic ancestor.

Awakening the Spirits: A Bullroarer

Bullroarers are powerful ritual tools that convey the totemic bond between living and dead members of an aboriginal (not necessarily Australian) group. A bullroarer has a hole at one end, and when the device is swung around on a string, air passes through, resulting in a booming-whirring sound. The sound waves vibrate at a frequency that affects the human viscera, evoking a strange feeling, one that conveys the presence of the totemic spirit.

A bullroarer painted with a serpent motif. Swinging the roarer produces a deep, piercing sound that elicits a feeling of numinosity in ritual participants.

the "kangaroos" in the group, on this one annual occasion, gather to renew their primordial identity and "become one flesh" again. How? By hunting down a kangaroo and ingesting its flesh. These rites are performed to increase the totemic species and give spiritual strength to individuals in the group. Here, again, in the animist belief system, humans and nature form a spiritual totality: although the design of the world was fixed once and for all in the Dreamtime, it is the task of humans, through their totemic rites, to maintain and renew this creation.

The French sociologist Émile Durkheim argued that totemism points to a key feature in all religious life. It is the sacred totem (here the kangaroo) that gives the group a singular focus and in so doing really stands for the group itself. For Durkheim, religion is at root a cultural means by which members of a society, however small or large, hold their own group's identity, survival, and worth as sacred. In other words, through their collective focus on a common symbol, and to explain the unseen but deeply felt inward-moving force of their own social group, humans instituted religion. Durkheim's influential theory is that whatever else has come to define religious beliefs across the world's human groups, religion's power to bind us together keeps it central in human life.

THE SHAMAN

Among the many fascinating scenes shown in prehistoric cave art are over fifty images of humans that suggest the depiction of no ordinary person. There is a bison hovering over a man, with a pole surmounted by a bird; there is a human seeming to morph into a composite animal that walks hidden among a large herd of deer. These ancient icons may be the first recorded depictions of the shaman, an individual with special powers, whose roles, even 30,000 years ago, may have included healing the souls and bodies of others, dealing with death, and venturing into the realm of the dead. The !Kung healers of today embellish walls with totemic paintings, and records of similar practices have been found in ancient caves in Europe and Asia. We imagine that the shamans shown on these prehistoric walls are discerning the movements of animal herds, guiding the hunters to success, and recalling errant souls of the living.

What happens if the group's band of skilled hunters come home empty-handed after a month? How to respond when debilitating illness marked by fever, chills, and physical weakness afflicts a growing number of villagers? Who can halt or reverse the series of misfortunes befalling a family that has let its ancestral shrine fall into ruins? Only a shaman, referred to variously as "medicine man," "folk healer," "spirit medium," "witch doctor," "mystic," and so on. These terms taken together designate some of the traits attributed to shamans. These include the ability to heal (both literally and metaphorically), as well as to injure or kill enemies. Shamans are ritual specialists, intermediaries who attempt to connect this world to another. By these activities, the shaman knits together the community in the face of the chaos of disease, death, and discord.

Scholars believe that prehistoric hunting group initiation ceremonies were held in undergound sanctuaries decorated with carefully rendered images of animals like this early masterpiece of cave art.

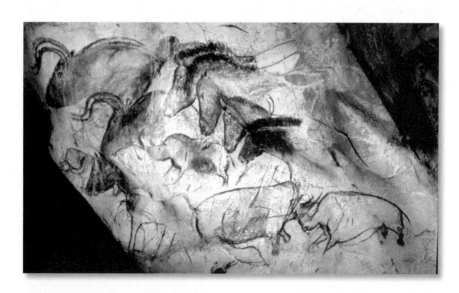

Shamans Across the World

The shaman remains the key religious specialist in many societies today. The term "shaman" (pronounced "SHAY-man" or "shah-MAN") comes from the Evenk, a group of hunters and reindeer herders in Siberia. The term was adopted for all similar practitioners, however, because early scholars thought that the Siberian shaman tradition had spread across Eurasia, and into the Americas, a theory that is disputed today.

Four religious figures are central to an understanding of the world's religions: the shaman, the prophet, the sage, and the priest. The first is our concern in this chapter, for the shaman is still found among peoples on every inhabited continent and in the earliest records of our direct forebears.

Though differing in details of clothing and techniques, shamans are found across the world today: left, a Yanomami shaman in the Amazon; center, a Korean shaman in Seoul; right, a Navajo shaman in North America.

Some shamans teach that the daily, ordinary world is not all there is, for a deeper spiritual order enfolds the known world. In the primal traditions, the living and the dead, the community and its sacred ancestors, form one community. Binding the community together is the shaman, who uses his body and soul as a bridge to connect the two worlds. If harmony in a primal community has been shattered, only the shaman, who is able to visit both worlds and communicate the needs of one to the other, can restore balance.

Shamans have been found in over a thousand societies, and their practices vary accordingly. A commonly held conception in the primal religions is that sickness can be due to the loss of an individual's soul, by accident or by theft. In some cultures, people believe that illness can be induced by an enemy inserting a piece of bone or an insect into a victim's body. The common characteristic of the shaman's intervention is that he or she enters an *altered state of consciousness* or *trance*, to communicate with unseen spirits, acquire awareness of the inner reality of a situation, and intervene on behalf of the afflicted party.

The trance state can be reached by drumming and singing alone, but in global perspective the agents for altering consciousness are very numerous. Fasting is common, but practices may also involve the inhaling of incense, snuffs, or smoke from psychoactive herbs, or the ingesting of mushrooms or plant concoctions. The shaman's trance may be marked by loud breathing, protruding eyes, insensitivity to heat, cold, and pain, convulsions, swooning, or trembling. In many traditions, the shaman's soul is thought to be able to leave the physical body, free to fly to the heavens, beneath the earth, or under the sea. On these "spirit flights" or "soul journeys," shamans attempt to locate another person's soul, perhaps because it has wandered off in this world or passed on into the afterlife and become lost. A common belief is that the dead need a shaman's assistance to reach the afterlife dwelling place of the clan's ancestors.

Shamans through initiation find connection with a protective, or *tutelary, spirit.* This supernatural being is a god or ancestral spirit whose help is required to perform heroic soul journeys, negotiate with evil spirits, compel a soul to return, or increase the individual's healing power. In many tribes, shamans have human helpers who watch over their unconscious bodies during trance states.

The shamanic world is one in which spirits coexist with humans in a layered cosmos, with humans occupying the earth between an upper and a lower world. The spirits reside in physical objects and actual places, and are particularly accessible to humans in special locations. As we saw in Chapter One, each culture regards these locations as being connected to the "center of the world" (*axis mundi*). Most commonly, such sites are actual or symbolic sacred mountains or sacred trees, revered as places of original revelations, intensely alive with spiritual power, or *numinous* presence. Several examples show how shamanic traditions from around the world today share common traits.

!Kung Healers

The !Kung San of southern Africa believe that the dead go to an afterlife, a "next world," populated by ancestors, that is similar to this world and is linked closely to the living. Souls that miss the living return to earth as ghosts and try to sicken friends and family members in an effort to hasten their arrival in the next world. The most accomplished !Kung shamans (*n/um kxausi*) have the ability to enter into a trance during night-long dances, in which everyone joins in ceremonies of rhythmic drumming and singing around a fire. With this group support and social purpose, anthropologists suggest, the !Kung shamans activate a natural force within their bodies, the *n/um,* a power that "boils" in and moves up the spine. The body shakes and sweats, and inhalations grow forced and deeper as the shaman slips into a trance state. Thus empowered, the shaman begins to touch the heads of others to transfer into them the healing force of the boiling *n/um.* Expert healers can also identify and suck out poisons from the bodies of the sick; some may massage the patient with a mixture of the shaman's own sweat and blood. Healers who perceive the ghosts of troublesome ancestors watching the dance outside the community circle may hurl stones at the uninvited spectators, or at deities in the shadows who are identified as causing difficulties. The most effective !Kung shamans are honored, but they are otherwise typical members of the tribe; most are men.

A !Kung healing ceremony. The trancing and healing performed by !Kung shamans depends on the community's participating in drumming, singing, and dancing.

CASE STUDY

A Siberian Shaman's Initiation: Death, Dismemberment, and Resurrection

(An account of the near-death, out-of-body initiation experience of a shaman)

Sick with smallpox, a future shaman remained unconscious for three days and so nearly dead that on the third day he was almost buried. His initiation took place during this time. He remembered having been carried into the middle of a sea. There he heard his Sickness (that is, smallpox) speak, saying to him: "From the Lords of the Water you will receive the gift of shamanizing. Your name as a shaman will be *Huottarie* (Diver)." The candidate came out and climbed a mountain. There he met a naked woman and began to suckle at her breast. The woman, the Lady of the Water, said to him: "You are my child; that is why I let you suckle at my breast. You will meet many hardships and be greatly wearied." The husband of the Lady of the Water, the Lord of the Underworld, then gave him two guides, an ermine and a mouse, to lead him. When they came to a high place, the guides showed him seven tents with torn roofs. He entered the first and there found the inhabitants of the underworld and the men of

the Great Sickness. These men tore out his heart and threw it into a pot. In other tents he met the Lord of Madness and the Lords of all the nervous disorders, as well as the evil shamans. Thus he learned of the various diseases that torment mankind.

Still preceded by his guides the candidate then came to the Land of the Shamanesses, who strengthened his throat and his voice. He was then carried to the shores of the Nine Seas. In the middle of one of them was an island, and in the middle of the island a young birch tree rose to the sky. It was the Tree of the Lord of the Earth. Beside it grew nine herbs, the ancestors of all the plants on earth. The tree was surrounded by seas, and in each of these swam a species of bird with its young. . . . After visiting the seas, the candidate raised his head and, in the top of the tree, heard voices: "It has been decided that you shall have a drum (that is, the body of a drum) from the branches of this tree." He began to fly with the birds of the seas. As he left the shore, the Lord of

The most skilled !Kung shamans enter into the deep trance state (*kia*) so that their souls can leave the body and journey to the "next world," to confirm the fate of the dead, investigate causes of sickness, or convey messages between the dead and living. The spirit flight is a practice attributed to shamans in all primal societies, past and present.

The shaman's role is universally regarded as mortally dangerous. The !Kung call entering trance "being half-dead" and with great care guard a shaman's physical body while the healer's soul is believed to be journeying to another world. Like many primal peoples, the !Kung are also careful not to startle sleeping individuals, for fear that souls wandering during sleep will not have time to return to a person who has been awakened suddenly.

the Tree called to him: "My branch has just fallen; take it and make a drum of it that will serve you all your life." . . . Clasping the branch, the candidate was ready to resume his flight when again he heard a human voice, this time revealing to him the medicinal virtues of the seven plants and giving him certain instructions concerning the art of shamanizing.

Then his two guides, the ermine and the mouse, led him to a high rounded mountain. He saw an opening before him and entered a bright cave, covered with mirrors, in the middle of which there was something like a fire. One gave him a hair, which was to be useful to him when he shamanized for reindeer. The second woman, too, gave him a hair. When he shamanizes he mentally turns toward the cave.

Then the candidate came to a desert and saw a distant mountain. After three days' travel he reached it, entered an opening, and came upon a naked man working a bellows. On the fire was a caldron "as big as half the earth." The naked man saw him and caught him with a huge pair of tongs. The novice had time to think, "I am dead!" The man cut off his head, chopped his body into bits, and put everything in the caldron. There he boiled his body for three years. The blacksmith then fished the candidate's bones out of a river, in which they were floating, put them together and covered them with flesh again. . . . He forged his head and . . . changed his eyes; and that is why, when he shamanizes, he does not see with his bodily eyes but with these mystical eyes. He pierced his ears, making him able to understand the language of plants. The candidate found himself on the summit of a mountain, and finally he woke in the yurt, among his family. Now he can sing and shamanize indefinitely, without ever growing tired.

Source: Mircea Eliade, *Shamanism: Archaic Techniques of Ecstasy* (Princeton, NJ: Princeton University Press, 1964), pp. 38–42.

Men and women who become shamans in the !Kung or other cultures must train through long apprenticeships. But in most groups it is common for shamans to feel that they were chosen for the role by a tutelary spirit, often in spite of their own resistance. In many societies, the novice shaman must prove his ability by surviving an initiation ordeal that entails going into trance, receiving the grace of a tutelary spirit, and providing evidence of superhuman powers. Many shamans feel that they wear out their bodies by repeatedly undergoing near-death experiences in the course of soul journeys, or the ingestion of spirit-infused herbs.

Sioux Vision Quests

Among the Lakota Sioux of North America, young men go to a sacred wilderness region on a "vision quest" where they seek a personal protector spirit. After preparatory training, the apprentices fast and purify themselves in a sweat lodge. Then each one ventures out alone into the wilderness. The Sioux believe, as do the !Kung, that every human being has the potential for supernatural connection and that all should be encouraged to develop this ability. Those contacted by strong spirit allies and have vivid visions of the ancestors may go on to become shamans after further training with an elder practitioner. As the Sioux shaman Lame Deer recalled his experience, "All of a sudden I heard the cry of an eagle, loud and above the voices of many other birds. It seemed to say, 'We have been waiting for you. We knew you would come. . . .³ Apprentices learn the techniques of trance, the myths of the tribe, the location of "power places" in the landscape, and other healing arts that involve the use of medicines.

In many primal traditions, the shaman encounters evil spirits that must be tricked, seduced, or killed to complete the healing task. Shamans are never the same after initiation; many receive a new name, a new identity, and in the myths they even obtain a new body. Becoming a shaman is often described as a death-and-rebirth experience.

Shamans and the Bear Sacrifice

In many primal religions, the shaman serves as a medium who brings the spirits down to earth for "ritual negotiations." An example of this practice is the bear sacrifice, once common across the upper Pacific Rim and the circumpolar region from northern Japan to North America. Shamans carefully manage such sacrificial rituals, offering gifts from humans in exchange for an animal's life. A common belief in hunter-gatherer societies is that animals are actually spirits in disguise, who assume animal bodies to interact with humans. This is perhaps the earliest example of the phenomenon of incarnation, the embodiment in earthly form of a spirit or god.

Among the Ainu people on Hokkaido Island in northern Japan, spirits that incarnate themselves as animals are called *kamui.* They dwell in an "other world" mostly, but can contact humans by coming to earth and assuming life in a bear's body. The Ainu conception is that humans and *kamui* are of equal status. Although the latter (when unencumbered by a body) can fly and have magical powers, only humans can give them what they really need and want: precious wine and *inau,* the earth's fragrant willow sticks. In the Ainu understanding the spirits don animal "clothes" to "trade," for they can get *inau* and wine, only if ritually hunted and dispatched in exchange for their own fur and meat.

The Ainu shaman performs special rituals to attract a spirit in its bear incarnation. A young animal, knowing that an exchange has been requested, and consenting to it if humans have kept up their part in earlier exchanges,

A bear raised from infancy is exercised in preparation for a community sacrifice by Ainu tribesmen in northern Japan.

leaves trail signs that allows hunters to track and capture it. Villages then raise the specially chosen animal until it becomes fully grown. Afterwards, the shaman addresses the bear respectfully, makes the proper offerings, performs a ritual execution, and releases the *kamui* spirit to return to the other world, happy with its gifts. The Ainu believe that if the sacred conventions of the exchange are duly observed, the *kamui* just released and other spirts will continue to assume animal form. Thus the shaman ensures that the people will have a continuous supply of meat and shelter.

Shamans Who "Repair the World"

Just as a shaman's expertise is credited with allowing the cycle of life to proceed without end, he alone can intervene effectively when trouble intrudes, as it inevitably does. The practices of the Inuit (who dwell in the polar region of Alaska) illustrate the shaman's role in "repairing the world." The Inuit believe that the great goddess Takanakapsaluk, Mistress of Sea Animals, lives on the ocean floor and releases the whales, seals, fish, and other marine creatures that humans may kill for their subsistence. But when the human community spoils any ritual or breaks a moral taboo, the Inuit believe that the goddess's hair "becomes soiled" and that she burns in anger, holding back all creatures in her domain. Takanakapsaluk can be mollified only if the shaman, in a trance, makes a soul journey to the bottom of the ocean to "wash the hair of the goddess" with flattery and apologies. Inuit legend has it that polar bear spirits often aid in the shaman's perilous journey.

The Yanomami of the Amazon rain forest also illustrate the role of shaman as medium who repairs community life by bringing spirits down to earth. Village leader, curer, and defender against evil spirits, the village shaman locates and returns the disoriented souls of the sick and the dying. If others have acted to weaken or steal someone's soul, the shaman can identify both the

A Séance: Shaman Combs the Hair of the Goddess on the Ocean Floor

When there is an incurable sickness or a famine, or after an unsuccessful hunt, the Inuit shaman is employed to descend to the seafloor. He sits behind a curtain and says again and again, "The way is made ready for me!" after which the audience responds, "Let it be so." Finally from behind the curtain, the shaman cries, "Halala-he-he-he halala-he-he!" then he drops down a tube, which is believed to lead straight to the bottom of the sea. The shaman's voice can be heard receding further in the depths, and finally it disappears. During the shaman's absence, the audience sits in the darkened house and can hear the faint sighing and groaning of the dead. As soon as the shaman reaches the seabed, he has to dodge three deadly stones which churn around and hardly leave room to pass. He also has to get past the father of the goddess, Takanakapsaluk and a fierce guard dog. Approaching the goddess, the shaman finds her angry, hair uncombed, filthy, and hanging over her eyes. The creatures of the ocean sit in a pool beside her. The shaman gently turns the goddess toward the animals and a nearby lamp, combing and washing her hair. He then asks why the animals are not coming and she replies that they are being withheld because the people have eaten forbidden boiled meat and because the women have kept their miscarriages secret, failing to purify their homes afterward. Mollified by praises and promises to make amends, Takanakapsaluk releases the animals and they are swept back in to the ocean. The shaman's return is marked by a distant, then louder call of "Plu-a-he-he!" as he finally shakes in his place, gasping for breath. After a silence, he says, "Words will arise," and then the audience members begin to confess their misdeeds. By the end of the séance, there is a mood of optimism.

Source: Summarized from Piers Vitebsky, *The Shaman* (New York: Macmillan, 1995), p. 125.

misdeed and the perpetrators. To be initiated as a shaman and to achieve such abilities, an individual must memorize chants, drum rhythms, and struts, and then attract the support of his ancestral spirits. He must also master the use of the hallucinogenic snuff called *ebene,* made from psychoactive plants that a teacher repeatedly blows into the student's nostrils as part of his training. This powerful substance is thought to be a spirit ally that is essential for opening the Yanomami shaman's body to see and contact the world's spirits.

The Yanomami shaman has the power to conduct the spirits into the human world. The spirits can then be induced to enter the shaman's body and respond to questions about matters of concern, small or great. At times and without invitation, the shaman's mouth may speak the spirit's messages about group origins, life's meaning, or hidden facts behind recent events.

The reliance on psychoactive substances to assist the shaman to achieve altered states of consciousness, as found among the Yanomami, is not the standard practice across the world. Drug-induced trances are limited mostly to the Americas, where the use of the cactus peyote, the vine extract ayahuasca, and plants such as jimson and datura have long been in the shaman's medicine bag. What is universal for shamans across the world, even among shamans utilizing psychoactive drugs, is reliance on the impact of fast rhythmic drumming, dancing, chanting, and fasting to induce trance experiences. Thus, the drum or the rattle is a universal symbol of the shaman's religious practice.

PRIMAL RELIGIONS AND THE CATACLYSMS OF COLONIALISM

A theme that runs throughout this book is the traumatic disruptions to life and religious traditions caused by modern European colonialism. For the primal societies of the planet, this coercive expansion of invading outsiders and the political dominance they imposed has been nothing less than disastrous.

This cataclysm had many facets. Native peoples of the New World and other remote regions were decimated by the diseases of Eurasia, to which they had no natural resistance. Often simultaneously, the disease-bearing outsiders plundered the native people's riches, utilizing horses and superior weapons technology to achieve their aims. In the early colonial era, millions of people in small-scale subsistence societies were killed or enslaved. In countless instances, the outsiders appropriated and transformed the native lands when natural resources were discovered there. Whole peoples were ruthlessly swept aside, and ways of life that had evolved over centuries were violently ended. Since religion is closely related to a community's way of life, the genocide and disruptions suffered by the world's indigenous peoples inevitably included the destruction and deformation of ancient religious traditions.

Over time, as the worst cruelties of colonial rule eased, the survivors and their descendants faced stark choices. Would they risk the chaos of migration by retreating into the receding natural frontiers of forests, and mountains? Would they acquiesce to a nineteenth-century government's program of forced resettlement on reservations? Or would the best choice be for individuals to go their separate ways, to assimilate with the dominant society and submit to national laws of others? Whatever the choice, the solidarity and cultural integrity of most of these displaced groups worldwide has weakened over every generation. It has inevitably been the young who have seen the limits of their minority status, rejected the old dialects and religious customs, and responded to the allure of the dominant culture by embracing assimilation.

Exposure to missionary religions and their alien exponents often contributed to the downfall of the primal religions. Beliefs and practices of many native peoples elicited much hostility and criticism. Missionaries accused shamans of being obstacles to the advance of the colonizing powers and often accused the native healers of combining evil with fakery: acting as "servants of the devil" while also being imposters or religious charlatans who exploited a naive, credulous people. For the Euro-Americans, for example, shamanism represented the wild, a source of disruptive chaos threatening the colonial order. Under these circumstances, native peoples in many cases had to hide their drums, medicines, and sacred images. They believed that the only way to preserve their culture was to take it underground.

Other native peoples, however, organized in attempts to restore their place in the world and give new life to their traditions. In North America, shamans rallied to attempt to revitalize native peoples in the nineteenth century through a movement called the Ghost Dance. After the decimation of the buffalo by white hunters, which greatly contributed to the destruction of the native way of life on the Great Plains, several elders had the same visionary revelation. Their tutelary spirits announced a way to restore the lost world by bringing back the ancestors and causing the whites to disappear. Native American prophets preached that this could be accomplished if all the people performed a new dance ritual as prescribed by the spirits. Soon the Ghost Dance was practiced with fervor across the Great Plains by those whose kin had died, with the dancers falling unconscious in hopes of experiencing reunion with their deceased relatives. One leader in this movement had his vision of the Ghost Dance recorded thus,

> All Indians must dance, everywhere, and keep on dancing. Pretty soon in the next spring, the Great Spirit come. . . . The game be thick everywhere. All dead Indians come back and live again. . . . White can't hurt Indian then. Then big flood come like water and all white people die, get drowned. After that, water go away and then nobody but Indians everywhere and game of all kinds thick.[4]

The pain of engagement with outsiders is unmistakable in this new religious movement, one that sought to bind a vision of ecological renewal with the restoration of traditional religious consciousness. Although similar prophetic revitalization movements arose later, the U.S. Calvary ended this nationwide movement in 1890 by massacring the men, women, and children gathered for the Ghost Dance at Wounded Knee, South Dakota.

PRIMAL RELIGIONS TODAY

In 2005, no primal societies remain on earth that have not been exposed to the world of outsiders with their missionaries, armies, nation-states, and corporations. Some have even been the targets of genocidal persecution. Most of the !Kung people have been relocated onto reservations, forced to give up hunting, and directed to adopt agriculture or simple crafts. The Ainu of northern Japan have suffered land seizures and legal discrimination, with few so stigmatized willing to profess knowledge of the old traditions and shamanic practices. Native peoples of the Amazon rain forest have been displaced by land-clearing settlers and threatened by multinational mining projects. The history of Native Americans since 1500 is a shameful story of genocide and land taking, made worse by legal discrimination against Native American religious

Cultural Survival

Founded by anthropologists in the 1970s in response to the serious problems affecting indigenous peoples all over the world. Cultural Survival works to promote the rights, voices, and visions of these small subsistence societies. As of 2004, there were 3,000 members from 150 countries supporting a diverse array of activities. These include the publication of two journals that report on problems and humanitarian interventions across the globe; an educational outreach program that provides curricula and experts for secondary schools worldwide; an Indigenous Action Network that uses the Internet to match indigenous peoples with experts in various development skills; a Law Initiative that provides legal research and support to indigenous peoples; and an undergraduate internship program that promotes education and engagement with specific global problems. Cultural Survival special projects are found on every continent and issues related to religious freedom are often cited in its publications. Further information is available at the organization's Web site (http://www.culturalsurvival.org).

practices. In every decade, hundreds of indigenous languages and religious traditions are declining in use and disappearing forever. It is hard for those centered in the dominant world civilization to absorb vicariously the shattering impact of the past centuries on the earth's "first peoples."

The indigenous groups that have survived most intact are those that live far from resources the modernizing world has sought: in the trans-Arctic zone, deep in the rain forests, high in the remotest mountains, or on isolated islands far from the continental landmasses. Those that have retained autonomy, resisted assimilation, and worked to revitalize their identities are remarkable and show both the adaptability of human culture and the resilience of the human spirit.

Unsurprisingly, shamans are still pivotal figures, leading their societies in facing the crises of modernity. Because traditionally they have been entrusted with mediating between spirits and humans, shamans are the natural choice to act on behalf of the group when the outside world intrudes. In the face of fierce repression, some shamans saw confrontation as the only hope and died in vain defense. Some, like Siberian and Mongolian shamans under Soviet rule, retreated to the wilderness and continued to practice there. Some have led creative responses, weaving together alien and indigenous religious beliefs and practices. In present-day Mexico, for example, shamans long ago integrated Christian saints and sacramental theology into their healing rites.

Primal religions have generally been vulnerable to centralized religious power such as that represented by the major world religions. In many colonized lands, rituals of the primal religions were banned. Possessing nether wealth, institutional power, nor prestige among the colonial rulers, shamans persisting in their practices were imprisoned, some in psychiatric hospitals. Many studies have found that even after an indigenous people's successful accommodation to a dominant colonial culture, what often survives as shamanic tradition is a partial practice, the most portable or applied elements such as healing services.

In a world turned upside down, one in which the ancestral spirits clearly failed to protect the group or safeguard its territory, change was inevitable. Over generations, many shamanic traditions themselves have been diminished or reformulated to match the new life circumstances. Under colonial conditions and until today, cultures that were thriving only a few centuries ago exist only in dimming memory. What has proven the most enduring is shamanism.

Shamanism in Asia: Division of Labor with the World Religions

Shamanism continues to exist as an integral part of the pluralistic religious cultures of Asia. In most settlements across the region, there is a shaman who can enter into the trance state, if called upon to heal or solve practical problems. Such shamanic practice today has been harmonized with the doctrines of the dominant religions and is tolerated by the Hindu, Buddhist, or Islamic religious establishment that also is deeply rooted in these areas.

This pattern of coexistence includes East Asia, where shamans augment popular Confucian beliefs and ancestral traditions, a tradition of pluralistic accommodation going back to the beginnings of recorded history, a relationship that will be discussed in Chapter Eight. Here we can say that given the widespread belief in deities inhabiting this earth and in the soul's afterlife destiny, it is not surprising that East Asians still recognize the utility of spirit mediums who attempt to communicate with the dead. Divination has provided answers to such problems as where grandmother's soul might be residing, whether the ghost of a dead child is causing family troubles, or what might be done to gain the favor of a god who could help end a drought. Unhappy spirits (*kuei*) were also thought to cause distress to the living, so here, too, shamans have had an important role in healing the sick.

Typically, a client approaches a spirit medium today because of the suspicion that an illness is due to ghost possession. The medium goes into trance in the sick one's presence and speaks or acts (sometimes writing on a slate or sandcovered board) after having made contact with one or more spirits. The medium's communications are usually interpreted by an assistant, who acts as the intermediary for the family and community members present. For example, contemporary mediums in Taiwan, called *dangki*, become possessed and rapidly write divinely inspired characters in red ink on yellow papers. Sometimes the objects become amulets for their patients; alternatively, they may be burned, whereupon their ashes are mixed with water that is drunk as medicine. The role of these spirit mediums has, if anything, *increased* with the modernization and rising prosperity of Taiwan. The same phenomenon has been reported in modern Korea as well.

Though in urban settings of China and Japan, shamans are regarded as marginal figures of low status, across South Korea, even among its large Christian minority, their practices are uniquely honored and sought by people of all faiths. Korean shamans called *mudang* tend to be predominantly women, drawn into the role from one of two backgrounds: troubling personal experiences that led them to initiation or inheritance of the role through kinship lines. An estimated hundred thousand Korean shamans practice their healing arts today, dealing with life's pragmatic problems. Their seances, called *kut*, are usually held to contact a deity to request economic blessings, healing, restoration of good marital relations, or help in becoming pregnant. The mudang enters a trance and then begins to speak with voices attributed to deities. Typically the first statements are complaints of deficiencies in the offerings laid out or about impurity, which Korean supernaturals particularly dislike. When sponsors apologize and promise to do better next time, the divinities entertain the sponsor's request(s). A second type of ritual has the mudang lead to the next world the soul of someone who has recently died or check the status of a newly departed soul.

Shamanism Expropriated: "White Shamans"

Traditional shamanistic practices now appeal to those in the dominant societies who are simultaneously repelled by and drawn to the mysteries of life. With their esoteric and primordial qualities, these practices are seen by the West as "uncontained," the last remaining spiritual frontier on earth. Now growing numbers of adventurers, romantics, and spiritual explorers from the urban civilizations seek out shamans as representatives of nearly lost worlds, hoping to recover something of value. Thousands each year sign up for tours to Siberia, the Amazon, or the Himalayas to observe and even be initiated by local shamans. Some native peoples regard this development as an attempt by the conquerors to take the last of their possessions. Ever zealous in guarding their traditional secrets, they distrust the outsiders and doubt their sincerity. Responding to these postmodern possibilities, the shaman is again mediating worlds in creative ways. As David Chidester has noted,

> Acting on behalf of a community, even when that community was displaced and dispossessed, shamans developed new religious strategies, not only for preserving archaic techniques of ecstasy, but also for exercising new capacities for memory, concealment, performance, translation, and transformation in negotiating indigenous religious survival under difficult . . . conditions.[5]

We will trace this now global arc of the interaction with primal religions, shamanism and "white shamans" further in the last chapter. We will also see how neo-shamanism has become one of the world's "new religions."

CONCLUSION

Evidence of religion in prehistory reflects the major concerns of our species as hunter-gatherers. Fertility was important for group survival, the need to hunt for prey was a constant and central fact, and there was ongoing concern to maintain group and gender boundaries. We can also discern the emergence of the first religious specialist, the shaman, who cultivates the universal human capacity for entering altered states of consciousness. Both serving and leading the people, the shaman gives them confidence and direction in dealing with the world's unseen forces.

Shamanism is widespread in the world today. Even where one or more of the great world religions has been adopted by a population, shamanic traditions continue to find patrons. In some cases, shamans express concepts associated with one of the now dominant world religions (e.g., the soul, hell, the force of karma). In other instances, a shamanic cosmos exists side by side with that of a world religion. Today, shamanism is practiced "underground" if there is reason to fear persecution. In some places, however, it is tolerated, perhaps even integrated with the dominant world religion.

In the next chapters, we can find repeatedly the imprint of primal religions, especially animism and shamanism. Soul beliefs remain nearly universal in the great religions, with East Asia's widespread ancestor veneration an important example of archaic practices still enduring. Death rites continue to be powerful expressions of religious tradition, and states of altered consciousness are still an important means for heightening spiritual experiences. The metaphor of human life existing on a plane between heaven above and a nether world below is found in all major world religions. Finally, sacred places that are believed to be at the center of the world (the *axis mundi*) in the primal traditions continue to be revered in the great world religions: divine revelations occur on mountains (as to Abraham, Moses, Muhammad, and the Daoist sages), and trees connect humans to life's sacred cosmic mysteries (Buddha was enlightened under a tree; Jesus was crucified on a wooden cross). As for the connection with shamans, when examining the lives of the founders of the world religions, both prophets and sages, we can notice the performance of miracles like healing the sick and ascending to the heavens on magical flights, in every case demonstrating the mastery of what began as a shamanic art.

This process of assimilating primal animistic and shamanistic traditions into urban-based civilizations is one that goes back to the very beginnings of recorded human history, as we saw in Chapter One. We will see in subsequent chapters how most world religions from antiquity onward were amenable to and often central actors in the absorption of primal peoples and "converting them" away from their ancient religions. It will also be seen in the final chapter that attempts have been made to use the "civil religions" of modern nations to legitimate the often violent work of unifying and assimilating primal peoples.

For at least the last 30,000 years, humans have evolved through culture, not anatomy. Art, religious practices, and complex symbols were all present among *Homo sapiens* from the beginning. And all three emerged simultaneously. What should we understand from this circumstance? Religion is an essential element in our species' evolution: it has helped humanity bond more tightly, face the unknown, hunt more effectively, and reconcile with death. Cultural historians see all these factors helping human groups maximize the quality of their diet, which in turn enabled them to better organize, and to better understand and adapt to their environment, as well as to each other. With more free time, there were greater possibilities for individuals to specialize and so introduce cultural innovations.

To the extent a group adopted religious beliefs and practices that abetted its survival, that group obtained advantages vis-à-vis other groups. As a force binding communities, as a means of "being careful" about the unseen, and as a decisive factor in helping human groups adapt to their environment, the world's primal religions point out the central issues we face in understanding the continuing role of religion in later human life.

Discussion Questions

1. What are the inherent problems in knowing and understanding the religion that existed before the development of written language?

2. How might the history of religions be written by a member of an indigenous people?

3. In many hunter-gatherer groups, the people often refer to themselves as "the true people." How would sudden awareness of the existence of other people in itself undermine the cosmos posited in such primal religious traditions?

4. Do you think that it is valid to generalize from modern hunter-gatherers back into the past to reconstruct the origins of religion? Why or why not?

5. How might a modern shaman explain the endurance of her tradition and the attraction of shamanic practices by those living in modern industrial societies?

6. Interpret the tradition of rock and roll festivals in the West and the range of behaviors displayed in them from the standpoint of an historian of primal religions.

7. Scholars who have studied subsistence peoples now counsel sympathetically imagining primal religions as "lived through the body" and involving the entire spectrum of human perception. Explain why this approach has value, given the practices of !Kung shamanism.

8. The scholar of comparative religions Joseph Campbell once suggested that the dominant world religions all differed from the primal religions by their requiring followers to distance themselves from the powerful personal religious experiences that were routine in many primal societies. While you are invited to test this assertion in the following chapters, can you see any problems with traditions that invite everyone to have regular immersions into the sacred as described in this chapter?

Key Terms

animism   numinous

cosmogony   totem

Suggested Readings

Eliade, Mircea. *Shamanism: Archaic Techniques of Ecstasy* (Princeton, NJ: Princeton University Press, 1964).

Gardner, Robert. *Gardens of War. Life and Death in the New Guinea Stone Age* (New York: Random House, 1969).

Grim, John. *The Shaman: Patterns of Religious Healing Among the Ojibway Indians* (Norman: University of Oklahoma Press, 1983).

Harner, Michael. *The Way of the Shaman* (New York: Bantam, 1972).

Harris, Marvin. *Our Kind* (New York: Harper & Row, 1989).

Hayden, Brian. *Shamans, Sorcerers and Saints: A Prehistory of Religion* (Washington DC: Smithsonian Institution Press, 2004).

Katz, Richard. *Boiling Energy: Community Healing Among the Kalahari Kung* (Cambridge, MA: Harvard University Press, 1982).

Kendall, Laurel. *Shamans, Housewives, and Other Restless Spirits* (Honolulu: University of Hawaii Press, 1988).

———. *The Life and Times of a Korean Shaman* (Honolulu: University of Hawaii Press, 1988).

Lame, Deer and R. Erdoes. *Lame Deer: Seeker of Visions* (New York: Simon & Schuster, 1972).

Mumford, Stan. *Himalayan Dialogue: Tibetan Lamas and Gurung Shamans* (Madison: University of Wisconsin Press, 1989).

Pfeiffer, J. E. *The Creative Explosion* (New York: Harper & Row, 1982).

Ritchie, Mark. *Spirit of the Rainforest: A Yanomana Shaman's Story* (New York: Island Lake Press, 1996).

Shostack, Marjorie. *Nisa: Autobiography of a !Kung Woman* (New York: Random House, 1982).

Taylor, Timothy. *The Buried Soul: How Humans Invented Death* (Boston: Beacon, 2002).

Vitebsky, Piers. *The Shaman* (New York: Macmillan, 1995).

Notes

1. Marjorie Shostack, *Nisa: Autobiography of a !Kung Woman* (New York: Random House 1982), p. 16.

2. Ian Tattersall, "Once We Were Not Alone," *Scientific American*, January 2000, 62.

3. Lame Deer and R. Erdoes, *Lame Deer: Seeker of Visions* (New York: Simon & Schuster, 1972), pp. 136–137.

4. Quoted in Sherman Alexie, *The Lone Ranger and Tonto Fight in Heaven* (New York: Atlantic Monthly Press, 1993), p. 104.

5. David Chidester, "Colonialism and Shamanism," in Mariko Walter and Eva Fridman, eds. *Shamanism: An Encyclopedia of World Beliefs, Practices, and Culture* (Santa Barbara, CA: ABC Clio, 2004), p. 48.

CHAPTER THREE

The Many Stories of Judaism
Sacred and Secular

Overview

In a neighborhood in Jerusalem, ultra-Orthodox Jews, dressed in black suits and hats, close off their streets and neighborhoods to traffic in strict observance of the rules of Sabbath. The majority of Jerusalem's inhabitants, secular Israelis in modern Western dress, who also consider themselves to be Jewish, choose to ignore the Sabbath and most other religious rules. Meanwhile, in a New York City neighborhood, a woman rabbi leads her Reform congregation in a Friday night prayer service; three blocks away, a male rabbi leads the traditional worship at an Orthodox synagogue. Secular Israelis reject the attempts of the ultra-Orthodox to impose their strict Sabbath observance on Israeli society and yet, at the same time, the state of Israel does not recognize either Reform or Conservative Judaism, the two largest of the three branches (along with the Orthodox) that dominate American Judaism. This paradox exists because of the influence of ultra-Orthodox Jews who dominate religious life in Israel despite their minority status. Since the Holocaust, the majority of Jews worldwide reside either in Israel or in the United States, yet one can still find communities of Jews throughout Europe and scattered throughout the Middle East, Africa, Latin America, and Asia, including India and China.

Behind this modern diversity and the conflicts it creates lies premodern *Rabbinic*, or *Talmudic, Judaism*, which provided the normative framework for Jewish life from about the sixth century CE until the emergence of modern forms of Judaism in the nineteenth century. Indeed, ultra-Orthodox Jews see themselves as preserving premodern Judaism against the onslaught of modern Jewish diversity. In this chapter, we shall try to understand the unity and diversity of Judaism by tracing its historical origins and the transformations associated with modernization.

Judaism is the smallest of the great world religions, comprising less than one-half of 1 percent of the world's population. Yet Jews have had, and continue to have, a major impact on history. Over the millennia, Judaism has been many things to many people in different times and places. Moreover, some people today who consider themselves to be Jewish do not identify themselves as religious. And yet, secular or ethnic ways of being Jewish, as we shall see, have had profound effects on the Jewish religion and so must be included in our survey to help us understand the religion of Judaism. We will find great diversity among the Jewish people, and yet we shall look for a common thread.

JUDAISM Timeline

2000 BCE	Abraham
1280	Moses, Exodus, and covenant
1240	Conquest of land of Canaan under Joshua
1004–965	King David
721	Fall of northern kingdom of Israel to Assyrians
586	Fall of southern kingdom of Judah to Babylonians
538	Return from Exile
198–167	Maccabean revolt against enforced Hellenization
63	Beginning of rule by Rome
c. 30 CE	Hillel and Shammai—first of the Tannaim
70	Destruction of the second temple
73	Fall of Zealot fortress at Masada
90	Emergence of Academy at Yavneh
90–200	Formation of the Mishnah
200–500	Formation of the Gemara
1070	Founding of Talmudic academy by Rashi in Troyes, France
1095	First Crusade—beginnings of pogroms—mass slaughter of Europe's Jews

Jews take as the highest reality the God of creation and history, who revealed himself at Sinai, and they believe that to act in harmony with the will of this God is the highest goal of life. Indeed, the monotheism of both Christianity and Islam is rooted in this most ancient of the three traditions. Christianity and Islam also follow Judaism in seeing the gravest problem in human life as sin—the failure to live in harmony with the will of a God who demands justice and compassion. The ideal of life is living in harmony with the will of God, and the problem of life is sin, which disrupts that life-giving harmony. In Judaism, one overcomes the problem and realizes the ideal by means of the study and practice of God's teachings or revelation: Talmud Torah.

The Christian concept of original sin, the idea that the sin of the first two human beings, Adam and Eve, was inherited by all descendants, does not exist in Judaism. Rather, each and every human being is free to choose good or evil because each person stands before God in the same relationship that Adam and Eve did. However, in creating the people of Israel, God gave them a gift to tip the balance between good and evil in favor of good. This was the

1306	Jews expelled from France, beginning of pattern repeated throughout Europe
1700–1760	Hasidic leader Israel ben Eliezer, the Ba'al Shem Tov
1729–1786	Moses Mendelssohn, leading figure in Jewish *Haskalah* (Enlightenment) movement/Reform Judaism
1808–1888	Samson Raphael Hirsch, leading figure in emergence of Orthodox Judaism
1860–1904	Theodor Herzl, founder of modern Zionism
1917	Balfour Declaration—proposal for Jewish homeland in Palestine endorsed by British government
1933–1945	Rise and fall of Nazi party; the Holocaust, 6 million Jews murdered
1939–1945	World War II
May 14, 1948	Birth of state of Israel
May 11, 1949	Israel admitted to United Nations
1967	Six-Day War, followed by emergence of Judaism of Holocaust and Redemption
1973	Yom Kippur War, followed by growth of ultra-Orthodox movements
1979	Camp David peace treaty between Egypt and Israel
1980s	*Intifada*: Palestinian uprising and escalation of conflict between Palestinians and Israelis
1993	*Oslo Accord*, developing increased autonomy for Palestinians and the framework for negotiating peace with Israel, followed by continued violence on the part of radicals on both sides who view compromise as betrayal. Also continued tension between secular Israeli Jews and ultra-Orthodox Haredim and also between Israeli Haredim and Conservative and Reformed Jews of the Diaspora

JUDAISM *Timeline*

dual Torah, the sacred oral and written teachings concerning God's revelation to his people. In giving Israel the Torah, God established a covenant (i.e., a binding agreement) with Israel, making them a holy people and reminding them: "I will be your God and you shall be my people, I will guide and protect you and you will obey my commandments." According to the story of Torah, God set before Israel the choice between life and death and made it possible for the people to choose life by choosing "to walk in the way of God." This could be accomplished by following the 613 commandments, which means God's law or commands, *halakhah*. These commandments require deeds of loving kindness, or *mitzvot*, by which the people would embody in their lives the justice and mercy of God as a model for all the world.

It would be misleading, however, to think that this summary sketch of the religious worldview of Judaism would be agreed to by all Jews. In the remainder of this chapter we shall try to understand both the unity and the diversity of Judaism as a religious tradition and the profound impact of the emergence of modernity on its development. We begin by discussing the

The interior of the Tuoro Synagogue in Newport, Rhode Island, the oldest synagogue in the United States, consecrated in 1763.

twentieth-century encounter of Judaism with modernity that gave rise to ultra-Orthodoxy. We then go back to the historical beginnings of Judaism and trace its history, to understand the sources of the diverse threads of contemporary Judaism and the ongoing struggle to define its future. Because our goal is to understand Judaism's encounter with modernity, we shall focus primarily on the aspects that reveal the diversity of Judaism today and show how that diversity developed.

ENCOUNTER WITH MODERNITY: MODERN JUDAISMS AND THE CHALLENGE OF ULTRA-ORTHODOXY

Premodern Rabbinic Judaism, as we shall see, was a world unto itself, embracing every aspect of life and offering safe haven from the non-Jewish world that largely rejected it, and greatly restricted the role of Jews in society. The modern world, by contrast, seems to offer Jews a new option—the possibility of sharing in its citizenship. Thus all modern forms of Judaism draw a line between the secular (i.e., non-religious) and the religious to allow Jews to participate in both worlds.

At the same time, each modern form of Judaism tries to preserve an essential core of Judaism while creating space for aspects of life not directly controlled by religion. For Reform Jews the essence is the ethics of Judaism. Consequently all the beliefs in supernatural phenomena and all traditional ritualistic requirements are seen as negotiable. For Conservative Jews the rituals are not negotiable but beliefs in supernatural matters are. The Orthodox say that neither is negotiable but still allow that some parts of a Jew's life (secular education, job, etc.) can be carried out in the secular world. The new, late-twentieth-century, ultra-Orthodox movements reject even this compromise with the world. They seek to create a Jewish way of life, totally separate from both the modernizing forms of Judaism and the surrounding gentile world. They accomplish this for themselves by means of segregation: creating Jewish communities where all of life (the way one dresses, how and where one works, how one spends one's leisure time) is governed by supernatural beliefs and traditional ritual.

The ultra-Orthodox seek to recapture, as far as possible, the way of premodern Jews. And they hope to see the day (at least in Israel) when all modern forms of Judaism will disappear and their own communities will be the model for the whole of society. The goal of deprivatizing Judaism, so that its religious vision can shape all of public life, sets ultra-Orthodox Judaism apart from other modern forms of Judaism. At the same time, ultra-Orthodoxy rejects pluralism, a key characteristic of what some call "postmodernity." Because they fear that pluralism leads to religious and ethical relativism, ultra-Orthodox movements fight a battle similar to that of Christian fundamentalists. Thus they rebel against the modern world by insisting that there is one truth, one way of life to which all Jews must return if they are not to drown in a sea of relativism that will undermine any sense of higher purpose for life. For the ultra-Orthodox there cannot be many ways to keep the covenant—only one way. And that one way is all encompassing. It does not permit a Jew to parcel out his or her life into separate secular and religious portions. Nor does it permit men and women to redefine their gender roles in new and "liberating" ways. Such redefinitions, they argue, will inevitably lead to moral chaos and the collapse of the family. Although only a minority of the world's Jewish population have opted for ultra-Orthodoxy, this way of being Jewish offers a challenge to Jews the world over to examine the implications of their modern spiritual and political beliefs: can one be both modern and Jewish, and remain the true Israel called forth by Torah?

The Conflict over Public Life: Religion and Politics in the State of Israel

The conflict created by ultra-Orthodoxy is most obvious in the state of Israel, where public life was shaped initially by secular Jews with a nonreligious socialist–Zionist worldview (about which we will say more later). In the 1990s 80 percent of Israelis remained secular. However, especially since the mid-1970s, the ultra-Orthodox have formed increasingly influential religious parties that seek to undo this secularity and place the public order under the religious commandments or laws of the premodern Talmudic tradition, the *halakhah*.

Although a minority with considerable diversity and disagreement among themselves, the ultra-Orthodox share in the desire to make the public life of the secular state of Israel more religiously observant. They insist, for example, that all businesses be closed on the Sabbath, and they succeeded in having the legislature, the Knesset, pass a law requiring that all marriages be done by Orthodox rabbis. In the eyes of the ultra-Orthodox, their secular, Reform, and Conservative brethren are not really Jews, and Orthodox Jews are not orthodox enough. All non-ultra-Orthodox Jews are urged to repent and return (*teshuvah*) to the true Judaism. Consequently both Orthodox and ultra-Orthodox Jews have campaigned to amend an Israeli law enacted in 1950, two years after Israel achieved statehood. The act called the law of return assures all post-Holocaust Jews that Israel is their homeland and grants automatic Israeli citizenship to all Jews, born of a Jewish mother, who apply. Orthodox and ultra-Orthodox partisans have repeatedly tried to have the law modified to prevent anyone who has not undergone an Orthodox conversion from being accepted for citizenship.

Ultra-Orthodox Minorities:
The Gush Emunim and the Neturei Karta

Religious political movements and religious parties in Israel are too diverse and complex to fully account for here, but we can understand something of the dynamics of their role in Israeli society by looking at representative groups. Beyond favoring segregation and opposing pluralism, the ultra-Orthodox are themselves quite diverse. The spectrum extends from religious Zionists like the Gush Emunim (Bloc of the Faithful), at one extreme, to the anti-Zionists such as the Neturei Karta (Guardians of the City) at the other. In between stand various compromise movements, like the Agudat Yisrael (Federation of Israel), founded in 1912.

The Neturei Karta emulate a centuries-old way of life that comes out of the traditions of the eastern European haredim, or "those of true piety." The Gush Emunim, while remaining rigorously ultra-Orthodox in their observance of Jewish law or *halakhah*, have developed a manner of dress (e.g., jeans, short-sleeved shirts, and skullcaps for the men) that distinguishes them from the haredim, in their wide-brimmed hats and long black coats. Rather, the Gush identify with the secular Zionists who founded the state of Israel, whom they see as their counterparts.

The Neturei Karta, and most of the ultra-Orthodox movements, have their roots in a strand of vigorously anti-Zionist eastern European Orthodoxy, which unlike most of western European Orthodoxy, made no compromise with modernity. It is because they seek to preserve the way of life of premodern eastern European Judaism that the haredim refuse to permit secular education and modern dress.

Unlike the more modern Reform, Conservative, and Orthodox Jews, the ultra-Orthodox haredim do not live in communities having gentile (i.e., non-Jewish) residents, nor are they willing to mix with modern Jews who do not share their views. Rather, they live in ghettolike communities typically led by a rabbi revered for his piety and Talmudic skill—communities where the faith is a way of life, untarnished by the compromises with modernity regarded as unavoidable by "modern" Jews. Certain that only the coming of the messiah in God's own time can bring about a true Jewish polity, the haredim reject the state of Israel as secular and profane. In this they continue the attitude of premodern Rabbinic Judaism, which from the beginning rejected political and Zionist messianic Judaism. That second-century political-messianic Judaism, which had interpreted the Torah as giving Jews a divine right to the land, had authorized holy war against the Romans but ultimately was crushed by them.

Paradoxically, at the other extreme of ultra-Orthodoxy, this rejection was itself rejected. The Gush Emunim, for example, do not accept the Jewish state in its secular form, but have firmly endorsed the emergence of the secular state as in accordance with the divine will, a step on the way to a genuine (*halakhah*-based) Jewish state. Coming into existence early in 1974, the Gush Emunim represent a distinct branch of ultra-Orthodoxy. Unlike the Neturei Karta, they sought to transform secular Zionism—to put this form of nationalism on the correct path by making public life in Israel conform to *halakhah*. Thus we see how difficult it is for ultra-Orthodoxy to keep historical change out of Judaism: even ultra-Orthodoxy finds itself developing modern forms of Judaism.

While religious Jews make up only about 20 percent of the population in Israel, and despite the anti-Zionist stance of most of them, the various political parties that represent them have managed to play a significant role in Israeli public life because typically neither of the major secular parties—Labor and Likud—is able to secure enough votes to form a majority government without entering into a coalition with at least some of the religious parties. This state of affairs has given such religious parties bargaining power out of all proportion to their numbers.

While some ultra-Orthodox, like the Neturei Karta, reject both the secular state and ultra-Orthodox religious Zionist movements, others, like the Gush Emunim, have sought to force secular Israeli society to conform to their political and religious vision of Jewish life. Still others, both religious Zionists like the members of the Mizrahi (Spiritual Center) party and those opposed in principle to religious Zionism, such as Agudat Yisrael, have been more moderate, willing to work with the secular state of Israel to find ways of constructive compromise.

Ultra-Orthodoxy as a Type of Fundamentalism

The ascendancy of ultra-Orthodoxy is a part of a larger religious resurgence that has been going on around the globe since the mid-1970s. The late 1960s and early 1970s were a time of radical cultural disruption in Western urban secular societies—a time when the youth of the Western world, the children of those who experienced World War II, were rejecting what they described as the emptiness of modern secular culture. In their rejection, large numbers turned to various religious movements as a way of recovering a sense of meaning and purpose in life. Indeed, the less modern and secular the movement, the more attractive it appeared.

One form that this religious resurgence took was distinctively fundamentalist. What all religious fundamentalist movements have in common is a desire to return to the foundations of belief and action that existed in their respective traditions prior to the coming of modernity. These movements see in contemporary culture, where many view all truth and all values as relative, the logical outcome of modernity. This outcome seems to them to prove the decadence of the modern period—a period in which human beings have lost their way and ended up in a world without standards and norms.

Much of the new strength of ultra-Orthodoxy is due to significant numbers of new adherents, former secular Jews and modern religious Jews whose dissatisfaction with life made them receptive to the ultra-Orthodox movements. These Jews have made a leap of faith out of a world that either did not ask them to give their heart to anything (pure secularism) or asked them to give only a part of their heart (modern religious forms of Judaism). They have chosen a form of Judaism that promises to bring order and meaning to the whole of life, not just to a part of it, that requires a full-time commitment, not just a part-time commitment. They have sought to return to the fundamentals of the Judaism of the dual Torah—that is, premodern Rabbinic Judaism.

CONTRASTING RELIGIOUS VISIONS

As the following contrasting visions indicate, every religious tradition is capable of generating both visions that encourage peace and understanding and visions that encourage conflict and violence.

Abraham Joshua Heschel, 1907–72, a great Hasidic Jewish scholar and rabbi who marched with Martin Luther King Jr. at Selma and championed the way of nonviolence.

Abraham Joshua Heschel, 1907–72

On June 16, 1963, Rabbi Abraham Joshua Heschel sent a telegram to John F. Kennedy. Heschel and other religious leaders were scheduled to meet with the president the next day to discuss race relations and civil rights in America. The rabbi proposed that the president declare a state of "moral emergency" to aid black Americans. "We forfeit the right to worship God as long as we continue to humiliate negroes. . . . Let religious leaders donate one month's salary toward a fund for negro housing and education. . . . The hour calls for high moral grandeur and spiritual audacity."

Abraham Joshua Heschel was born in Warsaw, Poland, on January 11, 1907. He was the son of a Hasidic rebbe and a long line of distinguished hasidic teachers who were deeply steeped in Jewish mysticism. Heschel was a child prodigy. By age fourteen, he had mastered the Talmud and was himself writing Talmudic commentaries. As a young university student he was expelled from Germany by the Nazis and fled back to Poland and then to America, by way of England, shortly before the invasion of Poland. He taught first at Hebrew Union College in Cincinnati and then, for most of his career, at the Jewish Theological Seminary in New York. He is the author of numerous books that have deeply influenced modern Judaism, including *Man Is Not Alone*, *The Sabbath*, *God in Search of Man*, *Man's Quest for God*.

Heschel's life demonstrates the capacity of Orthodox Judaism to embrace the pluralism of the modern world. As a great Jewish scholar and Hasidic rabbi, Heschel was the leading Jewish voice responding to social injustices in America during the civil rights/Vietnam War era of the 1950s and 1960s. An advocate of nonviolent civil disobedience, Heschel marched with Martin Luther King Jr. from Selma to Montgomery, Alabama, in the spring of 1965 in defense of civil rights for black Americans. "Any god who is mine but not yours, any god concerned with me but not with you" Heschel asserted, is an "idol" or false god. To segregate the races, he insisted, is nothing short of "segregating God."

As a leader of Clergy and Laymen Concerned about Vietnam, the Center for Nonviolent Social Change, and also the Jewish Peace Fellowship, Heschel convinced Dr. King to join the protest against the Vietnam war. To this end, the rabbi introduced the Baptist pastor to the leader of the Vietnamese Buddhist Peace Movement, the monk Thich Nhat Hanh. In this act Heschel showed himself to be a revolutionary not only in his advocacy for social justice of all peoples but in his openness to other religions, working closely with Christians and Buddhists to bring about social justice. Holiness, he insisted, is not to be limited to those of any one religion, not even Judaism. Holiness is defined by the intention of the heart and the righteousness of the deed. To equate God and any one religion is, for Heschel, the essence of idolatry, for God is the all-inclusive reality. The will of God is not to be found, he argues, in uniformity but in diversity. Thus whenever we meet and welcome each other as human beings, sharing a common humanity despite our differences, we encounter the presence of God.

Quotations from: Abraham Joshua Heschel, *Moral Grandeur and Spiritual Audacity* (essays edited by Susannah Heschel), New York: Farrar, Straus, Giroux, 1996.

Meir Kahane, 1932–90, did not share Rabbi Abraham Joshua Heschel's commitment to nonviolence. His party was banned from the Knesset (the Israeli governing body) in 1984 for inciting racism.

Meir Kahane, 1932–90

Meir Kahane was born in Brooklyn, New York, on August 1, 1932. The son of a rabbi deeply involved in the Zionist movement, he too became a rabbi. In 1968 he founded the JDL, or Jewish Defense League. Kahane was no advocate for nonviolence. On the contrary, he argued that Jews cannot depend on others to defend them and need to learn to protect themselves, using violence if necessary.

Kahane's life illustrates the insistence of ultra-Orthodoxy that there can only be "one way" for all Jews, a way that protects them from pollution by the secular world and all religious diversity. In 1971 he moved to Israel and founded the anti-Arab Kach party, which called for the forcible removal of all Arabs. This party attracted a strong following among the Gush Emunim and other religious Zionists. In 1984 Kahane was elected to the Knesset, but his party was banned before the next election, in 1988, on the grounds that Kach incited racism. Kahane was assassinated by an Egyptian Muslim radical in New York City on November 5, 1990, after a speech urging all American Jews to return to Israel to protect the land from the Arabs. In the speech he had warned of a coming apocalypse in which the American stock market would collapse, leading to a new holocaust against all Jews who were still in the country.

Kahane was an advocate of a messianic Zionism that was violently apocalyptic, expecting the messiah to come soon and lead the Jews in driving all Arabs out of Israel. He rejected the view of some religious Zionists that a secular state might be a stepping-stone to the final appearance of a genuinely religiously Jewish state. Kahane had little patience with the secular state of Israel and saw its secular leaders as the enemies of all religious Jews and hinderers of the creation of a genuine Jewish state. For Kahane, any act that elevated Jews and humiliated Arabs and all other enemies of the Jews, was viewed as sanctifying God's name and hastening the coming of the messiah.

In 1994 the Kach party and its offshoot, Kahane Chai, were designated terrorist organizations by both the Israeli government and the U.S. government. This labeling was largely in response to the 1994 attack on a mosque in Hebron during which a Kach member, Baruch Goldstein, killed thirty-four Muslims. Then in 1995 another Kahane admirer, Yigal Amir, assassinated the prime minister of Israel, Yitzhak Rabin, to put a stop to his attempts to make peace with the Palestinians. Rabin's willingness to consider compromising with the Palestinians on land issues was viewed as treason by these radical Zionists and, in their eyes, this justified his murder. While most Jews remember Kahane as a terrorist, some hold him up as a hero, martyr, and true revolutionary for a militant Zionism that preaches that by divine command, Israel is for Jews only.

The "fundamentalist" movements challenge modern forms of Judaism by refusing to reduce being Jewish to historical heritage, morality, and ethnicity. Ultra-Orthodox Jews attempt to recover what they believe has been lost to modern Judaism, namely, the centrality of God (as a living force), Torah (as divine revelation), and Israel (as an eternal people). Ultra-Orthodoxy rejects all forms of secular Judaism and the diversity found in Judaism today. The ultra-Orthodox wish to revert to a time when, in their view, there was one truth and one way. The total immersion in a deliberately premodern way of life represents to the ultra-Orthodox a definitive break with the decadence of Western civilization. And while the completeness of their immersion experience parallels that of the premodern tradition of Rabbinic Judaism, its self-consciousness does not. For these "new" Jews have chosen to engage in an experiment, and in this sense, their religion too belongs to the range of forms of Judaism of the modern/postmodern period. They, like all other religious persons of the modern era, have no choice but to choose. Their choice is between withdrawal from and involvement with the modern world, either back to what they somewhat romantically view as the "one way" of premodern Judaism or forward into pluralism. To understand the implications of this choice, we must return to the beginnings of premodern Judaism in the biblical period and work our way forward.

PREMODERN JUDAISM: THE FORMATIVE ERA

The Biblical Roots of Judaism

As we learned in Chapter One, Judaism, along with Christianity and Islam, is shaped by the myth of history. Indeed, the myth of history begins with Judaism. Judaism finds its roots in the story of the God who made promises to Abraham and his descendants that were fulfilled centuries later when this God sent Moses to deliver his people from slavery to the Egyptians and lead them into the "land of promise"—the land of Canaan. From these beginnings the story blossomed to tell of the God who acts in time (i.e., in history) and leads his people on a journey through time toward a day of final resurrection in which all injustice, suffering, and death will be overcome.

While all religious traditions pass on their vision of reality through stories, story plays a unique role in Jewish religion. All the great religions of the world have told stories that draw on the metaphors of nature to explain religious experience. For instance, the cycles of nature are used to explain the wheel of death and rebirth in the myths of liberation from India and the rhythms of yin and yang in the myths of harmony from the religions of China. Analogies from nature are not absent from Judaism, but there is a clear shift of emphasis from nature to history. That is, if you want to understand who the God of Israel is, you do not look primarily to nature but to history as the story of the people Israel's journey through time.

Indeed, for Judaism God is the divine storyteller, and the unfolding of creation in history is God's story. In the beginning God said, "Let there be light," and the story began. And the unfolding story will continue to play out in history until God brings it—after many trials and tribulations—to a happy conclusion at the end of time, when the dead are raised to enjoy a new heaven and a new earth.

The Story Begins

The story of the past, as it was imagined by the people Israel, proceeds from the creation of the first man and woman, Adam and Eve, to the near annihilation of humanity, as related in the story of Noah and the flood. Then came the division of humans into many language groups at the tower of Babel, God's call to Abraham to be a father of many nations, and God's promise to give the land of Canaan to the descendants of Abraham (Genesis 15). The story moves on to the migration of the family of Abraham's great-grandson Joseph into Egypt at a time of famine. It relates how the tribes of Israel, Abraham's descendants, became enslaved in Egypt and how God sent Moses to deliver them from slavery. In the story of the Exodus, God assists Moses by sending down ten plagues on the Egyptians and then parting the waters of the Red Sea to enable the Israelites to escape to the land God gives them, in keeping with a promise made to Abraham (Genesis 15:18–21). According to this story, on the way to this land of promise God brought the people to Mount Sinai, gave the Torah to Moses, and formed a covenant with the people. As the book of Exodus describes it:

> Moses went up to God, and the Lord called to him from the mountain [Mount Sinai], say-ing, "Thus shall you say to the house of Jacob, and tell the people of Israel; You have seen what I did to the Egyptians, and how I carried you on eagles' wings, and brought you to myself. Now therefore, if you will obey my voice indeed, and keep my covenant, then you shall be my own treasure among all peoples; for all the earth is mine; And you shall be to me a kingdom of priests, and a holy nation. These are the words which you shall speak to the people of Israel."
> —(Exodus 19:3–6)

This description of the delivery of the covenant at Mount Sinai is a climactic moment in a powerful and dramatic story about a journey that created a holy people—the people Israel. In fact, the Hebrew word for holy (*qadosh*) suggests that to be holy is to be "set apart." So Israel was chosen out of all the nations and set apart to be God's people.

The story goes on to tell how the tribes of Israel wandered in the desert for forty years, entering the land of promise, under the leadership of Joshua only after the death of Moses (see Map 3.1). For the next two hundred years they lived on the land as a loose confederation under military leaders called "judges." However, as threats of conquest from their neighbors became more frequent, many among the tribes began to demand to have a king like other nations, with a standing army to protect Israel. Some, however, argued that

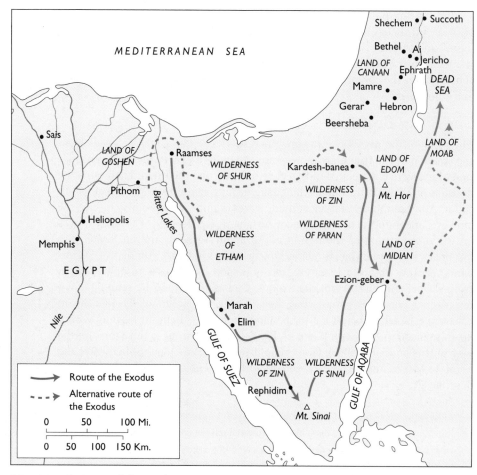

Map 3.1   The route of the Exodus.

there could be only one king over Israel—the God of Abraham, Isaac, and Jacob. God, according to the story, agreed to allow the people to have a king. And so Saul, chosen by God, was anointed with oil by a prophet, as a sign that the first king over Israel had been selected by God, not the people. Indeed, the concept of messiah (*mashiah*) has its beginnings here, for "messiah" means "anointed one," and it was understood that the one so anointed had been chosen to rule over the kingdom of God, the kingdom of Israel.

Saul, however, proved to be a weak king, for he lacked independent authority and had to depend on the cooperation of the tribes, which could be uncertain. It was David, the second king over Israel, who established Israel as a nation. Under David and later his son Solomon, Israel claimed, for a brief time, to be the greatest nation in the Middle East. Stories were told of David's rise to power—how even as a young boy he had saved the tribes by slaying the Philistine giant, Goliath. Indeed, Saul, who had virtually adopted David as a member of the royal family, soon became jealous and turned on him. Forced to flee and fearing for his life, David became a Robin Hood figure, leading a private army of loyal followers. When Saul died in battle against the Philistines, David was proclaimed by the people and anointed as their king. Later, the northern tribes, called Israel, visited David and asked him to be their king, too. Soon he would consolidate the monarchy, becoming known as the king of all Israel and Judah.

David used his army to capture Jebus, a Canaanite city, renaming it Jerusalem, or "Gods peace." Because Jerusalem had not belonged to any of the tribes, it gave David a neutral vantage point from which to rule over both Israel and Judah. David made his capital a holy city by bringing to it a sacred object, the gold-covered chest called the Ark of the Covenant, which contained the stone tablets inscribed with the commandments given at Mount Sinai.

Indeed, it was during David's reign that God is said to have promised David that his heirs would rule Israel into the far distant future (2 Samuel 7:16). After David's death his son Solomon succeeded him to the throne, and Israel was at the height of its power. It was Solomon who built the first temple so that God could dwell in a splendor greater than that of any of the gods of the other nations.

However, after the time of Solomon there was quarreling about the succession to the throne, and for over two centuries Israel, in the north, had one king and Judah, in the south, had another. Soon prophets like Amos and Hosea arose in Israel. The biblical prophets were revered persons believed to know God's will. They reminded the people that since abandoning their nomadic life to become farmers and city dwellers, they had been drifting further and further from the tribal values of the covenant made at Sinai. In the cities the people acted as if they were strangers to each other, and the rich mistreated the poor. The prophets warned that God would punish those who offered sacrifices in the temple while acting unjustly as citizens and neighbors. What God wants most of all, the pious believed, is the sacrifice of a pure heart committed to deeds of justice and compassion.

Jerusalem is often called the City of David. King David conquered the Canaanite city of Jebus and sanctified it by placing there the Ark of the Convenant. Renamed "Jerusalem" by David, the city has been holy for Jews through all times since.

The Story Continues with the Prophets

It is with the prophets that Jewish monotheism becomes fully formed. For in the tribal days of the time of Moses, Israel's commitment had been "henotheistic"—that is, to one God above all others. Thus the commandment "I am the Lord your God . . . you shall have no others beside me," did not mean that there were no other gods, only that Israel was forbidden to follow them. God was their tribal God. But after Israel was established as a great nation in the time of David, the prophets forced Israel to see that they did not own God, nor could they renege on the covenant once in the land of promise—that the covenant conferred not so much privileges as responsibilities. According to the prophets, Israel's God was the God of all the nations and he would use the other nations, if necessary, to punish Israel for any failure to keep the covenant.

Instructed by the prophets, Israel began to think of God in the manner expressed in the book of Genesis—as the creator of all things and all peoples. From the eighth century BCE forward, Israel would become progressively convinced that having "no other gods" required more than loyalty to a tribal deity. It required affirming that there were no other gods. Out of the prophetic experience came the pure and simple creed of Judaism, the *Shema*: "Hear O Israel, the Lord our God, the Lord is one" (Deuteronomy 6:4). This confession is completed by reminding the people to love this God with all their heart, soul, and strength; to pray the Shema on arising and retiring; and to bind the words on their hands, foreheads, and doorposts to ensure that the awareness of the one true God might permeate their every thought and action.

The prophets warned the people that if they did not return to the covenant, the God of Israel, Lord of all creation and history, would punish them. And that is exactly how the misfortunes of Israel and Judah came to be interpreted. For in 721 BCE the Assyrians conquered the kingdom of Israel and carried its inhabitants off into slavery. In 621, Judah's King Josiah is said to have discovered in the temple what he believed to be the long-lost book of the law (the biblical book of Deuteronomy). These writings echoed the teachings of the prophets about the need to practice justice to please God. On this basis Josiah initiated a reform that included a renewal of the covenant and designated the temple in Jerusalem as the only proper site for sacrifices. However, according to the biblical story, the reforms were not observed conscientiously, and God again allowed the people to be punished. In 586 the Babylonians conquered the Assyrians and their territories, destroyed the temple Solomon had built, and carried off the inhabitants of the southern kingdom of Judah into exile and slavery.

As the time of the Babylonian exile approached another generation of prophets arose—Jeremiah, Ezekiel, and Isaiah— spanning the time of exile and eventual return. These prophets asserted that God was indeed punishing Israel for its failure to keep the covenant, but added that the punishment would be temporary (to teach them a lesson). As it happened, the Persians soon conquered the Babylonians, and after only fifty years, in 538, the Israelites were permitted to return to the land. This turn of events was due to the benevolent policy of the Persian king, Cyrus. That a pagan king should so favor the Israelites was seen as miraculous, and Cyrus was declared a messiah, that is, one anointed by God to carry out God's will to return his people to their land (Isaiah 45:1–13). Cyrus himself was not aware of his role in the destiny of Israel. Thus we see that even in the biblical period, Judaism was capable of finding religious significance in secular political events.

The Story Becomes One of Exile and Return

When the first wave of exiles returned to the land (520–515 BCE), the leadership was weak and the people lacked a clear direction. It was not until Ezra, a priest, and Nehemiah, a gifted layman, led a second wave of exiles (458) in a return to the land of Israel that a clear pattern for a postexilic Judaism appeared. These leaders demanded that the people repent: they had married citizens of other nations and sacrificed to other gods, and now they must rededicate themselves to the covenant and repurify themselves as a holy people by separating themselves from their neighbors. It is with this priestly reform that Judaism adopted the experience of exile and return as the normative pattern through which to interpret all its future experiences. In this sense, the experience of exile and return gave birth to Judaism.

A model of the city of Jerusalem centered around the temple as it might have looked in 50 BCE.

In the fourth century BCE, Alexander the Great conquered the ancient world, and after his death in 323 his empire was divided among his generals. For over a century the Ptolemies ruled over Israel (301–198). They were replaced by the Seleucids (198–167), who began a policy of enforced Hellenization, requiring all their conquered peoples to adapt Greek customs and beliefs, including veneration of many gods. The Jews, who refused to abandon their worship of the God of Abraham, Isaac, and Jacob, were severely persecuted for their noncompliance. Thus in the middle of the second century, Judas Maccabaeus and his brothers led a revolt against the cruel Seleucid ruler, Antiochus Epiphanes IV. This effort, the Maccabean revolt, was successful in bringing about a status of semi-independence, which lasted into the first century CE. However, in a bid to resist new efforts at control by the Seleucids, the Jews in 63 BCE invited in the Romans to protect them. After the Exile, the temple was rebuilt on a modest scale and then later, between 20 BCE and 60 CE under the domination of Rome, the second temple was rebuilt on a grander scale.

The Historical Roots of Diversity

In the centuries after Alexander, there grew up considerable diversity within Judaism, leading to several first-century Jewish movements—the Sadducees, the Pharisees, the Hellenists, the Samaritans, the Zealots, the Essenes, and the Nazarenes—all of which were engaged in ongoing debate. Today we would be tempted to say the debate was the right way to be Jewish, but the idea of Judaism as a religion did not yet exist. Rather, the partisans of the first century saw the debate as about an attempt to define how one must live to be the "true Israel" or people of God. To understand this debate it is important to remember that at the beginning of the first century there was no official Bible and no set of practices and commitments accepted as normative by all Jews. It was only at the end of the first century that the Tanak, or Bible of Judaism as we have it today, came into existence, along with Rabbinic Judaism as the normative pattern of Judaism for the next eighteen hundred years.

More needs to be said about these movements. The Sadducees came from the wealthy upper class, were associated with the temple tradition that was exclusive to Jerusalem, and saw their task as keeping peace with Rome. They accepted only the five books of Moses as sacred scripture and insisted on literal adherence to the written Torah.

The Pharisees were teachers associated with the synagogues (houses of study and prayer) found in every city and village; they accepted not only the books of Moses but the historical and wisdom writings and those of the prophets. Both the Jewish Bible (Tanak) and the Christian Old Testament are largely derived from the Pharisees' selection of scriptural materials. The Pharisees taught that God revealed himself in the written Torah and through oral traditions that accompanied the giving of the Torah to Moses. Moreover, they insisted that the written word could not be properly interpreted without the oral traditions. In these teachings the Pharisees offered a precursor to the later Rabbinic doctrine of God's revelation through the dual Torah, the oral and the written. Politically, the Pharisees were neither cozy with, nor openly hostile to, the Romans.

Jews who were dispersed in the Roman Empire (i.e., outside the protectorate of Palestine) were known as the Jews of the Diaspora. The leaders of their synagogues were Hellenistic Jews who used a Greek translation of scriptures that closely corresponded to the Hebrew scriptures of the Pharisees, with some important exceptions. The Hellenists were the great missionaries of Judaism, who used Greek philosophy to explain the meaning of the biblical stories. They were anxious to promote Judaism as a religion that had a place for gentiles, and they adapted Judaism to Greek customs whenever feasible. They successfully encouraged large numbers of gentiles to come and worship the one true God of Israel.

Finally, there were sectarian movements like the *Zealots*, the *Samaritans*, the *Essenes*, and the *Nazarenes* (the followers of Jesus of Nazareth). Some, like the Zealots and Essenes, were openly hostile to the gentile world, whereas the Nazarenes, like the Hellenists, were very positive toward gentiles and sought their conversion. Adherents of these movements tended to be apocalyptic, believing that God would bring the world to an end soon, and so would send a messiah to judge all human beings and reward the faithful. In the first century there was no single clear definition of "messiah." A wide variety of speculations emerged, each sectarian group had its own ideas. Most were expecting a spiritual leader, but some, primarily the Zealots, looked for a military leader able to overthrow the Romans, whose rule in Palestine had become oppressive.

What was typical of these sectarian movements was a strong distrust of the Sadducees, who were viewed as having sold out to the Romans. The Zealots, the most hostile of all, had nothing but contempt for the Sadducees and chose to directly oppose them. If the Sadducees urged "don't rock the boat," the Zealots were committed to rocking the boat as often as possible. To this end, they staged random guerrilla attacks against the Roman legions. In the second century a Zealot, Simon bar Kokhba, claimed the title of messiah and was executed by the Romans.

Finally, at least some of the sectarian groups practiced baptismal rites, that is, ritual immersion and purification. Ritual immersion was already a requirement for any gentile convert to Judaism (along with circumcision of males). From the first century on, however, some groups insisted that not only gentile converts were to be immersed and purified, but also Jews, if they had strayed from the true path of Judaism as understood by the particular sectarian movement.

Exodus and Exile:
Story, History, and Modernity

The difference between premodern and modern is the difference between sacred story, or scripture, and secular story, or history. Fundamentalists fear the incursion of time and history into their sacred story, whereas modernists welcome it. The biblical writings as we have them are organized to tell a story of God's saving journey with his people. It is, as we have noted, the story of the God who acts in time and leads his people through time toward a final fulfillment. This is a grand story that answers questions of origin and destiny for the Jews as a religious people: Where do we come from? Where are we going? When modern historians read this story, they ask different questions. Primarily they want to know if things really happened as described in the sacred texts. They try to find out by comparing the stories with what else is known about the past through ancient writings, through literary analysis of stylistic changes in the writings, and through archaeological artifacts.

When historians began to read the biblical stories critically, they believed they could identify different layers of historical development in the scriptural writings. It is on this basis that they identified four major layers of historical materials: J&E (Jahwist and Elohist, from two different Hebrew names for God) from the period of the monarchy of David and Solomon (c. 1000 BCE), D (Deuteronomic, c. 621 BCE) associated with the prophetically rooted reforms of King Josiah, and P (priestly, c. 458 BCE) associated with the priestly reforms of Ezra and his administrative successor, Nehemiah. Today biblical scholars do not think that the historical materials can be sorted out quite that neatly, but the recognition of historical layers remains essential to the historical study of biblical writings.

The earliest stories (J&E) seem to have been written down in the courts of David and Solomon to tell the story of how God chose Israel, from humble beginnings, to become a great kingdom. Bringing together diverse ancient tribal narratives, the royal storytellers constructed a larger and more complex story that begins with the creation of the world and ends with the kingdom of Israel under David and Solomon as the greatest nation of the ancient Middle East. It is an unambiguous story of promise and fulfillment. However, the story had to be revised in light of the Babylonian exile. The Priestly revision describes Israel as a people shaped by seemingly broken promises that are unexpectedly fulfilled, at least in part, leading to new hope and new life—a story of exile and return.

If the Exodus was the founding event of Judaism, the Exile was its formative event. As one distinguished scholar of Judaism, Jacob Neusner, has noted, it was the great crisis of exile and the astonishment of return that set the mythic pattern of Judaic thought and experience ever since.[1] The exile and return provided a story pattern through which all past and future events, whether of triumph or of tragedy, could be meaningfully integrated into Jewish identity. "Exile and return" shaped the imagination of all future generations. No longer did Israel think of itself as David did (in 1 Chronicles 22:1–19), as having an unconditionally guaranteed existence. On the contrary, its existence was dependent on its commitment to the covenant.

Therefore, the fall of the second temple at the hands of the Romans in 70 CE was a trauma and a deep blow to those who wholeheartedly believed the story of the God who leads his people through time, but the crisis was not without precedent or without meaning. For although the power of leadership shifted once more, this time from the priests to the teachers (i.e., rabbis), the rabbis immediately reverted to the priestly pattern of explanation, arguing once more that the cause of the present misfortune was that Israel had not kept the covenant faithfully enough. Consequently, although the disasters that befell the first and second temples were two of the most traumatic events in the long history of Judaism, neither destroyed the faith of Jews. On the contrary, in each case Jews came to the conclusion that the loss of the temple was not a sign of God's abandonment but a call to the people Israel to be more fully observant of the covenant. Thus today Jews willingly recall these events on the holy day of Tisha B'Av, for remembering brings about not despair and hopelessness but repentance and renewal.

From Torah to Talmud

The Pharisaic Roots of Rabbinic Judaism

To follow the emergence of Rabbinic, or Talmudic, Judaism, we need to resume our discussion of the various Jewish sects and movements that existed in the first century. Such diversity was brought to an end by the destruction of the temple in 70 CE. Of the movements that had been vying to provide a model for Jewish life, only a few survived, and of these it was the Pharisees who provided new leadership. There were at least three reasons for this.

First, the political neutrality of the Pharisees in the period before the fall of the temple made them appealing to the Romans. Unlike the Zealots, the Pharisees seemed benign in their views toward the Roman Empire. So the Roman authorities gave them permission to establish an academy at Yavneh on the coast of present-day Israel. There began the task of reconstructing Judaism for a new period of exile apart from the land and the temple. Second, the Pharisees were already the leaders of the synagogue tradition and the teachers (rabbis) of the importance of the oral tradition. And finally, the oral tradition the Pharisees had espoused gave them the flexibility to interpret the requirements of Jewish life in changing circumstances. Thus when the temple priesthood disappeared, no new institutions needed to be invented. The Pharisees became the natural leaders by default everywhere in ancient Palestine.

The task of the new leadership was to transpose the priestly model focused on the temple in Jerusalem into a new key—one that would allow the people Israel, like their ancestors in Babylon, to survive as Jews apart from the land and the temple. The solution the Pharisees arrived at was a model in which the people Israel (not just the temple) were holy, and every male head of a Jewish household was in fact a priest, even as the table in every Jewish house was an altar. In this new model, the center of Jewish life shifted from written Torah to the oral tradition, from priest to rabbi, from temple to synagogue, and also from temple altar to family table.

The priestly tradition had insisted that Israel was a holy people, set apart for service to the one true God, and had established elaborate rules of ritual separation to keep the people from blending in with the general population. The Pharisees, drawing on the prophets, insisted that what God wanted more than cultic worship, with its sacrifices, was deeds of loving kindness (*mitzvot*)—that is, acts of justice and mercy. To this end, then, the Pharisees transferred the rituals of separation from the temple cult to a system of ethics. The prophets had issued sweeping demands, in the name of God, for justice and mercy. The Pharisees took these demands and made them the content for the priestly rituals of holiness, working out their application in all the details of everyday life according to the best insights of the oral tradition. Between the second and fifth centuries, Rabbinic Judaism, or the Judaism of the dual Torah, emerged as the insights of the oral tradition were written down and incorporated into what became known as the Talmud. And it was this Talmudic tradition, as we shall see, that shaped Jewish life from the sixth century until the advent of Jewish modernizing movements in the nineteenth century.

The heart of the teachings of the Pharisees was that God was a loving personal father who chose Israel to enter into the covenant revealed in the oral and written Torah, so that each and every individual who keeps this covenant can live in hope of resurrection from the dead. Although the Pharisees are depicted as legalists in the Christian scriptures, historians have shown that they taught that the sacrifices that God wants, deeds of loving kindness, are not merely a matter of external observance but must be rooted in a pure heart.

The Pharisees asked Jews to love God above all and their neighbor as themselves. They insisted that what is hateful to oneself must not be done to one's neighbor. They insisted that humans do not live by bread alone, and therefore one should trust in God rather than worry about tomorrow. They insisted that those who would seek the will of God would find it and that those who humbled themselves would be exalted. All these teachings were adopted by Christianity, as well.

The Rabbis and the Formation of the Talmud

Hillel and Shammai were the two leading rabbis, or teachers of oral tradition, in the first century of the Common Era. Their influence led to the development of two major schools: the house of Hillel (*Bet Hillel*) and the house of Shammai (*Bet Shammai*). The disputes between Hillel and Shammai, and their schools, eventually became the foundation of the Talmud and set the tone of disputation and dialogue that is characteristic of the Talmudic Judaism. Both Hillel and Shammai sought to apply the oral Torah tradition to the details of everyday life. In general it is said that Shammai interpreted the demands of Torah more strictly and severely. Hillel, who tended to be more lenient and compassionate in his decisions, is frequently quoted for this summation of the whole of the Torah: "What is hateful to you, do not unto your neighbor; this is the entire Torah, all the rest is commentary. . . . Go and study." In general, although not always, it is the teachings of Hillel that shaped the emerging Talmudic tradition. And it was the students of Hillel who were the primary shapers of the Mishnah—the writings that form the core of the Talmud.

It was the disciples of Hillel and Shammai and their descendants who led the Jews into the Talmudic era. A disciple of Hillel, Johanan ben Zakkai, had been chosen to initiate the academy at Yavneh. There the first task was to settle one of the key arguments that had been going on in Judaism at the beginning of the century—namely, which writings of the tradition to consider to be holy and therefore, revelations from God. The argument, of course, was settled by default. Since the Pharisees survived to reestablish Judaism, it was the writings they revered that were selected to comprise the canon, the official set of scriptures. Unsurprisingly, the Pharisees did not limit their choices to the Torah, that is, the books attributed to Moses. In addition to the five books called the Pentatouch (Genesis, Exodus, Leviticus, Numbers, Deuteronomy), the Pharisees included the books of the prophets (e.g., Jeremiah and Ezekiel, Amos and Hasea), some historical writings (e.g., First and Second Kings), and also the writings, or wisdom literature (e.g., Proverbs, Ecclesiastes, Job). Thus it was the academy at Yavneh that settled on the books that make up the Bible of Judaism, known as the *TaNaK*—an acronym standing for Torah (teachings), Neviim (prophets), and Ketuvim (writings).

In Western culture it has often been thought that to compare the teachings of Judaism and Christianity, all one need do is compare the Tanak or Hebrew Bible (which Christians call the Old Testament) with the New Testament. Such a view, however, is totally misleading. The Talmud and the New Testament are like two different sets of glasses for reading the Hebrew Bible. Through the

Talmud glasses, certain passages seem very clear and easy to read, while other parts are fuzzy and unreadable. And with New Testament glasses the fuzzy passages become clear, and vice versa. Both Jews and Christians read the Hebrew Bible through the eyes of a further revelation (Talmud and New Testament) that tells them how to read the Hebrew scriptures, including what is valid and what can be dismissed. Thus Jews and Christians who seem to be reading an important body of holy writings in common might just as well be reading two different books—which, in a sense, they are. Consequently to understand Judaism one must understand the Talmud and the central role it plays in Judaism.

With the Jewish people's sacred teachings committed to writing in the written Torah or Tanak, the *Tannaim* ("those who study") began the paradoxical process of writing down the vast and diffuse teachings of the oral tradition and transforming this material into the oral Torah. The process occurred in two phases.

First, the Tannaim, led by Hillel and Shammai, organized the wisdom of the Jewish oral tradition into categories, or seders, covering six areas of every-day life: agriculture, sabbaths and festivals, women and property, civil and criminal law, laws of conduct for cultic ritual and temple, and rules for maintaining cultic purity. Then the discussions of the rabbis recalling the wisdom of the oral Torah on each of these areas were written down. This collection of materials, known as the Mishnah, thus codifies the wisdom of the oral Torah. The Mishnah was intended to show Jews how they could sanctify life (i.e., make it holy) despite their loss of the temple and absence from the land of Israel.

In the second phase of Talmudic formation, the successors to the Tannaim, the Amoraim ("those who interpret"), set about developing a commentary on the Mishnah that would link the oral to the written Torah. The result of their work was called the Gemara, and these writings in combination with the Mishnah form the Talmud (meaning "learning" or "study" as related to Torah).

Even though the Talmud (Mishnah and Gemara) is said to have been completed by the sixth century, there is a sense in which the Talmud is never complete. For example, sages in the tradition, the Geonim (eminent scholars) followed up the work of the Amoraim by providing the Responsa—further commentaries on the Talmud. These writings constitute answers to requests from Jews throughout the Diaspora for insight and guidance in applying the teachings of the Talmud to the problems of everyday life. The tradition of commentary, which continues from generation to generation, is integral to Judaism, leaving the Talmudic traditions, as an expression of oral Torah, open to continuous development.

The Talmud records the ongoing discussion of Torah by the great Rabbinic minds across the ages and is meant to be studied and debated in a communal setting.

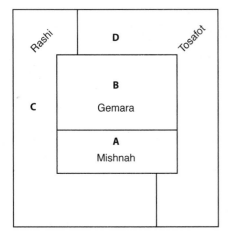

A page of Talmud.

Producing the Talmud by writing down the oral Torah surely seems like a self-contradictory task. And yet the genius of the Talmud is in preserving the oral character of the material in written form. To appreciate the uniqueness of the Talmud one really has to look at it and see how its pages are constructed. A typical page is made up of diverse and distinct parts, coexisting on the same piece of paper. These parts express the voices of the rabbis throughout the ages, and teachings about the same subject are juxtaposed on the same page. The Talmud is an ongoing dialogue among Jews not only of the same time period but from age to age. At the core of a page you may find statement (A) from the Mishnah of the second century outlining the opposing points of view of Hillel and Shammai on a question of appropriate behavior. Above this text, on the same page, might be a section of the Gemara (B) from a period two or three hundred years later, relating the Mishnah to relevant passages from the Tanak and to the diverse opinions of the Amoraim, who comment on the meaning of the Mishnah in light of the scriptures and of the opinions of the Tannaim. Typically, as well, there will be a section (C) devoted to the commentary of the greatest of the Rabbinic Talmudic scholars, Rashi. In yet another section (D), will be the commentaries of the students of Rashi from a collection known as the Tosafot. Each of these expresses views on the meaning of the passages of the Mishnah in the light of the comments of the others and in light of additional commentaries and writings that supplement the tradition. The sections on a given page of the Talmud might span a thousand years or more.

Although Talmudic decisions are made to guide the life of the Jewish community, it would be a mistake to think that the whole point of Talmud study is to reach a conclusion. For Talmudic study is a form of religious ritual whose purpose is nothing less than to bring the student of Torah to experience God through the thrust and parry of argument about the one thing that matters most in life—God's word. That is why it is not unheard of for a debating partner to help an opponent who is stumped for a response by suggesting a line of argument that might be able to refute the point the stronger partner has just made. In this way the Talmud sanctifies doubt and questioning as a medium of religious experience that brings one in touch with God. God is in the questions even more than in the answers. For this reason too, then, the Talmud is never finished as long as there is one more Jew ready to join the debate. It is a tradition of commentary upon commentary that guarantees that the Talmud is always both ancient yet ever fresh and new. The Talmud is always about how one is to make the new day holy.

This understanding of Talmudic debate echoes the Torah story that explains how Israel got its name. For according to Genesis (32:23–32), one night Jacob wrestled with a stranger who refused to tell his own name but rather blessed Jacob and gave him a new name, Israel, meaning "one who has wrestled with God and men and prevailed." As the sun arose, Jacob limped away, convinced that he had "seen God face to face."

So the Torah teaches that Israel is the one God has chosen to wrestle with, and that the way of Torah is to wrestle with the God who cannot be named (or for that matter, imaged). And it teaches that the one who wrestles not only with God (and God's Torah) but with other humans (about the meaning of Torah) can prevail. Indeed to wrestle with the Torah is to see God face to face, to be transformed and given a new name: Israel, or wrestler with God. Hence in Rabbinic Judaism there is no higher calling than to wrestle with others over the meaning of God's Torah. This activity is one that includes rather than excludes those who disagree. According to Talmudic tradition, when the rabbis disagree on the observance of *halakhah*, the majority opinion is to prevail for the good of order. Yet it is understood that the minority are not necessarily wrong. The Torah is large enough to embrace everyone.

According to the Talmud, "The world is suspended in space and has nothing to rest on except the breath of Torah study from the mouths of students— just as a man may keep something up in the air by the blowing of his breath."

Indeed, the story of the covenant at Sinai, through which God chose Israel, suggests just such a give-and-take relationship. For, according to the story, the covenant established that day was a *mutual* agreement between two parties, much like a marriage contract that is both a legal arrangement and an expression of mutual love and care. In this covenant the people promise to obey the commandments of God and walk in the way of the Torah, which gives life. And God promises to guide and protect them on their journey through time. Throughout this journey, God and Israel have wrestled with each other—at one moment God is reminding Israel that the people have strayed from the promise by their sins and at another moment, Israel is reminding God that he appears to have strayed from his promises. Within the bounds of the covenant, each party can be held accountable by the other.

It is this covenant that makes Israel Israel—that is, the chosen people. For the rabbis, the identity of the Jews lay not in their national or ethnic history, although within the myth, the symbolic story, of Torah they surely embraced that history. Nor is the people's Jewishness a function of their being, by choice, members of a religion called "Judaism"; in fact there is no word for "Judaism" in classical Hebrew. Instead, the Jewish identity lies in having been chosen, before all creation, to be God's beloved eternally. The rabbis reminded the people how God had brought them to himself on eagles' wings, to be a holy people (Exodus 19:3–6), set apart to be a witness to the holiness of life. In this setting apart lies the ultimate meaning of the rules for kosher dining that forbid Jews to eat pork, to mix meat and milk, and so on. Even what one eats and the way one eats should remind the world that life is not meant to be profane and meaningless. Rather, a holy life, one that is set apart, is not one's own but belongs to God. Indeed, every act of one's life, whether in work, in eating, in the bedroom, or in prayer, should be a witness to the One who alone is truly holy and in turn sanctifies all creation.

"Torah," in the Talmudic tradition, is a multidimensional word. In its narrowest sense, Torah refers to Pentateuch, the first five books of the Bible. In a broader sense it refers to the entire Bible, or Tanak. Broader still is its meaning as the dual Torah, comprising the entire Talmud. And ultimately Torah is the source and pattern for all creation. For according to the Talmud, when God created heaven and earth he did it by consulting the Torah, which was already with God in the beginning. Hence the Torah provided the pattern for the right order of the universe, a pattern revealed in the *halakhah*, given through oral and written Torah.

Finally, the Torah can be identified with the very being of the rabbi. The rabbi was viewed as a man so close to God that the meaning of Torah was revealed not only in the pattern of his life but also in his extraordinary powers to work miracles and healings. He was a charismatic figure, capable of drawing together a school of disciples for the purpose of studying Torah. He was also the organizer and leader of the community in which he lived, providing guidance and wisdom. Finally, he was a religious virtuoso to whom everyone looked for guidance. If Torah united heaven and earth in the will and presence of God, it was the rabbi who was that living link—Torah in the flesh.

Rituals of Jewish Identity and the Life Cycle

Bris or Brit Milah

In accordance with the teachings of the Torah (Genesis 17:10–14), every male child must be circumcised when he is 8 days old, as a sign of the covenant between God and his people. This ceremony is known as the *Bris* or *Brit milah* (derived from the Hebrew for "covenant" and for "circumcision"). During this ritual the child is named and the foreskin of his penis is cut as an external sign of the covenant. This ritual ties and binds every male child's life to the eternal covenant between God and his people, renewing that covenant with each generation, child by child.

Bar and Bat Mitzvah

When a boy reaches the age of adulthood, 13, he is eligible to become a *bar mitzvah* (son of the commandments, or covenant); to this end, he is expected to demonstrate the ability to carry out his responsibilities in maintaining the religious life of the community. After intense training by his rabbi in the study of Hebrew, and of Torah and Talmud, the young man is called forth at a synagogue service to recite the blessing that precedes the reading of the Torah. Then he reads the Torah portion for the week, and then a portion of scripture from the Prophets. He may also be asked to comment on the meaning of the passages. By doing this the boy shows that he is able to function as a full member of the religious community. Once he has completed this ceremony he is considered to be an adult, qualified to form part of the *minyan* (ten adult males) required for any Jewish worship service. In the modern period, Conservative and Reform Jewish communities have extended this ritual, now called the *bat mitzvah* (daughter of the commandments, or covenant), to female children as well.

PREMODERN JUDAISM: THE CLASSICAL ERA

The Premodern Rabbinic World: God, Torah, and Israel

If human beings are not only storytellers but also storydwellers, then the Torah story of the rabbis was a magnificent dwelling indeed. According to the Talmud, the existence of the world is dependent on the study of the Torah: the world "is suspended in space and has nothing to rest on except the breath of Torah study from the mouths of students—just as a man may keep something up in the air by the blowing of his breath." And if religion (*religio*) is about being "tied and bound" into the cosmic drama of life by one's story symbolically told (myth) and enacted (ritual), then Torah was, and is, just such

Marriage

A Jewish wedding takes place under a *huppah*, a sort of grand prayer shawl stretched over four poles that can be said to symbolize the heavens and God's creation, even as the bride and groom stand in the place of Adam and Eve, the first man and woman created by God. In the marriage ceremony, prayers and blessings sanctify the union of a man and a woman by binding them to each other and to the story of Israel's relation to God, from creation through exiles and tribulations to joyous redemption in the new Zion. Before entering the canopy the man places the veil over the bride's face. Under the canopy the marriage contract (*ketubah*) is witnessed, the couple are betrothed and married with an exchange of rings, and the words "behold you are sanctified to me by this ring in accord with the tradition of Moses and Israel" are followed by seven blessings said over a cup of wine. It is customary, at the end of the ceremony, for the groom to step on and break a glass, symbolizing the fall of the second temple. Great festivity and celebration follow.

Death

Jewish death rites are very simple. A person facing death is encouraged to say a prayer of confession, asking for forgiveness of sins and healing if possible. The prayer continues by asking that the person's death, if it is to come now, serve as atonement for all his or her sins. The prayer ends with requests ("grant me a share in the world to come" and "protect my beloved family") and commits the person's soul into the hands of God. Burial takes place on the day of death or the day after, without embalming. The community places the body in the ground with prayers binding the soul of the deceased to the Eternal One. The immediate family of mourners remains at home for seven days and will continue to recite memorial prayers (*kaddish*) for eleven months, and thereafter on the anniversary of the death.

Observant Jews, like this young man putting on tefillin, declare God's oneness by binding the Torah scrolls to their bodies before daily prayer.

a story. For the Torah story embraces not only every minute, hour, and day of Rabbinic Jewish life, providing a template to make it holy, but also the whole of time from the creation of the world to its ultimate messianic redemption.

In the premodern world, the right to live within this story accompanied being born of a Jewish mother (except for those who were converts). While women thus determined Jewish identity, the primary guardians of Rabbinic religious life were men. Males alone had to be confirmed in their religious status through two key rituals: circumcision shortly after birth and a ceremony, bar mitzvah, in which they demonstrated their knowledge of the faith as they entered adulthood at age 13.

The Jews of the Rabbinic age ate, drank, and slept Torah. The men began the day by dressing in garments with fringes (*tzitzit*) to remind them of the commandments of the covenant (Numbers 15:37–40). Before morning prayer, they wrapped the words of Torah (Deuteronomy 6:4–9) on their arms and foreheads, encased in small leather boxes known as tefillin, or phylacteries. Indeed, every act of the day would be couched in prayer. And every Sabbath (the seventh day of the week), all work ceased and eternity pervaded all things as the people both recalled the beginning of creation and contemplated its fulfillment, to come in the messianic era at the end of time. No matter what suffering history brought to Israel, on the Sabbath an eternal people dwelled with their eternal God, savoring a foretaste of that messianic day for which all creation was made—when God will be all in all.

The meaning of the Sabbath unfolded in the portion of Torah assigned for every week of the year, organized around a great cycle of festivals. From New Year's, which begins with the story of creation on Rosh Hashanah (literally, "head of the year") and concludes ten days later with stories of divine judgment on Yom Kippur (day of atonement), through Passover (liberation/redemption of the Exodus) to the Feast of Weeks (the giving of the dual Torah and the covenant) to the Feast of Booths (the wandering in the desert, awaiting the fulfillment of the promises) as well as the commemoration of disasters averted (Purim) and not averted (Tisha B'Av), the great story unfolded. The story of Torah stretched out over the lives of Jews from the beginning of the day until the end of the day, from the beginning of the year until the end of the year, from the beginning of their lives until the end of their lives, and from the beginning of time until the end of time. In the Torah story, God and Israel dwelled—sometimes in harmony and sometimes wrestling with each other—but always within a drama that gave life meaning in spite of brutal incursions of the profane world that surrounded and rejected the Jews.

The genius of this Talmudic Judaism was that instead of totally rejecting the messianic apocalypticism of the biblical period it transformed it, replacing political Zionism with an apolitical spiritual Zionism. The rabbis argued that Israel had been seduced by the Zealots into trying to force the coming of the messianic era by their own political activity. The truth is, the rabbis argued, that only God can initiate the messianic era, and God will bring the age of exile to an end and restore to Israel the land of promise only when all Israel is fully observant of *halakhah*. This view prevailed throughout the Middle Ages and was not seriously challenged until the coming of modern secular Zionism in the twentieth century.

The Medieval Journey of Judaism

Discrimination Against Jews in the Early Middle Ages

Dwelling in the great cosmic story of Torah, Israel survived its journey through the medieval world of persecutions and expulsions. It was splintered by the Jewish Enlightenment in the nineteenth century, however, and nearly shattered by the Holocaust in the twentieth century. That journey is a tale of tragic harbingers of the Holocaust; and yet it is also a story of amazing spiritual endurance and creativity that enriched and expanded the house of Torah in which Israel dwelled—especially through the contributions of Kabbalistic mysticism and Hasidic piety.

The situation of the Jews deteriorated with the decline of the Roman Empire and the rise of Christianity. While Jews in Palestine, the land of Israel, were under the colonial rule of the Romans in the first four centuries, they enjoyed a unique protected status as a legal religion, despite their refusal to

---

The Days of Awe and Passover

Rosh Hashanah and Yom Kippur

After the Sabbath, which sets the rhythm of Jewish religious life, the Jewish New Year (Rosh Hashanah and Yom Kippur) and Passover are the most prominent of the Jewish holy days or festivals. Unlike Passover, which is focused on the home and family, Rosh Hashanah and Yom Kippur are days of communal prayer spent in the synagogue. At Rosh Hashanah services, the story of creation is retold, and people are reminded that God is deciding who will and who will not be written in the book of life for another year, even as he will decide the fate of nations and of the whole world. So the new year raises questions of life and death and calls for self-examination. The process ends ten days later, on Yom Kippur, a day of total fasting and repentance. When Yom Kippur ends at sunset and the fast is broken, penitents consider themselves to be both cleansed and prepared to face the new year. The solemnity of Yom Kippur is intended to fill worshipers with the appropriate awe and respect for the Lord of the universe who governs the destiny of all.

(continued on next page)

The Days of Awe and Passover   *(continued)*

Passover

Passover, or *Pesach,* recalls God's deliverance of the tribes of Israel from slavery in Egypt (Exodus 1–15). Traditionally, Passover is celebrated in the home, usually with extended family and friends, with an event called a seder, during which Jews relive the story of the liberation from Egypt. The male head of the household presides at the retelling of the story, with extensive commentary from the sages of the Talmud, but members of the family are invited to participate, individually and collectively, in the recitation. Prominence is given to the youngest child, who must ask four key questions. The first one is "Why is this night different from all other nights?" In this way the story is passed on from generation to generation. The seder takes place around the dining table, and as the story is retold, certain symbolic foods are eaten to remind everyone of the events that led and still lead to liberation from slavery for every Jew.

This festival is also called the feast of unleavened bread (*matzah*), for the story indicates that the people left Egypt with little preparation and did not have time to make leavened bread (Exodus 12:31–34). To prepare for Passover all leavened bread must be removed from the premises and all utensils cleaned. Special foods used in the seder service include wine to celebrate the joy of deliverance; bitter herbs (e.g., horseradish) to recall the bitterness of oppression by the Egyptians; saltwater to recall the tears of the tribes in slavery; celery or parsley as a sign of spring, life, and hope; a roasted or boiled egg and a roasted shank bone to recall both the destruction of the temple and Israel's redemption at the Red Sea by the "outstretched arm" of God; and a mixture of apples, walnuts, and spices, called *haroset,* to recall the mortar used by Israelite slaves in building the Egyptian cities. The symbolic foods are consumed during the telling of the story, and then a full family meal of celebration is eaten, after which there are further prayers and recitations from the Passover portions of the Talmud. It is said that ordinary time is suspended during the Passover meal, and every Jew becomes part of the liberating event, able to say, "This day I too have been liberated from slavery."

To be rescued from peril is an experience that can transform the identity of a person or of a people. The Passover meal is a ritual meal, celebrated annually, to recall God's liberation of the tribes of Israel from slavery in Egypt. A Jewish family celebrates this great story of deliverance.

worship the gods of the official state cult. When the emperors and the empire became Christian, the colonial domination of the Jews became more severe. That domination did not really end until the establishment of the state of Israel in the twentieth century. In 380 the first Christian emperor, Theodosius, declared Christianity the official religion of the empire. All pagan religions were outlawed and Judaism, though not banned, was given a restricted legal status. Under the Theodosian law code of the early fifth century, Jews were not protected against severe discrimination in matters of religion and economics. In the sixth century the emperor Justinian produced an even more severe law code, under which Judaism had no legal protection at all, although Jews as individuals were granted some of the rights accorded other citizens. The view that Christians had superseded or replaced the Jews as God's chosen people led to what in later centuries would be called "the Jewish problem"—namely, the continuing existence of Jews. Jews came to be seen as an "obstinate" and "stiff-necked" people who refused to acknowledge the truth of Christianity and convert (or, in later modern secular culture, refused to give up their Jewishness and assimilate).

Their unfavorable legal status rendered Jews extraordinarily vulnerable to discrimination and persecution by the overwhelmingly Christian population that surrounded them. However, in the eighth century, an Islamic empire was created that stretched from India into Spain, subsuming the vast majority of Jews under Muslim rule. While Jews did not enjoy full equality under Islam, they usually fared better than under Christian rule. Nevertheless, they experienced sporadic periods of discrimination and persecution from Muslims as well. For example, it was under a Muslim ruler of Egypt, in the eleventh century, that Jews were first forced to wear special clothing as a "badge of shame" (a practice later adopted by the medieval Catholic church, and later still by the Nazis). Jews moved from agricultural village life into the new urban centers of the Muslim empire, where they became craftsmen or else capitalized on their Diaspora connections to prosper as traders and merchants. In the Christian West, Jews also embraced trading and selling, but out of necessity rather than choice. This was because only Christians were allowed to have slaves, and at that time slave labor was essential to success in agriculture.

The Carolingian Era of Tolerance

For a while in Europe, under the Frankish Carolingian kings, who founded the Holy Roman Empire, the life of Jews improved. Jews enjoyed high positions in the courts and in the professions and experienced new opportunities for wealth. Indeed, the court chaplain under Louis I converted to Judaism in 839. An attempted backlash of discrimination was squelched by the emperor, who is known to history as Louis the Pious. And while Jews were not considered full citizens, they prospered under so-called diplomas of protection from the king's court. They became "the king's Jews." This practice was a benefit as long as Jews were favored by the king. However, in later periods the arrangement resulted in sudden reversals of fortune whenever a king (or Holy Roman Emperor) found it convenient to rescind his protection.

Centuries of Persecution and Pogrom

In the late Middle Ages Jewish life became truly precarious in Europe. The tide turned against Jews with the launching of the first Crusade by Pope Urban II in 1095. The announced reason for the Crusades was to free Jerusalem and all of the Holy Land from the Muslims, who had taken Jerusalem in 638. As in Christianity and Judaism, Jerusalem is a holy city in Islam.

A "plenary indulgence," or guarantee of forgiveness of sins and entry into heaven was promised to anyone who participated in the Crusade. However, as the armies raised for this purpose passed through the cities and towns of Europe on their way to rid the Holy Land of infidels, they decided to use the opportunity to purge the Christian world of its other "enemy" as well.

The Christian armies passing through the Rhine Valley offered Jews the choice of conversion or death. Many responded by committing suicide; many others were massacred. Few converted. The pattern of persecution and violence against Jews continued in the centuries that followed. In 1251 the Fourth Lateran Council of the Catholic Church adopted the Muslim practice of forcing Jews to wear distinctive dress and to live in segregated quarters called ghettos. To the pattern of violence was added the periodic practice of expulsion. In 1306, in a single day, all the Jews of France were arrested and ordered to be out of the country within a month. Other countries followed suit, driving the majority of Europe's Jews into eastern Europe. In 1348, as the Black Death swept across the Continent, Jews were blamed and made the scapegoats, and the Jews of many communities were executed. In Strasbourg, for instance, two hundred Jews were burned alive in a cemetery on the Sabbath.

The first Crusade ended with the violent retaking of Jerusalem from the Muslims in 1099.

The Protestant Reformation, initiated in 1517, seemed to be characterized by a more positive attitude toward Judaism. At first, Martin Luther wrote favorably of the Jews. But toward the end of his life, the German religious leader realized that Jews were no more receptive to his interpretation of the Gospel than to the Catholic interpretation. Thereafter, Luther turned viciously anti-Judaic, advocating the abuse of Jews and the burning of synagogues. Nevertheless, the aftermath of the Reformation in the sixteenth and seventeenth centuries left Christians too busy fighting each other to make the Jews a central concern. This distraction, as well as a modification of ghettos that put Jews under lock and key at night, served to reduce the violence Jews experienced at the hands of Christians.

However, at the same time, as the Jewish population of eastern Europe grew by leaps and bounds as a consequence of the expulsions from western Europe, new waves of violence broke out against Jews in eastern Europe. Between 1648 and 1658, in organized massacres called pogroms, over seven hundred Jewish communities were destroyed. Jewish deaths numbered in the hundreds of thousands. Fueling this violence in Europe was an ethos of Jew-hatred that lent plausibility to the rationalization "Jews are our misfortune" and helped prepare the way for the Holocaust.

The skeletal horse and rider in this fifteenth-century fresco represent the devastation of the plague, or Black Death, throughout Europe in the 1300s.

From the Golden Age in Spain to the Spanish Inquisition

In the midst of this violent history stands the Golden Age of Spain as an extraordinary interlude, when Jews were welcomed as allies against the Muslims in the portions of Spain that had been reconquered by Christians. For a time in the twelfth and early thirteenth centuries, Jews were encouraged to settle in the reconquered territories and were given unusual freedom both socially and politically, achieving important roles in the royal court and in the professions. It was a period of unprecedented intellectual exchange between the great scholars of Judaism, Islam, and Christianity.

The period came to an end in the mid-thirteenth century as Christians reacted to the presence of Jews in high places with alarm. This fear of a "Jewish takeover" led to a new period of persecution, violence, and forced conversions, culminating in the Spanish Inquisition. Between 1480 and 1492 some thirteen thousand Jews, most of whom had been forcibly baptized as Christians, were condemned for practicing Judaism in secret. Many were tortured and burned at the stake. The Jews were expelled from Spain in 1492 (see Map 3.2).

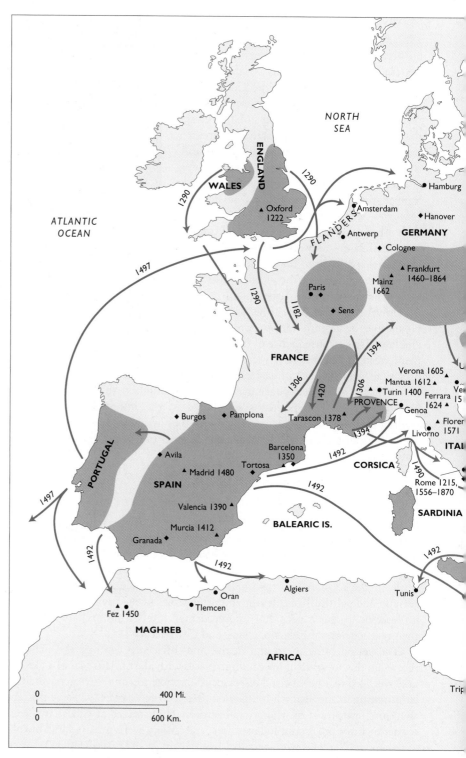

Map 3.2   Jews in Christian Europe.

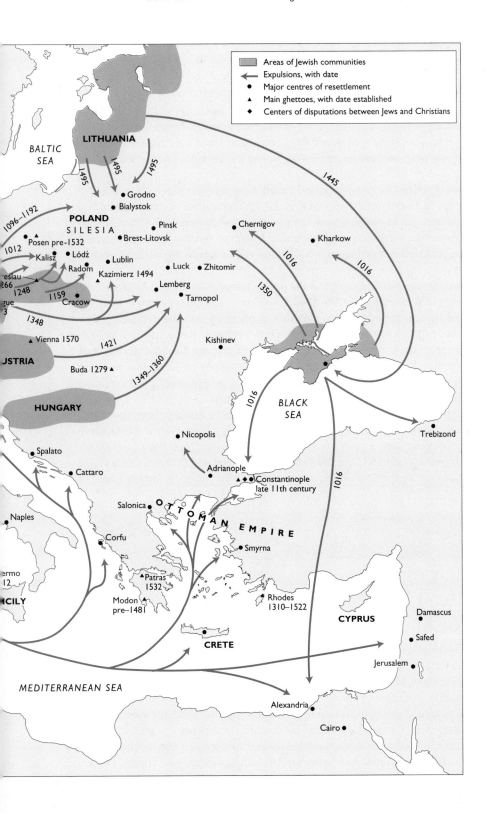

Areas of Jewish communities

Expulsions, with date

● Major centres of resettlement

▲ Main ghettoes, with date established

◆ Centers of disputations between Jews and Christians

BALTIC SEA

LITHUANIA

1495

1495

1495

1445

● Grodno

● Bialystok

POLAND
SILESIA

1096–1192

1012

▲ Posen pre-1532

● Pinsk

● Chernigov

● Kharkow

Kalisz

● Lódź

● Brest-Litovsk

1016

● Lublin

▲ Radom

Kazimierz 1494

● Luck   ● Zhitomir

reslau
266

1248

1159

Cracow

● Lemberg

1350

1016

gue
3

1348

● Tarnopol

▲ Vienna 1570

1421

● Kishinev

USTRIA

Buda 1279 ▲

1349–1360

1016

HUNGARY

BLACK SEA

Trebizond

● Nicopolis

● Spalato

Adrianople

● Cattaro

▲ ◆ ◆ Constantinople
late 11th century

Naples

Salonica ●

OTTOMAN EMPIRE

● Corfu

1016

● Smyrna

ermo
12

▲ Patras
1532

CILY

Modon
pre–1481 ▲

Rhodes
1310–1522

CYPRUS

Damascus

● Safed

Jerusalem ●

CRETE

Alexandria ●

MEDITERRANEAN SEA

Cairo ●

The Popes and the Paradox of "the Jewish Problem"

Throughout Christian history, the Jews of Italy, on the whole, fared much better than the rest of European Jewry. Rome is the only major city of Europe from which Jews were never expelled. Jews experienced no punitive taxes, were free to select their occupations, and were not forbidden by law to marry Christians. Nor were Jews persecuted in Italy during the Crusades and the years of the Black Death.

There were a number of reasons for this paradoxical thread in the religious history of Europe. For example, the medieval feudal system ended very early in Italy, permitting the development of free cities, with their many advantages. In addition, since usury was an allowable occupation for Christian financiers in Italy, Jews were not singled out for resentment. Later, the Renaissance brought a new openness toward the Jews as well. But perhaps the most influential factor was the relation between the popes and the Jews.

It was widely believed by medieval Christians that the gentile followers of Jesus had replaced the Jews as God's chosen people. To explain away "the Jewish problem"—why God nevertheless permitted Jews to continue to exist—the popes, from the sixth century on, turned to a theory developed by St. Augustine, the so-called negative witness theory. According to this theory, it was God's will for Jews to wander the earth without a home, their unhappy existence functioning as a "negative witness" that proved the superiority and truth of Christianity. Consequently, the popes preached that God had rejected the Jews, while at the same time, paradoxically, acting as the legal protectors and guardians of the original chosen people, insisting that they not be physically harmed.

Although the negative witness theory shaped papal strategy for dealing with the "Jewish problem" in medieval Christendom, during the Renaissance some popes took a less biased view. Pope Sixtus IV (1471–84), for example, commissioned a Latin translation of the Kabbalah. Later Pope Clement VII sought to develop a common translation of the Old Testament by Jewish and Christian scholars, and he suspended the persecution by the Spanish Inquisition of Jews who had been forcibly baptized in Spain.

Two Great Medieval Scholars: Rashi and Maimonides

The period of the late Middle Ages produced two of the greatest scholars in the history of Judaism: Rabbi Solomon ben Isaac (1040–1105), otherwise known as Rashi, and Moses ben Maimon (1135–1204), otherwise known as Maimonides. Rashi's commentaries on the Gemara of the Babylonian Talmud, which appeared in the first printed edition of the Talmud and have been in all editions since, are considered to form an essential component of the work. Rashi is hailed as the most unsurpassable teacher of Torah in the history of Talmudic Judaism. He founded an influential Talmudic academy in Troyes, France.

Maimonides is famous for his philosophical writings, in which he uses Aristotelian concepts to explain Jewish teaching. His *Guide of the Perplexed*, is well known today, and for over three centuries his compendium of Talmudic law, the *Mishneh Torah*, was the most influential guide to *halakhah* in Judaism. Although Judaism is not a religion that emphasizes dogma (right belief) as the test of true faith, Maimonides is credited with giving Judaism a credal statement known as the Thirteen Articles of Faith.

Kabbalah—Jewish Mysticism

Judaism, like all religions, has a mystical dimension. Not only in Judaism, but in the other two monotheistic traditions of Christianity and Islam, mystics have generally been viewed with an element of mistrust because mystical experience is direct and immediate and so tends to undermine traditional lines of authority. The mystic finds God without the guidance of either a priest or a teacher (rabbi). Moreover, the mystic often speaks of God in ways that are unconventional and sometimes seem contradictory to the nature of prophetic monotheism.

In the monotheistic traditions mysticism expresses itself in two dramatically different forms—the mysticism of love and union (the divine–human marriage) and the mysticism of identity. The place of the mystic in monotheism has always been an ambivalent one, more so for the mystics of identity than for those of unity. This is because mystics often speak not of the difference between God and the person but of their oneness. The mystics of identity sometimes seem to say they are not just in union with God but that they are God. Whenever mystics speak in this way they are in danger of being accused of confusing themselves with God and claiming to be God. Any such representation would be heretical and blasphemous in all three biblical religions, hence would be unacceptable by any of them. And yet, despite this seemingly ever-present danger, each of the monotheistic religions has chosen to maintain an uneasy peace with its mystics, neither denying the importance and validity of mysticism nor suppressing its practice.

Although Jewish mysticism goes back to the ancient world and reflects the influences of Neoplatonism and gnosticism, it did not become a decisive influence in Judaism until the explicit emergence of Kabbalah in the late medieval period. Kabbalism sought to explain the mystery of good and evil in the universe precisely at a time of intensifying persecution and pogroms. Jews could not help but seek an understanding of God that could sustain them through a new period of suffering.

The most important Kabbalistic work is the *Zohar* (Book of Splendor). For Kabbalists, the God beyond the God of the Bible is the *En Sof* ("limitless" or "infinite"), who manifests himself in the world through his *Sefiroth* ("fragments or emanations of the infinite") or qualities such as wisdom, mercy, and justice. The elements of the Sefiroth are fragments that emanate from the spiritual world and are encapsulated in the physical world, finally manifesting in the *Shekinah* ("divine presence"). According to Kabbalistic teaching, there was a time when God manifested himself in the world, allowing his *Shekinah* to be perceived in all things. However, because of the fall of Adam, evil entered the world and the divine presence has been exiled from its unity with the infinite (*En Sof*). Humans were created for *devekut* ("communion") with God, but this relationship was destroyed by Adam's sin and must be reestablished through mystical contemplation (*kavanah*) of the divine through prayer and the devout performance of the requirements of *halakhah*. The reunion of all with the infinite will bring about nothing less than the ingathering of all Jews from exile in the messianic kingdom to come.

The Kabbalistic tradition comprises a profound mystical variation on the theme of exile and return. It can be seen as a powerful religious response to the overwhelming tragedy of persecution and expulsion that marked Jewish life in Europe in the late Middle Ages and beyond. It explained the age of darkness in which Jews lived in exile and offered them a hope of transcending that darkness.

Hasidism

For the Hasidim there is no greater sin than sadness. The proper response to God's presence, hidden everywhere in creation, is joy. One expression of that joy is to dance with the Torah, as this Hasidic man in Jerusalem is doing, accompanied by other male dancers of all ages.

The mystical impulse of Kabbalism was given further embodiment in the Hasidic movement, which appeared in eastern Europe, partly in response to the pogroms endemic to the region. A hasid is a pious one, whose life is marked by great devotion. Piety has always been an important element in the observance of the way of Torah. As a movement of enthusiastic piety, however, hasidism really came into its own in eastern Europe at the beginning of the eighteenth century. It was at this time that the term acquired a new intensity of meaning.

The Hasidic movement emerged in Poland with the activities of Israel ben Eliezer, who was called "the Besht" by his followers. This title was a shortened form of Ba'al Shem Tov, or Master of the Good Name, where the "good

name" was understood to be the name of God. The Besht was an ecstatic healer who worked miracles using magic, amulets, and spells. He taught that joy is the appropriate response to the world no matter how much suffering Jews experience.

In fact, although Hasidism emerged in an era of pogrom and immense suffering in eastern Europe, the Hasidim say there is no greater sin than melancholy or sadness (atzut). For sadness, which stems from ignorance of the pervasive presence of God in all things, is the root of all sin. According to the Besht, God hides himself in his creation. Therefore, there is no distance between God and humanity for those who have the eyes to see. And once you do see, there can be no sadness but only simhah—deep, pervasive, passionate joy and celebration.

The Besht was a charismatic figure whose followers hung on his every word and gesture. Their prayer circles were characterized by ecstatic singing and dancing, and they looked forward to deeply moving spiritual talks by the Besht around the Sabbath dinner table. The Besht taught that the essence of the way of Torah is to be found in devotion (kavanah), burning enthusiasm (hitlahavut), and attachment or clinging to God (devekut) rather than in study of the Talmud.

The Besht became a model for the Hasidic notion of the Tzaddik or "righteous man." The Tzaddik's authority in each Hasidic community was every bit as powerful as that of the rabbi in a traditional Talmudic community. For the Hasidim, the Tzaddik was no ordinary person but one especially chosen by God as a direct link between heaven and earth. He was revered as a savior figure whose holiness was considered so powerful that, like Moses (Exodus 32:11–14), he could intervene on behalf of the faithful and literally change the mind of God. Like the rabbis, the Tzaddik was a religious virtuoso; however his virtuosity was of mystical piety and devotion, not of Talmudic scholarship. His holiness was said to be spontaneously contagious: just being near him, the Hasidim could catch his piety as a spark to light their own.

Hasidism garnered an enthusiastic popular following, for it offered even the poor and unlearned a way to move from the periphery into the heart of Judaism as they understood it. One reason for this was that in the early days, Hasidic Judaism rejected the elitism of Rabbinic Judaism. For the rabbis and their students were an intellectual elite, trained as Talmudic experts—something the average Jew could not hope to be. Hasidic Judaism offered ways to reach God other than Talmudic study: namely, devotion and prayer, which were within the reach of every sincere Jew. This path brought into popular practice the deep mystical piety of the Kabbalistic tradition.

What was most extraordinary about Hasidic mysticism was, and is, its communal nature. One cannot achieve this state of joy and selflessness by going off alone to a mountaintop but only by total immersion in the community life of the Hasidim organized around the festive worship made possible by the presence of the Tzaddik. It is this linking of deep mystical spirituality with community life that made Hasidism such a powerful force for renewal.

It was not immediately obvious to the rabbis that Hasidism would benefit Judaism, for Hasidism challenged the authority structure and hierarchy of religious virtues promoted by Talmudic Judaism. Rabbis who opposed the Hasidim were known as *Mitnaggedim* ("opponents"). However, despite fears that Hasidism would lead to excesses, the movement brought genuine renewal and rejuvenation to Judaism. In the nineteenth century, Hasidism moved toward reconciliation with Rabbinic Judaism by incorporating more emphasis on the study of Talmud and was accepted by the rabbis as an authentic expression of the way of Torah.

The Kabbalistic–Hasidic tradition was deeply influenced by Neoplatonism and gnosticism. The success of its integration with the Talmudic tradition demonstrates the extraordinary ability of Judaism to absorb and sanctify the "secular" and non-Jewish while reaffirming the practices of the tradition. This is a pattern we see repeated in the twentieth century, when many of the movements of modern and post-Holocaust Judaism have grown closer together. Judaism, despite inner tensions and conflicts, shows an amazing ability to absorb conflicting movements, which often catalyze transformation and renewal. This should not surprise anyone, for this has been true of Judaism from its very beginnings in the biblical period.

Having surveyed premodern Judaism, we are now in a position to look at the emergence of modern forms and to understand better how they are both like premodern forms of Judaism and different from them.

JUDAISM AND MODERNITY

The Emergence of Modern Religious Forms of Judaism

Reform Judaism

From the early days of Rabbinic Judaism, between the second and fifth centuries, until the French Revolution in 1789, Jews in Europe lived as a rejected minority in a world dominated by Christians in the political entity called the Holy Roman Empire. With Enlightenment secularization, the categories of human self-understanding underwent radical revision. Enlightened Europeans were secular universalists who defined their humanity not in terms of religious myths, which they believed created divisiveness, but in terms of reason, which they held to be universally accessible to humans. The ideal of this new orientation was to replace the categories of "Jew" and "Christian" with a single category: "human being."

For the first time in almost two thousand years, the dominant culture looked at Jews as rational beings, equal to all other human beings, and Jews were invited to participate as citizens alongside all other individuals in the modern capitalist nation-states (see Map 3.3). This message of inclusion was

Map 3.3   The Emancipation of European Jewry, 1789–1918.

widely accepted by the Jews of western Europe. It seemed that a new day was dawning. One of the leading Enlightenment scholars of the eighteenth century, Gotthold Lessing (1729–81), a gentile, wrote impassioned works proclaiming the humanity of Jews and of Muslims and arguing for their acceptance in society. Lessing befriended Moses Mendelssohn (1729–86),who became the leading figure in the Jewish Haskalah or Enlightenment movement, the eventual source of Reform Judaism, the first "modern" form of Judaism.

Like Hellenistic Judaism in the first century, the Haskalah movement favored partial assimilation into the gentile world, trying to show that in the 1800s, one could be an enlightened citizen of the secular world and a Jew at the same time. This required the leaders of the Reform movement to answer a question that all modern forms of Judaism (including Orthodoxy) have confronted: how can I be both a Jew and a citizen of a secular state? It had been pointless to ask this question earlier, when secular states did not exist and Christian states offered Jews no possibility of citizenship.

Reform Judaism, and all other forms of modern Judaism, however, have had to make a decision about how to relate to the larger secular society. They have had to determine what belonged to the essence of Judaism, treating other practices and beliefs as negotiable. Embracing the Enlightenment ideal of religion within the "limits of reason," the leaders of the Reform movement defined the essence of Judaism as a rational–ethical system rooted in the prophetic–ethical ideal of justice—an ethic that was Judaism's gift to humanity. Like their Hellenistic counterparts, they did not think that this ethic was for Jews alone but rather that Judaism was its source and purest form. This universal rational ethic was the essence; all other aspects of Judaism were open to discussion.

As Reform Judaism developed, it showed a remarkable openness to secular society. For instance, Jews could use the vernacular instead of Hebrew in worship; thus synagogue prayers and sermons could be spoken in the local language (German, French, English, etc.). As the movement developed in the late nineteenth century, it was also prepared to abandon the observance of kosher laws, restricting the foods Jews can eat, and other "historical accretions" as inessential to being Jewish. Indeed, it rejected the Talmud as revelation, seeing it instead as simply a human historical tradition. And it rejected belief in a literal coming of the messiah, replacing it with a belief in a messianic age that could easily be identified with the goal of the modern age of scientific and rational progress. Finally, it renounced any desire to return to the land of Israel, insisting that Jews were not a people tied to a specific land but a "religious community."

What especially marks the Reform movement as modern is its openness to secular learning and historical consciousness. In premodern Rabbinic Judaism (with such notable exceptions as Maimonides), the only learning worthy of consideration was the study of Torah and Talmud. But among enlightened Jews, secular learning not only was permitted but took precedence. For instance, in deciding what is and what is not essential to Judaism, Reform Judaism argued not from the "revealed will of God," as had premodern Judaism, but from the history of the development of Judaism as a religion. Thus "history" and "Judaism," not "God" and "Torah," became the defining categories. Religious disputes were to be settled primarily by appeal to the developmental history of Judaism. After all, what history reveals, Reform Jews argued, is that Judaism is a religion not of eternal, unchanging truths but of constant change. From this perspective, Reform Judaism is the true Judaism for the modern world and the logical successor, in the authentic unfolding of the historical tradition, to premodern Rabbinic Judaism.

Reform Judaism explained how one could be a Jew and still be part of a larger secular society. Reform Judaism, which initiated the journey of Judaism into the modern world, was the pioneer of all modern Judaisms. For some of these, Reform Judaism was a model to be emulated with modifications, especially the more secular forms of Judaism—ethnic Judaism, Jewish socialism, and Zionism (to be discussed shortly). Indeed, it would be hard to imagine the secular state of Israel without the path opened up by Reform Judaism. Yet other Jews believed that the Reform was heading in the wrong direction. Indeed, it was only after the bold statements of Reform Judaism that a second form of modern Judaism appeared: Orthodox Judaism, which vigorously rejected the claims of the Reform movement.

Orthodox Judaism

To call Orthodox Judaism a modern form of Judaism may seem contradictory, for orthodoxy claims that it continues the ancient tradition of premodern Rabbinic Judaism. Reform Judaism, of course, also claims to continue the same tradition. Orthodoxy, however, defined continuity in terms of resisting all change, whereas Reform Judaism thought it meant being true to the historical law of constant change. The issue between Reform and Orthodox Jews was whether, as Reform Jews held, God was acting through an ever-changing history, progressing toward an age of messianic freedom, or whether the Orthodox were correct in their view: that God revealed himself only in the eternal, unchanging covenant given at Sinai. This reflects the choice modernization puts to all religions—whether to embrace historical change or reject it out of faithfulness to a view of premodern unchanging fundamental truths.

Reform Jews argued for changes that would accommodate the modern world, while the Orthodox wanted to refuse all accommodation, although they seldom fully achieved this. Orthodox Jews wanted to present their choice of orthodoxy as if it were no choice. But clearly, the very appearance of the reform meant that one could no longer just be a Jew; one had to choose to be a Jew of a certain kind. In agreeing that it was necessary to choose, orthodoxy gave evidence that it too was a Judaism of the modern period. From now on, like Reform Judaism, it would have to think of itself as one religious community alongside others. Premodern Rabbinic Jews had no such dilemma, for there was no "Judaism" to choose, only God, Torah, and Israel, the givens of one's birth into the chosen people.

Orthodoxy became, in many ways, the mirror image of Reform Judaism, for mirror images reverse the original that they reflect. Thus if Reform Jews prayed in the vernacular, the Orthodox insisted that all prayers be in Hebrew. If Reform Jews insisted on historical change, the Orthodox insisted on eternal unchanging truth. If Reform Jews decided issues of religious practice on the basis of history, the Orthodox decided them on the basis of the eternal word of God given in the Torah and Talmud. If Reform Jews abandoned literal messianic beliefs, the Orthodox reaffirmed them. If Reform Jews dismissed the Talmudic requirements (*halakhah*) as historical accretions, the Orthodox insisted on continued observance of the requirements of the dual Torah (the written Torah and the oral Torah). And if Reform Jews abandoned any ambition to return to the land of Israel, the Orthodox prayed "next year in Jerusalem" while awaiting the deliverance of the messiah.

Women in Judaism

Talmudic Judaism shares with the emerging Judaism of the ancient biblical period a common assumption of premodern urban societies, transposed into a monotheistic frame of reference. Specifically, it was long assumed that there is a sacred natural order of the world, revealed by God, in which maleness is the normative pattern for full humanity. Traditionally, this assumption was validated by the second creation story presented in the Bible: Genesis 2:5–3:24 (as opposed to the first version, Genesis 1:1–2:4). Since in the second story God created Adam first and then Eve from the rib of Adam, men were accorded primary responsibility for the order of things, women having been created to help men. Indeed, women (like animals and slaves) are the property of men. A father could sell his daughter as payment for a debt (Exodus 21:7), for instance. Basically, a woman belonged to her father until she was given to the man who married her to whom she then belonged. Women had no role in the public worship in the temple, but at the same time women were honored as mothers and the mainstay of the family.

The biblical attitude toward women was continued in premodern Rabbinic Judaism. However, during the biblical period certain exceptional women were revered for their wisdom and their gifts of prophecy: Miriam (the sister of Moses), Deborah (one of the judges of Israel), and Huldah (a prophetess during the reign of Josiah). Both Rabbinic and later Hasidic traditions also present models of women who were exceptions, noted for their learning and piety. Beruriah, the wife of Rabbi Meir, was noted for her skill as a Talmudic scholar, and Oudil, the daughter of the Ba'al Shem Tov, was praised for her wisdom and joyous piety. Nevertheless, such women were not the norm. They remained the exception that proved the rule.

The Enlightenment brought with it a gradual change in the status of women in Western culture, and women have progressively claimed autonomy, that is, control of their own lives. Modern forms of Judaism tend to demythologize traditional Jewish gender roles as inessential historical accretions that may even contradict fundamental insights of Judaism concerning justice and human dignity. Thus, it is probably fair to say that the greatest equality for women has been among the secular forms of Judaism, especially Jewish socialism and Zionism, and among the most secular forms of religious Judaism—Reform first, then Conservative, and least among the Orthodox.

The ultra-Orthodox set out on a path of segregation, challenging the integrationism of the Reform Jews. East European haredim tried to shut out modernity altogether, but this meant doing what no premodern Rabbinic Jew had ever had to do—become a sectarian. In western Europe the Orthodox saw the futility of separating themselves completely from the secular world and allowed that in "inessentials," like clothing, secular education, and choice of job or career, Jews may be like everyone else. Indeed, Orthodoxy's first great intellectual defender, Samson Raphael Hirsch (1808–88), sought to show that one can live as a Jew in a secular nation-state and remain fully Orthodox.

The Declaration of Independence of the State of Israel, drawing on the nation's secular socialist and Zionist roots, asserts complete equality of men and women in social and political rights. The Equal Rights for Women law of 1951, guarantees women the same rights enjoyed by men to own property and to make decisions on behalf of their children. Among the explicitly religious forms of Judaism, the Reform movement has led the way. As early as 1846 a movement to declare women equal appeared in Germany. And about the same time women were admitted to Hebrew Union College in the United States. Nevertheless, the desire of women to become rabbis was not discussed seriously until the 1920s, and it was not until the 1970s that women began to be ordained (although one private ordination is said to have occurred in 1935 in a German Reform congregation).

Conservative and Orthodox Judaism have been slower to respond to issues of gender equality. For in these traditions Talmudic precedent carries more weight than it does among Reform Jews, and progress toward equality can be achieved only through skillful Talmudic arguments for change. Nevertheless, today it is not uncommon, in both Reform and Conservative synagogues in America, for a young woman to celebrate her bat mitzvah as a parallel rite to a brother's bar mitzvah. Nor is it unusual for women to read the Torah scrolls at a Sabbath service. And it is even becoming more common for women cantors to chant such services and for women rabbis to conduct them. All of this was unthinkable in premodern Judaism. And it remains unthinkable among the ultra-Orthodox.

Today in both Reform Judaism and Conservative Judaism women are ordained to the rabbinate. This rabbi works with 13-year-old twins as they rehearse for their b'nai mitzvah at the Jewish Community Center in Tucson, Arizona.

Therefore, above all, what makes Orthodoxy a modern Judaism is that, like Reform Judaism, it divides the world into the religious and the secular, separating religion and politics in a way that allows Orthodox Jews to be both Jews and citizens of a secular nation-state.

Conservative Judaism

Once the lines had been drawn between the first two modern ways of being Jewish, it was perhaps inevitable that a third option would emerge, seeking a compromise. That option was Conservative Judaism. The Orthodox saw Jewish life as the life of an eternal people, Reform Jews saw Jewish life as the life of an historical religious community. Conservative Jews saw Jewish life as the life of an historically ethnic people that included but was not limited to the religious dimension. Conservative Judaism arose among Jews who were deeply committed to the Orthodox way of life, yet sympathetic to the "modern" intellectual worldview of Reform Judaism.

The message of the leaders of Conservative Judaism was "Think whatever you like, but do what the law requires." Thus on the question of the relationship to the secular, Conservative Judaism focused on practice rather than belief. This compromise gave conservative Jews considerable intellectual freedom of interpretation—one could believe or disbelieve any or all elements of the supernatural worldview of premodern Rabbinic Judaism and still be a Jew, as long as one observed Talmudic law in everyday life (although modest compromises in this area were permitted). This position puts the emphasis on orthopraxy (right practice) as opposed to orthodoxy (right belief).

Largely of American origin, with intellectual roots in the German Haskalah, Conservative Judaism fits very well with the pragmatic attitude of modern (especially American) culture. Like Reform Jews, Conservative Jews see Judaism as an historically unfolding religion, but unlike the Reform Jews and more like the Orthodox, the Conservatives emphasize an organic continuity. Historical change does not produce abrupt reorientations but gradual development—a development of the unfolding essence of Judaism. And that essence is found not so much in belief as in practice. In this way, Conservative Judaism, like Reform and Orthodox Judaism, saw itself as the logical continuation of the tradition. Conservative Judaism, as the third option, has been the most influential and widely embraced form of modern Judaism in America.

Reconstructionism

In addition to the three main strands of modern Judaism is the movement known as Reconstructionism, founded in America in the 1930s by Mordecai Kaplan. Kaplan cast his understanding of Judaism in almost completely secular terms drawn from the modern social and historical sciences. Judaism was defined as the religion of Jewish civilization, where "religion" was understood not in supernatural terms but as the embodiment of the ideals and group identity of a culture. But for that very reason, the practice of the religious rituals of the tradition was an important means of preserving the identity and continuing vitality of Jewish civilization. For Kaplan, Judaism must not be about life beyond death but about improving the individual's life and working for the progress of society. Membership in the Reconstructionist movement is modest, but many of its themes are found in the three main types of secular Judaism that, as we shall see, found the need for religious ritual less compelling.

The Emergence of Secular Forms of Judaism

The dawning of the age of Enlightenment created an optimistic mood among Jews. But that mood did not last, for the promise of inclusion for Jews turned out to be false. The hidden premise of the new offer became apparent in the aftermath of the French Revolution, which offered full citizenship to Jews. The offer, however, gave *everything to Jews as individuals and nothing to the Jews as a people*. To be a citizen in the postrevolutionary secular society, one had to trade one's religious identity for a secular or nonreligious one.

But even the considerable number of Jews who paid the high price never were accorded the equality that had been promised. The ideals of the Enlightenment were genuine enough, but they quickly crashed on the rocks of the intractability of human prejudice. As more and more Jews were "secularized" in Europe, either abandoning or minimizing their Judaism, they entered into the political and economic life of their respective countries. As they achieved success, a backlash occurred. Throughout Europe, non-Jews began to fear that the Jews were taking over "their" society.

By the end of the nineteenth century a secular, supposedly scientific, definition had come to replace the old religious definition of the Jews. The Jews became defined as a race—an inferior race that had a biologically corrupting influence on society. With the introduction of the language of race, all the old Christian stereotypes of Jews as a rejected people were resurrected in a new guise. Theoretically, at least, the Jews as a religious people could be converted—hence, "the Jewish problem" could be solved. But race is perceived as a biologically unchangeable fact; people cannot convert from one race to another. Moreover, the advocates of the "scientific" theory of race viewed any attempt at assimilation through intermarriage as racial pollution. The attempt to designate Jews as a race fueled undercurrents of anti-Jewish feeling, never completely absent in twentieth-century Europe. As a consequence, in the 1930s the Nazi party, in Germany, could begin to exploit prejudice against "the Jewish race" to devastating effect.

In the United States, Jews fared better than in Europe. America was forged as a nation of many peoples fleeing religious intolerance in England and on the Continent. Anti-Semitism and other forms of religious bigotry were not absent from America's formative history, but Jews in America never experienced pogroms and mass expulsions. American individualism allowed more space for diverse ethnic and religious communal identities.

Jewish immigrants to the United States came in two waves. The first and more modest wave, dating from 1654, consisted of seekers of religious freedom, Jews of Spanish or Portuguese extraction, known as Sephordic Jews. The second and much larger wave began in the nineteenth century among the Ashkenazi, Jews of eastern Europe who were fleeing persecution and pogrom. By the beginning of World War II, approximately a third of the world's Jews lived in the United States. After World War II, twice as many Jews lived in the United States as in all of Europe.

While Jews in America were being integrated into society, in the late 1800s and early 1900s, the Jews of western Europe were once more being persecuted. Most of the Jews of eastern Europe never did sense that they had been invited to join a new Enlightenment order of equality and inclusion. On the contrary, the increase in persecutions and pogroms of the nineteenth century represented the continuation of an ancient pattern. The challenge was to devise a strategy for surviving in societies that were replacing religious anti-Judaism with secular anti-Semitism. And it was among the more fully assimilated and secularized Jews that the new responses emerged, responses that would form a bridge from the modern forms of Judaism (Reform, Orthodox, and Conservative) to the postmodern and postcolonial Judaism of Holocaust and Redemption. These new secular forms of Judaism were Jewish socialism, ethnic (Yiddish) Judaism, and Zionism, each one offering a distinct way of being Jewish. Yet they were capable of combining in interesting and powerful ways that set the stage for the emergence of the Judaism of Holocaust and Redemption.

Jewish Socialism

Some of the strongest currents of Jewish socialism came out of eastern Europe, where secularized Jews saw in socialism another way of resolving the tension between being Jewish and being modern. For, as noted in Chapter One, socialism, especially the later "scientific" socialism of Marx, offered an essentially secularized version of the Jewish and Christian myths of history. It was a view of history as a story of exile and return, in which human beings begin in paradise (primitive communism), only to be expelled from the garden into a world of selfishness and sin (class conflict). Socialism, however, promises a transformation, eventually, into a global, classless, society in which suffering and injustice will be overcome and all will live in perfect harmony— a vision very much like that of one kingdom of God. Perhaps it is no coincidence that Karl Marx, whose father was a convert to Christianity, was the grandson of a rabbi.

For the many "secularized" Jews of Europe, the socialist story of history offered a new, yet very familiar, framework in which to understand their place in the drama of history. And it offered a story that, like the ancient pattern of exile and return, both deferred yet continued the (Enlightenment) promise of freedom and equality for all (hence the end of anti-Semitism)—if not now, then in a future classless society, corresponding to the messianic age of Judaism and Christianity. In the meantime, this new secular story gave the Enlightenment-oriented secular Jews a secular way of being Jewish. In this, Jewish socialism adapted the spirit of Reform Judaism, opting for historical development as the key to continuity in Jewish history and for a secular vision of Judaism that favored the prophetic witness of the written Torah (redefined as socialist ethics) over that of the oral Torah traditions of the Talmud. And, like Reform Jews, the Jewish socialists did not need to regard their message as exclusive to Judaism. For them it was enough to see Judaism as the unique contributor of the ideal of social justice to an international ethic for the whole human race. However, unlike their Reform counterparts, Jewish socialists no longer represented themselves as "religious"—for religion belonged to the prescientific age that was passing away.

Who was attracted to this way of being Jewish? The message of socialism was directed to the proletariat—industrial workers with little chance of upward mobility. So the message naturally took deep root in a demographic that had resulted from the capitalist factory system: impoverished secular Jewish workers. In the wake of the Russian Revolution of 1917, socialism was especially attractive to the Jews of Russia and eastern Europe, and to the poor Jewish immigrants from these areas who came to the United States. These were Jews who were victims not only of anti-Semitism but also of economic depression and unemployment. The pivotal date for Jewish socialism is usually said to be 1897, the year of the formation of the Bund, or Jewish Worker's Union, in Poland.

Many secular Jews joined the socialist movement but rejected all connections with Judaism. They thought of themselves as purely secular, nonreligious persons. Some even vigorously disavowed their Jewish roots, going so far as to contribute to existing currents of anti-Semitism. Jewish socialists, by contrast, were not religious, yet wished to retain and affirm their ties to the history of the Jewish people. And so they turned to ethnicity as the key to Jewish identity—an ethnicity that was primarily identified with speaking the Yiddish language.

Yiddish Ethnic Judaism

Even secular Jews who no longer used or knew Hebrew knew Yiddish, the common language of European Jews that developed from about the eleventh century—an amalgam of Hebrew and German. The focus on Yiddish language, and especially Yiddish literature, which often echoes Talmudic and biblical stories, gave secular Jews a way to identify with Judaism without being "religious" and to draw on the wisdom of the tradition.

Yiddish was more than a language. It stood for a way of experiencing and interpreting the world that was still deeply rooted in Judaism. Indeed, ever since the first nation-states emerged in Europe, language had been the key to national identity. Through Yiddish, Jews, otherwise dispersed—without a land of their own—sought to sustain their identity as a people in a secular age. As the language of working-class Jews, Yiddish gave Jews a deep sense of "ethnicity," of being bound together in a common historical tradition that offered, as well, a unique identity. That ethnicity could easily be tapped by Jewish socialists to mobilize Jews, that is, to organize them for the workers' revolution that was part of the Marxian scheme of history.

From the end of the nineteenth century until the end of World War II, Jewish socialism was the predominant secular response to modernity among Jews, both in Europe and America. But it was not the only response, for there emerged in the nineteenth century another Jewish movement that, in the long run, would be even more influential—Zionism.

The Origins of Zionism

Zionism was born out of disenchantment with modernity and the promises of the Enlightenment. Unlike Jewish socialism, Zionism did not hold out much hope for a future in which Jews would be accepted as equals in society. In the Zionist view, the only viable solution for Jews in light of the long history of rejection, first by Christendom and then by modern secular society, was to have a state of their own where they could protect themselves.

"Zion" is a biblical term used to refer to the city of David—Jerusalem. The word "Zionism," coined in 1893, represents a longing virtually as old as Judaism itself: to return from exile, home to Zion. In premodern Rabbinic Judaism, this longing was expressed in a messianic belief that someday God would send a messiah and reestablish a homeland for his people in the land of Israel. For premodern Rabbinic Judaism, as well as for much of modern Orthodoxy and ultra-Orthodoxy, the return of Jews to their own land can only be the work of God. Any attempt by Jews to create a Jewish state on their own is presumptuous to the point of blasphemy. Thus when Zionism appeared at the end of the nineteenth century, this secular movement to organize Jews for the creation of a homeland in Palestine was vehemently rejected by the Orthodox and ultra-Orthodox. Reform Jews, having defined themselves as a religious community rather than as a "people," showed little interest in returning to the Middle East. In truth, Zionism did not come into its own until after the Holocaust, when it seemed clear to Jews everywhere that Jews could never count on being accepted as equals in Europe and that the only protection available to them would be in their own homeland—their own state.

A pivotal event in the development of secular (political) Zionism was the Dreyfus affair in France. The trial of a Jewish army officer on charges of treason had a profound influence on a young Jewish journalist, Theodor Herzl (1860–1904). The outcome of the trial—conviction of Dreyfus, who was innocent—convinced Herzl that assimilation would never be a feasible option for Jews. In 1896 he wrote *The Jewish State*, in which he rejected assimilation and proposed the creation of a Jewish state. Thus was born a movement that was destined to change the future of Judaism: political Zionism.

Theodor Herzl, founder of the Zionist movement to create a Jewish state.

Herzl convened the First Zionist Congress in Basel, Switzerland, in 1897, the same year as the formation of the Jewish socialist Bund in Poland. At this conference the World Zionist Organization was founded. In addition to Palestine, Herzl considered sites for a Jewish homeland in Cyprus. Later, the Sixth Zionist Congress rejected a British offer for a colony in Uganda, then a British protectorate. From that time forward Palestine became the sole option for Zionists. Herzl even wrote a utopian novel, *Altneuland*, imagining a Jewish state in Palestine.

Herzl's Dream and Its Ramifications

Theodor Herzl died in 1904, but not his dream. He left behind a thriving and committed body of political Zionists, the World Zionist Organization. In 1911 this organization began a modest but persistent program of colonizing areas in Palestine, which was then under British control. In 1917, as a result of Zionist efforts, the

Turning to the pulsing, steady beat of his drum and chant, a Mongolian shaman seeks to contact the spirits who can assist him in his spirit flight and healing mission.

In Africa and everywhere around the world, entry into the Christian faith is through the ritual of baptism.

In Peru, the Christian festival of Easter is celebrated with all the color of the local culture by these masked marchers.

This 1305 painting by the great Renaissance artist Giotto portrays family and friends mourning over the body of Jesus, which has just been taken down from the cross.

Ultra-Orthodox Jewish children celebrate the festival of Sukkot, which recalls the wandering of the tribes of Israel in the desert before entering the land of promise.

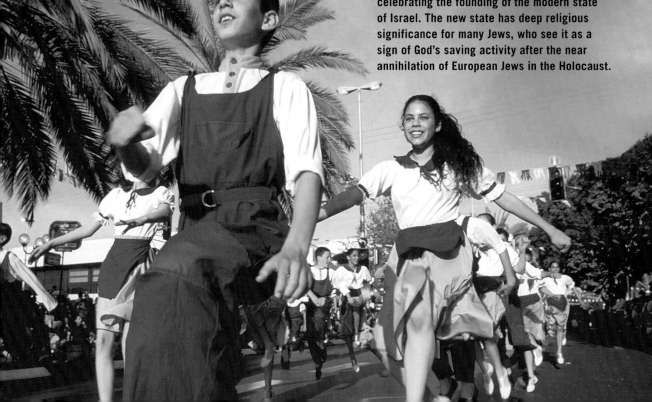

Children march in an Independence Day parade celebrating the founding of the modern state of Israel. The new state has deep religious significance for many Jews, who see it as a sign of God's saving activity after the near annihilation of European Jews in the Holocaust.

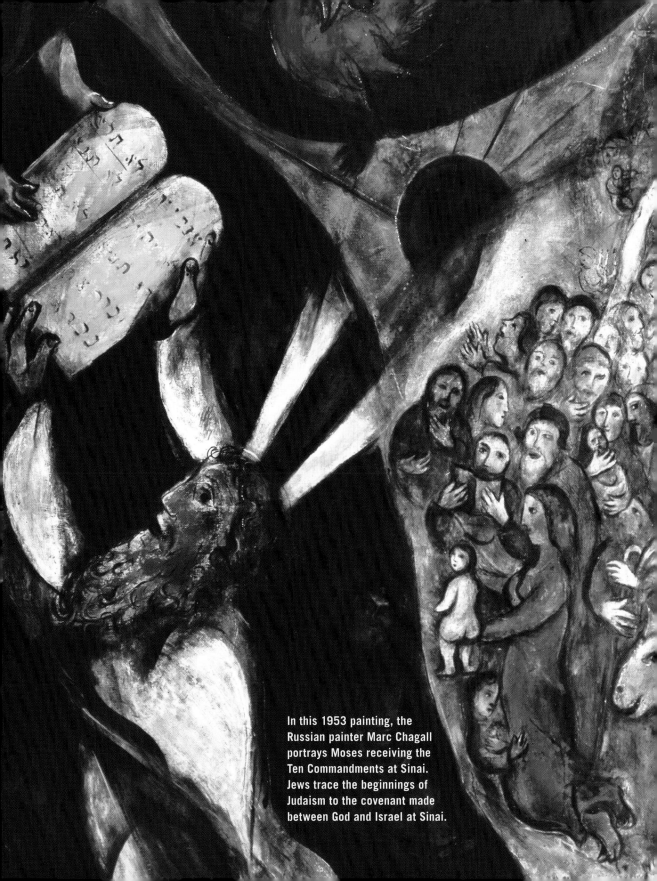

In this 1953 painting, the Russian painter Marc Chagall portrays Moses receiving the Ten Commandments at Sinai. Jews trace the beginnings of Judaism to the covenant made between God and Israel at Sinai.

Five times each day across the Muslim world, the faithful are called to prayer in Arabic by a muezzin.

As in other world religions, in Islam marriage is solemnized in a religious ceremony. This Baghdad wedding is an occasion for great joy and celebration among the couple's family and friends.

The Blue Mosque, Shrine of Ali bin Abi Thabit, cousin and son-in-law of Prophet Muhammad. Ali was the fourth caliph of Sunni Islam and the first imam of Shiah Islam. Built in the fifteenth century, the mosque has survived countless wars in near perfect condition. While some believe that it houses the tomb of Ali, most Shiah believe that he is buried in the Imam Ali Mosque in Najaf, Iraq.

The pilgrimage to Mecca is one of the Five Pillars of Islam. All Muslims, health and wealth permitting, are expected to make the pilgrimage at least once in their lifetime.

British foreign secretary, Lord James Balfour, wrote the letter now known as the Balfour Declaration, pledging Britain's support for a Jewish national home in Palestine. France, Italy, and the United States endorsed the idea. One cannot overestimate the tremendous importance of the organizational infrastructure developed in both Jewish socialism (embodied in the Bund) and in Zionism (embodied in the World Zionist Organization). The skills developed in these organizations and transferred to the early settlements in Palestine, with ongoing support from Jews all over the world, made possible the "sudden" emergence of the state of Israel in 1948 with sponsorship by the United Nations.

Like Reform Judaism, Zionism relied on history and historical change as its link to the premodern traditions of the Jewish people. But unlike Reform Judaism, political Zionism did not think of itself as a religious movement. Therefore, unlike Reform Judaism, Zionism sought continuity in the idea of the Jews as an historical people. Zionists reappropriated the biblical stories of the origins of Israel as part of their story, but the biblical narratives were to serve not as religious stories of God's actions in history but as "secular" stories of the Jewish people's struggles to achieve and preserve their national identity.

Therefore, Zionists retold the stories of origins from a perspective other than that of the premodern Rabbinic tradition of the dual Torah. That tradition had its beginnings in the failure of ancient militant Jewish political messianism (with the defeat of the Zealots) and success of a political policy of neutrality practiced by the Pharisees. The Zionists reacted to what they

This 1948 poster illustrates a vision of the strength and power of the Israeli Jew, a vision fostered by a Zionist movement prepared to defend the new nation of Israel.

The Dreyfus Affair

Alfred Dreyfus, a Jew, was a captain in the French army who was accused of having conveyed secret documents to Germany. In 1894 he was convicted and sentenced to life in prison on the basis of extremely weak circumstantial evidence. Moreover, the real traitor, a man by the name of Esterhazy, was acquitted in a later trial. Public protests were unable to override the tide of popular anti-Semitism that underlay this travesty of justice. In 1898, however, a famous novelist Émile Zola wrote an editorial protesting the wrong done to Dreyfus. Zola himself was imprisoned, but his words persuaded many that a great miscarriage of justice had occurred. Not long after the publication of the editorial, a French officer admitted having forged the documents used to convict Dreyfus and committed suicide. Dreyfus was given a new trial in 1899 and was again found guilty but with extenuating circumstances. The second trial, which proceeded in an atmosphere of high emotion that virtually tore the country apart, ended with a pardon for Dreyfus by the president of France. In 1906, when passions had abated, he was declared completely innocent and was allowed to finish out his career in the army.

An aerial view of Masada, where first-century Jews who had resisted Rome chose suicide rather than surrender. The defenders of Masada were an important symbol of courage and resistance to Zionists.

Some Sabras, secular Jews who led the Zionist movement to create an Israeli state, stand guard over their fields on a kibbutz in Israel in the early days of the new nation.

perceived as the failure (after almost two thousand years) of the Rabbinic strategy of accommodation and to the more recent Reform strategy of partial assimilation. They were not content to wait to be emancipated by others (whether God or modern gentiles). They were looking for Jewish heroes who were prepared to emancipate themselves. Thus they retold the stories of Moses and David as stories of nation builders and militant revolutionary political leaders.

For the Zionists, the interesting stories were the marginal ones of the Maccabean revolts of the second century BCE and those of the Maccabees' successors, the Zealots, who would rather kill themselves (as they did at Masada in 73 CE) than let the fight for their land end in surrender. The Zionists were looking for a militant hero who could serve as a prototype for a new kind of Jew, one prepared to fight to the last against all odds. This hero, they imagined, was the kind of Jew who would reestablish a homeland in Israel.

And yet, while calling for a new kind of Jew, Zionism was repeating the formative pattern of Judaism, telling a story of exile and return—a people who originated in the land of Israel, were forcibly dispersed for almost two thousand years, and now sought to return. Moreover, like Jewish socialism, Zionism offered secular Jews a powerful secular version of the goal of history. In the Zionist vision, however, the Jewish people were not incidental but essential. This vision recalls the biblical prophecies (Isaiah 65:17–18) that God will create not only a new heaven and a new earth but also a new Jerusalem, namely, a reestablished Jewish homeland. All in all, they made much more comprehensive and creative use of the stories of the biblical past than did the Yiddish-speaking Jewish socialists.

Like Jewish socialism, Zionism created a new way for secular Jews to be Jewish, reappropriating the tradition through story, language (which for Zionists was the recovery and reconstruction of Hebrew as a modern language), and social organization. While Jewish socialism had more adherents than Zionism before World War II, it was later eclipsed by a Zionism that absorbed and transformed its vision. For after the Holocaust and the destruction of nearly a third of the world's Jews, the validity and the urgency of the Zionist message seemed self-evident to the overwhelming majority of Jews, both religious and secular. If they were to survive, Jews must have their own homeland.

Zionism shaped a nation and turned a utopian dream into a reality—the state of Israel. Jewish socialism and Zionism together represented a powerful, if ambivalent, rejection of the modern era and its ideal of assimilation as defined by the Enlightenment. It was the amalgamation of these ways of thinking that made a natural bridge to the Judaism of Holocaust and Redemption. For without the socialist–Zionist revolution, there would be no state of Israel. And without the state of Israel, there would be only Holocaust and no sense of redemption—no sense of rescue from the forces of slavery and death as Jews were once brought out of Egypt.

The new state of Israel became a haven for Jews from around the world, including these Ethiopian schoolchildren.

JUDAISM AND POSTMODERN TRENDS IN A POSTCOLONIAL WORLD

The Judaism of Holocaust and Redemption

The Devastation of the Holocaust

In 1933 Adolf Hitler and the Nazi party came to power in Germany. By 1939 they had drawn Europe into World War II, a six-year war of expansion that was meant to give additional *Lebensraum* ("living space") to what the Nazis considered to be the superior Aryan race of Germany. Near the end, however, when Germany was losing badly and soldiers and supplies were desperately needed at the front, trains were diverted to the task of transporting Jews to the death camps. Hitler was more desperate to rid the world of Jews than he was to win the war.

The Holocaust was a singular event in human history that opened the postmodern era to the reality of mass death. "Holocaust," or burnt sacrifice, is the name given to the attempt by Nazi Germany to eliminate an entire people, the Jews. Unlike the millions of others who died on the battlefronts of World War II, the Jews were not military combatants (see Map 3.4). The Jews of Germany were not enemies of Germany, but citizens. There was no military or territorial advantage to be had by systematically killing them. They were marked for death simply because they existed. Germans, defeated and humiliated in World War I (1914–1918), and suffering from extreme economic depression as a result of war reparations, chose not to blame these troubles on the aggressive military actions of their government during the war. Instead, they said, "The Jews are our misfortune"—they are to blame. The Nazis rose to power partly by portraying the Jews as a racial pollutant or a diseased growth on the healthy body of the German people that had to be surgically cut out if the nation was to be restored to health and greatness.

When the Nazi party came to power, the Jews were stripped of their citizenship and all their legal rights; their homes and businesses were appropriated; and they were herded into boxcars that delivered them to an elaborate system of death camps where they were either worked to death as slaves or murdered in specially designed gas chambers made to order for mass killings. At the most infamous of the camps, Auschwitz, in Poland, it is estimated that 2 million Jews were executed.

One has to ask: why the Jews? Blaming a scapegoat for misfortune is not unusual in history, but what induced the Nazis to pick the Jews for this role? The answer takes us back in large part to the story of the beginnings of Christianity (see Chapter Four) as a Jewish sect that came to be dominated by others, gentiles who saw themselves as having superseded and replaced the Jews as God's chosen people. The establishment of Christianity as the dominant religion of the Roman Empire led to both legal discrimination and popular discrimination that often was expressed in violence against Jews as

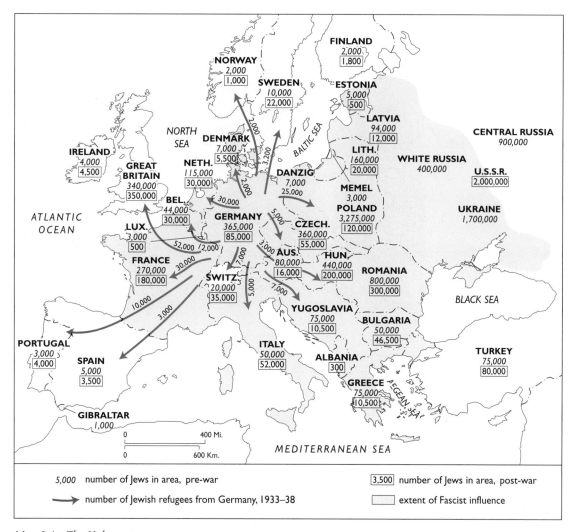

Map 3.4   The Holocaust.

"the children of the devil"—a people most Christians believed had been rejected by God for their role in the killing of Jesus, the Son of God.

Moreover the influential "negative witness" theory suggested by Augustine, portrayed the Jews as condemned to wander the earth without a home, their misery supposedly offering negative proof of the truth of Christianity. From the time of this early theologian forward, through the Middle Ages and into the modern period, Jews were the scapegoats, blamed for whatever misfortunes occurred in Western civilization. Indeed, Hitler played on popular Christian anti-Jewish sentiments to rise to the position of chancellor of Germany. Later, neither the Catholic nor the Protestant churches of Germany officially protested the Nazi treatment of the Jews—only the treatment of Jewish converts to Christianity. It took more than Christian

The Nazis rounded up European Jews and sent them to the death camps in boxcars. These Jewish prisoners, some of them children, were photographed at the infamous Auschwitz death camp.

anti-Judaism to make the Holocaust possible: for instance, the rise of secularism and scientific-bureaucractic forms of social control played an important part. Nevertheless, it is hard to imagine the Holocaust occurring without the significant contribution of Christian anti-Semitism.

The Holocaust as a Challenge to Jewish Faith

The Holocaust deeply challenges the faith stories of the exodus and exile traditions. For if these stories promised a God who would always be with the people of the covenant, guiding and protecting them, the Holocaust seemed to prove this promise a lie. God, it seemed to many Jews, had failed to keep his promises.

After the Holocaust, some of the most Orthodox of Jews wanted to treat the Holocaust as a tragedy of the same type as the fall of the first and second temples. In fact, they proposed that the best way to remember the Holocaust was to include it in the period of fasting and mourning of Tisha B'Av. But to many other Jews, both secular and religious, this seemed wholly inappropriate. For the main victims of the Holocaust were not the most liberal and secularized Jews but rather the most orthodox and observant population in Jewry, the Jews of eastern Europe. To many Jews, the scope of the tragedy was so great that failure to keep the covenant faithfully enough was inadequate to explain it.

How does one commemorate such an event? And how, after the Holocaust, could Jews go on believing the promises of God to guide and protect them on their journey through time? Indeed, a major debate is being carried out in contemporary Judaism in which a number of important authors offer suggestions on how Jews should respond to the Holocaust.

One author, Richard Rubenstein, says that God died at Auschwitz, and Jews will have to go on with their stories and their rituals without God. Emil Fackenheim argues that, on the contrary, God is still present in history. He justifies this view by suggesting that it is as if Jews had heard a silent yet commanding voice from Auschwitz, giving them a new commandment, a 614th commandment to be added to the 613 in the Torah. This commandment demands that Jews remain Jewish lest they allow Judaism to die, thus giving Hitler a posthumous victory.

Elie Wiesel, the Nobel Prize–winning author who is himself a survivor of Auschwitz, sees it somewhat differently. Only the Jew knows, says Wiesel, that one can have the *chutzpah* (audacity) to argue with God as long as it is in defense of God's creation—as Abraham argued with God over the fate of the innocent at Sodom (Genesis 18:22–33). After Auschwitz, Jews have a right to be angry with God, to call God into question, even put God on trial. After Auschwitz, says Wiesel, Jews have a right to conclude that this time it was not the Jews but God who broke the covenant. And yet, Jews have not despaired. Indeed, according to Wiesel, "Judaism teaches man to overcome despair. What is Jewish history if not an endless quarrel with God?"[2] Wiesel, who grew up in the Hasidic tradition in eastern Europe, insists that to be a Jew is to refuse all temptations to despair. Instead, he believes, Jews, who can no longer be required to keep a covenant broken by God, are choosing to keep the covenant of their own free will.

Another major Holocaust scholar, Irving Greenberg, argues that after Auschwitz Jews can only live a "momentary faith"—tossed back and forth between the stories of the Exodus and the stories of the Holocaust. In one moment a Jew might believe in the promises of Sinai, only in the next moment

Alzbeta Horovitzova, a Holocaust survivor, celebrating her 98th birthday at a retirement home in Prague.

to have them clouded over by memories of the smokestacks of Auschwitz. While, endorsing Wiesel's view that after Auschwitz Jews cannot be required to embrace the covenant and yet they do so freely, Greenberg observes that this embrace takes on a wide variety of forms, from the extremely orthodox to the extremely secular. And after Auschwitz, he insists, all Jews, from the extremely orthodox to the extremely secular, are obligated to accept each other as Jews, accepting contemporary Jewish pluralism as an authentic covenantal pluralism. For Jews to turn their backs on other Jews, as some of the ultra-Orthodox in the state of Israel do when they refuse to acknowledge the Jewishness of nonorthodox Jews, is another way of granting Hitler a posthumous victory. In a post-Holocaust and postcolonial world, Jews find themselves once more facing the question that arose in the first century of the Common Era: which of all the ways of being Jewish is the right way? What has changed after Auschwitz, says Greenberg, is that Jews are free to observe or not observe the covenant; they are not, however, free to reject Jews who exercise this freedom.

Post-Holocaust Judaism offers an alternative to the "one way" of ultra-Orthodoxy. This postmodern form of Judaism, in which there is not one single way to truth and to faithfulness but many, has taken the Conservative strategy of diversity in thought but uniformity in practice to a new level. Covenantal pluralism is affirmed in so far as great diversity in thought *and* practice, both secular and religious, is allowed. One practice, however, is not negotiable: the obligation of post-Holocaust Jews to accept one another in their diversity. Both ultra-Orthodoxy and the Judaism of Holocaust and Redemption seek a way out of what they see as the spiritual poverty of a modernism that made the Holocaust possible. The choice they offer to all Jews is either withdrawal from or involvement in the modern world, either back to what they view as premodern uniformity or forward to a new age of Jewish pluralism.

Finally, the post-Holocaust Jewish scholar Marc Ellis insists that Israeli Jews must never use the suffering of Jews in the Holocaust as an excuse for the oppression of their Palestinian neighbors. They must remember that the covenant relation of the Jews to the land includes the demands to ensure justice for all and to show compassion to the stranger. Not only must Jews accept other Jews in their diversity, they must accept their Christian and Muslim Palestinian neighbors in Israel in an environment of justice and peace for all. Such a task is not easy now, when extremists on all sides seek to undermine genuine efforts at compromise and cooperation, and yet many in the state of Israel continue the struggle to find that middle ground.

The Holocaust and the State of Israel: Exile and Redemption

This new Judaism of Holocaust and Redemption, which has proven very attractive to American Judaism, Israeli Judaism, and Israeli nationalism, has a postmodern and postcolonial orientation. That is, instead of seeking to return to some premodern orthodoxy emphasizing one truth and one way, it attempts to find unity in the diversity of religious and secular Jews. Even its new "holy days" or "holidays" display characteristics of both the holy and the secular. Indeed, two days that seem to be entering the Jewish calendar are recollections of seemingly secular events—*Yom Hashoah* (Day of Desolation), recalling the Holocaust, and *Yom Ha'atzmaut* (Independence Day), celebrating the founding of Israel.

The impact of the Holocaust on Jewish consciousness cannot be overstated. For those born after World War II often fail to realize that during the Holocaust the Nazis nearly succeeded in their goal of eliminating Jews from the face of the earth. Nearly a third of all Jews died in the Holocaust; nearly two-thirds of the Jews of Europe died. The eastern European Jewish communities were hit the hardest. Ninety percent of these Jews, and more than 80 percent of all the rabbis, Talmudic scholars, and Talmudic students then alive, were murdered.

Jews might have despaired after the devastation of the Holocaust, but the founding of the state of Israel by the United Nations in 1948 gave them hope. The counterbalancing of the Holocaust and the founding of the state of Israel fits the great formative story of Jewish existence—exile and return. After two thousand years without a homeland, many Jews experienced the ability to return to Israel as a Jewish state as a miraculous act of divine redemption akin to the return to the land of promise after slavery in Egypt or after exile in Babylon. That redemption made it possible for Jews to remember the Holocaust without despairing.

It is in this context that we review the history of the establishment and development of the state of Israel, which marks an important turning point in the demise of colonialism and the emergence of a postcolonial, post-Holocaust Judaism. In 1922 the League of Nations gave Britain a mandate over Palestine, which had been under Muslim control. Meanwhile, the Balfour Declaration of 1917 had already set the stage for the establishment of a homeland for Jews in the area, alongside the existing Palestinian population. In supporting this policy, Britain legitimated the goal of the international Zionist movement, while doing little to hasten its implementation. Thus at the conclusion of World War II, Palestine was still under the British mandate.

In 1947, as a member of the newly formed United Nations, Britain asked the General Assembly to establish a special committee on Palestine. The report of this committee, UNSCOP, led to a resolution to divide Palestine into two states—one Jewish and the other Arab (see Map 3.5). The state of Israel was established on May 14, 1948, the date on which Great Britain gave up official control of the area. Within a year Israel would be admitted to the United Nations.

The creation of a Jewish state was supported by two key UN member nations, the United States and the Soviet Union, and it represented the triumph of the Zionist movement. The Arab states, however, refused to accept the UN partition plan, and on May 15, 1948, the armies of seven Arab states invaded the newly formed nation and the war for independence was under way. The war was fought in two phases, with an intervening cease fire, and

Map 3.5   *The creation of the state of Israel.*

This Israeli Rosh Hashana card celebrates Moshe Dayan and Yitzhak Rabin as heroes of the victory of Israel in the 1967 Six-Day War.

ended in the defeat of the Arab forces and an armistice with the Egyptians in February 1949. Later agreements were signed with Jordan, Lebanon, and Syria; however, none was signed with Iraq. Relations with neighboring Arab states remained tense throughout the decades that followed, flaring again into the wars of 1967 and 1973.

It is hard to overstate the impact of the 1967 war on Judaism. In June of that year, the state of Israel was seriously threatened by four predominantly Muslim nations: Egypt, Jordan, Syria, and Iraq. Israeli forces were overwhelmingly outnumbered, and the country was surrounded by 250,000 troops, having at their disposal some 2,000 tanks, as well as 700 fighter planes and bombers. A UN Emergency Force had withdrawn in May, and Israeli diplomatic initiatives seeking intervention from European countries and America met with feeble responses. Israel perceived itself to be alone, without allies and doomed to what many feared would be a second holocaust. Israeli armed forces, under the leadership of General Yitzhak Rabin, staged a surprise air attack on the morning of June 5. In a brilliant series of military moves, Israel routed the combined Arab forces in a war that was over in six days.

At the end of the war, Israel occupied territory formerly under the control of the Egyptians and the Syrians—from the Suez Canal to the Golan Heights. In the process Israel had taken control of the entire area west of the Jordan River, including the Old City of Jerusalem (on June 7), recovering one of the holiest places for all Jews, the Western Wall of the Second Temple (destroyed by the Romans in 70 CE), which had been under Jordanian control (see Map 3.6). As the dust of the Six-Day War settled, Jews both in the land of Israel

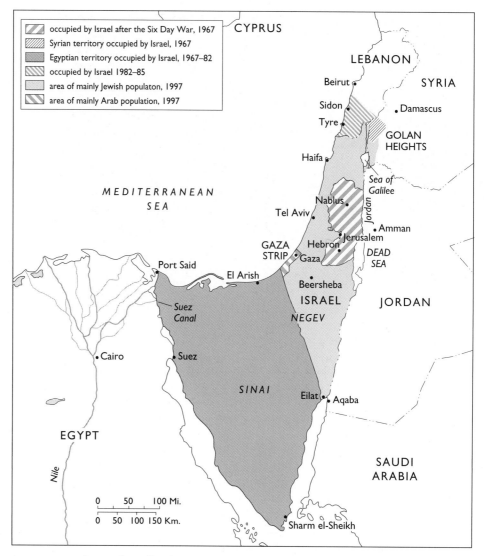

Map 3.6   Arab–Israeli conflict from 1967.

and in diaspora were overwhelmed with a sense of awe at their seemingly miraculous deliverance. Even among the most secular or nonreligious Jews, many could not help but see the redemptive hand of God in these events.

In response to this unexpected defeat, at a conference held in Khartoum in August 1967, Arab nations adopted a policy of no recognition or negotiations with Israel. Under new leadership, the three-year-old Palestinian Liberation Organization began a long and systematic policy of guerrilla warfare against Israel.

But the essential fact for Jews has been that Israel exists and has withstood all onslaughts against it. For many Jews the 1967 war was the turning point. From that time forward the meaningful connection between the Holocaust and the founding of the state of Israel could not be ignored. The two events became indissolubly linked in Jewish minds, and the days of remembrance of these two events became ever more prominent in the Jewish calendar.

The existence of the state of Israel represents for many Jews a redemption from two thousand years of powerlessness and exile. The state of Israel represents, for Jews, a new age of politics, power, and a capacity for self-defense in a world that has often been bent upon subjugating or destroying them. In the twenty-first century, Jews continue to struggle to find a way to live constructively with their own diversity in the Diaspora and to maintain the autonomy of the state of Israel, while seeking a just and lasting peace in the Middle East.

CONCLUSION

What we learn from the study of the diverse ways of being Jewish is that religion can either reject the secular or accommodate it. What form shall the life of the people Israel take in the modern world? That is the issue being debated among Jews as they move into the future. Those like the ultra-Orthodox, who reject the secular, see religion as being about a sacred, eternal, and unchangeable way of life that must not be profaned by accommodation with the world. Consequently they are segregationists. The ultra-Orthodox, like fundamentalists everywhere, see modern secular society as profane—a contradiction of the sacred order embodied in premodern religious forms. All modern and postmodern/post-Holocaust religious forms of Judaism, by contrast, see the holy and the secular less as opposites than as complementary, and they tend to see historical change as the medium through which God reveals himself in time.

For modernist and post-Holocaust Jews, knowledge of the historical development of Judaism (in varying degrees) became an inherent component in their self-understanding and has made it possible for each person to admit new levels of diversity and change into the tradition. The difference between the modernist forms of Judaism and the later Judaism of Holocaust and Redemption is that the modernist forms (Reform, Conservative, and Orthodox) tend to regard diversity as competition, in which one is right and others are wrong, whereas for the Judaism of Holocaust and Redemption, Jewish diversity reflects complementarity. To the ultra-Orthodox, by contrast, diversity is apostasy, and segregation from the non-Jewish modern world and from all forms of Judaism that compromise with that world is the only path to the true Israel.

For most ultra-Orthodox, to admit any change is to condone relativism, and with it unbelief. For modernist and post-Holocaust Jews, to admit change is a matter of intellectual integrity: since time cannot be stopped, some change is inevitable. Jews at the two ends of the spectrum disagree over how much change is permissible, with the Orthodox demanding a return to the

The 1973 Yom Kippur War and Its Aftermath

The Yom Kippur War of 1973 was less decisive than the 1967 war in military terms, but it sparked a resurgence of religious Zionism. On October 6, 1973, the Egyptian army penetrated the Israeli-occupied territory of the Sinai peninsula, while the Syrians invaded the Golan Heights. The surprise attack occurred on Yom Kippur, one of the holiest days in the Jewish calendar. Although caught off guard, Israel rallied and successfully rebuffed its attackers, but the event undermined confidence in the leadership of the Labor party. Thus the ground was prepared for the rise of the conservative Likud party with the election of Menachem Begin as prime minister in 1977. Another result was increased political influence from religious Zionists like the Gush Emunim.

The Gush Emunim were committed to the notion that none of the occupied territories from the 1967 War was to be given back in any peace agreement after the 1973 war. Believing strongly that the Jews were chosen by God to inherit this land, they were no more inclined to share it with their Palestinian neighbors than many Christian and Muslim Palestinians were to share it with the Jews. Consequently, the Gush Emunim began an intensive program of establishing settlements in the occupied territory, an activity that was not authorized by the Israeli government. When Menachem Begin came to power, however, he supported the settlements. In this fashion, religious Zionism began to play an important role in Israeli public policy.

While the settlements were in their infancy, however, Begin signed a peace treaty with the president of Egypt, Anwar Sadat. This agreement, signed at Camp David in 1979 with the encouragement of U.S. President Jimmy Carter, called for Israel to return occupied territory in the Sinai. The Gush Emunim saw the territorial rollback as a betrayal of God's will. The movement splintered in 1982, with the death of its spiritual leader, Rabbi Zvi Yehuda Kook, and some adherents began to wage guerrilla warfare against Palestinian militants. Some even planned to blow up the mosque on the Temple Mount in Jerusalem, but they were discovered before the plan could be carried out. The leaders were arrested in 1984, and the movement lost a large measure of the public support it had enjoyed.

fundamental truths and practices of premodern Judaism and the secular Judaisms accepting at least some integration into the non-Jewish world. For Reform, Conservative, and Holocaust and Redemption Jews, God reveals himself in the continued unfolding of history. For ethnicists, socialists, and Zionists, meaning is to be found not in the God of history but in the history itself. Such "secular" Jews are not "religious" in the traditional sense of biblical theism, but they do display one type of religious behavior commonly found in the history of religions—reverence for the ways of the ancestors, ways that are held sacred.

All but the ultra-Orthodox are convinced that to be the true Israel not only does not require Jews to go back but allows them to go forward. The strength of the modern/postmodern forms of Judaism is in their ability to adapt Jewish

The 1980s saw escalating violence between Israelis and Palestinians. In 1991 the United States, and the Soviet Union sponsored a peace conference in Madrid, attempting to bring about a negotiated settlement among hostile Middle Eastern parties, but the process stalled. In 1993 secret talks between Israeli scholars and officials of the Palestinian Liberation Organization led to a Declaration of Principles for negotiating peace between Israelis and Palestinians. At a ceremony in Washington D.C., hosted by President Bill Clinton, PLO chairman Yasir Arafat and Israel's prime minister, Yitzhak Rabin, signed the document. Radical terrorist elements on both sides have sabotaged constructive peace efforts ever since, and in 1995 Rabin was assassinated by a Jewish Zionist radical. At the beginning of the twenty-first century, many Jews in Israel search for a way to live peaceably with their Palestinian neighbors, while Jewish radicals continue to advocate violence on the basis of claims of divine privilege and Palestinian radicals continue to respond with violent acts of "holy war."

The signing of the Camp David Peace Accord on March 26, 1979. U.S. President Jimmy Carter at the center is flanked by President Anwar Sadat of Egypt on the left and Israeli premier Menachem Begin on the right.

life to new environments and situations. The strength of the Orthodox and ultra-Orthodox is in challenging those who would adapt to not sacrifice the heart of Jewish religious existence as a people—God, Torah, and Israel. They would argue that history and Jewish ethnicity are not an adequate substitute.

The adventure continues as Jews everywhere wrestle with each other and with the world around them over what it means to be a Jew—especially in the state of Israel, where there can be no peace unless accommodation both among Jews and with their Christian and Muslim neighbors is found. And yet the very struggle of Jews everywhere, whether secular or religious, among themselves and with the non-Jewish world around them, is very Jewish. We need only recall the story of how Jacob's name was changed to Israel (Genesis 32:23–32). For Jacob wrestled with the stranger who would not tell Jacob his name but instead blessed Jacob and changed Jacob's name to Israel, meaning "he who has wrestled with God and human beings and prevails." Throughout history, the drama of Judaism has been to wrestle with God and the stranger. Today, whether secular or religious, Jews are still deeply shaped by the stories of Israel, they still wrestle with the stranger, and they still prevail.

Discussion Questions

1 At what point in biblical history did the fundamental pattern of Jewish experience emerge, and what shape did it take? Give two examples from the history of Judaism, one secular and one religious.

2 What are the issues that separate premodern from modern and post-modern or post-Holocaust forms of Judaism?

3 How does the history of anti-Judaism in Western Christianity and Western civilization relate to the Holocaust. What was the impact of the Holocaust on the shape of modern and postmod-ern forms of Jewish life, religious and secular?

4 In what ways have secular forms of Judaism transformed the shape of contemporary religious forms of Judaism? Give examples and explain.

5 What is the Judaism of Holocaust and Redemption, and how does it relate to modern and premodern forms of Judaism? Also, why might it be seen as the alternative to ultra-Orthodoxy?

6 What does it mean to say that Judaism is a form of the myth of history? Give examples from both the biblical and postbiblical periods.

7 What is the Talmud, and what is its significance for the religion of Judaism?

8 Compare and contrast Enlightenment Judaism (Haskalah) and Hasidic Judaism.

9 Whom would you nominate as the three most important postbiblical figures in the history of Judaism, and why?

10 Is Zionism a secular form of Judaism or a religious form, or both? Explain, with historical examples.

Key Terms

bar mitzvah	gentile	Mishnah	Tannaim
bat mitzvah	*Halakhah*	*Mitzvot*	temple
circumcision	haredim	Rabbinic	Tisha B'Av
covenant	Hasidism	Shema	Tzaddik
Diaspora	Israel	synagogue	Zionism
dual Torah	Kabbalah	Talmud	Zohar
Gemara	kosher	Tanak	

Suggested Readings

Armstrong, Karen, *The Battle for God*. New York: Knopf, 2001.

Fackenheim, Emil, *What Is Judaism?* New York: Summit Books, 1987.

Fosching, Darrell J., *Narrative Theology After Auschwitz: From Alienation to Ethics*. Minneapolis: Fortress Press, 1992.

Greenberg, Irving, *The Jewish Way*. New York: Summit Books, 1988.

Isaacs, Ronald H., and Kerry M. Olitzky, eds., *Critical Documents of Jewish History: A Source Book*. London: Jason Aronson, 1995.

Johnson, Paul, *A History of the Jews*. New York: Harper & Row, 1987.

Keppel, Gilles, *The Revenge of God: The Resurgence of Islam, Christianity and Judaism in the Modern World*. University Park: Pennsylvania State University Press, 1991, 1994.

Lawrence, Bruce B., *Defenders of God: The Fundamentalist Revolt Against the Modern Age*. Columbia: University of South Carolina Press, 1995.

Neusner, Jacob, *The Death and Birth of Judaism*. New York: Basic Books, 1987.

Neusner, Jacob, *Self-fulfilling Prophecy: Exile and Return in the History of Judaism*. Boston: Beacon Press, 1987.

Notes

1. Jacob Neusner, *The Death and Birth of Judaism*. New York: Basic Books, 1987, p. 116.

2. Elie Wiesel, *A Jew Today*. New York: Random House, 1978, p. 146.

CHAPTER
FOUR

Christian Diversity and the Road to Modernity

Overview

In a storefront church in the Midwest of the United States, Christians—male and female, black and white—stand and raise their arms above their heads, their hands extended toward heaven. The eyes of many are closed; soon some begin to speak in an unknown language. These worshipers are Pentecostal or charismatic Christians who believe they have gifts or abilities, to speak a special spiritual language known as "speaking in tongues." They believe that the Holy Spirit of God has descended upon them and speaks through them, even as this Spirit guides their daily walk with Christ. Meanwhile in Rome, the leader of the largest Christian denomination in the world, the Roman Catholic Church, is carried on a chair into the great Cathedral of St. Peter escorted by a long line of men in flowing robes. The men carrying the chair make their way between the majestic rows of stone pillars led by one man carrying a processional cross. Incense bearers follow, swinging pots of richly aromatic incense whose smoke wafts through the air as if carrying the sounds of organ music and chanting up to heaven. Soon the pope will arrive at the altar to celebrate Mass.

For some Christians, worship is a powerful and physically involving emotional experience, as in this contemporary charismatic service in Manhattan, New York.

CHRISTIANITY Timeline

31 CE	Crucifixion of Jesus of Nazareth
48–60	Letters of Paul of Tarsus
70	Fall of the Jewish temple in Jerusalem to the Romans Gospel of Mark written
80–100	Gospels of Matthew and Luke and John written
313	Edict of Milan by Constantine permitting Christianity in Roman Empire
325	Council of Nicaea declares Word of God to be same as (*homoousios*) God
380	Christianity declared the official religion of the Roman Empire by Emperor Theodosius
451	Council of Chalcedon, doctrine of two natures and one substance in Christ
500s	Development of Benedictine monasticism in the West
590–604	Pontificate of Gregory the Great, first great pope of Middle Ages
732	Muslim invasion of Europe stopped at Tours by Charles Martel
800	Coronation of Charlemagne
1095	First Crusade against Muslims and mass violence against Jews
1184	Inauguration of church inquisitions by Pope Lucius III
1198–1216	Pontificate of Innocent III, most powerful pope in history
1224–1274	St. Thomas Aquinas, greatest theologian of Middle Ages
1414	Council of Constance—papal decadence and the declaration of conciliar rule in the church
1517	Luther's Ninety-five Theses posted on church door at Wittenberg, beginning of Protestant Reformation

In yet another place, somewhere in Africa, villagers gather to dance and sing tribal chants in praise of the risen Christ, even in a small unadorned room in England, a dozen Quakers sit in wordless prayer, waiting for the Holy Spirit to inspire one of them to speak a message to the rest. Back in the United States, at an inner-city Episcopal church in the Northeast, a woman priest consecrates bread and wine as the body and blood of Christ. Southward, in a small village in Latin America, a dozen campesinos sit in a circle on a hillside under the morning sun, preparing to share the bread and wine as the body and blood of Christ and studying the Gospel of Luke. Remembering that the word "gospel" means "good news," they are encouraged by Jesus' words of hope to the poor and the downtrodden. And in rural India, a small group of Christians, virtually indistinguishable from their neighbors who are Hindus, gather to pray and offer flower petals before a statue of Jesus. At the same time, an international television broadcast of the Billy Graham Crusade beams the American evangelist's call for the thousands who fill a sports stadium to come forward and declare themselves for Christ with the whole world watching.

1545–1563	Council of Trent, Catholic Counter-Reformation
1555	Peace of Augsburg—first attempt to end religious wars of the Reformation
1648	Peace of Westphalia—end of religious wars, quest for religious tolerance
1703–1791	John Wesley, founder of Methodism
1768–1834	Friedrich Schleiermacher, father of modern theology
1791	1st Amendment to US Constitution
1813–1855	Søren Kierkegaard, Christian existentialism
1851	Karl Marx publishes *Communist Manifesto*
1859	Charles Darwin publishes *On the Origin of Species*
1869–1870	First Vatican Council
1910–1915	Publication of *The Fundamentals* begins fundamentalist/modernist controversy
1939–1945	World War II and the Holocaust
August 6, 1945	Atomic bomb dropped on Hiroshima, Japan, leading to end of World War II
1947	India achieves independence; Church of South India is formed
1950s, 1960s	Emergence of civil rights movement under Martin Luther King Jr. Pope John XXIII and the 2nd Vatican Council
1970s–1990s	Religious resurgence of evangelical fundamentalism and emergence of liberation theology movements
2005	Death of Pope John Paul II

CHRISTIANITY *Timeline*

For some Christians, worship inspires hope for a world of justice and compassion. A liberation theology base community meets in Panajachel, Guatemala, to hear the good news from scripture that Jesus Christ has come to liberate the poor and the oppressed.

Young women praise Jesus as the British Christian rock band Delirious performs in a stadium in Anaheim, California, in July 2001.

Despite their incredible diversity, all these believers are Christians engaged in Christian prayer and worship. The challenge before us is to understand the unity and diversity among Christians, especially in the contemporary world.

Like Jews and Muslims, Christians believe that there is but one God, the God who made all things and rules over history. This God is the highest reality, and to act in harmony with the will of this God is the highest goal of life. Christians are unique, however, in believing that God is one God yet three persons (Father, Son, and Holy Spirit) and that the reality of this God is uniquely revealed in the life and person of Jesus of Nazareth. For Christians believe that the eternal Word of God was united to humanity through the person of Jesus, who suffered and died on the cross for the sins of the world. They believe that Jesus was raised from the dead three days later, and after forty days ascended to heaven, where he will reign until he comes again at the end of time to judge the living and the dead at the final resurrection.

Like Jews and Muslims, Christians believe that the gravest problem in human life is sin—the failure to live in harmony with the will of God. Sin has two dimensions: idolatry and injustice. Idolatry is more than worshiping the images of false deities. It is treating anything that is not God as if it were more important than God. Idolaters shift the focus from the God who seeks the good of all to their selfish desires, thus sowing the seeds of injustice. For if nothing is more important than achieving such selfish goals as wealth and power, treating other human beings unjustly can be seen as necessary to ensure that these ends are met.

However, Christians differ from Jews and Muslims in their view of sin and how it is to be overcome. For most Christians define "sin" in terms of the concept of *original sin*, which says that the will to do the good in all human beings was corrupted by the first human beings—Adam and Eve—and through their disobedience to God's will, sin and death came into the world. Thus most Christians believe that while human beings were created good, their good will (the desire to do what is good) was corrupted by the inherited consequences of the sin of Adam and Eve, so that humans feel compelled to act selfishly. Humans are enslaved to the power of sin and not fully capable of obeying the will of God. Out of compassion for human beings, God chose to send a savior, Jesus Christ, to redeem them by dying in reparation for their past sins and restoring human nature (recreating a good will in them) in order for obedience to the will of God to be possible and in order to restore human destiny to its true goal of eternal life with God.

God sent into the world his only son, to become incarnate—that is, fully embodied—in the person of Jesus of Nazareth. In doing so, God united his divine nature to human nature, healing its flaws. The primary means for Christians to overcome sin and live in harmony with the will of God is to die spiritually and be reborn through faith in Christ. The Christian who has undergone this conversion experience believes he or she has become a new person, one who is free to obey the word of God as revealed in the scriptures. Christians believe that during their earthly lives they are called to help bring about the Kingdom of God—the beginning of a new creation of love, compassion, and justice in which death will finally be overcome, even as Jesus overcame death on the cross.

In century after century, Christians have sought this "Kingdom of God," sometimes referred to as the kingdom of heaven in scriptures. Always, they have puzzled over the means whereby might it be established. This goal has forced Christians to try to understand the relationship between the church and the world, and how their faith and way of life should be related to the non-Christian world around them. Both Catholic Christianity, which took definitive shape in the early and medieval church, and the seventeenth-century Protestant movement to reform Catholicism have struggled with this question in every age, including the present one.

Despite the explanation of Christianity just given, it would be misleading to think that all Christians in all times and places would agree with it. Like all religions, Christianity is more than one thing. It has taken many forms and been many things to many people. In the remainder of this chapter we shall try to understand both the unity and diversity of Christianity.

Today Christianity is the largest religion in the world. With over 1,870,000,000 adherents, of whom a little over one billion are Catholic, all together Christians represent approximately one-third of the world's population. This 33 percent of the world's population breaks down roughly as follows: Catholics, 19 percent; Protestants, 8 percent; Orthodox, 3 percent; and other forms of Christianity, 3 percent. Our primary task in this chapter is to understand Christianity in all its diversity and to understand the unique role that this religion has played in the development of the modern society that presented such a formidable challenge to it and all other faiths. Since modernity grew up within the womb of Western Christian civilization, we will have to understand not only the history of Christianity as a religion but the way it has influenced and been influenced by modern social, political, and intellectual trends in Western history.

Within this history some Christians (fundamentalists) have argued that the alliance of Christianity with modernization is a mistake that could be corrected by returning to the "fundamentals" of the faith, as they believe these fundamentals were understood and practiced before the emergence of the modern scientific and secular view of the world. Others (modernists) have argued that modernization is itself evidence of the power of the Christian Gospel to transform the world and therefore should be embraced as the path to human dignity and liberation.

The Christianity of yesterday helped give birth to the modern world in all its diversity; and to understand the latter we need also to understand the former. We shall begin with the Protestant encounter with modernity and then look at Catholicism's struggle with the modern world. Then, to see how things came to be the way they are today, we shall return to the beginning in the first century and journey forward.

ENCOUNTER WITH MODERNITY: THE FUNDAMENTALIST–MODERNIST CONTROVERSY

The Protestant Confrontation with Modernity

The nineteenth century marked a critical turning point in the history of Christianity as it sought to coexist with an increasingly "modern" secular and scientific world whose views challenged many of the fundamental truths and practices of Christians. The central issue in modern Christianity has been the struggle between modernism and fundamentalism. Indeed, the term "fundamentalism" is a legacy of the American Protestant encounter with "modernism."

Modernization in nineteenth-century America was profoundly shaped by the growth of industrialization, which, in turn, fueled urbanization, drawing many people away from agrarian life to seek jobs in the cities. In this context the churches were growing dramatically. Between 1860 and 1900, Protestant churches tripled in numbers to about 16 million. Catholicism was growing even faster, especially as a result of emigration from Europe.

At the same time the United States was becoming more secular, especially in the areas of science and higher education. This was a major cultural shift, for in the mid-1800s, most colleges were under *evangelical* Protestant leadership. This form of Christianity emphasized the centrality of the powerful "born-again" experience of spiritual transformation and the primacy of the Bible as a source of true knowledge. By the end of the century higher education was more and more in the hands of universities modeled on the German scientific ideal of scholarship, in which each discipline has its own rational and empirical standards that make no direct appeal to the Bible or Christian beliefs. In this context, Charles Darwin's theories on the biological evolution of humanity from lower primates had caught the popular imagination. Less generally known but very much on the minds of evangelical preachers was the new "biblical criticism" that had come out of Germany. Although by "criticism" proponents meant analysis, not finding fault, this new scholarship, which looked upon the Bible as an historical, humanly created document, challenged many pious beliefs about its teachings.

The challenges stemming from Darwinism and biblical criticism were a double blow to Christian beliefs and elicited two opposing responses: the modernism of liberal Christian evangelicals, on the one hand, and the fundamentalism of conservative Christian evangelicals on the other. Liberal evangelicals developed a new theology to show how modernism and Christianity were compatible. They saw God at work in evolution and in history. Christians, they argued, have an ethical calling to cooperate with God's will, operative in evolution and history, to transform this world into the Kingdom of God. Out of this new theology the Social Gospel movement emerged, seeking to reconcile science and Christian faith. It drew on disciplines such as sociology and political science to understand the social problems accompanying modernization and to suggest solutions that entailed changing the structures of society. It saw both sin and salvation primarily as having to do with life in this world. The Gospel was about transforming a sinful society into the Kingdom of God.

By the end of World War I, liberal evangelical Christianity dominated the northern Protestant churches. However, in the eyes of many other evangelicals, the attempt to adapt Christianity to the modern world was doomed to failure. What one ended up with was a Christianity emptied of everything that made it Christian and filled with everything that was secular and modern.

It was modernization that split evangelical theology in two: opposing the Social Gospel was Protestant fundamentalism. Whereas the theologians of the Social Gospel believed they represented the next logical stage in the historical development of Christianity, evangelicals who responded in a fundamentalist mode were convinced that there could be no historical development in this respect. If there was a conflict between the scriptures and modern science, then it must be modern science, not the Bible, that was in error.

In a series of twelve paperback books entitled *The Fundamentals*, published between 1910 and 1915, champions of the fundamentalist movement spoke in defense of Bible-based religion and against the apostasy, as they perceived it, of modernism. Convinced that liberal theology and Darwinism were undermining American civilization, they took their stand on the inerrancy of the Bible, pure and simple. If you did not share these beliefs, the fundamentalists did not consider you to be a true Christian.

The development of two American schools of evangelical Christianity was paradoxical. Evangelical Christianity had originated as a strategy for transcending the theological disputes and religious wars that occurred in the aftermath of the Protestant Reformation. The original evangelicals, in Europe, believed that a true Christian was identified not by acceptance of the right doctrines but by an emotional transformation undergone that produced a life-style of love and compassion and enabled Christians to accept each other, despite disagreements over fundamental beliefs. One of the most influential proponents of evangelical Christianity, John Wesley (the founder of Methodism), was famous for insisting that doctrinal differences should not separate Christians: "If thou lovest God and all mankind, I ask no more: 'give me thine hand.'"

Many other evangelicals, however, feared that the shock of modernism threatened Christian faith to the core, and by the 1920s the movement dubbed "fundamentalism" by the popular press was understood to refer to militantly antimodernist evangelical Protestants. The event that decisively formed the public image of Christian fundamentalism in America was the Scopes trial held in Dayton, Tennessee, in 1925. John Scopes, a high school teacher, had been accused of breaking a law that banned the teaching of evolution in the state's public schools. Three-time candidate for president of the United States William Jennings Bryan appeared for the prosecution. The defense was led by the legendary Clarence Darrow, a favorite of the international press corps that attended the trial. Although Bryan won the case in court, he lost the cause in the media, which portrayed fundamentalism as the philosophy of ignorant backwoods hicks. Fundamentalism then lost popular support and Protestant liberalism, which sought to embrace modernity, held sway largely unchallenged until the surprising resurgence of fundamentalism in the last quarter of the twentieth century.

The Catholic Confrontation with Modernity

In 1864 Pope Pius IX issued a Syllabus of Errors listing eighty "modern" teachings that challenged the control of all knowledge and all politics by the church. Pius IX thought that such ideas could only lead to a godless society that would no longer heed the eternal and unchanging fundamental truths of the one true church, and he admonished Catholics to reject them. In 1869 Pius IX called the first Vatican Council of cardinals and bishops to shore up the teachings of the church against the threat of modernism. In 1870 the papacy was besieged not only by modern ideas but by modern secular politics. For in that year the new secular kingdom of Italy seized the papal estates from Pius IX and the Vatican lost the political power it had enjoyed for centuries.

Thus Vatican I, as the council is now known, was in session precisely at the time when the intellectual and political authority of the papacy was at its weakest and most vulnerable. In 1870, at the insistence of Pius IX, Vatican I declared the pope to be infallible. This meant that a pope's official declarations on faith and morals could not be altered, even with the consent of the church, including any future councils.

There is a striking similarity-in-contrast between Protestant and Catholic antimodernist responses. Both attempted to prevent modernization and historical change from entering the church by an appeal to an infallible or inerrant authority that they believed was higher than scientific and secular authority. For Protestants it was the Bible, for Roman Catholics it was the pope, as the final authority on how the Bible was to be interpreted.

It is all the more remarkable therefore, that almost a century later a new pope would seek to reverse many of the decisions of Vatican I and come to terms with the modern world. When Pope John XXIII called the Second Vatican Council in 1962, in one dramatic gesture he sought to reverse the more than four centuries of church attempts to reject the emerging modern world. And he sought to heal the bad feelings generated by religious divisions in Christianity going back to the Protestant Reformation and even earlier. Moreover, in its Declaration on the Relationship of the Church to Non-Christian Religions, the council expressed a new openness to the teachings of other world religions. Indeed, it declared: "The Catholic Church rejects nothing which is true and holy in these [non-Christian] religions."

Pope John XXIII, who opened the doors of the Roman Catholic Church to modernity by calling the Second Vatican Council, sits at his desk in the private library of the Vatican to record a radio and television address in September 1962.

The Second Vatican Council's meetings lasted from 1962 to 1965. John XXIII did not live to see them completed, but in his brief papacy (1958–1963) he unleashed a spirit that transformed the Catholic Church from a world-shunning institution into one that was open to the modern world. In the decades since Vatican II, Catholics have wrestled with their future, with some wanting to return to the fundamentals of the Catholicism of Vatican I, and others wanting to follow the road to modernization.

The Nineteenth-Century Historical and Social-Scientific Revolution

We have seen that in the recent past, both Catholics and Protestants have responded to the revolution in human thought that had marked the nineteenth century. This revolution was precipitated by the emergence of new academic disciplines, representing the final shock wave of modern consciousness.

The first wave had been created by the natural sciences. Copernicus had outraged the European world when he suggested in 1543 CE that the earth was not the center of the universe. Later, geologists had concluded that the earth was far older than had been calculated by anyone who used the Bible as a guide. Then in 1859 Charles Darwin published *On the Origin of Species*, rendering completely implausible the biblical account according to which human beings appeared on earth on the sixth day of creation. Darwin claimed that the operative force in the evolution that had been proceeding for many thousands of years was a struggle between members of the various species that resulted in the survival of the fittest.

The social sciences delivered the second shock wave, especially critical historiography, which showed that popular legends about the past did not accurately describe the events they purported to chronicle. The other social sciences did little to ease the shock. Sociologists and anthropologists who studied societies comparatively suggested that humanity had invented gods to make the ways of life of various cultures seem sacred. This view was reinforced by Sigmund Freud's suggestion that God was a projection or instance of wish fulfillment—an illusion that human beings needed to create to give them a feeling of security in an unstable world. Now human beings were asked to think of both society and human identity as created by human choices rather than by the actions and decisions of gods, as claimed by many traditional teachings.

This new awareness created a profound problem. The question that came to divide modern Christianity was whether to reject the developments of modernity, as did Protestant evangelical fundamentalism and Vatican I Catholicism, or accept them, seeing God at work in evolution and historical change, as did Protestant evangelical liberalism and Vatican II Catholicism—or strike some kind of compromise in between. Paradoxically, although modernity appeared to be a threat to Christianity, it had been nurtured, in significant part, by Christianity itself. Our task now is to return to the beginning of Christianity so that we can better understand the historical circumstances that led its adherents and its institution, the church, to contribute to the development of the modern world.

PREMODERN CHRISTIANITY: THE FORMATIVE ERA

Ancient and Modern: Contrasting Worldviews

When the first followers of Jesus of Nazareth looked up into the night sky in the first century, they did not see what modernists did when they looked upward in the nineteenth century. For modernists saw a cosmos with stars and planets scattered in infinite space. They knew that the earth is not at the center of the universe but just one of the planets circumnavigating a star (the sun) in one of many galaxies. When individuals in the first century looked up they saw a world shaped not by the modern imagination but by the imagination of the ancient Greeks. They accepted the Greek view that the earth was at the center of seven spheres. The higher spheres of the stars and the planets embodied spiritual beings (Paul of Tarsus called them the "principalities and powers") that governed the universe. Everything above the moon, they believed, belonged to the realm of the spiritual and eternal. Everything below the moon belonged to the realm of the physical and temporal. The Greeks thought that the souls of all humans had their origin in the spiritual realm and had descended into the material or bodily realm. But the spiritual goal, each individual's hope of salvation, was to return to the eternal realm above, beyond time, decay, and death.

In addition to the legacy of the Greeks, the worldview of the first Christians owed a debt to the Hebraic tradition of ancient Israel, namely, that creation is a story unfolding in time. In the beginning God spoke and the story began. The story has many dramatic ups and downs as it unfolds, but at last, God will bring the present world to an end, judge it, and transform it into a new creation. Today "modern" believers wrestle with the question of whether being a Christian requires adherence to the ancient worldview or can accommodate changing worldviews, including the modern scientific one.

The New Testament

The journey of Christianity from the ancient to the modern world begins in the first century with the life and teachings of Jesus of Nazareth as communicated in the Gospels of the New Testament. Being a Jew, Jesus participated in a religious tradition that went back another two thousand years before his time. This is acknowledged in the Christian Bible, which is made up of two parts. What Christians call the Old Testament is basically an adoption of the Pharisaic and Hellenistic Jewish collections of sacred writings that have been the official scriptures of Judaism since the end of the first century of the common era (CE). The scriptural writings of Christians call the New Testament did not assume the form of the twenty-seven books we have now until the year 367 CE—more than three hundred years after the death of Jesus. During those centuries there were in circulation many stories of the life and sayings of Jesus, most of which do not appear in the New Testament. What is striking is that the tradition did not settle on a single story of Jesus for its Bible but actually included four different stories—the Gospels of Matthew, Mark, Luke, and John. To these were appended letters by the apostle Paul and others, a short history of the early church (the Acts of the Apostles), and a vision of the end of time (the book of Revelation). Christians believe that these scriptures show that Jesus of Nazareth is the Christ—the anointed one, or messiah—whose coming was foretold by the Hebrew prophets.

According to tradition, the Gospels were written in the order of their appearance in the New Testament: Matthew, Mark, Luke, and John. After careful scrutiny of the literary structure and probable historical context of each Gospel, however, many modern scholars concluded that Mark's Gospel probably was written first (at the time of the fall of the temple in 70), and that both Matthew and Luke used Mark's material as a model in writing their versions (sometime between 80 and 90). The Gospel of John (written after 90) is so different in literary tone, content, and structure that it seems to have been a largely independent creation.

Christians in every culture tend to imagine the birth of Christ in terms of their own culture, as in this Chinese painting.

Also, according to tradition, the Gospels were written by disciples (or disciples of disciples) of Jesus. Taking advantage of historical and archaeological findings that shed additional light on the biblical period, modern scholars do not believe any Gospel had a single author. Rather, each one began in shared oral traditions as told in different communities of believers after Jesus' death on the cross and attested resurrection. These traditions were eventually written down and edited to place the sayings of Jesus in the context of different remembered events from Jesus' life.

As we have noted, the sacred scriptures of Christianity were first examined critically in the nineteenth century. Within Christianity the validity of this modern approach is in dispute. Fundamentalists reject it, while other Christians see it as helpful for understanding the development of faith in the early church. And yet for all their differences, and quite apart from historical questions of "what really happened," all forms of Christianity share a common reverence for the stories of Jesus as they are found in the New Testament.

The Stories of Jesus

The power of the Christian message is revealed in the stories of Jesus, especially the Sermon on the Mount (Matthew 5–7), with its message of loving your neighbor and doing good to everyone, including your enemy. It is that message of compassion and forgiveness that has moved millions. What the stories of Jesus tell is that God's true being manifested itself in the life of a human being, Jesus. Ancient philosophies often denigrated the human body as a prison to be escaped from and unworthy of association with God, who was thought of as pure spirit. The story of Jesus, in whom God's word was made flesh, affirmed that being human was not to be belittled, for God embraced it.

Jesus was born roughly at the beginning of the first century, possibly in Bethlehem or Nazareth. In any case he grew up in Nazareth in ancient Palestine, then under Roman rule (see Map 4.1). Little is known of his youth, but according to the scriptures he was raised by Joseph, a carpenter, and his wife, Mary, the child's mother. The birth of Jesus was said to have been miraculous, for Mary became pregnant through the power of God as announced by an angel rather than through marital relations with Joseph.

Around the age of thirty, Jesus had a traumatic experience. Someone he knew, admired, and was related to—John the Baptist—was arrested on orders from Herod and eventually beheaded. To everyone's surprise, soon after John's arrest Jesus began teaching the very message that had gotten John in trouble with Herod—"Repent, for the kingdom of heaven is at hand" (Matthew 4:17).

Map 4.1   Palestine at the time of Jesus.

While his family and childhood friends thought he had gone mad, Jesus soon attracted followers who thought otherwise and called him rabbi, which means "teacher." His teachings are exemplified in a passage from the Sermon on the Mount:

You have heard that it was said, "An eye for an eye and a tooth for a tooth." But I say to you, offer no resistance to one who is evil. When someone strikes you on (your) right cheek, turn the other one to him as well. If anyone wants to go to law with you over your tunic, hand him your cloak as well. Should anyone press you into service for one mile, go with him for two miles. Give to the one who asks of you, and do not turn your back on one who wants to borrow. You have heard that it was said, "You shall love your neighbor and hate your enemy." But I say to you, love your enemies, and pray for those who persecute you, that you may be children of your heavenly Father, for he makes his sun rise on the bad and the good, and causes rain to fall on the just and the unjust. For if you love those who love you, what recompense will you have? Do not the tax collectors do the same? And if you greet your brothers only, what is unusual about that? Do not the pagans do the same? So be perfect, just as your heavenly Father is perfect.
—(Matthew 5:38–48)

In addition to preaching repentance and love, according to the scriptures, Jesus began working miracles—healing the sick (Mark 1:40–45; Matthew 9:18–22), walking on water (Mark 6:45–52; John 6:16–21), casting out evil spirits (Mark 1:23–28; Matthew 8:28–34), miraculously multiplying a few loaves and fishes to feed a multitude, a story recounted in all four Gospels.

Illustration of Jesus healing a leper from a biblical manuscript found at Mount Athos Monastery in Greece.

As the fame of Jesus spread, Sadducees and Pharisees (see Chapter Three), according to the stories, grew jealous of him and began to plot his demise. They had him handed over to the Romans who had heard some call him "messiah." While the Gospels typically make it appear as if the Jews, not the Romans, are the cause of Jesus' crucifixion, historians have pointed out that only the Romans had that power. Moreover, for the Romans the term messiah was associated with their enemies the Zealots. A militaristic sect of Judaism that engaged in guerrilla warfare against the Roman legions, the Zealots openly announced their expectation that God would send a messiah, a political revolutionary who would overthrow the Roman Empire. Historically, the reason the Romans condemned Jesus to die nailed to a wooden cross was that they thought of him as an enemy of the state.

Throughout history the Crucifixion has captured the imagination of great artists such as Matthias Grünewald, creator of this sixteenth-century altarpiece now in Isenheim, Germany.

Whatever the political facts, the followers of Jesus have always found deep spiritual meaning in the Crucifixion. What is striking about Mark's account of the event (found also in Matthew 27:46) is the bleakness of Jesus' final words: "My God, my God, why have you forsaken me?" This is very different from the final words of Jesus reported in other Gospels: "Father, into your hands I commend my spirit" (Luke 23:46) and "It is finished" (John 19:30). Mark presents a Jesus with whom even a hearer in the depths of despair can identify.

And yet the Gospels do not allow despair to be the final word. For they offer the hope that just as Jesus was raised from the dead, so may the believer be who in faith embraces the life of the holy one who also knew despair and death. As the story is taken up in the Gospel of John (John 20), some of the disciples came to Jesus' grave on Sunday morning, the first day of the week, only to find an empty tomb; later Jesus appeared among them, displaying his wounds to prove it truly was he, risen from the dead. Now the disciples, who had been afraid, began to be filled with a new and bold spirit—the Holy Spirit of the God who had raised Jesus from the dead (Acts 2). Emboldened by this spirit they began to proclaim the message of the risen Lord who had conquered death and would return very soon. At this second coming, or Parousia, Jesus would raise the dead, judge the heavens and the earth, and inaugurate the Kingdom of God, in which all injustice would be overcome, and suffering and death would be no more.

In a world filled with injustice, suffering, and death under the oppressive rule of the Romans, such a message inspired hope and joy. In a world of pain it offered people a sense of having a destiny that transcended tragedy and death. In a world where everything seemed to be governed by chance and fate it suggested that a personal God guided the lives of individuals toward ultimate meaning and fulfillment. The world was not a cold and uncaring place, for the love of God nourished every creature. The life of Jesus presented people with a story of suffering and tragedy that was real yet not final, for suffering and death were overcome in the resurrection. In the life of Jesus, people could see their own lives reflected, leading to the hope that their own tragedies would not be final and that they too would be resurrected. To understand these things is to understand some of the reasons that Christianity is the religion of one-third of the world's population.

Christianity's Emergence from Judaism

Jesus was born a Jew, lived as a Jew, participating reverently in traditions that had originated two thousand years before his birth, and died as a Jew. His gentile followers, however, thought that Jews did not understand his message. As a consequence, what began as a new way of understanding Judaism was embraced almost exclusively by gentiles (non-Jews), who thought of themselves as practicing a new and improved faith—Christianity. These gentile Christians came to teach what some scholars have called the myth or story of supersession—that God had rejected the Jews and chosen gentiles instead. It was a myth that would endure until the twentieth century.

Christianity, in fact, began as a Jewish sectarian movement. After two thousand years of biblical history, especially after the Babylonian exile (586–538 BCE), a variety of movements (such as those of the Sadducees, Pharisees, Hellenists, Zealots, Samaritans, Essenes, and Nazarenes, discussed in Chapter Three) developed in Judaism. There was no agreement on a common set of sacred writings, however. Only at the end of the first century of the Common Era did the Hebrew Bible as we know it come into existence, largely owing to the influence of the Pharisees and the Hellenists. At the beginning of the century, however, these groups and others were engaged in an ongoing argument about the right way of life for the people of Israel.

Naturally, each movement saw itself as the model for the right way of life and all others as deviant. The result was a diverse set of sectarian movements, each proclaiming a message something like this: "We are the true Israel (i.e., the true Jews); you are not. The end of the world is at hand, when God will come to judge the heaven and the earth. Jews who have strayed, who are thus no better than pagans, must repent and be ritually immersed. Then they will become true Israel again—true Jews, who by definition live the way we do." The "we" here of course was a different "we" depending on who was preaching the message. Of course any Jews who were not part of that "we" were likely to find the message an insult, for traditionally the baptismal rite of ritual immersion and purification was required only of non-Jewish converts to Judaism (along with circumcision for males).

The Fall of the Temple

This whole picture of diversity changed dramatically in the year 70 CE when the Romans did just what the Sadducees (members of the Jewish upper class who had tried to keep peace with the Romans) had feared; and ceased to tolerate constant guerrilla attacks from the Zealots, marched into Jerusalem with thousands of troops, burned down the temple, and drove the Jews out of their holy city. In the aftermath of the fall of the temple, two movements emerged to shape Western religious history: the Pharisaic movement, which became Rabbinic Judaism, and the Nazarene movement, which became gentile Christianity.

The Pharisees survived the destruction of the temple because they were able to provide a flexible leadership under dramatically new conditions. Unlike Pharisaic Judaism, the Nazarene movement never had a large following among Jews. Its greatest success was a missionary movement for the conversion of gentiles. The Nazarenes were an apocalyptic movement, believing that the end of time was at hand and that their special mission was to convert the gentiles before the final judgment. In this they were inspired by the prophecies of Isaiah that in the last days all nations would be gathered into Jerusalem (Isaiah 66:18–20).

A critical issue for the Nazarenes was the status of new gentile converts. This was taken up around the year 48 at a meeting in Jerusalem. The Christian tradition refers to this meeting as the first church council or the "Council of Jerusalem." The conservatives from Jerusalem argued that gentile converts had to be circumcised and obey the whole Mosaic law as required of other Jews. Paul of Tarsus came to this meeting from Antioch where he and other Hellenistic Jews were converting large numbers of gentiles. Hellenistic Jews, the great missionaries of first-century Judaism, believed in adopting Greek culture and language to make Judaism attractive to gentiles. Paul and others sympathetic to the Hellenistic mission argued that gentiles should be exempt from the requirement of circumcision and from most of the ritual obligations, focusing instead on obeying the moral commandments of the Mosaic covenant. The faction led by Paul won the argument, and a letter urging these changes went out to all the mission communities (Acts 15:19–21).

This ruling was decisive for the growth of the Nazarene movement among gentiles. Released from those practices that gentiles were most reluctant to embrace, they flooded into the movement. By the second century Jewish-born people made up a smaller and smaller proportion of the total membership. And as the leadership fell more and more into the hands of gentiles, the movement lost its sense of identity as a Jewish movement and began to take on a separate identity as a new religion—Christianity.

Paul

It is one of the paradoxes of Christianity that the one person, after Jesus himself, who has most deeply influenced the tradition is a man who began as a persecutor of the Nazarene movement in the first century, treating it as a heretical form of Judaism. Paul, who came to be known as an apostle of Jesus, was not one of the original twelve apostles selected by Jesus and never met Jesus before his crucifixion. He came to know Jesus as the risen Lord, after an extraordinary encounter on the road to Damascus, an experience that led to his conversion. Paul became the first great missionary of the Christian movement, and we know of Paul's thoughts and actions primarily from his letters to the churches that he founded in places like the ancient Greek cities of Corinth and Ephesus. The letters form approximately one-fourth of the New Testament. Other accounts of Paul's ministry appear in the Acts of the Apostles, in the New Testament, a book attributed to the author of the Gospel of Luke.

Paul was both a Hellenistic Jew and a Pharisee who was born in present-day Turkey and educated in Jerusalem. Hellenistic Jews were the very successful missionaries to the gentiles in first century Judaism. They presented Judaism as open to Greek patterns of thought and behavior. When Paul became a convert to the Nazarene movement, he continued the missionary activity familiar from Hellenistic Judaism but with a new twist: he argued that this movement's task was to bring the gentiles into Judaism as a "wild olive branch" grafted onto a cultivated olive tree, by which he meant Judaism (Romans, 11:16–18). Through Jesus, Paul thought, the gentiles were now called to share with the Jews in the promises made to Abraham (Ephesians 2:11–22). Paul and others like him were responsible for the beginnings of the transformation of the Jewish Nazarene movement into a new religion—gentile Christianity. In later centuries major theologians, from the early church father, Augustine, to the Protestant Reformation leader Martin Luther, embraced Paul's thought. Thus Paul's teachings, especially on justification by faith, have greatly influenced Western Christianity. Tradition says that Paul was martyred in Rome, probably around the year 60 CE.

Renaissance painting depicting Paul visiting the apostle Peter in prison.

The Origins of Christian Anti-Jewish Sentiment

We are now in a position to discuss a problem that has plagued the relationship between Jews and Christians throughout the history of Western civilization. For the New Testament reflects the context of the Jewish sectarian arguments that had been going on in the first century, in which groups like the Zealots, the Essenes, and others were saying to each other: "We, not you, are the true Israel, the true Jews. Therefore repent, be baptized, and become Jews the way we are, for the end of time and God's judgment are at hand."

These first-century Jewish sectarian arguments were incorporated into the sacred writings of Christianity found in the New Testament. However, when these statements were read and repeated by the leaders of the "Christian" movement in the second and later centuries, they were no longer seen as exhortations from one Jewish group to another. Now gentiles who had come to identify themselves as Christians took up the refrain: "We are the true Israel, you are not." And thus was born the Christian myth of supersession or divine rejection. Christians now argued: "We Christians have replaced you Jews as God's chosen people. Because you did not recognize Jesus as messiah and had him crucified, God has rejected you and chosen us to supersede you."

Soon this logic was disastrously extended to include the claim that since "the Jews" had brought about the death of the very son of God who was sent to save them, not only had God rejected the Jews for all time, but it was the Christians' duty to punish them. It was a view that played a tragic role in the persecution of Jews throughout much of Western history. It was not until the time of Vatican II (1962–1965) that a commission created by Pope John XXIII condemned the teachings of supersession and divine rejection of the Jews and affirmed Paul's metaphorical view, that gentiles are a wild olive branch grafted onto the tree of Judaism to share in God's promises to Abraham. By the end of the twentieth century, most Protestant churches had renounced supercession as well.

Jesus as Son of God

In the first four centuries after the time of Jesus, as gentile Christianity separated itself from Judaism, Christians struggled to formulate an authoritative understanding (dogma) of who Jesus is and what his significance is. The essential problem that faced the early followers of Jesus who, like the apostle Paul, believed that they had a special mission to convert the gentiles, was how to translate an essentially Jewish message about a coming "messiah" into terms non-Jews could understand. These missionaries did not want pagans to confuse Christian claims about Jesus being Son of God with pagan myths in which divine beings come down to earth in humanlike bodies. The challenge was to speak correctly and clearly about the being and meaning of Jesus of Nazareth without claiming either too little (that Jesus was just a good man) or too much (that Jesus was not really human but rather a supernatural being like the gods of pagan mythology). For about three hundred years, Christians debated the various possible ways of thinking and speaking about Jesus and held several church councils. By the time the argument was settled, both extremes had been deemed heresy.

The most important councils were those of Nicaea in 325 and Chalcedon in 451. Some bishops and theologians argued that Jesus was a divine being with neither a mortal mind nor body. Some argued that Jesus had a human body and a divine mind, others said that although his mind too was human and mortal he had a divine will, and so on. Such views made Jesus a kind of half-man and half-god, not unlike other characters in pagan mythology. The Council of Chalcedon rejected all such views, insisting that Jesus had a human body and a human mind. He was fully and completely human, with a birth and a death like every other person. Jesus' humanity differed from that of others in only one way—he was without sin. Moreover, in this man Jesus God was wholly present. The formula arrived at to reconcile the apparent paradox was that in the "one person" of Jesus there were "two natures" (divine and human) united "without confusion" or mixture. That is, in the person of Jesus divinity and humanity were united yet completely distinct.

Two beliefs had to be held together in this formula, that of Nicaea—that the Word through which all things were created was the "same as" (*homoousios*) God (i.e., eternal)—and that of Chalcedon—that the man Jesus was a mortal human being to whom was united that eternal Word (which had existed before the incarnation of Jesus). If the Word was not eternal, it could not confer eternity; and if Jesus was not mortal, his resurrection offered no hope to other mortals. This formula was meant to combat views eventually declared heretical to the effect that Jesus was a divine (i.e., purely spiritual) being—a god who only appeared to be human and therefore could not have died on the cross, nor would it have been necessary for him to arise from the dead.

The formula of two natures in one person developed at Chalcedon was complemented by another unique doctrine or belief of Christians—the belief in a triune God, which had been affirmed earlier at the Council of Constantinople in 381. The doctrine of the *Trinity* asserts that God is one essence but three persons. The formula "three persons in one God, Father, Son, and Holy Spirit" is not really about mathematics. Rather, it means that God, the creator of the universe, can at the same time be present in the life of Jesus and in all things in the world through God's Word and Spirit—without ceasing to be transcendent or beyond the universe. The doctrine of the Trinity states that God is *in* all things without accepting the pantheistic notion that God *is* all things.

Jews and Muslims, with their theology of a prophetic monotheism, according to which God is one and not three, have typically misunderstood the meaning of the doctrine of the *Trinity*. But then so have many Christians, so this should not be surprising. Nevertheless, the intent of both the "two natures, one person" doctrine concerning Jesus and the doctrine of the Trinity concerning God is to affirm the uniqueness of a God who is both present in and transcendent to the cosmos. This true God who has no equals—the God of Abraham—the very same God affirmed by Jews and Muslims.

Constantinianism: The Marriage of Christianity and Empire

Perhaps the single most important political event in the history of Christianity was the conversion of the Roman emperor Constantine, the first monarch to champion the rights of Christians. Constantine, who issued the Edict of Toleration (also known as the Edict of Milan) in 313, was baptized on his deathbed. With the imperial declaration, Christianity went from being an often persecuted religion to a permitted (and eventually the favored) religion in the empire. Now a Roman ruler had placed the empire under the protection of the cross of Christ.

Heretofore, many Christians had tended to look at Roman civilization, with its imperialism and colonial domination of foreign territories, as the work of the devil. That is how it is portrayed in the book of Revelation, for instance. After Constantine, Christians began to see Roman imperialism as a good thing, as a way of spreading the Gospel throughout the world. This was a decisive step in shaping the Western religious vision of a Christian civilization. The Constantinian vision achieved the status of official political policy in 381, when Christianity became the official religion of the Roman Empire under Emperor Theodosius. Within ten years, pagan worship was declared illegal and all pagan temples were closed. Only Judaism was permitted as an alternative to Christianity, and it existed under severe legal restrictions, with Jews losing many of the freedoms they had had under pagan Rome.

The Greek-speaking churches of the East took Constantine's relationship to the church as a model of how things should be. There were four great centers

A Roman gold coin from the fourth century displays the head of Roman emperor Constantine.

The Constantinian unification of church and state is illustrated in this Roman mosaic showing the Roman emperor Justinian, accompanied by churchmen and court officials, bringing gifts to an altar.

of Orthodoxy, in Constantinople, Alexandria (Egypt), Antioch (Syria), and Jerusalem, each ruled by a patriarch. In the Eastern Roman or Byzantine Empire, centered in Constantinople, church and state existed symbiotically. The Christian emperor called church councils and even appointed the bishops. The emperor ruled over both church and state in the name of Christ.

However, the pattern of the Western civilization that shaped the road to modernity was not that of Eastern Christianity but an important modification of it that put church and empire in a precarious relationship combining cooperation and antagonism. The Constantinian model thrived in Byzantium until the fifteenth century, but in the West, Roman political rule collapsed after the time of Theodosius. The political vacuum created by the absence of an emperor in the West allowed the bishops of the Latin-speaking churches to assume much greater independence with respect to the state. This was especially true of the bishop of Rome, whose power and authority grew as secular political power and authority collapsed, leading to the idea of the primacy of this bishop of Rome as "pope" (father) over all other bishops. In the Latin church the idea of separation between church and state developed. The chief architect of this alternate vision was Augustine of Hippo.

Orthodox Christianity

While our main emphasis is on Latin (Western) Christianity, because that is the form of Christianity that fostered the emergence of modernity, the Eastern churches have great historical and cultural significance. Although subject to the emperor, internally these churches were conciliar, placing ultimate authority not in a single bishop (a pope) but in church councils as meetings of all the bishops. Each of the four great centers of Eastern Orthodoxy, Constantinople, Alexandria, Antioch, and Jerusalem, was ruled by a patriarch who was held to be equal to the others and to the bishop of the Latin church in Rome. The bishops of Rome and Constantinople were especially esteemed, but all the bishops together were seen as sharing authority.

Eastern Orthodox Christianity was distinctive for its mystical emphasis: Christ became human, it is said, so that humans could become divinized and share mystically in the eternal life of God—a process known as "theosis." Orthodoxy is also distinctive for its understanding of sin as ignorance rather than corruption of the will through Original Sin as put forward in Latin-Augustinian Christianity. For the Orthodox churches, Christ is the great teacher who comes to dispel human ignorance of oneness with God and to restore humans to mystical unity with the creator. The emphasis is not on Christ as the lord of History but on the cosmic Christ through whom all things are created, held together, and brought to fulfillment. From the beginning there was tension between the Eastern and Western churches, but a formal split did not occur until 1054.

Augustine, Architect of Western Christianity

From the fifth century on through the Protestant Reformation and the emergence of modernity, the West has been deeply influenced by the theological thought of Augustine of Hippo, whom Christians typically refer to as "St. Augustine." After Jesus and the apostle Paul, probably no other individual in history is more responsible for the shape of Western Christianity. Augustine's vision deeply shaped the development of Roman Catholicism from the fifth through the twelfth centuries. Then he was eclipsed by Thomas Aquinas, only to be recovered by the Protestant reformers Luther and Calvin in the sixteenth century who drew heavily on the writings of Augustine.

Constantine died in 337. Augustine, who was born in 354 and died in 430, lived through the time of Theodosius and witnessed firsthand the transformation of the Roman Empire from a pagan empire into a Christian one. This stunning reversal could not fail to impress contemporary observers. They could not believe that the pagan Roman Empire had become Christian through chance or good luck. They concluded instead that God intended to use the Roman Empire to provide the political unity and stability needed to spread the Gospel to the ends of the earth.

Augustine of Hippo is depicted reading the letters of St. Paul, just before his conversion to Christianity, in this fifteenth-century painting by Gozzoli Benozzo.

In century after century, Christians turned to Augustine's spiritual autobiography, *The Confessions* (400), as a model of conversion and piety. And in century after century, rulers of church and state turned to his book *The City of God* (423) as a model for the political order. Indeed, the first great medieval pope, Gregory I, used Augustine's vision to justify his exercise of power over the political order, and Charlemagne, who on December 25, 800, became the first Holy Roman Emperor, is said to have slept with a copy of *The City of God* under his pillow. The influence of the vision of personal life embodied in *The Confessions* and the vision of history embodied in *The City of God* on the history of European Christianity is so vast and profound that it is almost impossible to calculate.

The Confessions: Faith, Reason, and the Quest for Wisdom

A key turning point in Augustine's life, as he relates it, was the awakening of his mind and heart to a passion for wisdom when he was nineteen years old. Before that event, the young man had devoted himself to fulfilling selfish desires for wealth, fame, power, and sexual pleasure. About the time Augustine was completing his studies in Carthage in Africa, he came across a book entitled *Hortensius*, by the pagan author

Cicero. This book, says Augustine, set him on fire with a new kind of desire—the desire for wisdom. He was not encouraged by his reading of Cicero "to join this or that sect; instead I was urged on and inflamed with a passionate zeal to love and seek and obtain and embrace and hold fast wisdom itself, whatever it might be" (*Confessions*, III, 4). And so he resolved to follow his doubts and questions wherever they might lead him. Augustine doesn't say that *Hortensius* changed his thinking but rather that it "altered my way of feeling . . . and gave me different ambitions and desires" (III, 4). Augustine's wording here is very important. His experience changed his feelings and desires, which in turn changed his thinking and eventually led to his full conversion. Christianity is a religion of the transformation of the heart as the location of the emotions. In the first century of the Common Era, Jesus had called his hearers to undergo a change of heart, and virtually every great reform and renewal movement in Christian history has returned to this theme.

Augustine's story of his conversion became a model for understanding the relationship between faith and reason. Theology is "faith seeking understanding." Some interpretations to the contrary, this does not mean "you first have to believe to be able to understand." Rather, you will be led to deeper understanding if you have faith or trust that God is working through one's very own doubts to lead one to deeper understanding. In his *Confessions* Augustine says that only after his full conversion did he come to realize that when he had the faith to doubt he already had an implicit faith in Christ, who was leading him, through doubts, to true wisdom.

The City of God: Augustine's Tale of Two Cities

In the same way that *The Confessions* provided a model of faith and reason, *The City of God* provided a model of church and state. The meaning of history is unraveled for Augustine by a symbolic reading of the biblical stories as a history of two cities—the human city and the city of God, located in a world guided by two different loves, *cupiditas* (selfish love) and *caritas* (selfless love), respectively. These, of course, are the same two loves Augustine saw at war in his own life in his *Confessions*. Augustine's formulation of the appropriate relationship of these cities modeled relations between church and state, religion and politics, and sacred and secular for most of Western history.

For Augustine the story of the human city was the story of the history of civilizations going through endless cycles of progress and decline—a story without any clear purpose or meaning. But hidden within that history was another story—that of the city of God. This story, which is revealed in the Bible, has a clear purpose and direction. It is the story of a journey with God through time toward a final resurrection and eternal life for all who belong to the city of God. The city of God, however, was not identical with the church. Only at the final judgment will human beings come to know who truly belongs to the city of God.

In defining the relationship between the two cities Augustine argues that both state and church exist through God's will to serve God's purposes. God uses the state to establish the peace necessary for the spread of the Gospel by the church. In the journey through history each entity should serve the other. The state should be subject to the church in spiritual matters, and the church should be subject to the state in earthly matters. Neither should seek to dominate the other. However, in actual history the sides could never fully agree on where to draw the line between earthly matters and spiritual matters. And too often each side forgot the part about not dominating the other. Indeed, throughout most of Western history both popes and emperors maneuvered to upset the balance between the two by trying to dictate to the other.

Unlike the pure Constantinian vision, Augustine separates church and state (e.g., by expecting there to be both a pope and an emperor). Yet Augustine's vision is not yet the modern one that insists on a secular or nonreligious state, for he assumes that the two powers will work together to achieve a worldwide Christian civilization. Since the time of Augustine, most Christians have assumed that the task of Christianity is to transform every society into a "Christian society" comprising two branches: church and state. This pattern continued even after the Holy Roman Empire collapsed and the Protestant Reformation helped usher in the modern era. In more recent times, modern European culture replaced Roman civilization as the political order thought to be willed by God for the purpose of spreading Christianity around the world. Only gradually, after the religious wars the Protestant Reformation provoked, did Christians begin to explore an alternative—the modern idea of a secular, or nonreligious state as the guarantor of freedom to worship in a religiously pluralistic world. We will return to this observation when we discuss modernization.

PREMODERN CHRISTIANITY: THE CLASSICAL ERA

In 476 Romulus Augustulus, the last Roman emperor in the West, was deposed. Less than a century after the time of Augustine of Hippo, the Roman Empire and its civilization collapsed in the West. Most commerce ceased, for example, and the Roman money economy was replaced by a barter system. Over several centuries Europe was invaded by tribes from the north, and as tribal leaders upgraded themselves into lords of their domains, feudalism began to take shape. The feudal system was a network of loyalties established between a landholder (a king or a nobleman) and those who served him and his estates. It was a hierarchical arrangement with the nobility on the top, subordinates called vassals in the middle, and serfs and slaves at the bottom. The nobles were members of either a secular warrior aristocracy or the religious aristocracy consisting of bishops and abbots (the heads of monasteries), for the church was a major landholder and church officials too could be feudal lords.

The Middle Ages roughly spans the sixth through the fourteenth centuries. It was a world without printing presses, and so the few existing books were handwritten. Only the elite among the clergy and the nobility could read, in any event. The average Christian got his or her religious view of life from sermons delivered by priests and from images depicted in the stained glass windows and on the walls of the churches and cathedrals.

In this new world, the church carried civilization forward into Europe, accomplishing this primarily through the spread of Christian monasteries. It was monasticism that provided the bridge of civilization between the ancient world and the modern world, bringing technological development and the light of learning to a European period that has been otherwise described as the Dark Ages.

Monasticism was the first serious reform movement in the church. For once Christianity became the official religion of the Roman Empire, many who became Christians did so for reasons of expediency rather than piety. The practice of Christianity came to be more about social acceptability and worldly success for them. By the late third century, members of the Eastern (Greek) churches who wanted to lead an exemplary Christian life often felt they had to separate themselves from the corrupt world around them, moving into the desert to live simply, with much time for prayer. The first monks tended to be hermits, but gradually many of the pious, solitary men began to form monastic communities. The most out-standing of these monks, called the desert fathers, had a powerful influence on the church throughout the Middle Ages. For example, Gregory I, the first medieval pope, was born to aristocracy but abandoned his privileges to become a monk in the desert. It was the beginning of a pattern. Whenever Christianity tended to grow corrupt with worldly power and success, it was monasticism that provided reform movements to call the church back to its spiritual mission.

By the late fourth century, monasticism had spread to the Western (Latin) churches. Whereas Greek monasticism was supported by church and state, the Latin communities set up according to the model of Benedict of Nursia were self-supporting organizations for work and prayer under the leadership of an abbot. In the ancient world work was viewed as a task for slaves, but Benedict taught that "to work is to pray" and integrated physical labor into the daily schedule of group prayer and private

Before the printing press was invented, all books were written by hand. Depicted is a medieval monk transcribing a text at his desk.

devotions. Consequently, the Benedictine monasteries preserved and developed not only spiritual knowledge but also ancient learning and technology. The Benedictines were the great engineers of the Middle Ages, who developed impressive waterwheel and windmill technologies to improve the monks' productivity. The goal was to make work more efficient so that there would be more time for prayer. Thus, the monasteries brought to the West, not only spiritual renewal but also intellectual and technological advances, making profound contributions to the full flowering of technological civilization in the modern period.

The Medieval Worldview: Sacraments and Festivals

Sacraments

In the medieval world, life on earth was seen as a test and a place of waiting to enter one's true home in heaven, if one passed the test. Christians believed that when they died their souls would be separated from their bodies and would come before God for individual judgment. In the future (at an unknown time) the world would come to an end and Jesus would return to raise the bodies of the dead and unite them to their souls. Those who had been faithful and good would be rewarded for all eternity in heaven, enjoying the "beatific vision" or presence of God; the rest would be consigned to eternal punishment in hell.

The church was God's gift to this world to help Christians prepare for their final judgment. The church was founded by Jesus Christ, the Son of God, who had passed on leadership of the church to his chief apostle, Peter (Matthew 16:18). This apostolic succession was continued by the popes, who were seen as the direct successors of Peter, guaranteeing that the church would be divinely guided because the pope speaks with the authority of Christ on earth. The Catholic Church claimed that apostolic succession proved that it alone was the one true church.

Through the descending hierarchy of the pope, the bishops, and the lower clergy, as Christ's priesthood, the grace of God was conferred on humankind, mediated to every Christian through seven *sacraments:* baptism, confirmation, Holy Eucharist (communion), marriage, ordination (holy orders), confession, and extreme unction. These sacraments were taken to be the outward and visible signs of God's inward, invisible grace (forgiveness and assistance), helping Christians grow spiritually and morally toward holiness or saintliness. Grace, considered an undeserved gift from God, was also seen as an invitation to a renewed spiritual life that required human cooperation, accepting the aid offered by God, and consciously trying to use that aid for spiritual and moral improvement. Because the sacraments could be administered only by ordained clergy, every Christian was dependent on the priests and bishops of the church, under the rule of the pope, to be in a right relationship to God. Outside the institutional church, it came to be thought, there was no salvation.

The Seven Sacraments and the Life Cycle

The seven sacraments, which developed by the late Middle Ages, provided ritual assistance to the Christian at every stage of life, from birth to death. The concept of "sacrament" has its roots in the Greek word for "mystery," a term borrowed from first-century pagan cults known as "mystery religions." Cult rituals, which symbolized dying and rising with the pagan gods, were performed in the hope of achieving immortality.

The sacraments of Christianity, by uniting humans to God and eternal life, were said to guarantee salvation from sin and death. With the coming of the Protestant Reformation in the sixteenth century, only baptism and communion retained the status of sacraments. The other five rituals were rejected on the ground that they could not be found as such in the New Testament. However, many of these "rejected" practices are observed in some Protestant denominations as rituals, but not sacraments in the full sense.

Baptism

The early Christians followed the Jewish practice of ritual immersion for new converts in which the person's whole body was submerged in a river, lake, or special pool. For Christians, however, full submersion was seen as participation in Christ's death in the tomb; the emergence of the body from the water was equated with Christ's resurrection and departure from the tomb. The submersion was accompanied by the words, "I baptize you in the name of the Father, the Son, and the Holy Spirit." As the practice of infant baptism developed in later generations, pouring of water over the baby's forehead was adopted as an alternative. Both types of baptism are still performed today.

This ritual is believed to flood the soul with divine grace (divine love, forgiveness, and assistance), erasing all stain of original sin, the sin of Adam and Eve that is said to mark every newborn child. Baptism changed one's destiny from death to eternal life.

Communion

Equal in sacramental importance was the Eucharist, or Holy Communion. This practice seems to have been an adaptation of the Jewish blessing of the bread and wine at meals, especially as it was practiced at Passover, the Jewish remembrance of the people's deliverance by God from slavery in Egypt. In the Gospels, at Jesus' last Passover he broke the bread, blessed it, and said, "This is my body." He blessed the wine, too, and told his disciples, "This is the cup of my blood, shed for you and for many for the forgiveness of sins." By eating the bread and drinking the wine consecrated by a priest or minister who represents Jesus, Christians believe they are partaking of the body and blood of Jesus (for some literally, for others spiritually) who died for their sins on the cross and brought them to eternal life. Both baptism and communion were established well before the Middle Ages. However, to these, five other sacraments were added.

Confirmation

The first converts to Christianity were adults who made a conscious decision to be baptized and follow Christ. As the practice of infant baptism developed, so did a controversy over whether this was appropriate, since the infant was too young to make such a choice. Infant baptism, it was decided, signifies God is choosing the child rather than the child is choosing God. At some point, however, a young Christian was expected to make a conscious choice to live for Christ. In the ritual of confirmation, young people at about the age of 13 demonstrated their knowledge of the faith, were anointed on the forehead with oil, and made a public declaration of commitment to Christ. Thus, young adults were *confirmed* in the faith, accepting responsibility for the commitment made for them at baptism.

Marriage

During the Middle Ages, marriage was transformed from a civil proceeding into a sacrament. The union between a man and a woman came to be compared to the union between Christ and the church. As such it became more than a union between the couple for the purpose of raising a family. It became a ritual for uniting the spouses to each other in Christ. The husband and wife promised to love and care for each other as Christ loved and cared for his church.

Holy Orders

In the Middle Ages, a ritual also developed for inducting men in to the priesthood. Bishops, Christ's representatives in the community of the faithful, ordained others, priests, to assist them in their pastoral work. In the ritual of ordination, bishops anointed the new priests' hands with oil to symbolize their sacred role in conferring the grace of God upon their parishioners through the administration of the sacraments. Bishops themselves were consecrated to their new office by the laying on of hands by other bishops.

Until the late Middle Ages, ordained priests could also be married. In the Western church, later reforms established the requirement that priests remain unmarried, or celibate. From this point on a man had to choose between the sacrament of marriage and that of ordination. In the Eastern church priests have always been allowed to marry, but bishops must be celibate.

Confession and Extreme Unction/ Anointing of the Sick

Two additional sacraments were developed during the Middle Ages: confession, to mediate God's forgiveness for sin, and extreme unction anointing of the sick, to confer God's power of healing in times of illness. In the early church it was common for people to put off baptism until death was near for fear that sins committed after baptism could not then be washed away. To encourage baptism in infancy, the church developed a sacrament for the forgiveness of sins: the penitent would confess his or her sins and express true sorrow for them to a priest, who would then absolve the person that is, forgive the sins in the name of Christ thereby reconciling the sinner with God. The priest would also assign an appropriate penance for the absolved sinner to complete in reparation for his or her sins. Penance varied depending on the seriousness of the sin but most frequently required the penitent to repeat certain prayers or make a pilgrimage to a sacred place and resolve not to fall into sin again.

Closely associated with the practice of confession was the anointing of the sick with oil. In cases of serious illness, a priest would be called to anoint the Christian with oil in hopes of mediating God's grace to heal the person. Since this ritual of healing was administered to a person who was near death, it was called extreme unction and came to be thought of as the sacrament of the dying.

An Orthodox wedding ceremony at the cathedral of Minsk, Belarus.

Festivals

If the sacraments carried Christians from cradle to grave, the annual cycle of religious festivals carried them through the seasons of the year and created for them a world of stories in which to dwell. The early church saw itself as living in the time between Easter and the "advent" or "coming" (parousia) of Christ to raise the dead and judge the heavens and the earth. By the Middle Ages the times of the year corresponded more closely to human calendars. The church year began with Advent, whose stories evoke hope for the Second Coming. Gradually a concurrent theme of Advent as preparation for Christmas developed, overshadowing the earlier theme. Christmas and Epiphany were festival seasons designed to celebrate the stories of the birth of Jesus, the visit of the wise men from the East, and the baptism of Jesus. No one knew the date on which Jesus was born; December 25 was chosen to compete with a popular pagan festival honoring the sun god.

The season of Christmas/Epiphany is followed by Lent, a time of penitence, fasting, and prayer in preparation for Easter. Its stories recall the temptations, healings, and teachings of Jesus. Lent culminates in Holy Week, in which the stories of Jesus' trial and death are recalled. In the Easter season, the church retells the stories of the resurrection and the subsequent appearances of Jesus to his disciples. The final season of the church year, Pentecost, recalls the descent of the Holy Spirit upon the apostles and the birth and growth of the church. After Pentecost, of course, comes Advent again, and a new year of hope and expectation. Thus, for many centuries the cycle of festivals has allowed Christians to dwell in a world of stories that tie and bind them into the great cosmic drama in which God is bringing salvation to the whole world.

Medieval Christians grounded in the sacraments and oriented by the festivals and their stories also sought divine aid through prayers to the saints and angels in heaven. That is, they prayed that exemplary Christians (saints) who had died, and other spiritual beings, known as angels, would present their petitions to God in heaven. This was, after all, how things got done in medieval feudal society. If you wanted a favor from a member of the nobility or the king, it was best to ask someone at court to intercede for you. Hierarchies of saints and angels were believed to exist in heaven and to work in a similar fashion. On the other hand, it was believed that some angels who rebelled against God, the devil and his minions, exercised an evil influence over human beings that must be resisted through the power of prayer and the sacraments.

British children reenacting the nativity story.

In this medieval worldview, we have the full integration of the biblical worldview of life, death, and resurrection of the body with the Greek metaphysical worldview of the cosmos as a hierarchical order. It forms the essence of the Catholic worldview. Lacking the historical consciousness that came after the Renaissance, medieval Christians thought this amalgamated worldview was exactly what Jesus had proclaimed in the Gospels.

A depiction of the coronation of Charlemagne as the first Holy Roman Emperor by Pope Leo III on Christmas day in the year 800 CE.

The Two Cities Revisited

Throughout the Middle Ages there was a struggle between the two cities that Augustine had described. From the time of the Holy Roman Emperor Charlemagne (800–814), the emperors sought to dominate the church and the popes sought to dominate the state. A turning point in the development of the power of the papacy was its emulation of a monastic model of church discipline that originated in France. Because Benedictine monasticism had a strong work ethic, many monasteries became great centers of wealth, which in turn led to abuses. In 910 a new reform movement swept through monasticism, and a new monastery was founded at Cluny, in east central France. The Cluny reforms aimed at spiritual renewal and reorganization.

In addition to their emphasis on spirituality, the Cluniac monasteries provided an important organizational model for the development of colonialism, first adopted by the church, and later emulated by such secular institutions of modernity as the multinational corporation. Whereas each Benedictine monastery was a world unto itself, under its own abbot, all the Cluniac monasteries, regardless of location, were answerable to a central command—the monastic headquarters in Cluny. Under Pope Gregory VII (1073–1085), Rome adopted this form of organization, thus imposing papal authority over all the bishops in the church.

The height of papal power occurred under Pope Innocent III (1198–1216), who forced the kings of England and France into submission, authorized the fourth Crusade, and carried forward an immensely punitive inquisition against all heretics without interference from civil authorities. Innocent actually had the spiritual and temporal power to which the papacy had long aspired. The weakest moment of papal power, by contrast, occurred, as we have noted in connection with the First Vatican Council, under Pius IX in the late nineteenth century.

The Promise and Threat of Christian Mysticism

Like every great religion, Christianity has a long tradition of mysticism—referring, in this context, to beliefs and practices thought to lead to a direct and immediate experience of God in Christ. The meaning of this experience is communicated through the biblical claim that human beings are created in the image and likeness of a God who is without image. The closer one comes to being like God, the more one is emptied of self-identity.

Christian mysticism expresses itself in two dramatically different forms—the mysticism of love and union (the divine–human marriage) and the mysticism of identity. The former is exemplified by Spanish mystics of the sixteenth century, Theresa of Avila and her student, John of the Cross; the latter by the German mystic, Meister Eckhart. Unlike early Christian theology, Christian mysticism has for centuries been enriched by the contributions of women: Theresa of Avila, Catherine of Siena, Theresa of Lisieux, Julian of Norwich, to name a few. In part this is because mystical experience is viewed as a gift from God that cannot be institutionally controlled. Consequently, it unleashes a powerful impulse toward equality. The mystical experience is accessible to male and female without distinction—all are equally in the image of the God without image.

As with the Jewish tradition, so too in Christianity, mysticism has been viewed ambivalently. This is because some mystics seem to speak as if they are not just in union with God but, in some sense, are God. This is the claim of mysticism of identity. Yet despite this strain of what some consider to be blasphemy, Christianity has continued to affirm the validity and importance of mysticism.

Christianity, Judaism, Islam: Crusades and Inquisition

Islam, which seemed to appear abruptly in the Arabian desert in the early 600s, grew within the span of a century into a civilization larger than the Roman Empire had been. For a time they seemed poised to proceed east of Spain to conquer most of Europe. But Charles Martel, whose initiative led to the formation of the Carolingian dynasty and the Holy Roman Empire, turned the Muslims back at Tours in 732. Europe remained Christian, but its holy sites, in Palestine, were in the hands of Muslims.

The Crusades were meant to change that. There were four main Crusades, in 1095, 1147, 1189, and 1202. Armies were organized to march to the Holy Land (Jerusalem and surrounding territories) and free it from the Muslims. But as the crusading armies marched through Europe they unleashed devastating violence on the Jewish communities they encountered along the way, fed by ancient Christian stereotypes of Jews as a "rejected people," killing an estimated ten thousand Jews in Germany alone during the first expedition.

The Muslims were the Crusaders' primary targets, however. For the Muslims held the Holy Land in their possession and threatened the Eastern church, whose main center was Constantinople. Thus the Crusades were ostensibly for the purpose of driving back the Muslims, reclaiming Jerusalem, and reuniting the Eastern and Western branches of the church. Pope Urban II, who preached the first Crusade, promised that all soldiers who participated would have their sins forgiven and would enter heaven. In addition, Crusaders were promised that they could keep the lands they conquered. The Crusaders laid siege to Jerusalem in June 1099, and the city fell on July 15. Men, women, and children lost their lives in a bloody massacre.

The Crusades brought dramatic changes to Christendom, opening up new trade routes and fostering interactions between cultures, all of which stimulated economies. As a result of their exposure to new ideas and attitudes and new religious beliefs and practices, some Europeans embraced new forms of ancient heretical beliefs. For example, a religious movement known as the Cathari or Albigensians took root in southern France and began to spread. The Cathari believed in reincarnation, and their goal was to liberate the spirit from the evil of a fleshly body. This led Pope Lucius III (1184) to adopt the format of the inquisition, in an effort to stamp out heresy. The Fourth Lateran Council in 1215 authorized the punishment of all heretics by the state and also prescribed distinctive dress for Jews and Muslims (e.g., pointed hats or yellow badges) and restricted Jews to living in ghettos. Soon, inquisitions under church auspices would become infamous for their unfairness and cruelty.

The awe-inspiring Notre Dame Cathedral in Paris is considered to be one of the most magnificent examples of Christian architecture.

There were positive consequences of the Crusades as well. Most of Aristotle's work, lost to the West, had been preserved by Islamic scholars. The rediscovery of Aristotle led to new and controversial ways of thinking in the new universities of Europe in the twelfth and thirteenth centuries. And for a brief time Jewish, Muslim, and Christian philosophers, like Maimonides (1135–1204), Averroes (Ibn Rushd, 1126–1198), and Thomas Aquinas (1224–1274), all used a common philosophical language to learn from each other's traditions, even if only, in the end, so that each could argue for the superiority of his own.

CHRISTIANITY AND MODERNITY

The Emergence of Modernity

By the year 1500, Europe had been transformed from a primitive land of farms and undeveloped regions into a network of significant urban centers. In these cities, incorporation, a form of legal agreement that gave citizens the right of self-governance in exchange for taxes paid to the nobility, facilitated the emergence of individualism, an independent economy, and democratic self-governance. With increased craftsmanship and trade, corporate charters were also granted to the new craft guilds or "universities." These corporations mark the beginnings of the secularization of social institutions. Indeed, one of the defining characteristics of modernization is the existence of self-governing institutions that operate independently of direct religious authority (pope and bishops) and also of traditional medieval political authority (kings and lords). Education, too, declared its independence from the monasteries and cathedral schools, as scholars banded together to form their own universities. It was in these institutions of learning that intellectual secularization first appeared, as scholars began to think about their subject matters with a sense of independence from direct church authority. Now the infrastructure was in place for the development of the institutional and intellectual diversity characteristic of modern secular societies. And in this environment three trends converged to shape the modern West: the millennialism of historical progress, the *via moderna* of autonomous reason, and the *devotio moderna* of emotional transformation.

Millennialism: History as Progress

One strand of modernity had its roots in the apocalyptic visions of a man whose vision of history deeply influenced the modern age. A monk and abbot from southern Italy, Joachim of Fiore (1132–1202), suggested in his *Everlasting Gospel* that history can be divided into three ages corresponding to the three persons of the Trinity: the age of the Father (beginning with Abraham), which was superseded by the age of the Son (beginning with Christ), which would in turn be replaced by a third and final age, that of the Holy Spirit. Joachim thought of himself as living at the beginning of "millennium," the final age of the Spirit in which there would no longer be any need for the institutional church and its clergy—nor for any other institution, including the state. Joachim, a mystic, expected the Holy Spirit to direct the creation of a natural spontaneous harmony between all individuals, rendering existing institutions superfluous. The third age, which Joachim believed was predicted in Revelation, would be an age of perfect freedom and harmony, and was destined to last a millennium, a thousand years.

Joachim's version of the myth of history as proceeding through three ages profoundly shaped the modern view of history as a story of progress—history was seen as moving forward from the ancient period through the medieval, culminating in the modern age. For Joachim the third age was identified with the triumph of mysticism over the institutional church. But his three ages became increasingly secularized in the 1700s, during the Enlightenment in Western Europe. As a result, while the three-age model persisted, the Holy Spirit was no longer identified as the force behind the millennium. For instance, Gotthold Lessing, the great Enlightenment scholar, held that the education of the human race passed through three phases: childhood, adolescence, and adulthood. The last or third age he identified with the Age of Enlightenment in which the autonomy of reason (instead of the Holy Spirit) would lead to a natural and rational harmony among human beings. This vision of three ages was carried forward into the nineteenth century. Auguste Comte, the founding father of sociology, divided history into the ages of myth, philosophy, and science. One can find further parallels in the visions of other nineteenth-century philosophers such as Hegel and Marx.

The Via Moderna and Devotio Moderna

According to the greatest of the medieval theologians, Thomas Aquinas, faith complements and completes reason. For Aquinas the Prime Mover known through Greek philosophy (especially Aristotle) is the same as the God of the Bible. One can have some knowledge of God through reason, independent of faith, but scripture enriches this knowledge immeasurably. Faith and reason, rightly used, can never contradict each other. However, the generation of theologians that followed Aquinas, known as nominalists, radically disagreed with him. William of Ockham (1285–1349) and other nominalists rejected this view as "ancient" (they called it the *via antiqua*) and outmoded. Espousing instead a *via moderna*, or modern way, these later theologians argued that reason was of no help in discerning the will of God. The split between faith and science had made its appearance.

The "modern way" secularized the world by separating faith and reason. The only way to know what God wills is through faith as a deep emotional trust in God and a fervent reading of scriptures as the revealed word of God (the devotio moderna). The only way to know the world God has created is through rational empirical investigation of the world God has actually created. Thus, when it comes to knowledge of the world, faith requires the secular via moderna of rational scientific or empirical inquiry. And when it comes to knowledge of God, only revelation understood through "faith alone" will do. Protestantism and modernity are like two sides of the same coin, arising out of the *via moderna* and *devotio moderna* of the late medieval theology to flourish in the Renaissance and Reformation. Therefore, unlike all other religious traditions, Protestantism did not, at first, experience modernization as the intrusion of an outside force but rather as a form of experience nurtured from within. It was only as modernization and secularization took on lives of their own, independent of the Protestant Reformation, that they began to appear threatening.

The Renaissance and the Reformation are siblings that grew up together. The Renaissance began as a literary movement in the south of Europe, especially Italy, in the fourteenth century. It did not reach northern Europe (France, Germany, and England) much before the sixteenth century and the time of the Protestant Reformation. The intent of the first Renaissance thinkers was to recover the pre-Christian wisdom of the ancient world of Greece and Rome. The Reformation, in a parallel fashion, sought to reach back into antiquity and recover the original New Testament Christian vision as it existed before medieval theologians integrated it with Greek metaphysics. The new ideas of modernity were greatly facilitated by new technology, the printing press. With the introduction of movable type in 1454, a growing popular literacy made possible the rapid and wide dissemination of new ideas. The printing press also greatly accelerated the development of national identities by promoting a common language and shared ideas within a geographic area.

The initiator of the Protestant Reformation was Martin Luther (1483–1546), an Augustinian monk who embraced the new modern way of thinking. While Luther thought that reason could be useful in secular matters, when it came to matters of faith, Luther called reason a "whore" that could not be trusted to lead one to God. Knowledge of God, rather, can be obtained only through faith and scripture undistorted by reason. This, in fact, became the central doctrine of the Protestant Reformation, also embraced by the second major figure of the Protestant Reformation, John Calvin (1509–1564).

The Renaissance and Reformation fostered a new individualism in the new free cities by encouraging people to cherish their individuality and to have a sense of personal dignity and equality with others. This way of thinking could not be sustained without a shift from the established hierarchical view of authority to a democratic view. Knowledge through empirical inquiry and political authority based on the consent of the governed lie at the heart of the revolution called "modernization." It is the encounter with these modern notions of knowledge and power, throughout the nineteenth and twentieth centuries, that has placed anxiety in the hearts of traditional or premodern societies around the globe. Such societies, like those of premodern Europe, typically are imbued with a sense of sacred, cosmic hierarchical order in which those in power ruled with sacred authority from above. As suggested earlier, Protestantism was unique in that from the beginning it was part of the revolutionary shift away from divinely decreed hierarchies toward individuality, equality, and dignity.

Devotio Moderna and the Protestant Reformation

The devotio moderna is exemplified in Martin Luther's emotional experience of being born again. Luther grew up in a medieval Catholic world in transition toward the modern world of the Renaissance. At the insistence of his father he began to train in law as a young man, but after nearly getting hit by lightning in a rainstorm, he abandoned that path, became an Augustinian monk, and was ordained as a priest as well. His quest for moral and spiritual perfection drove him into feelings of great anxiety and hopelessness, for he felt that he could never live up to what was expected of him by God. Then, somewhere between 1511 and 1516, he had a powerful spiritual experience. While studying Paul's letter to the Romans, he suddenly came to see the meaning of the phrase often translated as "The just shall live by faith" (Romans 1:17).

What Luther came to realize, he said, was that he was acceptable before God with all his imperfections, as long as he had faith in Christ who had died for his sins. There is nothing one can do to be saved. God has done everything as the gift of grace. All sinners must do is have faith and because of that faith, God will treat sinners as if they were saints, as if they were without sin. As this realization came over him, Luther said: "Thereupon I felt myself to be reborn and to have gone through open doors into paradise. The whole of scripture took on a new meaning." In this moment Luther was overcome by a liberating and exhilarating experience of having been in the immediate presence of a forgiving and compassionate God. And he now knew that *justification* (i.e., being considered to be righteous in God's eyes) before this God was not by a person's works but by God's grace, as received through faith alone and understood through scripture alone—not, as the Catholic church had insisted, through grace *and* works, faith *and* reason, scripture *and* (hierarchical) tradition.

In 1516, Leo X authorized the selling of indulgences to raise funds to rebuild the Cathedral of St. Peter in Rome. That is, the pope promised that the sins of generous donors would be wiped away, so that after death, they would avoid all punishment due them for their sins. For Luther, this was the last straw. Salvation was not to be purchased, since it comes by grace and faith alone. On October 31, 1517, Luther posted *Ninety-five Theses Against the Sale of Indulgences* on the church door of Wittenberg Castle, calling for public debate. That event marks the symbolic beginning of the Reformation.

In this portrait of Martin Luther, by the sixteenth-century painter and eyewitness Lucas Cranach the Elder, the fiery reformer, once an Augustinian monk, appears peaceful and contemplative.

Luther's problem was how to reform a church tradition gone corrupt. His solution was to criticize the tradition by raising faith and scriptures to a higher level of authority than church tradition, using scripture to judge and reform the tradition. This was an option open to him that was not available to Christians before the canon, or list of books in the New Testament, had been agreed on (after 387). It was the Catholic tradition that picked the scriptures and created the Christian Bible, as Catholics would say, "under the guidance of the Holy Spirit." Without the success of Catholicism, Protestantism's "faith alone, scriptures alone" would not have been possible, and without the failures of Catholicism, Protestant reform would not have been necessary.

Luther started out protesting abuses in the church but he quickly moved on to challenge the entire mediating role of the church, the sacraments, and the papacy. Luther did not start out to create a new form of Christianity, only to reform the existing tradition. But events took on a life of their own that very quickly turned a reformation into a revolution, and Protestant Christianity was born in a radical break with the ancient medieval way. In addition to the ancient Catholic way of faith *and* reason, scripture *and* tradition, guided by papal authority there would be the new modern Protestant way of faith alone, through scripture alone, and the individual alone before his or her God.

Calvin and the Protestant Ethic

Protestantism was unique in that from the beginning it was part of the revolutionary shift away from sacred hierarchy toward not only secular rationality but also individuality and equality. In this, Protestantism, in conjunction with Renaissance humanism, laid the groundwork for the emergence in the West of the idea of human dignity and human rights. And yet, in the relation of Christianity to the state and to society, the basic assumptions of the Constantinian/Augustinian vision of the unity of church and state remained operative, at least for the major strands of the Protestant Reformation. The state should be a Christian state, only now that meant Protestant.

Next to Luther, John Calvin was the greatest of the reformers. Calvin spent his life transforming the city of Geneva in Switzerland into a model for Protestant civilization. Arguing that human sinfulness requires that all power be limited, he created a Christian democratic republic with a division of powers among its representative bodies. This institutional strategy served as a model for later secular democracies.

The Protestant work ethic associated with Calvinism really represents the secularization of the Benedictine motto "to work is to pray." Indeed, a major teaching of Luther and Calvin is the idea that work in the world (whether as a shoemaker or doctor, etc.) is as holy a task as praying in a monastery—indeed, a holier task. What makes work holy is not where it is done but doing it as a result of God's call. The Protestant ethic demanded that one live simply and work hard: "earn all you can, save all you can" to be able to "give all you can" for the greater glory of God. The early twentieth-century sociologist Max Weber suggested that this ethic helped to fuel the emergence of capitalism in Europe by encouraging hard work, which allowed individuals to prosper, and savings, which were needed for investment.

Calvinistic concepts are important to note here because in Europe and North America, it was Calvin's rather than Luther's vision of Protestant civilization that most influenced the future, not only of democracy but also Western capitalism and colonialism.

Other Reform Movements

If the via moderna split faith and reason apart and confined reason largely to the secular parts of life, the devotio moderna of mystical piety played a parallel role, making faith the domain of emotion. By the fourteenth and fifteenth centuries, a new kind of "this worldly" mysticism—the devotio moderna—was creating popular pietistic movements for spiritual renewal that grew up spontaneously and without official church approval. These "grassroots" movements focused on personal piety founded on intense, emotionally transforming religious experiences. The experiences fostered a new democratic spirit by emphasizing the equality of all before God and the spiritual benefits to be obtained from living simply. They were typically critical of the medieval Catholic church, its wealth and its hierarchical order.

The Anabaptist Rebellion
Against Both Church and State

We have described the Lutheran and Calvinist center of the Protestant Reformation. However, there were wings to the left and right of this center as well. On the left were the radical reformers and on the right the Anglicans. The radical reformers have deep roots in the mystical and millennial movements of the late Middle Ages, mentioned earlier in connection with Joachim of Fiore.

The Anabaptists were Christians who denied baptism to infants because the practice is not mentioned in the New Testament and because they believed that only those who freely choose to join the church should be baptized. The views of the Anabaptists alienated them from both the center of Protestantism and from Catholicism and led to their severe persecution by both. By 1535 over fifty thousand Anabaptists had been martyred.

Interestingly, the pacifist strands of this movement stand out in the history of Christianity because the Anabaptists do attempt to break with the Constantinian vision of a Christian civilization, rejecting both the authority of the hierarchical church and the authority of the state. This meant that pacifist Anabaptists have refused any role in public service on the grounds that the state condones killing and that taking an oath of office goes against one of Jesus' statements in the Sermon on the Mount: "No one can serve two masters" (Matthew 6:24). The Hutterites, the Mennonites, and the Amish are all products of the Anabaptist wing of the Reformation. The most pious of

The struggle to keep the premodern traditions pure is difficult. Even among the Amish, in-line skates and cell phones are making an appearance.

their twentieth-century descendants among the Amish are distinctive for refusing to compromise their principles by taking advantage of such conveniences of modernity as modern electricity and motor vehicle transportation.

The Anglican Reformation and the Puritan Revolt

At the other extreme, the English Reformation was initiated by the state rather than by Christians in the churches. Initially the English monarch championed Catholicism against Luther's views as "heretical." Indeed, Pope Leo X conferred the title "Defender of the Faith" on King Henry VIII. Problems arose, however, when Henry, who had no male heir to the throne, wanted to divorce his first wife, Catherine of Aragon, and remarry in hopes of fathering a son. Pope Clement VII refused to give his permission. So in 1534, Henry VIII nationalized the church, making himself the head of what was now the Church of England. Then the archbishop of Canterbury declared the marriage to Catherine invalid. Nevertheless, apart from breaking with the papacy, the English church remained essentially Catholic, and Henry continued to oppose and often punish those he considered to be heretics. Only after Henry's death were Protestant reformers safe in England.

As Protestants made inroads in Britain, the Church of England's doctrine did not seem pure enough for the Puritans, Calvinist radicals who were intent on returning to a New Testament Christianity shorn of all "popery." After a short period of dominance under their military leader Oliver Cromwell, Puritans became the object of persecution. Puritanism was a diverse and fragmented movement that had splintered into Congregationalists, Presbyterians (who prevailed in Scotland), Separatists, and Nonconformists, including Baptists—all rejecting the thirty-nine Articles of Religion, the official statement of doctrine of the Church of England. In 1620, 101 Pilgrims sailed for North America. Over forty-thousand Pilgrims fled England in the next two decades, bringing to the new colonies their propensity for sectarian diversity.

The Catholic Counter-Reformation

The Council of Trent was a series of meetings held between 1545 and 1563 for the purpose of responding to the reformers. The positions hammered out in these meetings reinforced the absolute power of the pope and made the medieval theology of Thomas Aquinas normative for the church. Trent froze Catholicism in its late medieval form. It affirmed that the Catholic "tradition" was equal in authority to scripture, that Latin should remain the language of the Bible and of worship. It also retained the seven sacraments (which Protestantism had reduced to two, baptism and communion), and the importance of the saints, relics, and indulgences. Indeed, the buying and selling of indulgences was not even discussed. At the conclusion of the meetings of the Council of Trent, Pope Pius IV declared that there was "no salvation outside the Catholic faith."

Religious Diversity:
Church and State in War and Peace

The Reformation led to political divisions and open warfare between Catholics and Protestants throughout Europe. Like Catholics, all Protestants except the Anabaptists, assumed that the goal of Christianity was a Christian civilization. For the most part, however, neither side considered the other side Christian. Each tended to think the other was doing the work of the devil. Consequently Christians resorted to warfare to settle whose religion would shape the public order. In Germany, a series of wars between Protestants and Catholics ended in the Peace of Augsburg in 1555, with its compromise statement *"cuius regio, eius religio"* (the religion of the ruler shall be the religion of the land). As a consequence, the splintering of the church seemed to match the splintering of Europe into nation-states. Another series of wars, known as the Thirty Years War, was brought to a conclusion with the Peace of Westphalia in 1648. This was a general settlement that reestablished the conditions of the Peace of Augsburg with additional protections for minorities and encouragement of religious toleration (see Map 4.2).

Clearly the Protestant Reformation created not a new and purer unity but a new and chaotic diversity. The more people learned to read the Bible for themselves, the more a diversity of interpretations emerged, leading in turn to more and more diverse forms of Christianity. The Protestant Reformation and the religious wars that followed had relativized and privatized religion, making the very act of interpreting the Bible seem more and more private and subjective. Thus the Reformation helped to create a key element in modern consciousness, the awareness of the relativity of one's understanding of the world and the need to choose one's identity. The result, after much bloodshed, was the gradual transformation of both Protestantism and Catholicism into denominational religions. Whereas in medieval Catholicism and the early sectarian movements of Protestantism, each group had seen itself as the sole repository of truth to which all in society should conform, denominational religions foster the establishment of religiously diverse communities, expressing the private views of their adherents.

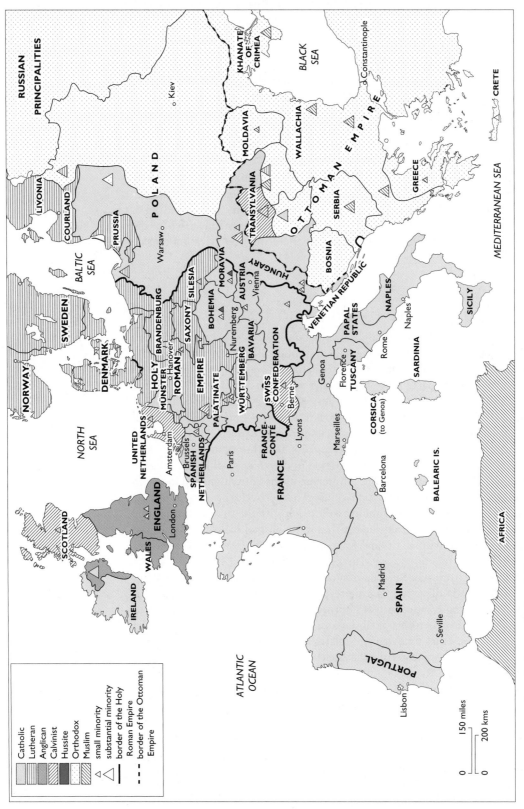

Map 4.2 *Europe after the Peace of Westphalia.*

With the emergence of denominationalism, Christianity was on a path leading to a new relationship to the public and political order of society. In North America first, and then in Europe, a new understanding of the state emerged—the state as a secular and neutral political institution that favored no religion. Hence, after the French and American revolutions, the secular, democratic nation-state that functioned by privatizing religion (restricting it to peoples' personal lives) increasingly became the normative model for the modern Western world. Paradoxically, this development coexisted with the continued assumption by many Christians that the task of Christianity was to Christianize the world. Consequently, as Europe's public order was becoming more and more secular in the nineteenth and twentieth centuries, European Christians were setting out to Christianize the world in concert with Western colonialism's political and economic attempts at global conquest.

Enlightenment Rationalism and Christian Pietism

Pietism and rationalism, two responses to the doctrinal, social, and political divisions created by the Reformation, were rooted in the split between faith and reason that we have already described. And both contributed to the development of Western notions of universal human rights.

Rationalism

The rise of modern science and technology was dramatic and impressive. Science came to express the most public and certain knowledge that people believed they had about their world. And the more public and certain scientific knowledge appeared to be, the more private and uncertain religious knowledge seemed to be. As science developed, scientists came to believe that they had less and less need to bring God into their explanations. In the nineteenth century, the French astronomer Pierre Laplace announced that he had no need of the "God hypothesis" to explain the world scientifically.

We have seen that in the model of Enlightenment philosopher Gotthold Lessing, human beings were entering the third age of history. Lessing called this era the age of reason, or the adulthood of the human race. People no longer needed to be told what to believe. To be "enlightened" was to discover the autonomous power of rationality for oneself. Enlightenment rationalism became the foundation of all scientific and public knowledge. The Enlightenment was built on four key concepts aimed at harnessing the courage to use one's own reason, freedom from tradition through the rational critique of the past, a view of nature as a finely tuned machine whose mechanisms can be understood, and the perception that history is guided by hidden laws of progress. The power of reason was assumed to be capable of freeing human beings from the irrationality of the past (including the irrationality of much of religion), of discovering how the universe really works, and of introducing a golden age of progress.

Enlightenment rationalism fostered the emergence of deism, which likened the world to a clock and God to a divine clockmaker. Just as a clockmaker makes a perfect machine that runs on its own without assistance from its maker, so God, as creator, does not actively guide or influence events in the world.

The Enlightenment promised to overcome the divisions among human beings that had generated the religious wars of the Reformation by reducing religion to its rational elements. By thus eliminating the emotion-laden "superstitions" of traditional religions, rationalists, believed they would create a more tolerant world. Enlightenment rationalists, who identified reason as the one universal that all humanity shared, expected the exercise of universal reason to lead people of every religion and culture into greater harmony. They hoped that as people became more enlightened and rational they would abandon the beliefs that had divided them and come to share a common rational morality. A rationalism of what was called enlightened theism was characteristic of denominations like the Unitarians and the Universalists, which played an important role in championing universal rights. Enlightenment morality contributed to the emergence of a modern ethic of human dignity and human rights by stressing the fundamental unity of the human race. And indeed, in England and elsewhere laws of toleration began to be passed.

Pietism

What was missing in the clockwork universe of deism was warmth or emotion. The alternative to the cold rationality of both Enlightenment rationalism and Protestant rationalism was supplied by Pietism, a new movement that gave rise to evangelical Christianity. In their search for a way of uniting people of faith, who had been divided since the Protestant Reformation, the Pietists explored the nonrational aspects of religion, those in the realm of emotion. Indeed, Pietism was a movement to recover the devotio moderna of the late medieval and Reformation periods.

Pietists sought to transcend religious differences by minimizing the role of sectarian dogma, which seemed to divide Christians, and maximizing the role of religious emotion, which they hoped would be a unifying factor. The true test of Christian faith, Pietists argued, is not found so much in right belief or dogmas as in a changed heart. Thus the goal of evangelical piety was in the beginning antisectarian and antidogmatic. One of its greatest representatives, John Wesley (1703–1791), believed passionately that doctrinal differences should not separate Christians. He saw the deep emotion of faith as the way to Christian unity.

The first wave of Pietism came in the seventeenth century. It included such groups as the Moravians and the Quakers. The greatest and most far-reaching expression of Pietism in the eighteenth century was the Methodist movement begun by John Wesley, who was deeply influenced by the Moravians as well as by Catholic and Anglican mystics. Wesley, whose conversion had "strangely warmed" his heart, rejected some of Calvin's ideas and questioned the doctrine of original sin by emphasizing freedom of choice, suggesting that humans were capable of achieving spiritual and moral perfection.

John Wesley, the founder of Methodism, often preached to the men, women, and children of the new working class during the Industrial Revolution.

Wesley's message was primarily aimed at the new working class created by the Industrial Revolution. Factory owners did not always pay just wages, and working conditions and hours were often inhumane. The Methodist movement was one of the first constructive responses of Christianity to these changing conditions. Methodist communities were committed to a morality of perfecting both self and society. Mystical piety is a great equalizer in social experience because it is contagious and can overtake anyone, without regard to social status, race, gender, or creed. Methodism's most striking accomplishments include leading roles in the abolition of slavery in England (1833) and in introducing women into the ministry. Both exemplify the importance of evangelical piety in the development of the modern commitment to human dignity, equality, and rights.

The tremendous power of the Methodist and other evangelical movements tapped a long tradition in the history of Christianity. This is the tradition of combining a simple regimen of prayer and devotion with life in small communities of discipline and mutual encouragement oriented toward improving the world, or at least part of it. This formula fueled the monastic movement that missionized the tribes of Europe and brought learning and the heritage of Greek civilization to Europe. This same spirit was carried forward in Calvinism and was transferred to evangelical Christianity primarily (but not exclusively) through Methodism. In these Protestant formulations, it would be carried around the world in the global missions of the nineteenth century. Thus, paradoxically, the Augustinian vision of a mission to Christianize the world that had had such consequences as Inquisitions and the excesses of the Crusades also afforded a model for promoting human dignity and equality. The arrogant side of Western colonialism brought with it the seeds of its own demise as it

Women in Christianity

Christianity (like Judaism, Islam, and the religions of Asia) arose in patriarchal (male-dominated) societies. Historically, women have played the greatest roles in forms of Christianity that valued direct and immediate religious experience (mystical piety) as more authoritative than the institutional authority of the bishops. Thus in the early church women played a greater role in Gnostic (mystical and otherworldly) and Montanist (apocalyptic and ecstatic) Christian movements than in Catholicism, which was institutionally hierarchical. And yet there were always some women who were exceptions to the rule. According to the letters of Paul, women had leadership roles in some of the early Christian communities. As the early church became institutionalized, however, prevailing customs of male dominance seemed to reassert themselves, and the pattern of excluding women from roles as priests and bishops took hold.

During the Middle Ages women found ways to exercise autonomy and independence by founding female monastic orders. With the Protestant Reformation, however, even that option was taken from them, and women were largely confined to the home and child rearing. This began to change in the nineteenth century, when the evangelical missionary movements with deep roots in the mystical traditions of piety (devotio moderna) offered new opportunities for women in leadership roles. The role of women in these missions played an important part in the political development of the woman's movement for independence and the right to vote. Also, among the more unusual forms of Christianity, with mystical or Gnostic roots, women founded new traditions. For example, the Shakers, the Unity School of Christianity, and Christian Science were begun by Ann Lee, Emma Curtis Hopkins, Mary Baker Eddy, respectively.

Another major source of women's autonomy was the via moderna as expressed in the denominations influenced by Enlightenment secularization and rationalism. Consequently, in the nineteenth century women began to be ordained in some Protestant denominations, the Congregationalists leading the way in 1853. They were followed by the Universalists, the Unitarians, and other denominations. The mainline Protestant churches (e.g., Methodist, Presbyterian, Episcopal, and Lutheran) did not follow suit until the twentieth century. The Roman Catholic and the Orthodox churches still do not ordain women, arguing that the maleness of Jesus and the apostles reveal the divine intent for an all-male priesthood.

spread around the world. Today (as we shall soon see), the base communities of liberation theology and the communities of indigenous (non-European) spiritual renewal among African and Asian Christians are touched by a postcolonial form of the evangelical missionary message.

The rationalism and Pietism of the Enlightenment shared a faith in the progress of the human race. Drawing on the myth of the three ages as formulated by Joachim of Fiore in the thirteenth century, members of these groups shared a millennial faith that they lived in the final age of history, when

The last four decades of the twentieth century saw the rise of a theologically based feminism. The issue that divides feminists and fundamentalists is whether God created a sacred natural order in which men's and women's roles are eternally defined. Fundamentalists say yes, feminists say no. Feminists say that fundamentalists confuse the cultural attitudes and common practices of premodern societies with the will of God. Fundamentalists turn this argument on its head, saying that feminists and other liberation advocates confuse the cultural attitudes and common practices of modern societies with the will of God.

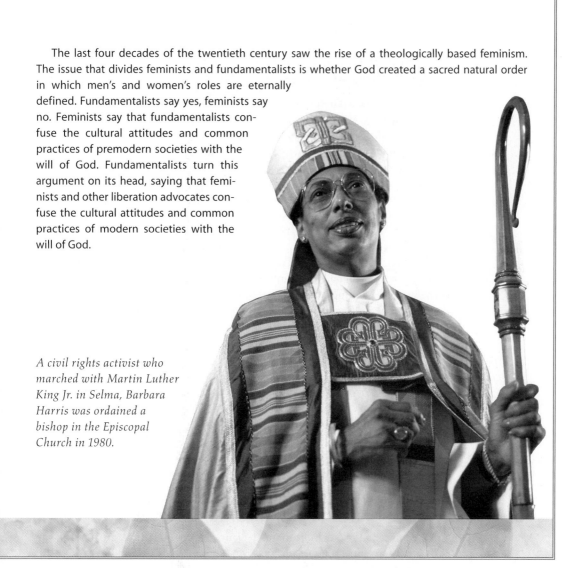

A civil rights activist who marched with Martin Luther King Jr. in Selma, Barbara Harris was ordained a bishop in the Episcopal Church in 1980.

people would throw off the authoritarianism of past tradition and institutions and be instead guided by a direct inner light that would bring with it progress and harmony. For this to come about, the rationalists relied on the via moderna of the light of reason. For the Pietists it was the devotio moderna— the warm emotional light of spiritual illumination, which comes from being born again. Thus both share the millennial mysticism (of Joachim of Fiore) that has driven the modern spirit of progress.

Nineteenth-Century Romanticism and Existentialism

The French Revolution in the Wake of the Failure of Reason

At the end of the eighteenth century economic conditions grew very bad in France, and they were not helped by the extravagance of the court of King Louis XVI. This led to a massive revolt, the French Revolution, which began in 1789. In addition to replacing the government, the new leaders created a revolutionary religion featuring a "Cult of Reason" and later a "Cult of the Supreme Being" (deism). The churches were transformed into "Temples of Reason" and statues the Virgin Mary were replaced by icons of "nature goddesses" and "the goddess of reason." King Louis and his wife, Marie Antoinette, were executed in 1793, and in the Reign of Terror that followed, thousands of clergy and nobility were arrested and beheaded.

The bloody events of the 1790s brought about considerable disillusionment with reason. Reason had been embraced at the beginning of the Enlightenment as the way of avoiding fanaticism, dogmatism, violence, and intolerance. And yet in the French Revolution reason had shown itself to be fanatical, dogmatic, violent, and intolerant. People grew weary of the violence and of the complexity of urban life and longed for the simplicity of nature uncorrupted by civilization. With the failure of reason, many people turned to emotion as the foundation for renewal of life. If the Enlightenment was rationalistic and mechanistic, the Romantic period that followed was emotional and organic. If the Enlightenment had sought to escape the suffocation of past tradition and enter a bright new future of scientific advances, Romanticism sought to return to the organic, familial, and deeply emotional connections of traditional agricultural or village society. An ambivalent struggle between these alternative visions is still very much a part of contemporary culture.

From Reason to Emotion: The Romantic Alternative to Enlightenment Rationalism

The German philosopher Immanuel Kant (1724–1804), the greatest of the Enlightenment philosophers, argued for religion within the limits of reason that focused on ethics, on the grounds that there is no rational way at arriving at belief in God. Friedrich Schleiermacher (1768–1834), considered to be the father of modern Christian theology, offered the Romantic solution to Kant's rationalist challenge, suggesting that knowledge of God does not come to people through reason (the via moderna) but rather through emotion (the devotio moderna). Consequently knowledge of God can coexist with scientific knowledge of the world: there is no conflict because the outer secular public sphere of reason is separate from the inner private sphere of faith.

Moreover, Schleiermacher disputed the opinion of some Christians that the affirmation of faith in the resurrection of Jesus Christ depends on historical proof. When a person does not believe in the resurrection one day and then confesses such faith the next day, the theologian argued, that person has had a powerful transformative emotional experience. The altered conviction did not result because the person had learned a new historical fact. This emphasis on transformative emotion places Schleiermacher directly in the tradition of the *devotio moderna* and evangelical Pietism.

Kierkegaard and the Existentialist Response to Cultural Relativism

Another important development in modern Christianity was existentialism, marking the start of the postmodern exploration of the implications of cultural relativism. Existentialism was responding to the new thinking that accompanied advances in historical and social scientific consciousness. The results of both historical and ethnographic studies made people aware that various cultures interpreted "human nature" differently. Cultural relativism entails the acknowledgment and examination of these differences.

According to the existentialists, one is not born with an essential human identity. Rather, "existence precedes essence"—that is the core insight of existentialism. When you plant an acorn, you know you will get an oak tree. The essence of the tree is there from its beginnings. But when a human child is conceived, biology is not definitive because human freedom enters into the equation. No one can predict who or what that child will become. The life task of a human being is to create a self through his or her choices.

Søren Kierkegaard (1813–1855) invented what came to be called Christian existentialism. Kierkegaard argued that if we have no innate human nature, each person must make a "leap of faith" inspired by faith in Christ to trust God to help him or her construct an identity as a loving and compassionate human being. Like Schleiermacher, Kierkegaard wrote that such faith does not depend on either logical reasoning or historical proof, but on a personal choice driven by powerful emotions that lead one to make the leap of faith.

Christian faith is not proved by scientific and/or historical facts, nor by metaphysical arguments, but by the emotional, moral, and spiritual transformation of the individual. In making this argument, Friedrich Schleiermacher became the founder of modern Protestant theology.

From the Holocaust to Hiroshima: The Global Collapse of the Modern Myth of History as Progress

The existentialist response to the social sciences and cultural relativism led some philosophers, like Friedrich Nietzsche (1844–1900), to conclusions quite the opposite of Kierkegaard's—namely, that history and ethnography show "God" to have been a human invention, who is now dead, a circumstance that obliges us to invent our identities without God.

For Nietzsche, the modern world was incompatible with belief in the biblical God: history had demythologized the sacred stories of the Bible and shown them to be false even as science had demythologized the biblical view of creation and replaced it with a Darwin's theories of evolution. As Nietzsche saw it, European Christians who acted as if Christianity and modernity were compatible would one day realize that in embracing modernity they had killed

God. Recalling the argument between fundamentalists and modernists at the beginning of this chapter, we can now see that Nietzsche and fundamentalists shared at least one conviction that belief in God is incompatible with modernity. But for fundamentalists this meant that Darwin's theories had to be rejected, whereas for Nietzsche it meant belief in God had to be rejected.

Nietzsche, having rejected the God of the Bible, believed that history is guided by a struggle for existence, and he proposed that there is a human "will to power." Like Kierkegaard, he argued human beings must choose who they will become, but he believed their choices should be preceded by a rejection of Christian values and beliefs. The problem with Christianity, said Nietzsche, is that it fosters ideals of compassion and equality. Biblical morality teaches weak values like forgiveness and pity, which ultimately lead to resentment against persons who are strong and courageous. They lead, the philosopher believed, to an ideal of "equality" that rewards mediocrity. Nietzsche therefore, called biblical values bad for civilization. The future, he believed, should belong to the strong—those superior and creative individuals who had the courage to "transvalue all values," and make their own morality.

Little more than half a century after Nietzsche announced the death of God, the Nazis came along to embrace Nietzsche's vision of a will to power. Nietzsche's model for a world ruled by superior persons was not that of the Nazis, who distorted the philosopher's ideas. They had cast themselves as those superior human beings destined to recreate the world. What Nietzsche's vision did have in common with that of the Nazis was a contempt for the ideals of equality and democratic rule that Nietzsche associated with Christendom.

Nietzsche, who had characterized Christians as weak because their religion taught them to show compassion and pity, might have been surprised by the number of churchgoers who showed themselves quite willing to abandon their weak values in exchange for the Nazi ideals of elitism and the will to power. Between 1933 and 1945, Hitler and the Nazi party ruled Germany and drew Europe and America into World War II (1939–1945).

One of the key factors in Hitler's rise to power was his successful appeal to anti-Semitism in German and Austrian culture. Hitler was able to achieve power, in large part, by appealing to long-standing prejudice against the Jews created by the churches over the centuries. By the time of the Middle Ages, Christians viewed Jews as deserving to suffer for rejecting and crucifying the messiah, the Son of God. Consequently the Nazis were able to strip the Jews of their citizenship, confiscate their property, and send them off in boxcars to concentration camps without serious resistance from the churches and often with their assistance. Over 6 million European Jews are estimated to have been killed, mostly in the gas chambers of the Nazi concentration camps.

The horrors of World War II made Nietzsche's claim that God was dead seem more feasible. For the killing of millions on the battlefields and in the camps, achieved by means of the latest science and technology, represented the death of what "God" had become for many in Western civilization, namely, the "God of progress." The millions upon millions of dead and the

Christianity and the Holocaust

The Christian churches might have been a powerful force against the Nazi attempt to exterminate the Jews but they were not. In Germany, by some estimates, only 20 percent of the Protestant churches resisted Hitler and the Nazi message. Even fewer took issue with the treatment of the Jews. Pope Pius XI signed a concordat with Hitler in hopes of protecting the autonomy of the German Catholic churches. Most Christians passively acquiesced in the Nazi program of genocide, and many actively cooperated.

A minority of Christians held fast to what Nietzsche called the "weak values" of Christianity (love and compassion) and rescued Jews, but with a few important exceptions they were lone individuals of conscience. Christians in Denmark were one notable exception, and most of Denmark's Jews survived because of collective resistance by church and state. Le Chambon sur Lignon in France is another such exception: this small village of mostly French Protestants saved over five thousand Jewish lives. Wherever the churches led resistance to the Nazis, Jewish lives were saved. Unfortunately that did not happen often. As the church historian Franklin Littell has noted, the irony is that more priests and ministers died in Hitler's armies than died resisting Hitler.

Reflection on the lessons of the Holocaust brought unprecedented change to Christianity in the last decades of the twentieth century. Since Vatican II and in response to the Holocaust, not only the Catholic Church but also the main Protestant denominations have sought to correct past teachings about the Jews as a rejected people and have replaced these teachings with an affirmation that the Jewish covenant is an authentic covenant with God—one that exists both prior to and apart from the Christian covenant. This public acknowledgement of the Jewish people as chosen by God and of the religion of Judaism as a valid expression of monotheism is unprecedented in the history of Christianity.

shameless reality of the Nazi death camps gave modern persons good reasons to question whether modernity and "progress" were truly worthy human ideals. Science and technology had become essential instruments in the propagation of mass death.

Finally, with the dropping of the atomic bomb on Hiroshima, Japan, at the end of World War II, and the accumulation of nuclear weapons in the second half of the twentieth century, by the USSR and USA, suggesting the possibility of a nuclear war that would destroy the planet, belief in the progress of history and a better future through science and technology began to disintegrate on a global scale. As the world moves beyond its modernist phase, thoughtful Christians are beginning to explore the possibility of separating the church's message from the myth of history as progress and from the assumptions of the cultural superiority of the West that reinforced colonialism.

CHRISTIANITY AND POSTMODERN TRENDS IN A POSTCOLONIAL WORLD

From Colonial to Postcolonial Christianity

The Christianity that fostered the rise of modernization and the myth of progress was not that of the Eastern Orthodox churches, which saw Christian civilization as a sacred unity of church and state. It was Western Augustinian Christianity, with its model of two cities, one sacred and the other secular. Indeed, the term "secular," comes from the Latin term *saeculum*, which means "worldly," refering to those who live in the world, in comparison with those who leave the world to seek God in the monasteries.

For most of its history Christianity has been predominantly a European religion. Europe gave birth to Roman Catholicism during the Middle Ages and to modern Christianity with the Protestant Reformation. In 1600 the overwhelming majority of Christians in the world lived in Europe. However, the invention of the modern three-masted sailing ship (c. 1500) had unleashed massive changes that began when the countries of Europe acquired their first colonies and seemed to be culminating in the birth of a global civilization. Colonial expansion was accompanied by worldwide missionary activity, first led by Catholic countries like Portugal and Spain and later by countries with new Protestant centers of power, especially England. By 1900 only half of all the Christians in the world lived in Europe, and by the end of the twentieth century the majority of the world's Christians resided elsewhere in Latin America, Africa, and Asia. Thus, Postcolonial Christianity is overwhelmingly non-European.

Even as church membership was waning in Europe, it was planting the seeds of its possible transformation and renewal in postcolonial forms elsewhere in the world. On the one hand, while birth rates among Christians declined in Europe, children born to Christians elsewhere increased dramatically. On the other hand, the secularization of Europe led to a large decline in the practice of Christianity there. Paradoxically, at the same time, through European colonial expansion, Protestant evangelical Christians engaged in a massive missionary enterprise whose aim was the Christianization of every part of the world touched by colonization (see Map 1.3 in Chapter One). This plan was justified on the grounds of the assumption that the political and economic colonization of the world by Europe was part of God's plan to make possible the spread of the Gospel to the very ends of the earth.

The feeling of the superiority and global destiny of European civilization that accompanied colonialism communicated itself through an attitude of paternalism. At first many in the premodern cultures were impressed with the wonders of Western science and technology. Before long, however, indigenous peoples came to feel demeaned and diminished by the Westerners' attitude toward them.

In former colonial areas, whether in Africa, Asia, or the Americas, resentment against Western Europeans inevitably led to a political backlash that typically coalesced around liberation movements. Activists called for rejection of some Western values, such as capitalism and individualism, in favor of political and economic independence and restoration of traditional values and customs. Paradoxically, at the same time, other values espoused by the West, such as dignity and equality, lent support to these indigenous liberation movements. We see this paradox for example in Gandhi's campaign to liberate India from English colonial domination, which appealed both to Hindu values and to modern Western values in just this way.

If colonialism brought modernity to the non-European world, the rejection of Western colonialism can be said to mark the beginnings of postcolonial and postmodern trends in Christianity. It is among postcolonial Christians that we might find the beginnings of a new postcolonial and non-Eurocentric form of Christianity, more open to coexistence with other religions and cultures.

Latin America

Latin America was colonized in the sixteenth century by Spain and Portugal, two Roman Catholic countries untouched by the Protestant Reformation. Thus the Spanish and the Portuguese brought to the New World medieval patterns of social order that were hierarchical and antidemocratic. By the mid-twentieth century, however, the forces of secularization and Marxism had taken their toll, and while 90 percent of Latin Americans were baptized, only about 15 percent were estimated to be practicing their faith. This situation set the context of the emergence of postcolonial movements of liberation theology and evangelical–charismatic Christianity.

In the last decades of the twentieth century, Christians (mostly Catholics) exposed to the Marxist analysis of European colonial exploitation criticized the traditional hierarchical order of society that reinforced privileges for the few and ensured poverty and oppression for the many. Their response was called liberation theology. These ideas, in turn, produced a backlash among some branches of evangelical and Pentecostalist Protestant Christianity, the movements that had inspired the missionary zeal of the nineteenth century. These evangelical and Pentecostal Christians saw liberation theologies as the ultimate sellout of Christianity to modern culture. In an effort to return to the premodern spiritual foundations of their faith, Pentecostalists and others down played issues of cultural and economic oppression. Rather, they focused on issues of personal conversion (being born again) and/or ecstatic experience (e.g., speaking in tongues). Their idea was to transform society through personal virtue, to be cultivated by spiritual means within the parameters of any social system, including capitalism, in which individual Christians happened to live.

For Christians in the liberation movements, the heart of the Gospel is love for the poor and the struggle for social justice. For evangelical Christians it is personal conversion, personal regeneration in the Spirit, and the shaping of a public order that will give priority to these goals. Despite their differences, however, both parties regard Christianity as the single appropriate means of shaping the public order of political and economic life.

Africa

For models of Christianity that break with both the premodern and modern visions of a "Christian civilization" one must look primarily to the African and Asian churches, where we see the emergence of a "diaspora" model of Christianity. A diaspora religion is one whose adherents are "dispersed" as minority communities among many nations and cultures.

Except for the ancient Coptic Church in Egypt and the Church of Ethiopia, Christianity in Africa is the result of missionary efforts primarily from the colonial period. At the beginning of the twentieth century there were scarcely any Christians in Africa. At the end of the century it was the fastest growing geographic area for Christianity, and more than a fifth of the world's Christians can be found there today. Almost half of the population of Africa is now Christian, with Islam a close second.

As the number of converts to Christianity grew, the people overcame the tight control missionaries had sought to maintain over African Christianity by developing indigenous forms. One of the most interesting of the African independent church movements is Isaiah Shembe's Nazareth movement, whose members openly long for a black Christ. Shembe is described as having a miraculous birth and being born of the Spirit—as one who came from heaven so that native Africans might know that God is with them. In general, in the twentieth century, even among the more traditional denominational native African congregations, Christianity became more and more African and less and less European. There are, however, strong syncretistic elements; that is, some aspects of the African churches today are Christianized versions of indigenous pre-Christian traditions.

There is a liberation theology in Africa but, as the leadership of retired Anglican bishop Desmond Tutu in South Africa illustrates, it is less on the model of Latin American Marxist theory and more on the model of the

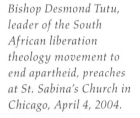

Bishop Desmond Tutu, leader of the South African liberation theology movement to end apartheid, preaches at St. Sabina's Church in Chicago, April 4, 2004.

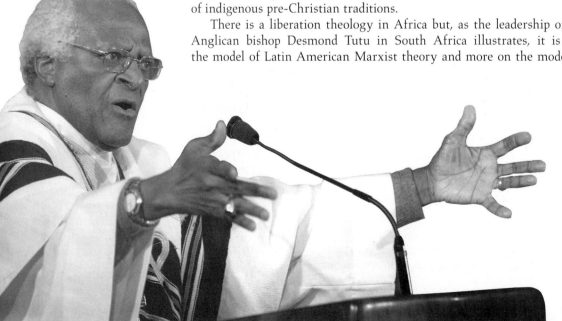

nonviolent civil rights movement in the United States. Indeed, the movement led by Martin Luther King Jr. is an interesting blend of the liberation passion for justice with an evangelical ecstatic piety. This type of evangelical/Pentecostalist piety has also left its stamp on African Christianity, commingling with the experiential/ecstatic elements of traditional African tribal religions. In the twenty-first century, African Christianity is likely to be a major contributor to the development of a postcolonial Christianity. In Africa, Christianity's success tempts believers to envision a "Christian Africa." It is in Asia, however, that Christianity is most clearly creating models that break free of the Augustinian civilizational model in favor of a diaspora model of creative coexistence with other religions and cultures.

Asia

European colonialism occurred simultaneously in Africa and in Asia, where there was a strong British presence in Ceylon (Sri Lanka), India, Burma (Myanmar), Malaysia, Singapore, Hong Kong, and various Pacific islands (also Australia and New Zealand). The French expanded into the Indochina peninsula, including Laos and Cambodia. As in Latin America and Africa, the spread of Christianity that accompanied this colonial expansion was driven by the same Augustinian sense of the providential link between the expansion of European civilization and the spread of the Gospel.

The Black Nazarene festival in the Philippines is illustrative of the indigenization of Christianity in local cultures.

In the West, Christianity had few rivals as a "world religion," and its two main competitors, Judaism and Islam, were variations on the same worldview—the myth of history. Asia presented Christianity with interesting new challenges, for unlike the local polytheistic and animistic religions encountered in the Americas and in Africa, the religions of Asia, like Christianity itself, had shaped whole civilizations. The traditions of the great nonbiblical world religions—Hinduism, Buddhism, Daoism, and Confucianism, were rooted in mythic worldviews as grand and powerful, as those inspired by Christian scriptures.

The expansion of a great world religion, it seems, can be stopped only by another great world religion. In Asia, Christianity is a distinct minority presence and seems unlikely to ever become the religion of civilizational order. Asia's contribution to the development of a postcolonial Christianity may well be the development of a diaspora model of Christianity, one that will transcend traditional Western civilizational and denominational boundaries and be open to creative coexistence with other religions and cultures. We shall briefly survey this movement as it is unfolding in South and East Asia.

Everywhere the story of Jesus has been told, believing artists have tried to present the events in terms of their own cultures. In this way the universal appeal of the story of Jesus is demonstrated, as in this depiction by the Indian artist Jamini Roy of the Holy Family's flight to Egypt.

India

According to ancient Christian traditions, Thomas, one of the twelve apostles of Jesus, brought Christianity to India. In the sixteenth and later centuries Jesuits, Dominicans, and representatives of other Catholic orders spread their faith in India and elsewhere in Asia. As in Africa and Latin America, the major Protestant incursion was the wave of mission activity that accompanied nineteenth-century colonialism. Once India had won its independence from British colonial rule in 1947, there was increasing pressure on the churches in India to become less European and more Indian. Indeed, Hindus often accused Indian Christians of being unpatriotic much as some European Christians had accused Jews of being unpatriotic. In response, Indian Christians began to move beyond European denominational Christianity.

In 1947 Anglicans merged with Methodists and other Protestant bodies to form the Church of South India. Much later, the Protestant Church of North India was founded and also a Protestant Church of Pakistan (1970). With these changes there was also a shift of emphasis from conversion to dialogue, with the goal of showing the compatibility of Hinduism and Christianity. Christians have had to learn how to live as a diaspora religion in a largely Hindu culture, renewing efforts to indigenize Christianity with the appearance of Christian ashrams (both Protestant and Catholic) and syneretistic trends resulting in Hinduized forms of worship.

China

Similar patterns of missionary activity by Catholics, followed by Protestants occurred in China and Japan. Nineteenth-century colonialism brought the first large-scale attempts to convert the Chinese. China did not welcome the missionary movements and permitted them only under the military and economic duress that accompanied colonialism. After the Communists came to power in 1949, many missionaries were either imprisoned or expelled. Chinese Christians were persecuted and often forced to undergo "reeducation." All ties between indigenous Protestant Chinese Christians and Western Christian organizations were severed in 1952. The break for Chinese Catholics came in 1958, when bishops began to be elected rather than appointed by the Vatican, despite the latter's protests.

With the coming of Mao Zedong's Cultural Revolution in 1966, churches were closed, Bibles burnt, and Chinese priests and ministers sent to work camps. All public worship was banned. Nevertheless, Chinese Christians persisted by secretly worshiping in private homes ("house churches"). When Western relations with China improved in the 1980s, it was discovered that indigenous forms of Christianity had survived and were still being practiced in that country.

Japan

Until the nineteenth century Japan was largely closed to all Western enterprises, including to missionary activity. While as early as the 1500s, the Jesuit Francis Xavier (1506–1552) had established a Catholic community in Japan, the Jesuits were driven out by severe persecution in the next century. Nevertheless, when missionaries returned in the mid-nineteenth century they found a thriving community of "hidden Christians" at Nagasaki. The believers were considered to be unpatriotic and subversive by Japanese rulers. Very quickly, Japanese Christians moved to assert their independence from Western forms of Christianity and to develop indigenous forms.

The Japanese Protestant leader Uchimura Kanzo is famous for having started the "nonchurch" movement. He saw Western church structures as culturally inappropriate to Japanese culture and sought to restructure Christianity on the Asian teacher–disciple model. He tried to demonstrate in his life that it was possible to be both a patriotic Japanese citizen and a Christian. Ironically, the atomic bomb dropped on Nagasaki destroyed the oldest center of Christianity in Japan. After the war Japanese Christians turned strongly pacifist and sought to break with the Japanese state by resisting any move toward government involvement with Shintoism.

Korea

Korea is the great success story of Christian missionary activity in Asia. A Catholic presence in Korea goes back to the eighteenth century. Protestant missionaries came in the 1870s, but significant growth did not occur until Korea began signing trade agreements with the West in the 1880s. Korean interest in Christianity mounted after the Japanese victory over China in 1895, which Koreans rightly felt was threatening to their own autonomy. Christianity became identified not only with modernization and Westernization but also with anti-Japanese sentiments, which increased in 1910, when Japan annexed Korea.

After World War II, the victorious Allies divided the country into North and South Korea, and civil war followed (1950–1953). Communists in North Korea have driven out Christians there, although house churches may survive. South Korea has the highest percentage of Christians of any nation in Asia except for the Philippines. Nowhere in Asia (except for the Catholic Philippines) has Christianity played as strong a role in public life as it has in South Korea, whose first two presidents were Christians. Since the 1970s a highly political liberation theology similar to that developed in Latin America, known as *minjung* theology, has emerged. And as in Latin America, Africa, India, China, and Japan, Korea too developed its own indigenous forms of Christianity, the most famous of which is the Unification Church of Sun Myung Moon, who is heralded by his followers as a new messiah—in this case an Asian messiah.

Given that the majority of Christians in the world are now non-European, it is likely that much of postcolonial Christianity will draw upon the experience of these "mission churches." The question remains whether the dominant model will be an African model, aspiring against the odds to Christianize the continent, or an Asian model of diaspora churches, creatively relating to the consequences of globalization and a world that is religiously diverse.

Postcolonial Christianity: Back in the United States

Although the first explorers and settlers in North America were the Vikings and then later and more successfully the Spanish, and although France extended its reach to the continent as well, the United States came to be primarily as a result of colonization by the British. Indeed, it was a revolt against British colonialism by the citizens of its colonies that led to the Declaration of Independence in 1776 and later to the Constitution of the United States of America as the foundation for a new nation as formulated in 1787.

The citizens of the thirteen colonies that became the United States of America were largely but not exclusively refugees from the political intolerance toward sectarian religious minorities experienced in Europe. At first the European pattern of sectarian rivalry continued in the New World, but it soon became clear to the colonists that the uniqueness of America as an alternative to Europe had to lie in toleration of diversity. Consequently, the very first amendment to the U.S. Constitution declares: "Congress shall make no law respecting an establishment of religion, or prohibiting the free exercise thereof." These words guarantee religious freedom to all Americans by forbidding the government to name any religion as the state religion. This amendment, which became effective in 1791, created a major break with the Constantinian and Augustinian models of Christian civilization and opened the door to diaspora models of Christianity. It was, however, a legal transformation that took on cultural embodiment only as non-Christian populations in America began to grow.

In the nineteenth and twentieth centuries Protestant denominationalism emerged as a new pattern for a culture characterized by religious diversity, and new denominations proliferated out of all proportion to Protestant divisions in Europe. Gradually, diverse religious communities in North America came to think of the church as an invisible reality embracing all Protestants, and denominations as voluntary associations that one joined according to one's preferred style of being Protestant.

Enlightenment rationalism and evangelical Pietism, both of which de-emphasized dogmatic divisions, deeply influenced the emergence of denominationalism. But this new perspective was, at first, developed around the notion of America as a Protestant nation. Therefore, it was very traumatic when, beginning in the latter half of the nineteenth century, Catholic and Jewish immigrants poured into the United States and tipped the balance away from a Protestant majority. This led to a strong reaction of anti-Catholicism and anti-Judaism, which did not disintegrate until the last half of the twentieth century when Protestant, Catholic, and Jew came to be seen as acceptable alternatives within the denominational pattern. In the twenty-first century, the modern equilibrium is being further challenged by influxes of immigrants from Asia and the Middle East. In an emerging global civilization, U.S. citizens who are Muslim, Hindu, or Buddhist are increasing in numbers and in prominence.

Consequently, the decision of whether to be a Christian civilization or adopt a diaspora model of Christian life is playing itself out not only in the developing world but in North American as well. Fundamentalism wants to create a public order focused on creating a "Christian America," yet a North American form of liberation theology seems to be embracing a diaspora model of Christianity. The liberation movement sees itself as one force among many, seeking social justice for all in a pluralist society. While drawing inspiration from the Marxist liberation theology of South America, North American liberation theology received much of its practical impetus from the civil rights movement, with its strategies of social protest and civil disobedience.

Not all Christian houses of worship in America have that New England look. This adobe mission church is in Taos, New Mexico.

CONTRASTING RELIGIOUS VISIONS

As the following contrasting visions indicate, every religious tradition is capable of generating both visions that encourage peace and understanding and visions that encourage conflict and violence.

Martin Luther King Jr. transformed the social landscape of American society by integrating the Sermon on the Mount with Gandhi's techniques of nonviolence to further racial and social justice in the United States.

Martin Luther King Jr.

On December 1, 1955, Rosa Parks, a black woman in Montgomery, Alabama, refused to move to the segregated section at the back of a public bus. Her subsequent arrest aroused the churches in the black neighborhoods of Montgomery to organize a boycott of the buses and to demand repeal of the state's bus segregation laws. The Reverend Martin Luther King Jr., pastor of the Dexter Avenue Baptist Church, himself the son of a Baptist minister, was elected to lead the boycott. The boycott came to a successful conclusion when the Supreme Court declared Alabama laws requiring segregated buses unconstitutional. The ruling, on November 13, 1956, took practical effect on December 21, 1956.

This boycott marked the beginning of the struggle to end segregation (c. 1954–1966). Dr. King and the Southern Christian Leadership Conference, which he founded in 1957, were at the forefront of these efforts. Perhaps the major accomplishment of the movement was the passage of the Civil Rights Act in 1964.

Martin Luther King Jr. lived and died by the teachings of the Sermon on the Mount, in which Jesus told his hearers to love their enemies. King argued that the way of violent retribution, "an eye for an eye," leaves everyone blind. Moreover, he was open to the wisdom of other religions, for he believed that God spoke to humanity in every time and in every culture. Indeed, he drew upon the principles of nonviolence and civil disobedience first perfected by great Hindu leader Mohandas K. Gandhi in his twenty-two-year struggle against British colonial discrimination in South Africa.

On April 4, 1968, at the age of thirty-nine, King was assassinated by a sniper in Memphis, Tennessee. His efforts to secure racial justice for black Americans are a valuable legacy for the churches. But King was also an early voice in protest against the neglect of the poor of every race and religion.

Michael Bray

In May 1989 the Reverend Michael Bray was released from prison after serving time for burning down seven abortion clinics in Delaware, Maryland, and Virginia. Bray is the author of *A Time to Kill*, a book presenting biblical arguments that support the killing by Christians of anyone who performs abortions or assists in providing them.

Michael Bray grew up in a military family and, as a young man, he experienced an evangelical conversion. After studying at a Baptist Bible college and seminary with a strongly fundamentalist orientation, he became assistant pastor of a Lutheran congregation. He soon left to form a splinter group, the Reformation Lutheran Church, arguing that the larger body was not faithful to the literal meaning of the Bible. Bray espoused reconstruction theology, a radical fundamentalist school of thought that rejects the secularization of society and the separation of church and state and seeks to rebuild society around a literal understanding of biblical law. Reconstructionists believe that there is only one truth and one way for all of society. The Christian task, they say, is to establish a Christian civilization in accord with this truth.

Michael Bray rejects the notion that Jesus teaches nonviolence as the appropriate response to injustice. On the contrary, he argues, Jesus demands the justice of "an eye for an eye," like the God of war in the Old Testament (e.g., Leviticus 24:19–20). Bray says that the Sermon on the Mount applies only to Jesus' life as a "suffering servant" up to and including his crucifixion, contending that now Jesus is "a man of war" who reigns from heaven as the divine warrior who will come again to administer justice by the sword.

Michael Bray insists that only those living in conformity with God's law have a right to life and since God's law forbids abortion, those performing abortions have no right to live. He says he does not advocate violence but rather defends the morality of those who feel called by God to engage in the killing of anyone who provides abortion assistance. Bray is considered to have been a decisive influence on a several persons who have stalked abortion providers, including Rev. Paul Hill, who killed Dr. John Britton and his escort, James Barrett, in front of an abortion clinic in Pensacola Florida on July 29, 1994.

Not all Christians have embraced Martin Luther King Jr.'s nonviolent Christian message. Michael Bray (center) argues that the book of Revelation shows Jesus to be a man of war who would approve of Christians who fight abortion by killing abortion doctors.

*Three generations of
a Minnesota Christian
family saying grace
before dinner.*

CONCLUSION

A significant gulf divides the fundamentalist and postmodern
ways of affirming Christian faith. Modern Christians tended
to privatize religion and segregate personal piety from public
life. Religion was a personal and family matter, public life was
to be secular and therefore free of religion. Neither fundamentalist nor postmodern Christians are willing to accept that
model. Both insist that their faith should affect public life.
But the form that public faith takes in each is very different.
Fundamentalism champions either a Constantinian or an
Augustinian vision of a Christian civilization and a Christian
world. Postmodern, postcolonial Christianity affirms a pluralistic world and
a diaspora model of Christianity, in which those who believe in Jesus seek to
cooperate with others, religious and nonreligious, in achieving a compassionate social order with justice for all. We should not expect that Christians
will eventually favor one view at the expense of the other. More likely, as in
the past, there will be diverse expressions of Christianity in diverse social,
historical, and political circumstances.

Discussion Questions

1 What are the *via moderna* and *devotio
moderna* and how did they contribute
to the development of modernization?
Explain by contrasting modernity
with the medieval Christian world.

2 It can be argued that Eastern
Christianity, Western Christianity,
and postcolonial Christianity offer
three different models for understanding the relationship between church
and state and the relation of
Christianity to the non-Christian
world: a Constaninian model, an
Augustinian model, and a diaspora
model. Explain these models and identify their strengths and weaknesses.

3 What is secularization, and how is it
related to the history of Christianity?

4 How did Western colonialism
contribute to the emergence of a
post-European or post-colonical
Christianity? Define and explain.

5 What were the issues that were
resolved by the development of
the doctrine of "two natures in
one person" (Council of Chalcedon)
and of the trinitarian nature of
God (Council of Constantinople)?
Do these doctrines put Christianity
into fundamental disagreement with
the prophetic monotheism of Judaism
and Islam? Explain.

6 What is original sin and why does
it lead to the need to expect a savior?
Is original sin a universal belief
among Christians? Explain.

7 How did the emergence of Protestantism contribute to the development of
the secular nation-state?

8 How did Luther's understanding
of Christianity differ from that of
the medieval church? What was the
political and religious significance
of this difference?

9 Why are Jesus, Paul, and Augustine often thought to be the three most important figures in the history of Western Christianity?

10 Explain the issues in dispute between fundamentalists and modernists. How is the argument between them expressed in contemporary Christianity?

11 The idea of "modernity" is deeply rooted in the Christian version of the myth of history as it was interpreted by Joachim of Fiore. Explain how this is so. Give examples.

12 What are the issues that separate pre-modern from modern and postmodern Christianity, and how do they exemplify the fundamentalist–modernist debate?

Key Terms

Augustinianism	fundamentalist	Kingdom of God	Second Coming
Catholic	Gospel	original sin	Trinity
Christ	grace	Pentecostal	two natures, one person
Constantinianism	heresy	Protestant	
deism	homoousios	Protestant ethic	Syncretism
evangelical	justification by faith	sacrament	

Suggested Readings

Augustine, *The Confessions*, Rex Werner, trans. (New York: Mentor-Omega, New American Library, 1963).

Bettenson, Henry, ed., *Documents of the Christian Church*, selected and edited by Bettenson, 2nd ed. (New York: Oxford University Press, 1963).

Capps, Walter H., *The New Religious Right: Piety, Patriotism and Politics* (Columbia: University of South Carolina Press, 1990, 1994).

González, Justo, *The Story of Christianity*, Vols. 1 and 2 (San Francisco: Harper & Row, 1984).

Johnson, Paul, *A History of Christianity* (New York: Atheneum, 1976, 1979).

Keppel, Gilles, *The Revenge of God: The Resurgence of Islam, Christianity and Judaism in the Modern World* (University Park: Pennsylvania State University Press, 1991, 1994).

Lawrence, Bruce B., *Defenders of God: The Fundamentalist Revolt Against the Modern Age* (Columbia, S.C.: University of South Carolina Press, 1995).

Littell, Franklin, *The Crucifixion of the Jews* (New York: Harper & Row, 1975).

Marsden, George M., *Understanding Fundamentalism and Evangelicalism* (Grand Rapids, MI: William B. Eerdmans, 1991).

McManners, John, ed., *The Oxford Illustrated History of Christianity* (New York: Oxford University Press, 1992).

Roof, Wade Clark, and William McKinney, *American Mainline Religion* (New Brunswick, NJ: Rutgers University Press, 1987).

Ruether, Rosemary, *Faith and Fratricide* (New York: Seabury Press, 1974).

———, *Liberation Theology* (New York: Paulist Press, 1972).

Stendahl, Krister, *Paul Among Jews and Gentiles* (Philadelphia: Fortress Press, 1976).

Tillich, Paul, *A History of Christian Thought*, Vols. 1 and 2, (New York: Harper & Row, 1967, 1968).

CHAPTER
FIVE

Islam
The Many Faces of the Muslim Experience

Overview

"Allahu Akbar. . . . There is no God but God. Come to prayer. . . ." Five times each day, Muslims throughout the world, in Algiers and Mindanao, in London and Paris, Bosnia and New York, are called to prayer. Shops are closed, office workers adjourn to a prayer room, professionals and laborers simply stop what they are doing and face Mecca to worship God.

On the streets of Cairo, Geneva, Kuala Lumpur, and Jakarta, Muslim women walk, some in stylish Islamic dress, some in dresses and veils that cover their faces and bodies. They join others adorned in Western fashions. While educated Muslim women in some sex-segregated countries are not visible in the workplace, in other countries they work as engineers, doctors, scientists, teachers, and lawyers alongside their male colleagues. All of these realities reflect the vitality and diversity of Muslim societies today.

Across the Muslim world in recent years, Muslim activists have marched beneath banners declaring that "Islam is the solution" or "The Quran is our constitution," as they press for the implementation of religion in state and society. Members of Islamic organizations have been elected to parliaments in Turkey, Algeria, Jordan, Egypt, Kuwait, Yemen, Pakistan, Thailand, and Malaysia. They have served in cabinet-level positions and as elected mayors and city councilors in Turkey and Israel and Malaysia. Other Islamic activists are elected officials in professional associations of doctors, lawyers, engineers, journalists, and teachers.

Although invisible a few decades ago, today Muslims are a significant presence in North America. This mosque in Toronto is an indication of this new status.

ISLAM *Timeline*

c. 570	Birth of Muhammad
610	Muhammad receives first revelation, commemorated as "Night of Power and Excellence"
620	Muhammad's Night Journey to Jerusalem
622	Emigration (hijrah) of the Muslim community from Mecca to Medina; first year of the Muslim lunar calendar
632	Muhammad's final pilgrimage to Mecca, farewell sermon, and death
632–661	Rule of the Four Rightly Guided Caliphs, formative period for Sunnis
638	Muslim conquest of Jerusalem
661–750	Umayyad Empire
680	Martyrdom of Husayn and his followers at Karbala, Iraq
750–1258	Abbasid Empire: height of Islamic civilization, patronage of art and culture, development of Islamic law, and rising trade, agriculture, industry and commerce
756–1492	Andalusia (Muslim Spain): period of interfaith coexistence of Muslims, Christians, and Jews
765	Death of sixth Shii imam, Jafar al-Sadiq; succession disputed, causing split between Sevener and Twelver Shiis
8th–9th centuries	Formation of major Sunni law schools
1000–1492	Christian reconquest of Muslim-ruled territories in Spain, Sicily, and Italy
1095–1453	Crusades
12th century	Rise of Sufi orders
1187	Saladin and Muslim forces reconquer Jerusalem
1281–1924	Ottoman Empire (Middle East, North Africa, and portions of Eastern Europe)

In the slums and many lower-middle-class neighborhoods of Cairo and Algiers, Beirut and Mindanao, the West Bank and Gaza, families that cannot afford state services, or live under governments that do not provide adequate social services, utilize inexpensive and efficient educational, legal, and medical services provided by Islamic associations.

In September 2001, terrorists attacked New York's World Trade Center and the Pentagon in Washington, D.C. The hijackers who committed these acts reflected a religious radicalism that has threatened many regimes in the Muslim world, as well as Western governments. In the 1990s, Muslim extremists were responsible for attacks and acts of terrorism in Egypt, Algeria, Lebanon, Israel/Palestine, Kenya, and Tanzania that killed and maimed

1453	Fall of Constantinople/Istanbul, capital of former Byzantine Empire, to Ottomans
1483–1857	Mughal Empire (South Asia)
1501–1722	Safavid Empire (Iran)
1876–1938	Muhammad Iqbal, Islamic modernist and ideologue for foundation of Pakistan
1897–1975	Elijah Muhammad, leader of the Nation of Islam in the United States
1903–1979	Mawlana Abu Ala Mawdudi, founder of the Jamaat-i Islami in India/Pakistan
1906–1949	Hassan al-Banna, founder of the Muslim Brotherhood in Egypt
1906–1966	Sayyid Qutb, radical, militant ideologue of the Muslim Brotherhood in 1950s and 1960s
1975	Wallace D. Muhammad (name later changed to Warith Deen Muhammad) succeeds his father Elijah Muhammad and progressively brings his followers into conformity with mainstream Sunni Islam
1979	Iranian Revolution and foundation of Iranian Islamic Republic under leadership of Ayatollah Khomeini; seizure of the Grand Mosque in Mecca by Muslim militants; Soviet Union invades Afghanistan
1989	FIS (Islamic Salvation Front) sweeps municipal elections in Algeria; Tunisia bars Renaissance Party (formerly MTI) from participation in elections; death of Ayatollah Khomeini in Iran
1990	FIS wins Algerian municipal and regional elections
1993	Bombing of World Trade Center in New York City by Muslim militants
1995	Welfare (Refah) party wins parliamentary; Dr. Necmettin Erbakan becomes Turkey's first Islamist prime minister
1998	US Embassies in Tanzania and Kenya bombed by Muslim militants
September 11, 2001	Terrorist attacks against the World Trade Center in New York City and the Pentagon in Washington, D.C. sparks U.S. led war against global terrorism and the hunt for Osama bin Laden and al-Qaeda
2004	French Parliament bans Muslim headscarf in schools and public places

ISLAM Timeline

Muslims and non-Muslims alike. Spokesmen for the groups denounced the victims as "enemies of God" and railed at "atheist" governments. Post 9/11, Osama bin Laden's al-Qaeda and other extremist movements were responsible for attacks from Spain and Morocco to Indonesia and the Philippines.

The images and realities of Islam and of Muslims are indeed multiple and diverse. This chapter will explore the challenges and struggles within the Muslim community in defining the meaning of Islam for modern and postmodern life. We will look at the history, tradition, and heritage of Islam in the context of its significance and impact on Muslim society and world events today.

The study of Islam and Muslim society, yesterday and today, is a fascinating trip across time and space. It requires a bridging of the gap between religion, history, politics, and culture. Let us begin by briefly answering the question: what is Islam and where is the Islamic world?

The word *islam* means submission or surrender. A Muslim is one who submits, who seeks to follow and actualize God's will in history. The Muslim community (*ummah*) is a transnational community of believers, God ordained and guided, whose mission is to spread and institutionalize an Islamic Order to create a socially just society: "You are the best community ever brought forth for mankind, enjoining what is good and forbidding evil" (Q. 3:110).

Islam belongs to the Abrahamic family of great monotheistic faiths. Jews, Christians, and Muslims all view themselves as the children of Abraham, whose story is told in the Old Testament and in the Quran. While Jews and Christians claim descent from Abraham and his wife Sarah through their son Isaac, Muslims trace their religious roots back to Abraham (Ibrahim) through Ismail, his firstborn son by Hagar, Sarah's Egyptian servant.

According to both Hebrew and Muslim scripture, when after many years Sarah had not conceived a child, she urged Abraham to sleep with Hagar, so that he might have an heir. The child who was the result of that union was a boy named Ismail. After Ismail's birth, Sarah finally became pregnant and gave birth to Isaac. She then became jealous of Ismail, who as firstborn would be the prime inheritor, overshadowing Isaac. So she pressured Abraham to send Hagar and Ismail away. Abraham reluctantly did this, after God promised to make Ismail the father of a great nation.

Despite specific and significant difference, Judaism, Christianity, and Islam share a belief in one God, the creator, sustainer, and ruler of the universe who is beyond ordinary experience. All believe in angels, Satan, prophets, revelation, moral responsibility and accountability, divine judgment, and eternal reward or punishment. For Muslims, Islam is the completion of earlier revelations.

Mecca is the holiest city of Islam: the birthplace of the Prophet Muhammad, where the earliest revelations occurred and toward which Muslims turn in prayer five times each day. Muslims on pilgrimage gather near Mecca's Grand Mosque following Friday dawn prayers.

Islam is the world's second largest religion. Its more than 1.2 billion followers can be found in some fifty-six predominantly Muslim countries, extending from North Africa to Southeast Asia (see Map 5.1). Because Islam has often been equated simply with the Arabs, only about 20 percent of the worldwide Muslim community, few realize that the vast majority of Muslims live in Asia and Africa: Indonesia, Bangladesh, Pakistan, India, and Nigeria. Islam's presence and impact extend beyond countries in which the majority of the population is Muslim, often referred to as "the Islamic world." In recent years, Islam has become a visible presence in the West as the second or third largest religion in

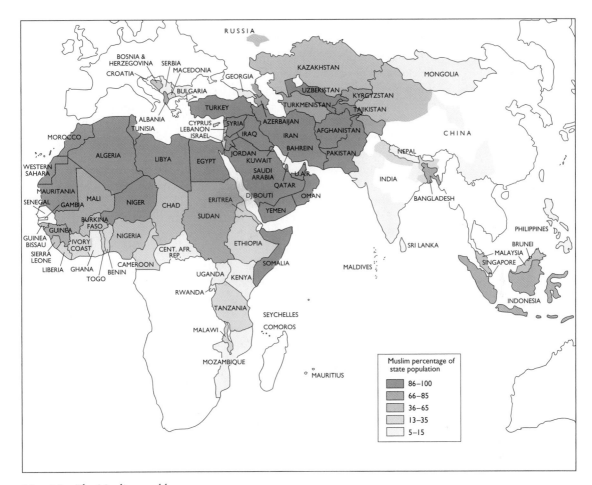

Map 5.1   The Muslim world.

Europe (in particular France, Germany, and England) and in North America. Today the capitals or major cities of Islam are not only exotic-sounding places like Cairo, Damascus, Baghdad, Mecca, Islamabad, and Kuala Lumpur, but also London, Paris, Marseilles, Brussels, New York, Detroit, and Los Angeles.

A dynamic religion that interfaces and at times competes with other faiths, Islam has had a significant impact upon world affairs. In contrast to the modern secular belief in the separation of church and state, Islam for many Muslims represents a more comprehensive worldview in which religion and society, faith and power, have been and are more closely bound. Throughout much of history, to be a Muslim was not simply to belong to a faith community or to worship in a given place but to live in an Islamic community or state, governed (in theory if not always in practice) by Islamic law. Many Muslims see their religion as much more than a personal faith. Historically, Islam has significantly formed and informed politics and civilization, giving rise to vast Islamic empires and states as well as Islamic civilization.

From Islam's origins to the present, Muslims have been engaged in a continuous process of understanding and interpreting the word of God (Quran), defining, redefining, and applying Islamic practices to the realities of life. The development of Islamic law, theology, and mysticism reflects the complexity of this process. Religious doctrines, laws, and practices result not only from clear prescriptions in sacred texts but also from fallible, limited human beings, whose conclusions reflect their intelligence, political and social environments, and customs. For example, since interpreters of Islam were males living in male-dominated societies, the development of Islamic laws relating to women and the family reveals a patriarchal mind-set. Of equal importance, Islamic doctrines and laws addressed the political and social questions and issues that arose in the first centuries of Islamic history. Thus, while it is correct to say that there is one Islam, revealed in the Quran and the traditions of the Prophet, as we shall now see, there have been many interpretations of Islam, some complementing each other, others in conflict.

Muslims today, like other people of faith, struggle with the relationship of their religious tradition to modernity and postmodernity. How does a faith revealing a God-centered universe speak to a modern, post-Enlightenment human-centered world focusing on reason and science? Like Judaism and Christianity, Islam contends with questions about a range of issues from evolution, birth control, artificial insemination, and organ transplants to ecology, nuclear energy, and chemical warfare. What is the relationship of Islam to secularization: should Islam today be restricted to personal life, or should it be integral to the state, law, and society? Is Islam compatible with modern forms of political participation such as democracy? With secularism, or the separation of religion and politics? In the twenty-first century, what should be the Islamic positions on treatment of religious minorities, non-Muslims, and women?

What is the relationship of Islam to the West? Many in the West see the religion of Islam in terms of the stereotypes of jihad and religious extremism. Muslims charge that the real culprit is a militant Judeo-Christian tradition, as seen in the Christian-initiated Crusades and inquisitions, European colonialism, and American neocolonialism. Critics of U.S. actions in the Muslim world condemn "anti-Muslim" policies. Not only do they point to the creation of Israel and a perceived bias toward Israel in the Palestinian–Israeli conflict; they also note U.S. support for authoritarian Arab and Muslim regimes that for decades has had the effect of excluding the Middle East and Muslim world from America's promotion of democracy and human rights. These issues have been reflected by what some on both sides regard as an impending clash of civilizations or global confrontation between Islamic countries and the West.

In recent years the presence and growth of large Muslim populations in America and Europe have required Muslims to address a host of questions and problems. Muslims have had to struggle to overcome stereotypes arising from the Iranian revolution of 1978–79, hostage-taking, and terrorism. Fallout from 9/11 and the threat of global terrorism have often made it more difficult for Muslim citizens in Western countries to gain recognition and respect for their faith and its practice. American society, however officially secular, recognizes

Christian and Jewish Sabbaths (Saturday and Sunday) and famously accords holiday status to Christmas. Muslims have had to seek accommodation for their Friday congregational prayer, celebration of holy days, and respect for women who wear the headscarf (hijab). Some communities have resisted the opening of mosques and Islamic schools, and the introduction of Muslim chaplains into the armed forces and prisons proved difficult. Muslims have fought for recognition of their dietary requirements, which include bans on alcohol, pork, and foods cooked with certain products. Like Jews who keep kosher, many Muslims will not eat meat from an animal that has not been killed in a religiously observant manner.

Muslim dietary law, like Judaism's kosher law, requires the ritual slaughter of animals permitted to be eaten. Today across America, halal butcher shops may be found, providing these religiously prepared meats for their Muslim customers.

ENCOUNTER WITH MODERNITY: THE CHALLENGE OF WESTERN COLONIALISM

The Islamic world has witnessed upheaval and renewal since the nineteenth century, as Muslims absorbed the impact of European colonialism. The twentieth century brought the creation of modern Muslim nation-states, the superpower rivalry between America and the Soviet Union during the cold war, and notable failures and challenges of Islamic societies, all in the religious, intellectual, and moral contexts of rapid change and globalization that continue into the 2000s.

The early and rapid expansion of Islam and Islamic empires extending from Africa to Asia and their continued success and power until the nineteenth century and the rise of European colonialism were seen as the result of God's guidance and pleasure with the Islamic community.

Yet by the nineteenth century, many Muslim areas were colonized by the West: the French in North, West, and Equatorial Africa and the Levant (Lebanon and Syria); the British in Palestine, Transjordan, Iraq, the Arabian Gulf, and the Indian subcontinent; and in Southeast Asia, the British in Malaya (Malaysia, Singapore, and Brunei), and the Dutch in Indonesia.

Muslims found themselves on the defensive against a European imperialism that threatened their political, religious, and cultural identity and challenged time-honored beliefs and practices. Muslim responses to such Western power and ideas varied from rejection and confrontation to admiration and imitation.

Islamic modernist reformers sought to restore the pride, identity, and strength of their debilitated Islamic community by bridging the gap between their heritage and modernity. They emphasized the compatibility of Islam with reason, science, and technology and the need for *ijtihad,* the reinterpretation of Islamic law to meet the needs of the modern world. However, these reformers failed to produce a systematic reinterpretation of Islam, nor did they develop effective organizations and institutions to preserve and propagate the reformist message. These failures led to the emergence of modern Islamic activist organizations (sometimes referred to as fundamentalist movements), the Muslim Brotherhood in the Middle East and *Jamaat-i-Islami* (the Islamic Society) in South Asia. Both these movements have criticized Islamic reformers for trying to westernize Islam. In particular, they have condemned the tendency of most Muslim countries to uncritically adapt Western models of development. Islam, they insist, offers an alternative path to Western capitalism and communism/socialism; Islam is a total, comprehensive way of life. These activist movements and their many offshoots, from mainstream social and political organizations to radical revolutionary groups, continue to be major forces in modern Islam.

During the post–World War II era, most of the Muslim world had regained its independence. However, the boundaries of modern nation-states like Syria, Sudan, Jordan, Iraq, Kuwait, Malaysia, and Pakistan were arbitrarily drawn by the European states that had colonized the areas. Indeed, many of the first twentieth-century Muslim rulers were appointed by colonial governments; others, often military officers or former officers, simply seized power. As a result, instead of elected governments, much of the Muslim world received a legacy of autocratic rulers not of their choosing.

Questions regarding the political legitimacy of rulers and issues of national identity or unity have plagued many of these nations to this day, and some governments have relied heavily for control and stability on internal security forces and America, Europe, and the former Soviet Union. Because the West provided the models for development, it was widely supposed that modernization and progress would depend on westernization and secularization. Iran's Islamic revolution of 1979–80 shattered this assumption.

Although Iran drew attention to the reassertion and power of Islam in society, in Egypt, Libya, and Pakistan, Islam had been reasserting itself in Muslim politics for more than a decade before 1979. The crushing military defeat of combined Arab forces in the Six-Day War of 1967, and the loss to Israel of major territories (the Sinai, West Bank and Gaza, Golan Heights and especially Jerusalem, the third holiest city of Islam) became "*the* disaster" in Muslim literature and consciousness. This key event triggered a period of doubt and self-examination.

Despite national independence, most Muslim countries had remained weak, underdeveloped, and dependent upon the West. What went wrong? To regain their past power and glory, many Muslims believed that they must return to the straight path of Islam. The 1973 Arab oil embargo and, later, the Islamic revolution in Iran, reinforced the belief that Muslim economic and political power could be attributed to the resurgence of Islam in contemporary Muslim politics and society.

During the late 1960s and 1970s, Islam enjoyed a higher profile in personal and public life, demonstrated by greater religious observance and Islamic dress as well as the growth of Islamic political and social organizations and institutions: banks, publishing houses, schools. In addition, many governments as well as their opposition political parties used Islamic slogans and language to mobilize popular support. Despite their differences, an array of Muslim rulers (Egypt's Anwar Sadat, Libya's Muammar Gadhafi, Sudan's Jaafar al-Nimeiri, Pakistan's Zulfikar Ali Bhutto, and Muhammad Zia ul-Haq) also turned to Islam in politics during the 1970s and 1980s. At the same time, Islamic activist organizations mushroomed in number and size throughout the Muslim world. Alongside Islamic organizations like the Muslim Brotherhoods of Egypt, Syria, Jordan, and Sudan, there were violent revolutionary organizations with names like Jund Allah (Army of God), *Hezbollah* (the party of God), and jihad (Holy War).

Yet by the late 1980s and 1990s, it was increasingly clear that a quiet (nonviolent) revolution had occurred. From North Africa to Southeast Asia, Islam was playing an increasingly more visible and important role in the social-economic and political life of society. In the twenty-first century, Islamic activists and parties are a significant factor in electoral politics in Egypt, Algeria, Sudan, Lebanon, Jordan, Turkey, Pakistan, Malaysia, Indonesia, and Central Asia. Many authoritarian rulers have experienced the power of religion in Muslim politics through ballots of Islamic supporters as well as bullets of the more radical groups. Islam has become a powerful force in confronting modernity and postmodernity.

Change is a reality in contemporary Islam and in every level of Muslim societies. The question is not whether there should be any change but rather—how much change and what kinds of change are necessary and permissible?

In contrast to the past, to speak of Islam in the twenty-first century is not only to speak of Islam *and* the West but also of Islam *in* the West. Islam is the fastest growing religion in North America and in Europe, the second largest religion in France, Holland, Belgium, and Germany, and the third in Britain and the United States. Even without increases in Muslim immigration and conversions to Islam, in several decades Muslim birthrates will result in Islam's replacing Judaism as the second largest religion in the United States.

Muslims in the United States, like other religious or ethnic minorities before them, face many questions about their faith and identity: Are they Muslims in America or American Muslims? Can Muslims become part and parcel of a pluralistic American society without sacrificing or losing their identity? Can people be Muslims in a non-Muslim state that is not governed by Islamic law? Is the U.S. legal system capable of allowing for particular Muslim religious and cultural differences?

In the West, it has sometimes been fashionable to speak of a post-Christian society, but for many Muslims, however, talking about a post-Islamic society is not relevant. For many Muslims, the debate is not over whether religion has a place and role in society, but rather what kind of Islam or Islamic presence should exist. Understanding Islam today requires an appreciation of the full spectrum of Muslim responses to the modern world, ranging from those who view Islam as a personal faith to others who wish to see it implemented more formally in state and society.

Throughout the ages, when Muslims have sought to define or redefine their lives Islamically, the starting point has always been an understanding of the past. Thus, we need to go back in order to go forward. To understand Islam's present and future, we must learn about the history and development of Islam and the Muslim community.

PREMODERN ISLAM: THE FORMATIVE ERA

Like all the world's religions, Islam places great emphasis on its early history. For Muslims, the formative period is the time of the Prophet, Muhammad, a period that included the revelation of the Quran and Muhammad's founding of the first community. Islam's formative period is often seen as the "best of times," the time of the purest and most authentic Islamic community, a society that was to be emulated by future generations, a model to return to for inspiration and guidance.

At the core of Muslim belief and faith are the messenger and the message. As Christians look to Jesus and the New Testament, and Jews look to Moses and the Torah, Muslims regard Muhammad and the Quran as the final, perfect, and complete revelation of God's will for humankind. In addition, because of the remarkable success of Muhammad and the early Muslim community in spreading the faith of Islam and the rule of Muslims, an idealized memory of Islamic history and of Muslim rule became the model for success, serving as a common reference point for later generations of reformers.

The foundations of Islam are belief in God (Allah) and in his messenger, Muhammad. Since God is beyond our ordinary experience or transcendent, Islam teaches that he cannot be known directly but only through his messengers and revelations. Thus, Muhammad and the Quran, the final messenger and message, were key in the formation and development of the Islamic tradition, its beliefs, laws, rituals, and social practices. Learning more about the messenger and the message will increase our understanding of Islam today and our insights about the sources Muslims use to guide their lives in the twenty-first century.

Muhammad's Early Life

Few observers in the sixth century would have predicted that Muhammad ibn Abdullah and central Arabia would come to play pivotal roles in world history and world religions. Most would have seen as limited at best the future impact of an orphan raised in a vast desert region marked by tribal warfare and divisions and bounded by two great imperial powers, the Eastern Roman, or Byzantine, Empire and Persian (Sassanid) Empire. And yet the message Muhammad brought from God and the force of his personality would quite literally transform Arabia and have a significant impact on much of the world, past and present.

Because Muhammad regarded himself as a religious reformer and not the founder of a new religion, it is important to understand pre-Islamic Arabian society and religion, which were tribal in structure and organization. Individuals lived in extended families; several related families constituted a clan; a cluster of several clans comprised a tribe. Al Ilah (Allah) was seen as the high god over a pantheon of tribal gods and goddesses who were believed to be more directly active in everyday life. Each city or town had its divine patron/protectors and shrine. Tribal gods and goddesses were respected and feared rather than loved, the focal points of the rituals of sacrifice, prayer, and pilgrimage. The tribal polytheism of Arabia was embodied in a cube-shaped building that housed the idols of 360 tribal gods and was a center of pilgrimage. Located in the ancient city of Mecca, this cube, *Kaaba*, would be rededicated to Allah in the seventh century.

Tribal polytheism was a very "this worldly" religion with little concern about or belief in an afterlife, divine judgment, or reward or punishment after death. Individual identity and rights were subordinated to tribal and family identity, authority, and law. The key virtue, "manliness," included loyalty to family and protection of its members, bravery in battle, hospitality, and honor. There was little sense of meaning or accountability beyond this life, however, no moral responsibility and accountability beyond tribal and family honor. This era, in which justice was guaranteed and administered not by God but by the threat of retaliation by family or tribe, is referred to as the *jahiliyya,* or period of ignorance of Islam.

Muhammad: The Final Messenger

No prophet has played a greater role in a world religion and in world politics than Muhammad. Both in his lifetime and throughout Muslim history, Muhammad ibn Abdullah has served as the ideal model for Muslim life. Some Muslims have called him the "living Quran," that is, the embodiment in his behavior and words of God's will. He is viewed as the last or final prophet who brought the final revelation of God. He is so revered that the name Muhammad (or names derived from it—Ahmad, Mahmud), is the most common Muslim name. In some Muslim countries, every male child has the Prophet's name as one of his forenames. Thus, the Prophet and his example or Sunnah are central to Islam and Muslim belief and practice. Muhammad is not only the ideal political leader, statesman, merchant, judge, soldier, and diplomat but also the ideal husband, father, and friend. Muslims look to his example for guidance in all aspects of life: eating; fasting; praying; the treatment of a spouse, parents, and children; the creation of contracts; the waging of war; and the conduct of diplomacy.

Monotheism was known in Arabia. Both Arab Christian and Jewish communities had long resided in the region. The Quran speaks of Arab monotheists, *hanifs*, descendants of Ibrahim. In addition, Arab traders would have encountered Judaism and Christianity, since Jewish and Christian merchants regularly came to Mecca, a major center for trade as well as pilgrimage. However, monotheism's powerful appeal to the Arabs came only when the Prophet Muhammad received his message from Allah, a message that would change the lives of hundreds of millions of peoples throughout Arabia and beyond.

While there is a great deal of information about Muhammad's life after he received his "call" to be God's messenger, the portrait of his early years is drawn from history, legend, and Muslim belief. Muhammad ibn Abdullah (the son of Abdullah) was born in 570 into the ruling tribe of Mecca, the Quraysh. Orphaned at an early age, Muhammad was among the tribe's "poorer cousins," raised by an uncle and later employed in Mecca's thriving caravan business. During the prime of his life, Muhammad had one wife, Khadija, for twenty-eight years, until her death. Much is recorded about Muhammad's relationship with Khadija, who was his closest confidante and comforter and strongest supporter. The couple had six children, two sons who died in infancy and four daughters. After Khadija's death, Muhammad married other women, all but one of them widows.

By the age of 30, Muhammad had become a prominent, respected member of Meccan society, known for his business skill and trustworthiness (he was nicknamed al-Amin, the trustworthy). Reflective by temperament, Muhammad would often retreat to the quiet and solitude of Mount Hira to contemplate his life and society. It was here during the month of Ramadan in 610, on a night Muslims commemorate as the Night of Power and Excellence, that Muhammad the caravan leader became Muhammad the messenger of God. Through a heavenly intermediary, identified by later tradition as the angel Gabriel, Muhammad at the age of 40 received the first message or revelation: "Recite in the name of your lord who has created, Created man out of a germ cell. Recite, for your Lord is the most generous One, Who has taught by the pen, Taught man what he did not know."

Muhammad became a link in a long series of biblical prophets, messengers from God who served as a conscience to the community and as God's messenger. Like Moses, who had received the Torah on Mount Sinai from the God of the Hebrews, Muhammad received the first of God's revelations on Mount Hira: "It is He who sent down to you the Book with the truth, confirming what went before it: and He sent down the Torah and the Injil ["Evangel," "Gospel"] before as a guidance to the people" (Q. 3:3). Also, like Amos and Jeremiah before him, Muhammad served as a "warner" from God who admonished his hearers to repent and obey God, for the final judgment was near:

Say: "O Men I am only a warner." Those who believe, and do deeds of righteousness—theirs shall be forgiveness and generous provision. And those who strive against our signs to avoid them—they shall be inhabitants of Hell. (Q. 22:49–50)

Muhammad continued to receive revelations for more than two decades (610–632); together these revelations constitute the text of the Quran (literally, "the recitation or discourse").

The first ten years of Muhammad's preaching were difficult. At first he revealed his religious experience to his wife and close friends only. When he finally began to preach God's message, critiquing the status quo, he encountered the anger of Mecca's prosperous, powerful political and commercial leaders. In the name of Allah, the one true God, Muhammad increasingly denounced polytheism and thus threatened the livelihood of those who profited enormously from the annual pilgrimage, which was the equivalent of a giant tribal convention. Equally problematic, Muhammad preached a message strong on issues of social justice, condemning the socioeconomic inequities of his time. The Prophet denounced false contracts, usury, and the exploitation of the poor, orphans, and widows. Muhammad claimed an authority and legitimacy, as God's prophet, that undermined the primacy of Mecca's rich and powerful masters. He called all true believers to join the community of God, a universal community that transcended tribal bonds and authority, a community led by Muhammad, not by the Quraysh.

As Muhammad continued to preach his message, the situation in Mecca became more difficult. He and his followers were persecuted harshly by the ruling Quraysh; they were beaten, denied food and drink, and exposed to the intense heat of the day to induce them to deny their beliefs. After ten years of rejection and persecution in Mecca, Muhammad and his followers migrated to Yathrib, renamed Medina, "city" of the prophet, in 622. Invited to serve as arbiter or judge, for Muslim and non-Muslim alike, Muhammad became the religious and political leader of the community. Medina proved a new beginning, as the Muslim community prospered and grew.

After the Hijra

The emigration (*hijra*) from Mecca to Medina in 622 was a turning point in Muhammad's life and in Islamic history. To appreciate the central significance of hijra and the birth of the Islamic community, the *ummah*, one has only to note that when Muslims devised their own calendar, they dated it not from the birth of the Prophet or from his first revelation but from the creation of the Islamic community at Medina. Thus, 622 CE is now called 1 AH, "after the hijra." This act reinforced the meaning of Islam as the realization of God's will on earth as well as the centrality of the Islamic ummah. Thus, Muslims, then and now, believe Islam is a world religion, a global community of the faithful with a universal message and mission.

Muhammad did not create a new religion; rather, he was a prophet and reformer. His message proclaimed monotheism, the unity (*tawhid*) or oneness of God. Polytheism and idolatry, putting anything in place of the one, true God—were to be condemned and suppressed. While Arabian polytheism was ignorant of and violated the doctrine of *tawhid*, Muslims believe that over time, the Jewish and Christian communities distorted

God's original revelation. Therefore, they see Muhammad (the last or "seal" of the prophets (Q. 33:40) and the Quran, the complete, uncorrupted revelation, as a corrective, a restoration of the true faith and message of God. All were called by Muhammad to repentance, to turn away from the path of unbelief and false practice and toward the straight path (*sharia*) of God.

Muhammad taught that submission (islam) to God was both an individual and a community obligation. Tribal identity must be replaced by identification with Islam, now the primary source of community solidarity. This belief was reinforced by the Quran's emphasis on social justice, social welfare, and protection of women, orphans, and the poor. Muhammad rejected or reformed some rituals, and introduced others. In addition, he reinterpreted the pre-Islamic Arabian pilgrimage to the Kaaba at Mecca. The Kaaba was cleansed of its 360 tribal idols and rededicated to Allah. Pilgrimage to the Kaaba in Mecca, like prayer five times each day, became one of the Five Pillars, or required practices, of Islam.

During the short decade that Muhammad led the community at Medina, he, in light of continuing revelations, defined its mandate and mission. He forged its identity, consolidated its political base, and established its basic religious law and practice.

Muhammad skillfully employed both force and diplomacy to defeat the Meccans and then to unite the tribes of Arabia under the banner of Islam. In 624 Muhammad and his followers successfully engaged and defeated the far greater Meccan forces at the Battle of Badr. For Muslims, then and now, this battle has special significance, a "miraculous" victory in which the forces of Allah and monotheism, were pitted against those of Meccan polytheism. Yet despite overwhelming odds, the army of God vanquished the unbelievers. The Quran itself tells of God's assistance (Q. 8:42ff, 3:123) in securing the victory. Quranic witness of divine guidance and intervention made Badr a sacred symbol that has been remembered and commemorated throughout history. The 1973 Egyptian–Israeli war was given the code name Operation Badr

The courtyard of the Mosque of the Prophet in Medina, the first mosque in Islam, is among the most sacred sites in Islam. The original structure has been rebuilt and expanded several times.

by President Anwar Sadat in an attempt to inspire and motivate his forces by means of this symbol of Islam triumphant.

After a three-year series of battles, a truce was struck at Hudaybiyah. In 630, charging that the Meccans had broken the truce, Muhammad led against them an army ten thousand strong; the Meccans surrendered without a fight. Muhammad rejected the options of vengeance and plunder and instead granted amnesty to his former enemies. The majority of the Meccans converted to Islam, accepted Muhammad's leadership, and became part of the Islamic community.

In his early preaching, Muhammad had looked to Jews and Christians as natural allies. As "People of the Book" who had received prophets and revelation, they had much in common with Muslims and so he anticipated the approval and acceptance of Islam by the Jews of Medina. Muhammad initially presented himself to the Jews of Arabia as a prophetic reformer reestablishing the religion of Abraham. However, the Jewish tribes of Medina, who had lived there a long time and had political ties with the Quraysh of Mecca, did not accept the reformer's message. While the majority of tribes converted to Islam, Medina's three Jewish tribes, half the population of Medina, did not. Until that time, Muslims had faced Jerusalem to pray and, like the Jews, fasted on the tenth day (Ashura) of the lunar month. However, when the Jews rejected Muhammad's claims and proved resistant to conversion, Muhammad received a revelation and changed the direction of prayer from Jerusalem to Mecca. Thereafter, Islam was presented as a distinct alternative to Judaism.

Because Muslims lived in close proximity to people of other faiths, Muhammad promulgated the Constitution of Medina, which set out the rights and duties of all citizens and the relationship of the Muslim community to other communities. Jews were recognized as a separate community, politically allied to the Muslims, but retaining internal religious and cultural autonomy. However, political loyalty and allegiance were expected. The Jews' denial of Muhammad's prophethood and message and their ties with the Meccans became a source of conflict. The Quran accuses the Jewish tribes of regularly breaking treaties: "Why is it that whenever they make pacts, a group among them casts it aside unilaterally?" (Q. 2:100). After each major battle between the Muslims and Meccans, one of the Jewish tribes was accused of having acted in bad faith, with escalating consequences. In the end, Muhammad moved to crush the remaining Jews in Medina, whom he regarded as a political threat to Muslim consolidation and rule in Arabia.

In 632, Muhammad led the pilgrimage to Mecca. There the 62-year-old leader delivered a farewell sermon in which he emphasized:

> Know ye that every Muslim is a brother unto every other Muslim, and that ye are now one brotherhood. It is not legitimate for any one of you, therefore, to appropriate unto himself anything that belongs to his brother unless it is willingly given him by that brother.[1]

This event continues to be remembered and commemorated each year by millions of Muslims who make the annual pilgrimage to Mecca, in modern Saudi Arabia.

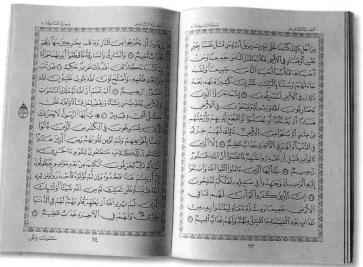

The Message of the Quran

Muslims believe that the Quran is the eternal, uncreated, literal, and final word of God revealed to Muhammad as guidance for humankind (Q. 2:185). Thus, for Muslims, Islam is not a new religion but rather the oldest, for it represents the "original" as well as the final revelation of God to Abraham, Moses, Jesus, and Muhammad. The Prophet Muhammad is seen as a conduit, an intermediary, who received God's message and then communicated it over a period of twenty-two years. The text of the Quran is about four-fifths the length of the New Testament. The Muslim scripture consists of 114 chapters (*surahs*) of six thousand verses, arranged by length, not chronology.

God's word, as revealed in the Quran, is the final and complete revelation. It provides the primary and ultimate source of guidance, the basis for belief and practice in Islam. Study, memorization, recitation, and copying of the Quran have been central acts of piety. The noble art of copying the Quran has produced a rich tradition of calligraphy. These manuscript pages provide a beautiful example.

The God (Allah) of the Quran is seen as the creator, sustainer, ruler, and judge of humankind. He is merciful and just, the all-knowing and all-powerful, the lord and ruler of the universe. The Quran teaches that God's revelation has occurred in several forms: in nature, in history, and in scripture. God's existence can be known through nature, which points to or contains the "signs" of its creator and sustainer (Q. 3:26–27). The record of humankind also contains clear examples and lessons of God's sovereignty and intervention in history (Q. 30:2–9). And finally, God's will for humankind has been revealed through a long line of prophets and messengers: "Indeed We sent forth among every nation a Messenger saying: 'Serve your God and shun false gods' " (Q. 16:36). As a result, throughout history, people could know not only that God exists but also his will, what God desires and commands, for humankind.

Muslims believe that the Quran, like the Torah and the Evangel (Gospel), is taken from an Arabic tablet, the source or mother of all scriptures, preexisting with God in heaven. From it, the teachings of the three Abrahamic faiths (Judaism, Christianity, and Islam) were taken and revealed at different stages in history. Indeed, many Muslims take their names from the biblical prophets Ibrahim (Abraham), Musa (Moses), Sulayman (Solomon), Dawud (David), Yahya (John), Mary (Maryam), and Issa (Jesus). Equally striking to many is the fact that the name of Mary, the mother of Jesus, is cited more often in the Quran than in the entire New Testament.

Throughout history, Jesus and Mary (Maryam), his mother, have been held in high esteem. Jesus enjoys a special place among the prophets in Islam. The Quran affirms the virgin birth of Jesus, the promised Messiah," who declared from his cradle: "I am God's servant; God has given me the Book, and made me a prophet" (Q. 19:30).

Because Arabic is the language of the Quran, all Muslims memorize, recite, and pray the Quran in Arabic whether they fully understand it or not. Much as the Roman Catholic Mass until the middle of the twentieth century was always said in Latin and the faithful responded to the priest in Latin rather than local languages, across the world Turkish, French, Pakistani, Malaysian, German, Indian, and American Muslims stop to pray in Arabic five times each day. Arabic is viewed as the sacred language of Islam; in a very real sense it is seen as the language of God. Whereas Christianity, at an early stage, translated its scriptures into Latin and Greek and after the Reformation translated the scriptures into local languages, which were also used in congregational worship, Muslims maintain Arabic as the language of the Quran, the primary source for religious learning and training, and of formal worship. Translations, which have occurred only in the past century, are usually accompanied by the Arabic text.

For many Muslims the clearest evidence of the Quran's power and uniqueness is its impact upon its hearers; indeed many have been moved to conversion after hearing the beauty of a Quranic recitation. The Quran, being sacred, is handled with reverence. A devout Muslim will not write in the Quran or mark it up in any other way. Memorization of the entire text of the Quran is a time-honored act of piety. Recitation or chanting of the Quran is a major art form as well as an act of worship. Muslims gather in stadiums and auditoriums around the world to attend international Quran recitation competitions as many in the West might attend an opera. To win an international competition can be a source of great national pride.

Because Muslims believe that the Quran is God's Word or revelation, from an early age children are taught to read the Quran.

A Golden Age of Expansion, Conquests, and Creativity

The rule of Muhammad and his first four successors, or caliphs, is seen as the normative, exemplary period of Muslim faith and history. After God sent down his final and complete revelation for humankind through his last prophet, the Islamic community/state was created, and the sources of Islamic law, the Quran and Sunnah of the Prophet, originated. Both reformers and Islamic revivalists today look to this period as the reference point for divine guidance and historical validation. Muslims believe that the revealed message of the Quran and the example of the Prophet and his successors were corroborated in the full light of history after "miraculous" victories at Badr and elsewhere by the spread of Islam to many converts and by the phenomenal geographic expansion that ultimately justified the term "Islamic Empire."

Through force and diplomacy, Muhammad united the tribes of Arabia under the banner of Islam. During the next century, the period of the four Rightly Guided Caliphs, Muslim armies were inspired by their new faith. There were also material rewards, in the form of bounty from richer societies, and spiritual rewards from obedience to God, such as the eternal home in paradise promised to martyrs. These highly motivated armies overran the Byzantine and Persian empires, which had been greatly weakened by internal strife and constant warfare.

Christendom experienced the early conquests and expansion of Islam as a threat to its religious and political hegemony. Muslim rule, and with it the message of Islam, quickly spread from the Byzantine and Persian empires to Syria, Iraq, and Egypt, and then swept across North Africa and into Europe, where Muslims ruled Spain and the Mediterranean from Sicily to Anatolia (see Map 5.2).

For non-Muslim populations in Byzantium and Persia, who had been sub-jugated by foreign rulers, Islamic rule meant an exchange of rulers rather than a loss of independence. Many in Byzantium willingly exchanged Greco-Roman rule for that of new Arab masters, fellow Semites, with whom they had closer linguistic and cultural affinities. Upon declaration of their alle-giance to the Islamic state and payment of a poll (head) tax, these "protected" (*dhimmi*) peoples could practice their faith and be governed by their religious leaders and law in matters of faith and private life.

Islam proved more tolerant than imperial Christianity, providing greater religious freedom for Jews and indigenous Christians. Under Muslim rule, most local or indigenous Christian churches, persecuted as schismatics and heretics by the "foreign" Christian orthodoxy of their rulers, could practice their faith.

The rapid spread and development of imperial Islam produced a rich Islamic civilization that flourished from the ninth to the twelfth centuries. Urban cultural centers emerged in Cairo, Baghdad, Cordova, Palermo, and Nishapur. With significant assistance from Christian and Jewish subjects, Muslims

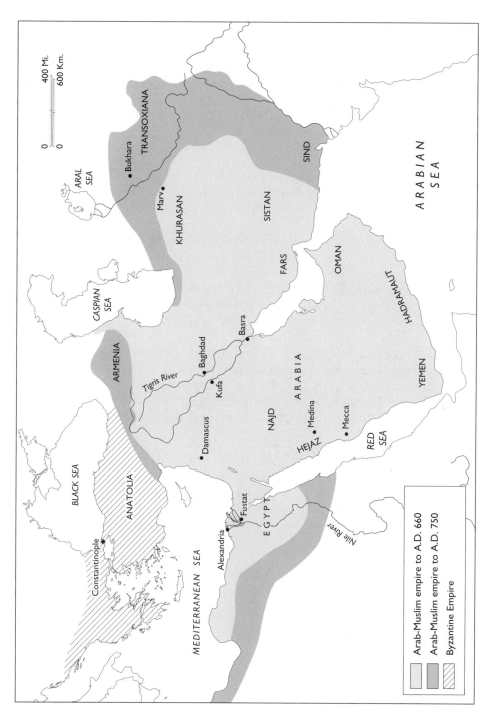

Map 5.2   *The Muslim Empire to 750.*

This enameled glass mosque lamp, made in the early 1300s, was dedicated to a Muslim ruler. Quotations from the Quran decorate the lamp.

collected the great books of science, medicine, and philosophy from the West and the East and translated them into Arabic from Greek, Latin, Persian, Coptic, Syriac, and Sanskrit. The age of translation was followed by a period of great creativity as a new generation of educated Muslim thinkers and scientists made their own contributions to learning in philosophy, medicine, chemistry, astronomy, algebra, optics, art, and architecture. These were true "renaissance men," multitalented men of genius who often developed mastery in the major disciplines of philosophy, medicine, mathematics, and astronomy. Avicenna (Ibn Sina), remembered as "the great commentator" on Aristotle, reflected this pattern:

> I busied myself with the study of Fusus al-Hikam (a treatise by al-Farabi) and other commentaries on physics and mathematics, and the doors of knowledge opened before me. Then I took up medicine. . . . Medicine is not one of the difficult sciences, and in a short time I undoubtedly excelled at it, so that physicians of merit studied under me. . . . At the same time I carried on debates with and controversies in jurisprudence. At this point I was sixteen years old. Then, for a year and a half, I devoted myself to study. I resumed the study of logic and all parts of philosophy. During this time I never slept the whole night through and did nothing but study all day long. . . . Thus I mastered logic, physics, and mathematics. . . . When I reached the age of eighteen, I had completed the study of all these sciences. At that point my memory was better, whereas today my learning is riper.[2]

The cultural traffic pattern was again reversed when Europeans, emerging from the Dark Ages, turned to Muslim centers of learning to regain their lost heritage and to learn from Muslim advances. The failures and reforms of Muslim societies today, as in the recent past, are often measured against this history, at times romanticized, of an earlier period of brilliant success.

Diversity, Division, and Dissent

The victories and accomplishments during the early history and spread of Islam were accompanied by deep division and dissent. During the lifetime of the Prophet, the community had been united by Muhammad's prophetic claims, his remarkable leadership skills, and the divine revelations he continued to receive. However, Muhammad's death precipitated crises, dissent, and civil wars.

Given the pivotal role of Muhammad in the life of the community, his death in 632 was a traumatic event. What was the community to do? Who was to lead? Issues of political succession and secession or civil war were to plague and threaten its survival.

Muhammad's senior followers, known as the Companions of the Prophet, moved quickly to reassure the community. In proclaiming Muhammad's death to the faithful, the Companion Abu Bakr declared: "Muslims! If any of you has worshiped Muhammad, let me tell you that Muhammad is dead. But if you worship God, then know that God is living and will never die." The Companions of the Prophet, the elders of Medina, selected Abu Bakr as caliph (*khalifah*, "successor or deputy"). A caliph was not a prophet but rather Muhammad's successor as political and military head of the community.

This next stage in the history of the Muslim community, the Caliphate (632–1258), has traditionally been divided into three periods: the time of the Rightly Guided Caliphs (632–661), followed by the Umayyad (661–750) and Abbasid (750–1258) dynasties. During these centuries a vast empire was created with successive capitols at Medina, Kufa, Damascus, and Baghdad. Stunning political and military success was complemented by a cultural florescence, resulting in powerful Islamic empires and a brilliant Islamic civilization. However, it was the earliest period, that of the Rightly Guided Caliphs and the Companions of the Prophet, that was to become the example for later generations of believers.

Abu Bakr (632–634), the first successor of Muhammad, was tested almost immediately when some Arab tribes attempted to bolt from the community, declaring their independence. Abu Bakr countered that all Muslims belonged to a single community and that the unity of the community was based upon the interconnectedness of religion and the state, faith, and politics. Abu Bakr crushed the tribal revolt, consolidated Muslim rule over the Arabian peninsula, and preserved the religiously based unity and solidarity of the Islamic-community state.

Abu Bakr's successor, Umar ibn al-Khattab (634–644), initiated a period of expansion and conquest. During the reign of the next caliph, Uthman ibn Affan (644–656), from the Umayyad clan, tribal factionalism resurfaced with a series of rebellions that would plague the Islamic community's development.

A second crisis of leadership occurred when civil war broke out during the reign of the fourth caliph, Ali. Although in 632 the majority of the community had supported the selection of Abu Bakr as caliph, a minority dissented, believing that leadership should stay in the family of the Prophet and thus pass to its senior male member, Ali. In addition to being Muhammad's cousin, Ali was the Prophet's son-in-law, having married Fatima, a daughter of Muhammad and Khadija. Shortly after Ali's accession to power, his authority was challenged by a triumvirate that included Muhammad's widow Aisha, who was the daughter of Abu Bakr. This was followed by the rebellion of Muawiya, the governor of Syria. Arbitration proved inconclusive but did lead to two results that have had a profound impact on the history of Islam.

First, a group of Ali's followers, the Karajites (those who "go out" or secede), broke away. They maintained an uncompromising faith, believing that Ali's failure to subdue his opponents rendered him no better than Muawiya. The Karajites held both Ali and Muawiya to be unbelievers whose revolt against God was punishable by death. Second, Muawiya remained recalcitrant in Syria. He bided his time until Ali was assassinated by a group of Karajites. Muawiya then seized power and established a monarchy, the Umayyad dynasty (661–750).

The Umayyad dynasty was responsible for the rapid spread of Islam and the emergence of imperial Islam with its capital in Damascus. However, opposition to what later Muslim historians would characterize as impious Umayyad caliphs also resulted in some important movements for renewal and reform. Some movements like the Karajites and the Shiah were revolutionary, while others led to the development of Islamic law and mysticism (Sufism).

The Karajites, who had broken with Ali, emerged as revolutionaries who, although unsuccessful in their own times, continue to inspire contemporary radical groups. Like some religious extremists today, the Karajites interpreted the Quran and the Sunnah literally and sought to follow their beliefs absolutely and to impose them on others. They viewed the world as divided into belief or unbelief, into Muslims, defined as those who agreed with the Karajites, and infidels, the enemies of God: those who differed with the Karajites and therefore should be excommunicated, or cut off from the community.

Like extremist groups today, who have taken such names as Jihad, the Soldiers of God, or al-Qaeda, the Karajites, claiming to follow the letter of the Quran and the example of the Prophet, adopted their own interpretation of Muhammad and the experiences of the early communities. Seeing themselves as the instruments of God's justice, God's righteous army, they believed that violence, guerrilla warfare, and revolution were not only legitimate but obligatory in their battle against the usurpers of God's rule. Other Muslims, however pious, who committed an action contrary to the letter of the law, as interpreted or understood by the Karajites, were guilty of grave (quite literally mortal) sin. According to the Karajites, they were apostates and thus had committed treason against the Islamic community-state. If they did not repent, they were to be fought against and killed. Many of the components of this early Islamic worldview may be found in twentieth- and twenty-first-century Muslim extremist writings including those of the Muslim Brotherhood's Sayyid Qutb and in the ideology of groups like Islamic Jihad, the Army of God, the Armed Islamic Group, Muhammad's Youth, Takfir wal Hijra (Excommunication and Flight), and al-Qaeda.

The Origins of the Sunni and Shiah Split

A second major revolutionary movement spawned by opposition to Umayyad rule was the rebellion by the followers of the fourth caliph, Ali. The results of this violent disagreement would lead to the two great branches of Islam, the communities of the Sunni majority and the Shiah, or Shii minority.

The followers (*shiah*, "partisans") of Ali had been thwarted twice: when Muhammad's cousin was not appointed as the first caliph, and later when Muawiya seized the caliphate from Ali, who had been the Prophet's fourth successor. In 680, when the Umayyad ruler Yazid, the son of Muawiya, came to power, Husayn, the son of Ali, was persuaded by a group of Ali's followers in Kufa (a city in modern Iraq) to lead a rebellion. However, the support promised to Husayn did not materialize, and Husayn and his army were slaughtered by the Umayyad army at the city of Karbala (also in modern Iraq).

The memory of Karbala and the "martyrdom" of Husayn resulted in a Shii worldview, a paradigm of suffering, oppression, and protest against injustice. The mentality encouraged by this paradigm was reinforced by the Shiis' minority status and discrimination against them through the centuries.

It sustained the community throughout history and became a major source of inspiration and mobilization during Iran's "Islamic" revolution of 1978–79.

Sunni Muslims constitute 85 percent and Shiah approximately 15 percent of the global Islamic community. Although united in their common confession of faith in God, the Quran, and the Prophet Muhammad, their notions of leadership and history differ.

The reality of the dynastic Umayyad and Abbasid caliphates notwithstanding, in Sunni Islam, the caliph ideally is the selected or elected successor of the Prophet. He serves only, however, as political, military leader of the community, not as prophet. In Shiah Islam, the imam, or leader, is not selected from among the members of the community but must be a direct descendant of the Prophet's family. He is not only the political but also the religiopolitical leader of the community. Though not a prophet, he is the divinely inspired, sinless, infallible, final authoritative interpreter of God's will as formulated in Islamic law.

Sunni and Shiah also developed differing interpretations of history. For Sunni, the early success of Islam and the power of its rulers were signs of God's guidance, rewards to a faithful community that were seen as historic validation of Muslim belief and claims. In contrast, the Shiah saw the same events as the illegitimate usurpation of power by Sunni rulers. Therefore, for Shiah history is the theater for the struggle of a minority community, righteous, but historically oppressed and disinherited, who must restore God's rule on earth under his imam.

PREMODERN ISLAM: THE CLASSICAL ERA

A critical issue faced by all religious believers today is the connection or continuity of current religious practice with centuries-old sacred traditions. Muslim believers tend to legitimate or justify their belief and practice, or their calls for renewal and reform, in light of their Islamic tradition and heritage.

Law and Mysticism: The Outer and Inner Paths to God

Dissatisfaction with Umayyad rule, in which wealth led to abuse of power and corruption, resulted in the development of two nonrevolutionary reform movements or institutions: the ulama (religious scholars, or learned ones), with their Islamic law, and the Sufis, whose Islamic mysticism we shall discuss later.

In contrast to Christianity's emphasis on doctrine or theology, Islam, like Judaism, places primary emphasis on what believers should do, on religious observance and obedience of God's law. Muslims are commanded by the Quran to strive or struggle (the literal word for struggle is "jihad") in the path (sharia) of God, to realize, spread, and defend God's message and community.

The faithful are to function as God's vicegerents or representatives on earth, promoting the good and prohibiting evil (Q. 3:104, 3:110). All Muslims are responsible as individuals and as a community for the creation of the good society. The good will enjoy eternal happiness in heaven, and the evil will suffer eternal damnation in hell. Despite vast cultural differences, Islamic law has provided an idealized blueprint that has instilled among Muslims throughout the ages a common code of behavior and a sense of religious identity.

The development of Islamic law during the Umayyad dynasty in the eighth and ninth centuries was a response to real religious and political concerns and issues. Law was standardized by legal experts, with a view to taking control out of the hands of the caliph or his appointed judges. Law continued to flourish during the tenth century under the Abbasid caliphs, who overthrew the Umayyads and legitimated their revolution by becoming the patrons of Islam and Islamic law. It is important to note that law did not develop primarily from the practice of courts or from government decrees but through the interpretation of scholars, the ulama who set out a religious ideal or blueprint based upon four official sources of Islamic law: The Quran, the Sunnah, *qiyas,* and *ijma.*

The Quran, the very word of God, is the primary material source of Islamic law, God's will for humankind: "Here is a plain statement to men, a guidance and instruction to those who fear God" (Q. 3:138). The Quran contains approximately eighty proscriptions that would rank as legal in the strict sense of the term, but the majority of Quranic texts provide general principles and values, reflecting what the aims and aspirations of Muslims should be.

The Sunnah (example) of the Prophet comes from the Quran, early biographies, and especially prophetic traditions, the richest sources of information about Muhammad and his times. The Sunnah consists of the volumes of hundreds of thousands of narrative stories or reports (*hadith*) about what the Prophet said and did. The material seemingly covers every situation. The centrality of the Sunnah and hadith, yesterday and today, cannot be over estimated. As a distinguished contemporary Muslim scholar has noted: "They are associated with the person who is 'alive' here and now and who is as revered and loved by all Muslims now as he was fourteen centuries ago."[3]

The third source of law, qiyas, means analogical reasoning. When confronted by a question or issue not addressed specifically and clearly, in the Quran or Sunnah, jurists looked for similar, or analogous, portions of scripture to identify principles that could be applied to a new case. For example, there is no specific text dealing with the use of mind-altering drugs, but from qiyas, jurists can justify the condemnation of such substances on the basis of sacred texts that plainly forbid the consumption of alcohol.

Finally, ijma, or *consensus* in theory was based on a statement traditionally attributed to the Prophet: "My community will never agree on an error." In reality, consensus has generally amounted to acceptance or consensus about an issue from the majority of religious scholars who represented religious authority.

The two main divisions of Islamic law concern a Muslim's duties to God (*ibadat*), which consist of obligatory practices such as the Five Pillars of

Islam, and duties to others (*muamalat*), which include regulations governing public life, from contract and international law to laws on marriage, divorce, and inheritance.

Islamic law is a source of unity and guidance, but individual jurists and legal scholars from diverse social backgrounds and cultural contexts have ever differed in their interpretation of texts, in their personal opinions, and in their notions of equity and public welfare. Acceptance of contrasting views is reflected in a doctrine that acknowledged the validity of different (*ikhtilaf*) opinions.

We see these differences in official legal opinions or interpretations (*fatwas*) of legal experts (*muftis*) who advised judges and litigants in recent times. Salman Rushdie, the author of *The Satanic Verses*, a novel, was condemned to death by a fatwa from the Iranian Ayatollah Ruholla Khomeini, who found Rushdie guilty of blasphemy. With a price on his head, Rushdie went into hiding. Some muftis, however, while deploring the book, called for the writer to be tried by Islamic law. In the Gulf War of 1991, some muftis supported Iraq and others supported a U.S.-led armada that included troops from Egypt, Kuwait, and Saudi Arabia. Similarly, sharp differences have existed among religious leaders over the religious legitimacy or illegitimacy of suicide bombing in Israel–Palestine. However different and contentious interpretations of Islam have been throughout Islamic history, the Five Pillars of Islam unite all Muslims in their worship and following of God.

For many years, Islam and other religions were suppressed and persecuted in Albania by a communist regime that declared the state officially atheist in 1967. Many mosques in this Muslim, majority country were closed or destroyed, and religious symbols were banned. In 1990 the ban was lifted, and this and other mosques were rededicated and opened.

The Five Pillars of Islam

If God, the Quran, and the Prophet Muhammad unite all Muslims in their common belief, the Five Pillars of Islam provide a unity of practice in the midst of the community's rich diversity.

1. *The Declaration of Faith.* A Muslim is one who bears witness that "There is no God but the God and Muhammad is the messenger of God." One need only make this simple statement, known as the *shahadah*, to become a Muslim. The first part of the shahadah affirms Islam's absolute monotheism, an unshakable and uncompromising faith in the oneness or unity (*tawhid*) of God. The second part is the affirmation that Muhammad is the messenger of God, the last and final prophet, who serves as a model for the Muslim community.

   The action or doing orientation of Islam is illustrated by the remaining four pillars or duties.

2. *Prayer.* Five times a day (dawn, noon, midafternoon, sunset, and evening), Muslims throughout the world are called to worship God. In many cities of the world, the quiet of the night or daily noise of busy city streets is pierced by the call of the *muezzin* from atop the tower (*minaret*) of the mosque: God is Most Great (Allahu Akbar)!, God is Most Great!

I witness that there is no god but God (Allah) . . .
I witness that Muhammad is the Messenger of God . . .
Come to prayer . . . come to salvation . . .
God is Most Great! God is Most Great! There is no god
but God!

Prayer (*salat*) is preceded by a series of ablutions to cleanse the body and to symbolize the purity of mind and body required for worshiping God. Facing the holy city of Mecca, Islam's spiritual homeland where the Prophet was born and received God's revelation, Muslims recall the revelation of the Quran and reinforce a sense of belonging to a single, worldwide community of believers. Muslims may pray in any appropriate place wherever they happen to be: at home, in an airport, on the road. They may do so as individuals or in a group. For Muslims, salat is an act of worship and adoration of God and remembrance of his word, not one of request or petition.

On Friday, the noon prayer is a congregational prayer that usually takes place in a mosque (*masjid*, "place of prostration"). A special feature of the Friday prayer is a sermon (*khutba*), preached from a pulpit (*minbar*). Since there is no priesthood in Islam, any Muslim may lead the prayer. In many communities, larger mosques do have an imam who leads the prayer and is paid to look after the mosque.

3. *Almsgiving.* The third pillar of Islam is the *zakat*, almsgiving. As all Muslims share equally in their obligation to worship God, so too they all are duty bound to attend to the social welfare of their community by redressing economic inequalities. This is accomplished through an annual contribution of 2.5 percent of one's accumulated wealth and assets, not just

These Uzbek Muslims, like fellow believers across the world, perform their prayers five times each day.

Breaking the fast of Ramadan. Muslims are required to abstain from food and drink from dawn to dusk during the month of Ramadan. At dusk each day during Ramadan, families gather to break the fast and share a meal. This practice is called "breakfast."

on income. Strictly speaking, zakat is not charity, since almsgiving is not seen as voluntary but as a duty imposed by God, an act of spiritual purification and solidarity. Just as the Quran condemns economic exploitation, it warns against those who accumulate wealth and fail to assist others (Q. 3:180). Those who have benefited from God's bounty, who have received their wealth as a trust from God, are required to look after the needs of the less fortunate members of the Muslim community.

In most countries, Muslims determine to whom they will pay the zakat. However, in recent years, some governments such as those of Pakistan, Sudan, and Iran, in the name of creating a more Islamic state, have collected and distributed the zakat. This has proved to be a point of contention, for some charge that the central government misappropriates funds, and others prefer to have the freedom to distribute it themselves to needy relatives, friends, or neighbors.

4. *The Fast of Ramadan.* Muslims are required to fast during Ramadan, the ninth month of Islam's lunar calendar. From dawn to dusk, all healthy Muslims must abstain from food, drink, and sex. The primary emphasis is less on abstinence and self-mortification as such than on spiritual self-discipline, reflection, and the performance of good works.

The fast is broken at the end of the day by a light meal, called breakfast. In the evening, families exchange visits and share foods and sweets that are served only at this time of the year. The month of Ramadan comes to an end with a great celebration, the Feast of the Breaking of the Fast, Id al-Fitr, one of the great religious holy days and holidays of the Muslim calendar. Family members come from near and far to feast and exchange gifts in a celebration that lasts for three days.

5. *Pilgrimage to Mecca.* The pilgrimage season follows Ramadan. Every adult Muslim who is physically and financially able is expected to perform the pilgrimage (*hajj*) to Mecca in Saudi Arabia at least once in his or her lifetime. Those who are able may go more often. Just as Muslims are united five times each day as they face Mecca in worship, each year believers make the physical journey to this spiritual center of Islam, where they again experience the unity, breadth, and diversity of the Islamic community. In the twenty-first century almost 2 million Muslims gather annually from every part of the globe in Saudi Arabia for the hajj.

The focus of the pilgrimage is the Kaaba, the cube-shaped House of God that Muslim tradition teaches was originally built by the prophet Ibrahim (Abraham) and his son Ismail to honor God. The black stone is believed to have been given to Abraham by the angel Gabriel. Thus the stone is a symbol of God's covenant with Ismail and, by extension, with the Muslim community. Like salat, the pilgrimage requires ritual purification; no jewelry, perfume, or sexual activity is permitted. Pilgrims wear white garments, symbolizing for everyone, rich and poor alike, the unity and equality of all believers before God.

As the pilgrims near Mecca, they shout: "I am here, O Lord, I am here!" When they reach Mecca, they proceed to the Grand Mosque that houses the Kaaba. There they pray at the spot where Abraham, the patriarch and father of monotheism, stood, and they circumambulate the Kaaba seven times. Another part of the hajj is a visit to the Plain of Arafat, the site of Muhammad's last sermon, where pilgrims seek God's forgiveness for their sins and for those of all Muslims throughout the world.

The pilgrimage ends with the celebration of the Feast of Sacrifice (Id al-Adha). The "great feast" commemorates God's testing of Abraham by commanding him to sacrifice his son Ismail (in the Jewish and Christian traditions it is Isaac who is put at risk). Commemorating God's final permission to Abraham to substitute a ram for his son, Muslims sacrifice animals (sheep, goats, cattle) not only in Mecca but across the Muslim world. While some of the meat is consumed, most is distributed to the poor. The three-day Feast of Sacrifice is a time for rejoicing, prayer, and visiting with family and friends.

The Kaaba. The pilgrimage (hajj) to Mecca, one of the Five Pillars of Islam, takes place during the first ten days of the twelfth month of the lunar calendar. The focus of the pilgrimage is the Kaaba, "the cube," also known as the House of God, which tradition says was built by Abraham and his son Ismail. Pilgrims circumambulate the Kaaba, located within the Great Mosque of Meccaa. This is a ritual act that many believe symbolizes the angels' circling of God's throne in heaven.

Jihad: The Struggle for God

Jihad, "to strive or struggle," is sometimes referred to as the sixth pillar of Islam, although it has no such official status. In its most general meaning, jihad refers to the obligation incumbent upon all Muslims, as individuals and as a community, to exert (jihad) themselves to realize God's will, to lead a virtuous life, to fulfill the universal mission of Islam, and to spread the Islamic community through preaching Islam to convert others or writing religious tracts ("jihad of the tongue" and "jihad of the pen"). Thus, today it can be used to describe the personal struggle to keep the fast of Ramadan, to lead a good life, to fulfill family responsibilities. Popularly it is used to describe the struggle for educational or social reform—to establish good schools, to clean up a neighborhood, to fight drugs, or to work for social justice. However, it also includes the struggle for or defense of Islam, holy war. Although jihad is not supposed to include aggressive warfare, this tactic has been invoked by early extremists like the Karajites, by rulers to justify their wars of conquest and expansion, and by contemporary extremists such as Osama bin Laden and his jihad against America as well as jihadi organizations in Lebanon, the Persian Gulf, and Indonesia.

Women and Muslim Family Law

Few topics have received more popular attention than women and the family. If many Muslims speak of Islam as liberating women, others in the West as well as in Muslim countries decry the continuing oppression of women. The position of Muslim women must be viewed within the dual context of their status in Islamic law and the politics and culture of their societies. Islamic law itself reflects both the Quranic concern for the rights and protection of women and the family (the greater part of its legislation is devoted to these issues), and the traditions of the male-dominated society within which Islamic law was developed.

The Quran introduced reforms affecting the status of women both through new regulations and by teachings that led to the modification of prevailing customs. The Quran recognized a woman's rights to contract marriage, to receive and keep her dowry, and to own and inherit property. No equivalent rights existed in Christianity or in Judaism during or long after the lifetime of the Prophet. In fact, women in the West did not gain inheritance rights until the nineteenth century. These Quranic reforms and others would become the basis for Muslim family law.

As the Five Pillars are the core of a Muslim's duty to worship God (ibadat), family law is central to Islam's social laws (muamalat). Indeed, Muslim family law has often been described as the heart of the sharia, reflecting the importance of the family in Islam. Because of the centrality of the community in Islam and the role of the family as the basic unit of society, family law has enjoyed pride of place in the development of Islamic law and in its implementation throughout history. Similarly, though the emergence of modern Muslim states has often seen the adoption of Western-oriented civil and commercial laws or legal systems, in most countries Muslim family law has remained in force. While in some countries family law has been reformed rather than replaced, often this reform has generated considerable conflict and debate. In the 1980s, the resurgence of Islam was often accompanied by attempts to return to the use of classical family law and to reverse modern reforms. Thus today, as in the past, the subject of women and the family remains an important and extremely sensitive subject in Muslim societies.

The status of women and the family in Muslim family law is the product of many factors: Arab culture, Quranic reforms, foreign ideas and values assimilated from conquered peoples, and the interpretation of male jurists in a patriarchal society. Regulations developed in the early centuries of Islamic history regarding marriage, divorce, inheritance, and bequests have guided Muslim societies, determining attitudes toward women and the family.

The Quran teaches that men and women are equal before God in terms of their religious and moral obligations and rewards (Q. 33:35). However, husbands and wives are seen as fulfilling complementary roles, based on differing characteristics, capacities, and dispositions and their traditional roles in the patriarchal family. Men function in the public sphere, the "outside" world; they are responsible for the financial support and protection of the family.

A woman's primary role is that of wife and mother; she is responsible for the management of the household, raising her children and supervising their religious/moral training. In light of women's more sheltered and protected status and men's greater experience in public life and broader responsibilities, the Quran (and Islamic law) teaches that wives are subordinate to husbands (Q. 2:228), and in Islamic law the testimony of one man is worth that of two women. Similarly, because men in a patriarchal system were responsible for the economic well-being of all women and other dependents in the extended family, the male portion of inheritance was twice that of a female.

Marriage is a primary institution in Islam, regarded as incumbent upon all Muslims. It is a civil contract or covenant, not a sacrament. It safeguards chastity and the growth and stability of the family, legalizing intercourse and the procreation of children. Reflecting the centrality of the family and the identity and role of individual family members, marriage is not simply an agreement between two people but between two families. Thus, marriages arranged by the two families or by a guardian are traditional, although the majority of jurists agreed that a woman should not be forced to marry a man against her will.

Many non-Muslims are ignorant or unaware of Quranic reforms affecting women; indeed, most equate Islam with polygamy, or more accurately, polygyny. The Quran explicitly permits a man to marry four wives, while in the same verse (Q. 43) noting that if all cannot be supported and treated equally, then only one is permitted. The purpose of this provision is not to discourage all men from practicing monogamy but to afford protection to unmarried women, as well as to limit and regulate the unfettered rights of men. Islamic modernists in recent years have used this same spirit and another verse ("You are never able to be fair and just between women if that is your ardent desire," Q. 4:129) to argue that the Quranic ideal is monogamy and that plural marriages should be restricted or eliminated. In particular they note that the original revelation was given to a premodern community in which losses in battle left many widows who needed protection. More important, many maintain that the demands of modern life make it extraordinarily difficult for any man to provide equally for more than one wife, especially in terms of time and affection.

Islamic law, reflecting the spirit of the Quran (Q. 4:35) and a saying of the Prophet ("of all the permitted things divorce is the most abominable"), regards divorce as permissible but reprehensible. One authoritative legal manual calls divorce: "a dangerous and disapproved procedure . . . nor is its propriety at all admitted, but on the ground of urgency of relief from an unsuitable wife."[4] Islamic law itself, as if to underscore the seriousness of divorce, prescribes that a man must pronounce the words or formula of divorce three separate times to make it irrevocable.

The strong influence of custom can be seen in the more limited rights to divorce afforded women. The Quran had declared: "Women have rights similar to those (of men) over them; while men stand above them" (Q. 2:228). For example, while the ulama extended more limited divorce rights to women, in contrast to men women had to go to court and present grounds for divorce far more specific than unsuitability; they were limited to charges like physical abuse, abandonment, and failure to provide adequate maintenance. Beginning in the 1920s, some Muslim governments relaxed these and other legal restrictions on women.

Historically, divorce rather than polygamy has proved to be the more serious social problem, especially since women have often been ignorant of their legal rights or unable to exercise them in male-dominated social environments. Historically, a woman's Quranic and legal rights to contract and dissolve her own marriage, to receive and control her dowry, or to inherit often disappeared under the pressures and mores of strong patriarchal societies. Thus custom tended to prevail over Islamic law as well as the letter and spirit of the Quran.

A major example of the interaction of custom and scripture is the veiling or covering and seclusion (*purdah*) of women. These customs, assimilated by Islamic practice from the conquered Persian and Byzantine empires, have been viewed by many, though certainly not all, as appropriate expressions of Quranic principles and values. The Quran does not stipulate the veiling and seclusion of women, although it does say that the wives of the Prophet should speak to men from behind a partition. It tells women to dress and behave modestly (Q. 24:30–31), but the admonition applies to men, as well.

Veiling and seclusion have varied considerably across Muslim societies and in different historical periods. Originally veiling had been meant to protect women in upper-class urban surroundings, where they enjoyed mobility and opportunities to socialize. Village and rural women were slower to adopt the measure, which interfered with their ability to work in the fields.

Over the centuries, as the practices of veiling and seclusions spread, there were deleterious effects upon the status of women religiously and socially. The institution of purdah served to cut off many women's access to the mosque, the social and educational center of the community, an isolation that further lowered their status. Poorer women were often restricted to small houses with limited social contacts. The serious negative impact of purdah in modern times was attested to in the 1940s by an Egyptian scholar and religious leader who bore the name of a distinguished predecessor. The twentieth-century Muhammad al-Ghazali (d. 1996) said: "Ninety percent of our women do not pray at all; nor do they know of the other duties of Islam other than their names."[5]

Although debate rages today in many Muslim societies about the status and character of "the Muslim woman," with greater opportunities for women's education and employment have come reforms to address the inequities of some Muslim laws that affect women only. Modernizing governments from the 1920s to the 1960s reformed Muslim family laws in marriage, divorce, and inheritance.

Reforms included measures that restricted a male's right to unilaterally divorce his wife as well as to practice polygyny. In fact, a wife was permitted to specify in her marriage contract that a husband must obtain her permission before taking another wife. A wife's grounds for divorce were increased, as well. These reforms were partial and were imposed from above through legislation. They were often resisted or reluctantly accepted by the ulama. Moreover, with the resurgence of Islam, more conservative religious forces and many Islamic activists have rejected family law reforms as Western inspired, calling instead for a return to classical Islamic laws and seeking to again limit and control women's role in society.

The Interior Path: Islamic Mysticism

Islamic mysticism, like Islamic law, began as a reform movement. With the phenomenal success of Islam uniting the tribes of Arabia and conquering the Byzantine and Persian empires, the ummah entered another phase in its development. In a new capital, Damascus, the Umayyad caliphs set up a court characterized by an imperial lifestyle and material luxuries. Increasingly, pious Muslims in many locations saw these changes as evidence that God and submission to his will were being replaced in the royal courts of dynastic rulers by concerns for power and wealth. To counter this trend, the critics began to study the Quran and traditions of the Prophet, and the performance of religious duties, in a spirit of asceticism that rejected the comforts of the material world and reemphasized the centrality of God and the Last Judgment.

The term "Sufism" comes from the coarse woolen garment (*suf*, "wool") worn by many of these early ascetics. The reformers did not reject the world so much as dependence on the things of this world; they did not wish to allow creation to obscure the Creator, or to forget the Absolute Reality in the course of being swept along and away from God by material realities. Desiring a more faithful return to the purity and simplicity of the Prophet's time, men and women pursued a path of self-denial and good works. The Sufis were known for detachment from the material world, which they viewed as ephemeral, a transient distraction from the divine; repentance for sins; fear of God and the Last Judgment; and selfless devotion to the fulfillment of God's will.

Over the years, a variety of ascetic and ritual practices were adopted as part of the mystic way, including fasting, poverty, silence, and celibacy. Among the Sufi techniques to "remember" God, who is always present in the world, are rhythmic repetition of God's name and breathing exercises that focus consciousness on God and place the devotee in the presence of God. Music and song as well as dance are also used to express deep feelings of love of God, to feel or experience his nearness, and to show devotion to God and Muhammad. The most well-known use of dance is that of Turkey's "whirling dervishes," who circle their master to imitate the divinely ordained motions of the universe.

Turkish Sufi order (Mawlawi Tariqah), founded by Jalal al-Din Rumi (d. 1273), one of the most famous Sufi mystics. These men are popularly known as "whirling dervishes" because of one of their meditation rituals, a dance in which they revolve to the music of Sufi songs.

One popular practice of Sufism is the veneration of Muhammad and Sufi saints as intermediaries between God and humanity. Despite the official Islamic belief that Muhammad was only a human being and not a miracle worker, his central role as the ideal model of Muslim life had generated stories of the Prophet's extraordinary powers. In Sufism these stories mushroomed and were extended to Sufi saints, the friends (*wali*) or protégés of God, who are said to have had the power to bilocate, cure the sick, multiply food, and read minds. The burial sites or mausoleums of Sufi masters became religious sanctuaries. Pilgrims visited them, offering petitions for success in this life and the next, and miracles were reported.

Though Sufi spirituality complemented the more ritual and legalistic orientation of the ulama and the sharia, the relationship between the two was

The Sufi Path

At the heart of Sufism's worldview and spirituality is the belief that one must die to self to become aware of and live in the presence of God. For guidance in the way Sufis relied on a teacher or master (*shaykh* or *pir*), one whose authority was based on direct personal religious experience. The master leads his or her disciples through the successive stages of renunciation of the transient phenomenal world, purification, and insight. Along the way, God is believed to reward and encourage the disciple through special blessings and certain religious experiences or psychological states.

often tense. The ulama tended to regard Sufi masters and the mystic way as a challenge to their authority and interpretation of Islam. Sufis tended to regard the ulama's legalistic approach to Islam as lesser, incomplete, and subordinate to the Sufi way.

By the eleventh and twelfth centuries, Sufism seemed to be on a collision course with orthodoxy. With the Abbasid Empire apparently unraveling, many feared that Islam was in danger. The universal caliphate at Baghdad had disintegrated into competing states. In the ensuing debates over the relationship of reason and revelation, Muslim philosophers, indebted to Hellenism and Neoplatonism, espoused a rationalism that tested the ulama's belief in the primacy of faith over reason. Sufism had become a mass movement with a strong emotional and devotional component and an eclectic tendency to incorporate local non-Islamic superstitious practices. The majority of the ulama reacted to these challenges to their authority and worldview by condemning both Islamic philosophy and Islamic mysticism in the name of Islamic orthodoxy. At this critical juncture a prominent Islamic scholar, Muhammad al-Ghazali (1058–1111), emerged to save the day.

Al-Ghazali spent many years traveling to major Sufi centers in Arabia and Palestine, practicing and studying Sufism. During this time, he wrote *The Revivification of the Religious Sciences,* in which he showed that law, theology, and mysticism were neither incompatible nor inconsistent with one another. This brilliant tour de force reassured the ulama about the orthodoxy of Sufism and countered the rationalism of the philosophers. In al-Ghazali's great synthesis, law and theology were presented in terms that the ulama could accept, but they were grounded in religious experience and interior devotion (Sufism). Rationalism was tempered by the Sufi emphasis on religious experience and love of God.

One of the great scholars of Islam, al-Ghazali reconciled the ulama and the Sufis, producing a religious synthesis that earned him the title "Renewer (*mujaddid*) of Islam." While the tension between many of the ulama and Sufism continued, and as we shall see in later centuries led to attempts to reform or suppress Sufism, al-Ghazali had secured an important place for Sufism within Islam. Indeed, Sufism in the twelfth century and later swept across much of the Islamic world. Sufi orders became the great missionaries of Islam, and Sufism became integral to everyday popular religious practice and spirituality.

However, the strength of Sufism as a popular religious force also proved to be its weakness. Its flexibility, tolerance, and eclecticism, which enabled it to incorporate local religious practices and values as Islam spread to new regions, also led at times to the indiscriminate incorporation of superstitious and otherwise non-Islamic activities ranging from magic and fetishism to drunkenness and sensuality. Sufism's healthy concern about the dangers in the ulama's religious legalism and ritual formalism gave way to rejection, by some, of the official practices of Islam in favor of a highly individualistic and idiosyncratic brand of devotion. Emphasis on the limits of reason and importance of religious practice and experience devolved into an anti-intellectualism that rejected all Islamic learning and authority and promoted superstition, passivism, and fatalism. Premodern reformers and modernists, both secular and Islamic, have blamed Sufism for the ills of the Muslim world, yet throughout much of the ummah, Sufism has remained a vital spiritual presence and force.

Islam and the State

From Muhammad's establishment of the first Muslim community at Medina in 622 CE and down through the centuries, the faith of Islam became a central force in the development of state and society. The soldiers, traders, and Sufis of Islam spread God's word and rule, creating a vast land or region of Islam (*dar al-Islam*). The caliphate with its centralized Islamic empires, the Umayyad (661–750) and Abbasid (750–1250) dynasties, was followed by an extensive series of Muslim sultanates extending from Timbuktu in Africa to Mindanao in Southeast Asia. During this period great medieval Muslim empires emerged: the Ottoman in the Middle East (1281–1924), the Safavid (1501–1722) in Iran, and the Mughal (1483–1857) in South Asia.

However different these empires and sultanate states, Islam constituted the basic framework for their political and social life. Islam provided legitimation, a religiopolitical ideology, and law, informing the state's political, legal,

The Taj Mahal, the mausoleum built (1631–47) by the grief-stricken emperor Shah Jahan for his beloved wife Mumtaz Mahal, who died in childbirth. Situated in a 42-acre garden, it is flanked by two perfectly proportioned mosque complexes. This crowning achievement, landmark of world architecture, symbolizes the wealth and splendor of the Mughal Empire. The project brought together craftsmen and calligraphers from the Islamic world who worked with Muslim and Hindu craftsmen from the empire.

educational, and social institutions. The caliph or sultan, as head of state, was seen as the political successor of Muhammad. Though not a prophet, he was the protector of the faith who was to implement Islamic law and to spread Islamic rule. The ulama were the guardians of religion, its interpreters, and as such often served as advisers to caliphs and sultans. They were not an ordained clergy, nor were they associated with organized "congregations." Rather, they were a major intellectual and social force or class in society. They played a primary role in the state's religious, legal, educational, and social service institutions. The ulama were by this time theologians and legal experts, responsible for the application of the law and the administration of sharia courts. They ran the schools and universities that trained those who aspired to public as well as religious office. They administered funds that were applied to a broad range of services from the construction and maintenance of mosques, schools, student hostels, and hospitals to roads and bridges. In time, they came to constitute a religious establishment alongside and often dependent upon the political establishment. Indeed, in many empires the ruler appointed a senior religious leader, Shaykh al-Islam, as head of religious affairs, a post that exists in many Muslim countries today.

In an Islamic state, citizenship, or perhaps more accurately degree of citizenship, was also based on religious affiliation. Muslims were full citizens, enjoying all the rights and duties of this position. As discussed earlier, Jews and Christians, as People of the Book, were also citizens, but had the status of protected people (dhimmi). Islam also informed the international relations of the state. The spread of Islam as a faith and a religiopolitical system was legitimated by the Quran and by the teaching and example of Muhammad. Muslims sought to create a "Pax Islamica," much like the "Pax Romana" and what U.S. policy makers would later speak of as a "Pax Americana." Conquest and diplomacy, force, persuasion, preaching, and alliances were its means.

The obligation to strive (jihad) to follow and realize God's will entailed opposition to evil and injustice and included jihad as an armed struggle to defend Islam or the community and to spread Muslim rule and empire. As such, jihad became part and parcel of Islam's doctrine of war and peace. As Islamic empires spread, non-Muslims were offered three options: to convert to Islam, to become "protected people" and pay a poll tax, or to become enemies to be fought.

For the believer, the role of Islam in state and society was mirrored in the continuum of Muslim rule, power, and success from the time of the Prophet Muhammad to the dawn of European colonialism. Despite the contradictions of life, civil wars, impious rulers, and dynastic usurpers, the presence and continuity of an Islamic ideology and system, however different the reality might at times be from the ideal, validated and reinforced a sense of a divinely mandated and guided community with a purpose and mission. Thus for many Muslims the history of Islam is that of a vibrant, dynamic, and expansive faith. Islam and Muslim rule were extended over major areas of Africa; the Middle East; South, Southeast, and Central Asia; Spain; and southern Italy. As a result, Sunni Muslim history contains the belief that following the

Islamic community's divine mandate to spread God's guidance and governance will lead to prosperity and power in this life as well as the promise of eternal life in heaven.

Islam and the West (Christendom): The Crusades

Despite common religious roots and instances of cooperation, the history of Islam and Western Christendom has been marked more by confrontation than by peaceful coexistence and dialogue. For the Christian West, Islam is seen as the religion of the sword; for many Muslims, the spirit of the Christian West was epitomized first by the Crusades and centuries later by a movement seen as largely equivalent, European colonialism.

Unlike Judaism or any other world religion, Islam constituted an effective theological and political challenge to Christendom and its hegemonic ambitions. Muslim armies overran the Byzantine Empire, Spain, and the Mediterranean from Sicily to Anatolia. At the same time, Islam challenged Christian religious claims and authority. Islam appropriated Christianity's insistence that the New Testament describes a new covenant and revelation superseding that of the Jews. Rather, Muslims claimed, there had been a third major stage in God's revelation, a third covenant. Therefore, Christians and Jews should acknowledge that they had corrupted their original revelations from God and that the one, true God in his mercy had sent his revelation one final and complete time to Muhammad. Islam now claimed to have a divinely mandated universal mission to call all to worship God and to join the Islamic community and live under Islamic rule. From the seventh to the eleventh centuries, Islam spread rapidly, extending Muslim rule over Christian territories and winning Christian hearts, in time creating large numbers of converts. Christianity and Islam were on a collision course.

By the eleventh century, Christendom's response to Islam was twofold: the struggle to reconquer Andalusia Spain (1000–1492), where the coexistence of Muslims, Christians, and Jews had produced a cultural florescence, and the undertaking of the Crusades (1095–1453).

Jerusalem had been taken by Arab armies in 638. Thereafter, for five centuries, Muslims lived in peaceful coexistence with Christians and with Jews. Although banned by Christian rulers, Jews were permitted by Muslims to return to live and worship in the city of Solomon and David. However, in the eleventh century political events and an imperial–papal power play that pitted

Courtyard of the Lions, Alhambra Palace, the fourteenth-century residence of the Nasrid dynasty in Granada, Spain. One of the remarkable monuments remaining from the several centuries of Muslim rule in Andalusia, when Muslims, Jews, and Christians coexisted and produced a high culture.

Christendom against Islam began a period of misunderstanding and distrust that has spanned nearly a millennium.

In 1071, the Byzantine emperor Alexius I, whose army had been decisively defeated by a Seljuq (Abbasid) army, feared that all Asia Minor would be overrun. He called upon other Christian rulers and the pope to come to the aid of his capital, Constantinople, by undertaking a "pilgrimage" or crusade to free Jerusalem and its environs from Muslim rule. For the leader of the Western church, Pope Urban II, Jerusalem provided an opportunity to gain recognition of papal authority and the pontiff's role in legitimating the actions of temporal rulers. In addition, Christian rulers, knights, and merchants were driven by the promise of booty, as well as trade, and banking opportunities, coming from the creation of a Latin kingdom in the Middle East. This enthusiastic response to the call for help by Alexius served to unite a divided Christendom, in a holy war against the "infidel," ostensibly to liberate the holy city. The appeal to religion captured the popular mind and gained its support. This was ironic because as one scholar has observed, "God may have indeed wished it, but there is certainly no evidence that the Christians of Jerusalem did, or that anything extraordinary was occurring to pilgrims there to prompt such a response at that time in history."[6]

Few events have had a more shattering and long-lasting effect on Muslim–Christian relations than the Crusades. Three myths pervade Western perceptions of the Crusades: that Muslims were the protagonists; that Christendom triumphed; and that the sole purpose of the Crusades was to liberate Jerusalem. In fact, the Crusades were launched by Urban II and secular Christian rulers for causes as much political and economic as religious, and on balance Muslims prevailed.

For Muslims, the collective memory of the Crusades lives on as the clearest example of militant Christianity, an early harbinger of the aggression and imperialism of the Christian West, a vivid reminder of Christianity's early hostility toward Islam. If many regard Islam as a religion of the sword, Muslims down through the ages speak of the West's Crusader mentality and ambitions. While historians in the West speak of Richard the Lion Hearted, Muslims remember Richard as the conqueror who in 1099, having promised to spare women and children, took Jerusalem and slaughtered all its Muslim inhabitants on the way to establishing the Latin kingdom. They contrast the behavior of the King of England with that of Salah al-Din (Saladin), the great Muslim general, who in reconquering the holy city in 1187, spared noncombatants.

By the fifteenth century the Crusades had spent their force. Although ostensibly launched to unite Christendom and turn back Muslim armies, the opposite had occurred. One unintended result of the Crusades was the deterioration of the position of Christian minorities in the Holy Land. These minorities had had rights and privileges under Muslim rule, but, after the establishment of the Latin Kingdom, they found themselves treated as "loathsome schismatics." In an effort to obtain relief from persecution by their fellow Christians, many abandoned their beliefs, and adopted either Roman

Catholicism, or—the supreme irony—Islam.[7] Amid a bitterly divided Christendom, the Byzantine capital, Constantinople, fell in 1453 to Muslim armies, was renamed Istanbul, and became the seat of the Ottoman Empire.

For Muslim–Christian relations, what actually happened in the Crusades is less important than how the period has been remembered. Each community (Islam and Christianity) sees the other as militant holy warriors, somewhat barbaric and fanatic in their religious zeal, determined to conquer, convert, or eradicate the other, and thus an enemy of God—an obstacle and threat to the realization of God's will. As we shall see, the history of their contention continued through the next wave of European colonialism and finally in the superpower rivalry that began in the twentieth century.

How do we get from a centuries-long history of Muslim vitality, creativity, power, and success vis-à-vis the West to a time in which much of the Muslim world is part of the developing rather than the developed world? How do we get from the confrontations of the past, on the one hand, and the coexistence and tolerance of Andalusia, on the other, to contemporary concerns about a clash of civilizations? Why is Islam equated by many with violence, religious extremism, and terrorism: from hostage taking and hijackings to holy wars, assassinations, and bombings?

Understanding Islam today requires an appreciation of key historical events from the eighteenth to the twentieth centuries as well as of the causes and nature of premodern and modern reform movements. Sacred texts and long-held religious beliefs, combined with the specific sociopolitical contexts of Muslim communities, have been critical factors in producing a diversity of Muslim experiences and interpretations of Islam.

Premodern Revivalist Movements

From the eighteenth to the twentieth centuries, the Islamic world witnessed a protracted period of upheaval and renewal. In many countries Muslim societies, already threatened by European colonialism, failed and declined for internal reasons, as well. Such crises sparked responses from religious social/political revivalist movements that quite literally spanned the breadth of the Islamic world: from the Mahdi in the Sudan, the Sanusi in Libya, the Fulani in Nigeria, the Wahhabi in Saudi Arabia, to the Padri in Indonesia. Though their political and socioeconomic conditions varied, all were concerned about the religious, political, and social disintegration of Islam, and all were convinced that the cure for the societies was a renewal of the Islamic way of life.

Islamic revivalist movements draw on a long and rich history and tradition of revival (*tajdid*) and reform (*islah*). Throughout Islamic history, the failures of and threats to Muslim societies have given rise to individual reformers and to reformist movements led by scholars or mystics. Islamic revival and reform involve a call for a return to the fundamentals, the Quran and Sunnah, and the right to interpret (*ijtihad,* or use of independent judgment) these primary sources of Islam.

Geometric design plays a major role in Islamic art. Artists use circles, triangles, hexagons, and squares to create ornate patterns to express and reinforce the unity of the Islamic world vision. This striking illustration comes from a Moroccan Quran tablet.

Islah is a Quranic term (Q. 7:170, 11:117, 28:19) that describes the vocation and activities of prophets. As in Judaism and Christianity, prophets are reformers who call upon wayward or sinful communities to return to God's path. Thus, Muslim reformers called for the realignment of individual and community life with the norms of the sharia. This Quranic mandate, coupled with God's command (Q. 3:104, 110) to enjoin good and prohibit evil, provides the time-honored rationale for Islamic reformism.

The tradition of renewal (tajdid) is based on a saying of the Prophet that "God will send to this umma at the head of each century those who will renew its faith for it."[8] That is, at the beginning of each century, many Muslims expect God to send a renewer, or mujaddid, to purify and restore true Islamic practice. A mujaddid like al-Ghazali is able to regenerate a community that over time has strayed or been distracted from the straight path of Islam. In the eighteenth and nineteenth centuries, this belief took on popular religious forms. While such Islamic renewers or revivalists claimed to simply return to the original teachings of the Quran and the Prophet Muhammad, in fact each one produced new religious interpretations and cultural syntheses needed to guide his age. We shall discuss the Wahhabi movement in Arabia and the Mahdiyya in Africa, perhaps the best known of the postmedieval revivalists. Each exerted a formative influence on modern Muslim states: the Wahhabi in what is now Saudi Arabia and the Mahdists in Sudan.

A religious leader, Muhammad ibn Abd al-Wahhab (1703–1792), and a local tribal chief, Muhammad ibn Saud (d. 1765), joined forces to produce a united, militant religiopolitical movement. Ibn Abd al-Wahhab was dismayed by the condition of his society, which he saw as having degenerated to that of pre-Islamic Arabia, the *jahiliyya* or period of ignorance of Islam. He was appalled by such popular religious practices as the veneration of Sufi saints, which he believed compromised the unity or oneness of God, and he was very critical of the Islamic community in Arabia, which had fallen back into tribalism and tribal warfare. He condemned some devotional rituals as idolatry, the worst sin in Islam, and dismissed others as pagan superstitions. Abd al-Wahhab wished to purify Islam from all foreign un-Islamic practices.

The Wahhabi movement waged a rigorous holy war to subdue and once again unite the tribes of Arabia. Muslims who did not go along were declared enemies of God who must be fought. Unlike other revivalist movements, the Wahhabi chose to completely suppress rather than merely reform Sufism.

The Mahdi of the Sudan, on the other hand, was a charismatic Sufi leader who initiated a militant reformist religiopolitical movement. The founder of the Mahdiyya order, whose name was Muhammad Ahmad, proclaimed himself Mahdi ("divinely guided one") in 1881. Thus, he went beyond most other revivalist reformers who claimed the right to interpret Islam and instead said that he was a divinely appointed and inspired representative of God.

The Mahdi established an Islamic community, uniting his followers, who like the Prophet's Companions were called Ansar ("helpers"). He also justified waging holy war against other Muslims, declaring Sudan's Ottoman Muslim rulers infidels who "disobeyed the command of His messenger and His Prophet . . . ruled in a manner not in accord with what God had sent . . . altered the sharia of our master, Muhammad the messenger of God, and blasphemed against the faith of God."[9] During this period, sufism was reformed and alcohol, prostitution, gambling, and music were outlawed as foreign un-Islamic practices that had corrupted society. After a four-year struggle, Mahdist forces overcame Egyptian forces of the Ottoman Empire, and an Islamic state was established in Khartoum in 1885.

ISLAM AND MODERNITY

By the nineteenth century, the internal decline of Muslim societies made them vulnerable to external powers. Sharing the fate of many, they fell victim to European imperialism, which ultimately did much to shape the modern Muslim world politically, economically, and religioculturally. When Europe overpowered North Africa, the Middle East, South Asia, and Southeast Asia in the nineteenth century, reducing most Muslim societies to colonies, many Muslims experienced these defeats as a religious crisis as well as political and cultural setbacks.

Colonialism brought European armies and Christian missionaries, who attributed their conquests not only to their military and economic power, but also to the superiority of Western civilization and the truth inherent in Christianity. The French spoke of a "mission to civilize" and the British of "the white man's burden." Thus the missionaries who accompanied the armies of bureaucrats, soldiers, traders, and teachers were quick to spread the message of the superiority of the culture they represented.

Muslim responses to Europe's political/religious penetration and dominance varied significantly, ranging from resistance or warfare in "defense of Islam" to accommodation to Western values, if not outright assimilation. Some advocated following the example of the Prophet Muhammad, who in the face of rejection and persecution in Mecca chose initially to emigrate from Mecca to Medina and later to fight. However, the military defense of Islam and Muslim territory generally proved fruitless in the face of the large modernized weapons of superior European forces; and emigration to a "safe, independent" Muslim territory was logistically and physically impossible for most.

The response of many Muslim rulers, from Egypt to Iran, was an attempt to emulate or adopt that which had made the West triumphant, its knowledge, science, and technology as well as its culture. From Muhammad Ali, an early nineteenth-century ruler of Egypt, to the shahs of Iran in the twentieth century, the goal was development of modernized societies with modern militaries. Even Muslim rulers who sought an end to Western hegemony seemed convinced of the superiority of the culture and were drawn by its accomplishments and power. Students were sent to the West to study, to learn the sources of its success. "Modern" schools and institutions, based on European models and curricula, were created in many parts of the Muslim world to provide a "modern" education for a new generation. Alongside traditional Islamic schools and great mosque-universities like Egypt's al-Azhar University, new universities, which offered a modern, Western-based curriculum, were founded: Cario University, Baghdad University, Damascus University, and the University of Malaya, among others. As a result, a modern, Westernized elite quickly emerged.

Most members of the modern Mulsim elite, intellectually and culturally influenced by, if not dependent on, the West, regarded the traditional Muslim religious establishment, the ulama or scholars who interpreted Islam, as relics of the past, incapable of inspiring and responding to the demands of the day. Most advocated a Western, secular model of development, and to this end they favored appropriating Western political, economic, and social institutions. In addition, however, they wanted to introduce a process of secularization, entailing separation of church and state and the restriction of religion to private, rather than public, life.

Islamic Modernism

In the late nineteenth and early twentieth centuries, Islamic reformers sought to bridge the gap between conservative religious leaders and modernizing secular elites, to demonstrate that Islam was not incompatible with modernization. Islamic modernists advocated a bold reinterpretation (ijtihad) of religious doctrine and practice in light of the needs of modernizing societies through programs of religious, educational, and social reform. They rejected the tendency of the ulama to cling blindly to past traditions and religious interpretations no less than the indiscriminate Westernization promoted by many secular modernists.

Islamic modernism asserted the compatibility of faith and reason, of Islam and modernity. It provided an Islamic rationale for the reinterpretation of Islamic doctrine and law, for the adoption or adaptation of modern ideas, science, technology, and institutions. Declaring Islam to be a religion of reason, science, and progress, reformers called upon Muslims to reclaim the beliefs, attitudes, and values that had made the Islamic community so successful in the past, contributing to the creation of Islamic empires and a world-class civilization.

Maintaining that the decline of the Muslim community was not due to Islam but to Muslims' departure from the dynamic faith of Muhammad, Islamic reformers advocated a process of purification and reconstruction, of renewal and reform, to overcome what they viewed as the prevailing static medieval religious worldview. Centers of Islamic modernist thought sprang up across the Muslim world from Cairo to Jakarta.

Islamic modernism challenged both the doctrines and the leadership of the conservative religious establishments, rejecting blind acceptance of the authority of the past. These reformers were not traditionally trained religious scholars but modern educated "laymen" who claimed for themselves the right to interpret and reinterpret Islam. They repudiated the authority of the ulama as the sole "keepers of Islam," as well as the tradition that the ulama's legal doctrines/interpretations were binding.

The rationale of Islamic modernism was simple: the corpus of Islamic law consisted, on the one hand, of divinely revealed and thus immutable laws and, on the other, of laws that were human interpretations that met the needs of past historical and social contexts and were therefore subject to change to accommodate modern circumstances and conditions. Thus, they distinguished between the unchanging laws of God (observances governing prayer, fasting, pilgrimage) and social legislation or regulations that were capable of reformulation and change.

Islamic modernism inspired movements for religious reform and national independence but remained primarily attractive only to an intellectual elite. Its major contribution was to provide much of the vocabulary for Islamic reformism and to legitimate a modernist agenda. In particular, it stressed the compatibility of religion and reason, the need for reinterpretation of some traditional sources, and thus the need for religious, political, and social reforms. Islamic modernism provided the precedent for Islamizing "modern" ideas and institutions (from the nation-state and parliamentary government to women's education) as well as the notion that those qualified to interpret Islam should be extended beyond the monopoly exercised historically by the ulama. However, it failed to produce a systematic reinterpretation of Islam or to develop effective organizations to preserve, propagate, and implement its message. These failures contributed to the emergence of Islamic organizations like the Muslim Brotherhood in Egypt and the Islamic Society in South Asia.

Modern Revivalist (Fundamentalist) Movements

The continued presence and power of Europe in the Muslim world and the seeming failure of reformers to effectively block Western political and cultural penetration spawned two major Islamic revivalist movements in the Middle East and South Asia in the 1930s, the Muslim Brotherhood (Ikhwan al-Muslimi) and the Islamic Society (Jamaat-i-Islami). Islamic activist organizations have been the driving force behind the dynamic spread of the contemporary Islamic resurgence. Their trailblazers, Hassan al-Banna (1906–49) and Sayyid Qutb (1906–66) of the Brotherhood and Mawlana Abul Ala Mawdudi (1903–79) of the Jamaat, have had an incalculable impact on the development of Islamic movements throughout the Muslim world. Both movements constructed an ideological worldview based on an interpretation of Islam that informed social and political activism. They are the architects of contemporary Islamic revivalism, men whose ideas and methods have been studied and emulated by scholars and activists from the Sudan to Indonesia.

Hassan al-Banna, a schoolteacher, established the Muslim Brotherhood in Egypt in 1928, and Mawlana Abul Ala Mawdudi, a journalist, organized the Jamaat-i-Islami in India in 1941. Both leaders combined traditional Islamic educational backgrounds with a knowledge of modern Western thought. They believed that their societies were dominated by and dependent on the West, politically and culturally. Both al-Banna and Mawdudi posited an "Islamic alternative" to conservative religious leaders and modern elites, whose orientation was Western and secular. The ulama were generally regarded as passé, a religious class whose fossilized Islam and co-optation by governments was a major reason for the backwardness of the Islamic community. Modernists were seen as having traded away the very soul of Muslim society out of blind admiration for the West.

The Brotherhood and the Jamaat proclaimed Islam to be a self-sufficient, all-encompassing way of life, an ideological alternative to Western capitalism and Marxism. These movements did not simply retreat to the past. Joining thought to action, they provided Islamic responses, ideological and organizational, to their twentieth-century Muslim societies to address such issues as how best to respond to European colonialism and to revitalize the Muslim community and its fortunes. In contrast to Islamic modernists who justified adopting Western ideas and institutions because they were compatible with Islam, al-Banna and Mawdudi sought to produce new interpretation, using Islamic sources.

For Hassan al-Banna and Mawlana Mawdudi, the penetration of the West in education, law, customs, and values, which threatened the very identity and survival of the Muslim community, was far more dangerous in the long run than political intervention.

Though they opposed Westernization, the Brotherhood and the Jamaat were not against modernization per se. They engaged in modern organization and institution building, provided modern educational and social welfare services, and used modern technology and mass communications to spread their message and to mobilize popular support. Their message itself, though rooted in Islamic revelation and sources, was clearly written for a twentieth-century audience. It addressed the problems of modernity as seen through Muslim eyes: government accountability, the relationship of Islam to nationalism, democracy, capitalism, Marxism, modern banking, educational and legal reform, women and work, Zionism, and international relations.

Organizationally, the Brotherhood and the Jamaat believed that, like Muhammad and the early Muslim community in Mecca, they were a vanguard, righteous communities within the broader ummah of Islam. Both organizations recruited followers from mosques, schools, and universities: students, workers, merchants, and young professionals, primarily city dwellers from the lower middle and middle classes. The goal was to produce a new generation of modern educated but Islamically oriented leaders prepared to take their place in every sector of society. However, while al-Banna worked to develop a broad-based populist movement, Mawdudi's Jamaat was an elite religious organization having multiple levels of membership; its primary goal was to train leaders who would come to power.

While al-Banna and Mawdudi viewed an Islamic revolution as necessary to introduce an Islamic state and society, they did not mean a violent political revolution. To establish an Islamic state required first the Islamization of society through a gradual process of social change. Both the Brotherhood and the Jamaat maintained that Muslims should not look to Western capitalism or communism and that faith in the West was misplaced. Western democracy had not only failed to check but also had contributed to authoritarianism, economic exploitation, corruption, and social injustice. These early Islamic activists believed that the inherent fallacy of Western secularism, separation of religion and the state, would be responsible for the moral decline and ultimate downfall of the West. Finally, the Brotherhood maintained that years of Arab subservience to the West had not prevented the West from betraying Arabs by supporting Israeli occupation of Palestine.

Ideological Origins of Contemporary Revivalism

Despite differences, Hassan al-Banna and Mawlana Mawdudi shared the following ideological worldview based on an historical tradition that has inspired and guided many contemporary reform movements.

1. Islam is a comprehensive way of life, a total, all-embracing ideology for personal and public life, for state and society.

2. The Quran, God's revelation, and the example (Sunnah) of the Prophet Muhammad are its foundations.

3. Islamic law (the sharia, the "path" of God), based upon the Quran and Sunnah, is the sacred blueprint for Muslim life.

4. Faithfulness to the Muslim's vocation to reestablish God's sovereignty or rule through implementation of God's law results in success, power, and wealth of the Islamic community (ummah) in this life as well as eternal reward in the next.

5. Muslim societies fail and become subservient to others because they have strayed from God's divinely revealed path, following the secular, materialistic ideologies and values of the West or of the East—capitalism or Marxism.

6. Restoration of Muslim pride, identity, power, and rule (the past glory of Islamic empires and civilization) requires a return to Islam, the reimplementation of God's law, and the acceptance of God's guidance for state and society.

7. Science and technology must be harnessed and used within an Islamically oriented and guided context to avoid the Westernization and secularization of Muslim society.

Radical Islam

The worldviews and interpretations of Hassan al-Banna and Mawlana Mawdudi were shaped by social context as much as by faith. The Muslim Brotherhood had a confrontation with the Egyptian state in the late 1950s and 1960s that caused the ideology of Islamic revivalism to become more militant and radicalized. The chief architect of this transformation, Sayyid Qutb, recast the ideological beliefs of Hassan al-Banna and Mawlana Mawdudi into a rejectionist revolutionary call to arms.

Like Hassan al-Banna, Sayyid Qutb had studied at a modern college established to train teachers. A devout Muslim, he had memorized the Quran as a child. Like many young intellectuals of the time, he studied Western literature and grew up an admirer of the West. Qutb was a prolific writer and an active participant in contemporary literary and social debates.

In 1949, a turning point in his life, Qutb traveled to the United States to study educational organization. Although he had come to the United States out of admiration, Qutb's experiences convinced him that the sexual permissiveness, moral decadence, and anti-Arab bias, which he perceived in U.S. government and media support for Israel, had corrupted all of Western civilization. Shortly after his return to Egypt in 1951, Sayyid Qutb joined the Muslim Brotherhood.

During the 1950s, Qutb emerged as a major voice of the Muslim Brotherhood, especially influential among the younger, more militant members. Government harassment of the Brotherhood and Qutb's imprisonment and torture in 1954, for alleged involvement in an attempt to assassinate Egyptian strong man Gamal Abdel Nasser, increased his radicalization and made his worldview even more confrontational. During ten years of imprisonment, he wrote prolifically. In his most influential Islamic ideological tract, *Signposts*, or *Milestones*, he took the ideas of Hassan al-Banna and especially Mawlana Mawdudi to a militant radical revolutionary conclusion.

For Qutb, the present Muslim governments were primarily repressive and anti-Islamic. Society was divided into two camps, the party of God and the party of Satan, those committed to the rule of God and those opposed to it. There was no middle ground between the forces of good and of evil. Qutb advocated a vanguard, a group of true Muslims within the broader corrupted society. The Islamic movement was a righteous minority adrift in a sea of ignorance and unbelief. Muslim governments and societies alike were seen as un-Islamic, atheist or pagan entities.

Qutb maintained that the creation of an Islamic system of government was a divine commandment, and therefore an imperative, not an alternative. Given the authoritarianism of many regimes, Qutb concluded that jihad as armed struggle was the only way to implement a new Islamic order. Islam, he declared, stood on the brink of disaster, threatened by repressive anti-Islamic governments and the neocolonialism of the West and the East. Qutb went beyond his predecessors when he declared Muslim elites and governments atheists, enemies of God, against whom all true believers should wage holy war. Many later radical groups have used Qutb's formulation of the two options to bring about change: evolution—a process that emphasizes change from below, or revolution—violent overthrow of established (un-Islamic) systems of government.

In 1966, Qutb and several other Muslim Brotherhood leaders were executed. Thousands of Brothers were arrested and tortured, while others went underground or fled the country. Many concluded that the Brotherhood had been crushed, a prediction that was to prove false a decade later.

It is difficult to overstate the impact of Hassan al-Banna, Mawlana Mawdudi, and Sayyid Qutb. Their worldviews and organizations became formative influences for contemporary Islamic movements. Combining religio-political activism with social protest or reform, contemporary Islamic movements represent a spectrum of positions from moderation and gradualism to radicalism and revolutionary violence, from selective criticism of the West to rejection and attacks upon all that the West stands for. Indeed, these movements reflect the multiple issues facing Muslims in their struggle to determine the relationship of Islam to modern state and society: countering Western political and cultural hegemony; dealing with the seeming challenge of modernity to Islamic belief; redefining Islam and its relevance to modern life and society; and addressing the clash of cultures not only between the West and the Muslim world but within Muslim societies over religious and national identity and development.

ISLAM AND POSTMODERN TRENDS IN A POSTCOLONIAL WORLD

The Impact of the Islamic Resurgence

Since the last decades of the twentieth century, the Muslim world has experienced the impact of the contemporary resurgence of Islam. This Islamic reawakening remains visible in society, as evidenced by mosque attendance, Islamic dress, and a renewed emphasis on family values and social justice. It is seen, as well, in Muslim politics, and in international affairs.

New Islamic governments or republics were established in Iran, Sudan, and Afghanistan. Rulers, political parties, and opposition movements used Islam in attempting to attract supporters. Islamic activists have led governments, served in cabinets and in the elected parliaments of Turkey, Jordan, Kuwait, Egypt, Sudan, Pakistan, Malaysia, and Yemen, and served as senior officials in professional associations. At the same time, radical Islamic organizations in Egypt, Algeria, Lebanon, the West Bank, and Gaza have engaged in violence and terrorism to topple governments or to achieve related goals. Extremists have left a legacy of kidnapping, hijacking, bombing, and murder from the Middle East to Southeast Asia, from Paris to New York and Washington. Understanding this complex and multifaceted phenomenon is often difficult and requires an awareness of its roots and sources. What were the causes and conditions that led to the contemporary resurgence of Islam?

Islam in Modern State and Society

A map of the modern Muslim world reveals both old and new realities and begins to visually explain the upheaval in Muslim societies. During the twentieth century, former Islamic empires and sultanates were replaced by modern nation-states, carved out by European colonial powers after World War I. By World War II, most of these newly designated states had won their independence, but it was an independence of artificial creations, and the new rulers, in Jordan, Syria, and Iraq had been placed on their thrones by Britain or France. Moreover, European education, culture, and values strongly influenced the elites in most states and societies. As a result, issues of government legitimacy as well as of national and cultural identity remained unresolved. After World War II, stability of many rulers was due more to Western or Soviet support and strong military-security apparatus than to supportive indigenous culture or widespread political participation.

Once these modern nation-states had been created in the Muslim world, it was expected that they would generally follow a "modern," that is, Western, secular path of development. Outwardly, this seemed to be the general case. While Saudi Arabia proclaimed itself an Islamic state, based upon the Quran and sharia law, most new nations adopted or adapted Western political, legal, social, economic, and educational institutions and values. In contrast to Saudi Arabia, Turkey positioned itself at the opposite end of the religion versus secularism spectrum. Under the leadership of Mustafa Kemal Ataturk, it suppressed Islamic institutions, banned Islamic dress and Islamic law, and transplanted Western secular laws and institutions to create its own version of a secular state.

However, Egypt, Syria, Iraq, Pakistan, Malaysia, and Indonesia created what may be called "Muslim states." In these and most other countries in the Islamic world, the majority populations are Muslim, but despite some religious prescriptions, Western-inspired institutions have been adopted: parliaments, political party systems, legal codes, educational systems and curricula, banks, and insurance companies. Western dress, movies, and culture became prominent and pervasive among the wealthy and powerful in urban centers.

Throughout much of the twentieth century, progress and prosperity in Muslim societies were regarded by most governments and by those with key positions in government and society as dependent upon the degree to which Muslims and their societies were "modern." The degree of progress and success for individuals, cities, and governments was measured in terms of conformity to Western standards and values. Based on these criteria, Turkey, Tunisia, Egypt, Lebanon, and Iran were often seen as among the more modern, advanced, and "enlightened," that is, Westernized and secular, countries. Saudi Arabia, the states of the Persian Gulf, Afghanistan,

Bangladesh, and Pakistan were generally regarded as more traditional, religious, and thus "backward."

The Failure of Modernity and the Islamic Revival

The 1960s and 1970s shattered the hopes and dreams of many who believed that national independence and Western-oriented development would usher in strong states and prosperous societies. These were decades that proved a powerful catalyst for a religious resurgence and revival. The crises of many Muslim societies underscored the failure of many governments and societies to become strong and prosperous, even after national independence. The realities of many Muslim societies raised profound questions of national identity and the political legitimacy of rulers, as well as of religious faith and meaning. Such pervasive conditions as poverty, illiteracy, failed economies, high unemployment, and maldistribution of wealth, could not be blamed entirely on Western influences.

The signs of these profound problems would not become fully appreciated in the West until the Iranian revolution of 1978–79. There were previews, however, during the preceding decade: the 1967 Arab–Israeli war, Malay–Chinese riots in Kuala Lumpur in 1969, the Pakistan–Bangladesh civil war of 1971, and Lebanon's civil war of the mid-1970s. Such catalytic events triggered a soul-searching reassessment among many Muslims. Their disillusionment and dissatisfaction were accompanied by an Islamic revival, a quest for self-identity and greater authenticity, as many reaffirmed the importance of Islam and Islamic values in their personal and social lives. Along with a reemphasis on religious identity and practice (prayer, fasting, dress, and values) came an equally visible appeal to Islam in politics and society made by governments as well as Islamic political and social movements. Islamic ideology, discourse, and politics reemerged as major forces in the development of the Muslim world, forces that both Muslim and Western governments have had to accommodate or contend with for several decades.

The return of Islam as an international political force was seen by many as signaling a return of God's guidance and favor. However, the fall of the shah and a ulama-led revolution were as threatening for many Sunni Muslim governments and elites, especially those in Gulf states like Iraq, Saudi Arabia, Bahrain, and Kuwait, which have significant Shiah populations, as these events were to the West, America and Europe.

Perhaps the most significant symbolic event, which sparked Muslim disillusionment and dissatisfaction, was the 1967 Arab–Israeli war, now often called the Six-Day War. Israel defeated the combined forces of Egypt, Syria, Iraq, and Jordan in a "preemptive" strike, which the Israeli government justified as necessary to counter a planned Arab attack. The Arabs experienced a massive loss of territory: Sinai, Gaza, the West Bank, and in particular Jerusalem, the third holiest city (after Mecca and Medina) of Islam.

Muslims, like Jews and Christians, for centuries have looked to Jerusalem, a city central to Muslim faith and identity, a place of religious shrines and pilgrimage. Muslims hold Jerusalem to be sacred because of its association with prophets (from David and Solomon to Jesus) and because of its central role in the Prophet Muhammad's Night Journey and ascension.

When Muslim armies took Jerusalem without resistance in 635, they built a large mosque (al-Aqsa) and then a magnificent shrine, the Dome of the Rock, on the site associated with the Night Journey and the biblical site of Abraham's sacrifice and Solomon's temple. Muslim loss of Jerusalem in the 1967 war was a traumatic experience, which made Palestine and the Arab–Israeli conflict not just an Arab Muslim and Arab Christian issue but a worldwide Islamic issue. Many who asked what had gone wrong also wanted to know why Israel had been able to defeat the combined Arab forces. Were the weakness and failure of Muslim societies due to their faith? Was Islam incompatible with modernity and thus the cause of Arab backwardness and impotence? Had God abandoned the Muslims? These were questions that had been raised before.

As we have seen, from the seventeenth to the nineteenth centuries, internal threats to Muslim societies were followed by the external threat of European colonialism. The mid-twentieth century; however, was a period of independence and Muslim self-rule. The failures of the "modern experiment" led many to turn, or perhaps more accurately to return, to a more authentic, indigenous alternative to modern nationalism and socialism. Despite significant differences from one country to the next, many Muslims worldwide sought an Islamic alternative to Western capitalism and Soviet Marxism. In this context, Islam became a rallying cry and symbol for political organization and mass mobilization.

The Dome of the Rock in Jerusalem, a major holy site and place of pilgrimage erected by the Umayyad caliph Abd al-Malik, was completed in 692. The famous shrine is built on the spot from which Muslims believe Muhammad ascended to God and then returned to the world. In this story, one of the grand themes of Islamic scholarship and popular piety, the Prophet, in the company of the angel Gabriel, was transported at night from the Kaaba in Mecca to Jerusalem. From there, he ascended to the heavens and the presence of God.

The Religious Worldview of Contemporary Islamic Activism

Islamic activists shared the following beliefs or points of ideology:

1. Islam, a comprehensive way of life, is and must be integral to politics and society.

2. The failures of Muslim societies were caused by departing from the path of Islam and depending on Western secularism, which separates religion and politics.

3. Muslims must return to the Quran and the example of the Prophet Muhammad, specifically by reintroducing Islamic laws in place of Western laws.

4. Modern development must be guided by Islamic values rather than those that would lead to Westernization and secularization of society.

As Islamic symbols, slogans, ideology, leaders, and organizations became prominent fixtures in Muslim politics, religion was increasingly used both by governments and by opposition movements. Libya's Muammar Gadhafi, Pakistan's Muhammad Zia ul-Haq, Egypt's Anwar Sadat, and Sudan's Jaafar al-Nimeiri appealed to Islam to enhance their legitimacy and authority and to mobilize popular support. At the same time, Islamic movements and organizations sprang up across the Muslim world. Opposition movements appealed to Islam: in Iran Ayatollah Khomeini led the "Islamic revolution" of 1979–80; militants seized the Grand Mosque in Mecca in 1979 and called for the overthrow of the Saudi government; religious extremists assassinated Anwar Sadat in 1981. Afghan freedom fighters (*mujahideen*, "holy warriors") in the late 1970s and early 1980s led a resistance movement against the Soviet Union, which had invaded and occupied their country. Other Islamic movements and organizations throughout the 1980s created or extended their influence over religious, educational, social, cultural, and financial institutions, as well as professional schools.

The leadership of most Islamic organizations (particularly Sunni groups) was and remains outside the control of the ulama. Islamists have earned degrees in modern science, medicine, law, engineering, computer science, and education. Most Islamic organizations have attracted individuals from every stratum of society. While the majority of Islamic organizations work within the system, a minority of radical extremists insist that Muslim rulers are anti-Islamic and that violence and revolution are the only way to liberate society and impose an Islamic way of life.

From the Periphery to Mainstream Politics and Society

The 1980s were dominated by fear of "radical Islamic fundamentalism," embodied in Iran's announced desire to export its "Islamic fundamentalist revolution" and the activities of clandestine extremist groups. Feeding these fears were disturbances by Shiah militants in Saudi Arabia, Kuwait, and Bahrain; Iran's strong backing of a Lebanese Shiah group, Hezbollah, which emerged in response to the Israeli invasion and occupation of Lebanon; and a series of hijackings, kidnappings, and bombings of Western embassies. Although Muslim rulers and Western leaders alike were on edge, no other "Irans" occurred.

By the late 1980s and early 1990s, it was increasingly clear that a quiet, or nonviolent revolution had taken place in many parts of the Muslim world. Islamic revivalism and activism had in many contexts become institutionalized in mainstream society. From Egypt to Malaysia, Islam played a more visible and important role in socioeconomic and political life. Islamically inspired social and political activism produced schools, clinics and hospitals, and social service agencies such as day care, legal aid, and youth centers. Private mosques were established, alongside those controlled by governments, and financial institutions such as Islamic banks and insurance companies appeared. In addition, an alternative elite emerged consisting of modern educated but Islamically (rather than secularly) oriented doctors, engineers, lawyers, business people, university professors, military officers, and laborers. Perhaps nowhere was the impact of the Islamic revival experienced more visibly than in political elections.

The majority of Muslim countries are under authoritarian rule, a legacy of premodern Muslim history, European colonial rule, and postindependence Muslim governments that have not fostered the growth of participatory or democratic governments, institutions, and values. During the late 1980s, however, in response to "food riots," protests, and mass demonstrations over the economic failures of governments, elections were held in Jordan, Tunisia, Algeria, and Egypt. Participating Islamic organizations such as the Muslim Brotherhoods of Jordan and Egypt, Tunisia's Nahda (Renaissance) party, and Algeria's Islamic Salvation Front (FIS) emerged as the major political opposition.

In Algeria, the FIS swept municipal and later parliamentary elections and thus was poised to come to power peacefully, through the electoral process. The Algerian military intervened, however, installing a new government, canceling the election results, and imprisoning and outlawing the FIS. This set in motion a spiral of violence and counterviolence that polarized Algerian society and produced a civil war costing more than 100,000 lives.

By the mid-1990s, Islamic activists could be found in the cabinets and parliaments of many countries and in the leadership of professional organizations. In Turkey, the most secular of Muslim states, the Welfare (Refah) party swept mayoral elections and in 1995 elected its first Islamist prime minister and also the leader of the Welfare party, Dr. Ecmettin Erbakan. The Turkish military, claiming the need to save Turkish secularism, brought about the resignation of Erbakan and was influential in having the party outlawed and some of its leaders imprisoned.

The Road to 9/11

Also in the 1990s, radical extremist groups like Egypt's Gamaa Islamiyya (Islamic Group) and Islamic Jihad attacked Christian churches, businesses, foreign tourists, and security forces. Other extremists were convicted in the United States and Europe for terrorist acts such as the 1993 bombing of the World Trade Center in New York. Terrorist attacks against American institutions continued throughout the decade, causing many casualties.

September 11, 2001, would prove to be a watershed, signaling the extent to which Muslim extremists had become a global threat, in particular emphasizing the role of Osama bin Laden and al-Qaeda in global terrorism.[10] The wealthy son of a multimillionaire, bin Laden was suspected of involvement in the bombing of the World Trade Center in 1993 and bombings in Riyadh in 1995 and in Dhahran in 1996.[11]

In February 1998, bin Laden and other militant leaders had announced the creation of a transnational coalition of extremist groups, the World Islamic Front for Jihad Against Jews and Crusaders. His own organization, al-Qaeda, was linked to a series of acts of terrorism: the truck bombing of American embassies in Kenya and Tanzania in August 1998 that killed 263 people and injured more than 5,000, followed in October 2000 by a suicide bombing attack against the U.S.S. *Cole*, which killed 17 American sailors.

Bin Laden's message appealed to the feelings of many in the Arab and Muslim world. A sharp critic of American foreign policy toward the Muslim world, he denounced U.S. support for Israel and sanctions against Iraq, which he said had resulted in the deaths of hundreds of thousands of civilians. He dismissed as the "new crusades" the substantial American military presence and economic involvement in his native Saudi Arabia. To these messages were added other populist reminders of Muslim suffering in Bosnia, Kosovo, Chechnya, and Kashmir.

Al-Qaeda represented a new global terrorism, associated at first with the Muslims who had gone to Afghanistan to fight the occupying Soviets in the 1980s. It was also reflected in the growth of extremism and acts of terrorism in Central, South, and Southeast Asia, where it has often been attributed to the influence of Saudi Arabia and Wahhabi Islam. Bin Laden and other terrorists transformed Islam's

The ethnic warfare that accompanied the breakup of Yugoslavia had tragic effects in Bosnia, one of the oldest Muslim communities in Europe. Refugees of all ages, at Mihatovici, near Tuzla, line up to receive food.

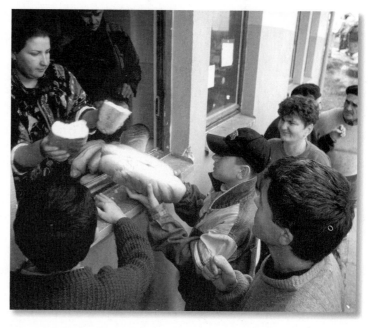

CONTRASTING RELIGIOUS VISIONS

As the following contrasting visions indicate, every religious tradition is capable of generating both visions that encourage peace and understanding and visions that encourage conflict and violence.

Muhammad Iqbal (1876-1938)

Educated at Government College in Lahore, Pakistan, he studied in England and Germany where he earned a law degree and a doctorate in philosophy. Iqbal's modern synthesis and reinterpretation of Islam combined the best of the East and the West, his Islamic heritage with Western philosophy. Both admirer and critic of the West, Iqbal acknowledged the West's dynamic spirit, intellectual tradition, and technology but was sharply critical of European colonialism, as well as the materialism and exploitation of capitalism, the atheism of Marxism, and the moral bankruptcy of secularism.

The Reconstruction of Religious Thought in Islam succinctly summarizes Iqbal's reformist vision, which can also be accessed in his extensive writings and poetry. Like other Islamic modernists, Iqbal rejected much of medieval Islam as static and stagnant. He saw Islam as emerging from five hundred years of "dogmatic slumber" and compared the need for Islamic reform now to that confronting Christianity at the time of the Reformation. Iqbal emphasized the need to reclaim the vitality and dynamism of early Islamic thought and practice, calling for a bold reinterpretation (ijtihad) of Islam. He attempted to develop alternative Islamic models for modern Muslim societies. Thus, for example, drawing on Islamic traditions, he sought to "rediscover" Islamic principles and values that would provide the basis for Islamic versions of Western concepts and institutions such as democracy and parliamentary government.

---

norms about the defense of Islam and Muslims under siege to legitimate the use of violence, warfare, and terrorism. Their theology of hate espouses a bipolar view of a cosmic struggle between the armies of God and of Satan, the forces of good and evil, right and wrong, belief and unbelief. Those who are not with them, whether Muslim or non-Muslim, are judged to be against them. These extremists have "hijacked" the Islamic concept and institution of jihad in an attempt to lend legitimacy to their acts of violence and terror.

Globalization and Hijacking of "Jihad"

Since the late twentieth century the word "jihad" has gained remarkable currency. On the one hand, the term's primary Quranic religious and spiritual meanings became more widespread: jihad was the "struggle" or effort to follow God's path, to lead a moral life, and to promote social justice. On the other hand, the idea of jihad as armed struggle has been widely used by resistance, liberation, and terrorist movements alike to legitimate their cause and recruit

Osama bin Laden (b. 1957)

Born in Riyadh, Saudi Arabia, bin Laden received a degree in public administration in 1981 from King Abdul-Aziz University. A major turning point in bin Laden's adult life occurred in 1979 when the Soviets occupied Afghanistan. From 1979 to 1982, he used his financial resources to vigorously support the jihadi resistance against the Soviets, providing construction materials, building roads and airfields, and then moving to Afghanistan to set up his own camps and command Arab mujahideen forces, who became known as "Arab Afghans." He later created al-Qaeda, "the base," to organize and track the fighters and funds being channeled into the Afghan resistance.

Bin Laden's opposition to the American-led coalition in the Gulf War of 1991 placed him on a collision course with the Saudi government and the West. In 1994 the kingdom revoked bin Laden's citizenship and moved to freeze his assets because of his support for militant fundamentalist movements. Bin Laden joined other dissident activists and religious scholars, moving to Sudan and then back to Afghanistan. Assuming a vocal leadership role in international terrorism, in 1996, he issued a Declaration of Jihad created to drive the United States out of Arabia, overthrow the Saudi government, liberate Islam's holy sites of Mecca and Medina, and support revolutionary groups around the world. In 2000 he was among the founders of the World Islamic Front for the Jihad Against Jews and Crusaders, an umbrella group of radical movements across the Muslim world, and issued a fatwa emphasizing the duty of all Muslims to kill U.S. citizens and their allies.

followers. Thus the Afghan Mujahideen waged jihad in Afghanistan against foreign powers and among themselves; Muslims in Kashmir, Chechnya, the southern Philippines, Bosnia, and Kosovo have fashioned their struggles as jihads; Hezbollah, HAMAS, and Islamic Jihad Palestine have characterized war with Israel as a jihad; and Osama bin Laden, speaking as head of al-Qaeda, has declared global jihad, targeting Muslim governments as well as the West.

Bin Laden and other terrorists go beyond classical Islam's criteria for a just jihad and recognize no limits but their own. They reject the tenets of Islamic law regarding the goals and means of a valid jihad: that the use of violence must be proportional; that innocent civilians, noncombatants, should not be targeted; and that jihad can be declared only by a ruler or head of state. Today, extremists from Madrid to Mindanao legitimate unholy wars in the name of Islam itself, by passing the Quranic requirement that authorization for jihad be given by a nation's ruler.

While bin Laden and al-Qaeda have enjoyed support from a significant minority of Muslims and religious leaders, other Islamic scholars and religious leaders across the Muslim world, such as the Islamic Research Council at al-Azhar University, regarded by many as the highest moral authority in Islam, have issued authoritative declarations against bin Laden's initiatives: "Islam provides clear rules and ethical norms that forbid the killing of non-combatants, as well as women, children, and the elderly, and also forbids the pursuit of the enemy in defeat, the execution of those who surrender, the infliction of harm on prisoners of war, and the destruction of property that is not being used in the hostilities."[12]

Post 9/11: Impact and Response

9/11 highlighted the struggle for the heart and soul of Islam that has been going on in recent decades, a war not only within Muslim societies but also across national borders. Subsequent terrorist attacks from Madrid to Bali led many to ask, "Why?" and "What is the relationship of Islam to global terrorism?" President George Walker Bush, like numerous other political and religious leaders, carefully distinguished between the religion of Islam and Muslim extremism, but many others did not. Some prominent leaders of the Christian right, including Franklin Graham, Pat Robertson, and Jerry Falwell, disparaged the religion of Islam and the Prophet Muhammad, charging that the roots of extremism and terrorism were in the Quran or the teachings of Muhammad and Islam. Still others, however, spoke of the need to look for the root causes of terrorism, citing the authoritarianism and repression of many Muslim governments, as well as economic and social environments characterized by poverty, illiteracy, maldistribution of wealth, and rampant corruption. Also conducive to the growth of radicalism and the appeal of bin Laden and other terrorist leaders and their theologies of hate was anger at U.S. and European policies in the Muslim world: uncritical support for regimes, Palestinian–Israeli policies and to the West's double standard in promoting democratization.

The fact that Osama bin Laden and many of the 9/11 hijackers were from Saudi Arabia, as well as Saudi support for some Islamic groups and madrasas in countries like Afghanistan and Pakistan have raised questions about the role of Wahhabism in global terrorism. Wahhabi Islam, the official form of Islam in Saudi Arabia, is among the most ultraconservative interpretations of Islam.

As we have seen, the Wahhabi movement takes its name from Muhammad Ibn Abd al-Wahhab and eighteenth-century revivalist movement. Over time, the ideas of many uncompromising interpreters of Wahhabi Islam have resulted in an ultraconservative, "fundamentalist," brand of Islam: literalist, rigid, puritanical, exclusivist, and intolerant. Wahhabi's believe that they are right and all others (other Muslims as well as people of other faiths) are wrong. Presenting their version of Islam as the pristine, pure, unadulterated message of the Prophet, Wahhabis have sought to propagate and sometimes impose throughout the world their strict beliefs and interpretations, which are not shared by the majority of Muslims.

Since the last half of the twentieth century, domestic and foreign provocations have led to the emergence of militant, violent interpretations of Islam. In 1979, when militants seized the Grand Mosque in Mecca, they called for the overthrow of the Saudi monarchy. After a bloody battle, the rebels were crushed, their leaders killed or executed. At the same time, Islamic activists from Egypt and other countries, often fleeing their home governments, had found refuge in Saudi Arabia, teaching in universities and religious schools, or working in government ministries and organizations. As a result, alongside the puritanical Wahhabi Islam of the establishment, a radical brand of Islam, having both internal and external sources, infiltrated Saudi society. Its theology and worldview was one of militant jihad, domestic and global.

Both government-sponsored organizations and wealthy individuals, Saudis, like bin Laden, exported Wahhabi Islam, in its mainstream and extremist forms, to other countries and communities in the Muslim world and in the West. They offered development aid, built mosques, libraries, and other institutions, funded and distributed religious tracts, and commissioned imams and religious scholars.

Wahhabi theology, funding, and influence were exported to Afghanistan, Pakistan, the Central Asian Republics, China, Africa, Southeast Asia, the United States, and Europe. At the same time, some wealthy businessmen and organizations in Saudi Arabia and the Gulf provided financial support to extremist groups that actively promote a holy war ("jihadi") culture. The challenge is to distinguish between those who preach and propagate an ultraconservative Wahhabi theology and militant extremists and terrorist organizations. Similar divisions between mainstream Muslims and violent extremists exist in other religions, with Jewish, Christian, and Hindu fundamentalists sometimes acting in ways not condoned by the majority of their coreligionists.

Questions for Postmodern Times: Issues of Authority and Interpretation

Muslims in the twenty-first century, as throughout Islamic history, are called by their faith to worship God and, by their lives, to implement God's will for humankind. The sources and sacred texts of Islam, the Quran and the Sunnah of the Prophet, remain the same, but the political, social, and economic contexts have changed. While all Muslims continue to affirm belief in God, Muhammad, and the Quran, Muslim interpretations of Islam today vary significantly. Some believe that Islam, like most faiths in the modern age, should be primarily a private matter; many others have struggled to implement Islam in public life as well. Although categories are not clear-cut and overlap at times, four general Muslim orientations or attitudes toward change may be identified: secularist, conservative, Islamist or neofundamentalist, and Islamic reformist or neomodernist.

Like their counterparts in the West, secularists believe religion is a personal matter that should be excluded from politics and public life. Calling for the separation of religion and the state, they believe that Islam belongs in the mosque, not in politics, and that the mosque should solely be a place of prayer, not of political activism.

Conservatives emphasize following past tradition and are wary of any change or innovation that they regard as deviation, or *bida*, the Christian equivalent of heresy. Conservatives are represented by the majority (though certainly not all) of the ulama and their followers, who continue to assert the primacy and adequacy of centuries-old Islamic law. Advocating the reimplementation of Islamic law through the adoption of past legal doctrine, they resist substantive change. They argue that since Islamic law is the divinely revealed path of God, it is not the law that must change or modernize but society that must conform to God's law as formulated in past centuries.

Islamic activists or Islamists (often commonly referred to as fundamentalists) are in some respects similar to conservatives though more flexible. They represent a broad spectrum, from ultraorthodox, literalist, and puritanical movements to more flexible and reform-minded believers, from militant extremists to those who hold mainstream political and social positions. In contrast to conservatives, they are not wedded to the classical formulations of law. In the name of a return to the Quran and Sunnah, fundamentalists speak of purifying Muslim belief and practice by a rigorous and literalist embrace of the past, while more mainstream Islamists are prepared to interpret and reformulate Islamic belief and institutions.

In contrast to modernizers, Islamic activists emphasize the self-sufficiency of Islam over compatibility with the West. Few of their leaders are religious scholars or imams. Like the Muslim Brotherhood and other Islamic revivalist organizations from the twentieth century, their comprehensive understanding of Islam fosters social and political activism, often challenging the political and religious status quo. Their Islamic ideology is less innovative than that of today's Islamic reformers, or modernists, and thus they have boldly reformulated Islamic responses in sensitive areas like Islamic law and the status of women and minorities.

Neomodernists, despite some overlap with mainstream Islamists, are more open to substantive change and to borrowing from other cultures. Like Islamists, they root their reforms in the Quran and Sunnah and are not wedded to classical Islamic law. However, their approach to change is different: they distinguish more sharply between the principles and values of Islam's immutable revelation and certain historically and socially conditioned practices and institutions, which they believe can and should be changed to meet contemporary circumstances.

At the heart of reformist approaches to Islam is the core issue, the relationship of the divine to the human in Islamic law. Thus reformers focus on the need to distinguish between the sharia, God's divinely revealed law, and *fiqh* ("understanding"), including the areas of human interpretation and application that are historically conditioned. Reformers go further than conservatives or traditionalists in their acceptance of the degree and extent to which classical Islamic law may be changed. They place more emphasis on the finite nature of early doctrines. They argue that just as early Muslim jurists applied the principles and values of Islam to the societies of the past, again today a reinterpretation or reconstruction of Islam is needed. Many reformers, after an early traditional or Islamic education, have obtained degrees from major national and international universities in the Muslim world and the West, combining an appreciation of Islam with modern academic disciplines and knowledge.

The primary question is not change, for most accept its necessity. Rather, it is how much change is possible or permissible in Islam and what kinds of change are necessary. This issue is central to virtually all the questions that Muslims face with respect to their faith in contemporary life: the relationship of Islam to the state, political participation or democratization, reform of Islamic law, promotion of religious and political pluralism, and the rights of women.

As in the past, both the ulama, the religious scholars of Islam, and Muslim rulers continue to assert their right to protect, defend, and interpret Islam. The ulama persist in regarding themselves as the guardians of Islam, the conscience of the community, its only qualified interpreters. They continue to write religious commentaries, and to run schools and universities. Many rulers, through co-optation and coercion, combine their obligation to protect and promote Islam with the state's power to influence, control, and impose certain "brand" of Islam. Governments control and distribute funds used to build

Islam and Democracy

A primary example of Islamic reformism and its method today is the debate over the relationship of Islam to democracy. Some Muslims reject any discussion of the question, maintaining that Islam has its own system of government. Others believe that Islam and democracy are incompatible, claiming that democracy is based upon un-Islamic Western principles and values. Still others reinterpret traditional Islamic concepts like consultation (*shura*) and consensus (*ijma*) of the community to support the adoption of modern forms of political participation or democratization such as parliamentary elections. Thus, just as it was appropriate in the past for Muhammad's senior Companions to constitute a consultative assembly (*majlis al-shura*) and to select or elect his successor through a process of consultation, Muslims now reinterpret and extend this notion to the creation of modern forms of political participation and government, parliamentary governments, and the direct or indirect election of heads of state. This process is sometimes called "Islamization." Similarly, in legal reform some Muslims believe that Islam is totally self-sufficient; they demand the imposition of Islamic law, and reject any outside influences. Others argue that Islamic law can be reinterpreted today to incorporate new interpretations or formulations of law, as well as laws from elsewhere that do not contradict the Quran and Sunnah.

mosques and to pay the salaries of religious officials and functionaries. Even topics or outlines for Friday mosque sermons are subject to government approval. Governments appoint religious leaders and judges.

Today, many argue that it is not rulers or the religious scholars but the laity and parliaments that should be major actors in the process of change. While the ulama base their authority on their training in traditional Islamic disciplines, lay Muslims counter that they possess the legal, economic, and medical qualifications necessary to address contemporary issues and should be counted among the "experts" along with the ulama.

Islam in the West[13]

As noted earlier, as members of the second or third largest religion in Europe and America, Muslims have become part and parcel of the American and European landscapes. Today, the major cities of the world of Islam include Paris, Marseilles, London, Manchester, New York, Chicago, Detroit, and Los Angeles, in addition to Cairo, Damascus, Islamabad, and Kuala Lumpur.

Muslims were long an invisible presence in the West. Most came as immigrants. Many wanted to fit into their new societies, to be accepted, gain employment, raise families, and live quietly in their adopted countries. Others wished to live apart, to avoid any prospect of loss of identity or assimilation into a Western, non-Muslim society. Political events in the Muslim world reinforced a desire for a low profile in a country to which Muslims had relocated; in some cases Muslims found themselves on the defensive. Images and stereotypes of camels and harems from the past were replaced by modern impressions of violence and terrorism associated with the threat of militant "Islamic fundamentalism." The result has often been Muslim bashing and what some have called Islamophobia.

Today, Muslims in Europe and America no longer live primarily in clusters of immigrants; rather they are members of second- and third-generation communities, participating in professional and civic life. Yet many continue to face issues of faith and identity as a religious minority.

The Muslims of Western Europe

More than 18 million Muslims may be found in Europe, half in western Europe and half in the southeast. Because many, though certainly not all, wish to retain their religion, culture, and values, the presence and citizenship of Muslims in western Europe, as in America, have made assimilation, acculturation, integration, and multiculturalism major religious, social, and political issues.

In contrast to America, in western Europe the Muslim presence is due in large part to immigration based on a vestigial colonial connection. After independence, many professionals and skilled laborers from former European colonies in Africa, South Asia, and the Arab world immigrated to Europe seeking a better life. In the 1960s and 1970s, unskilled workers flooded into European countries whose growing economies welcomed cheap labor.

In addition, from the 1970s onward, increasing numbers of Muslim students came to Europe, as they did to America, to study. While many returned home, others chose to stay for political or economic reasons.

The largest Muslim population in western Europe, is in France, with 5 million Muslims, many of whom come from North Africa. They may be found in most major cities and towns. The Muslims of France, comprising almost 10 percent of the population, now exceed Protestants and Jews in number and are second only to France's Catholic community. There are grand mosques in Paris and Lyons and more than a thousand mosques and prayer rooms throughout the country. Britain's 1 million to 2 million Muslims come primarily from the Indian subcontinent; more than six hundred mosques serve as prayer, education, and community centers in Britain.

The issue of Muslim identity has been particularly acute in France where, after a long battle, the government took a firm stand in favor of total assimilation or integration rather than the more multicultural approaches of Britain and America. The issue was symbolized in a celebrated case in which the wearing of a headscarf by Muslim female students was outlawed. The government's ministry of education united with the teachers' union in claiming that wearing the hijab violated France's secular constitution and traditions. In October 1996, after several years of bitter debate, the French Constitutional Council ruled that students could not be expelled for wearing headscarves if no proselytizing occurred. Then, in February 2004, France's National Assembly ignored protests and criticism from around the world and voted 494–36 to approve the controversial ban in public schools. Although the new law was primarily aimed at Muslims wearing the hijab, other religious apparel (large Christian crucifixes and Jewish skullcaps or yarmulkes) was included; violators face suspension or expulsion. The government argues that a law is needed not only to protect France's secular traditions but to ward off rising Islamic fundamentalism.

Islam in America

Islam is the fastest growing religion in the United States; more than a million Americans have converted to Islam. Estimates of the number of American Muslims vary significantly, from a low of 4 million to a high of 12 million. Many believe that in the first half of the twenty-first century, Islam will become the second largest religion in America after Christianity.

Muslims were present in America prior to the nineteenth century. Perhaps 20 percent of the African slaves brought to America from the sixteenth to the nineteenth centuries were Muslim. However, most were forced to convert to Christianity. It was not until the late nineteenth century, with the arrival of waves of immigrant laborers from the Arab world, that significant numbers of Muslims became a visible presence in America. In recent decades many more have come from the Middle East and South Asia. In contrast to Europe, which attracted large numbers of Muslims as immigrant laborers in the 1960s and 1970s, many who have come to America in recent decades have been well-educated professionals, intellectuals, and students. Many have come for

The diversity of Muslims in America. The Muslim community in America is a rich racial, ethnic, and cultural mosaic of indigenous believers, the majority of whom are African American, and immigrant Muslims. Thousands of Muslims from New York's varied ethnic communities praynext to Coney Island's landmark Parachute Jump to celebrate the Feast of Sacrifice (Id al-Adha). This major religious holiday commemorates God's command to Abraham to sacrifice his son Ismail.

political and economic reasons, leaving behind the constraints of life under authoritarian regimes and failed economies.

Unity of faith is tested by the U.S. Muslim community's rich diversity. About two-thirds (60%) of America's Muslims are immigrants or descendants of immigrants from the Middle East, Africa, and South and Southeast Asia. The rest are primarily African American converts to Islam, plus a smaller percentage of white American converts. The majority of American Muslims are Sunni, but there is a strong Shiah minority. Racial, ethnic, and sectarian differences are reflected in the demographic composition and politics of some mosques, as well: many houses of worship incorporate the diversity of Muslims in America, but the membership of others is drawn along ethnic or racial lines.

African American Islam

African American Islam emerged in the early twentieth century when a number of black Americans converted to Islam and established movements or communities. Islam's egalitarian ideal in which all Muslims belong to a brotherhood of believers, transcending race and ethnic ties, proved attractive. Whereas Islam was seen as part of an original (African) identity, Christianity was associated with the legitimation of slavery and thus a legacy of white supremacy and oppression of black Americans that extended into the twentieth century. The early twentieth century saw the appearance of quasi-Islamic groups, combining a selective use of Islamic symbols with black nationalism. The most prominent and lasting movement, the Nation of Islam, was associated with Elijah Muhammad (formerly Elijah Poole, 1897–1975).

Elijah Muhammad had been a follower of Wallace D. Fard Muhammad, who preached a message of black liberation in the ghettos of Detroit in the early 1930s. After Fard mysteriously disappeared in 1934, Elijah Muhammad became the leader of the Nation of Islam. Adopting the title of the Honorable Elijah Muhammad, he claimed to be the messenger of God. Under his leadership, the Nation of Islam, popularly known as the Black Muslims, was redefined and transformed into an effective national movement. Elijah Muhammad preached black liberation and nationalism, black pride and identity, strength and self-sufficiency, black racial supremacy, and strong family values. The spirit and ethic of the Nation of Islam was embodied in the phrase, "Do for self," a doctrine of economic independence that emphasized self-improvement and responsibility through hard work, discipline, thrift, and abstention from gambling, alcohol, drugs, and eating pork.

The Nation of Islam differed significantly from mainstream Islam in a number of basic beliefs. It claimed that Allah (God) was human, a black man named Wallace D. Fard, and that Elijah Muhammad (not the Prophet Muhammad) was the last messenger of God. The Nation taught black supremacy and black separatism, whereas Islam teaches the brotherhood of all believers in a community that transcends racial, tribal, and ethnic boundaries. The Nation did not subscribe to major tenets of the faith, such as the Five Pillars of Islam.

Three individuals epitomize the development and transformation of Elijah Muhammad's Black Muslim movement: Malcolm X, Wallace D. Muhammad (Warith Deen Muhammad), and Louis Farrakhan.

Malcolm X (1925–1965), born Malcolm Little, exemplified the personal and religious transformation for which the Nation of Islam was noted. His experience of racism and prejudice led to his alienation from and rejection of American society. A prison sentence was the result of an early life of drugs and crime in the ghettos of Roxbury, Massachusetts, and later in New York's Harlem. It was during his incarceration (1946–52) that he became self-educated, reading widely in history, politics, and religion. Malcolm became convinced that Christianity was the "white man's religion" and that the Bible "[in the] white man's hands and his interpretation of it, have been the greatest single ideological weapon for enslaving millions of non-white human beings."[14] In 1948 he formally turned to Elijah Muhammad and accepted the teachings of the Nation of Islam. Malcolm Little became Malcolm X.

Malcolm X (d. 1965): also known as El-Hajj Malik El-Shabazz, African American Muslim leader, civil and human rights advocate. An early disciple of Elijah Muhammad, chief minister of the Nation of Islam, he became one of its most prominent leaders and spokespersons. He withdrew from the Nation in 1964, becoming a follower of Sunni Islam. He was assassinated in 1965 by members of the Nation of Islam.

Muhammad Ali: renowned heavyweight boxing champion of the world. Born Cassius Clay in 1942, he revealed in midcareer that he had become a member of the Nation of Islam and changed his name to Muhammad Ali. He became the most prominent and popular Muslim public figure in America and globally.

A gifted speaker, dynamic and articulate, and a charismatic personality, Malcolm X rose quickly through the ranks of the Nation of Islam to national prominence in the 1950s and early 1960s. He organized many of the Nation's temples, started its newspaper *Muhammad Speaks,* and recruited new members, including the boxer Cassius Clay, renamed Muhammad Ali.

However, Malcolm's increased involvement in domestic and international politics, as well as his contacts with Sunni Muslims in America and in the Muslim world, led to a gradual shift in his religious/ideological worldview. This development put him increasingly at odds with some of Elijah Muhammad's teachings. While Elijah Muhammad advocated separation and self-sufficiency that excluded involvement in "white man's politics," Malcolm came to believe that "the Nation of Islam could be even a greater force in the American Black man's overall struggle if we engaged in more action."[15] He spoke out forcefully on a variety of issues: the civil rights movement, the Vietnam War, solidarity with liberation struggles in colonial Africa. Such statements made him an easy target for those within the Nation who were jealous of his prominence, and as a result he found himself increasingly marginalized.

In March 1964 Malcolm X left the Nation of Islam to start his own organization and a month later went on pilgrimage to Mecca. Here Malcolm underwent a second conversion—to mainstream Sunni Islam. The pilgrimage brought Malcolm and the religious/separatist teachings of the Nation face to face with those of the global Islamic community, vividly exposing their conflicts and contradictions. Malcolm was profoundly affected by the Muslim emphasis, which he experienced at firsthand during the hajj, on the equality of all believers: "We were truly all the same (brothers)—because their belief in one God removed the 'white' from their minds, the 'white' from their behavior, and the 'white' from their attitude."[16] He returned a Muslim rather than a Black Muslim, changing his name to El Hajj Malik El-Shabazz. On February 21, 1965, Malcolm Shabazz was assassinated as he spoke to an audience in New York.

The 1960s were a transitional period for the Nation of Islam. Not only Malcolm X but also Elijah Muhammad's son, Wallace D. Muhammad, each in his own way, questioned the teachings and strategy of the senior Muhammad. At one point, Wallace was excommunicated by his father. Despite their disagreements, however, Elijah Muhammad had designated his son as his successor, and in February 1975, Wallace D. Muhammad succeeded his recently deceased father as supreme minister. With the support of his family and the Nation's leadership, Wallace set about reforming the doctrines of the Nation and its organizational structure. He simultaneously integrated the Nation within the American Muslim community, the broader American society, and the global Islamic community.

The Nation and its teachings were brought into conformity with orthodox Sunni Islam, and the organization was renamed the World Community of al-Islam in the West (WCIW). Wallace Muhammad made the pilgrimage to

Mecca and encouraged his followers to study Arabic to better understand Islam. The community now observed Islam's Five Pillars. Black separatist doctrines were dropped as the community proceeded to participate in the American political process. The equality of men and women believers was reaffirmed; women were given more responsible positions in the ministry of the community. In 1980, as if to signal his and the community's new religious identity and mission, Wallace changed his name to Warith Deen Muhammad and renamed the WCIW the American Muslim Mission.

The transformation of the Nation of Islam under Warith Deen Muhammad did not occur without dissent. Louis Farrakhan (born Louis Eugene Walcott, in 1933), a bitter foe of both Malcolm and Wallace, broke with Wallace in March 1978. Farrakhan retained the name and organizational structure of the Nation of Islam as well as its black nationalist and separatist doctrines. However, from 1986 onward, while using many of the political and economic teachings and programs of Elijah Muhammad, he moved the Nation closer to more orthodox Islamic practices.

While Farrakhan's militancy and anti-Semitic statements brought condemnation and criticism, the effectiveness of the Nation in fighting crime and drugs in ghettos and in rehabilitating prisoners earned the Nation praise. Farrakhan's leadership of the Million Man March on Washington in 1995 received widespread media coverage and support among Christian as well as Muslim leaders and organizations. Though the Nation of Islam has far fewer members than Warith Deen Muhammad's American Muslim Mission, Farrakhan's persona and actions gave him a disproportionate amount of visibility and recognition as the twentieth century drew to a close.

Issues of Adaptation and Change

Islam and Muslim identity in North America reflect the diverse backgrounds of the community: from immigrants who came to America in pursuit of political, religious, or economic freedom to native-born African Americans seeking equality and justice. Muslims have been challenged by an America that, despite separation of church and state, retains a Judeo-Christian ethos. Jewish and Christian holidays are officially recognized holidays; Judeo-Christian values are regarded as integral to American identity. The tendency of some in America, as in Europe, to contrast American "national culture" with Islamic values further complicates the process of Muslim assimilation. Finally, the American media's frequent portrayal of Islam or Muslims as militant, the identification of Islam as a global threat, and talk of a clash of civilizations in the post–cold war period has often led to the equation of Islam with extremism and terrorism. Despite their numbers and religious heritage as one of the three branches of the Children of Abraham, Islam and Muslims have yet to be fully recognized as fellow citizens, neighbors, and equal partners in American society.

Islam in America provides many examples of significant change and reform. Both mosques and their leaders, or imams, have been transformed by the American experience. In contrast to many parts of the Muslim world, mosques in America serve not only as places of worship but also as community centers. Because Friday is a work day and a school day in America, many Muslims are not able to attend the Friday congregational prayer. Therefore, for many, Sunday at mosques and Islamic centers is the day of congregational prayer, religious education ("Sunday school"), and socializing. Imams in America not only are responsible for the upkeep of mosques and leading of prayers, but often take on the duties of the clergy of other faiths, ranging from counseling to hospital visits.

Many American residents raised in Muslim majority countries are troubled by the question of whether they should, or indeed can, live in a non-Muslim territory. Muslim jurists writing during the days of expansionist Islamic empires had encouraged Muslims to migrate from non-Muslim areas lest they contribute to the strength and prosperity of non-Muslim states. However, while the ideal was to live in a Muslim territory, Islamic jurisprudence did allow Muslims to live outside the Islamic territory provided they were free to practice their religion. In the twenty-first century, Muslim minority communities have become a global and permanent phenomenon. If some religious leaders continue to counsel emigration from non-Muslim territories back to Muslim lands, many others have redefined the conditions under which Muslims can live permanently as loyal citizens in their new homelands while preserving their faith and identity.

Today, American Muslims increasingly seek to empower themselves, participating in rather than simply reacting to life in America. Like American Jews and other minorities before them, Muslims are developing grassroots institutions that are responsive to their realities. Attempts to adapt and apply Islam in America can be seen in mosque architecture that reflects the landscapes of American contexts, and the appointment of imams from the local population, rather than bringing in native speakers of Arabic. In addition, mechanisms are being set up to obtain legal opinions (fatwas) from local rather than overseas muftis, and Muslim advocacy and public affairs organizations promote and lobby for Muslim rights and community interests.

Teaching materials and syllabi on Islam and Muslim life are available for the instruction of children and adults at mosques and in schools. Moreover, Muslim educational associations monitor textbooks and the teaching of Islam to assure accuracy and objectivity. Public affairs organizations monitor publications and respond to misinformation in the media and to objectionable policies and actions by legislators and corporations. Islamic information services develop and distribute films, videos, and publications on Islam and Muslims in America to further better understanding. Some communities have primary and secondary Islamic schools.

ISLAM: POSTMODERN CHALLENGES

Islam and Muslims today are again at an important crossroads. The struggle today, the world over, is one of faith and identity. What does it mean to be a Muslim in contemporary society? What is the relevance of Islam to everyday life?

Islamic schools. Like catholic and Jewish communities before them, which created their own schools to safeguard and preserve the faith and identity of the younger generation, some Muslim communities have created Islamic schools that combine a standard academic curriculum with training in Arabic and Islamic studies.

Secularism and Materialism

Like the other Children of Abraham, their Jewish and Christian cousins, Muslims facing the challenges of secularism and materialism, of faith and social justice, bear witness to the fact that monotheism is not monolithic. Whereas the process of reform occurring in contemporary Islam is often seen through the prism or lens of explosive headline events, of radicalism and extremism, the quiet (nonviolent) revolution in Islamic discourse and activism is often less noticed. As in the past, and as in all faiths, the unity of Islam embraces a diversity of interpretations and expressions, a source of dynamism and growth as well as contention and conflict among believers and, at times, with other faith communities. The challenge for all believers remains the rigorous pursuit of "the straight path, the way of God, to whom belongs all that is in the heavens and all that is on the earth" (Q. 42:52–53) in a world of diversity and difference.

While the Quran and Sunnah of the Prophet Muhammad remain normative for all Muslims, vigorously debated questions have been raised in the areas of interpretation, authenticity, and application. If some Muslims see little need to redefine past approaches and practices, others strike out into new territory. Some Muslim scholars distinguish between the Meccan and Medinan *surahs* (chapters). The former are regarded as the earlier and more religiously binding; the latter are seen as primarily political, concerned with Muhammad's creation of the Medinan state and therefore not universally binding. Still other Muslim scholars say that whereas the eternal principles and values of the Quran are to be applied and reapplied to changing sociopolitical contexts, many articles of past legislation addressed conditions in specific historical periods and are not necessarily binding today.

Although the example (Sunnah) of the Prophet Muhammad has always been normative in Islam, from earliest times Muslim scholars saw the need to critically examine and authenticate the enormous number of prophetic traditions (hadith). In the twentieth century, a sector of modern Western scholarship questioned the historicity and authenticity of the hadith, maintaining that the bulk of the Prophetic traditions are pious fabrications, written long after the death of the Prophet. Most Muslim scholars and some from outside the Islamic world have taken exception to this sweeping position. If many of the ulama continue to accept the authoritative collections of the past unquestioningly, other Muslim scholars have in fact become more critical in their approach and use of tradition (*hadith*) literature.

Contemporary Muslim discussion and debate over the role of Islam in state and society reflect a broad array of questions: Is there one classical model or many possible models for the relationship of religion to political, social, and economic development? If a new Islamic synthesis is to be achieved that provides continuity with past tradition, how will this be accomplished? Will it be imposed from above by rulers and/or the ulama or legislated in populist fashion through a representative electoral process?

Islamization of the Law

The debate over whether the sharia should be part of or the basis of a country's legal system raises questions, as well. Does Islamization of law mean the wholesale reintroduction of classical law as formulated in the early Islamic centuries or the development of new laws derived from the Quran and Sunnah of the Prophet? Or can it include the acceptance of any laws, whatever their source (European, American etc.), that are not contrary to Islam? Who is to oversee this process: rulers, the ulama, or parliaments?

Queen Rania of Jordan at prayer with other Muslim women. The queen also fulfills an important role in society by participating in events in the secular world.

The implementation of sharia, where it has occurred, has not followed a fixed pattern or set interpretation even among those countries dubbed conservative or fundamentalist, such as Iran, Sudan, Afghanistan under the Taliban, Pakistan, and Saudi Arabia. Women in Saudi Arabia cannot vote or hold public office. In Pakistan and Iran, despite other strictures and problems, women vote, hold political office in parliaments and cabinets, teach in universities, and hold responsible professional positions. However, Islamization of law has underscored several areas that have proved particularly problematic: the *hudud* (Quranically prescribed crimes and punishments for alcohol consumption, theft, fornication, adultery, and false witness), the status of non-Muslims and minorities, and the status of women. All potentially involve changes in Islamic law.

While many conservatives and Islamic activists or fundamentalists call for the reimplementation of the hudud punishments, other Muslims argue that such harsh measures as amputation for theft and stoning for adultery are no longer suitable. Among those who advocate imposition of the hudud, some want it introduced immediately and others say that it should be contingent on the creation of a just society in which people will not be driven to steal to survive. Some critics charge that while appropriate relative to the time they were introduced, hudud punishments are unnecessary in a modern context.

Women and Minorities

The reintroduction of Islamic law has often had a particularly pronounced negative impact on the status and role of women and minorities, raising serious questions about whether the gains made in many societies have been rolled back. During the postindependence period, changes occurred in many countries, broadening the educational and employment opportunities and enhancing the legal rights of Muslim women. Women became more visible in the professions as teachers, lawyers, engineers, and physicians, and in government. However, these changes have benefited only a small proportion of the population, and the number of women who advance has varied from one country or region to another. Women's status and gender relations continue to be strongly influenced by religious and local traditions, economic and educational development, and government leadership.

As we have seen, one result of contemporary Islamic revivalism has been a reexamination of the role of women in Islam and, at times, a bitter debate over their function in society. More conservative religious voices among the ulama and many Islamists have advocated a return to veiling and sexual segregation as well as restrictions on women's

Benazir Bhutto, former prime minister of Pakistan, is one of several Muslim women to have served as president or prime minister in an Islamic nation.

Women and Empowerment

Muslim women in the twentieth century had two clear choices or models before them: the modern Westernized lifestyle common among an elite minority of women and the more restrictive traditional "Islamic" lifestyle of the majority of women, who lived much as their grandmothers and great-grand-mothers had lived. The social impact of the Islamic revival produced a third alternative that is both modern and firmly rooted in Islamic faith, identity, and values. Muslim women, modernists, and Islamists have argued on Islamic grounds for an expanded role for women in Muslim societies. Rejecting the idea that Islam itself is patriarchal and distinguishing between revelation and its inter-pretation by all-male ulama in patriarchal settings, Muslim women have reasserted the right to be primary participants in redefining their identity and role in society. In many instances, this change has been symbolized by a return to the wearing of Islamic dress or the donning of a headscarf, or hijab. Initially prominent primarily among urban middle-class women, this new mode of dress has become more common among a broader sector of society. For many it is an attempt to combine religious belief and Islamic values of modesty with contemporary freedoms in education and employment, to pair a much-desired process of social change with indigenous Islamic values and ideals. The goal is a more authentic rather than simply Westernized modernization.

Women's attire.
The Quran and Islamic tradition enjoin modesty, and thus everyone is required to wear modest dress. The diversity of attire found across Muslim world is reflected by this group of young Muslim women in the United States. Though all are dressed modestly, some wear a headscarf (hijab) while others do not.

education and employment. Muslim women are regarded as culture bearers, teachers of family faith and values, whose primary role as wives and mothers limits or prevents participation in public life. The imposition of reputed Islamic laws by some governments and the policies of some Islamist movements rein-forced fears of a retreat to the past. Among the prime examples have been the enforcement of veiling, closure of women's schools, restriction of women in the workplace in the Taliban's Afghanistan; Pakistan's General Zia ul-Haq's reintroduction of hudud punishments and a law that counted the testimony of women as worth half that of men; restrictions on women in the Islamic repub-lics of Iran and Sudan; and the brutality of Algeria's Armed Islamic Group toward "unveiled" or more Westernized professional women. In fact, the pic-ture is far more complex and diverse, revealing both old and new patterns.

Modern forms of Islamic dress have the practical advantage of enabling some women to assert their modesty and dignity while functioning in public

Indonesia has the largest Muslim population in the world. These women from the province of Aceh, contestants seeking to become Miss Indonesia, learn how to perfect the application of makeup.

life in societies where Western dress often symbolizes a more permissive lifestyle. It creates a protected, private space of respectability in crowded urban environments. For some it is a sign of a real feminism that rejects what is regarded as the tendency of women in the West, and in many Muslim societies, to go from being defined as restricted sexual objects in a male-dominated tradition to so-called free yet exploited sexual objects. Western feminism is often seen as pseudoliberation, a new form of bondage to dress, youthfulness, and physical beauty, a false freedom in which women's bodies are used to sell everything from clothing to automobiles to cell phones. Covering the body, it is argued, defines a woman and gender relations in society in terms of personality and talents rather than physical appearance.

New experiments by educated Muslim women to orient their lives more Islamically have also resulted in more women "returning to the mosque." In the past, when women were restricted to the home and allowed only limited education, they did not participate in public prayer in mosques. While some attended the Friday congregational prayer, sitting separately from the men; it was more common for women to pray at home and to leave religious learning to men. Today, in many Muslim countries and communities, particularly those that have been regarded as among the more modernized such as Egypt, Jordan, Malaysia, and the United States, women are forming prayer and Quran study groups, which are led by women. To justify these public activities, women cite the examples of Muslim women in early Islam who fought and prayed alongside their men and of women who were held in high repute for their knowledge and sanctity. Women from the United States to Malaysia, as individuals and in organizations, are writing and speaking out for themselves on women's issues. They draw on the writings and thought not only of male scholars but also, and most importantly, a growing number of women scholars who utilize an Islamic discourse to address issues ranging from dress to education, employment, and political participation.

Contemporary Muslim societies reflect both the old and the new realities. Old patterns remain strong and are indeed reasserted and defended by those who call for a more widespread return to traditional forms of Islamic dress and segregation or seclusion of women (purdah). However, at the same time, Muslim women have become catalysts for change. They have empowered themselves by entering the professions, running for elective office, and serving in parliament, becoming students and scholars of Islam, and establishing women's professional organizations, journals, and magazines. Women's organizations such as Women Living Under Muslim Laws, based in Pakistan but international in membership, and Malaysia's Sisters in Islam, are active internationally in protecting and promoting the rights of Muslim women.

Islamic Reform

The perversions of Islam represented by the terrorist activities of Osama bin Laden and al-Qaeda symbolize and underscore the urgency of Islamic reform. Formidable challenges and obstacles must be overcome including the discrediting of militant jihadist ideas and ideologies and the reform of madrasas and universities that perpetuate a "theology of hate" and train jihadis. Another obstacle to reform, however, is the ultraconservatism of many (though not all) ulama; which hinders reform in the curriculum and training of religious scholars, leaders, and students.

Like the Christian Reformation of the sixteenth century, Islamic reform is a process not only of intellectual ferment and religious debate but also of religious and political unrest and violence.

Today it is critical to distinguish between the religion of Islam and the "hijacked" version promoted by extremists. The struggle of Islam is between the competing voices and visions of over a billion mainstream Muslims and a dangerous and deadly minority of terrorists like Osama bin Laden and al-Qaeda. While the extremists dominate the headlines and threaten Muslim and Western societies, the vast majority of Muslims, like other religious believers, pursue normal everyday activities.

For decades, quietly, persistently, and effectively, a group of reform-minded Muslims have articulated a variety of progressive, constructive Islamic frameworks for reform. These intellectual activists represent voices of reform from North Africa to Southeast Asia and from Europe to North America. They respond to the realities of many Muslim societies, the challenges of authoritarian regimes and secular elites, the dangers of religious extremism, and the dead weight of well-meaning but often intransigent conservative religious scholars and leaders.

Islam, like all religious traditions, is an ideal that has taken many forms historically and has been capable of multiple levels of discourse, conditioned by reason or human interpretation and historical/social contexts. For example, much of the debate over the relationship of Islam to women's rights must be seen in terms not only of religion but also, as in other religions, in the light of a patriarchal past, when a male religious elite, the ulama, were the interpreters of religion.

The lessons of the Protestant Reformation, the Catholic Counter-Reformation, and more recently Vatican II demonstrate that religious reformations take time and are often fraught with conflict and even danger. Generations of reformers, often a minority within their communities, struggle today against powerful forces: conservative religious establishments, with their medieval paradigms, authoritarian regimes able to control or manipulate religion, education, and the media; and political and religious establishments that sometimes see reformers as a threat to their power and privilege.

CONCLUSION

The history of Islam in the contemporary world, as throughout much of history, continues to be one of dynamic change. Muslim societies have experienced the impact of rapid change, and with it the challenges in religious, political, and economic development. Muslims continue to grapple with the relationship of the present and future to the past. However, in contrast to Judaism and Christianity, Muslims have had only a few decades to accomplish what in the West was the product of centuries of religious and political revolution and reform. This is because during the period that included the Enlightenment, the Reformation, the Counter-Reformation, and the French and American revolutions, Muslims were subject to European colonial dominance and rule.

Yet as for believers in other faiths, the critical question facing Islam and Muslim communities globally is the relationship of faith and tradition to change in an ever transforming, pluralistic world. Across the Muslim world today, many have taken up the challenge articulated by Fazlur Rahman, a distinguished Muslim scholar, who noted that Islamic reform required "first-class minds who can interpret the old in terms of the new as regards substance and turn the new into the service of the old as regards ideals."[17]

Discussion Questions

1. Identify and describe the Five Pillars of Islam.

2. Describe the diverse meanings of *jihad*. How has the concept been used by different Islamic movements to justify their activities?

3. What are the differences between Sunnis, Shiites, and Sufis?

4. What is the difference between the sharia and *fiqh*? What impact have these aspects of Islam had on modern revivalism and reformism?

5. What are the origins of the Crusades? Explain their long-term effects on Muslim-Christian/Western relations.

6. Discuss the impact of European colonialism on the Muslim world. What are some of the ways in which Muslims responded to it?

7. What are *taqlid* and *ijtihad*? Why are these concepts at the heart of the question of the relationship between Islam and modernity?

8 Describe the different themes and techniques used for the revival and reform of Islam in the eighteenth century.

9 Discuss the basic tenets and significance of the Muslim Brotherhood and the Jamaat-i-Islami.

10 What are the causes and conditions that led to the contemporary resurgence of Islam?

11 How is Islam used both to support and to oppose the state? Give examples.

12 Discuss the origin and development of the Nation of Islam. Do African American Muslims differ from mainstream Muslims?

13 How has Islam affected or changed the status of women? How are women influenced by Islamic movements today? How are they influencing these movements?

14 What are some of the issues facing Muslims living in non-Muslim majority countries today, particularly in Europe and America?

Key Terms

Allah	hijab	People of the Book	Sufism
ayatollah	hijrah	Quran	Sunnah
caliph	ijtihad	Ramadan	Sunni
dhimmi	jihad	salat	tawhid
fatwa	mahdi	shahadah	ulama
hadith	mosque	sharia	ummah
hajj	mufti	Shiah	zakat

Suggested Readings

Armstrong, Karen, *Muhammad: A Biography of the Prophet* (San Francisco: Harper, 1993).

Asad, Muhammad, *The Message of the Quran* (Gibraltar: Dar al-Andalus, 1980).

Esposito, John L., *Unholy War: Terror in the Name of Islam* (New York: Oxford University Press, 2000).

———, *What Everyone Needs to Know About Islam* (New York: Oxford University Press, 2002).

———, ed., *Islam: The Straight Path*, 3rd rev. ed. (New York: Oxford University Press, 2005).

———, *The Islamic World: Past and Present*, vols. 1–3 (New York: Oxford University Press, 2004).

———, ed., *The Oxford History of Islam* (New York: Oxford University Press, 2000).

Haneef, Suzanne, *What Everyone Should Know About Islam and Muslims* (Chicago: Kazi Publications, 1996).

Lings, Martin, *What Is Sufism?* (London: I. B. Taurus, 1999).

Nasr, Seyyed Hossein, *Ideals and Realities of Islam*, 2nd ed. (Chicago: Kazi Publications, 2001).

————, *The Heart of Islam: Enduring Values for Humanity* (San Francisco: Harper, 2002).

The Quran: A Modern English Version, translated by Majid Fakhry (Berkshire: Garnet Publishing, 1996).

Notes

1. Ibn Hisham, quoted in Philip K. Hitti, *History of the Arabs*, 9th ed. (New York: St. Martin's Press, 1966), p. 120. For the text within the context of a major biography of the Prophet Muhammad, see Ibn Ishaq, *The Life of Muhammad*, A. Guillaume, tr. (London: Oxford University Press, 1955), p. 651.

2. Bernard Lewis, ed., tr. *Islam: From the Prophet Muhammad to the Capture of Constantinople* (New York: Harper & Row, 1974), pp. 179–181.

3. Seyyed Hossein Nasr, *Muhammad: Man of God* (Chicago: Kazi Publications, 1995), p. 90.

4. The Hedaya, Charles Hamilton, tr., 2d ed. (Lahore, Pakistan: Primier Books, 1957), p. 73.

5. As quoted in Rueben Levy, *The Social Structure of Islam* (Cambridge: Cambridge University Press, 1955), p. 126.

6. Francis E. Peters, "Early Muslim Empires: Umayyads, Abbasids, Fatimids," in *Islam: The Religious and Political Life of a World Community*, Marjorie Kelly, ed. (New York: Praeger, 1984), p. 85.

7. Roger Savory, "Christendom vs Islam: Interaction and Coexistence," in *Introduction to Islamic Civilization*, Roger Savory, ed. (Cambridge: Cambridge University Press, 1976), p. 133.

8. John O. Voll, "Renewal and Reform in Islamic History: Tajdid and Islah," in *Voices of Resurgent Islam*, John L. Esposito, ed. (New York: Oxford University Press, 1983) p. 33.

9. John O. Voll, "The Sudanese Mahdi: Frontier Fundamentalist," *International Journal of Middle East Studies* 10, 1979, 159.

10. For perceptive discussions of Osama bin Laden, see A. Rashid, *Taliban: Militant Islam, Oil, and Fundamentalism in Central Asia* (New Haven, CT: Yale University Press, 2000) and J. K. Cooley, *Unholy Wars: Afghanistan, America and International Terrorism* (London: Pluto Press, 2000).

11. Transcript of Osama bin Laden Interview, CNN/Time, *Impact: Holy Terror?* August 25, 1998.

12. *Al-Hayat*, November 5, 2001.

13. This section is adapted from John L. Esposito, *Islam: The Straight Path*, 3d ed. (New York: Oxford University Press, 1998) and *Muslims on the Americanization Path* (New York: Oxford University Press, 1999).

14. Malcolm X with Alex Haley, *The Autobiography of Malcolm X* (New York: Ballantine Books, 1973), pp. 241–242.

15. Quoted in Clifton E. Marsh, in From *Black Muslims to Muslims: The Transition from Separatism to Islam, 1930–1980* (Metuchen, NJ: Scarecrow Press, 1984), p. 76.

16. Malcolm X, *Autobiography of Malcolm X*, pp. 316–317.

17. Fazlur Rahman, *Islam and Modernity* (Chicago: University of Chicago Press, 1982), p. 139.

CHAPTER SIX

Hinduism
Myriad Paths to Salvation

Overview

"Namaskar." Millions of Hindus every day extend this ancient Sanskrit greeting to holy seekers and other respected individuals, as well as to their gods. In a suburb of Calcutta, devotees lead a goat toward the small temple where a priest sprinkles pure water on its head; after seeing it "consent" to its fate by shivering, the priest skillfully wields a sharp knife to slit the animal's throat, severs the head, and pours the spurting blood from it on the icon of goddess Kali, saying, *"Om namaskar Kali-Ma"* (*"Om* homage to Mother Kali"). In a desert oasis town in western India, a sadhu who has renounced all family ties in quest of salvation walks slowly down a narrow byway, wearing a humble robe and carrying an alms bowl; a white cotton cloth covers his nose and mouth, indicating the sadhu's vow of nonviolence (that precludes even the unintentional inhaling of insects). A housewife offers some fruit, bows, and says, *"Namaskar baba-ji"* ("Homage to respected father"). Despite the apparent contradiction, no one would dispute that both animal sacrifices to Kali and absolutely nonviolent ascetics are following ancient and legitimate Hindu traditions. Nor can we ignore the fact that other venerable Hindu traditions empower holy men to take up weapons to defend their faith, or that in countless temples across the Hindu world today priests accept only the purest vegetarian offerings designed to nourish and please the deities.

From this bewildering set of examples, we can see that Hinduism is unlike the great world religions surveyed already. In addition, it lacks both a single canonical text accepted by all followers and an elite who exert control over the development of its fundamental beliefs and practices.

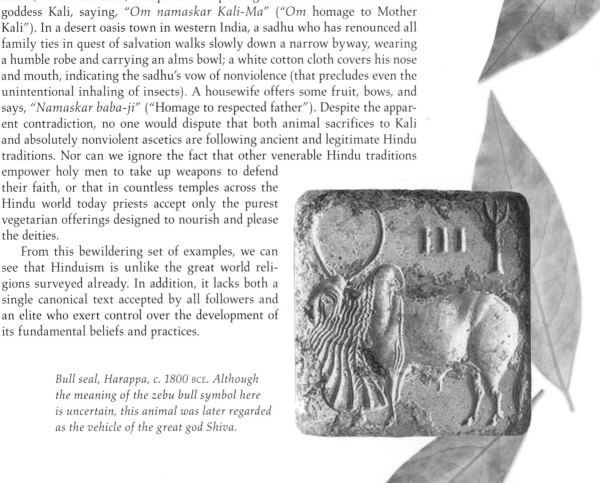

Bull seal, Harappa, c. 1800 BCE. Although the meaning of the zebu bull symbol here is uncertain, this animal was later regarded as the vehicle of the great god Shiva.

HINDUISM *Timeline*

ca. 3500–1800 BCE	Indus Valley civilization in northwestern South Asia
1500 BCE	Decline of major Indus cities; populations migrate east to Gangetic plain
1500–500 BCE	Period of Vedic civilization
900–400 BCE	Shramana period of wandering ascetics and composition of the Upanishads
300–100 BCE	Texts of brahmanical orthodoxy formulated (e.g., *Laws of Manu*)
100 BCE–400 CE	Composition of devotional texts and epics *Ramayana* and *Mahabharata*
50 BCE–300 CE	Composition of the *Bhagavad Gita* and Patanjali's *Yoga Sutras*
100 CE–700 CE	Hinduism established along rim of Indian Ocean in Southeast Asia
320–647	Classical temple Hinduism established
500–ff	Development of Advaita *Vedanta* school; textual expressions of Hindu tantrism as counterculture
788–820	Life of Shankara, *Vedanta* school exponent of Advaita Vedanta and creator of Hindu monasticism
800–1200	Six brahmanical schools established as divisions in elite philosophical Hinduism
1025–1137	Life of Ramanuja, philosophical defender of *bhakti* faith
1200–1757	Muslim rule of North India; Buddhism virtually extinguished in South Asia
1420–1550	Era of great devotional saints (e.g., Mirabai, Ravidas, Kabir, Chaitanya, Surdas)
1469–1539	Life of Nanak, the founder of the Sikh faith
1526–1707	Mughal dynasty; Muslim rulers alternate between anti-Hindu and ecumenical policies
1708	Death of tenth guru, Gobind Singh; Sikh text *Adi Grantha* declared guru of the community
1757–1857	British East India Company dominates Indian political life
1815	Christian missionaries present in most cities and towns of British India

A FAR-RANGING SPIRITUAL TRADITION

Ancient Hindu traditions continue to thrive today amid all the changes brought by colonial rule, independence, and the advent of science. There are newly built monasteries for study (mathas) in the traditional way, at the feet of recognized masters, or gurus. And there are also yoga centers in the major urban centers, catering to India's new middle class, that resemble those found in London or Chicago. New Hindu sects have arisen, usually around charismatic teachers, that combine classic doctrines with ideas from other

1828	Founding of the Brahmo Sabha (later Brahmo Samaj) by Ram mohan Roy
1834–1886	Life of Ramakrishna, charismatic guru with ecumenical teaching
1858–1947	After uprising, British crown assumes direct rule over India; South Asian ethnic groups recruited for government service spread Hinduism globally
1863–1902	Life of Swami Vivekananda, Ramakrishna's disciple, who led global Ramakrishna Mission
1875	Foundation of the Arya Samaj by Swami Dayananda Saraswati
1893	Speeches by Swami Vivekananda inspire interest at Parliament of World Religions in Chicago
1920–1948	M.K. Gandhi (1869–1948) leads civil disobedience campaigns, articulating ecumenical Hindu reformism influenced by Western culture
1923	Founding of the Rastriya Svayamsevak Sangh (RSS), Hindu nationalist group
1940	Ashram established by Sathya Sai Baba, beginning of large global movement
1947	Independence of India from Britain; prime minister, J. Nehru, declares India a secular state
1948	Gandhi assassinated by Hindu extremist
1964	Vishva Hindu Parishad (VHP) founded to unite Hindu leaders and devotees worldwide
1964	International Society for Krishna Consciousness (ISKON) established by Bhaktivedanta (1896–1977)
1984	Sikh extremists occupy Golden Temple in Amritsar; armed removal by Indian army; assassination of the prime minister, Indira Gandhi
1987	Weekly Indian television series *Ramayana* inspires rising sentiments of Hindu nationalism
1992	Hindu agitation in Ayodhya culminates in destruction of Babri Mosque; Hindu–Muslim riots across South Asia
1998	The Bharatiya Janta party (BJP), a Hindu nationalist political party, wins parliamentary majority for the first time; rules until 2004

HINDUISM *Timeline*

Asian traditions or the West, using video and Internet media to extend their outreach. Yet in India today there are also communities in which very conservative priests memorize, recite, and pass down orally and in secrecy to their sons the earliest hymns and rituals, some dating back three thousand years.

In the great centers such as Varanasi and Hardwar, pilgrims come by the hundred thousand each year to make offerings and see the deities enshrined in their magnificent temples, while musicians and dancers in traditional training studios nearby continue to perfect their dramatic renditions of religious themes. In many villages across the Indian subcontinent, where 75 percent of the population still lives, ritual practices within families and in local temples remain vigorous. What we label "Hinduism" ranges from monotheism to polytheism to atheism; from nonviolent ethics to moral systems that see as imperative elaborate blood sacrifices to sustain the world; from critical, scholastic philosophical discussion to the cultivation of sublime, mystical, wordless inner experiences. In this chapter, we will survey this broad spiritual tradition, one that spans almost every conceivable religious orientation—in belief and practice—that has ever been recorded in human history.

Religious Unity Underlying Diversity?

"Hinduism" is the term used to indicate the amalgam of spiritual traditions originating in South Asia that comprise the third largest world religion today. The term owes its origins to *Sindhus,* the Persian word for the great Indus River. Conquering Muslims used "Hindu" to designate people who lived east of the Indus, and later the British applied the term to the non-Muslim natives of the region.

The term "Hinduism" was never in vogue in South Asia, and it never stood for a single way of being religious. Some South Asian intellectuals and politicians did adopt it to stand amid the apparent singularities of the Muslim and Christian. What is meant, or what should be meant, by "true Hinduism" has remained contested throughout history, especially in the modern and postcolonial eras.

Religion in South Asia has been the most pluralistic and least centrally organized in the world, a characteristic dating back at least a millennium, when the Arab geographer Alberuni identified forty-two discrete "religions" in South Asia. While conservative religious ideology still is used to justify the caste system and social inequality, there are other ancient traditions that argue forcefully—in ways similar to those in the Western prophetic faiths—for the reform of society and for "God-given" egalitarianism. Hinduism itself thus incorporates differences at least as fundamental as those between Judaism, Islam, and Christianity. Therefore, it is only by distinguishing the various "Hindu" traditions from the more general and monolithic term "Hinduism" that we can compare this tradition with other world religions.

The Geography and Demography of Modern Hinduism

Though the great majority of Hindus live on the South Asian subcontinent, an important postcolonial development has been the global diaspora of South Asians. Their transplantation to other parts of the world has made Hinduism a global faith today. The estimated number of Hindus had surpassed 800 million by the turn of the millennium; after Islam, it is the second fastest growing world religion.

Among the contemporary nation-states, India remains the heartland of Hinduism (see Map 6.1). The modern state of India has been a secular democracy since its inception in 1947. It has over eighteen major culture regions, whose ethnic groups speak over a thousand distinct languages. These regions

Map 6.1   *India with major ancient and holy places.*

each have distinctive religious traditions as well. The most profound differences are seen between the traditions of North and South India.

Among the other South Asian states, Nepal is the world's only Hindu nation, with a majority of its 23 million people identifying themselves as "Hindu." Two Muslim nations, Pakistan and Bangladesh, contain Hindu minorities (3 and 16%, respectively), most of whom remained despite the chaos and bloodshed occasioned by partition of British India in 1947. Fifteen percent of Buddhist Sri Lanka's population of 20 million is Hindu. Five to 10 percent of Malaysia's large population is Hindu. Small communities of Hindus are also found in Myanmar (Burma), Indonesia, Fiji, and the Caribbean.

In North America there are over a million Hindus, mostly immigrants. In the United States, as across Europe, Hindu temples serve as centers of religious teaching and ritual practice. The yoga traditions that involve training the body for flexibility and mental peace have been the most influential vehicle for spreading Hinduism among non-Indian peoples. The most well-known Hindu tradition that has attracted Euro-American converts since the 1960s has been the so-called Hare Krishna movement (ISKON), established by Swami Bhaktivedanta.

ENCOUNTERING MODERNITY: HINDU CHALLENGES TO INDIA AS A SECULAR STATE

Religion in South Asia has undergone a continuous, additive development process throughout its history, one that has tended to preserve the past even amid striking innovations. Hindu traditions have thrived and multiplied without any single priestly group, theologian, or institution ever imposing a universal or reductive definition of the core beliefs. Hindus have since antiquity respected the remote past as a more refined era of spiritual awareness. There have been no heresy trials or inquisitions in South Asia's long history; in fact, debating spiritual truths, often with great subtlety, was a regular feature of premodern court life and in society at large.

This pattern continues to the present, with the result that Hinduism's multiplicities are continuously extended: very ancient traditions are preserved alongside those originating in the medieval era, and these threads exist in interaction with the traditions introduced by nineteenth- and twentieth-century reformers.

Although in many respects South Asia preserves elements of premodern religious culture with a vigor matched in few other places across the globe, there is no "unchanging East" in South Asia—or anywhere else! Religions have changed as the circumstances of individuals and societies have changed: the scientific ideas associated with the Enlightenment have affected nearly everyone through education, technology, and medicine; the views and practices of Christian missionaries, as well as the political practices of the modern state, impacted most regions as well. Most important, the pattern of reform and synthesis that has kept Hinduism so flexible and fluid has continued, as leading Hindus have entered the global religious arena and adopted mass media to serve the faith. Classical and reformed Hinduism alike, as well as political movements emphasizing religious identity, have proven extremely successful at attracting the loyalty of believers of every sort, from highly educated intellectuals to illiterate villagers.

Visionaries such as M.K. Gandhi and Jawaharlal Nehru, who led South Asia to independence, subscribed to the prevailing norm in Western political thought, insisting that for India to be modern it should be a secular democracy, formally favoring no religion. In the last decades of the twentieth century, however, this stance was questioned by an increasing number of Hindu citizens.

In reacting to perceived threats from modern secularism and non-Hindus, Hindu revivalist groups have created new organization styles based on Western prototypes. Among the many responses to British colonial rule and the changes it brought to South Asia, one of the most enduring has come from institutions calling for thoroughgoing reform of "Hindu-ness" (*Hindutva*) in national life and the reconstitution of India as a Hindu state (*Hindu rashtra*). With roots among nineteenth-century reformers, this ideology began to be forcefully articulated in 1923 across the nation by the Rashtriya Svayamsevak Sangh ("National Union of [Hindu] Volunteers"). This group, known as the RSS, proposed a nativist definition of "Hinduism" as devotion to "Mother India." Members have worked in the political arena to promote candidates wishing to repeal the secular rule of law India instituted in 1947, when the country gained independence from Great Britain. By 1989, RSS membership had grown to an estimated 3 million.

It was only with the most recent incarnation of an RSS-allied political party, the Bharatiya Janata party (BJP), that Hindu nationalists finally found success in electoral politics across the nation. In the elections of 1995, the BJP won more seats than any other party in the national parliament, defeating the Congress party that had dominated Indian politics since independence. In the 1998 elections, the BJP became India's ruling party, a position it held until 2004.

The BJP is controlled by high-caste politicians and appeals primarily to middle-class urbanites. It rose in prominence as its leaders sought to symbolize the unity of a militant and revived Hindu India through a series of motorized "chariot festivals" across the nation, culminating in reworked traditional rituals in which the waters from all the country's sacred rivers were brought together and merged. The BJP and its allies also stoked popular resentment over government-sponsored affirmative action initiatives that set quotas for hiring the most disadvantaged or "scheduled caste" members, a move aimed to break high-caste control over the nation's civil service and educational institutions.

Most stridently, the BJP also fomented confrontations with South Asian Muslims by accusing the secular government of favoring them in its civil laws and of protecting medieval-era mosques that were purportedly built on North Indian sites sacred to Hindus. The BJP today seeks to have the Hindu majority strike back to undo acts of centuries past and repress Islamic activism. The first and most violent focus was on Ayodhya, where in 1528 the Mughal ruler Babar built a Muslim house of worship known as the Babri Mosque. Modern BJP partisans claim that the site was the birthplace of Rama, a human incarnation of the god Vishnu. Responding to the call made by many Hindu groups, one that was dramatized in a widely distributed video production suggesting that the activists had been miraculously given Rama's blessing for this "service," thousands of volunteers converged on the site in December 1992. They attacked and subdued government troops protecting the site, then broke up the Babri Mosque with hammers, steel rods, and crowbars. In the aftermath, rioting broke out between Muslims and Hindus in other Indian towns and in Pakistan. Over two thousand people perished.

The RSS- and BJP-led movements, labeled as "fundamentalist–nationalist," advocate paths to religious modernization found elsewhere in the world: they adopt the latest technological media, yet reject the Enlightenment-inspired critiques of religious belief and insist that the secular political systems established in the colonial and postcolonial eras give way to a religious state. They have used the ancient idea of Mother India to express symbolically their sense of the "rape" of the Mother Goddess during years of colonial and postcolonial secular rule. Guru Golwalkara, the RSS chief between 1940 and 1973, put it this way:

> When we say this is a Hindu nation, there are some who immediately come up with the question, "What about the Muslims and Christians?" But the crucial question is whether or not they remember that they are children of this soil. . . . No! Together with the change in their faith, gone is the spirit of love and devotion for the nation. They look to some distant holy land as their holy place. It is not merely a change of faith, but a change even in national identity.[1]

Beyond declaring loyalty to the land and the Hindu state, however, fundamentalist–nationalist literature remains elusive and necessarily vague on what exactly "Hindu-ness" means, and for good reason: Hindus have remained divided on this question since antiquity, and certainly throughout the era of colonial rule and up to the present.

Yet the appeal of the Hindu-India movement has grown stronger, providing a political expression for the guru-oriented sects with their emphasis on personal devotional enthusiasm (discussed later in this chapter), and for the yoga centers of today, with their rigorous challenge of mastering inner discipline (also discussed later), both of which offer their own versions of "essential Hinduism." By contrast, the fundamentalist–nationalist groups appeal to the simplest level of religious identity. As the American scholar Daniel Gold has concluded, "If personal religion entails among other things the identification of the individual with some larger whole, then the Hindu Nation may appear as a whole more immediately visible and attainable than the ritual cosmos of traditional Hinduism."[2] To better understand the significance of the Hindu nationalism's challenge to modern secular India, we must go back to the beginning and trace the historical development of Hinduism.

PREMODERN HINDUISM: THE FORMATIVE ERA

The Aryans and Religion in the Vedic Era

The recounting of South Asian history until recently included legends of an invasion of the subcontinent by an aggressive, light-skinned people who called themselves "Aryans" and spoke an Indo-European language. These warriors in their horse-drawn chariots, were imagined destroying cities of the Indus Valley nearly as ancient as those of Egypt and Mesopotamia, subduing the darker skinned speakers of Dravidian languages that presently inhabit the southern subcontinent. This rendition of history was used to explain the modern distribution of "north" and "south" India as separate linguistic and racial zones. The Aryans, supposedly culturally superior, allegedly forced the invaded people to migrate southward over the Vindhya Mountains to settle in the lower peninsula.

Built on very forced readings of thin textual evidence, this view of history contained a racial assumption welcomed by early European scholars and by high-caste Hindus in the modern and postcolonial era. Then, when Sanskrit, the language of Hinduism's Vedic hymns, was discovered to be related to most languages of Europe, it was also concluded that the ancestors of the modern Hindu elite were distantly kin to the British. Western archaeologists and the British colonial government supported such research and found this imagined history attractive. The British, in particular, welcomed support, however tenuous, for their view of modern Indians as superstitious and modern Hindu priests as corrupt.

Although migration in prehistory is accepted by objective historians as explaining the linguistic geography of Eurasia, such scholars now find no justification for understanding "Aryan" as a racial term, and they reject utterly any suggestion that the ancient Aryans, or their descendants, were or are culturally superior to darker skinned people. The Indus Valley cities likewise are now thought to have declined not through conquest but owing to regional climatic changes. There are also signs that the Indus Valley culture in fact shared many continuities with subsequent "Aryan" culture. Indeed, "Aryan" in social terms really had no meaning beyond designating participants in early Vedic sacrifices and festivals. By 700 BCE, "Aryan culture" had been adopted by most politically dominant groups across the Indo-Gangetic plains, but most of the religious beliefs and ritual practices of Hindus today are those recorded from texts that were composed *after* the original four Vedas, to which we now turn.

A brahmin priest in Nepal prepares a sacrificial fire pit for his patrons.

Vedic Religion

Knowledge of early Indic religion comes from the four Vedas, a collection of over a thousand hymns of praise and supplication addressed to the gods, the oldest of which is the *Rig Veda*. Composed in archaic language and set in complicated poetical form, these hymns show no systematic development, ordering, or single mythological framework. It is likely that the Vedic hymns were collected and appreciated by only the most elite social groups of that earlier millennium (1500–500 BCE).

Early Vedic religion was centered on the fire sacrifices (*yajna* or *homa*). The sacrifice depended upon the knowledge of a special, hereditary group of priests called brahmins, who chanted the Vedic hymns and orchestrated highly intricate and time-consuming rituals intended to gratify the numerous Aryan deities. Accompanied by carefully cadenced chants, the brahmins placed grain, animal flesh, and clarified butter in a blazing fire, thereby transforming the offerings into fragrant smoke to nourish and please the gods. The entire universe was thought to be maintained by this sacrifice: if kept happy, well fed, and strengthened through the offerings, the deities would sustain creation and ensure the prosperity of the Aryan sacrificers.

The language of the Vedic hymns, called Sanskrit, was thought to be divine in origin. The hymns were memorized by brahmin priests and taught to men in succeeding generations. The Vedas existed for over two millennia in oral form; the earliest extant written manuscripts, which date back only to the eleventh century of the Common Era, include annotations showing proper accents and supplying ritual contexts.

The major deities of the Vedic world, all male, were those connected to sacrifice, martial conquest, mystical experience, and maintenance of moral order. Agni, the fire god whose flaming tongue licks the offerings, was essential for the successful ritual. The Aryan warrior deity par excellence was Indra, and he has the greatest number of hymns dedicated to him. It was Indra who subdued alien deities, and it was Indra who was called upon to lead the Aryan men into battle. Soma was conceived to be a divine presence dwelling within a psychoactive substance of the same name, which was drunk by humans and deities before battle and at the end of major ritual celebrations. Another strong deity, Varuna, was thought to enforce the moral order of the universe and to mete out punishment or reward. The hymns indicate that humans would approach Varuna with personal petitions for forgiveness.

Death and afterlife in the early Vedic era were envisioned as two alternative destinies. There was the possibility of becoming an ancestor (*pitri*) and reaching a heavenly afterlife (*pitriloka*) if one lived morally, but only if one's family, in the first after-death year, performed special memorial rituals (*shraddha*). These were designed to embody the initially disembodied spirit in its arduous journey to become, as several hymns poetically describe it, one of the twinkling evening stars. Alternatively, those whose deeds were immoral or whose families failed to do the proper shraddha rituals lost their individual identity and merely dissolved back into the earth.

Vedic religion was marked by faith in the power of the gods, ritual acts to influence them, and the spiritual resonance of Sanskrit words. The Aryans believed with absolute certainty in the primacy of their deities. In later eras, however, all the central deities of the earliest pantheon fade into minor roles: Indra is the king of the minor heavenly hosts, Agni is confined to be a guardian of ritual, Soma is seen as the deity residing in the moon, and Varuna becomes the lord of the ocean. Similarly, the Vedic concept of *rita*, the natural human order that the gods enforced, is replaced by three dominant themes in subsequent Hinduism: reincarnation, the law of karma, and the concept of dharma (duty).

Karma, Yoga, and the Quest for Liberation

Scattered references in later Vedic hymns indicate that a very different spiritual orientation had entered the Aryan world. The practice of asceticism—involving retreat into the forest, silent introspection, and the cultivation of trance states—was likely the first indigenous spiritual tradition absorbed into the dominant religion. Such practices found a receptive community in certain circles among the Aryans, and their synthesis of this spirituality emerges clearly in the Upanishads, the remarkable tracts that began to be appended to the Vedic hymns after 1000 BCE. The dialogues themselves and the name they are given—*upanishad* means "sitting near devotedly"—convey a context of disciples learning at the feet of masters who have gone beyond the Vedic sacrificial framework to adopt ascetic practices. These gurus developed new teachings and practices aimed at realizing the more fundamental realities underlying all existence.

The central idea they introduced is that of *samsara*, "the world," in which all phenomena are really only secondary appearances. But blinded by illusion (*maya*), humans act foolishly and thereby suffer from samsara's "fire," its pains and privations. These last until the realization dawns that the underlying reality is everywhere the same, and it is the unchanging spirit (*Brahman*). The individual soul (*atman*) wanders from birth to death again and again until it finds release (*moksha*) from the cycle by realizing that it is nothing other than Brahman.

An individual's destiny in samsara is determined by actions (deeds and thoughts) the person performs. Good deeds eventually bear good consequences, while bad deeds ripen into evil consequences. This natural law, which operates throughout samsara and affects the destiny of the atman, is called *karma*, a complex term whose meaning is often oversimplified. It is important to note that all the world religions that emerged in India accept the samsara paradigm: the "orthodox" traditions that accept the authority of the Vedas as well as the "heterodox" religions, primarily Buddhism, Jainism, and Sikhism that do not. Although all three hold different doctrines about the precise nature of the soul and the mechanisms of karma, each advocates specific yoga practices designed to realize the highest truth and achieve moksha.

The teachers in the Upanishads argue that the ultimate reality of the world is the universal spirit called *Brahman*.[3] Through a process that is inexplicable, this unitary ultimate reality in the process of the world's creation became subdivided into myriad atmans. Atmans are the truly real entities in the world, however subtle and difficult to perceive they may be. Flesh and blood individual human beings are ultimately illusory. All beings, then, have a spiritual center, sharing with one another and the forces that move the universe a common essence. This truth is stated concisely in the Chandogya Upanishad when the teacher simply states, "That [i.e., Brahman] thou art." As we will see, it is not enough simply to know intellectually that Brahman equals atman: one must realize this truth in one's own life through yoga.

Yoga

Yoga refers to the disciplined practices by which human beings can unify and focus their bodily powers for the purpose of realizing their true spiritual essence, the atman within. First surfacing clearly in the late Upanishads, these practices were codified in a text, the *Yoga Sutras*, attributed to a sage named *Patanjali*. The yoga meditation tradition is for the highly advanced spiritual elite, for those attempting to escape *samsara* by ending or "burning up" all past karma.

The *Yoga Sutras* assume that yoga can be performed properly only by individuals of high moral character, who have renounced most material possessions, live in simplicity (including vegetarianism), and study the teachings regarding the "inner reality." Advanced practice then turns to first postures (*asana*) designed to make the body flexible and free its energies, and breath control (*pranayama*) to harness and direct the body's primal energy. Then, after focusing on a single object for long periods (*dharana*), the person experiences a series of increasingly refined states of consciousness as the mind is withdrawn from external sensation. These experiences culminate in a trance state (*samadhi*). It is in samadhi that the yogin, or adept practitioner, develops a direct and unbroken awareness of the luminous origin of consciousness itself: the life-giving, pure, and blissful atman.

The *Yoga Sutras* assume that the progressive sensing of the commanding reality of the soul within weakens the power of ignorance and egotistic desire to distort human consciousness. The ultimate goal in yoga meditation is to dwell for extended periods in trance, reaching the highest state, *kaivalya*, an awareness that is perfectly at one with and centered in the atman. The yoga practitioner who reaches this state is said to put an end to all past karma and experience moksha, or release. This adept, freed from desire and ignorance, is thought to be omniscient and capable of supernormal feats such as telepathy,

*Seeking to discern
Brahman within
themselves, ancient
Hindu holy men
practiced many
forms of austerity,
as shown in this
Punjabi painting
of yoga positions.*

clairvoyance, and extraordinary travel. This "enlightenment" experience and
the capacity to know others' tendencies and thoughts makes the yogic sage an
ideal spiritual guide for seekers.

The great majority of Hindus from the formative period onward have oriented their religious lives around the reality of karma. Although subject to
various interpretations, Hindu karma doctrine asserts that all actions performed by an individual set into motion a cause that will lead to a moral effect
in the present and/or future lifetimes. This belief holds that a natural mechanism functions to make the cosmos orderly and just. One Sanskrit name for
India—karmabhumi, "realm of karma"—reflects the doctrine's centrality in
Hindu life. This has meant that inclinations to do good and avoid evil were
backed up by the belief in karmic retribution for one's actions. Since old karma
is coming to fruition constantly and new karma is being made continuously, it
is—in most explications—incorrect to see karma doctrine as fatalism. Further,
not all events in life are due to karmic accounting; Indic religious philosophies
and medical theory have also recognized natural causalities as part of the
human condition.

First appearing in the Upanishads, where it is described as the "seed sound" of all other sounds, OM (also written in full phonetic rendition as AUM) is one of the most prominent symbols of Hinduism. Repeated as part of almost every mantra for offerings and meditation, as well as written calligraphically on icons and other symbols, OM has become an ever-present and multivalent symbol, often reflecting sectarian differences. Upandishadic interpretations were carried on and developed in, for example, yoga where OM is seen as a symbol of cosmic origination and dissolution, and past–present-future–dissolution (A/U/M/ silence) in its one resonating sound. OM's components also include all four states of consciousness in yoga theory, with A as waking, U as dreaming, M as dreamless sleep, and the syllable as a whole "the fourth" OM is the sound-form of *atman-Brahman*. Repeating OM is thus the key to meditation that leads to *moksha*.

The theological schools discussed in the text have suggested yet further meanings: the three letters AUM representing Brahma, Vishnu, and Shiva; Vaishnavites identify OM with Vishnu; Shaivites see Shiva as Lord of the Dance creating from OM all the sounds for musical notes from his drum. OM adorns all the major deities as represented in the popular art forms.

What is implicit in karma theory for typical human beings is that one's karma in daily life is in fact unknown. In practice, this uncertainty principle (similar to the belief of some Protestant Christians that no one can be certain about his or her salvation) has sustained a strong tendency for Hindus to resort to astrology for guidance at times of important decisions, such as when to first plant the fields, the choice of marriage partner, or when to set off on a journey. As Indian society developed, other ideas were tied to karma, weaving tighter the socioreligious fabric of classical Hinduism.

PREMODERN HINDUISM: THE CLASSICAL ERA (180 BCE–900 CE)

There were very few periods in South Asian history when expansive empires unified the subcontinent. The first great empire was that of the Mauryas (300–180 BCE), whose emperors helped to spread Buddhism and its ideal of compassion as a principle of just rule. As Buddhism expanded and thrived, it competed with early brahmanical tradition.

Classical Hinduism, the product of response to Buddhism by the orthodox brahmin priests and spiritual teachers, absorbed and synthesized aspects of this missionary faith while also embracing pre-Aryan deities and other indigenous Indic traditions. As a result, nonviolence and vegetarianism became ideals of high-caste religiosity, Hindu monasteries for training and meditation were begun, and a distinctive theistic dimension of Hinduism (not part of early Buddhism) found vast elaboration and increasingly popular acceptance. Classical Hinduism in North India reaches a high point in the Gupta dynasty (320–647 CE), when wealth and cultural expressions of devotional Hinduism flowered in all the fine arts. This tradition was so compelling that by 1200 CE, by which time Hinduism had slowly absorbed the Buddha within its panoply of gods, Buddhism had virtually disappeared from South Asia except for the Himalayan (Nepal) and Sri Lankan peripheries. The brahmins in the classical age composed Sanskrit literature that codified and disseminated expressions of this new synthesis in the realms of philosophy, theology, and law. These texts and leaders gave the subcontinent a source of unity through one fundamental paradigm: an individual's place in society is defined in terms of karma.

The Reality of Karma and Caste

As we have seen, the idea of karma provided a way of explaining the destiny of a being according to its moral past. Evil deeds lead to evil destiny and vice versa; people get what they deserve, although not necessarily in a single life-time. This idea of karmic retribution had become widely accepted by the classical era, and brahmin social thinkers built upon it to formulate the basis of the ideal Hindu society in a series of texts called the *Dharmashastras* (*Treatises on Dharma*). These texts, the most famous of which is known by the English title *The Laws of Manu*, make a series of arguments about karma, while also charting practices and social policies designed to keep the world in order.

The *Dharmashastras* assume that one's birth location is the most telling indication of one's karma. They also argue that high-status birth gives one a higher spiritual nature, reflecting one's good karma past. Rebirth, then, is assumed to fall into regular patterns, and this cyclicity justifies seeing society, like the animal kingdom, as broken down into groups with very separate natures and capacities. These groups have come to be called "castes" in English; one Sanskrit word for them is *jati*.

Hindu social codes, which became the law of the land in India in the early classical period, prescribed that those born into a caste should marry within that group. Such individuals were believed to have closely matching karma, so that if they segregated themselves to bear and raise children, reincarnation patterns should be maintained consistently and clearly. Those born into a caste were also expected to perform the traditional tasks of that group. The four main groups were called *varnas*, or classes: *brahmins*, who were to master the Vedic and ritual practice; *kshatriyas*, who were to rule justly and protect society, especially the brahmins; *vaishyas*, who were to specialize in artisanship and trade, multiplying the wealth of the society; and *shudras*, the workers needed to perform laborious and menial tasks for those in the upper jatis.

The *Dharmashastras* also identify the top three classes as *dvija*, or twice born, meaning "born again" through a Vedic initiation. Despised groups such as *chandalas* were assigned to perform polluting tasks such as street sweeping and carrying dead bodies. Under each varna, hundreds of caste subgroups were arrayed, and to this day these vary regionally in their surnames and traditional social functions. It is also important to note that in antiquity (as in real life today), intercaste marriages, political events, and local history resulted in much more social flexibility than is prescribed in the brahmanical texts.

Each caste was thought to have a singular proper duty to perform in life; the term for this, *dharma*, is central throughout the subsequent history of Hinduism. The *Dharmashastra* texts argue that one must live in accordance with one's place in the world, which has been assigned from all earlier lives. Only by doing so does one make the good karma needed to move "upward" in samsara. As one famous passage in *The Laws of Manu* [10:97] warns, "Better to do one's own dharma badly than another caste's dharma well."

Hindu religious law, therefore, does not see all human beings as having the same social and religious status, nor as being subject to the same legal standards. While religious views underlie this system of social inequality, Hindu social theorists argued that in the fullness of time—beyond a single-lifetime framework—samsara and its law of karmic retribution allow for certain, inescapable cosmic justice, matching karmic past to social function. In the end, every soul will move upward through samsara to be reborn as a brahmin male and reach salvation. Individual freedom is sacrificed for harmony and for society's ultimate and eventual collective liberation.

Thus, in theory, the religious underpinning of the caste system has served to legitimate the social hierarchy beyond Vedic times. It preserves the purity and privileges of the highest castes and argues that society depends upon brahmins: if they live in purity and use their ritual mastery to worship the gods properly, they ensure that divine grace will sustain a fruitful society and a nonthreatening environment.

Consistent with this belief system, Hindus, like Jews, Christians, and Muslims, came to regard themselves as "chosen people." The next logical step was to use religious doctrine and caste ideology to justify their efforts to convert and subjugate other groups in their midst. As we shall see, this sanctioning of high-caste privilege had early critics among Buddhists and Jains, and later Hindus as well. Some modern reformers from the lowest social groups point out that these Hindu doctrines were and are an intellectual justification for the high-caste minority to rule over the low-caste majority. As Bhimrao Ambedkar, one of the legal reformers of the early twentieth century, stated,

> To the untouchables, Hinduism is a veritable chamber of horrors. The sanctity and infallibility of the *Vedas*, *Smritis* and *Shastras*, the iron law of caste, the heartless law of *karma* and the senseless law of status by birth are to the Untouchables veritable instruments of torture which Hinduism has forged against the Untouchables.[4]

The classical Hindu writers also prescribed other endeavors to realize the ideal Hindu life. To explain the extraordinarily precise attention shown to detail and to the ideal human lifetime, we must consider the individual's quest to fulfill his or her dharma fully.

The Four Stages of Life

The twice-born man becomes a full person only after he has passed through the stages known as student, householder, forest dweller, and homeless wanderer (sadhu). A student studies in the house of his teacher, learning to the extent appropriate to his caste and individual aptitude a curriculum that formerly included memorizing major portions of Vedas as well as acquiring proficiency in archery, medicine, astrology, and music. Upon completing the student phase, a man returns to be married; as a householder, his duty is to perform the traditional rites and raise children in the proper manner to continue the father's lineage. The *Dharmashastras* require women to subordinate themselves to men, although husbands are supposed to respect their wives and maintain happiness within the household. Marriage is treated as a sacrament, and divorce is not allowed.

A holy man (sadhu) with matted locks, prayer beads, and wristwatch.

Once a couple notices their hair turning white, "sees their son's sons," and finds the household well handled by their male descendants, they are directed to become forest dwellers. In this stage, they focus on spiritual matters by retreating to the forest living only on wild foods and with bare necessities; they renounce sensuality and sex, with rituals and meditation becoming their chief concern. The fourth portion of life, the homeless wanderer, builds on the third, on the supposition that knowledge and discipline have led the forest dweller to the gateway of moksha realization. Persons now wander alone; no rituals need be done, and they renounce all but what can be carried, as the remaining days are devoted to pilgrimages to holy sites and to yoga practice. From the classical era onward, the widespread dissemination of teachings about caste and stages in life, called *varnashrama Dharma*, has given "Hindu doctrine" its area of strongest consensus.

The bow asana, as demonstrated by the yoga master and guru Swami Satchitananda.

*A sadhu Hindu ascetic,
coated in ash, consults
a ritual text.*

The Four Aims of Life

Since individuals differ in their karma-determined capabilities according to caste and stage of life, the classical Hindu theorists in the *Dharmashastras* also identified four legitimate aims or ends that could be the focus of human striving. The first, *artha,* can be translated as material gain or worldly success. South Asian folk literature of animal stories and human parables imparts instructions toward this goal in life, an indication that belief in karma has never stifled pious Hindus' interest in "getting ahead."

The second aim, *kama* ("sensory pleasure"), was seen as an acceptable goal for embodied beings, especially householders seeking to fulfill the duty of propagating the family line. Although the *Kama Sutra,* the text that treats the cultivating of pleasure explicitly, is known in the West as a sex manual, many chapters are devoted to achieving "the good life" in other spheres as well. The third aim, *dharma,* fulfilling the duty prescribed by one's caste, we have already discussed; the other ends of life are justly pursued only if they remain consistent with one's caste and gender-appropriate duties. The last of the four goals, *moksha*—release from the cycle of future rebirth and redeath—is adopted by few, but the texts counsel that true ascetics pursuing this goal should receive everyone's respect and support through almsgiving. Hindus still venerate the sadhu saints, who follow this path of spiritual wandering.

Epics and the Development of Classical Hinduism

For the majority of Hindus, the ideals of the law books and the theologies of classical Hinduism are conveyed in the plots and characters of the great epics. By the classical era, the two great Hindu epics had been composed from oral sources that doubtless originated in heroic accounts of early battles fought by warriors in the Aryan clans. The longer of the two, the *Mahabharata,* records an escalating and ultimately devastating feud between rival sides of a family as they vied for control of the northern plains, each one aided by supernatural allies. The moral element of this story—one side has usurped power from the other, but the rightful heir has no desire to shed the blood of his kin to take it back—is explored with great subtlety. The *Mahabharata,* through the perspectives and destinies of its many characters, conveys a vast panoply of existential dilemmas, invoking situations (family relations, gender conflicts, caste duty versus individual wishes, etc.) that have touched Hindus in every station of life. Through textual recitations, dance dramas, art, and now comic books, Hindus have "dwelled in these stories" and subplots. This rivalry ended in a war of immense carnage that in theological interpretation marks the onset of the current age, the Kali Yuga. The *Mahabharata* and its most famous portion called the *Bhagavad Gita,* allowed for diverse and nuanced evaluations of dharma, especially that pertaining to warriors, kin, and women, and regarding the role of divinity in human affairs. The epic reveals the many difficulties, paradoxes, and ambiguities that face those who wish to apply the lofty religious ideals of the *Dharmashastra* to real-life circumstances.

The same quality of "speaking with many voices" is true of the second great epic, the *Ramayana.* Here, the underlying historical circumstance is the rivalry between Aryan clans—symbolized by the hero Rama—and the non-Aryans of the south, portrayed as powerful demons subject to unbridled lust, who rudely disrupt the Vedic sacrifices. Rama does succeed in defeating the demon Ravana and establishing a unified Hindu kingdom. The tale has proven very malleable in giving groups across South (and Southeast) Asia a narrative to express their own views on ethnic relations, the good king, gender relations, and the relationship between northerners versus southerners. In fact, there is no one *Ramayana* today, as through its tellings and retellings hundreds of groups have claimed their particular version as sacred and central to their own Hindu ideal.

The Circles of Time in Hindu Thought: *Cosmic Eras*

The Hindu view of time expressed in the ancient texts represents a web binding beings together to the eternal dance of life, death, and rebirth. The Vedic texts contain a multitude of creation accounts, and later texts combine them in a more circular vision of successive eras of cosmic dissolution followed by equally long eras when the created world undergoes a regular series of transformations. Once creation has begun, the earth evolves through four eras called *yugas.*

The first and longest era, the *Krita Yuga,* is a golden age without suffering or wants: meditation and virtue come naturally to all beings. In the second and third *yugas,* people are strongly inclined to proper duty (*dharma*); yet the inclination to virtue slowly wanes, and eventually there is the need for castes to be formed to keep order and the *Vedas* to be composed to aid those striving for truth and goodness. But in the *Kali Yuga,* which in the current cycle began in 3102 BCE, human life moves from bad to much worse: brahmins become unworthy, the Vedas are forgotten, castes mix unlawfully, and life spans decrease as a result of war and famine. Certain bhakti groups, however, proclaim a dissenting, triumphal alternative to this pessimistic scenario, and the grip of evil on this era has been (or will be) ended through the devotional practices of true believers. The Kali Yuga ends with the destruction of the earth after a series of natural disasters culminating in a great flood, when Vishnu will again sleep on the waters. Some texts recount that after one thousand of these four-era cycles, a greater destruction will take place, one in which all matter will be consumed in fire, reducing all reality to pure spirit.

Mainstream Hinduism and the Rise of Devotion to the Great Deities

The deities who dominated Hindu life by the classical age differed in name and conception from those of the earliest Vedic hymns. An entirely new collection of Sanskrit texts called *puranas* was composed to extol the glories of the emerging deities, specify their forms of worship, and celebrate the early saints. The purana stories recount examples of human incarnation, instances of divine omniscience, and episodes of grace. Heroes in these stories become models of exemplary devotional faith, or *bhakti*. Just as Hanuman the monkey king serves Rama, or Radha the consort loves Krishna without limit, so should one devote the full commitment of heart and mind to one's own bhakti practice.

All the puranas—which many Hindus revere today as the "fifth Veda"— share an important assumption about humanity living in the Kali Yuga, the post-Vedic age: this era, said to have begun in 3102 BCE, is defined as a period of degeneration in which human spiritual potential is declining. In view of this, the puranas declare that the deities have extended their grace to humanity in ever-increasing measure in return for their devotees unselfish devotion. While the ascetic practices of yoga do not end (and not all Hindus accepted Kali Yuga theory), this ideal of bhakti became the predominant one for Hinduism throughout the centuries until the present day.

Hinduism's shift toward bhakti follows its characteristic "add-on pattern" in merging a new theology with the fundamental ideas of the formative era: samsara, karma, and moksha. The devotional tradition accepts the early cosmic model but builds upon it by asserting that the great deities like Shiva, Vishnu, and Durga have the power to reward devotion by altering the karma of the *bhakta* (devotee). Though these deities are omnipotent and omniscient, they are seen as augmenting the earlier tradition, not challenging it. By absorbing human karma, they can bring their grace to persons seeking liberation from worldly suffering and ultimately from samsara. This view is most dramatically expressed in the *Bhagavad Gita*, where the deity Krishna argues that desireless action is possible only through ego-less bhakti faith and that the true suspension of all action (which produces additional karma) is impossible.

By the classical era, purana texts asserted the existence of 330 million deities. How could the theologians account for such mind-numbing diversity? The bhakti gurus argued that polytheism reflected the grace of the divine, since the diverse needs of a humanity comprising innumerable individual karmas could only be met be a diverse set of gods. The crucial goal facing each Hindu is to find and focus upon the one deity whose form is most appropriate to his or her level of spiritual maturity.

The common principle of simplification in later Hinduism was that each devotee should choose a personal deity (*ista deva*) to be at the center of his or her religious life, a focus for personal communion through an emotional relationship. Although most teachers (and families) believed that "good Hindus" should respect all the great deities as well as the lesser spirits thought to dwell in each locality, it was nonetheless essential for each person to establish a single divinity to meditate upon and venerate as a channel for grace. Among theologians, the terms and mechanisms of salvation vary; in many of the puranas, rebirth in one's chosen deity's heaven—not exit from samsara—is proclaimed as the highest human goal.

The concept of "chosen deity" entailed commitment to knowing extensively and loving selflessly that particular god. This meant making offerings (*puja*, to be discussed later), meditating, and studying the purana stories to be able to discern as completely as possible the divine personality. One formula for the stages of bhakti progress described the stages of devotion moving from listening, singing, and worshiping to self-surrender.

Each of the great deities of Hinduism has come to be known through the purana texts, and theologians provide different explanations for how and why the divine beings have manifested themselves to save humanity from mundane dangers and to bestow ultimate salvation.

Ganesh

Judged by the number of shrines and the universality of his image, the elephant-headed Ganesh is the tradition's most popular divinity. Most Hindus worship Ganesh, not as a divinity who will help them achieve salvation but more to secure his aid in worldly well-being. With a potbelly and love of sweets signaling his sensual orientation, Ganesh, who is commonly honored with offerings at the start of most rituals and journeys, is regarded as the kind, "fix it" god in the pantheon.

Shiva

The *Shaivite*, or one whose chosen deity is Shiva, focuses on two beliefs: that Shiva's essence is found in all creative energies that saturate this world, and that one can find one's own divine nature by dedicating bhakti practice to this lord. Shiva's identity in the puranas merges opposing sides of Hindu life: he is the ideal ascetic revered by yogins, the god who in the Himalayas underwent long penances while dwelling with cobras, clad in deer skin, and covered in ash. He is also conceived of as a divine householder who marries the goddess of the snow mountains (Parvati) and fathers divine sons Ganesh and Kumara.

In Hindu legend, Shiva saves the world repeatedly and requites devotion with his grace. However, Shiva also has a wrathful side and will punish humans as well. The puranas attribute to Shiva the periodic cosmic upheavals that return the universe to a formless, empty resting state. The sectarian Shaivite theologians see the linking of world creation, fertility, and destruction as signifying Shiva's omnipresence, making him the supreme "Great God."

A linga, the image commonly used to worship Shiva.

Vishnu and His Avataras

Although they may respect Shiva, Vishnu devotees (*Vaishnavites*) believe that their chosen deity is the one who truly underlies all reality. Vishnu alone sleeps atop the cosmic ocean in the universe's eras of dissolution, and he alone begets the god Brahma, who then begins another cycle of creation.

The great theme of Vishnu theology is that of incarnation. The puranas dedicated to him recount many episodes in the earth's history when demons or evil threatened creation. At these times, Vishnu assumed the form of whatever was needed to smash the threat. Some of these incarnations, or *avataras*, were animals and most were local heroes.

Vishnu remains alive and connected to the human community of devotees through temple icons and rituals and through the singing of songs recounting

The Dance of Shiva

One of the most lyrical and evocative symbols of Hinduism, especially in the sweeping design of South Indian artisans, is that of Nataraja, Shiva as Lord of the Dance. The upper right hand holds the twin-sided drum, from which sacred sound emerges, counting time and originating sound's creative resonance. The opposite hand shows on it a flame so that in Shiva's holding a fire, he points to his being a refuge in the fires of *samsara*. Fire also alludes to this deity's role as destroyer at the end of a great world era. Both hands move together in Shiva's great dance, ceaselessly integrating cosmic creation and destruction, including all the gods. Another hand shows the "fearnot" gesture, and the fourth points to his upraised foot, the place Hindu devotees touch most often in ritual. Shiva dances while treading on a demon who symbolizes heedlessness. Thus, to enter into the Dance of Shiva means to brave the circle of rebirth, transcend the limitations of time and apparent opposites, and join with the divine powers of the great deity whose grace and eternal energy can remove spiritual obstacles. Because the cosmos has become a manifestation of Shiva's power, a dance done simply for the purpose of his own entertainment, wherever individuals can cultivate artistic pleasure, they can find union with Shiva.

Shiva Nataraja, Lord of the Dance: twelfth-century bronze image from southern India.

his greatness. The texts also sense his being poised for humanity's future salvation, and one avatara, Kalki, is expected to come riding on a white horse to guide humanity as the Kali Yuga turns darker.

Vishnu avatara theory thus provides the most systematic example of Hinduism's theological pattern that spawned a profusion of sects, moving readily from the acceptance of multiple particular deities to arrange them in ordered hierarchies. But most Hindus, whether intellectuals or commoners, will assent to the same theological understanding, namely, that "ultimately all the gods are one." There is also a long history of Hindus (and Buddhists) refraining from staking out one final dogmatic position, since many traditions hold that Ultimate Reality is beyond all human naming or philosophical comprehension. Accepting this limitation has given Hinduism its flexible strength and its adherents an openness to ongoing revelation.

Rama

We have already encountered Rama, hero of the *Ramayana*, who slays the demon Ravana and reveals the ideal of proper filial obedience to parents, loyalty to brothers, and the exemplary conduct of Hindu kings. His alliance with the monkey leader Hanuman also signals the ideal of harmonizing the divine with the natural world. A second form of Rama is one dedicated to destroying any evil kings who would molest brahmins or their rituals.

Krishna

The most complex and multifaceted of the Vishnu avataras, Krishna is revered in many forms: the infant trickster god, whose every prank and gesture reveal his underlying divinity; the child who as "the butter thief" also steals the hearts of the world's mothers and fathers; the brave youth who rescues villagers from the poison of evil serpent deities (*nagas*) and from the cruel rains sent by the Vedic god Indra; and the divine paramour and consort of the female cowherds (*gopis*). Finally, Krishna is the mature guru who offers counsel about the necessity of serving the world according to one's dharma, clarifying choices among the many spiritual practices. Many of his sectarian devotees believe that Krishna is in fact the reality from which all the gods originate.

Devis

The consolidating pattern in Hindu theology is readily apparent in the development of the myths of the goddess. Hindu goddesses are born of the earth and can bestow its wealth. Rivers are all goddesses. From ancient times onward each locality had its own *devi* who protected it. Early Indian art depicts the fertile, creative power of the universe in scenes where a young woman touches a tree, her innate energy (*shakti*) causing it to burst into bloom. Those who predominantly worship goddesses are thereby called "shaktas" and theirs is the third major group among Hindu deity worshipers alongside Vaishnavites and Shaivites.

The earth goddess may be addressed as Ambika ("Mother"), Sita ("[born of the] tilled furrow), or Sati ("the Virtuous"). All these forms draw upon the

Bearing a mace, a discus, and a conch, Vishnu is represented as Lord of the universe.

Durga, riding her vehicle, the tiger, carries the weapons of the male gods.

creative, mothering female force. Another widespread and primordial sense of female divinity is that associated with destruction; this has been primarily in the form of the smallpox goddess, called in the north Shitala or Ajima. Yet other related female forms are the goddesses who destroy demons, Durga and Kali. Those needing to confront death to arrive at mature spirituality can make Kali their "chosen deity": to visualize the dance of Kali means seeing that life inevitably becomes encircled by death and so always keeping in mind that the gift of human life should not be frittered away.

Hindu theology also views the pantheon as balancing the distinct powers that are uniquely those of male and female. The cosmos, like the human species, is seen as created and sustained by the same combination of gender energies: the male shakta and the female shakti. Each is incomplete and even dangerous without the balancing influence of the other. Thus, the Hindu deities are married. Shiva is married to Parvati, or Uma, Vishnu to Lakshmi (important as the wealth goddess), Brahma to Saraswati (goddess of learning), Krishna to Radha, Rama to Sita, and so on. We shall see later how tantric Hinduism carries on the implications of this theology into individual yoga practice.

PREMODERN HINDUISM: THE POSTCLASSICAL ERA (900 CE–1500 CE)

The Formation of Hindu Schools of Thought

During the late classical era, the brahmin elite concerned with philosophical views (called *darshana*) consolidated their positions in systematic expositions, which became and have remained authoritative for the tradition. Every school's texts sought to explain the nature of the physical world, the boundaries of individuality, the basis for establishing human knowledge, and the means to salvation.

The orthodox schools formed in response to the heterodox, or nonstandard, schools of Buddhism and Jainism. Some of them were confined to small circles of high-caste scholastics, but others, discussed here, came to dominate the Hindu intellectual tradition.

Sankhya

One of the first systematic schools to appear, and closely aligned to the Yoga classical school, the Sankhya school's ideas were especially important in subsequent Hindu thought. The Sankhya school (literally, "analysis") posits a dualistic universe of matter (*prakriti*) bonded in various combinations with spirit (*purusha*). Both matter and spirit are eternal, with an infinite number of purushas eternally distinct from one another.

Sankhya admits the reality of gods but denies the existence of a transcendent God. The purpose of spiritual life is isolating purusha from prakriti. Although its goal is to go beyond the material world, the Sankhya nonetheless developed a powerful analysis of material formations, specifying twenty-five *gunas*, qualities, by which matter can be clearly understood. Sankhya's differentiation of spirit–matter combinations, which has informed Hindu culture to the present, is applied to the analysis of human personality, gender, species, the seasons, aesthetics, and even foods.

One typical use of Sankhya theory is to assess the spiritual status of human beings. All beings are combinations of three primary material qualities or "strands" that bind spirit to the material world: *sattva* (associated with purity, goodness, subtlety), *rajas* (passion, raw energy), and *tamas* (darkness, inertia, grossness). In the Sankhya view, too, even the gods are qualitatively similar to humans, different only by having more sattva. This school thereby sees the incarnation of divinities in human form as part of the universe's natural processes.

Advaita Vedanta

The Advaita Vedanta school is monistic; that is, it regards the singular reality of the universe as impersonal spirit, a view that draws upon the Upanishads' formula Brahman = atman. This school of thought began at the time of the Buddha and became the prevailing scholastic philosophy of South Asia after 500 CE, and it is often emphasized by modern Hindu reformers as well. Advaita Vedanta's enduring central place among Hindu philosophies was due to the brilliance of the great religious virtuoso Shankara (c. 788–820). His succinct commentaries and original works received additional exposure through public debates with proponents of other schools (including Buddhists).

Shankara argued that the apparent difference between the material and physical worlds is pure illusion (*maya*). Only study and yoga practice can enable a seeker to gain true knowledge, reversing the "superimposition" on pure spirit of deluded perceptions of two worlds. This path the Vedantins called *jnana yoga*, "union through discriminating knowledge."

Shankara admitted that one could in elementary and intermediate stages of spiritual development relate to Brahman as a personal divinity with characteristics ["*sa-guna*"] such as power and grace (saguna Brahman). But ultimately, moksha can be achieved only by going beyond this projection of a deity in terms of human characteristics to experience Brahman by merging one's own soul with nirguna Brahman, that reality "without characteristics."

Shankara also organized the first great network of Hindu monasteries (*mathas*) that supported male ascetics whose rule of conduct specified vegetarianism, dress in an ochre robe, use of a walking staff, and horizontal forehead markings. At monasteries established originally at Dvaraka in the west, Puri in the east, Badrinath in the north, and Shringeri in the south, this order grew, expanded, and survives to this day.

The Theology of Qualified Monism: Vishishta Advaita

While Shankara's monistic thought and practice appealed to intellectuals and ascetics, it was quite distant from the religious experience of most devotees who revered the gods. It remained for later theologians, particularly Ramanuja (c. 1025–1137), to link scholastic theology with popular theistic practice. Ramanuja argued that human beings could not really recognize the divine, except in the perceivable world. Why? Since Brahman pervades all reality, the religious path to moksha cannot and need not proceed beyond saguna Brahman. Like Shankara, Ramanuja wrote his own commentary on the Upanishads, but he reached a very different theistic conclusion about their ultimate spiritual truth. He emphasized Vishnu as the form of Brahman most effectively worshiped.

Ramanuja asserted that each individual is ultimately a fragment of Vishnu, wholly dependent upon him, and that a perfect continuous intuition of this could be realized only through concentrated and intense devotion (*bhakti yoga*). This theology also holds that souls do not ultimately merge with Brahman, maintaining a "separate nondifference" even in moksha.

Tantric Hinduism

Post–classical era Hinduism produced two major innovations: sectarian monasticism and *tantra*. Like the bhakti theology already mentioned, the tantric tradition built upon earlier ideas and practices but advocated new forms of spiritual experience. The name "tantra" relates to weaving, signifying "warp and woof," in this case likely indicating the interweaving of teaching and texts. The emergence of tantra can be seen in both Hinduism and Buddhism, indicating how thoroughly these later traditions affected each other.

Tantric teachers accepted Kali Yuga theory, and their texts typically begin by underscoring how the tantric path to salvation in this lifetime is suited for the Kali Yuga age, when individuals and the world itself are in spiritual decline. The assumption is that what worked for the Vedic sages is too subtle for today. Similarly, what was prohibited to the seeker then is needed today for spiritual breakthrough. Still, tantric teachings are not given openly or universally, but are bestowed by teachers only to those deemed capable of practicing methods that, as we shall see, contradict the dharma-based morality of the upper castes. The method of transmitting the teachings from guru to student, of course, goes back to the ancient period. However, the vows not to reveal to noninitiates the lessons of the teacher are more highly restrictive than in earlier practice.

Shri Yantra, symbol of the goddess used in meditation

There are many tantric schools, each deriving from an enlightened saint called a *siddha*, who discovered in an intensive personal quest a method of meditation and understanding that culminates in moksha. This personal lineage was passed down in small circles following specific beliefs and practices derived from the original master. All the tantric paths are rooted in the ancient yoga traditions we have discussed. *Tantric yoga,* too, regards the body as a microcosm of the universe; adepts believe that all bodily energies, if harnessed and focused, are capable of producing a transformative religious experience. What is distinctive in tantric yoga is that the energies of male and female become essential and focal. Thus, tantra incorporated the devotional worship of female deities in union with their consorts. Many tantric teachings prescribe the practice of ritualized sexual union during which both partners visualize themselves as divinities, cultivating in each other an enlightened awakening through the transformative energy that arises through their union. The goal is realization of the one blissful spirit that is beyond gender and is universal.

Most tantric traditions invite practitioners to experience this ultimate reality, one that can be found only by suspending the norms imposed by the Hindu social law and caste-determined individual conduct. Tantric yoga entails mastering complex rituals and practices that invert status and gender hierarchy norms, breaking down a person's construction of his or her identity on such conventional lines. Thus, one can select a tantric partner from a lower caste, and practitioners perform rituals that involve ingesting foods such as meat, fish, and alcohol that are otherwise unacceptable for high-caste groups. Places of tantric practice include cremation grounds, the most polluted ritual sites; ritual implements include human bones and skulls. The sexual elements and the use of gruesome items shocked orthodoxy, but they were deployed for the highly traditional goal of realizing moksha.

The six centers of the tantric body, displayed in relation to a yogin.

Ritualized union in Hindu tantra seeks to arouse an otherwise dissipated primal power conceived of as a serpent coiled at the base of the spine; this force, called the *kundalini,* is made to rise up the spine through a series of centers (*cakras*) visualized as wheels or lotuses. These centers are found proximate to the genitals, navel, heart, throat, eyes, forehead, and the top of the skull. If the energy can be raised to this topmost center, the "thousand-petaled lotus," one's spirit is perfected and a host of supernormal powers unfold. The unorthodox practices and extraordinary experiences were thought to be dangerous for those unready for them; this made the siddha teachers wary of instructing unproven individuals and led them to prescribe dire penalties for any initiate who revealed anything about tantric practice to outsiders.

While early on tantra grew to become a "counterculture" juxtaposed against orthodox Hinduism, its influence slowly grew even among the high castes. Later, tantric ideas shaped Hindu life-cycle rites and temple ritualism, as priests over the centuries who delved into tantric practice revised rituals to be multidimensional, adding meaning for the general public as well as for those attuned to more esoteric tantric symbolisms.

The Early Islamic Era:
Delhi Sultanate (1192–1525)

Soon after the conversion of central Asian and Turkic peoples to Islam in the first centuries after the death of Prophet Muhammad (632 CE), South Asia began to absorb Islamic influences. Muslim traders entered through caravan and port towns, built mosques, and eventually brought religious scholars and clerical authorities to guide their slowly growing communities. Missionaries preaching the tolerant and mystical tradition of Sufi Islam won an especially strong reception in some quarters. The conquest of northern India by Ghuride armies from central Asia (1192) ended resistance from the Hindu ruling class, the kshatriya, and resulted in Muslim armies destroying many religious monuments. The conquest was the most devastating to Buddhists, whose monasteries on the Gangetic plain were leveled and whose monks fled to bordering lands.

Over five hundred years of Muslim rule followed. It was an era of strong, increasingly centralized government. In many areas, Muslims displaced kshatriyas as heads of regional states; in many other places, Hindu rulers continued as their vassals. The Delhi sultanate was the Muslim administrative unit, including the northern sections of modern Pakistan and India, from the Indus to the Upper Ganges. In general, authorities of the sultanate did not attempt to regulate indigenous traditions in their own regions or in kshatriya-ruled states, and Hindu traditions continued strongly. Indeed, the great saints who rose to prominence in this era have dominated the popular Hindu devotional imagination ever since. The devotional songs of Ravidas (1450), Kabir (1440–1518), Nanak (1469–1539), Chaitanya (1486–1533), and Mirabai (1540–?) are still sung today.

Religion in the Mughal Era (1526–1707)

The great Mughal Empire that controlled northern and central India from 1526 until 1707 represented the second era of Muslim rule across much of South Asia. In its first century, Mughal rule was prosperous and peaceful, ushering in an efflorescence of Indo-Islamic culture in architecture and the fine arts. The Taj Mahal in Agra is the most famous among hundreds of magnificent buildings erected in this period. There was a significant rise in converts to Islam across North India.

Guru Nanak and the Rise of Sikhism

One of the principal bhakti saints, Guru Nanak, achieved unparalleled success as founder of the last great religious tradition to originate in India, Sikhism. The disciples committed to this faith now number over 20 million, eclipsing the number of Buddhists in South Asia and the number of Jews globally.

Guru Nanak was born in 1469, before the beginning of Mughal rule. He was a civil servant with a wife and two children who, at age 30, underwent a three-day religious experience that changed his life. His first pronouncement as a spiritual man was definitive and indicated the path he was about to embark upon as founder of a new faith: "There is neither Hindu nor Muslim, so whose path shall I follow? I shall follow God's path. God is neither Hindu nor Muslim and the path that I follow is God's."[5]

For the next twenty years, Nanak wandered far and wide as an ascetic. His teachings, many conveyed in song form, record encounters with animals, rulers, commoners, and holy men, Hindu sadhus and Muslim Sufis alike. Legendary accounts of Nanak's life describe his visiting Tibet and setting forth to Mecca, where his spiritual understanding and supernormal powers surpass those of all others. Sikh tradition avers that Nanak's mission was to reveal the full spiritual truth and the proper path to realize it, correcting the mistaken practices and partial truths of both Hinduism and Islam.

When he returned home from his wandering at age 50, Nanak set out to do just this. Back in the Northwest Indian region known as the Punjab, he taught all who were interested and soon attracted many disciples—"Sikhs"— who were drawn by the charismatic guru as well as by the community whose rules and rituals he established. Many disparate Hindu groups were drawn to this community, which offered an indigenous monotheistic alternative to Islam. After designating a successor, Nanak died in 1539.

The Ten Gurus and the Development of the Sikh Community

After Nanak there were nine other gurus, who managed the burgeoning communities being established across the region. They gathered the songs and sermons composed by Nanak, adding hymns attributed to other like-minded saints, forming a text called the *Adi Granth*. This work, 1,430 pages in its final form, remains the unique focus of Sikh worship to this day. The gurus also refined the community liturgies, making the group a compelling alternative to and socially separate from similar Hindu groups. The town of Amritsar was built and became a second center of the faith; its Golden Temple set in a lake is the crown jewel of Sikh architecture. The tenth guru, Gobind Singh (1666–1708), declared that in the future, the guru of the Sikhs in spiritual matters would be the holy text itself, which thus became designated the Guru Granth Sahib. Political leadership would be the province of an elite group called the Khalsa.

In the early years of Mughal rule, the Sikhs gained popularity and were welcomed at court. The emperor Akbar (1561–1605) found in the faith a tolerant monotheistic theology and regarded the followers as a disciplined moral community. Akbar's successors, however, felt distrustful about the Sikhs' growth and political influences. The fifth guru, Arjan (1581–1606), was killed on the order of one emperor, and in 1669 when another Mughal ruler ordered all Hindu temples and schools demolished, Sikhs resisted, and many were martyred. It was in response to this growing persecution that the Khalsa was formed, dedicated to struggling for the defense of the faith (*dharma yudha*, much like the doctrine of *jihad* in Islam). The Khalsa, who adopted a strict and determined lifestyle as guardians of the faith, marked themselves by their appearance: uncut hair (covered with a turban), short trousers, steel wristlet, comb, and sword. Sikhs in the Khalsa also adopted the names Singh ("lion") for men and Kaur ("princess") for women, to eliminate caste distinctions within the community.

*The Golden Temple
in Amritsar, Punjab.
This great landmark for
Sikhs worldwide, and the
faith's chief pilgrimage
center, was occupied in
the early 1980s by mili-
tants seeking Punjab's
secession from India.*

Sikh Theology and Spiritual Practices

Nanak's spiritual path contained elements of both Hindu and Muslim traditions. As in Islam, Nanak taught that there is only one "God" who never walked the earth as a man (i.e., had not had an incarnation). Nanak also set his teaching firmly in the Hindu nirguna tradition, mystically affirming that this God is entirely beyond form and human categories. To specify this god, Nanak introduced the terms Om-kara ("Divine One") and Sat Guru ("True Teacher").

Anticipating reformers of colonial and postcolonial Hinduism, Sikhs deny that asceticism is necessary or of value, holding that householders are perfectly capable of realizing the highest goal of salvation. Similarly, they say that ritual acts and pilgrimages have no spiritual effect. In addition, they reject the authority of the Vedas and the innate sanctity of the brahmin caste. As we have seen, the Sikhs' non-Vedic orientation has caused high-caste Hindus to regard them as heterodox.

Residing in the human heart and communicating with those who live rightly and develop their spiritual faculties, Sat Guru freely bestows grace that ends individual karma and rebirth. In Sikh spiritual understanding, the human struggle involves rejecting ego-centered living and embracing the inner life of opening to the divine Sat Guru within. Revelation occurs through the effect of divine sound on one's consciousness. Therefore, Sikh religiosity is centered on listening to and congregationally singing the hymns, composed by Nanak and other saints, whose very words both reflect and impart this grace.

Consciously rejecting the norms of caste society while living among a Hindu majority, Sikhs have had to make accommodations yet establish separate boundaries through their rituals. Festivals mark the birth or death of the Ten Gurus, but Sikhs join Hindus in observing the major Hindu festivals. Instead of Vedic or brahmanical texts, passages from the Adi Granth are used in community life-cycle rites for naming, marriage, and death. Sikhs find their salvation in combining public and private worship with social action, earning an honest living, giving alms, and doing community service. These activities are centered in Sikh temples, called *gurudwaras*.

HINDUISM AND MODERNITY

Hinduism Under British Colonialism

The first Europeans known to have settled in South Asia in Mughal times were Roman Catholic missionaries, initially the Dominicans in the Portuguese colony of Goa by 1510 and, after 1540, the Jesuits, led by Francis Xavier. Early merchants also arrived by sea to trade for spices, silks, indigo, and cotton goods. Although they had competitors among early Dutch, Portuguese, and French traders, the British under the East India Company eventually were the most successful at establishing themselves permanently. As the Mughal Empire over its last fifty years slowly disintegrated and the region's "Hindu states" asserted their independence, civil disorder increased, causing trade and tax revenues to decline. In this unstable atmosphere, the British transformed their trade missions into garrisoned fortresses, and by 1730 military detachments were integral to the British mercantile presence. From these centers, the British leaders were drawn into conflicts; when they defeated local rulers in battle, they made alliances and extended their command and control inward. South Asia soon became a patchwork of British territory and "princely states" that submitted to the British but were still ruled in their internal affairs by Hindu royalty or Muslim sultans.

Modern scholarship on India and Hinduism originated in this context of Europeans seeking to learn about native peoples in order to tighten imperial control. British officials believed that it was their duty as white Europeans to spread enlightened civilization to the "primitive peoples" of South Asia. This message was, in turn, repeated back in Europe to justify the expanding colonial enterprise.

British schools were established to train young Indians to serve in the lower echelons of the colonial bureaucracy. In large part, it was this new class of Indians that made first in-depth contact with modern ideas from Europe, especially in political thought, the natural sciences, and Christianity. This process unfolded in the colonial urban centers, the first of which was Calcutta. English quickly became the lingua franca of the subcontinent; knowing the English language and culture became the necessary path for any ambitious Indian subject in the British domain.

By 1813 missionaries had arrived from every major Christian denomination, challenging Hinduism on every front, from theology and ritual practices to morality and caste norms. Many ministers suggested that the British triumph in India represented God's judging Hinduism to be an idolatrous and demoniac heresy. Many South Asians came to regard the missionaries as in league with the colonialists.

In 1857 widespread civil disturbances swept across British-held territories. During this period, called "the mutiny" by the British and regarded by many Indians as "the first war of independence," Indian troops and peasants gave vent to resentments over colonial law and administrative insensitivities, executing some British officers and murdering their families. Colonial troops and loyal mercenaries put down the rebellion and exacted brutal reprisals against Indian citizens. When order had been restored, in 1858, the British parliament dissolved the company that had held the royal charter for trade with Asia and declared the Queen's rule over India directly. India became "the jewel in the crown" of the British Empire and so remained for nearly ninety years.

Challenges and Responses to Colonialism

The early modern era thus presented individual Hindus and Hindu institutions with a series of challenges that they shared with other colonized peoples across the globe. Powerful outsiders were arriving in significant numbers, proclaiming new truths and boldly denouncing Hindu beliefs. This ideological challenge appeared simultaneously in several forms: the scientific worldview of the European Enlightenment, humanistic critiques of religion, racial theories of European superiority, and the triumphalist Gospel teachings of outspoken Christian missionaries.

The early Christian missionaries from Britain were largely Protestant. As a result, the ideas of nineteenth-century Protestantism had a distinctive impact on Hindus who sought to reform their own traditions. Protestant emphases that were significant among Hindu reformers included the use of historical and scientific methods in the search for core scriptures and doctrines, and criticism of ritual that was not consistent with these doctrines. Other Protestant perspectives were distrust of traditional priests as purveyors of "blind superstition" and the promotion of spiritual individualism, whereby each person is responsible for his or her own spiritual destiny. Hindu reformers were further influenced by the Protestant reliance on new lay-run institutions to organize new religious movements, the linking of social uplift initiatives with religious reforms, and the prestige of monotheism. (With the exception of monotheism, the same ideas had an impact in the colonial Buddhist territories of Asia, as we will see in the next chapter.) In colonial India, too, "Protestant Hinduism" mobilized the colonized to protest against British imperialism.

Although most South Asians did not convert to Islam or Christianity, the states in which Hindus lived were ruled by non-Hindus (Muslims and the European successors). This state of affairs was distressing because texts conquest by outsiders suggested that the power and grace of the Hindu deities had been eclipsed. Further, the economic dislocations due to imperialism in many instances undermined the traditional channels of financial support for Hindu temples and monasteries.

The colonial government's political practice was to use religious identity as the basis for official dealings with "native constituencies." Thus, "Muslim,"

"Hindu," and "Sikh" became politically defined identities. This created a problematic postcolonial legacy, although it gave the British a convenient manner in which they could divide and conquer groups that arose to oppose their policies, or (eventually) their very presence as overlords of South Asia. As a result, too, Hindus, Muslims, and Sikhs competed against one another for favorable treatment at the hands of the colonial government. Since 1947, tensions between these groups defined by religion have resurfaced, sometimes tragically.

The nineteenth century saw a variety of Hindu responses to colonialism, making it an era of tremendous cultural vitality and synthesis. The early influential leaders were mainly brahmins, the traditional priestly caste that had long emphasized literacy and education, and whose rank-and-file caste members supported old-fashioned, change-resistant orthodoxy. Yet among this elite group, especially those in areas of most intense contact (Bombay and Calcutta), the initial reaction to the British shifted from indifference to more engaged positions: either hostility or curiosity. Some Indians quickly developed a genuine interest in European civilization, and increasing numbers traveled to Europe for education. We turn now to examine prominent examples among these Hindu responses.

The First Reformist Generation: Rammohan Roy and the Brahmo Samaj

The widespread issue that Hindus were forced to confront, one shared elsewhere by Muslims and Buddhists, centered on a question: how could it be that the world-preserving great deities have allowed non-Hindus to so utterly overshadow Hindus and defame Hindu society? Some Hindus gave an answer similar to that heard from time to time in Islam and in other faiths struggling under colonialism: Revelation has not failed, but the community has lost true belief and practice. Therefore, the community needs to be reformed. The first to articulate this position for Hinduism was Rammohan Roy (1772–1833), who is regarded as the father of modern India. Roy called for the reform of certain Hindu beliefs and practices prevalent across India, including superstition, caste discrimination, and the practice of widow immolation (*sati*). He was equally outspoken in defending Hinduism against missionary attacks, drawing on his study of the Bible and rational analysis to critique Christian dogmas.

In 1828 Roy founded Brahmo Sabha, an organization to further his reformist views. In 1841 the name was changed to the Brahmo Samaj, whose official English title—Fellowship of Believers in the One True God—expresses its goal of uniting Hindus of all castes to proclaim a reformist, monotheistic ideology. The Brahmo Samaj's importance lies in its strong influence on subsequent generations of Hindu reformers and revivalists.

More Strident and Sectarian: Dayananda and the Arya Samaj

Similar in many respects to the Brahmo Samaj but centered in Bombay and Lahore, the Arya Samaj was founded in 1875 by the brahmin teacher Swami

Dayananda (1824–1883). Dayananda held the fundamentalist view that only the four Vedas were valid sources for true Hinduism and that they were in fact "infallible," containing all knowledge, even the root ideas of modern science. For him, as for Roy, the essential Hindu theological idea was monotheism. Accordingly, he rejected post-Vedic scripture and saw later polytheism as the reason for Hinduism's decline. Dayananda tirelessly denounced practices such as child marriage, untouchability, and the subjugation of women. He composed his own simplified list of ethical norms and a description of properly reformed Vedic rituals.

Dayananda's successors made the Arya Samaj especially influential once the organization developed village institutions and schools. The many Dayananda Anglo-Vedic colleges and high schools continue the Arya Samaj revivalist tradition to the present day. Many of the current Bharatiya Janata party members and leaders have been influenced by the Arya Samaj. Its work spread globally by emigrés from South Asia.

Sikh Reform and Resurgence

Through their resistance to the Mughals, the Sikhs eventually carved out their own kingdom in western India that lasted from 1799 until 1849, when it was absorbed into British India. After this, Sikh men were recruited into the colonial army from 1870 to 1947, becoming renowned for their disciplined character and martial abilities. Sikhs also entered into many of the new colonial educational institutions, finding success as civil servants, educators, and businessmen. Soon, Sikhs were serving across the British Empire, and upon retirement many settled outside India, from Singapore and Hong Kong to England. These migrants brought their faith with them, making Sikhism a large global faith today.

Sikhs also responded to the religious challenges posed by South Asia's colonial situation and the aggressive Christian missionaries who appeared in the Punjab. A Sikh reformist organization, the Singh Sabha (Lion Society), was formed in 1879 to implement socioeducational uplift programs and defend the faith. The Singh Sabha sought to vitalize Sikhism through educational and literary activities as well as political agitation; it founded a college in Amritsar and sponsored magazines and newspapers that encouraged religious pride among the Sikh communities that were spreading across India and abroad.

Ramakrishna and Vivekananda: The First Global Hindu Mission

A brahmin like Roy and Dayananda, but with a much more humble educational background, Ramakrishna (1834–1886) was a charismatic guru who attracted reform-minded Hindus. In Ramakrishna's revivalism, however, the teacher emphasized mystical experience and ecumenical theology. His spiritual experiences included long periods of trance in which he reported being possessed in turn by Kali, Sita, Rama, Krishna, Muhammad, and Jesus. Ramakrishna's teaching emphasized that the entire universe is permeated

The Same Water, Different Names

The following parable by Ramakrishna was found in a pamphlet from the Ramakrishna Mission in Calcutta, dated 1976.

God is one only, and not two. Different people call on Him by different names: some as Allah, some as God, others as Krishna, Shiva, and Brahman. It is like the water in a lake. Some drink it at one place and call it "*jal,*" others at another place and call it "*pani,*" and still others at a third place and call it "water." The Hindus call it "jal," the Christians "water," and the Muslims "pani." But it is one and the same thing. Opinions are but paths. Each religion is only a path leading to God, as rivers come from different directions and ultimately become one in the ocean.

by the paramount divine spirit, a reality that is called different names by the world's different people, but whose essence is one. In articulating this view, Ramakrishna was updating to a global scale the interfaith ecumenical teaching of the classical Hindu school we have already discussed, that of Vedantic Hinduism.

It was Swami Vivekananda (1863–1902), Ramakrishna's foremost disciple, who became a guru in his own right and presented this theology in a forceful and systematic manner. Vivekananda was the first great missionary representative of Hinduism on the global stage. His popularity grew through lectures on Hinduism across America and Europe. Most Westerners' first acquaintance with Hinduism is largely a product of the teachings of Vivekananda and his later followers.

Vivekananda organized the Ramakrishna Mission, whose institutions spread across India. The mission advocated reformist traditions and embraced a global ecumenical awareness. Its highly organized order of monks cultivated inner spiritual development through yoga, taught "the Gospel of Ramakrishna," and established educational institutions, hospitals, and hospices open to all. Some monks trained as doctors. In 2004 there were 18 mission hospitals, 120 dispensaries, and 6,500 educational centers in India.

The Ramakrishna Mission became the first great global Hindu organization with a vision of ecumenical Hinduism as the savior of the world, not merely of India. The mission's disciples in the West now support its global reach. By 2004 it had published many books and built retreat centers, libraries, and sanctuaries in major cities in seventeen countries.

The Work of Gandhi:
Hindu Elements in Indian Nationalism

By the turn of the twentieth century, Britain's command over the subcontinent had grown with increasing trade, and the presence of Christian missions and the colonial government's bureaucracy had expanded. Indian leaders and organizations seeking to strengthen and reform Hinduism were also multiplying through this period, however, and religious reformism and political activism frequently converged.

The growing independence movement often drew upon religious identity and pride. An important player in the independence movement was the Indian National Congress, founded in 1880 in Bombay. Although dominated by brahmins and a few Muslims who were urban, English-educated lawyers, the Congress sought to speak for all Indians. While it proclaimed loyalty to the Raj, as the British colonial government was called, the Congress increasingly agitated nonviolently for greater economic development and the incremental growth of self-rule. Thus, it gained acceptance as the party to articulate an Indian voice vis-à-vis the colonial government.

The spiritual background motivating many of the Congress leaders was that of the reformists who sought to regenerate Indian culture (both Hindu and Islamic). Indeed, many were convinced that India had a spiritual message for the future of humanity. Such a sentiment was heightened, of course, by the great world wars, whose devastation suggested that neither science, European political systems, nor Christianity was to be triumphant in global history.

It was Mohandas K. Gandhi (1869–1948) who became the most significant leader to guide South Asia to independence. Gandhi himself embodies the changes and syntheses affecting South Asia as the era of globalism under colonialism was brought to an end. As a paradigmatic reformist Hindu who merged European and Indian cultures, Gandhi became one of the greatest world figures of the twentieth century.

Mohandas K. Gandhi. A great political leader who merged European ideas with reformist Hindu teachings to lead India to independence.

On the national stage, Gandhi linked the Congress elite with the masses. Although some disagreed with his stands, he was a nationally venerated guru, an activist who creatively reinterpreted Hinduism in an ethical, this-worldly manner. Gandhi went on hunger strikes to move British officials (or, at times, other Indian leaders) to reconsider their positions. The honorific "Mahatma" applied to his name, meaning "great-souled [one]," expresses the profound spiritual respect he garnered in his lifetime.

Carrying on the work of earlier reformers, Gandhi decried high-caste discrimination toward others, and he especially highlighted untouchability as a blight on Hinduism. He also extended the Hindu and Jain notion of *ahimsa* (nonviolence) to articulate an entire way of life guided by this ideal. Through following ahimsa in all spheres, Gandhi argued that the modern Hindu could find the truth in humble daily work. It was a principle that could transform the individual and society, imbuing each with a spiritual center.

Gandhi

M.K. Gandhi was born in a merchant family in the western region of Gujarat. As a young man he was interested in secular subjects, and he traveled to London to study law. While there he encountered for the first time the classical Hindu texts, all in English translations. He was introduced to them not by an Indian *guru* but through meetings at the Theosophical Society, a group of European mystics interested in the secret doctrines they felt were at the root of all world religions. While in England, Gandhi also read the Bible avidly, as well as books by European intellectuals like Tolstoy and Ruskin, and the American Thoreau.

After becoming a lawyer, Gandhi settled in South Africa, then a British colony with a large Indian minority. He was soon drawn into political activism in opposition to the racist and discriminatory imperial practices directed toward South Asians as "coloreds." From experiences with protests and community organization, Gandhi developed his central principle, one that guided his future life. He called it *satyagraha* ("grasping the truth"). This concept has roots in the Hindu and Jain doctrine of nonviolence (*ahimsa*) and in Christianity's injunctions to love one's enemy and turn the other cheek (as a reaction to being struck in the face). Gandhi required those opposing the government to confine their protests to nonviolent acts, accept suffering for the cause, to love the opponent, and to be disciplined in personal life. Gandhi's work in South Africa among Indian immigrants transformed him and drew attention to his teachings back in India, where Congress leaders urged him to return. He did so in 1915.

Although Gandhi always retained respect for British law and the moral ideals articulated in Western religions, back in India he abandoned the dress of the Western barrister for the humble *dhoti* (loincloth) of the Indian peasant. Gandhi's greatness as a political leader was likewise built upon his connection with the Indian masses, a relationship that developed through his wide-ranging tours of the countryside, his involvement with a series of peasant protests, his self-imposed poverty, and an effective organization (including a daily newspaper) that he developed with those who lived in his *ashram*.

Gandhi's life work was crowned in 1947, when India finally gained its independence. However, celebration of this long-anticipated moment was shattered by the violence that accompanied it. The British allowed no time for the orderly implementation of their partition, which divided India, a new secular nation, from the new Muslim state of Pakistan. A civil war broke out in which an estimated 4 million people perished. Nearing the age of 80, Gandhi traveled to many of these areas in an attempt to quell the chaos, but largely in vain. He was murdered in 1948 by a member of a fundamentalist Hindu group that had opposed partition and accused Gandhi of "concessions" to Muslims and the lowest castes.

India in many respects abandoned Gandhi's concept of spiritually centered development. Only in civil law has India continued to embrace Gandhi's vision, albeit haltingly, in its rhetorical commitment to eradicate caste discrimination and by holding fast to India's fundamental identity as a secular—not Hindu—nation. Even this last legacy of Gandhism has been under attack by the high-caste-dominated Hindu parties that have enjoyed increasing success during the last decade of the twentieth century, as witnessed by the rise of the BJP.

HINDUISM AND POSTMODERN TRENDS IN A POSTCOLONIAL WORLD

The Persistence of Traditional Religious Understandings

Despite the modernization of India that daily reaches ever further into the rural regions, there has been a remarkable persistence of traditional beliefs and practices in postcolonial India. While no single school or theology is representative of "Hinduism" in all its many forms, it is possible to trace broadly shared understandings and central ideas among the traditions that have remained influential to the present.

The Presence of the Divine

Whatever specific doctrines or practices an individual Hindu follows, what gives the tradition a measure of unity is the widely held conviction that there is something underlying the material world seen by our ordinary consciousness. For humans, therefore, life entails more than satisfying the needs dictated by survival. A divine reality enfolds human reality, interpenetrating the material world and human experience; this occurs primarily through the soul (atman), which animates an embryo in the womb and energizes human life.

In traveling across the villages of South Asia, one senses that the culture is unique in its veneration of the sacred in the daily rhythms of life. Rituals honor the rising and setting sun, temples have been erected at any unusual or aged natural feature (stones, trees), and reverence is shown to rivers, mountains, and animals (elephants, snakes, monkeys, and of course cows). There are shrines for the protectors of houses, families, artisans, and castes; there are guardian deities of the settlement and of the agricultural fields. Goddesses control outbreaks of disease; possession by ghosts and demons explains certain illnesses. Even the distant deities who appear in the night sky as planets are thought to be immanent, able to influence human destiny.

There is, thus, little acceptance of the deist notion made popular in post-Enlightenment Western theology that God set up creation as a mechanism and then, like a detached watchmaker, retreated to let it tick away. Across Hindu South Asia, the immanence of spirit is respected and the gods live next door. It is the human task to find harmony with them and eventually to seek salvation from rebirth by finding the spirit in whatever guise one is most suited to discover. Even in modern cities and among individuals who are highly educated, the wish to connect with and worship the divine remains strong today.

There is likewise a widespread view that through the key moments in one's life—especially birth, coming of age, marriage, death—one should strengthen one's own and one's family's collective spirit by seeking divine blessings. As a result, Hindu life-cycle rites are extensive undertakings. Full marriage ceremonies, for example, last two weeks. In fact, to whatever extent traditional Hinduism has unity, it is not belief but the ritual practices that sustain it.

Hindu Inclusivity Accommodates Wideranging Sectarianism

Another distinctive and enduring characteristic of Hinduism today is the broad range of ideas about the sacred and the widespread tendency for individuals to accept alternative, opposing views. The coexistence of so many competing theologies and religious practices, and even the toleration of nonbelievers, have been based upon two notions. First is the belief that a human understanding of the highest truth, whatever that is held to be, is never complete or perfect. Second is the expectation that as individuals learn and practice more deeply, they will see reality more clearly. From these twin perspectives, persons thought to hold false views are simply located on a lower rank in a hierarchy, not rejected. A wrongheaded person may be ignorant, immature, or incomplete, but not evil. Beginning with Islam, and extending into the modern era with other "Western" religions, Hinduism's acceptance of pluralism has certainly endured. Though Hindu nationalists have rejected an accommodationalist stance, even questioning the loyalty to India of Muslims and Christians, the inclusivist religious attitude is still shared by many. It has encouraged ever new spiritual searches and the appearance of new religious sects that combine beliefs and practices from various traditions, including astrology, Buddhism, and "secular" traditions such as psychology.

The fact that Hindu groups accept others, Hindu and non-Hindu, and acknowledge their value should not cloud the recognition that many Hindus are indeed sectarian in their religious orientation. While the view "all the gods are one" is widely expressed, it is not a view shared by everyone. Adherence to the ecumenical strategy of inclusivity, of accepting the legitimacy of competing religious standpoints, does not oblige one to abandon one's own sect's truth claims. Inclusivity is ultimately a means of subordinating other truth claims, be they Vaishnava theism, Vedanta monism, or Christian trinitarianism. Thus Hindu worldviews have held their primacy throughout modern times and into the postcolonial era; it has mainly been in reforming and modernizing their social institutions that Hindus have adopted non-Hindu ideas.

Hindu priest offers tika *powder, an essential part of the daily worship service for every god. The powder will later be retrieved and used to mark the foreheads of devotees.*

Contemporary Hindu Practices

The Guru–Disciple Relationship

Dating from the time of the Upanishads, one central Hindu tradition has been the relationship connecting gurus and disciples. Just as Hindus perceive the divine in their natural and settled environments, they find spirit alive in its realization by those who reach moksha, achieve spiritual powers, and share their experiences for the benefit of humanity. Charismatic saintly gurus still hold a central place in both traditional and reformist Hinduism. There is even a festival day each year for honoring one's spiritual guide. *Guru Purnima*, or teacher's full moon, is a day for disciples to make the year's largest material donation to the guru and, ideally, to pay a visit to the teacher.

We have noted the lasting forms of organized Hinduism that emerged in the postclassical era. Then as now, numerous spiritual teachers have emerged in the traditional manner of undergoing long periods training with independent gurus, then attracting their own disciples. Guru residences called *ashrams* sustain the community that performs rituals, meditates, and learns together under the guru's direction. Many Hindu guru-centered institutions tend to be short-lived, and the "school" that emerges lasts only as long as the charismatic teacher lives or only through his first generation of designated successors. Others continue, and in these cases we see the central Hindu notion of *parampara*, meaning "lineage, tradition, pedigree," that is, the belief that today's teachers are connected to earlier gurus, back to the first enlightened sage in the line.

The circle of intimate disciples must master the guru's instructions on the key spiritual practices (meditation, worship, etc.), most often memorizing them through intensive repetition. They may also collect their guru's teachings, sometimes only in memory, sometimes through writing, or today, on video! Eventually, the tested and trusted disciples are also designated gurus by the teacher, usually once he or she has reached an advanced age, and so the parampara, the succession, continues.

The true guru is one's soul-mate, but the disciple can expect the guru's full grace and loving guidance only through the complete abandonment of ego. Accepting a guru entails assuming a new identity, which is symbolized in the widespread practice of receiving a new name. For example, Western university researcher Richand Alpert took on the name Ram Dass when he became the disciple of the guru Maharaj-ji.

Given the many material and psychological rewards bestowed upon gurus, it is small wonder that there has been no shortage of clever charlatans who have cultivated followings and fortunes. This possibility, too, has been long recognized by the Hindu community. Yet even up to the present, most will show respect for all who conform to the role, acknowledging that, as one proverb goes, "Only Lord Shiva can say who is the true ascetic."

Meeting the Guru

In the postcolonial era, Americans and Europeans who have sought Hindu teachers have left rich accounts of their first encounters. Richard Alpert, the former Harvard researcher who became a popular Western interpreter of Hinduism as Ram Dass, describes his initial meeting with his guru Maharaj-ji in this manner:

Some time later we were back with the Maharaj-ji and he said to me, "Come here. Sit." So I sat down and he looked at me and said, "You were out under the stars last night."

"Um-hum."

"You were thinking about your mother."

"Yes." ('Wow,' I thought, 'that's pretty good. I never mentioned that to anybody.')

"She died last year."

"Um-hum." . . .

"Spleen. She died of spleen."

Well, what happened to me at that moment, I can't really put into words. He looked at me in a certain way at that moment, and two things happened—it seemed simultaneous. The first thing that happened was that my mind raced faster and faster to try and get leverage—to get a hold on what he had just done. . . . And at the same moment, I felt this extremely violent pain in my chest and a tremendous wrenching feeling and I started to cry. I cried and cried and cried. And I wasn't happy and I wasn't sad. . . . The only thing I could say was it felt like I was home."

Ram Dass with his guru, Maharaj-ji.

Source: Ram Dass, *Be Here Now* (Kingsport, TN: Hanuman Foundation, 1978), p. 55.

Living with Karma: Rituals, Astrology, and Rebirth

The classical doctrines associated with karma, reincarnation, and salvation are the center of Hindu (and Buddhist) belief, regardless of the school one follows or one's focus on a particular chosen deity. Karma is thus the most important spiritual force in the universe, determining one's place in the cosmos (as an animal, member of a human caste, etc.). What one does in a particular incarnation, however, then influences future destiny so that, properly speaking, Hindu belief does not posit a closed fatalistic worldview. Nonkarmic causalities (natural forces, biological reactions, chance) also shape human life, so that Hindus can say, like many Americans, "It was meant to be," as well as "Things just happen." Only enlightened saints are thought to be capable of knowing their karmic past and future; everyone else remains uncertain. For this reason, a steady menu of meritorious ritual is a sensible approach to living with karma, as is consultation with astrologers (again, a practice some Americans incline to).

Karma doctrine assumes that a natural causal mechanism conditions individual destiny; but a person's destiny can be shaped by group actions, too. Husbands and wives worship together and act together in many ways. Marriage ritual ties couples for life and can include a vow to be reborn together in future incarnations (a popular motif in South Asian folklore). Entire families are thought to be shaped by the actions of elders.

Hindus today may explain their individual and collective destiny in terms of karma causality. For example, stretches in life may seem to be inexplicable except in terms of karma accumulated in the past, and some individuals do indeed see everything in life as fated from earlier lifetimes. But the great majority of Hindus believe that their destiny today and in future lifetimes is also determined in significant part by their moral actions and ritual acts. The puranas and guru parables often state that being human and being Hindu are rare incarnations in samsara and should not be wasted. People may be reborn

A Hindu astrologer. Astrology provides suggestions about when to act in the world, in harmony with the gods and one's own karma.

Namaskara or namaste. The gesture of respectful greeting directed to the gods and humans

as other beings inhabiting this world, into purgatories (*naraka*) that receive evil human beings, or into heavenly realms (*svarga*) created by each great deity as dwelling places reserved for good and devout devotees. Indeed, many Hindus today regard being born in heaven, not in the disembodied realm of moksha, as the highest destiny.

Gestures of Respect for the Divine

Despite the attraction of many middle-class Hindus today to the neotraditionalist movement, which we shall discuss later, there is much more unity among Hindus in their ritualism than in their beliefs. Respectful gestures and puja are the means by which Hindus relate to the divine wherever and in whatever form they find it. Stylized, formal greetings, prostrations, and a circumambulation are among the best-known ritual gestures.

Hindus greet each other by raising the joined palms to shoulder level and repeating *"Namaskara"/"Namaste"* ("salutation"/"greetings"), sometimes bowing. Some gurus teach that saluting other humans in this way is a theological statement: "I center my physical self in the atman located in my heart, and salute your same holy center."

The core gesture of namaskara can be multiplied into any number of prostrations (*pranam*), principally either with the knees touching the ground or fully prone. This gesture, too, is one humans may do to other humans by, for example, grasping the feet of the one honored such as a guru, a priest, an elder in the family, a mother-in-law (for a daughter-in-law), a husband (for a wife), or parents (for children).

Another Hindu perception of the body involves the differentiation between its two sides: the right side is the pure side and one eats with the right hand;

the left hand is used to wash after calls of nature and is regarded as impure. As an extension of this, *pradakshina,* the circumambulation of an icon or temple, should be performed in a clockwise manner, keeping one's right side closest to the sacred object.

Puja

The concept of puja, or homage, is also built on the assumption that humanity and the divine must maintain an intimate connection, one marked by respectful hierarchy. For humans, the great deities (such as Shiva, Durga, and Vishnu) are superiors. Puja involves all the expressions by which an inferior can welcome, show respect for, and entertain a distinguished guest. Ideally, all ritual acts express a faithful bhakta's submissive, adoring, and self-negating service to the divine.

One doing puja seeks to please the deity as if the divine personage were human, that is, possessed five senses. All that Hindus offer as puja can be classified accordingly: incense pleases the sense of smell; flowers please the senses of sight and smell; foods gratify the taste; mantras and music please the hearing; cloth and pastes please the deity's tactile sense.

The inseparability of otherworldly and mundane blessings is seen in the full process involved in making a puja offering and then receiving back the remains, *prasad.* These substances, having been proximate to the image, carry

Hindu puja. Ritual is the means of expressing individual devotion and soliciting divine grace.

a subtle infusion of divine blessing, turning all prasad into "medicine." Food can be eaten, flowers can be worn in the hair, incense smoke wafted around the body, and holy water (*jal*) sipped. Colored powders that decorate an icon are carefully collected, mixed with water, and used to mark the forehead with a *tilak,* a spot in the center of the forehead above the eyes.

While the norms of different dharmas and of following one's own chosen deity have led Hindus to accept differences in religious orientation even among close family members, this "spiritual individualism" is balanced in most instances by the widespread and daily custom of families sharing from the same plate the prasad returned from the common family puja.

A good Hindu today, like a good Muslim, need never worship in public and may make all puja offerings to icons in a home shrine. In temples with priestly attendants, devotees usually place on the puja tray coins or uncooked rice to be taken by the priests, a meritorious service donation. It is through the medium of puja therefore that Hindu householders contribute to the subsistence of their priests and temples.

It is literally true that all the fine arts of South Asia developed as offerings made to the gods: instrumental and vocal music, dance, sculpture, and painting are all connected to temple rituals. Hindu temples are simply homes for ritually empowered icons that have been given "life" by brahmins chanting their heart mantras and by ritual painters who carefully paint in their eyes. They can be humble thatched buildings sheltering crude stones with no resident priests, or magnificent palaces built to house jeweled images attended by hosts of priests and other temple servants. Great temples may be surrounded by monasteries, music pavilions, pilgrim hostels, and sacred ponds; these are the preeminent centers of Hindu culture, and to visit them is to see all these cultural forms directed toward serving the gods with beauty, grace, and dedication.

Hindu Samskaras: Life-Cycle Rites

Being Hindu means following the proper path in life determined by the dharma codes set forth by the ancient sages. An individual's life—like society's groups—should be properly organized. The *Dharmashastra* lists over forty life-cycle rituals, *samskaras;* they are most observed today by families at the top of the caste hierarchy. We summarize the most popular contemporary practices briefly here, using terms and culture of northern India as representative.

Birth Rituals   Pregnant women are given empowered charms to protect the fetus and are made to stay within the family, isolated from demons and from sources of pollution. Despite the spilling of the mother's blood and bodily fluids, birth is a time of "happy pollution," and for the period of the mother's recovery (up to ten days), the family abstains from puja and does not eat with outsiders. A special "release from birth pollution" ritual (*chati*) must be done in which the house is cleaned and purified, mother and family bathe, the father shaves, and the family holds a feast.

Early Childhood Rituals   The ritual called *namkaran* serves to give an infant its formal name. Naming children after the deities is a common practice and this can be done according to a parent's chosen deity, for the day on which the child is born, or simply for auspiciousness. The carefully noted birth time must be used to construct a horoscope, which will be kept for lifelong consultation. Before the first birthday, the final early childhood rite of first rice feeding introduces the baby to solid food.

Coming of Age   Boys and girls are led on different ritual paths emphasizing male dominance and female fertility. The rites marking adulthood for both sexes establish expectations and responsibilities of full Hindu personhood; most significant is the assumption of accountability for actions, as these now "count" in karmic retribution. Since the *Dharmashastra* forbids teaching Vedic verses to women, adult females are not assigned brahmanical rites but participate in their husbands' rituals. Women's ritual customs have nonetheless developed.

Girls are initiated as women when they have their first menstruation, usually by going through a week of strict isolation, in which they are prohibited from seeing the sun or males. During this time, elder females in the family tell stories of the deities and instruct the girls on aspects of adult religious practice and the duties of Hindu women.

Boys of the top three castes are ceremonially given a sacred thread, after which they receive the first teachings from the family guru, including the rituals associated with the wearing of a multistranded thread (*janai*) over the left shoulder and right hip, a burden taken on from this day until death. (In modern times, this "wearing the thread" is maintained most consistently among brahmin families only.) Boys are also given their first mantra to memorize, the Rig Vedic Gayatri (3.62.10), to be repeated daily at the rising and setting of the sun:

> We meditate on that excellent light of the divine sun
> > May he illumine our minds.

In adult initiation, boys become "twice-born" through this second birth into the knowledge of the Veda and Vedic ritual.

Householder   Marriage is usually arranged by the couple's families, although many young people today can veto a choice proposed for them. The relatives setting up the match must be satisfied that the individuals' horoscopes match harmoniously, to ensure that their characters and karmas are compatible. This is a judgment usually requested of an astrologer.

Upon marriage, a Hindu woman leaves her home, often with a dowry, to live with her mother-in-law, shifting forever her ritual center to the husband's family line. (This pattern is breaking down today in the urban middle classes, where employment patterns require transfers; also, among the rural population that is drawn to migrate to cities in search of jobs and education, nuclear families are common.)

Death   Death produces a crisis in the family and a state of corporate pollution that for immediate kin endures for an entire year. When someone dies, the family out of love wishes to perform all the rites carefully to ensure that the soul will go to its best possible rebirth. However, the death of a loved one also produces fear that the soul might be reincarnated as a dangerous ghost. This concern has given rise to the custom of cremating a corpse as soon as possible after death, and before sundown. Carrying the body to the cremation site, the *ghat*, is men's work, with the eldest son lighting the pyre for the father and the youngest doing so for the mother. Hindus believe that when the heat of the cremation fire causes the skull to burst, the soul has been released to go to its next birth. The women, who stay at home during the cremation, must remove their ornaments and sweep the house, beginning to repurify the house polluted by death. The men who cremate must collect the burned remains so that the family can immerse them in a holy river.

After-Death Rites   Before the family may reestablish purity in their homes and resume social life, they must perform the first rites of feeding the departed soul who is thought to wander as a ghost (*preta*) from twelve days up to one year. Here, Hindu tradition is preserved in the performance of the ancient Vedic rites: the mourners offer *pinda* puja, ritual rice ball offerings, to feed the soul and build up its intermediate-state body to be a preta and continue on its afterlife journey. Shraddha rites for parents and especially fathers are done yearly on the death anniversary.

HINDUISM IN PRACTICE

Many Hindus today carry a small pocket almanac that organizes the Western, lunar, and solar succession of days. Why are these so popular? Since the year is punctuated by a succession of great and small festivals, or *utsavas*, some lasting only a day, others stretching over ten days, Hindus must harmonize personal, family, and business affairs with the religious celebrations. Being a Hindu today entails celebrating this yearly cycle of festival observance: doing special rituals, recalling acts of divine grace, and feasting with family.

Part of the reason for this elaborate festival agenda is that across South Asia, it is customary for each important deity to have a special day and procession (*jatra*) that is the occasion for extraordinary acts of devotion. At these times, the god or goddess is felt to be more accessible to devotees and more inclined to extend grace to those who demonstrate their faith. The Hindu utsavas offer the chance to live in a profoundly different and sacred time, when the great salvific deeds known from legend and myth are retold by religious scholars (*pandits*) or enacted through live cultural performances. In many of the utsavas, special foods, drinks, and decorations are made that appear at no other time. Some festivals are reserved for fasting, ascetic acts, or other penances.

Festivals

The greatest festivals celebrated in the notable religious cities of India are immense spectacles, and arranging for the myriad cultural performances and sideshows requires the participation of thousands. The gatherings can create a marvelous sense of community among *bhaktas*, drawing pilgrims from afar to witness and to seek blessings. The time chosen to visit the great pilgrimage sites often coincides with the major festival celebrations.

Diwali

In India, the new year begins around the vernal equinox, a date also marking for Hindus the moment when creation in each world era begins anew. But across the north, the year begins with *Diwali*, the festival around the autumnal equinox that focuses on Lakshmi, goddess of wealth. On the main day families wear new clothes, sweep their houses clean, arrange a special altar with puja laid out for the goddess, and set up lamps (now, most are "Christmas lights") to guide her. On a subsequent day, brothers and sisters honor their kin ties, and individuals may do other special pujas to strengthen their health for the year ahead. Middle-class families now send "Diwali cards," akin to Christmas cards.

Sri Panchami

The festival of Sri Panchami is dedicated to Saraswati, the goddess of learning and the fine arts. Students, scholars, and artists all will flock to her temples. Some temples set up a whitewashed wall on which young children are to write their first letters, for traditional Hindu parents wait until this day to begin to teach their offspring to read and write.

Shiva Ratri

Shiva's Night, Shiva Ratri, is the end-of-winter festival, one of two festivals each year dedicated to Shiva. This festival emphasizes fasting and grand offerings to Shiva's phallic icon, the *linga*. Shiva Ratri also in some localities connects with the god's identity that imagines him controlling the myriad ghosts and goblins that occupy the lower portions of the Hindu pantheon. It is also the time for ascetics to make offerings at Shiva's great temples, which accordingly fill with thousands of sadhus and yogins who meditate, instruct devotees, receive donations, and demonstrate their powers.

Sacred Cows and Hinduism

One of the striking first impressions of South Asia is the free-ranging movement of cows in villages and on city streets. Up through the 1960s, when India suffered its last major famine, many in the West said, "If only Hindus would eat beef, all their food needs could be met." What is certainly true is that cows are integral to Hinduism in many respects: one *purana* text suggests that all the divinities exist in the cow, and another sees the cow as an incarnation of the goddess Devi. Killing a cow is thus unthinkable. The cow's centrality is further seen in ritual practice: to mark and purify any space and make it suitable for *puja*, cow dung is a necessary ground coating; in addition, the five products of the cow (milk, curds, butter, urine, dung) are one of the most potent sources for the inner purification for humans when they are ingested.

Anthropologists have also sought to link the logic of "mother cow" veneration with its crucial contributions to South Asia's subsistence agriculture. Dried cow dung is an essential cooking fuel; composted cow dung is irreplaceable in the reinvigoration of the soil for intensive growing of rice and wheat crops. Cows are also capable of eating nearly everything and recycling chaff, odd roadside vegetation, even garbage. Finally, oxen, the gelded offspring of cows, are the most reliable beasts of burden for plowing deep enough to turn over the soil. Thus, for a subsistence farming family to harvest its (typically) sole cow at times of food shortage risks its long-term survival. Here, argues the cultural ecologist Marvin Harris, lies the reason for the cow's sacrality: it is holy because it promotes survival. And besides, the initial supposition is in fact false: tanner castes (ranked as untouchables because they collect dead cows) do eat beef. Modern fundamentalist groups have chosen the cow to symbolize "Mother India" and agitate for a ban on cow slaughter to define their religionationalist goals.

Holi

Hinduism's "feast of love," or holi, is the year's primary festival honoring Krishna in his guise as the playful trickster god. In harmony with the theology called *lila* (divine play), devotees establish a set period for honoring the youthful Krishna. For the primary three or so days, all of society is at play, and normal caste and gender rules are suspended. In imitation of Krishna and to find harmony with his spirit that transcends the mundane, all society should join in the lila, inverting established hierarchies and expectations. Women may sing lewdly in public or douse male passersby with buckets of water, and public officials such as policemen suffer usually playful insubordinations; in villages, an untouchable may be declared "headman" for the duration of the festival. On the last day, bonfires are lit to consume evil, commemorating Krishna's defeating a female demon who sought his demise.

Tij

Tij is the festival for women, who can act in imitation of Parvati, one form of Devi, who fasted, meditated, and underwent purification in the hopes of winning the husband she deserved. In her case, this was Shiva; for unmarried women, the hope is for a good human husband; for those already married, it is for the long life of one's spouse. For Tij, some women join to spend the night at a temple, one ideally situated beside a river or having a large bathing tank, where they sing devotional songs and dance to secure divine blessings. As they pass the night they also fast, listen to stories associated with Parvati and other exemplary women, then immerse themselves in the sacred waters to repurify themselves before sealing their vows.

Dashara

In many places the largest yearly Hindu celebration, Dashara usually falls just before the first rice harvest. It has become the occasion for marking two separate divine events. For Rama bhaktas, this festival is *Rama Navami* (Rama's Ninth) the time for celebrating both Rama's birth and his victory over the demon Ravana, when he rescued his consort Sita and instituted an era of proper Hindu rule. *Durga Puja* similarly enfolds the community in Durga's "Nine Nights" of struggle against Mahisha, the demon who could not be killed by a man and so threatened the gods and all creation. The "Victory Tenth Day" commemorates Durga's slaying of Mahisha, who had taken the form of a buffalo demon. To imitate the goddess in her moment of triumph and to bathe her images in the blood offerings that she most loves, devotees perform animal sacrifices at her temples, beheading primarily goats, fowl, and water buffalo. Durga Puja ends the festival year at the time of the rice harvest: tradition evolved so that divine and human feasting on animal meat coincides with the time that farmers need to cull their herds, especially of old and young males, who can wreak havoc in the luxuriant rice paddies if they escape the confinement imposed by humans.

A middle-caste priest prepares to sacrifice a goat to the goddess Durga.

Pilgrimage

From earliest times, Hindus believed the land bounded by the Himalaya mountains and the oceans to be holy. Thus the mountains and rivers of this region were imagined to be abodes of the deities and the places where sages have realized the highest truths. From then until now, devotees have gone on pilgrimage to see these sacred persons and places (for *darshan*, viewing the divine) and to dwell in the precincts blessed with spiritual powers. On their journeys today, Hindus do the rituals described for temples, make elaborate offerings and countless expressions of respect, and bring home treasured prasad. Modern transport has facilitated the expansion of pilgrimage in modern times.

Himalayas

The most dramatic and famous among the myriad Hindu sacred sites are located in the Himalayas, the world's highest mountain chain, where the very names of the snow-clad peaks reflect the perception of divine residence. According to one passage in the *Skanda Purana*, seeing any of the Himalayan peaks will transform one's karma: "As the dew is dried up by the morning sun, so are the sins of mankind by the sight of Himalayas."

Ganges

Rivers are also focal areas for pilgrimage. The Ganges and its tributaries that flow down from the Himalayan glaciers all are associated with divinity: the Ganges itself, conceived as a goddess, was sent by the gods to succor humanity in the midst of a horrific drought. The Ganges is thus a divine entity; and as such, many bathing rites are done along its banks, where devotees hope to draw upon her capacity to "wash away" bad karma. Ganges water is seen as the best source for purifying a ritual space, so that pilgrims collect it and store it for future ritual use.

All rivers in South Asia are identified with the Ganges. A common legend known across the continent states that each river shares a subterranean connection with it. The points on the river best suited for human pilgrimage and ritualism are tributary confluences called *tirthas*. The literal translation of the word (ford, or river crossing) also indicates metaphorically that it is easier to cross the great river of samsara to reach heaven or moksha at a tirtha. Many of the great religious cities of South Asia are located along rivers.

The Kumbha Mela

The largest single religious gathering on earth in the early twenty-first century was not Muslims assembling in Mecca for the hajj but Hindus congregating at a tirtha for the Kumbha Mela in 2001. At least 30 million Hindus gathered to bathe at Prayag ("place of sacrifice"), the tirtha near modern Allahabad, where the Ganges, Yamuna, and invisible Saraswati rivers meet. The pilgrims entered the water at the exact auspicious moment connected with a story in the puranas in which the gods battled the demons over possession of a pitcher (*kumbha*) containing an immortality-giving elixir. After a long struggle, the gods won and became immortal; during the course of the battle, however, four drops of the elixir fell to earth at four places, and the site of the Kumbha Mela, which occurs every twelve years, rotates among them in a prescribed order. The Kumbha Mela draws hundreds of thousands of sadhus from their retreats to immerse themselves in the hyperdivinized river waters, where they are joined by millions of pilgrims seeking an infusion of grace.

Pilgrimage in Hinduism is not a requirement of the faith as in Islam, but the benefits are elaborately outlined in the later Hindu texts: healing, good karma, personal transformation. Pilgrims can go alone on foot or in highly organized groups traveling on airplanes and buses. The goal may be to perform a ritual, such as a mortuary rite for a kin member. The more typical goal, however, is to seek general benefit through darshan and puja.

The Religious Institutions of Contemporary Hinduism

Although there is no single formal institution that unifies all Hindus, there are standard relationships that support the regular practice of ritual and the transmission of religious ideas. Most families have a relationship with a brahmin family priest whom they call upon when there is the need for a life-cycle rite or when someone wishes to perform a special puja.

Pilgrims at the Amarnath Cave. Devotees worship the ice lingam of the great god Shiva found within this Himalayan hillside.

The predominant religious institution of Hinduism, however, is the temple, and it is thought highly meritorious to build one that houses an empowered icon. Hindus from all classes, alone or collectively, have done so, but the temples built by the great kings enable the most complete expressions of Hindu religious culture. Yet the major temples are more than shrines: they include lands given to the deity and are supported by endowment funds that are continually augmented by the cash offered with puja.

Temple lands are usually rented out to tenant farmers, with part of the harvest going to the temple; other properties adjacent to the temple are often rented to merchants or artisans. Both rentals provide income for the upkeep of the temple buildings and payment for the priests. Through these relationships, Hindu temples have been integral to the local economies of South Asia, sometimes as the major landowners. Modern land reform has cut back on many of these holdings, forcing temples to find other means of support.

The more organized sects and sadhu orders rely on the matha, or monastery, to serve as a venue for schooling and training for ritual service under an abbot (*mahant*). Some modern groups such as the Ramakrishna Mission have built their panregional reform movement through a network of mathas. Another familiar institution is the *ashram*, a retreat dedicated to supporting gurus and their disciples, thereby maintaining the relationship that is one of the central lifelines of Hindu culture.

The Himalayas. Each year tens of thousands of devotees climb high into the snow-clad mountains to visit dozens of pilgrimage places associated with all the major gods.

Ritual bathers in Varanasi, also known as Kashi or Benares. Located on the western bank of the Ganges and with its riverside ghats dominating the urban settlement, Kashi is the sacred city where pilgrims congregate.

Changing Continuities:
Examples of Postcolonial Hinduism

Across the Hindu world each day, brahmins memorize, recite, and pass on to their sons the millennia-old Vedic rituals and hymns, as well as devotional songs composed centuries ago. Ancient rituals are vigorously practiced in millions of households. Certain gurus are regarded by thousands as divine incarnations. Increasing numbers of pilgrims flock to the great temples, consulting the institutions' Web sites for guidance. Ascetic communities in ashrams train in yoga and engage in silent meditative retreats. Religious innovations among Hindus have multiplied further through the colonial period and after independence, with recent teachers and globalization adding yet newer strands to the fabric of Hinduism. A 1986 gathering of nearly a thousand abbots of Hindu monasteries, one of the first ever held, assembled teachers representing 165 different organized spiritual traditions.

Yet modern medicine, mass media, and expanding transportation technology have changed how millions of Hindus understand and encounter Hindu doctrines and myths, and how they perform the rituals. Within major Indian cities today, a middle class is emerging, whose lifestyle and experience have been highly influenced by Euro-American media culture, education, and connections. Institutions and "yoga centers" among this middle-class elite are developing newly synthesized approaches to Hindu spiritual practices, in forms similar to those found in European and American cities. The global

Temple in Madras. Large temples are complex institutions with landholdings, charities, and resident priests.

spread of Hinduism now impacts the faith in South Asia. Cassettes and videos with sermons by gurus reach the middle class, affording traditional doctrinal teachings far wider exposure than was ever possible by word of mouth.

Thus, Hinduism has assumed more forms today than ever in its history, and the linkage of religion to politics is growing. Since there is no one version or center of Hinduism that can stand alone, we will draw upon a series of representative case studies to suggest the broad sweep of Hinduism in the postcolonial era. First we will discuss the modernizers; second, those who have *not* been influenced by science; and finally those proponents of Hindu nationalism who would end India's postindependence character as a secular state.

Some teachers and movements begun in the modern era (such as the Ramakrishna Mission) make strong assertions about the compatibility between scientific thought and venerable Hindu doctrines. The "big bang" hypothesis of creation, relativity theory, and the cosmological theories of multiple universes are referred to by these modernizers as compatible with—even anticipated in—the ancient scriptures. Hindu exponents have also proposed scientific explanations for rebirth and karma doctrines. Even the Vedas have been interpreted to credit the seers with awareness of contemporary technological possibilities (e.g., airplanes, genetics, brain waves). Hindu confidence that the traditional teachings will stand up to whatever science discovers is striking among modernists. Just as many scientists around the world (including many in India) refrain from suggesting that their discoveries are ever likely to disprove the existence of God or the reality of spirit, many educated Hindus have found no reason to abandon the essentials of their faith. Those with technological savvy have energetically expressed their faith on the World Wide Web, and by 2004 almost ten thousand Web sites were dedicated to the many sides of Hinduism. A sample of recent events and developments indicates how Hinduism has endured so strongly among such modernists.

Ganesh's Milk Miracle

A deity who attracts the devotion of nearly all Hindus is elephant-headed Ganesh, divine son of Shiva and Parvati. Ganesh is beloved for his earthy character, his potbellied silhouette, and his reputation as a remover of life's obstacles. Ganesh temples are found in nearly every locale where Hindus live. On September 21, 1995, at temples across North India, priests and devotees reported that icons of Ganesh had begun to drink the cows' milk that was being offered to them as part of the daily puja. The stories soon spread across the subcontinent by telephone and in press accounts, so that thousands of Hindus from all walks of life rushed off to visit their local temples to offer milk, hoping to witness the phenomenon. Telephone and the Internet just as quickly spread the news across the globe, and Hindus in London, Jersey City, Los Angeles, and Toronto began to report similar experiences.

For believers, this was merely the latest in a long-running series of demonstrations that the divine is alive, connected to humanity and capable of conferring grace upon those who serve the gods. From uneducated peasants to brahmin priests, people were citing the reports of disappearing milk as ample proof of the existence of a Supreme Being who accepts the offerings of his disciples. Whatever else this incident reveals about the role of media and the Hindu diaspora, it also demonstrates that modern believers hold the conviction that the divine is immanent, a traditional view that has shifted little amid all the changes of the modern era.

The reaction was interesting, too: the "miracle" gave rise to widespread public debate and rallies organized by Hindu societies (such as New Delhi's "Guru Busters") whose purpose is to expose charlatans and promote rational faith. Predecessors for these modern skeptics and atheists can be traced as far back as the time of the Buddha (fifth century BCE). Although the popular Western imagination about India and Hinduism has been informed by romantic accounts highlighting mysticism and exotic theistic spirituality, it is important to note that there is an equally long-established South Asian tradition of hard-nosed skepticism.

Ganesh, the most popular Hindu deity, beloved for his potbelly and his ability to help with everyday problems

Comic Books and Televised Epics

The modern printing press gave early Hindu reformers a means to reach a mass audience across the subcontinent more quickly than ever before. Ritual manuals, vernacular translations of texts, tracts on saints, interreligious debates, or even reformers' reductive definitions of "true Hinduism" (such as that proposed by the Arya Samaj or modern fundamentalists) reach the literate masses through such publications. South Asia's religious environment during the modern era has also been unified by the lithography of religious poster art, which has spread common inexpensive images of the deities.

An important mass media format appearing well after the end of colonialism is the religious comic book. Adopting reformist doctrines and linking far-flung Hindu communities is the Amar Citra Katha series of over two hundred titles, in which newly standardized versions of the great stories of Hindu scripture are offered in colorful illustrated formats; the text is written in English and in various vernaculars. Under the editorship of Anant Pai, more than 280 million copies of Amar Citra Katha texts have been sold. These have emphasized for middle-class readers that "true Hinduism" is rational, opposed to violence and superstition, upheld by heroic devotees, and based upon the respectful accommodation of other spiritualities (Hindu and non-Hindu) in the interest of national integration.

Television broadcasts of religious epics have also been pivotal cultural events. In 1987 India's national broadcasting system, Doordarshan, began showing in weekly installments its Hindi version of the *Ramayana*, one of the two great religious epics that date back to the early classical era. Although most Indians do not own television sets, groups crowded into tea stalls or banded together to rent TVs and view the series. Many treated the experience of viewing the transmitted image like a visit to a temple. Bathing beforehand, they arrived carrying incense and garlanded the television sets. Some watched

In India, there are countless comic books devoted to describing the stories of the Hindu gods and human saints. Most are printed in the vernacular languages of the subcontinent, as well as in English. Here, a scene from the great epic, the Ramayana.

with their hands joined together, using the namaste gesture directed to the divinities on screen, and some muttered prayers as the sacred scenes unfolded, weekly for over a year.

An estimated audience of 80 million watched the one-hour Sunday morning program, and the pace of life on India's streets visibly slowed. The media's *Ramayana* gave the nation its first "national version" of the epic, one that celebrates the glories of the legendary Hindu king Rama and his struggle to establish a just and prosperous Hindu nation. Doordarshan had to extend the series to meet popular demand. It has subsequently produced and broadcast an even longer series on Hinduism's second great epic, the *Mahabharata,* as well as dramatizations of other devotional stories centered on the great deities such as Krishna and Shiva.

The accessibility of lavishly produced TV productions of religious epics, complete with special effects, has in places undercut the relation between priest, teacher, and laity. Many argue, however, that Hindu nationalism has been strengthened by the common experience of viewing these sacred scenes.

The Dilemmas of Reform:
A Young Bride Commits Sati in 1987

Following Hindu traditions, Roop Kanwar, an 18-year-old bride, went to live with her husband's family in Deorala, in the western Indian state of Rajasthan. But seven months later, on September 4, 1987, her husband, Mal Singh, died suddenly. Following ancient custom, the young man's kin prepared to cremate him on a pyre outside the town boundaries immediately before sunset. What happened next shocked India: Roop Kanwar was burnt alive atop her husband's funeral pyre, becoming a *sati* ("virtuous [one]"), one of forty-two known cases since 1947. Five hundred people reportedly witnessed the act. What remains unclear were the widow's motivations and how freely she went to this death.

Rajasthan state officials were called to act on the basis of India's National Penal Code that holds widow immolation under any circumstances to be illegal. Reformers argued that those connected with Roop Kanwar's death should be prosecuted as murderers. Eventually, under pressure from national politicians and women's groups, members of Mal Singh's immediate family were arrested and an investigation ensued. Several months later the family members were released on bail, but no charges were ever filed. Few witnesses could be found who were willing to testify.

Sati is one of the few Hindu practices that the British had sought to reform through explicit legal prohibition. The immolation of widows was held up for ridicule by many Hindu modernizers as evidence of how Indian society needed to break with blindly followed traditions and to reform its ways. Yet in 1987, over fifty thousand devotees gathered for a commemorative ceremony for Roop Kanwar held thirteen days after her death. The site of the burning pyre has been transformed into a shrine, outside of which artisans sell ritual photos of the site and other mementos. Since 1987, the Singh family has received many thousands of rupees from donations. Throughout the town, the young widow is now celebrated by drummers and chanting youth as a brave Sati-ma, a divine figure who was blessed by and merged with the mother goddess, Devi. This act put Roop Kanwar, her husband's family, and Deorala in the tradition of devout adherents. As a Sati-ma, she became identified with part of the Hindu pantheon, a righteous suicide like the goddesses Sita and Savitri.

All India became caught up in the debate about whether Roop Kanwar's death was truly voluntary, as the Singh family maintains, or whether murder was being concealed under the veil of religion. Should the role of the secular state be to regulate this religious practice? Should the state enforce its legal code that defines sati as barbaric and prohibits the custom, as reformers urged? Or as Hindu traditionalists insisted—and many in this camp were local citizens and state politicians—should the state respect freedom of religion and allow Hindus to follow whatever path they choose to seek salvation?

The Spiritual Marketplace for Neotraditionalism:
Popular Guru-Based Movements

Most conspicuous over the last decades has been the rise of cults and sects catering to the urban middle class. What is it like to live in the urban middle class today in South Asia? It involves confronting conflicting claims on one's identity and loyalty, as loyalty to one's "primordial" allegiances (caste, kin, region) clash with the cosmopolitan and socially fluid urban culture that aspires to "be modern" and join the global culture of CNN, the Internet, and designer clothing. Traditional ties are to be honored at some level, but they no longer can fully contain the individual's deepest feelings of belonging.

Focused on sadhus and drawing inspiration from the reformists and revivalists of the nineteenth century, most of the new sects that have attracted the support of this new middle-class elite have proclaimed their own view of "essential Hinduism" as more belief oriented and less ritualistic. Just as modern technology has undercut to some extent the roles of priest and guru, the new sects have diminished the relevance of caste and regional social identity to spiritual seeking. Several utilize mass media to promote the teacher's message and link distant adherents. A number of the new sects have quickly built an international membership. In some cases they have benefited from praise and support for Hindu gurus active abroad, which has whetted an appetite for their teachings back home in South Asia. Most also emphasize women's participation. All engage their society and include community development, medical service, and educational initiatives, combining various traditional Hindu doctrines and practices with certain tactics adopted from Protestant missionaries.

Sathya Sai Baba   No modern Hindu saint has drawn devotees from as far and wide across India's urban middle classes as Sathya Sai Baba, a teacher known as much for the miraculous feats credited to him as for his instruction. A vigorous opponent of Western cultural influences on Hindu civilization and individual Hindus, Sai Baba advocates an active life informed by scriptural study and charitable giving; he teaches a form of classical silent meditation involving fixing one's gaze on a flame.

Sai Baba's trusts have established a vast network of service organizations: there are junior and senior Service Corps whose members feed the poor, act when disaster strikes, visit the sick, and so on. There are at present four Sai Baba colleges (three for women, one for men) that include educational outreach programs aimed to help small children. The ashram he established in 1923 marked the beginning of a large global movement toward neotradtionalism.

Sai Baba's fame and stature are based on accounts of his supernormal feats of multiple presence, miracle cures, and materializing out of the air items, including sacred ash, food, books, and even Swiss watches. Devotees see these powers of the traditional yogin saint as evidence that Sai Baba is an avatara of a divinity. Indeed, he has said that he is Shiva and his consort in a single body. Through Sai Baba, disciples can see one of the perennial themes nurtured in the myriad South Asian traditions: that the divine is alive and appears in human form, and that this world is still enchanted with grace.

Brahma Kumari   In India today, the most ardent sectarian proselytizers (especially across the northern states) are from the group called Brahma Kumari. Their Raja Yoga centers, also called "spiritual museums," are the organizing points around which each local chapter draws interested individuals and publicity, primarily among urban dwellers. The museums display doctrine-oriented pictures with a member providing commentary; visitors who show interest are invited to attend meditation sessions and classes. In 1997 these institutions were being maintained by eight thousand full-time priests.

This is another group that stems from a charismatic teacher. The visions and spiritual experiences of the founding guru Lekhraj (1876–1969), a jeweler from Hyderabad, inspired an early following. In 1936 Lekhraj established the Brahma Kumari sect and turned his entire wealth over to the first community.

Lekhraj attributed his vibrant visions portending the end of the world cycle to the grace of Shiva, the deity who commands the group's ritual attention. He also insisted that individuals must engage in radical purifications to survive and to inherit paradise. Such cleansing could come only through celibacy, vegetarianism, abstinence from tobacco and alcohol, and specific yoga practices. These traditional disciplines became the core practices of the Brahma Kumaris. The vow of celibacy, long an ideal for Hindu ascetics, is extended to all householders. As a result, married couples who become disciples have to transform their marital relations to be expressions of pure, noncarnal spiritual love. This teaching created serious domestic strife in the early community, forcing Lekhraj and his initially small circle of devotees to move to Karachi and later, after partition (1947), to Mount Abu in western India. Once there, the movement was transformed from a reclusive sect to an aggressively outgoing one. Soon missionaries had established centers across the major North Indian cities. Suspicion endures to the present over the group's claims of celibacy, and some have accused the Brahma Kumaris of providing refuge for women who abandon their husband's households.

Although its bhakti doctrines and cosmology could be characterized as drawn from premodern Hinduism, Brahma Kumari social practices are reformist. The sect was founded by a man and admits men as members, but it remains focused on women. Brahma Kumaris challenge Hindu society's patriarchal doctrines and ethical norms; the sect invites women to awaken to their divinity through a feminist reading of the texts describing the powers of traditional Hindu goddesses. In recent years, the Brahma Kumaris have won recognition from India's leading politicians for supporting the establishment of a "value-based society," as members work with U.N. agencies on educational projects across South Asia. In the last decade, the Brahma Kumaris have claimed status as an independent religion, rejecting the label of "Hindu." In 1997 the group counted membership at 450,000. Five thousand Brahma Kumari centers are found mostly in India, but eighty other countries have centers, as well.

Religious Nationalism:
Secular India and Its Discontents

As we noted earlier, many of India's anticolonial nationalist leaders were educated in England, and more than a few were unalterably committed to creating modern India as a secular democracy. They knew that religious strife in Europe had led to the formation of most modern Western in nations, and they wanted to avoid the problems among the complex and competing religious communities in India that would inevitably result if any sectarian favoritism were shown. Indeed, most of the early political leaders, who were high-caste Hindus, feared what civil and partisan strife the Hindu majority might bring to the subcontinent. In the end, they succeeded, with British help, in marginalizing groups such as the RSS that wanted to establish India as a Hindu nation.

In practice, however, the democratic and secular Indian state has proved to be an ally of the high castes, particularly brahmins, in comparison with its British predecessor. This has led to the suggestion that in fact India's "secular state" really amounts to a form of "neo-Brahminism." Under British rule, brahmins held 3 percent of government jobs, a figure almost exactly equal to their proportion in the population. In 1990, however, their hold on civil service positions was as high as 70 percent, while their representation in the general population remained much the same as in 1947.

Yet in a curious and paradoxical development, and despite the state's administration being heavily skewed toward their interests, high-caste politicians have convinced growing numbers of citizens that Hindus have been discriminated against by the laws and policies of secular India. Thus, throughout the 1990s, the BJP, the party controlled by members of the upper castes, campaigned on the basis of promises to establish a strong Hindu nation. Victories in state and national elections came in 1998.

The first year-long national BJP government (1998–1999) led India to explode its first atomic bomb and encouraged rhetoric by Hindu leaders questioning the patriotism of Indian Christians. There have been incidents across the nation in which Hindu terrorists have burned down churches and murdered Christians.

The BJP and its high-caste supporters also want to reverse the secular state's successful efforts to promote low castes and introduce democratic elections into India's villages. Recently, in regions where dominant and rich landholding, high-caste elites control most local politics, lower castes have mobilized, using their great demographic plurality, to elect their own members, including many women, to become village council leaders. As we have seen, this is an inversion of ancient Hindu caste law norms and traditional karma theory. During the first months of BJP rule, massacres in lower caste settlements were reported across North India; in most cases investigated, the killings were found to represent efforts to intimidate groups that had voted against high-caste candidates or had sought state intervention to enforce lower caste rights. Will such incidents of communal violence, like earlier attacks directed against Muslims and mosques, convince the Indian electorate that the imposition of a Hindu state portends a descent into chaos and national disintegration? Did the BJP's defeat in the 2004 national elections signal that the allure of strident Hindu nationalism will wane?

The VHP: Hindu Leaders in Search of a Religious Nation

Linked to the RSS and the Bharatiya Janata party, the Vishva Hindu Parishad (Council of All Hindus) was founded in 1964 as an organization of religious leaders who, while retaining their own disciples and spiritual agendas, wished to promote the interests of Hindus and a general kind of spiritual Hinduism. In agreement with earlier reformers and actually internalizing some of the criticisms made by European colonialists, the VHP accepts the decline of Hinduism as fact, seeks the roots of the faith in the earliest texts, and considers the *Bhagavad Gita* to be Hinduism's preeminent scripture.

Although we have spoken of the lack of a central institution as a characteristic of Hinduism, one measure of the VHP's rise is its increasing success at securing unity among hitherto fiercely independent spiritual leaders. Projects undertaken in common include religiopolitical festivals, missionary projects in tribal areas (including campaigns to "reconvert" some Indians from Christianity or Islam), and uplift initiatives among the "untouchable" castes. Critics have noted that such VHP efforts serve to add to the number the group can count as members of the "Hindu majority" in the state of India. But VHP supporters point out that uplift projects among the "untouchables" act on Gandhi's exhortation of Hindus to work to end the "evils of caste society."

The VHP argues that the era before Muslim rule (1200 CE) was a golden age for Hinduism, a time of social egalitarianism, prosperity, just rulers, and a wealth of enlightened seers. But with the Muslim conquest and such actions as the razing of temples to build mosques, Hindu culture declined; subsequent British domination of India made matters worse, causing further stagnation and division among all groups. The VHP views the secular state of India created in 1947 as a further means of dividing Hindus and thwarting the establishment of a great civilization centered on "Vedic spirituality." It further argues that if this secularism can be overthrown, and with it a mindset of inferiority induced during the colonial period, another golden age can begin. Accordingly, the VHP has voiced support for dismantling any mosques that were (in the party's historical determination) built over Hindu temples in centuries past. The destruction of the mosque in Ayodhya in 1992 attracted attention to the group and support from ultranationalists, as did the VHP's marketing scheme to raise funds by selling bricks for the construction of the new Hindu temple planned for the site. The VHP leaders still express their wish to see other Muslim shrines removed from Benares and Mathura.

Sikh Separatism and Globalization

Because the British invested heavily in irrigation and infrastructure in the Punjab, by the postcolonial era the Sikh home territory had become one of the most productive agricultural regions of India. But partition forced many Sikhs to flee to India and abandon holy sites; subsequently, Indian politicians divided Punjab politically and in development initiatives that were regarded as discriminatory against the Sikh majority. Although Sikhs became one of the wealthiest ethnic groups in postcolonial India, there were many who were left out and felt aggrieved by these events.

Following up on agitations, dating back to 1925, aimed to win British support for allowing Sikhs (not brahmins) to administer their own temples, the community had established a reformist modern organization, the Shiromani

CONTRASTING RELIGIOUS VISIONS

As the following contrasting visions indicate, every religious tradition is capable of generating both visions that encourage peace and understanding and visions that encourage conflict and violence.

Peacemaker: Pandurang Shastri Athavale and the Swadhyaya ("Truth Seekers")

Pandurang Athavale, born in 1920, grew up in a family that was active in movements sponsored by M.K. Gandhi, the Mahatma. In 1956 he began organizing social uplift programs for the poorest low-caste groups, drawing as well upon a modernist reading of Hinduism's great spiritual classic, the *Bhagavad Gita*. Living modestly as a householder, Athavale prefers to be called Dadaji ("Elder Brother"), resisting the usual trappings of the title *"guru."* His social programs have reached an estimated 20 million people living in 100,000 villages. The scope of this movement is due to the practice of *bhaktipheri,* or devotional visits, in which he or his followers spread the message of human service to new communities. His message is simple:

> It is my experience that awareness of the nearness of God and reverence for that power creates reverence for self, reverence for the other, reverence for nature and reverence for the entire creation. And devotion as an expression of gratitude for God can turn into a social force to bring about transformative changes at all levels in the society.

Acting on this conviction, members of Athavale's organization, called Swadhyaya, help build new temples that are ecumenical, open to all, and community centers for cooperative activities. Swadhyaya has become a worldwide movement, with 350 centers in the United States alone. The magnitude of the work and the authentic spirituality of the movement were the reason Athavale was awarded the 1997 Templeton Prize, the "Nobel Prize" for excellence in religious pursuits.

Source of quotation: Hinduism Today, June 1997, p. 35.

Gurudwara Pradandhak Committee. This body acted in consort with the Akal Takht, a group whose leaders manage the Golden Temple in Amritsar, the crown jewel of Sikh culture.

Despite Sikh prosperity, radical leaders in the 1980s revived a preindependence demand for a Sikh homeland in Punjab, following the logic that had led to the creation of Pakistan as the homeland for South Asian Muslims. Guerrillas tried to transform this region into a de facto separate state they called Khalistan, extorting contributions they identified as "taxes" from Sikh farmers and merchants while randomly murdering Hindus living there. The movement had support in the Akal Takht and was funded as well by contributions from Sikhs abroad.

In 1984, after armed secessionist leaders occupied the Golden Temple in Amritsar, the Indian government sent troops to invade this shrine, killing many and declaring martial law in Punjab. Later in the year the prime

Confrontationalist: Voices from the Vishva Hindu Parishad

Arguing that Hindus have suffered from disunity, mindless pacifism, and Muslim predations over the last millennium, leaders associated with the "Council of all Hindus'" have argued for revival by means of changing these old and decadent religious habits. An official inquiry on the Hindu–Muslim rioting in Bombay in 1993 reported that the responsibility lay in gangs of Hindus led by the Shiva Sena ("Shiva's Army"), a VHP ally. Members of this group went on a rampage, setting gasoline fires that burned Muslim businesses and homes. In the end, at least twelve hundred Muslims died. A Shiva Sena leader commented several years afterward, "Who are these Muslims? If the Shiva Sena comes to power, everybody will take an initiation of the Hindu religion [to become Hindu]."[a] Similar uncompromising sentiments were expressed by the woman ascetic Uma Bharati, who proclaimed in 1991, "Declare without hesitation that this is a Hindu country, a nation of Hindus. We have come to strengthen the immense Hindu shakti [force] into a fist. Do not display any love for your enemies. . . . The Qur'an teaches them to lie in wait for idol worshipers. . . . But we cannot teach them with words, now let us teach them with kicks. . . . Tie up your religiosity and kindness in a bundle and throw it in the Jamuna. . . . Any non-Hindu who lives here does so at our mercy."[b]

[a]: *India Today*, January 15, 1996, p. 25.
[b]: Thomas Hansen, *The Saffron Wave: Democracy and Hindu Nationalism in Modern India* (Princeton, NJ: Princeton University Press, 1999), p. 180.

minister, Indira Gandhi, was assassinated by two Sikh bodyguards, who had been outraged by the sacrilege. The murder triggered waves of violence: in 1987 and 1988, over 2,700 Sikhs were murdered in anti-Sikh rioting, and anti-state terrorist attacks in Delhi and other large cities resulted in the death of over 3,000 Hindus. By the turn of the millennium, the separatist agitation had largely dissipated as moderate Sikhs came back into power in national politics and international support for an independent state declined.

Through the last decades of the twentieth century, the Sikh global migration continued, and now almost 10 percent of Sikhs live outside India. With over 20 million followers worldwide, including a growing number of Western converts, Sikhism is slowly being recognized for its distinctive spiritual development and as the youngest of the three great heterodox faiths, the others being Buddhism and Jainism, that originated in India.

Poster at a political rally suggests that veneration of the cow provides the basis for unity among Indians of every religious group.

A Growing Global Tradition

Hinduism has entered into Western awareness strongly. As we will also see in the case of Buddhism, this interest is selective, centered on yoga and meditation, with much less focus on ritual. Many Westerners have been trained as yoga teachers by Indian masters, and nearly every major American city and college town has centers where one can go to practice. For many, of course, this interest is confined to the athletic or health benefits, with the religious beliefs underlying the practices often downplayed or tailored to fit into the customers' existing belief system. To see the panoply of traditions and applications of yoga in the West, one need only pick up a copy of *Yoga Journal*, a magazine that in 2005 counted over four hundred thousand subscribers!

The ubiquitous Indian diaspora is increasingly important in the process of Hindu globalization. First and second generations of Indians settled in the United States are the nation's richest ethnic group in terms of per capita income, and the majority who are Hindu has supported the internationalization of the faith. For example, the Hindus of the Greater Boston area have organized and collected several million dollars to build a large South Indian–style temple in Ashland, Massachusetts. They hired artisans from Madras and had the chief icons made to order; they also created an endowment that pays for the lodging and full-time employment of two brahmin priests, who are recruited for long-term assignments to serve patrons of the temple. Similar institutions exist in Austin, Texas, Los Angeles, and elsewhere.

As India has become an important player in the global computer and software business, older Hindu institutions and new movements have adopted the Internet technology. For example, a famous Ganesh temple in Bombay has set up a worldwide Web site in which viewers can have live darshan of the main icons, hear hymns being sung, and with a few additional mouse clicks, make credit card contributions to sponsor pujas. The Web site of a Vishnu shrine in the northern state of Jammu offers similar scenes and services, adding maps, regularly updated weather reports, and hostel bookings to aid the estimated 4 million pilgrims who visit the temple annually in person.

CONCLUSION

Recalling the initial caution about taking any religious tradition as standing for all of "Hinduism," we can only generalize about the broad patterns of change affecting the religion in South Asia. There is no doubt that India is changing just as other parts of postcolonial Asia are. Newly built roads,

transport systems, education, mass media, and industrialization are contributing to the rapid development of the economic system of the country, drawing
migrants from rural settlements to burgeoning urban areas and transforming
the life experiences of individuals. In these settings, the Hindu traditions of
the premodern world are in decline as new institutions and teachers arise to
meet the needs of those living under the new circumstances.

But even with so much change, the belief in the spiritual presence of the
gods, in yoga, in the guru-centered spiritual life remains strikingly strong.
It is easy to misinterpret surface changes as modifications to the religion:
Do cement buildings replacing cut stone temples or electric lights replacing
the butter lamps set out in the Diwali festival represent Westernization
and the decline of traditional values? Or simply the transposition of new
technologies in the service of the centuries-old wish to please the deities with
artful decoration?

In the cities, among the rapidly expanding middle class as well as among
slum dwellers, there are numerous new incarnations of "organized Hinduisms."
Hitherto independent groups such as sadhus from different regions are forming new organizations to work for common interests. Likewise, laity and
priests associated with major temples have pressed for the establishment of
management committees to orchestrate rituals and festivals as well as for
supervising temple accounts.

Thus, what in rural India was a largely preordained relationship with a
family priest and local guru, in urban settings has become a matter of individual choice. Hindus in ever-increasing numbers, then, are faced with the
"heretical imperative" (as discussed in Chapter One) of making their own
choices about their own religious paths. Media-savvy gurus appear on television, use video recordings and Web sites to link far-flung communities, and
draw upon a global network of disciples to build their movements. One of the
most popular English-language magazines dedicated to promoting reformist
Hinduism in India and abroad (*Hinduism Today*) is published in Hawaii.

The Connection of Religion with Social Reform

The impact of Christianity on Hinduism, as we noted earlier, was not primarily doctrinal but more in the arena of modeling the role of modern religious
institutions and the scope of religious service in society. Just as Christian
missionaries had shown that churches could be linked with schools and hospitals, Hindu reformers (e.g., the Ramakrishna Mission and Sai Baba) who have
begun spiritual movements almost without exception include social welfare
initiatives to address the nation's undeniable needs. Initially, perhaps, this was
done in competition with the Western missionaries; but the idea also found
support from Hindu theologies promoting the spiritual power of selfless,
compassionate service and extolling individuals to engage in humanitarian
merit-making.

As a result, most Hindu mathas have started educational institutions and many, like the Ramakrishna Mission, continue to expand networks of clinics and hospitals staffed by their own trained monks. Hindu gurus cite a variety of reasons for the motivation that mathas now display for social work. A swami influential in the early VHP remarked long ago that the Indian people required inspiration from leaders who do not merely retreat to caves and meditate. Likewise, the leader of one of India's largest monasteries described his work in education as necessary to make democracy a success. Another prominent swami, while acknowledging a desire to serve the people and foster humanitarianism, admits that his monastic order engages in social work primarily to dispel the impression that only other religions do it.

One might propose, then, examining what Hindu reformers collectively are *doing*. One case study would be the Ganges River, which flows from the high slopes of the Himalayas into the highlands through sites associated with all the great gods. The Ganges has a central place in the Hindu religious imagination, and every confluence with a tributary is considered to be a sacred site. Texts describe the Ganges as a gift from the gods to humanity and symbolize it by a goddess; in practice, its holy waters remove bad karma and receive the ashes of one's dead kin. In addition, this great river flows through the most densely populated states of India, from which countless farmers draw water directly to irrigate their fields and grow the food that feeds several hundred million people.

But as elsewhere in the industrial world, companies have used the river as a sewer and dumping place for factory wastes. The Ganges has been increasingly polluted over the last several decades, with dangerous water toxicity and pollutant levels recorded in many sections. In 1985 a coalition of religious and political leaders announced with great fanfare a campaign to restore the purity of the Ganges, with a multimillion dollar budget and international support. Here ostensibly was a powerful convergence of spiritual need and ecological necessity, with the moral goal of protecting the health of millions.

Yet twenty years later, few of the planned water filtration plants have been completed, funds have been misspent, and raw sewage and untreated wastes still flow directly into the river from most cities. If anything, the Ganges has gotten worse as new industries and burgeoning cities have added their discharges to the flow. To pose a question that environmental crises have raised globally, are religious convictions any match for the power of modern business interests?

As middle-class South Asians have raised their educational level, experienced rising prosperity, and encountered religions and societies elsewhere, they have been inevitably forced to consider "Hinduism" in comparison to these other belief systems and cultures. This process was very poignant in the summer of 1997, when the Indian elite was drawn into thinking about where their nation had traveled in the fifty years since independence and how the country now measured up both against earlier expectations and in comparison to the other great nation founded at roughly the same time, China.

Immersing himself in the divine Ganges River, a Hindu devotee offers water to the gods as he chants sacred mantras.

Children enjoying Holi, the festival when humans join Krishna in living life as a divine sport.

Elephant-headed Ganesh, Hindu god of success, is found in every Hindu community. He is always worshiped first and before any major undertaking.

A Tibetan monk in the rain. The communal life of the Buddhist sangha has its challenges and pleasures.

Mi-Lo-Fo, the future Buddha. Chinese Buddhists depict the next Buddha as jovial and corpulent, visiting humanity to observe the world and spread compassion.

Monastics and householders of the modernist Dhammakaya school reside in individual tents of mosquito netting on a mass meditative retreat in Thailand.

The eight immortals of Daoism, depicted in a Qing dynasty hanging scroll, with the Three Stars and the Queen Mother of the West. These were the chief divinities enshrined in Daoist temples from the Ming period onward.

Dressed in fine silk robes, a renowned Korean shaman conducts a seance in which she will bargain with ancestral spirits on behalf of her patron family.

Beatles with Maharishi Mahesh Yogi in India. Hindu yoga and mysticism were major influences on these musicians, and their enthusiasm sparked a broader Western interest in the religions of India.

Hare Krishna devotees parade on Fifth Avenue in New York City, seeking to spread communion with Krishna, one of the principal Hindu deities.

The widespread opinion expressed in the popular press was that while democracy was treasured and never to be surrendered, there was also the hard truth to be faced that Hindu culture and religion have failed to transform Indian society in many of the positive ways evident in contemporary China. How could caste discrimination endure? How could India's extreme poverty be tolerated among the masses while the rich get richer? How could the nation's leaders, drawn largely from the high castes, accept these failures? While no uniform answer emerged, and while not only religion was blamed, the frequent and often intense debates that swirled through that year signaled support for the view that Hinduism is part of the problem and needs reform. One representative example of this self-scrutiny, by the Nepali social critic Dipak Gyawali, incorporates many of the issues we have discussed, perhaps foreshadowing the direction of future change:

> In the social field, several things need to be done. The first is that modern Hindus need to rediscover the origins and rationale of Hinduism and its rituals because they are as ignorant as anyone. This is probably easier to do for a modernist Hindu because Hindu literature is now more readily available in English than in native languages or in incomprehensible Sanskrit. The second is that modern Hindus need to reject the archaic, the irrational, and the inefficient to make living a Hindu life less full of contradictions. The third is that they need to redefine the religion's core in a manner that is not exclusive but allows non-Hindu neighbors to participate as well. Finally, and most important, there is a need to reassert moral outrage rather than escape into flaccid tolerance whenever justice is being denied.[6]

Among the many voices of Hinduism today, those speaking against secularism and for reform have garnered unprecedented political power. Their daunting task in India is to demonstrate how Hindu values, beliefs, and conscience can serve the needs of all its citizens, who now number one billion.

Discussion Questions

1 What reasons might be suggested for the transformation of the polytheism of the early Vedic peoples into the monism and theism of later Hinduism?

2 Compare and contrast the spiritual practice of the shaman (Chapter Two) with that of the yoga practitioner. Is it possible to know exactly how different their experiences are?

3 Why would the lowest castes regard the doctrines of karma, caste, and duty as a system designed to subjugate them?

4 What reasons would a woman have for abiding by her dharma?

5 To what extent can karma theory be considered to be a doctrine of fatalism? Do humans still have freedom of action?

6 If you were an Islamic judge in medieval India, how would you advise the local sultan who asks if his subjects who follow Krishna (as depicted in the *Bhagavad Gita*) are in fact monotheists?

7 No Hindu religious group has ever acquired the power to define what was true doctrine and what was heresy. In this context, what are the strengths and weaknesses of the Hindu tradition?

8 How does ritualism relate to the ideals of bhakti Hinduism?

9 Why was the influence of colonialism on the religions of India powerfully conveyed by the phrase "Protestant Hinduism"?

10 What reasons are Hindu nationalists giving to support their view that secularism is the perpetuation of colonialism and a betrayal of the great modern Hindu reformers?

11 Explain why M.K. Gandhi's biography contains a paradigmatic study of the factors shaping modern Hindu reform.

12 Critique the following statement, coming from an ecumenical Hindu organization: "We can follow Jesus without contradiction, for he is none other than another *avatara* of Lord Vishnu."

13 What does it say about the power of ideas regarding the sacred versus the power of profane modern economic interests that Hindu leaders and politicians have been unable to prevent their most sacred river, the Ganges, from becoming a nearly dead and toxic waterway?

Key Terms

ahimsa	dharma	*puranas*	Shankara
atman	guru	Ramakrishna Mission	tantra
avatara	Kali Yuga		Upanishads
Bhagavad Gita	karma	Ramanuja	Vedas
bhakti	matha	RSS	yoga
BJP	moksha	saguna Brahman	*Yoga Sutras*
Brahman	nirguna Brahman	samsara	
brahmin	puja	satyagraha	

Suggested Readings

Babb, Lawrence, *The Divine Hierarchy* (New York: Columbia University Press, 1975).

————, *Redemptive Encounters: Three Modern Styles in the Hindu Tradition* (Berkeley: University of California Press, 1986).

Dass, Ram, *Be Here Now* (Kingsport, TN: Hanuman Foundation, 1978).

de Bary, William Theodore, ed., *Sources of Indian Tradition*, 2nd ed., 2 vols. (New York: Columbia University Press, 1988).

Dimmitt, Cornelia, and J. A. B. van Buitenen, *Classical Hindu Anthology: A Reader in the Sanskrit Puranas* (Philadelphia: Temple University Press, 1978).

Hawley, John, and Mark Juergensmeyer, *Songs of the Saints of India* (New York: Oxford University Press, 1988).

Hopkins, Thomas, *The Hindu Religious Tradition* (Belmont, CA: Wadsworth, 1982).

Jaffrelot, Christophe, *The Hindu Nationalist Movement in India* (New York: Columbia University Press, 1996).

Jones, Kenneth W., *Socio-Religious Reform Movements in British India* (Cambridge: Cambridge University Press, 1994).

Larson, Gerald James, *India's Agony over Religion* (Albany: State University of New York Press, 1995).

Zimmer, Heinrich, *Myths and Symbols of Indian Art and Civilization* (Princeton, NJ: Princeton University Press, 1970).

Notes

1. *India Today*, January 15, 1996, p. 22.

2. Daniel Gold, "Organized Hinduisms: From Vedic Truth to Hindu Nation," in *Fundamentalisms Observed*, M.E. Marty and R. Scott Appleby, eds. (Chicago: University of Chicago Press, 1991), p. 581.

3. For the sake of simplicity, in this text we use *brahmin* to indicate the priestly caste and *Brahman* to indicate the "world spirit," although in fact they are similar Sanskrit words: *brahman* and *brahmana*, respectively.

4. Bhimrao Ambedkar, *What Congress and Gandhi Have Done to the Untouchables* (Bombay: Thacker and Company, 1934), pp. 307–308.

5. W. Owen Cole, "Sikhism," in *A Handbook of Living Religions*, John R. Hinnells, ed. (New York: Penguin, 1984), p. 240.

6. Dipak Gyawali, "Challenged by the Future, Shackled by the Past," *Himal South Asia*, May 1997, p. 19.

CHAPTER
SEVEN

Buddhism
Ways to Nirvana

Overview

For over two thousand years, a simple recitation of "going for refuge" has been used to mark conversion to Buddhism, to affirm one's devotion, and to start Buddhist rituals:

- *Buddham Saranam Gacchami*   I go for refuge in the Buddha
- *Dharmam Saranam Gacchami*   I go for refuge in the teachings
- *Sangham Saranam Gacchami*   I go for refuge in the community

Today these three phrases are repeated across Asia and increasingly beyond, in Japan and Nepal, from Mongolia to Thailand, by immigrants and converts from Moscow to San Francisco. But for the student first encountering Buddhism, how different those who "go for refuge" appear. High in the Himalayas, a Tibetan monk wearing a humble red woolen robe seals himself into a cave retreat for three years and three months of meditative solitude. In the heart of urban Seoul, Korea, a layman wearing a stylish three-piece suit declares the opening of a twenty-four-hour Buddhist cable TV channel at a press conference in the ultramodern headquarters of a major Buddhist reform organization. In tropical Singapore, as householders gather to view 2,500-year-old bone relics of the Buddha, monks in yellow robes chant and extol the blessings of worshiping these mortal remains.

For Mrs. Wang of Taiwan, being a Buddhist means chanting set phrases in hopes of rebirth in the heaven of a Buddha. For Mr. Khatt of Cambodia, being a Buddhist means bestowing charity and doing good in order to achieve a better life in his next rebirth. For Mr. Vajracarya of Nepal, being a Buddhist means performing intricate rituals to honor the gods and Buddhas who out of their boundless compassion can bless his community. For forest monks in Thailand and American disciples of a Japanese Zen master practicing in his monastery in the Catskills, being a Buddhist means reaching enlightenment by meditation alone. It is true that each of these Buddhists reveres an image of the Buddha who is seated in meditation, serene and exemplary, but one cannot help but wonder what the historical Buddha might say if he heard how differently these disciples now construe his teachings.

BUDDHISM *Timeline*

563 BCE	Birth of Siddhartha [some traditions give 483 BCE]
528	Enlightenment of Shakyamuni, the Buddha; creation of the *sangha*, the monastic order
c. 510	Establishment of nuns' order
483	Death of the Buddha [some traditions give 360 BCE]
482	First Council collects and organizes oral accounts
383	Council of Vaishali leads to the first split in the sangha
273–232	Reign of Ashoka, convert to Buddhism, who spread Buddhism throughout India and beyond (Afghanistan, Burma, Ceylon)
250	Council of Pataliputra leads to division in "18 schools"
240	Sanchi *stupa* and other *stupas* built across India; relic cult at *stupas* central to community
c. 100	Origins of the Mahayana school, beginning with *Prajnaparamita* literature
80	First collections of written canon begun, beginning with the Vinaya, the monastic code; Pali Canon collection begun in Ceylon
c. 85 CE	Composition of the *Lotus Sutra*
50–180	Spread of Buddhism into central Asia via the Silk Road
124	Buddhist monks in western China
c. 200	Writings of Nagarjuna, the most influential Mahayana philosopher; Madhyamaka school formed
220–589	Buddhist missions reach Southeast Asia, Java, Sumatra, Korea, Japan, Vietnam; Buddhist monasteries established throughout China in era of weak central state
c. 300	Rituals and visualization meditations dedicated to bodhisattvas developed by Mahayana monks
c. 300	Origins of Pure Land school in India
320ff	Development of Yogacara school, led by monastic brothers Asanga and Vasubandhu
c. 425	Writings of a monk who shaped the Theravada school, Buddhaghosa, in Ceylon
c. 500	Rise of the Vajrayana Thunderbolt school in India, which eventually dominates Buddhist communities in Northeastern India, Nepal, and Tibet
c. 600	Formation of the Ch'an school in China inspired by teachings of the Indian monk Bodhidharma
700–1270	Buddhism dominates Sri Vijaya kingdom on Sumatra–Java; rulers build Borobodur *stupa*
749	First Buddhist monastery in Tibet
760–1142	Pala Dynasty rules North India, patronizes Buddhist monasteries and promotes Mahayana traditions; tradition in decline elsewhere in India
841–845	Extensive destruction of monasteries in China and defrocking of Buddhist monks and nuns
900ff	Restoration of Chinese Buddhism, principally the Pure Land and Ch'an schools

c. 1000	Second introduction of monastic Mahayana Buddhism into Tibet from India
1192	Muslim rule established across northern India; final destruction of Indian monasteries and decline of Bodh Gaya as center of Buddhist pilgrimage
1193–1227	In Japan, formation of new schools: Zen brought from China by Eisei (1141–1215) and Dogen (1200–1253); Pure Land by Honen (1133–1212) and Shinran (1173–1262), and school founded by Nichiren (1222–1282)
1000–1400	Era of Pagan Kingdom in Burma, establishing one of the great centers of Buddhism
1642–1959	Tibet dominated by Gelugpa monastic school under the Dalai and Panchen lamas
1815–1948	Era of British colonial rule. Conflicts in Ceylon lead to reformist movement styled "Protestant Buddhism" that influences Buddhists across Asia.
1851–1868	Rule of King Monghut in Siam, who revived the sangha and placed it under state control
1864–1933	Anagarika Dharmapala, Ceylonese reformist, founder of the Mahabodhi Society who spread reformism across Asia
1871–1876	Heavy Meiji persecution of Buddhism; 70% of monasteries lost as 75% of monks defrocked
1871	Fifth Buddhist Council held in Burma
1877–1945	Buddhist establishment in Japan supports nationalism, militarism, and seizures of Korea, Taiwan, and northern China
1893	Parliament of World Religions in Chicago; speeches by Zen monk and Dharmapala stir interest
1944	Buddhist Churches of America, a Pure Land organization, founded in California
1945	Soka Gokkai established in Japan, a branch of Nichiren school until 1991
1949–1976	Chinese Communist government persecutes Buddhists and seizes 250,000 monasteries and temples, with the Cultural Revolution (1966–1969) a period of intense destruction
1954–1956	Sixth Buddhist Council in Rangoon, Burma, culminating in the marking of the 2,500-year anniversary of Shakyamuni's death
1956	Foundation of the Mahasangha Sahayaka Gana in central India, a Buddhist organization
1959–present	Exile of the fourteenth Dalai Lama from Tibet and the era of the globalization of Tibetan Buddhism
1976–present	Slow restoration of Buddhist institutions in China
1982–present	Civil war against Tamil minority in Sri Lanka polarizes Buddhist community
1987	Founding of Shakyaditya, a worldwide organization of Buddhist women
1989	Foundation of the International Network of Engaged Buddhists by Thai activist Sulak Sivaraksha
1990	Revival of Buddhism in Mongolia after 88 years of suppression
1991	Founding of *Tricycle*, a Buddhist mass market magazine in America
1998–present	Full ordination taken by Theravada nuns in Chinese monasteries, reviving a lost tradition

BUDDHISM *Timeline*

The oldest of the world's missionary religions and perhaps the most accommodating in adapting to its widely varying communities in a wide-ranging global diaspora, Buddhism is in modest revival in most areas of the world today after having suffered debilitating setbacks throughout the modern era. Understanding Buddhism thus entails knowing about most of the peoples and cultures of Eurasia: from the homeland on the Ganges in South Asia into the high Himalayas, across the tropical states of Southeast Asia and over the central Asian deserts, and throughout the imperial domains of China, Korea, and Japan.

Buddhists today are becoming ever more aware of this diversity of Buddhist paths. Although modern activists and intellectuals may contest exactly "what the Buddha taught," Buddhism's basic teachings about life, mortality, and spiritual development have remained compelling amid the often traumatic changes of recent centuries. In every land, venerable institutions and reformist groups alike are seeking to adapt the faith to the changing world and to revive the essential practices that lead to Buddhism's perennial threefold goals: establishing moral community, securing worldly blessings, and realizing nirvana. This chapter will examine how Buddhism in its creative diversity has sought to direct devotees to secure these goals.

The Global Diaspora Today

Rough estimates place the number of Buddhists at 350 million, making it the fourth largest among world religions. Over 98 percent live in Asia. Globally, there are as many Buddhists as there are Protestant Christians. Among Buddhists, these sources estimate that 62 percent are adherents of the Mahayana and 38 percent are Theravada followers. With most Mahayanists located in the countries north of the tropics, the label "Northern Buddhism" is also used for this grouping, as opposed to the "Southern Buddhism" of the Theravadins. In a half-dozen Asian states (Sri Lanka, Myanmar, Thailand, Laos, Cambodia, Japan), Buddhists comprise the overwhelming majority of the population. They are significant minorities in Nepal, China, South Korea, and Singapore, while their presence in Malaysia (10%), Indonesia (3%), and India is less marked. (It should be noted that specific percentages, figures taken from Western almanac sources, are at best rough estimates, with wide margins for error.)

A recent survey of ordained Buddhist monks and nuns estimated that there are about 700,000 worldwide. Officially, monks outnumber nuns by six to one.

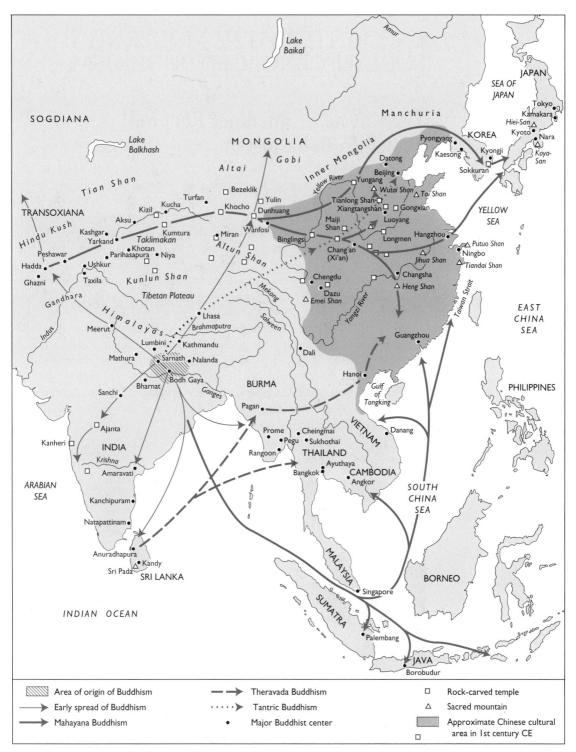

Map 7.1   The spread of Buddhism.

ENCOUNTER WITH MODERNITY: SOCIALLY ENGAGED BUDDHISM

The Karma of Buddhist Renewal: "Engaged Buddhism"?

With the end of World War II and, soon after, the demise of colonialism, most Asian nations faced the need to reinvent their societies politically and culturally. Yet in post–World War II China, Mongolia, Vietnam, and North Korea, those who sought the rebuilding and renewal of Buddhism faced crippling hostility from rulers who regarded Buddhist doctrine as superstition and Buddhist institutions as parasitic on society. These nations engaged in "revolutionary campaigns" aimed at disbanding the community of the faithful, destroying their buildings and images, and discrediting all forms of Buddhist belief and practice. There were other pressures as well, many of which have ultimately exerted more benign effects.

As Asia's rapid industrialization and urbanization created new forms of social dislocation and wealth, for example, there were dramatic increases in the numbers of landless wage-dependent workers and an unprecedented rash of ecological crises. At the same time, Asia saw an expansion of higher education and the rise of educated classes alongside new commercial elites. As a result of these changes, Buddhism was transplanted and drawn into entirely new social contexts, political struggles, and global dialogues.

Protesting the Vietnam war, a Vietnamese monk commits suicide.

One image of modern Buddhism came in the aftermath of the December tsunami that struck the Indian Ocean on December 26, 2004. Myriad press accounts of the first humanitarian responses reported that small groups of Buddhist householders immediately gathered what medicines, bandages, clothes, and food they could and headed to the coastal area to render compassionate assistance. Those interviewed in Sri Lanka and Thailand typically explained in a self-effacing way that they were strengthened and motivated by their Buddhist tradition's teachings—that suffering is sad but inevitable in life and that acting compassionately is a central duty. This unprecedented tragedy showed how strong—"at the grassroots level"—that adherence to basic Buddhist doctrines is today as they are applied to situations of human suffering.

Another image of modern Buddhism is that of a Vietnamese monk sitting cross-legged, engulfed in flames. This and other suicides in 1963 protested the South Vietnamese government's failure to respect Buddhism and to adopt a policy of national reconciliation. Among the many Buddhist monks who challenged the corrupt South Vietnamese state was Thich Nhat Hanh, who argued that when faced with immense suffering, Buddhists must take action and engage their society. While Buddhism's ascetic traditions advocate renunciation of the household life and retreat to nirvana-seeking meditation, Nhat Hanh drew upon other sides of the tradition to urge Buddhist monks and nuns to defer solitary individualistic practice in favor of staging nonviolent confrontations with the governments and other agencies responsible for profound suffering.

Inspired by the monks of Vietnam, contemporary Buddhist activists in Asia and now in the West are responding to crises posed by environmental despoliation, political corruption, and global hunger. Accordingly, they are identified as "engaged Buddhists," and they refuse to turn away from suffering, counseling instead "mundane awakening." In this way, engaged Buddhists hope to elicit compassion, which is as ancient and as fundamental to Buddhism as the ascetic and solitary practices of the spiritual elite, on the part of individuals, villages, countries, and eventually all people.

Buddhists engaging with society in political arenas now span the world, offering examples of revival from India to Japan: the Trailokya Bauddha Mahasangha Sahayaka Gana of India that has worked since 1956 to convert from Hinduism low-ranked castes in India and help raise them out of poverty; the Sarvodaya Shramadana movement in Sri Lanka seeks to promote rural development through harnessing the service commitments of lay volunteers; various postwar Japanese Buddhist groups such as the Soka Gakkai work to transform society through political activism informed by Buddhist ideals. On the ecumenical front, monk reformers such as Buddhadasa of Thailand and the Tibetan Dalai Lama have connected with those of other faiths to mobilize mutual seeking of the common good. In the late twentieth century, Sulak Sivaraksa, a Thai lay activist, formed the International Network of Engaged Buddhists to foster connections and develop this latest interpretation of traditional Buddhism.

The last major development in Buddhism since World War II has been the global diffusion of the tradition on a scale unprecedented in world history. Buddhist social activism has made the tradition more attractive to many in the West. In Asia, engaged Buddhists have no shortage of traumatic provocations given the region's rapid industrialization, the explosion of urban slum settlements, the alarming degradation of forests and watersheds, the predations of corrupt politicians, and the bloodshed from ethnic conflicts and civil wars. These profound changes and crises have disrupted the regions' rural societies, including many of the communities that harbor established Buddhist institutions.

The engaged Buddhists, predominantly in the urban centers, now offer new understandings of Buddhism and Buddhist action, often confronting politicians and corporations. Can this movement revitalize the tradition from the capitals to the rural hinterlands and mitigate suffering without reducing or compromising its principal values? To discover the "engagement" this movement advocates, to understand its importance, we must start with the founder and trace the historical development of his teachings.

Socially Engaged Buddhism: Some Examples

Thai activist Sulak Sivaraksa puts the ancient Buddhist concept of suffering into the framework of today's World: In Buddhist terminology, the world is full of *dukkha* ["suffering"], i.e., the dangers of impending world destruction through nuclear weapons, atomic fallout, air, land and sea pollution, population explosion, exploitation of fellow human beings, denial of basic human rights, and devastating famine. . . . World dukkha is too immense for any country, people, or religion to solve. We can only save ourselves when all humanity recognizes that every problem on earth is our own personal problem and our own personal responsibility. . . . The language of Buddhism must offer answers which fit our situation. Only then will Buddhism survive, today and tomorrow, as it has in the past, influencing humankind positively and generating love, peace, and nonviolence.[a]

An even more forceful exhortation is provided by the Vietnamese monk Thich Nhat Hanh: The word "Buddha" comes from the root budh, which means "awake." A Buddha is one who is awake. Are we really awake in our daily lives? That is a question. . . . Society makes it difficult to be awake. We know that 40,000 children in the Third World die every day of hunger, but we keep forgetting. The kind of society we live in makes us forgetful. That is why we need exercises in mindfulness. . . . Our earth is like a small boat. Compared with the rest of the cosmos, it is a very small boat, and it is in danger of sinking. We need a person to inspire us with calm confidence, to tell us what to do. What is that person? The Mahayana texts tell us that you are that person.[b]

[a] Sulak Sivaraksa, "Buddhism in a World of Change," in *The Path of Compassion: Writings on Socially Engaged Buddhism,* Fred Eppsteiner, ed. (Berkeley, CA: Parallax Press, 1988), pp. 16–17.

[b] Thich Nhat Hanh, "Call Me by My True Name," in *The Path of Compassion: Writings on Socially Engaged Buddhism,* Fred Eppsteiner, ed. (Berkeley, CA: Parallax Press, 1988), pp. 34–37.

PREMODERN BUDDHISM: THE FORMATIVE ERA

The Buddha: Context and Biography

We saw in Chapter Six that North India during the Buddha's lifetime (563–483 BCE) was a place of spiritual questioning and ascetic searching unmatched in the history of religions. The dominant Aryan society was evolving from small pastoral settlements to city-states and a more diverse economy. In the context of this transformation, the old religion controlled by members of the brahmin caste was becoming for some much less plausible as an explanation of humanity's deepest connection to the universe. In remote retreats and near to the emerging urban centers, there were many seekers called *shramanas* who pursued ascetic practices (yoga) to realize the true essence of life, reality, and consciousness. The society in which the Buddha was born was ordered by caste and brahmin ritualism. In addition, however, there were ardent, nonconformist shramana seekers who questioned almost everything brahminic tradition asserted about spirit, morality, and social hierarchy. Some lived naked, in silent retreat, or even sealed in clay pots; most explored various trance states and adopted renunciatory lifestyles. Still other ascetics advocated materialism, nihilism, agnosticism, or fatalism.

The Buddha's birth, depicted in a Chinese sculpture.

Like certain devotees of the Upanishadic seers, most shramanas believed that life consists of a countless series of rebirths, that these are determined by an individual's karma, a natural and moral causal force that accrues from one's deeds, and that rebirths continue until through moral perfection and yoga practices one "burns off" one's karma to reach a state of liberation, which in Buddhism is termed *nirvana*, or *sambodhi*. Shramanas differed widely on the exact means of reaching this goal, and they debated the details of personhood and universe. They were contrasted with the priestly brahmins in terms of two mortal enemies from the animal world, the cobra and the mongoose.

Siddhartha's Early Life

The most famous man ever to become an ascetic was born the son of warrior-caste parents who ruled a small state in the Himalayan foothills. According to legendary accounts, Siddhartha's birth was accompanied by auspicious celestial signs and a wise man's prediction that the child would be successful as either a universal monarch or a great ascetic. Thus the infant was named Siddhartha, which means "the one who attains the goal." The young prince, whose mother

The Buddha encountering the "Four Passing sights" that inspired his religious quest and eventual awakening.

died a week after giving birth, grew up in a palace where his father did everything in his power to ensure the first destiny. The son was trained in the martial arts, isolated from life's unpleasantness, and pampered with all the pleasures of rule, including marriage, a harem of concubines, and every form of artistic distraction.

Siddhartha's life changed when he followed an inclination to go with his faithful chariot driver to see the world beyond the palace walls. All the textual legends describe the profound impact of seeing a sick man, an old man, a dead man, and a shramana. These "four passing sights" overturned Siddhartha's rosy assumptions about life and also offered an idea about the personal path he could take to escape the spiritual emptiness he now felt in his sheltered existence. Within days, Siddhartha slipped away, abandoning his palace and family, including a newborn son. He began at that moment his search for a teacher among the forest-dwelling ascetics. The legends state that he was 29 years old.

Siddhartha Begins His Quest

Siddhartha found a shramana guru, Arada Kalama, whose way of meditation allowed one to achieve a "state of nothingness." Siddhartha soon mastered this technique, but he also recognized that the accomplishment was limited in value. His quest led to a second teacher, Udraka Ramaputra, who taught a method of attaining trances that brought an experience of "neither perception nor nonperception." But again Siddhartha found that fast-won mastery of a form of yoga still left him short of the highest goal.

He set forth alone again and soon joined five other men who vowed to explore together a rigorous ascetic practice involving fanatical fasting (down to a few rice grains daily), breath control, and long periods seated in unmoving meditation. He adopted this lifestyle for several years but rejected it also as too extreme, much to the dismay of his fellow seekers, who then ridiculed and abandoned him. Through this experiment, Siddhartha came to understand that the spiritual life is best undertaken as a middle path between the extremes of sense indulgence (the life in the palace) and asceticism so zealous that it weakens the body. One name for Buddhism, "the Middle Way," stems from this insight.

Although physically weakened and spiritually dismayed, Siddhartha did not quit. He was buoyed by a gift of rice and barley gruel from a village woman, and he came to sit beneath a great ficus tree by a river outside the town of Gaya. He vowed to find either success or death. The legends relate that his revitalized meditations were disturbed by Mara, a supernatural being regarded by Buddhists as the personification of death, delusion, and temptation. Mara summoned spirits who appeared as armies to provoke fear and as alluring females to elicit lust, but Siddhartha touched his right hand to the earth, asking it to bear witness to his merit and eventual success. This earth-touching gesture, seen often in depictions of the Buddha in art, brought forth earthquakes and a cooling stream that washed away Mara and his hordes.

The Bodhi Tree and the Deer Park

Later that night, after resuming his meditations, Siddhartha reached more subtle and blissful perceptions and then the attainment of superfaculties such as memory of former lives and psychic vision that allowed him to survey the destinies of all beings according to their karma, as well as the powers of levitation, telepathy, and superhearing. Finally he completely extinguished all desire and ignorance by fully realizing his capacity for insight (*prajna*). This "awakening" to the nature of reality under the *bo* (or *bodhi*, "enlightenment") tree, poetically recounted as occurring just as the dawn broke, provides the root meaning of the term "Buddha" that from this moment onward we can properly apply to Siddhartha. He is also referred to as "Gautama Buddha," using his family surname, and Shakyamuni, "the sage," or *muni*, from Gautama's clan, the Shakyas.

Buddha in earth-touching gesture, a frequently encountered icon that alludes to his calling upon the earth to bear witness to his fitness for enlightenment.

For seven weeks the Buddha remained in the vicinity of the bodhi tree, enjoying the bliss of nirvana. The texts recount a story that his very first disciples were householders, merchants who made offerings and received his benediction for their continued worldly success. He also received the veneration of *nagas*, the snake deities, whose submission symbolized Buddhism's claim of "spiritual conquest" over all deities in every locality. Then Mara returned to tempt the Buddha to remain isolated, enjoying his solitary nirvana. In his attempt to prevent the Buddha from continuing to teach, the evil one cited humanity's hopeless stupidity. But the high gods also intervened to request that the Buddha live on to share his doctrine because, they assured him, there were people everywhere capable of realizing enlightenment by means of his teachings, or Dharma. This request stoked the Buddha's compassion, and he vowed to return to the world, thus providing the ultimate model of the engaged Buddhist.

He walked for days to distant Sarnath, a deer park outside the city of Varanasi, where he found his former ascetic colleagues, who still disdained him as a quitter. Their disdain turned to awe, however, after the Buddha had enlightened each of them by imparting the "Four Noble Truths," which end in the Eightfold Path. The five ascetics became the first members of the sangha, and they were instructed to travel to different places in the four directions for the purpose of sharing the Dharma with them.

The Buddha's Life Work

For the next forty or so years, the Buddha empowered his enlightened disciples, called *arhats*, to act on his behalf, to admit qualified seekers into the sangha, guide those who wished to meditate, and teach the Dharma to any who would hear it. Shakyamuni converted other ascetics, sometimes whole assemblies of them, as well as solitary shramanas, householders, and rulers. Buddha's faculty of psychic knowledge allowed him to preach according to the exact capacity of his audience.

As the Buddhist movement grew, new situations arose that required adaptation, so that in addition to his skill at teaching, the Buddha succeeded in creating an entirely new institution in ancient India. The sangha was established on the basis of an extensive set of rules that adapted it to the many environments it reached.

After much urging (at least in some legends), Shakyamuni also gave permission, around 510 BCE, for the creation of a sangha for female renunciants, bequeathing a mixed message by emphasizing that women are capable of realizing enlightenment but also specifying rules forcing the nuns, or *bhikkhunis*, to subordinate themselves to the monks in personal power and in matters of social etiquette. When admitting nuns, the Buddha also predicted that the tradition would decline. In subsequently allowing the sangha to receive lands, buildings, and other donated communal resources, the Buddha established a framework in which the sangha could shift its focus over time from wandering to settled cooperative communal existence. This development, which also gave householder disciples a fixed focus for their patronage, in turn strengthened support for the sangha.

Late in life the Buddha began to suffer from various ailments, and he died in Kushinagar, a rural site, at the age of 80. His body was cremated and the remains, divided into eight portions, were enshrined in relic mound shrines (*stupas*) that became the focus of Buddhist ritual and the visible symbol of the Buddha's presence across the world.

Shakyamuni's life story became for Buddhists a paradigmatic example of an individual's quest for enlightenment, and his exemplary role for subsequent generations was elaborated in hundreds of stories that describe incidents from his previous incarnations as human, animal, or spirit. These narratives, called *jatakas,* along with stories of his path to Buddhahood, inspired arts and literatures across Asia that conveyed the essential doctrines in explicit, personified form. The Buddha, thus, embodies the Dharma, which as in Hindu practice is understood as the ultimate truth, as well as the teachings that lead to it.

Buddhism as the Path to Nirvana

The spiritual tradition we refer to as "Buddhism" arose from the Buddha's wish to help others realize the transformative experience of nirvana. The Buddha emphasized the practical goal-directed orientation of his way and urged his disciples not to engage in idle speculation or mere intellectualism. He taught that humanity comprises persons of very different kinds who bear different forms of karma. According to whether they are "ordinary persons," "learners," or "adepts," each is to be instructed differently. Regardless of an individual's level, to be born as a human at all, instead of an animal, is a rare opportunity. A human life is not to be wasted; rather, people should live with purpose. Unlike the other world religions, Buddhism has but a few universally

The Sanchi stupa with gateway and pathway for ritual circumambulation. This shrine, in Madhya Prodesh state, in central India, was a major Buddhist pilgrimage site in ancient India.

accepted doctrines. Beyond the three refuges cited at the beginning of the chapter, Buddhists have adopted varying subsets of the Buddha's teachings and many rituals, always keeping the monastic community (the sangha) as its central institution. How could a world religion accommodate such pluralism in the course of establishing its essential doctrines?

First, Buddhists (like Hindus) assume that since humanity contains persons of many sorts, many different spiritual avenues are needed to reach everyone. Teachers, therefore, formulated myriad practices, and philosophers offered multiple interpretations of the truth the Buddha had revealed.

The second reason for Buddhism's pluralism lies in an instruction from the Buddha himself: after his death, no one person or institution was to be allowed to fix a single canon or set a single norm of orthodoxy in doctrinal interpretations (the opposite extreme of premodern Christianity). As a result, by six hundred years after the death of Shakyamuni Buddha, five canons of collected teachings were made and the sangha aligned under two main divisions: the "elder traditionalists" and the Great Vehicle. The elders, or Sthaviravadins, were less numerous, and their sole surviving school is called *Theravada*. Since about 100 CE, only Theravadins have designated Buddha's most enlightened followers as arhats. *Mahayana* is the name given to the Great Vehicle division, and many schools survive today, including Pure Land and Zen, each with a great diversity of subgroups. Thus, in many respects it is quite artificial to posit a single "Buddhism" based upon a common code, text, or catechism of belief. Buddhism in popular practice among the laity, however, does show many continuities, as we will see. The first topic is the highest ideal.

Nirvana

The word *nirvana* is based upon the Sanskrit verb meaning "to cool by blowing" and refers to one who has "cooled" the feverish *kleshas* ("hindrances," "poisons") of greed, hatred, and delusion. It is the kleshas that inflame desire, create karma, and bind the individual into *samsara*, the world of rebirth and suffering. Buddhists often present the concept of nirvana realization by likening it to the extinction of a fire, for as this phenomenon was understood in ancient India, the flames of an extinguished fire had been released to return to a diffuse, unagitated, and eternal state. The state of nirvana thus carries similar associations: freedom and existence in an eternal state beyond all material description. Both men and women, by moral living and mastering meditation, can realize nirvana through the cultivation of *prajna*, the direct "insight" into the nature of existence.

The Four Noble Truths

The earliest and most enduring formulation of the Buddha's doctrine, the Four Noble Truths, provides a definition and analysis of the human condition as well as a diagnosis: the path toward nirvana. The biographies recount that through the realization of these truths in his own experience, Shakyamuni reached final enlightenment.

The first Noble Truth, "All life entails suffering," instructs the Buddhist not to deny the inevitable experience of mortal existence: physical and mental disease, loss of loved ones, the bodily degeneration of old age, and the inescapability of death. The intention of this first truth is not to induce pessimism but to encourage clear, realistic observation. Even pleasure and good times, however enjoyable, have a fundamental inadequacy because they are only temporary. The appropriate response to this truth is to make the most of the spiritual opportunities of human birth and to show compassion (*karuna*) and loving kindness (*maitri*) to alleviate the suffering affecting all other beings.

The second Noble Truth states, "The cause of suffering is desire." The term for "desire" (trishna) literally means "thirst," a term that covers possessions, power, sex, and all that human beings "thirst after," far beyond mere food and drink. (At the advanced stages of Buddhist practice, desire for doctrinal learning and even the wish for one's own enlightenment must also be rejected to reach the final goal.) The emphasis on desire in the second truth makes plain the need for renunciation, detachment, and asceticism.

The third Noble Truth, "Removing desire removes suffering," is rooted in the central Buddhist idea of spiritual causation: the same pattern of cyclical cause and effect by which desire leads to further suffering can also be reversed and eventually extinguished in nirvana. Later we shall present a more extended treatment of this important and universally accepted Buddhist doctrine of causality, which is known by its Sanskrit name, *pratityasamutpada*. The emphasis on renunciation also signals the importance of the sangha as a refuge for individuals who wish to remove themselves from the world of desire.

The fourth Truth, "The way for removing desire is to follow the Eightfold Path," specifies the treatment that will "cure" the human condition, the continuous cycle of rebirth, suffering, and redeath. As the Buddhist progresses toward enlightenment, moving through moral practice, meditation, and the cultivation of the prajna, his or her understanding of the Four Noble Truths deepens. There are eight specific elements in the progressive path to nirvana

The Eightfold Path

Among the many doctrinal lists compiled to describe Buddhist practices, The Eightfold Path has been the most widely disseminated. It outlines the necessary means for achieving the realization of nirvana. The usual order is as follows:

1. *Right Views,* especially of the Noble Truths

2. *Right Thought,* or thought that is shaped by detachment from hatred and cruelty

3. *Right Speech,* which refrains from falsehood, gossip, and frivolity

4. *Right Action,* defined negatively, as action free of killing, stealing, and harming

5. *Right Livelihood,* the refusal to earn a living through astrology, casting magic spells, or careers that involve inflicting harm or killing

6. *Right Effort,* to clear and calm the mind

7. *Right Mindfulness,* the distinctive form of Buddhist meditation that observes clearly the mind and body, and cultivates detachment

8. *Right Concentration,* another form of advanced meditation that attains the mastery of trance states

Another important arrangement of the Eightfold Path was organized according to three central categories of Buddhist practice:

Morality (Shila) entails Speech, Action, and Livelihood

Meditation (Dhyana) entails Effort, Mindfulness, and Concentration

Insight or Wisdom (Prajna) entails Views and Thought

The Ceylonese Theravadin commentator Buddhaghosa (fifth century CE), who refers to the two legs of Buddhism as Morality and Meditation, upon which the body of Insight stands, organized his entire summary of the faith on the basis of this division. The Eightfold Path emphasizes that moral progress is the essential foundation to successful meditation and that the measure of successful meditation is the awakening and deepening of prajna. Thedifferent elements of the path underscore Buddhism's practical emphasis on effectiveness, whether in the foundational goal of improving moral standards, good conduct, and the material welfare of society, or in the service of the more advanced ideal of deconditioning desire-driven behavior, restructuring cognition, and focusing consciousness on enlightenment realization.

The First Community and Its Development

Life in the Buddhist sangha was a true refuge for "sons and daughters of the Buddha" (as monks and nuns were called) who wished to leave behind their homes and live for spiritual purpose. The ideal was simple: material needs were managed by the institution and by householders, thus allowing the renunciants to meditate and study without encumbrances.

Texts regulating the early monks and nuns, called *Vinayas,* record how the rules developed. For example, because the Buddha was sensitive to the state laws under which he lived, he declared criminals, runaway slaves, or army deserters ineligible to join the sangha. He also specified principles to govern the community (by seniority, as reckoned from the time since ordination) and insisted that the group meet every two weeks so that each monk or nun can certify his or her personal compliance. This fortnightly ritual became a central feature of life in the sangha. The Buddha's organizational genius can be seen as well in his cultivation of a householder community that provided for the needs of the sangha. It was good Buddhist householders who joined the sangha, and it was the patronage of other good Buddhist householders that established the faith's monasteries and shrines across India and, over time, throughout Asia.

After the Buddha's death, in accordance with his instruction that authority over his community was not to reside in a single person or institution, the monks and nuns settled in separate monastic colonies, which became the centers that perpetuated the faith. The renunciants repeated and memorized the sets of sermons they had heard and worked out a distinctive form of communal life. Within the first three centuries there were several councils, which met to focus on the exact rules of monastic practice.

Although the early sanghas also found considerable common ground, no council ever achieved exact consensus on matters of discipline or doctrinal formulation. Dissenters went off to practice as they felt proper in their own monasteries, but the monastic codes in the *Vinayas* are remarkably similar, and the disagreements that led to schisms seem to have involved relatively minor points. This early fact of sangha autonomy and divergent understandings of the Dharma became precedents that shaped the continuation of regional pluralism found across the Buddhist world right up to the present. As Chinese pilgrim Fa-Hsien noted in 400 CE, after traveling extensively in India, "Practices of the monks are so various and have increased so that they cannot be recorded."[1]

How Buddhism Became a World Religion

In the first two centuries after Shakyamuni's death, Buddhist monks and converts spread slowly across the Gangetic plain as simply another one of the many shramana groups that emphasized asceticism and rejected the brahmin caste's privileged status, its ritual system, and especially its claim to hold a monopoly on advanced spiritual practice. It was Ashoka (273–232 BCE), an emperor of the powerful Maurya dynasty, who shaped and propelled Buddhism's emergence as a broad-based religion that reached beyond the ascetics. Now the faith was in a position to unify the social classes of a civilization and link the householder population with its monastic elite.

Just as the Mauryan Empire extended across most of the subcontinent, Ashoka through his personal prestige and imperial edicts, as well as the patronage of notable monks, helped spread Buddhism from Afghanistan to the Bay of Bengal, from the Himalayan foothills to the island of Ceylon (Sri Lanka). As a result, the first definite traces of Buddhist monuments (monasteries, and stupa shrines) can be dated to this era, as can the first systematic oral collections of the teachings. Within a century after the end of the Mauryan period, Buddhist institutions dotted the major trade routes going north and south, east and west from the Buddhist holy land, with major shrines, monasteries, and pilgrimage traditions developing at sites associated with the Buddha.

Buddha from Gandhara, in the upper Indus River region, where icons were made by artisans skilled in the Hellenistic style.

The expansion northwest into the upper Indus River, in the region called Gandhara and into the Kashmir Valley, and then beyond them up the trade routes crossing the mountains north into central Asia, made these areas a Buddhist stronghold for the next millennium. It was here that the Indic world had already met the Hellenic, for hundreds of settlements across the upper Indus were populated by descendants of the troops of Alexander the Great (356–323 BCE). Indeed, the expansion of the Mauryan Empire was enabled in part because Alexander's campaign of world conquest had faltered on the Indus. Stranded far from home, veterans of Alexander's army settled in the area, where their descendants established small states and became prominent regional traders. Many converted to Buddhism.

To understand Buddhism's successful rise to popularity among kings and commoners, however, we must comprehend how the sangha became the center of Buddhism across Asia.

Sangha and Monastery: The Institutional Vehicles of Buddhism's Expansion

Living in community, Buddhist monks, nuns, and devout lay followers established monasteries and shrines that rooted the faith in every locality. When Buddhist monasticism spread across Asia, it introduced independent, corporate institutions that transformed local societies and regional polities. In ancient India, the early sangha admitted new members without regard for caste as a limiting spiritual or social category. In Buddhism's subsequent missionary migrations, acceptance into the sangha offered ordinary citizens an opportunity for spiritual seeking and educational advancement that was otherwise unavailable.

Buddhism could not have existed in society at large without the support of the householders, for it was the laity that ensured the viability of the monastic institution. Throughout the Buddhist world, lay people made donations to the sangha to "earn merit" as a means of improving their karma and garnering worldly blessings for themselves, their families, and their communities. It was this central exchange, maintained between sangha and society, that kept Buddhism vibrant.

Varieties of Buddhist Monasticism

The typical Buddhist community had its center in a monastery (*vihara*), where monks or nuns would take their communal vows, meditate, study, and confirm their compliance with the monastic code fortnightly. These institutions also supported monks who practiced medicine, performed rituals essential to the Buddhist lifestyle of the locality, or managed the institution. Over time, distinctions developed within Buddhist monasticism: there were forest monasteries, where meditation and optional ascetic practices (*dhutanga*) could be undertaken (often under the leadership of a charismatic monk teacher), and monasteries, in village and urban settlements, which offered the opportunity to blend compassionate service to the community with individual cultivation and study. A Buddhist monk or nun typically moved between village and urban monasteries, often going out for periods "in the forest."

In many areas, the focus and inspiration for followers was a monk whose spiritual charisma and exemplary teaching ability drew ascetic disciples and donations from the laity. The common biography of such monks mirrors that of Shakyamuni (the Buddha): disillusionments, renunciation, retreat to the wilderness, nirvana realization, then a return to society to teach.

Practical Mechanisms of Expansion

Many successful monasteries expanded. The pattern was to send out monks to establish satellite institutions following the teachings of the charismatic founder, thereby perpetuating the monastic lineage. This template of Buddhist expansion created "galactic systems" that extended Buddhism into unconverted frontier zones. The resulting network of "mother–daughter" monasteries shaped alliances of all sorts, religious and otherwise, providing the pattern of new Buddhist institution building found from Ladakh to Bali, and more recently from Bangkok to Los Angeles, Dharamsala to New York. This institutional system also resulted in the tendency for aristocratic/dominant caste families to control local monastic lineages, a pattern of ethnic group dominance that was visible until recently in Buddhist Tibet and continues in the Kathmandu Valley, in Japan, and in Sri Lanka. In other contexts, Buddhist viharas broke down ethnic and class boundaries, blurred divisions between peoples, and created transregional communities.

Rulers across Asia were drawn to support Buddhism because of its emphasis on individual morality, its rituals designed to secure prosperity for the state

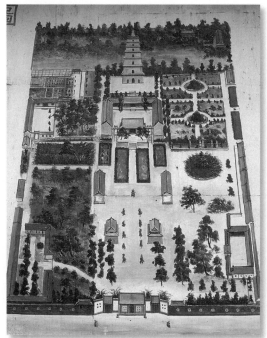

Buddhist monastery estate in China. By the end of the first Buddhist millennium, major monasteries had become complex institutions whose wealth helped popularize the tradition.

as well as for its head, and the powerful legitimization that respected monastics could bestow on a regime. History has also shown that states favoring Buddhism often placed controls on the sangha's development. For example, to orchestrate the early expansion of Buddhism in China and Japan, emperors ordered each provincial governor to build a monastery. This command was eventually reissued to the subunits in each province, as Buddhist institutions came to mirror the state's own administrative networks. Buddhist exponents, in turn, held up as a model for the ideal Buddhist ruler Ashoka, who today would be called a benevolent dictator. A fair, generous king (governor, local official, etc.) could be called a "future Buddha." The most praiseworthy title was *cakravartin*, a zealous protector and devotee. Thus leading monks in the sangha could offer those wielding political power the highest form of legitimation in the eyes of the faithful. In this manner, Buddhist doctrines, officials, and patrons permeated the secular and political lives of the societies Buddhism entered.

In places where Buddhism thrived, some monasteries in cities and villages evolved into complex institutions that were much more than refuges for ascetics. The monastery often housed the only local school, and members of the sangha served their societies by spreading literacy. Many urban monasteries also became lending institutions, appointing treasurers to see that when monies donated at shrines exceeded the sangha's requirements, the overage was reinvested (usually in trade loans) into the secular community. Interest earned through this practice was reinvested as well. On the trade routes especially, this practice, combined with profits from renting monastery-owned buildings to warehousing or retailing enterprises, garnered considerable income for the monastery treasuries. Such developments, which are attested from 200 CE onward in India and China, explain how Buddhism traveled across the Asian landscape on the basis of trade, supported by traders, and in cities along the commercial routes.

Another component in the spread of vibrant Buddhist institutions across Asia was the accumulation of lands donated by individuals and the state as perpetual endowments. Since monks were forbidden to till the soil, the sangha (as typically organized by lay managers) would rent out the cultivated lands it was acquiring. Whether its laborers grew rice and wheat or cultivated orchards, the monastery derived the food or cash needed for the sangha's upkeep. Until the twentieth century, in fact, many of the large Buddhist institutions were given indentured workers or slaves (usually entire families). Finally, shrines located within the monasteries would also earn income for the sangha in the form of offerings and from levies imposed upon artisans who sold icons and votive amulets. All these elements made running a major monastery a demanding job and ensured that the manager wielded considerable influence in the community.

These practices of "monastic landlordism," banking, and shrine management were also central to Buddhism's successful missions across Asia, creating the means to endow the faith with reliable income and a strong material culture. Buddhists attracted a following with their spiritual teachings but also with well-constructed, often remarkable buildings, shrines, and image halls that complemented the Dharma. Tied to the productive base of society, Buddhist monasteries were ornamented with masterpieces of art, their libraries grew with manuscript production, and their leaders could develop an effective presentation of the Dharma. Many viharas also organized endowed charities that fed the poor and dispensed free medical care.

But there was one problem. As a practical matter, monastery autonomy and the lack of an overarching authority to regulate the monks' and nuns' obedience to the *Vinaya* norms made political leaders the arbiters of the integrity of Buddhist institutions. These officials had to "purify the sangha" periodically—that is, remove those who were acting contrary to the Vinaya norms or perhaps had not entered the vihara through the proper channels. For Buddhism's strength through concentrating wealth and human resources was also its historical weakness: viharas were vulnerable to the vagaries of state patronage and royal protection, as well as to the devastating effects of internal corruption and civil disorder.

PREMODERN BUDDHISM: THE CLASSICAL ERA

The Pan-Asian Expansion of Buddhism

In his first sermon after receiving enlightenment, Shakyamuni Buddha told his former companions, the five ascetic monks, to spread the new teaching universally and to use the local dialects in these communications. Thus, from its inception Buddhism has been a missionary religion, teaching a message directed to and thought suitable for all peoples. As the first missionary religion in the world, Buddhism initially spread to places not unlike the urban and trading centers where it had begun. Within the first millennium of the Common Era, Buddhism was found throughout South Asia and well into central Asia on the overland routes. Monks also traveled on the maritime trade routes to Ceylon and across Southeast Asia. Monasteries welcomed all who would observe the rules of residence. By this time, small circles of philosopher monks had divided into more than twenty schools of doctrinal interpretation. What gave the religion unity was a common reverence for the Three Refuges; however, Buddhism has never been a unified faith either doctrinally or institutionally.

By the year 100 CE, Buddhism had entered China through central Asia on the silk routes. As it grew more popular and spread across East Asia over the next six centuries, monks and pilgrims traveled on the land and oceanic routes between the two great ancient civilizations of Asia. The taking root of Buddhism in this region constitutes one of the greatest instances of cross-cultural transmission and conversion in world history, parallel in scope only by the transformations wrought by the world's other great missionary faiths, Christianity and Islam. Buddhism added original conceptions of space, time, psychology, and human destiny that challenged indigenous notions. It also introduced a new social institution that fostered its missionary success: the land-grant monastery whose members could be drawn from diverse social classes.

The Core Doctrines

Textbooks always emphasize the division between traditionalists (Theravada) and adherents of the Great Vehicle (Mahayana), which grew among intellectuals in Buddhism's first millennium. For the lay majority who focused on morality, merit, and blessings, however, doctrinal disputes were mostly irrelevant. For householders, the sangha's conformity to the Vinaya code was the major concern because upright monks and nuns could be relied on for proper performance of rituals that benefited individuals and the community. In addition, householders would earn merit by making donations to the sangha itself.

We have suggested that an individual's beliefs and meditation practices were largely personal matters, and indeed, from the earliest days, monks (or nuns) following very different interpretations of the Dharma coexisted under the same monastery roof. We first consider doctrines and ethical norms that all Buddhists shared, then move on to discuss teachings that differed from school to school.

Prajna *and* Nirvana

Necessary for the attainment of nirvana and often translated as "wisdom," prajna refers to the active capacity for deep spiritual discernment. The term is better rendered as "insight," however. In Buddhism it means "seeing into" reality as it truly is, characterized by suffering, impermanence, and supporting the existence of these traits known as the Three Marks of Existence. Buddhist salvation is often referred to as "enlightenment" because this fullness of prajna eliminates ignorance and completely clears the mind to see reality.

The state a Buddha or an arhat, a fully enlightened follower in Theravada tradition, achieves at death is referred to as *parinirvana* ("final nirvana"), although the texts say that strictly speaking this after-death state is beyond conception. Nirvana has been described in both negative and positive terms: a deathless realm where there is neither sun nor moon, coming nor going, but also a state that is tranquil and pure. Most of the early scholastic treatises recognized nirvana as the only permanent reality in the cosmos. It is not, as erroneously depicted by early Western interpreters, to be seen as "annihilation," which is an extreme position rejected by the Buddha.

Non-Self Doctrine

The concept of *anatman* ("no-*atman*" or "non-self") is used to reject any notion of an essential, unchanging interior entity at the center of a person. The "atman" the Buddha rejected is the indestructible soul posited in the Upanishads and subsequent Hinduism, as described in Chapter Six. Buddhist philosophers argued that the universal characteristic of impermanence, one of the Three Marks of Existence, most certainly applies to human beings. As a result they regarded the human "being" in terms of the continuously changing, interdependent relationship between the five aggregates called *skandhas*.

Buddhist analysts begin with the person as a collection of the skandhas: the physical body, which is made of combinations of the four elements (earth, water, fire, air); feelings that arise from sensory contact; perceptions that attach the categories good, evil, and neutral to these sensory inputs; habitual mental dispositions (*samskaras*) that connect karma-producing will to mental action; and the consciousness that arises when mind and body come in contact with the external world.

The spiritual purpose of breaking down any apparently unchanging locus of individuality is to demonstrate that there is "no thing" to be attached to or to direct one's desire toward. The no-self concept, however, presented exponents of Buddhist doctrine with the perpetual problem of explaining moral causality: how can the doctrine of karma, with its emphasis on compensation for one's good and bad moral decisions, operate without the mechanism of the soul, as in Hinduism or Christianity? Early texts show that this question was clearly posed to Shakyamuni Buddha: if there is no soul, how can the karmic "fruits" of any good or evil act pass into the future of this life or into a later incarnation? The standard explanation given is that karma endures in samskaras that are impressed in the fifth skandha, consciousness. Although always evolving and so impermanent, one's consciousness endures in this life and passes over to be reincarnated in the next.

While the no-self or no-soul doctrine was at the center of Buddhist thought for the philosophical elite, householders across Asia nonetheless typically conceived of themselves in terms of a body and a soul. This contradiction may indicate how peripheral philosophers were to the mainstream of popular Buddhist understanding.

Impermanence and Interdependence

Another universally accepted doctrinal formula in Buddhism is one that specifies the causal pattern of psychic and bodily states conditioning a person's bondage to suffering and rebirth. Known as dependent, or conditioned, origination (*pratityasamutpada*), this doctrine views reality as an ongoing, impermanent, and interdependent flux in the form of a circle divided into twelve parts. Whatever point of entry you take, the next clockwise element is the experience conditioned and the adjacent element in the counterclockwise position is that condition directly affecting the present. Without spiritual exertion, we spin around, life after life, under these conditioning patterns. Used in this way, the twelvefold formula reiterates the basic doctrines already cited:

craving and ignorance are the two chief causes of suffering (Noble Truths Two and Three); and the human being has no soul, only changing components of bodily life units (skandhas). Conditioned origination also dismisses the role of God or gods in shaping human life, rejects merely materialist theories of reality, and undermines the assumption that life "just happens" in random fashion.

Diagram representing the formula of dependent origination, including several interpretative schemes.

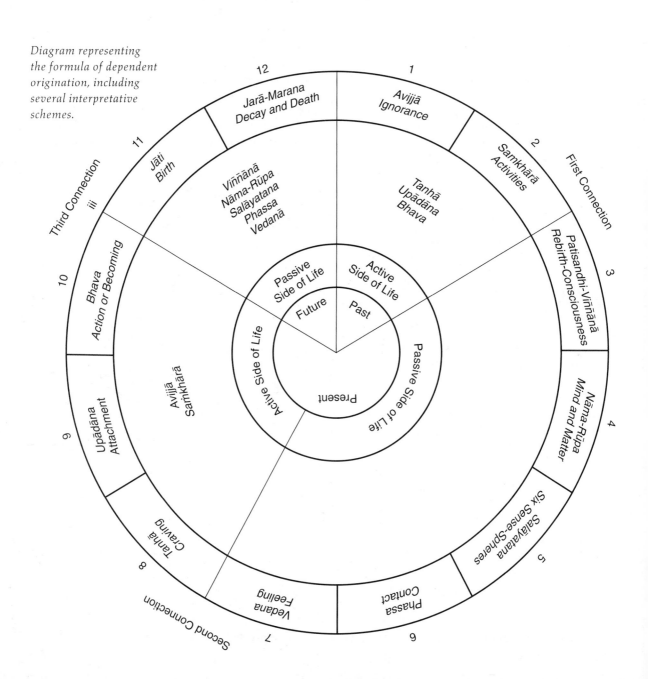

Buddhist Moral Precepts

The early Buddhists specified that moral practice is the first and necessary foundation for moving further on the path toward nirvana. Buddhist ethics entails an "ideology of merit" in which making good karma and avoiding bad is the only sensible approach to life. Popular Buddhist stories focus on imagining the reality of rebirth, which leads to the realization that since all contemporary beings have been one's parents and children throughout a vast number of rebirths, acting morally toward them should be natural and logical. Buddhist morality emphasizes the wisdom of cultivating detachment, discernment, and compassion (karuna).

The earliest moral rules the Buddha established consisted of five precepts. In South and Southeast Asia, they are chanted regularly in modern Theravada rituals by both monks and laity. In these communities, the precepts are regarded as general ideals applicable to everyone. Mahayana schools tended to regard the precepts more as vows, to be chanted only if one intends to follow them completely. (One can omit reciting a precept if one does not expect to be able to observe it.) The five precepts listed here are paired with corresponding positive traits that can be developed to counteract the inclination to violate a precept.

1. Not to destroy life intentionally → kindness and compassion

2. Not to steal → generosity and renunciation

3. Not to have sexual misconduct → seeking "joyous satisfaction with one's spouse"

4. Not to lie → loving the truth, seeking it, pursuing discernment and insight

5. Not to become intoxicated → mindfulness, contentment, awareness via meditation

Later in the history of Buddhism, people began to observe eight precepts, which entail a stricter interpretation of the original five along with three additional renunciations:

6. Not to eat (solid) food after noon

7. Not to participate in shows, dancing, singing or to wear garlands, perfumes, jewelry

8. Not to sleep on high or wide beds.

In addition to the eight precepts, usually taken and rigorously observed by householders on holy days, there is a set of ten precepts, observed by novice monks and undertaken as a long-term commitment. They comprise the eight, but split one of these into two parts and add a final prohibition against handling money. This final rule was made to ensure that begging for food would be the norm for monks and nuns and this exchange between laity and sangha binds the Buddhist community.

Karma and Causality

One can make the case from textual sources that karma doctrine is not fatalistic because one is continually making new *punya* ("merit") or *pap* ("demerit") to change the ongoing calculus of karmic destiny. Buddhist philosophy does stress the potential for certain strong karma effects to set off mechanistic causal connections between past and future. Nevertheless, a person's karma, like all phenomena, changes every instant.

Further, the Buddhist understanding of causality is that not all contingencies in life are karma dependent. In fact, according to the Theravadins, events are more likely than not to have had causes other than karma. Since only Buddhas can ascertain whether karma or other contingencies are at work in ongoing life, individuals are faced with uncertainty in evaluating events. Buddhists make a "general reading" of karma from birth station and biography. To be prepared for the future, however, the logic of the karma doctrine has motivated Buddhists everywhere to cultivate a life-long practice of seeking guidance through astrology and making punya. Indeed, texts for householders emphasize that accumulation of wealth is the fruition of good past karma and that giving away wealth to earn merit is the best human expenditure. This giving, of benefit to all, is in a sense the social application of the Buddha's teaching about interdependence. These principles have been incorporated into "Four Conditions" and "Four Good Deeds," doctrinal statements that have been as influential for the laity as the Four Noble Truths were for the philosophers:

> *Four Conditions (to seek)*
> Wealth gotten by lawful means
> Good renown in society
> Long life
> Birth in heaven

> *Four Good Deeds (to use wealth for)*
> Make family and friends happy
> Ensure security against worldly dangers
> Make offerings to family, friends, gods, and ghosts
> Support worthy religious people

The core doctrines we have discussed—prajna and nirvana, anatman or non-self, impermanence and interdependence, and karma causality—comprise the most common foundation for Buddhist belief. For householders, these ideas translate into fostering family ties, striving for economic success, making offerings to hungry ghosts and local gods, pursuing worldly happiness and security, nurturing faith, and seeking heaven.

Now we consider how in specific places and times individual Buddhists and Buddhist communities have focused on the fatalistic or free-will elements affecting individual life.

The Classical Ideal: Buddhist Civilization

Buddhist civilization was sustained by ritual exchanges between householders and renunciants, the monks and nuns whose advanced ascetic practices entailed abandonment of worldly comforts. Many formulations of proper Buddhist practice were made in the course of early Buddhist history to guide the faithful among the spiritual alternatives specified by the Buddha. The triad of moral practice (*shila*), meditation (*dhyana*), and insight cultivation (*prajna*) was an early organizing schema, as we noted in our discussion of the Eightfold Path.

Buddhist monasticism arose to provide refuge and support for renunciants seeking enlightenment, but the tradition survived by building multifaceted relationships with lay followers who provided for the monks' and nuns' subsistence. Eliciting the loyalty of a cross section of all classes, Buddhists articulated the foundations for a society with spiritual and moral dimensions. Buddhism adapted to myriad local traditions, yet still—when vital—its community remained focused on the Three Refuges: the Buddha, the Dharma, or teachings, and the Sangha, the monastic community.

The general ideals of Buddhist civilization were in place very early. Monks and nuns served the world through their example of renunciation and meditation, by performing rituals, and by providing medical services. As preservers, transmitters, and exemplars of the Dharma, the sangha's duty was to attract the lay community's merit-making donations by being spiritually worthy; complementing this, sangha members were to follow the *Vinaya* rules and seek out dedicated sympathizers and generous donors. Based upon these guidelines, Buddhist societies came to exhibit an array of common traits: relic shrines as centers of community ritual and economy; monasteries as refuges for meditation, study, and access to material resources; and sangha members who assumed leadership of the community's spiritual instruction and ritual life.

Thus, Buddhism successfully developed a broad vision of the spiritual community and of proper practice. Texts speak of the devout layman's duty to help others grow in faith, morality, knowledge, and charity, to live a life worthy of his or her family heritage, and to make offerings to the spirits of the dead. The Buddha also revealed several short texts (called *mantra* and *paritta*, later *dharani*) that, when chanted, could help householders achieve blessings and protections needed for a good worldly life. All Buddhists are instructed to listen to the Dharma and try hard to resist its decline. Given the variety of possible practices, the only sound definition of a "good Buddhist" is simple: one who takes the Three Refuges and practices accordingly.

The Mahayana: Philosophies and East Asian Monastic Schools

Despite their prolific writings, Mahayana philosophers and followers were in fact a minority in ancient South Asia, as monks of this persuasion lived in monasteries alongside Sthaviravadins, the predecessors of today's Theravadins. Mahayana first became the Great Vehicle, the dominant strain of Buddhism, outside the heartland, being a vibrant subculture in postclassical India (700 CE until its extinction), Burma, the Khmer, Indonesian, and Funan regions of medieval Southeast Asia.

The contrast between traditionalists (Theravadins) and Mahayanists seems to reflect a universal human tendency to divide religious communities between those inclined to a literal approach (holding to the letter within a conservative tradition) and those inclined to a more open-ended, experimental, and expansive approach to spiritual matters. The Mahayana in this light might be compared to the Sufis in Islam, opposed to the strict scholars of the law (ulama); the Christian analogy would be the mystics in opposition to the official church.

On the philosophical level, there were fiercely contested disagreements between the Theravadins and Mahayanas that we know of chiefly from the Mahayana side. For the most part, the traditionalists ignored the Mahayanas' polemics, dismissing proponents with the derogatory term "Illusionists" (*Vaitulika*). The pejorative label the Mahayanists applied to their opponents, the "Lesser Vehicle" (*Hinayana*), suggested diminished religious effectiveness, commitment, and vision.

We shall discuss the Madhyamaka and Consciousness Only schools of Mahayana thought, as well as some minority schools that happen to be well known today and an esoteric tradition called the Thunderbolt Vehicle.

The Madhyamaka

Among the earliest texts expressing Mahayana ideas are those called the *Perfection of Wisdom* (*Prajnaparamita*). In these texts of varying length, comments attributed to the Buddha or notable monks poke fun at the Theravadin arhats and poke holes in their scholasticism. More importantly, however, the *Prajnaparamita* texts represent a search for the ultimate truth behind the words of the oldest scriptures. Since Mahayana thought emphasizes interdependence, its exponents saw the Theravadins' focus on an individual's pursuit of nirvana as "selfish" and reflecting ignorance of the Buddha's highest teaching. The Mahayana exponents held that the laity as well as monks could attain enlightenment.

Opposition to the Theravadins coalesced in the writings of the monk Nagarjuna (born c. 150 CE), one of India's greatest philosophers and founder of the Madhyamaka school. Nagarjuna developed a deconstructive method that reduces all assertions to arbitrary propositions and applied the system to a wide-ranging subject matter. In one of the most courageous explorations in the history of religions, he argued that all language is conventional and all classifications set up by it are mere constructions, including all Buddhist constructs, even "nirvana" and "samsara." It is through understanding how humans construct reality arbitrarily from no-thing-ness (*shunyata*) that one is released from all illusions and desires, and from the cycle of rebirths. Nagarjuna's deconstructive philosophical effort was religious. His aim was to clear away all false assumptions and even the subtle attachment to language and scholastic categories, thus opening the way to meditation practices that transcend words, the only viable means of finding true refuge and final enlightenment.

"Consciousness Only" School

The other major school of Mahayana thought continued to develop the Great Vehicle from Nagarjuna's standpoint. The "Consciousness Only" (*Cittamatra*) school largely agreed with the Madhyamaka critique of experience as empty but asserted that the real arena of spiritual transformation can therefore be further specified within human consciousness. This school's great thinkers were the brothers Asanga and Vasubandhu (active c. 380 CE), who developed intricate theories of consciousness and causality. They described how karma works within the stream of consciousness, where past actions may block pure, passionless seeing. Further, the spiritual life must be devoted to purifying mind or consciousness, since this is all that truly exists. Again, the practical effect of such theories was to promote the traditional Buddhist practice of meditation, as indicated by another name often applied to this faction: Yogacara or "yoga practice" school).

Buddha Nature School

Another Mahayana philosophy grew later from Madhyamaka roots in East Asia: the Buddha-nature (*tathagatagarbha*) school. Its proponents held that if it is true that nirvana and samsara cannot be separated in any meaningful way, then nirvana must interpenetrate all reality. And if this is so, one might say that all beings have a portion of nirvana and so possess the latent potential for its realization. Among the many metaphors developed to convey the interdependence of all reality with the Buddha nature, that of Indra's jeweled net had widespread appeal. Just as each jewel in the net reflects every other one, including the reflections of the reflections, even the tiniest thing contains the mystery of the universe. Although support for this school eventually declined in China, its ideas and metaphors influenced the Buddhist practice called Ch'an in China and Zen in Japan. The Buddha-nature doctrine appeared to some as a reversion to belief in the soul; but it, too, reinforced the need for traditional meditation practices.

Manjushri, the bodhisattva of scholars, who cuts through ignorance and delusion.

*Tara, the popular
female bodhisattva,
who is believed to have
arisen from the tears
of compassion from
Avalokiteshvara.*

The Lotus Sutra and Its Schools

One of the most popular Buddhist scriptures in East Asia was the *Lotus Sutra*. Originally written in Sanskrit by 100 CE, this work was later translated into every East Asian language spoken by Buddhists. Through parables, accounts of astounding magical display, and hammering polemics, the *Lotus* develops the Mahayana doctrine of cosmic Buddhahood. It recounts how amazed and confused the arhats became when Shakyamuni Buddha revealed that the human Buddha to whom they were so attached is in fact the embodiment of a more universal Buddha reality that can materialize in many forms simultaneously throughout the cosmos. The *Lotus* describes how the Buddha's preaching skillfully adapted the Dharma to suit the level of the audiences. Even his dying was a show, performed to encourage the active practice of devotees so that they would take seriously the shortness of mortal life. The *Lotus* asserts that the nirvana of arhats is incomplete, merely a preliminary stage in enlightenment seeking. Rather, all beings are destined for Buddhahood through eons of rebirth in samsara.

The religious ideal in the *Lotus Sutra* and in other Mahayana texts shifts from the arhat to the *bodhisattva*, or "future Buddha." Disciples following the Great Vehicle are encouraged not to be satisfied with the arhats' limited nirvana, when Buddhahood is the proper, final religious goal for all. Why? Mahayana teachers point out that given the reality of interdependence, no individual can be an enlightened "being" somehow independent of others. Bodhisattvas should therefore not imagine ending their careers until all beings are enlightened, a mind-boggling and very long-term commitment.

The *Lotus Sutra* is only one among a large class of texts that focus on bodhisattvas who have garnered the merit necessary to earn rebirth as divinities. These "celestial bodhisattvas" continue to serve humanity by offering compassionate intervention to secure worldly blessings and even the means to salvation. In the popular imagination, by the end of the faith's first millennium they had become the Buddhist parallels to Hindu or Chinese deities. The most popular and universal celestial bodhisattva was Avalokiteshvara, who came to be known as Guanyin in China, Kannon in Japan, Chenrizi in Tibet, and Karunamaya in Nepal. Wherever Mahayana Buddhism spread, texts recounting the local deeds of this and other heavenly beings were commonly disseminated through storytellers, art, and popular texts. For the great majority of householders, being a Mahayana devotee meant performing rituals and asking for blessings from these compassionate divinities.

Pure Land Schools

Perhaps as an extension of the Buddha's injunction that the sangha should "show the householders the way to heaven," Pure Land Buddhism arose in India, around 300 CE, as yet another "cabin" within the Great Vehicle. This school's texts describe how certain bodhisattvas vowed to create celestial paradises upon reaching Buddhahood. In these "Pure Lands," there existed all the conditions needed for the individual to be reborn and enlightened. The popularity of this Buddhist orientation, which deferred enlightenment seeking from the human state until rebirth in a heaven, probably had its origins in Shakyamuni's predictions of Buddhism's decline after a thousand years. This expectation legitimated a new spirituality to match the changed times.

The most important and highly developed of the Pure Land schools was that associated with the western paradise called *Sukhavati*, skillfully created by a Buddha named Amitabha in Sanskrit (Amitofo in Chinese, Amida in Japanese). An ordered system of Pure Land doctrine and practice, developed in China, featured chanting Amitabha's name (*Namo A-mi-t'o Fo*) as a meditative act and communal ritual. Exponents assured Pure Land followers that by drawing upon this Buddha's distinctive cosmic power through chanting and other devotional practices, even those with bad karma could be reborn in Sukhavati. It was the Chinese monk Shan-tao (613–681) who effectively brought Pure Land teaching to its widest audience, preaching to court officials and to the masses.

In Japan, Pure Land Buddhism continued to evolve as devotees were taught that their own "self power" was insufficient to reach nirvana and only the "other power" of celestial Buddhas and bodhisattvas could be relied upon. Rituals at death were dedicated to having an individual's lifetime accumulation of merit (punya) be directed to attaining rebirth in the Pure Land. Over the years these schools expanded, and hopes for Pure Land rebirth became extremely popular among the laity. Pure Land schools were also the first to de-emphasize the requirement of monastic celibacy by its ordained sangha.

The Meditation School

By about 600 CE, a Mahayana school called Ch'an had formed in China. In contrast to the Pure Land emphasis on "other power," the Ch'an took a position on the "traditionalist" end of the Mahayana spectrum, insisting that individual effort to reach nirvana was the Buddha's true teaching. Ch'an masters stressed meditation, this-life realization, and "self power." This school still bases its authority on an unbroken line of enlightened teachers from Shakyamuni onward, with each subsequent enlightened master, in turn, transmitting enlightenment to his key disciple wordlessly, "mind to mind."

Less concerned with a single text and formed in close association with Daoist concepts and aesthetics, covered in Chapter Eight, Ch'an lineages respected the Mahayana scriptures but preferred to use texts recounting the teachings of their own patriarchs and masters, including their approaches to unlocking the gates of nirvana realization. This school also developed the use of paradoxical word problems called *koans* ("cases") that masters forced their disciples to ponder and answer. Resolution of the koans—with words, roars, bodily gestures, or composed silence—could lead to small awakenings of prajna or even complete nirvana realization. Ch'an masters also insisted on the necessity of mindfulness meditation.

The paradigmatic figure of this school is Bodhidharma, the patriarch who reputedly brought the mind-to-mind transmission tradition from India to China, early in the seventh century of the Common Era. He is depicted as a fierce meditating monk dispensing terse spiritual admonitions. Later known as Zen in Japan, the Ch'an school also developed in monasteries upholding strict monastic rules. Its lineages eventually split on the lines of those believing in gradual versus sudden enlightenment.

The Thunderbolt Vehicle

One additional branch of elite doctrine and practice that emerged among Mahayana Buddhists was the Vajrayana, the Thunderbolt Vehicle, a tradition that some scholars would consider to be distinct from the Mahayana school. Also called "tantra," and similar to the Hindu practice of that name, it developed after the faith's first millennium in South Asia. Initially the Thunderbolt was the province of wandering mendicants whose spiritual seeking on the fringes of society began in the Buddha's era. Perhaps in reaction to the complacency stemming from the mainstream view that final enlightenment would not be achieved until after many future lifetimes, the tantric traditions emphasized realizing salvation speedily and in this lifetime.

Tantric Buddhism used Indian yoga techniques and unconventional means under the guidance of an accomplished teacher, and it drew upon the Mahayana philosophy that equated samsara with nirvana. It agreed that all beings partake of the Buddha nature, the tathagatagarbha doctrine, and identified the essence of the Buddha's teaching as the pursuit of unshakable diamondlike insight by whatever means brought immediate success.

The descent of the cosmic Buddha at the time of a devotee's death, ushering the deceased to the western paradise.

Milarepa, the great tantric saint of Tibet, whose songs are beloved for conveying the struggles of solitary meditation and the joy of enlightenment.

The central experience of tantric Buddhism is *sadhana*, communion with a celestial Buddha or bodhisattva through the experience of identification with his or her body, speech, and mind. Dozens of sadhanas emerged. The sage who discovered each path is thought to have experienced the deity as the embodiment of enlightenment. Thus an initiate is taught to place the deity in his or her mind's eye, repeat mantras that resonate with that form, and build an existential connection with it, performing *mudras* (hand gestures) and other rituals that help to solidify the identification. When complete, one's identification ultimately implies the attainment of enlightenment equal to that of the divine form.

Some tantric traditions consciously break the norms of orthodox caste society. Men and women assume identities as divine, enlightened consorts, and their sexual union is developed as a unifying experience of the dual energies of *prajna* (the feminine, as insight) and *upaya* (the masculine, as means of practice). Sexual consort yoga was doubtless once an element in some tantric traditions. (In modern Nepal and Tibet, consorts are often spouses.) But as these traditions were systematized in textual form by Buddhist monks after 900 CE in North India, the requirement of literal sexual yoga practice was reinterpreted to allow its replacement by symbolic visualization.

PREMODERN BUDDHISM: BUDDHIST EXPANSION

As Buddhism expanded across Asia up to the early modern era, in each cultural region monks, nuns, and disciples adapted the traditions to local cultural conditions. Across Asia, all the sanghas developed Buddhist rituals to help individuals through their lives, from birth to death. In applying the faith's resources to fulfilling the religious needs of the householders, monks and nuns from all Buddhist doctrinal schools served their lay communities in a similar manner. We now survey the wide-ranging pilgrimage of Buddhism by geographic region, then note the distinctive beliefs and practices that gave the faith its local appeal.

Tantric icon showing visualization of salvific insight and skillful practice as the union of male and female siddhas.

South Asia

With the decline of the great Gupta dynasty in North India by 650 CE, small regional polities controlled the Hindu–Buddhist societies of South Asia. Buddhism survived mainly in the northeast under imperial patronage, its presence confined largely to monasteries at the major universities. Nalanda and Vikramashila, for example, fostered a vigorous articulation of Mahayana Buddhist philosophy, meditation, and popular piety. Ties to Tibet, Nepal, and centers in the Srivijaya kingdom of Sumatra–Java extended the influence of the Great Vehicle.

After Buddhism's successful transplantation in China, Ceylon, and Southeast Asia, monks and householders traveled to study in South Asia and to acquire texts. They also completed pilgrimage visits, venerating the "sacred traces" (cremation relics, begging bowls, etc.) of the Buddha and arhats that were entombed in the stupas. The Buddha's enlightenment tree in Gaya and the temple erected nearby were at the center of such visits. Distant rulers

Selections from a Merit Account Sheet

100 Merits: Save one life; save a woman's chastity; prevent a child from drowning; continue a family lineage

50 Merits: Prevent an abortion; provide for a homeless person; prevent someone from committing a serious crime; give a speech that benefits many

30 Merits: Convert another to Buddhism; facilitate a marriage; take in an orphan; help another do something virtuous

10 Merits: Recommend a virtuous person; cure a major illness; speak virtuously; save the life of a good animal; publish the Buddha's teachings; treat servants properly

5 Merits: Prevent a lawsuit; cure a minor illness; stop someone from slandering; make an offering to a saintly person; save any animal; pray for others

3 Merits: Endure ill treatment without complaint; bury an animal; urge those making a living by killing to stop

1 Merit: Give an article to help others; chant a Buddhist scripture; provide for one monk; return a lost article; help repair a public road or bridge

100 Demerits: Cause a death; rape; end a family lineage

50 Demerits: Induce an abortion; break up a marriage; teach someone to do great evil; make a speech that harms many

30 Demerits: Create slander that dishonors another; disobey an elder; cause a family to separate; during famine, fail to share food grains

10 Demerits: Mistreat an orphan or widow; prepare a poison; kill an animal that serves humans; speak harshly to parent or teacher

5 Demerits: Slander spiritual teachings; turn away a sick person; speak harshly; kill any animal; write or speak lewdly; not clear an injustice when possible

3 Demerits: Get angry over words spoken; cheat an ignorant person; destroy another's success; be greedy

1 Demerit: Urge another to fight; help another do evil; waste food; kill insects; turn away a begging monk; take a bribe; keep a lost article

Source: Guide formulated by Liao-Fan Yuan (1550–1624), a Zen master of Jiang-su Province. Translated in *The Key to Creating One's Destiny* (Singapore: Lapis Lazuli Press, 1988), pp. 43–46. Passages edited and in places paraphrased.

from Ceylon and Burma had been obliged to send funds and artisans to renovate the Gaya site, however. By 1296, when the last such donations were recorded, many Buddhist monasteries across North India had been abandoned for centuries and many shrines had been left to decay. The decline of the faith in South Asia was due partly to the successful development of popular devotional Hinduism and by the Hindu monasticism organized by the saint-scholar Shankara, whose Advaita Vedanta school we discussed in Chapter Six.

Another factor in Buddhism's decline was the arrival in South Asia of Islam, another missionary faith that slowly spread throughout the region. By 750 CE, Muslim conquests and conversions to Islam in central Asia and in northwestern India were undermining Buddhism. As we have seen, Buddhist monasticism was strongly tied to trade and mercantile patronage, and as the trade moving along the silk routes was overtaken by Muslim merchants, the monasteries lost a major source of support. In addition, an era of raids into North India culminated in 1192 in the first period of Muslim rule from Delhi. Across the Gangetic plain, almost all remaining Buddhist institutions were plundered, and the destruction dispersed Indian monks into the Himalayas, to coastal urban centers, and across the seas. In the southern peninsula of the Indian subcontinent, Buddhism declined slowly, and scattered monasteries existed as late as the seventeenth century.

Buddhism's dominant region shifted to East Asia after its sacred centers on the Gangetic plain were ravaged. Because many early versions of the first Buddhist textual collections had been lost, each school settled on surviving texts and scholastic traditions to establish its own doctrinal authority. Once Bodh Gaya was no longer accessible, pious donors built "replica Bodh Gaya temples" now found across Asia to accommodate regional pilgrims. In Southeast Asian states, Ceylon was regarded as the center of Theravada scholarship and disciplined practice. In East Asia, China became the prime center of Mahayana tradition, although after 1250 Tibetan Buddhists at times exerted strong influences within China, south into the Himalayas, and north into Mongolia.

The island of Ceylon embraced Buddhism, and its early kings after 100 BCE supported the sangha and built monuments to express their devotion. Although both Mahayanists and Sthaviravadins practiced there throughout the first millennium, the Theravada school eventually prevailed. The "reforms" instituted by various Southeast Asian kings in the 1300s drew upon respected Ceylonese monks, and these ensured the dominance of Theravada traditions of Burma, Siam (now Thailand), and the Khmer Empire (now Laos and Cambodia) that continues to the present day.

China

In East Asia, Buddhist schools formed around charismatic teachers whose interpretations favored one or another of the many texts as the Buddha's highest teaching. Mahayana Buddhism alone flourished, translated in terms compatible with Daoist mysticism, the indigenous gods, and aspects of Confucian morality and state governance (see Chapter Eight).

Under the weak states of the pre-T'ang era (up until 645 CE), Buddhism found widespread support. Indian and Central Asian monks had begun a determined project of translating the hundreds of Buddhist texts into Chinese. In addition, monks, merchants, and rulers had obtained many precious relics and had them enshrined in monasteries across China. Finally, Chinese Buddhists came to recognize Wu Tai Shan, one of China's sacred mountains, as the home of Manjushri, one of Mahayana Buddhism's chief celestial bodhisattvas (a topic discussed earlier in the chapter). This belief grew as devotees by the thousands ventured to this extraordinary site and had powerful meditative visions of this future Buddha. So strong was belief in Wu Tai Shan's Buddhist holiness that by the beginning of the T'ang dynasty, its fame spread back to India; the Chinese annals note that hundreds of Indian pilgrims traveled to China in subsequent centuries to seek Manjushri's spiritual blessings at Wu Tai Shan. Through textual transmission, the location of relics in monastic shrines across the country, and recognition of this (and other) sacred mountains, by 600 CE all of mainland Asia was unified by Buddhism as China itself was integrated into its sacred realm. With the consolidation of the T'ang state in Chang-an (modern Xian) and its revival of the traditional Confucian literati class, the destiny of Buddhism rose and fell according to the degree of support from the reigning emperor. Despite the generosity of imperial patrons and wealthy donors who profited from trade along the legendary Silk Road, many Confucian officials who manned the permanent state bureaucracy criticized Buddhism. They argued that monks and nuns were disloyal to parents, country, and ancestors, asserting as well that the rising wealth of the monasteries weakened the overall economy.

Anti-Buddhist sentiment culminated in the great persecution of 841–845. Nearly every Buddhist monastery was dismantled, metal images were melted down for the state treasury, and renunciants were ordered to return to lay life. Buddhism eventually rebuilt and rebounded, but the faith never permeated Chinese society so thoroughly again, nor did all the early Chinese doctrinal schools truly recover. From the Sung era onward, it was the Ch'an and Pure Land schools that survived, being less dependent on official recognition or aristocratic patronage. Leading monks repositioned the faith in Chinese society by emphasizing their disinterest in politics and their insistence that renunciants maintain a disciplined lifestyle. In addition, they stressed the compatibility of Buddhism with Daoism and Confucianism.

During the short-lived Mongol conquest of China marking the Yuan dynasty (1271–1368), Tibetan Buddhism became the state religion and its distinctive Mahayana–Vajrayana traditions were granted strong support across the empire, primarily in imperial strongholds. The Mongols' conversion to Buddhism, soon after their thirteenth-century campaigns of violent conquest and rule across Eurasia, marks another point at which Buddhism changed world history, in this case by undercutting Mongol martial values and expansionism.

With the return of native Chinese rule under the Ming (1392–1644), Mahayana traditions were embraced by a large sector of the population: worship of the celestial bodhisattva Guanyin (known as Avalokiteshvara in India); veneration of the sixteen saints designated as protectors of Buddhism until the coming of the next Buddha; and the practice of releasing animals (typically fish or birds) to earn merit. From the early Ming, too, the practice of householders keeping detailed merit account books gained in popularity. In China as elsewhere, merit making and ritual observances dominated the religious scene in most Buddhist communities.

Southeast Asia

Southeast Asia after 1200 was ruled by regional states that sought their legitimacy in supporting the Theravada Buddhist monastic system introduced from Ceylon. Buddha relics were imported as well, and stupas in the Ceylonese style were built across the region. The "reforms" already mentioned effectively reduced the presence of the Mahayana to a few isolated communities, and all of these eventually disappeared. The Khmer state for several periods was ruled by kings who favored Mahayana Buddhism, and they constructed magnificent temples and monasteries.

From the early eighth century, the Shrivijaya Empire in Sumatra and Java also supported the efflorescence of both Hinduism and Mahayana Buddhism. These rulers created the colossal stupa at Borobodur, the crowning monument of this era. But with the empire's decline in the thirteenth century, the smaller states ruled by regional kings favored local religions or (later) the mystical schools of Islam originating in India.

Yet in the majority of the Southeast Asian polities, it was Theravada Buddhism that thrived under rulers who claimed legitimacy under the cosmic law of karma, whereby they were reaping past merit to rule. Their states supported the sangha and sponsored rituals designed to have the powers of the Buddhist universe continually regenerated. In turn, they expected the people to emulate their example by following the Dharma, supporting a just Buddhist order in the territory, and accepting their place in the karma-determined social hierarchy. The many hundreds of grand stupas, image halls, and monasteries built in these prosperous states show the success of premodern Theravada Buddhism. The great Buddhist monuments legitimated the state, created spectacular sanctuaries, employed artisans and the masses, and lent prestige to the sangha. Across Theravadin Southeast Asia, this form of "state Buddhism" survived even after the kingdoms of the premodern era gave way to smaller regional states. However, this form of traditional, hierarchical Buddhism was to be challenged in the modern era, as new ideas and political systems emerged.

Avalokiteshvara, the most popular celestial bodhisattva in the Mahayana tradition.

Japan

Mahayana Buddhism was adopted across East Asia. By 1230, Japanese monks again had traveled to China to undertake the last transplantations of Chinese schools: two forms of the Ch'an became the Soto Zen school (instituted by the monk

Dogen [1200–1253]) and the Rinzai Zen school (under the monk Eisai [1141–1215]). Both vied for popularity among the aristocrats and warriors who controlled Japanese society in the post-Kamakura era (after 1350).

The Pure Land school also found widespread popular acceptance through the public preaching campaigns undertaken by charismatic monks. Since their simplification of Buddhist practice entailed only the *nembutsu*, the chant of *Namo A-mi-t'o Fo*, the honorific repetition of Amitabha Buddha's name imported from China, householders could hope for nirvana in Pure Land rebirth. A thirteenth-century monk named Shinran continued the basic rituals and textual interpretations imported from Chinese Pure Land teachers and added emphasis on *mappo*, the so-called decadent age doctrine, reflecting acceptance of Shakyamuni's prediction of a decline in popular devotion. Shinran argued that human beings were completely dependent upon the Buddha's grace to reach nirvana and had simply to acknowledge their grateful acceptance of it to enter the Pure Land. Shinran's school, the Jodo Shinshu, became a vital separate lineage, and its sangha was the first in Japan to drop the requirement of celibacy.

Images of the corpulent and happy Maitreya, the next Buddha, called Mi Lo Fo in China, are popular in East Asia.

A third track in this era of new Japanese schools is represented by Nichiren (1222–1282), a prophetic and charismatic monk who taught that the *Lotus Sutra* is the only true Buddhist text. Like Shinran, Nichiren subscribed to the doctrine of mappo and argued that the instability of the turbulent times confirmed it. He also accepted the ultimate reality of an omniscient cosmic Buddha immanent in the world and in persons.

Practice in the Nichiren school was simplified to three devotional acts: a short honorific repetition of the *Lotus Sutra*'s title (*Nam-Myoho Reng-e Kyo*), meditation on an image of the cosmic Buddha designed by Nichiren, and pilgrimage to the school's national shrine. Later, the monk's followers taught that Nichiren himself was a bodhisattva. Their interpretation of Buddhism emphasized Japan's special significance in leading Buddhism through the declining stage of history, a visionary view that endured to inspire several splinter movements in the modern and postwar eras.

The Himalayan Region

In Tibet, Mongolia, and Nepal, Mahayana schools again found supremacy. Across the highland frontiers, Vajrayana traditions came to be regarded as the Buddha's highest teaching, and the monks who introduced Buddhism there taught that Buddhist belief and practice have both outer and inner levels of understanding, the highest of which was accessible only through tantric initiation and practice. In these regions, Vajrayana traditions developed in rich elaboration, and dedicated elites practiced exhaustive meditation regimens. Tibetan scholars translated a vast corpus of Sanskrit texts, commented upon them, and composed their own interpretive tracts. Ritual masters also applied the texts and teachings to many aspects of life, designing rituals to promote the best possible rebirth. Even flags, watermills, and hand-turned wheels were adapted to broadcast the Buddha's teaching, continuously earning merit for individuals and communities.

In Tibet, too, the celestial bodhisattva doctrine was made more accessible to the laity: extraordinary monks and nuns came to be identified as their incarnations (*tulku* in Tibetan) of these divinities. Indeed, after 1250 as these

Archaeological remains of Pagan (Myanmar), one of the greatest Buddhist cities in the world between 1000 and 1400 CE.

"incarnate lineages" became institutions endowed with lands and households, some tulkus assumed power as both religious and political leaders of their regions. With the aid of the Mongols, leaders of the major Tibetan monasteries ascended to rule over central Tibet, a situation unprecedented in any other Buddhist society. With the triumph of the Gelugpa school under the Dalai and Panchen Lamas in 1642, Tibetan polity assumed its modern form that was dominated by large monasteries (joined by roughly 15% of the male population).

BUDDHISM AND MODERNITY

Early Modern Buddhist Polities: Monks, Nuns, Householders, Kings

One decisive factor in Buddhist history has been the relation between the institutional religion and political power, a recurring source of controversy from the colonial period until the present, as we will see again shortly. Buddhists have always looked to the legend of Ashoka (273–232 BCE) to define their exemplary relationship with rulers as protectors and patrons. Only with such support can the sangha's integrity be assured, the Buddha's monuments maintained, and the teachings passed down. In premodern Ceylon, the king appointed a senior monk as the *sangharaja* ("ruler of the sangha"); in every Theravada country today, leadership and jurisdiction over the sangha are found in the form of a single monk or monastic council appointed by the state.

"Nichiren confuses his enemies," a woodcut print by Utagawa Kuniyoshi (1798–1861). Nichiren's disciples followed the teacher's example of practicing aggressive missionary exposition, a trend that has marked the school up to the present.

The Potala in Lhasa, Tibet, was the palace of the Dalai Lamas from 1649 until 1959, when the fourteenth Dalai Lama went into exile.

A dramatic modern instance of this exemplary royal support was Burma's King Mindon, who convened the Fifth Buddhist Council (by Theravada reckoning) in 1871. The only complete version among the early collections of the Buddha's teachings was recited and corrected at this conference. These writings, revered today as the Pali Canon, were then inscribed in their entirety on large marble slabs set up in the city of Mandalay. Postcolonial Buddhist governments across the world sponsored similar activities in 1956 on the occasion of the 2,500-year anniversary of Shakyamuni's parinirvana.

For most of its history, the Buddhist sangha has existed in polities ruled by kings or emperors. As a result, a mutually beneficial tradition developed: the sangha adopted rules in harmony with those of states and would applaud exemplary moral leadership on the part of the monarch. In premodern times, monastic Buddhism usually served to promote social stability, accommodating itself to local traditions. The monks also chanted mantras and performed merit-making rituals on behalf of rulers, a custom that continues in modern Japan, Thailand, and Nepal.

Buddhist Monasticism

A monastery (vihara) can be of humble construction or built to imperial, aristocratic standards. Each, however, must have a place for the monks to sleep and a building in which they gather for reception into the sangha, fortnightly recitations, and other proceedings. Monasteries may also have one or more stupas, a "bodhi tree," a meditation hall, and an image hall.

The subsistence of the monks and nuns has remained dependent upon the donations of food and shelter by the lay community. Originally, all sangha members gathered their food in morning begging rounds, and the day's solid food had to be eaten by noon. By the modern period, however, Buddhists had developed other routines: in some places members of the laity would come to the monastery on a rotating schedule with food donations; in other places, monks cooked their own foods. Many Mahayana monasteries of East Asia interpreted the moral rules to require vegetarianism of the monks and nuns, but in recent centuries the restriction against alcohol was taken by most to mean "no intoxication," not complete abstinence.

A formal division that endured within the sangha was that between village monks and forest monks. Village and forest were the two poles of the monastic orientation. Generally, male and female renunciants in the former domain were dedicated to service and study, while forest dwellers fasted and meditated.

Meditation Practices

As we have noted, meditation remained essential for all aspirants, lay and renunciant, seeking to move on the final path to nirvana. This practice by monks and nuns, even if only by a few, certifies Buddhism's continuing spiritual vitality, inspiring layfolk to respect and take refuge in the sangha. Until late into the modern era, however, it was almost entirely the elite among monks and nuns who practiced meditation.

Buddhism inherited and extended the spiritual experiments of ancient India. The practice of trance (*samadhi*) is accepted, even encouraged, but this state does not lead to nirvana realization, hence is not given highest priority. The key practice is called mindfulness meditation (*vipashyana*): a careful attending to, or being mindful of, the three characteristics of existential reality—suffering (*dukkha*), impermanence (*anitya*), and non-self (*anatman*). The practice as taught today is simple: while remaining motionless, the practitioner seeks to focus all awareness on the breath, letting go of all intervening thoughts that arise. Attention to, and comprehension of, these realities opens up an awareness of the "inner life" we normally ignore. With such heightened awareness, mindfulness meditation has other critical effects: it shows how suffering and change are inevitable, it nourishes personal detachment that stills desire, and it cultivates the spiritual insight (*prajna*) that dispels ignorance. The development of *prajna* and the removal of ignorance eliminate bad karma and create good karma. Perfection eventually leads to the fullness of *prajna* in a breakthrough, transformative experience of an enlightened mind (*bodhi*).

Mahayana meditations elaborated upon these precedents. Ch'an or Zen mindfulness meditation, like Theravada vipashyana practice, focuses first upon the breath. Given the Mahayana teaching that all beings possess the Buddha nature (*tathagatagarba*), meditation can comprise any activity practiced with mindfulness, from walking to class to sipping espresso, or (more traditionally) from engaging in martial arts to arranging flowers.

In Pure Land meditation, the fervent wish to attain nirvana in an otherworldly western paradise (*Sukhavati*) encourages devotees to visualize that extraordinary paradise as described in the texts. These practices are especially important as death nears, for individuals who can visualize this realm are promised painless passage into heavenly rebirth through the boundless grace of the Buddha Amitabha.

Schools devoted to esoteric Vajrayana innovations developed yet other forms of meditation under the heading of *sadhana*. These *tantric* practices are based upon mind's-eye visualizations of enlightened bodhisattvas and mantra recitations to jump-start spiritual development. By controlling the appearance of mental images, one sees all experience as mind-constructed and thus empty (*shunya*) of any ultimate reality.

Again, however, it is necessary to emphasize that most Buddhists concentrated their devotional activities on rituals and on accumulating merit rather than on meditation, and so we turn to gift giving as the foundation of Buddhist practice.

Punya and Dana: The Fundamental Buddhist Exchange

The Buddha set out a "graded teaching" to order the spiritual teachings to be given to disciples. This framework begins with the merit-making donations that enable a Buddhist community's diverse cultural activities. Still used as a guide for modern Buddhist teachers, the sequence counsels progression through the following stages of religious striving:

1. *Dana* ("self-less giving" to diminish desire)

2. *Shila* ("morality")

3. *Svarga* ("heaven")

4. *Dharma-deshana* ("instruction on doctrine") on the Four Noble Truths

This hierarchy of progressive practices defines a "syllabus" for advancing in spiritual attainment. Stages 1 and 2 lead to heaven birth (3), the fruit of merit; the doctrines in stage 4 are the instructions concerning reaching enlightenment, beyond good karma making.

Just as merit, or punya, has provided the chief orientation point and goal in the Buddhist layperson's worldview and ethos, dana has always been the starting practice for accumulating it. Meritmaking for most Buddhists, including most monks and nuns, is the central measure of spiritual advancement. Merit making remains the universal, integrating transaction in Buddhist settings through the modern era, regardless of the respective intellectual elite's orientation toward competing Theravada, Mahayana, or Vajrayana doctrinal formulations or spiritual disciplines.

The wish for merit leading to rebirth in heaven has remained the most popular and pan-Buddhist aspiration; indeed, monks from the beginning of the faith were instructed to "show the laity the way to heaven" by acting as a "field of merit." Householders can "plant" donations in this field, and the "harvest" in good Karma they earn will be great. Punya is needed for a good rebirth, and although Buddhist doctrine holds that heaven is a temporary state, the reward of heavenly rebirth has motivated many to be "good Buddhists."

Merit making can lead one close to nirvana, but it also has practical, worldly consequences, impacting destiny both now and across future lifetimes. Therefore, Buddhists seek punya to change the karma "account" that affects them in this life as well as to modify future rebirth destiny.

To maximize punya and so enhance the course of spiritual advancement, popular texts urge all disciples, monastic and lay, to cultivate such practices as venerating images, fasting, taking extra precepts (as described at the very beginning of this chapter), organizing compassionate actions and charitable institutions, arranging public recitations of the texts, and encouraging meditation.

The most universal expression of lay Buddhist faith and punya seeking has been through dana. Making donations for spiritual purposes and setting aside time for moral observances, like saving an animal or returning a lost object, remained the foundation for householder practice; these still comprise the most visible Buddhist activity today. Passages in the Mahayana texts also articulate the value of dana to the individual as an expression of compassion (*karuna*) and as a renunciatory practice that undercuts desire and attachment.

Another popular pan-Buddhist practice is merit transfer—an idea that philosophers have struggled to rationalize. Texts exhort persons doing something meritorious to share the good deed's karma effects with family, community, and all beings simply by announcing the intent; such sharing is believed to increase the initial merit earned by helping others.

Western nuns reciting from texts at a Tibetan center in London.

Rituals

Buddhist monasteries developed ritual procedures and a yearly festival calendar for the purpose of imposing some uniformity on the widespread sangha network. The monk's vocation came to include priestly duties, performing rituals that linked the Buddha's spoken words with simple gestures. In the simplest (and still most popular) universal Buddhist ritual, monks pour water into a vessel as they chant words revealed by the Buddha. Now imbued with healing powers, the liquid can be drunk or sprinkled over the bodies of those needing assistance. All Buddhist schools also offer food, incense, and flowers to Buddha images, bodhi trees, and stupas.

Mahayana rituals are seen as an important part of a bodhisattva's service to others, and most emphasize mastery of word chains called mantras, known for their spiritual powers. A mantra can be spoken to bless and protect the speaker, the sangha, and an entire settlement. Ritual chanting of the Buddha's own sayings is thought to further the foundations of spiritual practice and infuse towns and families with good karma. Ritual service thus came to dominate Mahayana Buddhism in its missionary program, especially mantra recitations that expressed the faith's spiritual ideals and activated the unseen cosmic Buddha powers promised in the Mahayana texts.

The key Buddhist holiday called *uposatha* occurs each fortnight on the new moon and full moon days. On uposatha, sangha members privately recite the details confirming that they are Buddhists in good standing according to the Vinaya rules. This recitation follows a private confession, to the renunciant's superior, of any transgressions of the rules during the period. Uposatha continues in the modern era to serve as the regular occasion to review, correct, and certify the proper standards of monastery discipline in Theravada societies. Emphasizing the fundamental interdependence between sangha and lay community, householders visit the local vihara on these days to make dana offerings. On these days, too, devout layfolk take the opportunity to don white robes, camp on the monastery grounds, and observe eight of the ten monastic rules. They join with many more layfolk who have come simply to release animals or to make offerings to Buddha images, and remain to hear monks preach the Dharma. Thus, the lunar fortnight rhythm dominates the festival year. The regular succession of uposathas and the two half-moon days are when Buddhists typically undertake meritorious actions, perform rituals, and engage in meditation practices. Thus, each week has a special day for Buddhist observances.

Householders releasing animals earn merit by bestowing the gift of freedom and life.

Festival Traditions and Public Religious Observances

Like other great world religions, Buddhist cultures developed ways of ordering and shaping time through regular monthly and yearly festivals. Some festivals orchestrate the reliving of classical Buddhist events "in the beginning": celebrations of the Buddha's birth, enlightenment, and nirvana are universal, although occurring in different seasons. Other more regional sacred events likewise mark the year. These include Shakyamuni's descent from heaven to preach to his mother, events marking a key point in a popular bodhisattva's life, or the death anniversary of a local saint.

The Universal Buddhist Shrine

For all Buddhist schools, the stupa (or *caitya,* a term that can also signify any Buddha shrine) became a focal point and singular landmark denoting the tradition's spiritual presence. Buddhism eventually recognized "eight great relic caityas" for pilgrimage and veneration in South Asia. Stupa worship thus became the chief focus of Buddhist ritual activity, and this has continued through the modern era to the present. The Buddhist relic cult began early, inspiring monks, nuns, and householders to circumambulate the shrines (in the clockwise direction) and to have their own cremated remains deposited in the same great stupa or in smaller votive stupas located nearby.

Theravada monk sprinkling a lay woman with water over which the sacred words of the Buddha have been chanted.

Throughout Buddhist history, the stupa has served as a place to go to recall the Buddha's great acts, a "power place" tapping the Buddha's (or saint's) relic presence and its healing potency, a site to earn merit through joyful, musical veneration, and a monument marking the conversion and control of local gods and spirits. In the Mahayana schools, the stupa was also thought of as a symbol of Buddhahood's omnipresence, a center of Mahayana text revelation, and a perfect form showing the unity of the natural elements (earth, fire, air, ether) with the Buddha nature.

Later Buddhists identified stupas as the physical representations of the eternal teachings. They also expanded the possible sacred objects deposited in them to include Buddha's words in textual form. Despite these many understandings, Buddhists at every level of sophistication believe that ritually correct veneration of stupas will earn them merit. In practice, believers of every school converge at stupas to mark events associated with the Buddhas or saints. Stupas thus remain the natural sites for Buddhist festivals of remembrance and veneration.

Death Ritualism

In all Buddhist countries today, despite many regional differences, death rituals are the exclusive purview of the sangha and a key time for monks to expound core teachings and receive dana. Buddhist mourners carefully dispose of the corpse, relying on ritual to ensure that the dead person does not become a hungry ghost (*preta*) or, worse, a demon (*yaksha*). They also seek to avert bad destiny for the deceased by making punya, then transferring it to the dead person. In adopting such practices, Buddhists straddle both alternatives to the ancient Indic question of whether destiny is based strictly upon an individual's own karma, or whether the proper performance of rituals during and immediately after death can override unfavorable karma and manipulate rebirth destiny. Since Buddhism is conceptually centered on the doctrine that the cosmos is governed by karmic law, ritual traditions naturally surround death, the critical time in the operation of such causal mechanisms. Both Theravada monks and—more expansively—Mahayana ritualists apply ritual expertise to this time. The tradition's dependence on after-death ritual service for sangha donations is evident in all modern Asian traditions; even when people are otherwise hardly observant in modern urban areas of Japan, death rituals performed by Buddhist monks endure.

Buddhism Under Colonialism

The modern era was one of widespread decline for Buddhism across Asia. Medieval states either lost their autonomy or were destabilized by colonialism, first by European powers (the British in Burma, India, Ceylon, Tibet, and China; the French in Indo-China; the Portuguese and Dutch in Ceylon; the Dutch in Indonesia) and later, in the early twentieth century, by Japanese expansionism that lacked any pretense of compassion. In East Asia, the imperial Chinese state was weakened by the colonial powers (primarily Britain)

Buddhist stupa being whitewashed by a monk in Ladakh, in northern India near the Tibetan border. Monks,nuns, and laity have built these shrines since the Buddha's death.

whose aggressive trade practices backed by military intervention disrupted the Chinese economy. The civil disorders that followed also undermined Buddhist institutions. (These events are discussed in Chapter Eight.)

The impact of European colonialism on Buddhism can be summarized under two broad domains, institutional and doctrinal. Although Dutch, British, and French colonial governments had somewhat different ideologies guiding their rule in Asia, all administrations eventually declined to fulfill the traditional native king's role of patron and protector of the local religions, including Buddhism. As a result, the means of accommodation that had evolved over the centuries to perpetuate Buddhism ceased to exist, sometimes without warning, in every colonized polity. When the Portuguese and Dutch took power in Ceylon (1505–1658), for example, they seized the ports and lowlands, destroyed monasteries, persecuted Buddhists, forcibly converted many to Catholicism, and caused the Sinhalese king to flee to the central highlands. When all the island had become Britain's colony (1815), the British moved to end state support for the sangha and discontinued patronage dedicated to the upkeep of Buddhist buildings everywhere. Colonial administrations also typically ceased enforcement of indigenous land tenure relations and taxation, withdrew from supervision of monastic ordination, and halted ceremonies according respect to venerable monastic leaders, sacred symbols, and temples. The roots of modern crisis and Buddhism's decline across the region are easily traced to this abrupt deprivation of resources and political support.

Challenges from Colonialism, Communism, and Modern Critics

In the realm of ideas, the colonial powers introduced two alien and often contradictory systems of thought: on the one hand, the scientific notions derived from the Enlightenment, and on the other, theories of racial, cultural, and religious superiority that were used in attempts to legitimate the triumphant expansion of Euro-Christian peoples. European medicine, often effective where folk remedies and rituals had unpredictable results, presented another challenge to every local culture's worldview.

The fruits of the Enlightenment—democracy, modern science and technology—were imported into Asia through schools built by the colonial governments. One motivation for establishing the schools was to provide trained native people who spoke the language of the colonizer. The reach of the colonial governments was broader, however, for in fact they were the official and secular extensions of the European home states. In addition, the colonial administrators were for the most part supportive of the expansion of the Christian missionary presence. (For example, in many places colonial law recognized as legitimate only marriages conducted by Christian ministers.) It was with such backing that the first modern global missions were created: across Asia, lay and ordained Christians built churches and established educational institutions, hospitals, and charities; some proselytized aggressively through public preaching and pamphlets attacking Buddhist beliefs and practices.

After the fall of the Ching dynasty in 1912, socioeconomic conditions remained unstable under the Republic of China, only to worsen further with the rise of communism and the Japanese invasion, first in Manchuria (1931), then southward into the Chinese heartland. Throughout the twentieth century, the traditional Buddhist schools and Buddhist thought were subject to criticism not just by the communists but also by leaders of a modernizing faction called the May 4th Movement. Though critiqued fiercely by the elites, the Chinese sangha endured: in 1930, there were 730,000 monks and nuns who maintained 267,000 registered monastic temples. The sustained Communist party policy of thoroughgoing destruction, denigration, and disestablishment that began in 1949, however, had no precedent in modern Buddhist history.

Although at first disturbed and demoralized, Buddhists recovered from and responded to colonial-era challenges in various ways. Few converted to Christianity, however, despite such obvious inducements as access to charitable services and gaining an inside track to promotions into government service.

Although hampered by the disruption of their institutions, Buddhist intellectuals and preachers emerged to engage in the dialogue with science and Christianity. In Ceylon, for example, early Protestant missionaries, having assessed Buddhist monks as uniformly indolent and ignorant, felt themselves on the verge of mass conversion. Yet a series of public debates ended badly for missionaries, a reversal that restored public faith in the ongoing relevance of Buddhist doctrine.

In Ceylon, the dialectic between the West and Buddhism was most intense, and decisive new directions for Buddhist modernization were identified in the island nation. Reformers involved the lay society more fully in Buddhist institutions and spiritual practices (primarily meditation), motivating some among the laity to take the place of former royal patrons. The lay reformers, in turn, insisted that monks respect the sangha rules and discipline, and they supported the revival of monastic meditation practice, usually in newly created reformist monastic schools. Finally, Buddhist intellectuals carried out historical investigations, offering modern demythologized reinterpretations of the

Buddha and Buddhist doctrine analogous to the scholarly "search for the historical Jesus" that was emerging within Protestant Christianity at the same time. To publicize these reforms, Buddhists adopted one aspect of Christian missionary methodology: they began by investing in printing technology and undertaking publications that defined reformist doctrines and practices. They also rediscovered the practice of public sermonizing.

Reformers in Siam, as in Ceylon, also articulated new interpretations of "true Buddhism." They taught that Buddhism in its pure form was not concerned with communal rituals or harnessing the cosmic powers of Buddhism to support the secular kingdom. Rejecting the adaptive local traditions that had developed in the process of the globalization of Buddhism, reformers insisted that the only genuine center of the faith was the individual's quest for mind cultivation and salvation. Doctrines describing the interdependent and impermanent nature of existence were emphasized, while the teachings about hungry ghosts and snake gods were rejected. Most reform leaders were critical of—even hostile to—"superstitions," rituals, and other local accommodations. Meditation was now the heart of "true Buddhism," and it was not restricted to monks and nuns: all Buddhists could and should feel capable of seeking nirvana.

The Buddhist Revival Gains Strength

By the early twentieth century, reformers had created new institutions to advance the revivalist goals directly. Also supporting the revival process in Asia was the first generation of Europeans sympathetic to Buddhism, who saw in the faith a nontheistic spirituality that was a compelling alternative to dogmatic monotheism. Many Western seekers interpreted Buddhism as encouraging spiritual experimentation through meditation rather than requiring blind faith. Its philosophy was seen as ancient wisdom marvelously preserved and still accessible.

The exigencies of imperialism had resulted in easier travel for Westerners, and this development enabled sympathetic Europeans and North Americans to assist native Buddhist modernists as they argued back against Christian ministers. Westerners both educated native intellectuals on Christianity and shared with them Enlightenment critiques of Christian dogma. Members of the Theosophical Society, a European group formed to pursue the secret, mystical teachings thought to underlie all the world religions, created new institutions including English-medium Buddhist schools and lay organizations such as Buddhist teaching programs modeled after Christian Sunday schools. Buddhist nationalists also became involved in politics, seeking more favorable relations—and eventually independence—from the European colonial governments. This experience in Ceylon was eagerly shared across Asia with modernists from Japan to Burma.

Early Western scholarship also added to the awareness of modern Asian Buddhists. Indeed, sites associated with Ashoka and many long-forgotten early monuments were discovered in the course of archaeological expeditions under the auspices of the British colonial government. European scholars used modern critical methods to translate and interpret the earliest canonical texts and then disseminated them globally. In fact, it was common for the newly educated indigenous intelligentsia in Buddhist countries to read their first passages from a canonical Buddhist text in English translation. (As in medieval Europe, only the elite among monk–scholars could read the original sacred texts.)

As Buddhist literature in English became available and was assimilated, voices from outside the sangha joined the contested discussion of "what the Buddha really taught." Thus, throughout the Buddhist world, the leaders of the old Buddhist establishments were often challenged to conform to the standards of discipline set forth in the monastic texts. In most Buddhist countries, colonial and postcolonial governments sought to eliminate sources of political dissent by imposing on the sangha regulations supposedly designed to "keep pure" the local Buddhist institutions.

Buddhism Reduced for Western Consumption: Meditation and Atheism

The efforts by the colonial powers to control Buddhism and Buddhists had a paradoxical effect. The global diaspora of Buddhism flowed "backward" on the networks of empire and through Western converts who became aware of Asian religions as a result of expanding communications and travel. For some Euro-Americans, the Enlightenment-based critiques of the Western monotheistic religions were persuasive and led to a search for religions that did not depend upon belief in a personal God. By 1920, Buddhist centers in the West had been established by Euro-American converts and immigrants. As depicted in early popular and sympathetic accounts, the Buddha was a rationalist who rejected ritual and also a heroic social reformer. Buddhism was seen not as a religion but as an atheistic philosophy, compatible with science. Buddhist meditation, however, was regarded as an authentic, ancient spiritual practice, an aspect that attracted Westerners interested in the new field of psychology.

Euro-American contact with Mahayana Buddhism came strongest and earliest with Japanese Zen. Westerners were drawn to the spirit of iconoclasm and to meditation, and to Zen's connection with the fine arts conveyed by early exponents such as D.T. Suzuki (1870–1966). In the years immediately following the Second World War, Zen Buddhism particularly attracted segments of the bohemian and intellectual Western society, leading to a revival in interest that has grown throughout our day. It was in the years leading up to World War II, however, that Japan embarked on an imperialistic course that obscured the peaceful face of Zen Buddhism for decades.

Effects of Japanese Imperialism on Buddhism and on Asia

The role of Japan in twentieth-century Asia was undeniably pivotal. Once the country opened itself to the modern world with the restoration of the emperor in 1868, Japan's leaders sought to create a modern industrial state based on nationalism. Shinto was promoted as the shared national faith, and the emperor was revered as a living god. The nationalist movement also involved the deliberate diminishment of Buddhism. Despite its 1,400 years in Japan, Buddhism was criticized as "a foreign religion" inferior to Shinto. Many Buddhist monasteries and temples had their lands confiscated and state patronage withdrawn. Buddhist doctrines and practices were critiqued as "unnatural." In response to these changes, some Buddhist organizations instituted reforms that involved undertaking social work, educational initiatives, and the renewal of global missions. Some schools such as Zen even issued strong public pronouncements in favor of nationalism and militarism, with prominent monasteries raising money for armaments. Many new Buddhist movements also began outside the older schools.

Japan's rapid and successful modernization effort encouraged not only nationalism but imperialism as well. Led by former samurai and others who had studied in Western countries, Japan annexed neighboring Korea (1910) and northern China (1934), and eventually invaded more distant Asian countries (Indochina, 1940; Burma, 1942). Soon after the Pacific phase of World War II began with the attack on the U.S. base at Pearl Harbor in 1941, the Japanese occupation extended from Manchuria, Korea, and China south to Micronesia and as far west as the borders of India through Southeast Asia.

BUDDHISM AND POSTMODERN TRENDS IN A POSTCOLONIAL WORLD

By the mid-twentieth century, Asians had begun to recover from World War II and many conquered or colonized peoples were reclaiming their independence. The place of Buddhism in these new societies is as varied as ever. Buddhist movements today make use of the same approaches seen across the globe in other faiths. Some leaders reject modernity, seeking to return to practices that had been identified as "corrupted" by modernizers in the colonial era. Others strive to move Buddhism to an entirely new plateau to adapt to the global realities of the postcolonial world. Still others blend traditionalism and reform, "rescuing" from the past what in their view is the essence of Buddhism, while employing modern technologies to propagate the Dharma. New institutions have been created to champion strict adherence to monastic norms, scholastic learning, and meditation. Most commonly, organizations led by laypersons have been the most active and effective in adapting Buddhist teachings and practices to the world today.

South Asia

South Asia is the "holy land" where the Buddha was born, was enlightened, and died and where Buddhism has endured over 2,500 years. Among the contemporary countries of the region—India, Pakistan, Bangladesh, Sri Lanka, Bhutan, and Nepal—only in the Himalayan regions of the north and on the island of Sri Lanka to the south has Buddhism remained strong.

The Remnants of Buddhism in India: Reconstruction in the Land of Origin

Today, Buddhism is found in India only in very small communities. Most important for the faith's revival in the land of its origins are the sacred sites that were unearthed during the British-led archaeological digs of the nineteenth and early twentieth centuries. Among the hundreds of sites that were abandoned or had sunk into oblivion after the Muslim conquest of South Asia (since 1200 CE), the site where the Buddha was enlightened under the bodhi tree became the most significant and controversial. Identified by British officials in the mid-1800s and "restored" through colonial excavations and constructions (in the modern city of Gaya, Bihar), the "Great Enlightenment" temple built at the site, called the Mahabodhi, has again become a focal point for Buddhists. Religious reformers in the colonial era focused on reestablishing the sanctity of this temple as their first step in reviving Buddhism. In recent decades, over twenty Buddhist monasteries from around the world have erected branches in Gaya, as well as libraries, study centers, and pilgrim hostels. Reformist Buddhists are also attempting to reestablish the site as Buddhism's holiest center and pilgrimage destination, a shrine that unifies all Buddhists. Despite hard work by generations of reformers, this remains a distant goal.

Even after decades of negotiations, control over the Bodh Gaya temple has eluded the Buddhist organizations, as Hindu priests and politicians have failed to turn over ownership of the shrine. (The Hindu nationalists mentioned in Chapter Six also had a role in this conflict.) By 1992, frustrations at unfulfilled promises peaked, and resident monks were moved to take extreme measures. Two threatened to immolate themselves, and several others began fasts unto death. The provocation for this confrontation was severe: Hindu priests had enthroned a *lingam*, the phallic icon of Shiva, on a Buddhist altar and treated five Buddha images in the temple as deities celebrated in the Hindu epic, the *Mahabharata*.

The All-India Action Committee that has led the movement to reclaim Bodh Gaya has drawn many of its members from the country's activist Buddhist communities "untouchable" Mahar caste communities from Maharashtra, intellectual Buddhists from urban areas attracted to reformist institutions, and Tibetan refugees who have settled in India since fleeing Chinese rule after 1959. Modern Pakistan and Bangladesh, regions that were South Asian strongholds of Buddhism in antiquity, have almost no adherents today.

"Protestant Buddhism": An Enduring Colonial-Era Re-Formation of the Faith

Anthropologist Gananath Obeyesekere has described the modern re-formation of Buddhist tradition begun in colonial Ceylon as "Protestant Buddhism." He uses the term to convey two distinct but connected historic trends. The first is intuitively obvious: the adoption of aspects of missionary Protestant Christianity into the Buddhist framework to revitalize its institutions, practices, and doctrines. The second is a deeply ironic reference to a past marked by the arrogance of missionaries and British colonial discrimination against Buddhism.

The early influential mediator of such "Protestantism" in Ceylon was the American convert Henry Steele Olcott (1832–1907), who came to the country and helped activist Buddhist leaders organize their efforts. Olcott emphasized the importance of the laity in revitalization and the founding of Buddhist publications and schools. He also composed a *Buddhist Catechism* (1881) and invented a five-color Buddhist flag, both of which are widely used across the world today. Modern Protestant inclinations were evident in the reformist insistence that spiritual and scientific truth must be compatible and that the only true practice was meditation, not the mindless observance of ritual. Furthermore, the reformers believed—in agreement with the Protestant missionaries—that the practice of Buddhism in Ceylon had been corrupted by idolatry, Hindu polytheism, and an undisciplined and corrupt monastic "priesthood." The laity, however, could reestablish "true Buddhism" through adhering to the pure philosophy and meditation practices taught by the human Buddha. Popular texts and village traditions were strongly critiqued, and two new sangha schools were started with ordination lineages from Burma, both requiring strict adherence to Vinaya rules.

A Ceylonese protégé, who adopted the name Anagarika Dharmapala (1864–1933), continued Olcott's initiatives and went beyond them, preaching and publishing tracts to spread his vision of revitalized Buddhism. At the age of 29, Dharmapala addressed an ecumenical conference, the Parliament of World Religions, held in Chicago in 1893. He impressed hearers from all over the world with his definition of modernist Buddhism as compatible with science, free from dogma and superstition, tolerant of other faiths, and committed to social reform.

Dharmapala also found an enthusiastic reception among the Ceylonese laity, especially among the newly educated professional elite and the merchant middle class, who owed their rising positions in the world to the changes wrought by the colonial modernization of the country. Dharmapala energized the Buddhist reformers in Ceylon; his speeches and writings also contributed to the linkage between the faith and the nationalist struggles.

Dharmapala celebrated Ceylon as a uniquely pure Buddhist country, elevated the Sinhalese ethnic group as a "chosen Buddhist people," and harshly demonized those opposing the country's Buddhist restoration. Scholars today see these influences as having set in motion the cultural forces that have made the postindependence state, Sri Lanka, a zone of extremes where bloody conflict has taken deep root alongside uncompromising reform.

Dharmapala's founding of the Mahabodhi Society in Calcutta extended "Protestant Buddhist" reform into other countries in Asia. In recent times, "Protestant Buddhism" has fostered an individualist ethos among those whose ties to a village or traditional sangha have been broken through urban migration. Those influenced by these reformist ideas see it as their own responsibility to practice meditation and study the Dharma (usually in English translations) in the quest for nirvana. Joining the sangha or seeking spiritual guidance from an ordained monk is also not necessarily the norm for those whose view of Buddhism has been affected by "Protestantism."

Buddhism in the Himalayas: Shangri-La?

Many Westerners first became aware of Buddhism through fictional works such as *Lost Horizon*, the film version of which was set in an idyllic, tropical valley amid the scenic, snow-blown Himalayan peaks. It is true that, in fact, Tibetan Buddhist communities have survived in the remote and picturesque settlements nestled among the world's highest mountains, but this region has hardly been a utopian zone for Buddhism in the post–World War II era. Along the southern Himalayan region, the isolation of the states on the Tibetan frontier (Ladakh, Sikkim, Bhutan) enabled them to retain their independence until the end of the Second World War. Since, however, religious conservatism also kept the monks and leaders of these states isolated and ignorant about the modern world, there was little impetus for reform or adaptation to the postwar international political order.

In 1949 most of the territories on the Tibetan plateau ruled by the Gelugpa school's Dalai Lama were declared part of the People's Republic of China, which sent its army to enforce its claims. The peripheries once oriented to Lhasa were soon annexed into adjacent states, while central and western Tibet have been ruled by China as "the Tibetan Autonomous Region." Until the bitter end of China's Cultural Revolution (1976), all religious practices in the region were repressed and most Buddhist temples, monasteries, and shrines were destroyed. Thousands of Tibetans have died since 1949 in conflicts that set Chinese against Tibetan and Tibetan against Tibetan. The fourteenth Dalai Lama, Tenzin Gyatso, went into exile in 1959, and 10 percent of the population has left the country as well.

After 1980, official toleration of limited worship and monastic ordination returned, as did state-sponsored rebuilding of select monasteries. But increasing Tibetan protests since 1987 have been met with further restrictions and arrests, while increasing Chinese migration into the region has reduced Tibetans to a minority in their homeland.

Three nations have remained refuges of the faith. *Nepal*, the world's only Hindu kingdom but one of the world's poorest nations, has several million Buddhists among the highland-dwelling Tibeto-Burman peoples, in its settlements of Tibetan refugees, and among the Newars of the Kathmandu

Valley. Kathmandu is the modern capital of Nepal, and this valley is also Asia's largest center for international institutions connected with the major schools of Tibetan Buddhism. Tibetan Buddhism also has survived in mountainous areas of northern India (in Ladakh, Himachal Pradesh, and Arunachal Pradesh).

India has likewise accepted Tibetan refugees, for since 1959 the Dalai Lama's government in exile has been located in picturesque Dharamsala. Finally, there is Bhutan in the eastern Himalayas, a nation formed in 1907 as the royal kingdom ruled by the Wangchuck family. It is the world's only nation that has Tibetan Buddhism as its state religion.

Most regions where Tibetan Buddhism still flourishes have lost political autonomy. The central, northern, and eastern portions of Tibet were absorbed by China, while Ladakh and Sikkim were absorbed into modern India; Bhutan alone remained independent from India, but only in its internal affairs. In exile and in the isolated enclaves, Tibetan Buddhist institutions have sustained the faith, but these Buddhists struggle as refugees in poverty and as resident aliens within the larger states.

Yet amid the destruction of tradition and the tragedies of exile, there has been a paradoxical development: the end of independent Tibet, the persecution of the faith, and the exile of many Tibetans have also led to the extensive migration of Tibetan Buddhist teachers into almost every country of the world. Now publishing houses, learned lamas, Internet Web sites, and charismatic meditation teachers cross the globe to spread Buddhist teachings. While their predecessors were completely out of touch with the modern world and its spiritual challenges, contemporary monk-scholars and meditation teachers are now leaders in "bringing the Dharma to the West." The Fourteenth Dalai Lama, Nobel Peace Prize winner in 1989, is well known as a world leader and is certainly the most recognized Buddhist in the world.

Theravada Buddhism Today in Southeast Asia

The first regions missionized in antiquity by Buddhist monks have remained the stronghold of Theravada Buddhism. In Ceylon and Burma, a new era began with the withdrawal of the British (1947). Buddhism became a pillar of the new nations' identity, and the Buddha was elevated to the status of cultural hero and ancestor.

While supportive of the respective struggles for independence, Buddhism in these states had also been enriched and enlarged by revival movements throughout the colonial period. Most of these involved the laity in the administration of its institutions and saw the establishment of new monastic schools emphasizing revival through strict discipline, meditation, and social service. Buddhist leaders in the first decades after World War II were also at the forefront of addressing the relationship between socialism and communism, the political ideologies that had risen to popularity as alternatives to capitalism in guiding the newly independent states. Some monks were highly suspicious of communism and allied themselves with aggressive anticommunist campaigns; some political activists and high civil servants, however, used Buddhist rhetoric quite creatively to justify participation in communist regimes.

A Tooth Relic Visits Myanmar

The Buddha's cremation relics have been the most sacred and precious objects for devotees from the faith's very beginnings. Not only are they the sole remnants of the enlightened one, a "sacred trace" of his earthly existence; they are also thought to be infused with immense power, and mere proximity to them is believed to confer spiritual and worldly blessings.

In 1994 the Chinese government loaned a tooth relic to Myanmar. Placed in a jewel-embellished palanquin and conveyed from the Boeing 757 to a silk-draped float pulled by an elephant, the relic was taken to its shrine in the Maha Pasana cave in Rangoon, where over the next six weeks a half-million devotees came to pray and make offerings. SLORC, the country's ruling junta, who had sponsored the visit, used the state-controlled media to emphasize that its members were exemplary Buddhists. In 1995 the junta underwrote the construction of a new temple in the capital where the relic has been displayed in later visits. Displaying and respecting Buddha relics have been recognized as signs of just rulers in Buddhist states since antiquity, and the SLORC generals no doubt intend their sponsorship of tooth relic veneration to win popular approval and counter dislike of their authoritarian rule. After regaining independence from the British Empire in 1948 and undergoing a short period of experimentation with "Buddhist socialism," Myanmar's government has often dealt harshly with persons suspected of fostering dissent. After allowing elections in 1989 but not liking the results, the junta put the winner, Nobel laureate Aung San Suu Kyi under house arrest, where she remains today.

The tooth relic arrangements represent ironies of a kind not uncommon today. The Communist party of China found it politically expedient to utilize a Buddhist relic for advancing its goals in international relations. For their part, the junta ruling Myanmar has been supplying many of the images China now requires to rebuild the temples demolished by Red Guards during the most destructive years of the Cultural Revolution (1966–1969).

Three Contemporary Faces of Thai Buddhism

A constitutional monarchy since 1932 and a country never ruled by a European nation, Thailand is another predominantly Theravada country. Thai Buddhism remains one of the most dynamic faiths in the world today. The society supports traditional and reformist scholarship, the ancient spiritual practices of forest monks, and pioneering reformist initiatives. Thai reformers have assumed active roles in working for the modernization of the country through government development programs in infrastructure building, agricultural innovation, education, and health care. Several notable independent monks have opposed the state's toleration of corruption, pollution, and environmental destruction. However, Thai Buddhist monastic institutions have benefited from royal patronage and the rising wealth that accompanied the economic boom of the late twentieth century. Certain charismatic monks and a host of new lay-oriented independent Buddhist institutions are active in offering leadership to revitalize the faith. The burgeoning urban areas, where neither old community ties nor traditional monasteries effectively meet the needs of the new city dwellers, have been fertile ground for such reformists. Three examples suggest the gamut of reformists active in contemporary Thai Buddhism: the Dhammakaya, Santi Asoke, and the work of Phra Boonsong.

The Dhammakaya   The Dhammakaya is the fastest growing Buddhist reform group in Thailand, attracting the well-educated and newly affluent classes, as well as the royal family. Founded by the charismatic monk Phra Monghon Thepmuni in 1978, Dhammakaya spreads its teachings and meditation practices through the sophisticated use of publications and mass media. The movement has established a presence in every major city and town across the country, where its very highly educated monks administer a program of rigorous training for the laity. Another binding force of Dhammakaya is Phra Thepmuni's meditation technique, one that has more in common with Mahayana practices of the Himalayas than with traditional Theravada methods. For its followers, the Dhammakaya has reduced the ritual complexity of the traditional monastery to a few simple practices. It has also emphasized that

Gathering of devotees at the southern shrine of the Swedagon stupa, a Burmese temple in present-day Myanmar.

making money is compatible with Buddhism and has translated utopianism and interdependence teachings through the slogan, "World Peace Through Inner Peace." As of 2005, the group numbered its supporters at over one million, with branches in fourteen countries.

Santi Asoke   Santi Asoke differs in many respects from Dhammakaya: it has won a much smaller following (perhaps 130,000 in 2000) and has garnered much less wealth. Since its founding in 1976, however, movement activists have played the role of prophetic critics of the complacent established monastic schools and the compromises members feel Buddhists are making in modern Thailand. Santi Asoke ("People of Ashoka") are named after the first lay ruler in Buddhist history, the Indian emperor who (in Buddhist accounts) spread the faith across India and ruled according to the Buddha's ethical norms. Accordingly, this group seeks to reform Thai Buddhism through a return to austere ethical practices such as abstaining from meat, alcohol, and tobacco as well as avoiding gambling and hedonistic entertainment. Santi Asoke grew out of the work of forest monk reformers who in the 1920s and 1930s sought to revitalize the sangha by a return to an ascetic lifestyle for monks, complemented by rigorous meditation schedules. Santi Asoke's monks wear white robes instead of the traditional yellow because their founder, the charismatic but confrontational Phra Bodhiraksa, was defrocked by the Thai government's monk-monitoring body in the 1980s. The "Protestant" influence is evident in Bodhiraksa's criticisms of traditional rituals as "superstition and magic" and his outspoken rejection of the custom of worshiping Buddha images.

Phra Boonsong   Not all reformers in Thailand have been new institution builders. Phra Boonsong (1941–), who has been the head monk of Phranon Wat in central Thailand since 1972, is a dedicated environmentalist who is also an effective lobbyist. When he arrived in the area, the ecosystem was sick. Runoff from the Chin River, which flows by the monastery, was polluting paddy fields, and declining agriculture and fishing yields were causing men and women to seek employment in the cities. Phra Boonsong has worked tirelessly to improve the region's ecological balance. Appealing to the traditional Thai prohibition against killing inside a monastery, he began by declaring the river adjacent to it a "pardon zone" for all water creatures. Next, from profits made by selling fish food to local Buddhists (who in turn gave it to the fish, earning merit), he was able to add fish stock. The fish multiplied in that nearby stretch of the river, slowly adding to the breeding population available for harvest by many fishermen living along the river. This success enabled Phra Boonsong to convince the National Assembly to enact laws allowing monasteries nationwide to establish similar breeding zones, and over one hundred have done so. More recently the monk has begun planting fruit trees on long-deforested hills and having the orchards reduce the use of expensive, watershed-polluting chemicals. The expertise of the Phranon Wat monks in species use, grafting, fertilizers, and marketing is now being shared across the region, allowing other monks to spearhead similar efforts and promote environmental awareness across Thailand's rural hinterlands.

Buddhist Revival in Postwar Indochina

By 1985, all the countries of the Indochinese peninsula had begun to liberalize their economies and relax restrictions on religious observances. As communist governments retreat from dogmatism to pragmatism and accept the enduring popular attachment to Buddhism and indigenous religions, civil authorities in Vietnam, Laos, and Cambodia are accepting the place of Buddhism in national culture and politics.

A French colony until 1953, Cambodia suffered through the Vietnam wars with the French and the United States, and in the aftermath (1975–1979), the genocidal conflicts under the rule of the Khmer Rouge led by Pol Pot. Under Pol Pot's Communist regime, Buddhist monks and institutions were targeted for murder and destruction. While several Cambodian Buddhist centers were relocated among refugees over the border in Thailand, only after the withdrawal of the Vietnamese in 1989 did the restoration of Buddhism begin. Several prominent figures seeking national reconciliation have been Theravada monks.

Vietnam has increasingly tolerated the restoration of Buddhist monasteries and temples since north and south were reunited in 1975. Nevertheless, the government has imprisoned monks it regards as too involved in politics, and the officially sanctioned (and so-named) Vietnam Buddhist Church has won only minimum popular acceptance. Vietnam's population of 75 million resembles China in its religious orientation, with Buddhism the most widespread tradition existing alongside Chinese Daoism and Confucianism, indigenous cults, and Roman Catholic and Protestant Christianity. Vietnamese Buddhism today is predominantly Mahayana in the north, with Theravada monasteries found in the south.

The modern state of Indonesia contains the largest Muslim population in the world, though its western islands of Sumatra and Java were once at the center of an empire that supported both Hinduism and Buddhism. Under a constitution that officially protects all faiths, Indonesian Buddhists are a small minority (2% of 205 million), but the faith has undergone a vigorous revival since 1950. Small communities dedicated to predominantly Mahayana Buddhism likewise exist among minority ethnic Chinese communities in Malaysia and in Singapore, the city-state that separated from Malaysia in 1965.

East Asia

Guanyin Rises Again in China

Mahayana Buddhists have for fifteen centuries shared a common faith in Avalokiteshvara, whose cult was found from central Asia to Japan in shrines located in almost every settlement and home. The celestial bodhisattva has come to be called Guanyin in China and Kannon in Japan. Originally depicted as a male, this divinity is now usually represented in female form. With

Buddhism's missionary transplantation across East Asia, she became the refuge for all who desired rebirth in the western Buddhist paradise, for those who met dangerous life circumstances, and especially for women who wanted safe childbirth and sons. As Daoism organized and was systematized in response to Buddhism in China by the T'ang era (617–907), Guanyin was so popular (and Daoism so eclectic) that icons of Guanyin were accepted sights in Daoist temples or in clan temples otherwise dedicated to the veneration of ancestors.

The violently iconoclastic phase of Mao Zedong's Cultural Revolution (1966–1969) nearly eliminated Guanyin from public places all across China, and from private shrines as well, since Red Guards who found icons in their house-to-house searches claimed them as sure indicators of "reactionary elements." When icons were discovered, householders were in danger of being declared "enemies of the people," publicly humiliated, and even killed. Since the mid-1980s, however, Guanyin has returned to favor, and state-run factories have produced a large variety of images for sale, many at newly opened temple votive supply stores. Pilgrimage sites have been opened for Guanyin as well. Indeed, it is evident that even party members, especially among the younger and professional generations, tend to believe in the efficacy of worshiping this Buddhist divinity. Even so, the government's acceptance of the revival of Buddhist devotionalism stands in contrast to its harsh repression of other faiths that have taken root in China, from Christianity to the popular sect Falun Gong.

Since the death of Mao Zedong and the end of the Cultural Revolution in 1976, the Communist government of China has slowly allowed many Buddhist institutions to be reopened, including monasteries that train monks and nuns in traditional ritual and meditation practices. It also has allowed lay devotees to set up home shrines and undertake pilgrimages.

Buddhist Revival in South Korea

The formerly unified Korean culture area, artificially split into North Korea and South Korea after World War II, was strongly influenced by Chinese cultural borrowings, including Buddhism, throughout its history. As South Korea experienced rising economic prosperity from the 1970s onward, it has attracted patrons and activists who have sought to build the spiritual programs of the monasteries, present the Buddha's teachings in modern media, and try to reverse the slide of Buddhism in the face of Christian proselytizing and government discrimination.

Despite many setbacks over the last century, the surviving Korean Buddhist institutions remain well endowed with landed income and have established an important niche in Korean society through the many schools its monasteries and lay institutions have established. As in other Buddhist countries undergoing successful economic modernization, Korean Buddhism is experiencing a renewal. Its modern institutions are upgrading monastic education, creating mass media publications, and developing an urban, middle-class Buddhist identity based upon householder rituals, meditation, and youth organizations. The latest Korean innovation is the cable channel All-Buddhist

Network Television, whose programs offer a mix of sermons, chants, rituals, and chefs teaching vegetarian cooking.

Buddhism in Japan Recovers After World War II

Japan, like the United States, is a country of ever-broadening religious expression. Buddhism has contributed to this through its classical monastic institutions and by its doctrines providing starting points for many of Japan's "new religions." In the mid-nineteenth century, the Meiji state's ultranationalist governments deliberately weakened Buddhism through ideological campaigns

Boke Fuji ("Senility") Kannon: A New Incarnation of a Buddhist Deity

The late 1980s, saw the appearance of icons that depicted the goddess Kannon holding a flower in one hand and opening the other in a gesture of mercy to two elderly people, one male and one female, who clutch at her robes in supplication. Consistent with her renown developed over one and a half millennia for compassionately "mothering" her devotees and bestowing this-worldly boons to those who call upon her, this new form of the bodhisatva has arisen as senility or Alzheimer's disease has caused great emotional distress to many in Japan (as elsewhere). Both for the elderly and their families, who share a Confucian responsibility for parental care at this stage of life, old-age suffering has surfaced as a weighty problem, suggesting a creative Buddhist response. Thus temples have established social and spiritual programs, developing amulets, shrines, and pilgrimage routes for devotees to visit in search of preventive blessings. Buddhist priests, aware of physician's counsel, that the best way to keep senility at bay is for the aged to keep active, are encouraging this approach. By organizing pilgrimages, for example, they make available to the elderly enjoyable, stimulating, and hopeful activity, in which the pilgrims can both articulate their worries and acquire peace of mind.

A contemporary Boke Fuji ("Senility") Kannon amulet from Japan.

and institutionally. By the 1930s, many abbots of co-opted "establishment schools" were in fact actively fanning the flames of war. World War II left monasteries in ruins and prominent clergy in disgrace. But after the war, the sanghas of the oldest schools retained their nationwide presence under a system of head and branch monasteries developed in the late Tokagawa era (1600–1857), and some communities worked to restore their spiritual integrity. Today, most Japanese families are registered as *danka* ("parishioners") of a monastery branch of one or the other Buddhist schools for, at the very least, the performance of family death rituals.

But for many Japanese, Buddhism has remained in their lives. The great number of individuals undertaking pilgrimage circuits across the heartland of historical Japan to honor the Mahayana bodhisattva Avalokiteshvara, here called Kannon, attests to the importance of this deity in modern Japan. The Saikoku route, which is a sacred journey organized as far back as the thirteenth century, still attracts pilgrims to visit its many sites, including some of the greatest and most magnificent temples in Japan. This route has risen from postwar obscurity to host thirty thousand participants in the late 1960s and over ninety thousand by last count in the late 1990s. This "pilgrimage boom," as the popular religious revival has been labeled by journalists, was aided by the proliferation of pilgrim facilities. Moreover, the example of the Saikoku Kannon pilgrimage inspired the formation of thirty-three-stage Kannon pilgrimage routes in at least seventy-two other regions of Japan. There is some debate about how much of this rapid increase in pilgrimage is due to religious dedication to Kannon and how much to a less pious "cultural tourism."

Examples of recent revival show the continuing relevance of Kannon in Japanese life. One is lighthearted: the Zenshoji temple northwest of Tokyo has paired the bodhisattva with the Japanese craze for golf by erecting a 6-foot Kannon who holds various golf clubs in her hands. Hundreds of golfers come daily to pray for the mercy of lower scores. More serious is the recent creation of a thirty-three-stage pilgrimage route with a focus on worship of a completely new form of this bodhisattva: *Boke Fuji Kannon* ("Senility Kannon").

A final example of a new form of Kannon devotionalism in Japan is the cult organized to seek the forgiveness of the spirits of aborted fetuses (*mizuko*). Buddhist temples throughout Japan have seen a revival in rituals on their memorial grounds as women have set up icons to which they offer food and other ritual gifts to spirits to whom they denied birth in human form. Kannon and another popular bodhisattva named Jizo, are the main focuses of worship at many temples. Japanese women typically request that the compassionate deities guard and bless these wandering spirits until they fulfill their destiny and continue on to another human rebirth, as in classical Buddhist teachings. The mizuko cult has spread widely, promulgated by many temples that benefit from the income derived from the special ritual services they provide.

Buddhism Today in Diaspora and in Asia

Buddhism in the West

The economic boom that swept Asia in the 1990s and the global migration of Asians are the most recent developments affecting Buddhism today. To a large extent, newly affluent Buddhists have done what Buddhist householders have always done with a portion of their surplus wealth: make merit through pious donations. This infusion of new wealth has been used to rebuild venerable monasteries and temples, support new reform sects, and modernize Buddhist institutions by establishing schools, starting periodicals, and creating mass media outlets. The most affluent and internationally minded, particularly those in East Asia, have shifted the traditional missionary ideal from national to global outreach, building on the migration of the home ethnic group (e.g., Taiwanese, Thai, or Japanese), but often seeking a wider audience beyond. One exception to the trend of new Asian affluence pushing the international expansion of Buddhism is the Tibetan diaspora, which has depended largely upon donations by affluent Euro-American supporters, including Hollywood actors and rock stars.

The global migration of Buddhist monastic institutions and ideas has been so great that a representative of every major Asian school can now be found on every continent, and numerous non-Asians have been accepted for ordination into the various sanghas. In addition, awareness of the basic Buddhist doctrines of karma, nirvana, and Buddhahood, formerly confined to the educated classes of the world, is now accessible to all via the global mass media.

In the Zen and Tibetan schools in North America, especially, converts now speak of the emergence of new "Western schools of Tibetan (or Zen) Buddhism." An explosion in publications, educational programs, and meditation sessions marks the unmistakable deeper adaptation of the faith within Western societies. Such Euro-American Buddhist schools are selective in their adoption of Buddhism: they have eschewed celibate monasticism, featured meditation, and downplayed ritualism, much like the "Protestant Buddhists" of Asia. In 2005 a search for "Buddhism" on the Web elicited over 2 million connections.

The modern diaspora of Buddhism in some respects can be seen as the global continuation of the faith's ancient missionary spirit. In North America, Buddhist missionaries have been led by teachers of Japanese and Korean Zen, all lineages of Tibetan Buddhism, Theravadins emphasizing vipassana meditation with ties to the countries of Southeast Asia, Japan's Soka Gakkai sect, and the various Pure Land schools (in rough order of importance).

In the 1950s the perceived iconoclasm of Zen—its nonconformist appeal—attracted Americans who participated in the Beat Generation culture of jazz, poetry, and experimental literature. The lure of Zen meditation practices has drawn Western practitioners from the 1960s onward. Zen's connection with Japanese fine arts and martial arts also helped Zen-oriented teachers and their institutions across the globe to reach a wider artistic and athletic audience.

"Change Your Mind Day" in Central Park

Each year in late May, the Buddhist magazine *Tricycle* sponsors a gathering in New York's Central Park that draws a variety of teachers who are active in America. Other attendees—"longtime practitioners, meditators-for-a-day, Dharma bums, and dog-walkers"—are led through a series of guided spiritual exercises in the half-day program. In 2004, following 108 gong strikes, American abbots from Zen monasteries and Westerners initiated as teachers in Tibetan lineages gave sermons, Japanese monks led chants, and an American meditation master directed the group in Theravadin-style vipassana meditation. A friend of the late Allen Ginsberg read poems by this famous convert to Buddhism. A perennial favorite followed: a spirited debate in Tibetan scholastic style punctuated by hand-slapping exclamations between a Tibetan lama and an American convert who argued about the nature of nirvana. A T'ai Chi teacher directed a group exercise using martial arts and Japanese dance movements. After a musical interlude, a Tibetan monk gave teachings on loving-kindness, a Sri Lankan abbot discoursed on discipline in Buddhist practice, and a Chinese monk talked about the centrality of compassion. Another round of gongs ended the extraordinary inter-Buddhist ecumenical event attended by three thousand people. By 2005, eleven cities had begun similar "Change Your Mind" events.

The Japanese Soka Gakkai, a modern religiocultural offshoot of the Nichiren school, has an international following eager to reinterpret Buddhism and take political action to foster the development of a more enlightened world civilization. Pure Land Buddhism has been transplanted among East Asians who have migrated to urban areas worldwide, particularly the West Coast of North America. Indeed, migrants from every Buddhist country in the world have contributed to the globalization of their faith by establishing temples and monasteries in their adopted homelands. The largest block of Asian Buddhists in America has emigrated from Southeast Asia.

Outside Asia, Buddhists remain a small minority in the census figures and usually are found in urban areas. Among today's immigrants and Western converts, as in Asia, "being a Buddhist" does not necessarily imply an exclusive identity. Thus, the census figures, which show, for example, roughly a million Buddhists in North America as a whole, do not describe accurately the penetration of Buddhist concepts and practices in certain areas.

With intellectuals worldwide, however, awareness of Buddhist thought and practice is widespread. Advertising agents now deploy Buddhist ideas and practices routinely to promote materialistic attachments: popular advertising since 1999 found the Dalai Lama's image being used to sell Apple computers, a Nike sneaker called "Nirvana," and a designer sandal called "Buddha." The word "Zen" is now appended to hundreds of objects, certain to elicit consumer curiosity despite the absurdity.

The Reshaping of Buddhism in Asia

In the postcolonial period, then, Buddhists have had to determine how to situate their tradition in the new secular polities. The effort has entailed reconstructing sangha–state relations after colonial neglect of the religious institutions, responding to scientific thought and modern medicine, reckoning with the religious pluralism introduced by Christianity and other faiths, and revising law codes in relation to national minorities. The results have been mixed. In Bhutan and Sri Lanka, the dominant ethnic groups have promoted Buddhist nationalism at the expense of non-Buddhist minorities, while in Myanmar and Thailand, members of the military have used Buddhist monks and symbols in a manipulative way to impose or attempt to legitimate authoritarian regimes. Yet Buddhists in each country have led democratic movements resisting repressive policies and violence.

Reformist monastic schools and lay movements begun in the modern era have continued to the present, with recent initiatives arising to address problems confronting the widely differing national contexts: forest monks in Thailand respond to environmental crises, lay organizations in Japan campaign in elections to insert Buddhist values into the political culture, Mongolian leaders rebuild monuments and restore monastic education and ritual expertise, and Sri Lankan monks run for the national parliament vowing to keep their country's Buddhist identity strong.

As ethnic identity has held the loyalty of local communities, often against the demands of modern secular states, "being Buddhist" has drawn individuals to value, rediscover, and embrace Buddhism across Asia. In many cases, the postcolonial web of global interaction has shaped the process: the "Buddhism" that reformers discover has been filtered through and influenced by the thinking of Euro-American teachers and scholars.

An interesting and early example of this phenomenon occurred in Maharashtra, the modern state in central India. Since 1956, Mahar caste groups relegated to the bottom of the caste system have held mass ceremonies to convert to Buddhism, declaring their rejection of Hinduism and its institutionalization of social inequality. The Mahars' knowledge of Buddhism was informed in part by colonial scholarship; the presence in Maharashtra of ancient Buddhist sites revealed by British archaeology has obvious importance as well. The founder of this movement, Dr. Bhimrao Ambedkar (1891–1956), learned about Buddhism from his studies in the West, particularly at Columbia University, where Euro-American scholarship on Buddhism then held up the image of the Buddha as a social reformer. Statues of Ambedkar abound in Maharashtra villages today, monuments to the reinvention of tradition in the service of a late-twentieth-century social reform movement.

Buddhism's Elective Affinity for Modernization

At the beginning of this century, Western scholars such as Max Weber questioned whether Buddhism could prove compatible with economic modernization. Since the end of the Second World War, such skepticism has been laid to rest by the success of nations strongly influenced by Buddhism. We can now see that Weber erred in exaggerating the "other-worldliness" of mainstream Buddhism. He was not acquainted with the unambiguous early doctrinal emphasis on "good Buddhists" attaining worldly success, an ethos that traveled well across the trade routes of Asia and, it seems, into the twenty-first century. Modern reformers have had many canonical texts to draw upon to promote the compatibility between economic development and Buddhism. As an influential reformist monk of Thailand asserted generations ago, "Education breeds knowledge, knowledge breeds work, work breeds wealth, and wealth promotes happiness."[2]

The economic boom in Asia since World War II has clearly benefited Buddhism as newly wealthy patrons have sponsored various renewal initiatives. Moreover, these works almost never involve the sangha's leadership. For example, Thai and Korean projects are now under way that have transcribed canons into electronic media form (CD-ROMs), a new mode of spreading the Dharma locally and globally to all with computer technology. Translation of the sacred texts into the global medium of English is another innovation. The Buddhist Publication Society, founded in Ceylon in 1956, has offered hundreds of translations and interpretive tracts on the Pali texts; its work overlaps with that of the Pali Text Society founded in nineteenth-century England—a group that continues to extend its translations into the southern Buddhist tradition of extracanonical commentary.

Today each of the four Tibetan monastic schools has a modern publishing house that yearly prints dozens of texts promulgating explanations of Buddhist doctrine by its own teaching lamas. An even larger-scale project was initiated in 1991 by the Japanese industrialist Yenan Numata. His foundation, the Bukkyo Denko Kyokai, is underwriting the scholarly translation into English of the entire Chinese canon. To do all 3,360 scriptures, the project is estimated to span the next one hundred years!

State Buddhism and the Poison of Ethnic Passion

Few areas of Asian Buddhism have been removed from the crises and changes of the modern era: scientific thought and technology derived from the European Enlightenment challenged traditional doctrines, cosmologies, and medical theories; the impact of European colonialism forced economic transformations that undermined traditional rulers and patronage; the ideologies of Christian missionary triumphalism and racism conflicted with indigenous beliefs about the superiority of Buddhism.

With colonialism now gone, shifts in the political, socioeconomic, and intellectual spheres have changed individuals and caused Buddhists to adapt their beliefs and practices to a transformed world. Countries with Buddhist majorities now must decide how to shape society—in economic and political spheres—to best realize the Buddha's ideal of a compassionate civilization. Exponents still debate whether Buddhism should endorse military

CONTRASTING RELIGIOUS VISIONS

As the following contrasting visions indicate, every religious tradition is capable of generating both visions that encourage peace and understanding and visions that encourage conflict and violence.

Peacemaker: Thich Nhat Hanh

Since his early involvement in the peace movement in his native Vietnam, the Zen monk Thich Nhat Hanh (1926–) has projected a strong and ecumenical Buddhist voice. From exile in the West, he has been a firm advocate of toleration and the necessary centrality of peacemaking when facing both personal challenges and international policy. A leading advocate of "engaged Buddhism," and author of several dozen books, Nhat Hahn has for decades argued that Buddhists must participate in social and cultural activities, with activism informed by the clarity arising from meditation. As he once affirmed, "In times like this, when people suffer so much, the bodhisattvas don't stay in the temple; they are out there." His "12 Precepts of the Order of Inter-being" attempts to express universal principles of life beyond Buddhist sectarianism, rejecting absolutely killing, coercion, dogmatism, and untruthfulness, while advocating a meditation-centered life.

Quote source: Sallie B. King, "Thich Nhat Hanh and the Unified Buddhist Church," in Christopher S. Queen and Sallie B. King, eds. *Engaged Buddhism: Buddhist Liberation Movements in Asia* (Albany, NY: State University Press of New York, 1996), p. 351.

authoritarianism (on the model of the benevolent dictator Ashoka) or representative democracy (on the model of the sangha's democratic norms). Is it more compassionate to establish a "pure Buddhist state" that privileges Buddhism and Buddhists or to opt for a secular state that is evenhandedly tolerant of a multireligious and multiethnic society? Can Buddhist ideals be more effectively implemented in a socialist or a free-market system?

In countries such as Myanmar and Sri Lanka, where adherence to Buddhism was a powerful force against colonialism, reform movements within the sangha introduced state supervision and weakened the older institutional lineages. In modern China, Myanmar, and Vietnam, Buddhist monks have been called upon to withdraw, study, and meditate. In India, Sri Lanka, and Thailand, on the other hand, monks have become leaders in political reform movements and in the implementation of economic development projects.

In revolutionary China and Outer Mongolia, Buddhism was identified with the old feudal order and was fiercely disestablished. Across China's Tibetan and Inner Mongolian regions, the policy of the People's Republic of China, especially during the Cultural Revolution, was to destroy Buddhist

Confrontationalist: Political Monks of Sri Lanka's Maha Sangha

Drawing upon some of the nationalist pronouncements of reformists such as Anagarika Dharmapala, some monks have formed an entity called the Maha Sangha to engage in political action. These activist monks have urged their government to reply with relentless military action, not negotiated compromise, to resolve the Tamil revolt that has fueled Sri Lanka's tragic civil war since 1983. Arguing that "politics is the monks' heritage" and that Sri Lanka has special virtue as a Buddhist homeland, the Maha Sangha supports violence as the only solution. One poet has distilled their support of aggressive religious nationalism:

> My brave, brilliant soldier son
> Leaving [home] to defend the motherland
> That act of merit is enough
> To reach Nirvana in a future birth. . . .
> Country, religion, race are my triple gems. . . .
> The sangha is ever ready
> At the front
> If the race is threatened.

Quote source: H. L. Seneviratne, *The Work of Kings: The New Buddhism in Sri Lanka* (Chicago: University of Chicago Press, 1999), pp. 272–273.

monasticism, punish believers, and repress any public expressions of devotion. Just reestablishing stupas, ordination lineages, and traditional sangha life has been a challenge over the last decades in these nations. It was not until 1990 that Buddhism in Mongolia experienced a revival after nearly a century of suppression.

In Sri Lanka, once the nationalistic Buddhist movements had ushered in independence, they turned their efforts inward. By seeking to legislate a "purer Buddhist state" and a restoration of past glories, they created an environment in which activist monks enflamed unprecedented ethnic conflict with non-Buddhist minorities long resident on the island. Paradoxically, Buddhist universalism and the ideology of compassion have coexisted with modern attempts at "ethnic cleansing" there as well as in Burma and Bhutan. Some social historians see the further weakening of Buddhist ethics in the future. As populations rise and resources grow scarcer, they argue, politicians will be increasingly tempted to use Buddhism to unify majorities that will then repress religious minorities.

CONCLUSION

As a refuge of intellectual freedom and spiritual imagination, Buddhism historically nurtured and enriched the civilizations of Asia through teachers who analyzed the Buddha's Dharma. Surveying the belief patterns of the world's Buddhist communities, one is still challenged both by the sheer diversity of doctrinal expression and by the complexity of Buddhism's systematic thought. Such an outpouring of conceptualization from a tradition that held the ultimate to be beyond words! Buddhism's subsequent domestication across Asia and beyond has entailed the translation of texts, ideas, and rituals into non-Indic languages and cultures. In becoming a world religion, Buddhism in practice has promoted compassionate, medically advanced, disciplined, mercantile, and literate societies. Like other great religions today, Buddhism has shown that its definition of the human condition and its prescribed ways of addressing suffering and mortality have enduring value, even in the midst of changes that have shaken the world.

Sri Lankan monks march in support of the Marxist Party, the JVP, in May 2003.

The Sangha: Adaptive Reformism?

Given the repeated emphasis placed on the role of the sangha in maintaining the traditional goals of Buddhism in every society, it should not be surprising that we underline the role that spiritual exemplars, scholars, teachers, and

meditators could play in determining Buddhism's future into the third millennium of the Common Era.

Arguing that the sangha cannot keep Buddhism alive unless the monks keep pace with the educational level of the nation's population, countries like Thailand have invested in making higher education available to individuals in the sangha. This opportunity attracts young men from poor rural backgrounds to take ordination. Paradoxically, becoming a monk gives many individuals the chance to live in better material circumstances than their parents were able to achieve and to gain skills that can be taken back into lay life. But at the same time, modern states have bureaucratized their sanghas, scrutinized the preaching and personal lives of monks, and controlled the political activities of the monasteries. In recent times as in antiquity, the freedom accorded to one "in the robes," the refuge afforded by the monastery, and the high regard extended to charismatic monks brought unwanted attention from political leaders. Seeing clearly the threat that the Buddhist Dharma represents to unjust or uncompassionate regimes, politicians have sought to weaken Buddhist institutions even while honoring them. In Myanmar, Vietnam, and China, monks and nuns cannot escape the fear of repression or hope to exert meaningful political influence. It is hard to imagine Buddhist monks regaining the power they once enjoyed at the expense of the modern politicians across Asia.

Since World War II, many developments have undermined the classical patterns and exchanges within Buddhist societies. Whereas formerly, monastic schools were an important part of the sanghas' service to local communities and a source of their recruitment, today public education has been removed from the monastery almost everywhere. If connection with and awareness of modern changes are essential to an institution meeting the needs of the lay majority, is the traditional Buddhist sangha capable of keeping Buddhist ideas and identity vibrant in the whirl of changes sweeping modern Asian societies?

Many progressive Buddhists think not. Noting that the modern sangha has a hierarchy of authority unknown in earlier times, they see little opportunity for young monks to fashion innovative applications of the Dharma in thought or action. Noting how powerful elder monks typically lack vision, purpose, or inspiration beyond the guardianship of ceremonies and tradition, many Asian householders look to lay institutions for more promising avenues to keep Buddhism vital.

The number of men taking monastic vows across Asia has fallen far short of what population increases would predict. As a result, many village monasteries are understaffed, a trend reflecting the breakdown of rural communities that has contributed to the urbanization of Asia. While some Buddhists in Nepal, Korea, and Japan have countenanced sanghas of the "married ordained" to solve the problem of recruitment, these schools on the whole have actually shown even less inclination to revitalize or innovate. Again, it is easy to see why Buddhist reformers have almost always gone outside the boundary of the modern sangha to move ahead with their programs, at times having to face opposition from the established monastic community.

A Role for Buddhist Women?

Related to the issue of the sangha's adaptability and leadership is the status of Buddhist women renunciants. In 1987, at an international conference held in Bodh Gaya, 150 devout women formed a worldwide organization called Shakyaditya. The "Shakya Daughters" are dedicated to the restoration of the full ordination of bhikkhunis (nuns) among the Theravadins, a lineage most Buddhist monks of this school view as having died out almost a millennium ago. Throughout the Buddhist world today, there are several hundred thousand highly committed women who have adopted an unofficial and unheralded ascetic lifestyle involving meditation, service, or study. In every country there is also a male-dominated sangha that controls the Buddhist institutions, and the great majority of monks strongly resist changes in the gender status quo.

Yet some women who have adopted the lifestyle of the nun do not even wish to take the full bhikkhuni ordination. Why? According to the *Vinaya* rules, fully ordained women admitted into the sangha must accept the formal supervision of the senior monks. Presently, in their unofficial status, these renunciants enjoy near-complete autonomy to manage their living arrangements and spiritual training. They argue that since their real loyalty is to the Dharma and their true concern is nirvana-seeking discipline, it is pointless to seek formal recognition. Yet remaining "unofficial" places severe limitations on the women's ability to build their institutions, since they are not recognized for state patronage, and householder donations to them do not yield the same prestige or merit return that comes from donations to the monks. As a result, most of the unofficial "nuns" remain impoverished, without special honor in their societies at large, and marginal to the dominant Buddhist community.

Since 2000, over four hundred women practicing in all the Theravada countries have gone to Chinese Mahayana monasteries (in mainland China or Taiwan) to receive full nun's official ordination, as nuns, much to the consternation of the traditionalist monks. Can Buddhist traditions facing so many future challenges afford to relegate to the margins of their societies the energy, compassion, and merit of such women?

Globalization of Buddhism: Monks, Migrants, and Transnational Culture

The global migration of Asian Buddhists in the postcolonial era is another source of revival for the faith. As these groups grow and prosper in their new societies, they naturally channel a portion of their savings back to the home region. But these immigrants have also paid to sponsor monks and build storefront monasteries in the West and in the process, internationalized the home country's institutions through a slow grassroots process of development. As Buddhist priests, monks, and expatriates move between their new and old countries, innovations and resources are being shifted as well. This immigrant-induced exchange also includes the cross-fertilization of ideas moving between

Buddhist schools from distant areas of Asia and their Western exponents. It may well be that the future success—or perhaps even survival—of the modern national lineages and schools of Buddhism in Asia will depend upon an international membership, providing worldwide sources of funding and interpretive awareness. Through the 1990s, only the Tibetan Buddhists in exile have been truly successful at linking the material support and ritual practice by Western converts to their traditional schools; otherwise, most Asian Buddhists and converts practice their religion completely separate from Westerners who have converted to Buddhism.

Tibetan monks engaging in debate training, testing their ability to consistently expound the Buddha's teachings.

An especially promising development may be the growing presence of Buddhism in the emerging global culture. In the area of human rights, Asian Buddhist exponents have made impressive contributions. Buddhist doctrine offers many traditional ideals that have been rearticulated powerfully by reformists and activists who style themselves as "engaged Buddhists." These ideals include compassion, nonviolence, selflessness, interdependence, and detachment. There is no shortage of examples today of the existential "poisons" that Buddhists have always located at the center of their wheel of life—human greed, anger, and delusion. Yet the very compassion and selflessness that Buddhists have always embraced offer the means to lessen suffering of individuals, of communities, and of the earth itself.

An example of this determined insistence on applying Buddhist norms to modern crises is seen in the writings of the Thai activist Sulak Sivaraksa, founder (in 1989) of the International Network of Engaged Buddhists:

> When Prince Siddhartha saw an old man, sick man, a dead man, and a wandering monk, he was moved to seek salvation, and eventually he became the Buddha, the Awakened One. The suffering of the present day, such as that brought about at Bhopal and Chernobyl, should move many of us to think together and act together to overcome such death and destruction, to bring about the awakening of humankind.[3]

Engaged Buddhism is uniting Asian Buddhists with Western converts, bringing together the energies of householders, monks, and nuns, and finding issues that connect Buddhist activists with similarly committed reformers from other faiths. It remains to be seen whether Buddhist revivalists can offer a compelling interpretation of the Dharma as Buddhists find themselves drawn into the marketplace of multinational capitalism, with its doctrines of individualism and competition and its vigorous encouragement of consumerism.

Discussion Questions

1 Buddhists past and present have looked to the incidents in Gautama Buddha's life for inspiration. Pick three major episodes in the Buddha's life and discuss what lessons they impart to a typical Buddhist householder.

2 Many modern Buddhists regard the Buddha as a reformer. What teachings can be used to support this interpretation? What historical arguments can be made against this position?

3 Which of the Buddha's teachings are shared with post-Vedic Hinduism?

4 Explain how Buddhist doctrine can argue for reincarnation but against the existence of an "immortal soul."

5 Why is compassion a human ideal that is a logical extension of core Buddhist doctrines?

6 What is the relationship between the Three Marks of Existence, prajna, and nirvana?

7 In what senses can the Buddha be called the Great Physician?

8 Why is Buddhism known as the "Middle Way"? Give at least three reasons.

9 How might the Vajrayana school be viewed merely as an application of basic Mahayana Buddhist doctrines?

10 Why is the *Lotus Sutra* so important in China and Japan?

11 How does Mahayana Buddhism resemble and differ from devotional Hinduism?

12 How is the Mahar revival of Buddhism in India indicative of the effects of "Protestant Buddhism" and backlash from the colonial era within the Buddhist world?

13 Name five aspects of Protestant Christianity that were adopted by Buddhist reformers, shaping the nineteenth- and twentieth-century revitalization movements called "Protestant Buddhism."

14 In your opinion, how would a modern Buddhist revivalist present the Dharma and argue that it remains a religion relevant to life in the twenty-first century?

Key Terms

Amitabha/Amida	dependent origination	Mahayana	skandha
anatman	*Dharma*	mizuko cult	stupa
arhat	Eightfold Path	nirvana	Theravada
bhikkhuni	"engaged Buddhism"	Pali Canon	Three Marks of Existence
Bodh Gaya	enlightenment	prajna	Three Refuges
bodhisattva	Four Good Deeds	"Protestant Buddhism"	Thunder Vehicle
Buddha	Four Noble Truths	punya	Vajrayana
Buddha nature theory	koan	Pure Land	vipassana meditation
caitya	*Lotus Sutra*	sangha	Zen
dana	Madhyamaka	shramana	

Suggested Readings

Bechert, Heinz, and Richard Gombrich, eds., *The World of Buddhism* (New York: Thames-Hudson, 1987).

Gombrich, Richard, *Theravada Buddhism: A Social History from Ancient Benares to Modern Colombo* (New York: Routledge, 1988).

————, and Gananath Obeyesekere, *Buddhism Transformed: Religious Change in Sri Lanka* (Princeton, NJ: Princeton University Press, 1988).

Harvey, Peter, *An Introduction to Buddhism: Teachings, History, Practices* (Cambridge, UK: Cambridge University Press, 1990).

Heine, Steven, and Charles S. prebish, eds. *Buddhism in the Modern World.* (New York: Oxford University Press, 2003).

Lopez, Donald, ed., *Buddhism in Practice* (Princeton, NJ: Princeton University Press, 1996).

Queen, Christopher, and S. King, eds., *Engaged Buddhism* (Albany: State of New York University Press, 1996).

Rahula, Walpola, *What the Buddha Taught* (New York: Publishers Resource, 1978).

Reynolds, Frank E., and Jason A. Carbine, eds., *The Life of Buddhism* (Berkeley: University of California Press, 2000).

Rhys-Davids, Caroline A. F., tr., *Stories of the Buddha* (New York: Dover, 1988).

Robinson, Richard, and Willard Johnson, *The Buddhist Religion: A Historical Introduction,* 4th ed. (Belmont, CA: Wadsworth, 1997).

Seager, Richard, *Buddhism in America* (New York: Columbia University Press, 1999).

Snellgrove, David, *Indo-Tibetan Buddhism* (Boulder, CO: Shambhala, 1987).

Strong, John S., ed., *The Experience of Buddhism* (Belmont, CA: Wadsworth, 1995).

Swearer, Donald, *The Buddhist World of Southeast Asia* (Albany: State University of New York Press, 1996).

Trainor, Kevin, ed., *Buddhism: An Illustrated Guide* (London: Duncan-Baird, 2001).

Wijayaratna, Mohan, *Buddhist Monastic Life* (Cambridge, UK: Cambridge University Press, 1987).

Williams, Paul, *Mahayana Buddhism: The Doctrinal Foundations* (New York: Routledge, 1989).

Notes

1. Quoted in Samuel Beal, Si-Yu-Ki, *Buddhist Records of the Western World* (New Delhi: Munshiram Manoharlal, 1983), p. xxix.

2. Phra Kummsaen, quoted in Kenneth Landon, *Thailand in Transition* (Chicago: University of Chicago Press, 1939), pp. 67–68.

3. Sulak Sivaraksa, *Seeds of Peace* (Berkeley, CA: Parallax Press, 1988), p. 9.

East Asian Religions
Traditions of Human Cultivation and Natural Harmony

Overview

On public holidays and lunar days traditionally deemed favorable for approaching the gods, temples in China, Japan, and Korea are packed with morning visitors, the air thick with incense smoke. In Beijing, newly married couples flock to the White Clouds Daoist temple to light candles, requesting divine aid to ensure the birth of a son; at family shrines in Seoul, honor students approach ancestral altars to report their applications to study at universities abroad; in rural Japan, farmers gather at the village Shinto shrine for the annual harvest festival, clapping their hands to punctuate their prayers of thanks, then offering sake and purifying the sacred sumo wrestling grounds with salt. Buddhist monasteries have also attracted new patronage as economic prosperity has enriched the region: old women hoping for medicinal cures sip water that has been blessed, executive trainees sent by corporations for "toughening up" sit in meditation, and children desperate for assistance on an upcoming exam light incense sticks.

At a shrine atop the sacred mountain Tai Shan, in southern China, devotees light incense and candles to honor the local gods.

EAST ASIAN RELIGION *Timeline*

1766–1122 BCE	Shang dynasty in China; cult of departed ancestors and oracle bone divination practiced
1122–221	Zhou dynasty in China; yin-yang theory develops; era of intermittent civil disorder
c. 551–479	Life of Master K'ung (Confucius)
c. 520–286	Era of first Daoist sages, philosophers Lao Zi (d. 500 BCE?) and Zhuang Zi (365–290 BCE)
450–223	Era of Confucian sage scholars, Master Meng (Mencius, 371–289 BCE), Master Xun (298–238 BCE); origins of Confucian *Analects* and compilation of the *Five Classics*
221–206	Qin dynasty, the first to unify China; Great Wall completed
200 BCE–220 CE	Han dynasty in China; civil service based upon Confucian teachings
220–588 CE	Period of weak central state and the growth of Daoism and Buddhism
c. 450	"Three Caves" of Daoist scriptures collected
618–907	T'ang dynasty in China; period of Confucian revival; translations of Indian Buddhist texts
668–918	Silla dynasty in Korea, centered on Buddhism as state religion
710–784	Nara period in Japan; Shinto tradition organized; Buddhism made state religion
794–1185	Heian period in Japan, ends with emperor removed from rulership
918–1392	Koryo dynasty in Korea, with ecumenical development of Mahâyâna Buddhism
960–1279	Song dynasty in China; period of neo-Confucianism (the "Second Epoch")
c. 1150	Goddess Mazu becomes popular in China, recognized by the state
1130–1200	Life of Zhu Xi, leading neo-Confucian exponent, who reestablished the tradition as preeminent among the Chinese literati
1185–1333	Kamakura era in Japan, era of civil disorder and the rise of new Buddhist schools
1279–1368	Yuan dynasty in China, era of Mongol rule
1336–1600	Ashikaga period in Japan; era of Shinto–Buddhist syncretism, popularity of Pure Land Buddhism adoption of Zen among the literati
1368–1644	Ming dynasty in China, the last era of Han Chinese rule; doctrine of harmonizing the "three faiths"
1380ff	In China, *The Canonization of the Gods* fixes folk pantheon in hierarchy mirroring state bureaucracy
1392–1910	Yi dynasty in Korea, an era marked by state-favored Confucianism
1472–1529	Life of Wang Yangming, a neo-Confucian who promoted mind cultivation and character development

1501–1570	Life of Yi T'oegye, important Korean neo-Confucian
1534–1582	Life of Nobunaga, Japanese shogun who persecuted Buddhism and gave support to Christianity
1592	Publication of *Journey the West* written by Wu Cheng-en
1600–1867	Tokugawa era in Japan, with capital in Tokyo; Buddhism under strong state support
1644–1911	Qing (Manchu) dynasty in China; era promoting Confucianism
1815–1888	Oldest new religions in Japan: Kurozumikyo (1814), Tenrikyo (1838)
1850–1864	Taiping Rebellion in China, led by Hong Xiuquan (1814–1864)
1860	Ch'ondogyo movement founded in Korea by Ch'oe Suun (1824–1864)
1868–1945	Return of emperor's rule in Japan and the rise of state Shinto; Japan adopts Western calendar, technology, imperialist political views
1871–1945	Japanese Buddhist establishment joins Shinto nationalists and Christians in support of militarism
1880–present	Best and brightest individuals across the East Asia region studying Western learning, technology to seek rapid modernization
1889–1890	New constitution and Japanese government initiatives draw heavily on Confucian doctrines
1912	Fall of Qing dynasty in China, ending state patronage of Confucianism
1900–1945	Founding of "new religions' in pre-War Japan: P.L. Kyodan in 1924; Reikukai Kyodan in 1925, Soka Gakkai in 1930, Rissho Koseikai in 1938
1946–present	Founding of "new 'new religions'" in post-War Japan: Sukyo Mahikari in 1963, Agonshu in 1971, Aum Shinrikyo in 1989
1949–1976	People's Republic of China established; Communist party persecutes monks, priests, institutions
1966–1976	Cultural Revolution brings renewed persecution of religions and adherents in China
1984–present	Buddhist monasteries and Daoist temples reopen, many with newly trained monks and nuns in residence; pilgrims visit major sites to perform traditional rites
1994	Study of Confucianism officially supported by Chinese state
1995	Aum Shinrikyo sect in Japan launches poison gas attack in Tokyo
1996–present	Return of traditional ancestor veneration to China; images of Mao Zedong and other deceased Communist party leaders found on popular religious amulets
1999	Falun Gong, a syncretistic Buddhist–Daoist group founded by Li Hongzhu claiming 100 million followers in 30 countries, protests in Beijing; within months, Chinese government bans the group and begins persecution of practitioners

EAST ASIAN RELIGION *Timeline*

It is more difficult to find public shrines for the sage Confucius, but there is no doubt that Confucian tradition has survived the wars, political tumult, and scathing denunciations of the twentieth century. In the colonial era, Confucianism was blamed for retarding the region's development. Now its emphasis on education, strong families, individual discipline, and harmonious group relations is seen as holding the center of East Asia's stable societies and orchestrating this region's ascendancy in the world economy.

This religious pluralism sets East Asia apart. Throughout the region's history, the great majority of East Asians regarded Confucianism, Daoism, deity cults, and Buddhism as complementary, dealing with different aspects of life. Most felt that these interrelated beliefs and practices enriched their spirituality, offering them the chance to meld the traditions harmoniously to solve personal problems and address life's questions. It was rare for individuals—elite or common folk—to feel that "being religious" meant choosing one tradition to the exclusion of the others. This openness stands in contrast to the common Western belief that religious conviction means signing on to an exclusive creed or seizing upon one either/or alternative.

East Asia, more than in South Asia, exhibits a popular and strikingly common tradition that is rooted in the ancestor veneration and spirit worship of earliest antiquity. Over time these practices became blended with basic elements of Daoism, Buddhism, and Confucianism, comprising what is called *"diffuse religion."* Given that roughly 40 percent of humanity is East Asian, no full reckoning of human religious life can be made without taking into account China, Korea, and Japan.

Modern East Asian Countries and Their Religious Orientations

What is today referred to as China is the People's Republic of China (PRC). With over 1.2 billion citizens, it is the country with the largest population in the world. Different dynasties up to the present have struggled to unify the dozens of minority peoples of the periphery regions with those of the core region who have called themselves Han and whose descendants speak the Chinese dialect Mandarin. Although spoken Chinese contains over twenty major dialects, the literate culture of China has used the same written language for more than two thousand years. This has made the classical literary tradition (including all religious texts) accessible to the learned throughout the entire East Asian region (see Map 8.1). Mandarin language and Han culture effectively wielded by state officials did prove capable, at times, of unifying vast domains.

The formerly unified Korean culture area, artificially split into the separate countries of North Korea and South Korea since the end of the Second World War (1945), was most strongly influenced by Chinese cultural borrowings, including Buddhism. In the early modern period until the end of the Yi dynasty (1392–1910), Confucianism was the state religion, and the cult of ancestor worship became central in Korean society. Shamanic traditions, which are today stronger in Korea than elsewhere in East Asia, are found throughout the peninsula and are practiced by most individuals regardless of any institutional religious affiliation. Little traditional religious activity is sanctioned or reported among the 24 million people of the modern isolationist and communist state of North Korea.

China also generated wave after wave of influence over the island nation of Japan, but beginning later and penetrating less intensively overall than in Korea. Now a constitutional monarchy headed in practical governance by a prime minister, Japan had for centuries been ruled by an emperor and a single imperial line claiming mythological origins that are distinctively Japanese. Since the end of World War II, however, Japan's 128 million people have produced the world's fourth largest national economy. As elsewhere, this rapid transition has worked in contradictory directions, enriching devotees of every persuasion who have rebuilt institutions and created new ones, while changing the society profoundly and so leaving individuals seeing the world in ways previously unimagined. This explains why "new religions" continue to spring up in East Asia, offering creative spiritual responses to life in today's fast-moving societies.

The Chinese Core and the Periphery of East Asia

China has been the formative center of the East Asian region from earliest antiquity. The emergence of a central state there predates the unification of Korea and Japan by at least twelve and fifteen centuries, respectively. Most modern national boundaries that demarcate the region date back to the pre-modern era. The two Koreas, the region of Tibet, and the republic of Taiwan are exceptions.

In the broadest terms, all regions beyond China's early core can be seen as the periphery of Chinese civilization, where states and individuals selectively and creatively adapted the essential Chinese cultural forms. These forms encompass the full range of what "culture" entails: the written Chinese characters used to record the spoken languages, the fundamental material technologies needed for subsistence (intensive rice production, the making of iron, and porcelain pottery), and the beliefs and practices of its great religious traditions. As we have seen, even Buddhism, which the Chinese themselves adopted despite its origins in India, was transmitted to the East Asian periphery in the same pattern, through China.

Yet despite the overwhelming magnitude of Chinese culture and the nearly irresistible size and power of the Chinese states, Korean, Japanese, and Vietnamese peoples established and preserved their own separate identities. While importing and synthesizing much from China, each nonetheless developed a distinct spoken language, mythology, and spiritual connection to its geographical territory. In all these periphery states, too, the national cultures inspired people to identify with being separate culturally and politically from China, however much their elites admired Chinese culture. (In some cases,

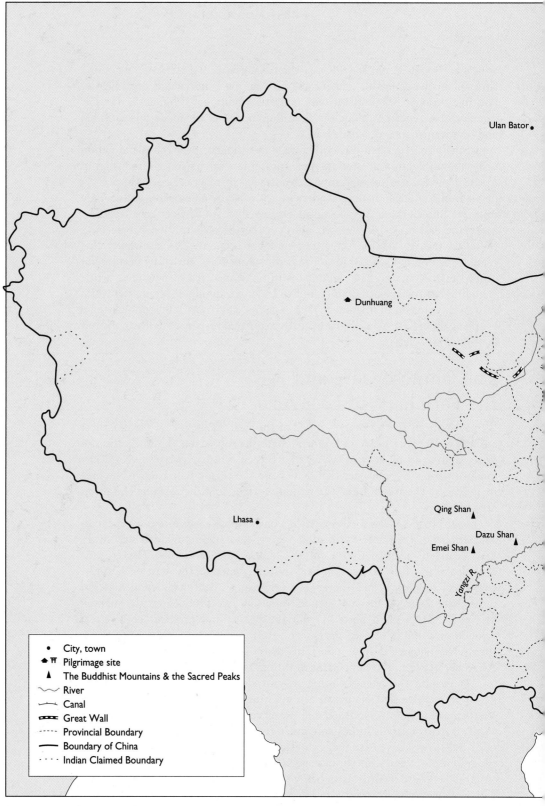

Map 8.1   Modern political map of East Asia showing important religious sites.

Yellow R.
Yungang
Miaofeng Shan
Beijing
Heng Shan
Tianjin
Wutai Shan

Dalian

Pyongyang
Kumgangsan

SEA OF JAPAN

Tokyo
Kamakura
Fuji

Seoul

Okyoto
Nara

Izumo
Tenri
Ise

Jinan
Tai Shan
Taian
Qufu
Lao Shan

Kwangji

Tóngdo-Sa

Hiroshima

Longmen
Layang
Kaifeng
Shan
Song Shan
Chang-an (Xi-an)
Xionger Shan
Nanwictai Shan

Grand Canal

Nagasaki

Amaterasu Jinja

Wudang Shan

Nanjing

Suzhou
Shanghai

Upper Tianzhu Monastery
Putuo Shan
Ninpo
AyuWang Monastery

Jinhua Shan
Poyue Shan
Hangzhou
Huang Shan
Tiantai Shan

Lu Shan

Longhu Shan

Shao Shan
Heng Shan
Wuyi Shan

Jinggang Shan

Nanhua Monastery

Caoxi Shan
Lofu Shan
Guangzhou

Hong Kong

TAIWAN

PACIFIC OCEAN

0   500   1000 km

especially given the destruction and changes that have swept modern China, Chinese cultural forms of earlier eras are now best preserved in Korea or Japan.) Further, as is all too plain in the modern era, the extensive and long-standing cultural ties connecting East Asian peoples did not prevent expressions of enmity between the modern states that have ranged from colonization to genocide.

ENCOUNTER WITH MODERNITY: POSTCOLONIAL CONFUCIAN ECONOMICS

The Postcolonial Challenge of Confucianism

By 1980 it was clear that modernity theorists who had predicted the decline of religion with the advent of science were incorrect in every instance. Nowhere have the flaws of this analysis been more striking than in East Asia, where indigenous intellectuals and reformers since the mid-nineteenth century blamed Confucianism for the region's decadence and failure to defend itself effectively against the imperialist West. The region's political despotism, social disintegration, economic retardation, scientific stagnation, poverty, and disease were all ascribed to blind adherence to Confucian ideals and practices.

The more quickly Confucianism could be abandoned in favor of Western cultural borrowings, reformers argued, the sooner East Asia would be on the road to prosperity. For this reason, many welcomed the fall of the Chinese (1912) and Korean (1910) imperial states, and with them the domination of Confucian officials and intellectuals. Yet as events transpired, not only has religion survived, it has revived and expanded, often in surprisingly strong forms.

For example, early modernity theorists once attributed Japan's postwar prosperity to its successful and rapid Westernization. Although the war fomented by European-styled fascism destroyed many of Japan's material accomplishments through the country's first era of modernization (1868–1945), the Japanese after World War II were still able to rebound and build what is today one of the world's strongest economies.

Scholars now see the success of Japan as the result of much more than its early and rapid Westernization: the Meiji era (1868–1912) facilitated the region's first union of Western technology and reformed Confucian social policy, one that was accomplished, too, in postwar South Korea, Taiwan, and Singapore and is now under way in post-Mao mainland China.

Thus, the socioeconomic analysis has been completely reversed. That is, we now find many scholars *attributing* the East Asians' success to the region's family-centered "bourgeois Confucianism" (as distinguished from the "high Confucianism" of the Mandarins, the former ruling elite).

The East Asian revival has also been realized in each instance by a strong post–World War II state that defines its duty in terms of providing leadership for the national economic agendas. This recent reinvention of Confucianism has produced societies marked by low crime rates, social harmony, and efficient economic behavior, which in turn has led to unprecedented success. Given the disastrous state of the region right after World War II, the overall accomplishment has been called an "economic miracle."

Now what reformers had identified as Confucianism's intractable flaws have been reanalyzed in positive terms: family-based businesses efficiently maximize scarce capital; tightly woven kin/family relations are excellent building blocks for supply and product distribution; an education system that fosters group cooperation, memorization, and imitation has proven adept at producing individuals able to work hard and master existing technologies. With strong states dedicated to achieving collective economic success, it was clear by 1990 that East Asian peoples with this reformed Confucian orientation had risen to top global positions in all the major manufacturing sectors of the postmodern world. Thus, after East Asians had acquired Western know-how, they effectively drew upon Confucian elements in their cultures to mobilize indigenous social resources and create political systems that ensured the social cohesiveness needed to promote national prosperity.

Not only does this success challenge the West's historical monopoly of wealth and economic power, it raises doubt about another tenet of modernity theory: is Westernization an inevitable consequence of modernization? Stated differently: Must all nations Westernize to modernize? Or is the Confucian route through strong authoritarian states an alternative for Asia, heralding a Third Confucian Epoch? To better understand the significance of this encounter with modernity, we must go back to premodern times and trace the historical development of religion in East Asia.

EAST ASIAN RELIGIONS IN THE PREMODERN ERA

East Asia is extraordinary among the world's regions because many beliefs and practices documented from earliest antiquity (1500 BCE) survive there in the present. To convey just how strong this conservatism has been, consider the example of deities worshipped by China's imperial court: a list of the gods receiving sacrifices from the last Qing emperor in 1907 exactly matches the gods mentioned in a very early record (c. 1100 BCE), with the sole exception of Confucius (who lived almost six hundred years after the Shang court). Therefore, it is important to survey the emergence and early development of Chinese religions to discern religion's pivotal importance in Chinese civilization and to see how its religious beliefs and practices spread to other East Asian societies.

Defining Terms

Our treatment of East Asian religions in the same chapter calls for a brief explanation of the central terms. Each topic highlighted here is developed in the chapter.

For convenience, we use *Confucianism,* a Western term originating in eighteenth-century Europe, instead of the corresponding Chinese term *rujia,* meaning "literati tradition." The tradition of the literati (or intellectuals) is rooted in the system of moral observance and ritual performance established in the sixth century BCE by Master K'ung (or, in English rendering, Confucius), whose teachings were commented upon and extended by subsequent sages. The Confucian tradition, which was made China's state ideology over two millennia ago, became noted for its wisdom books, political institutions, social teachings, and attention to self-cultivation. In this cumulative form, and as adapted by medieval scholars influenced by Buddhism, the rujia became the most common shared spiritual tradition of China, Korea, and Japan. The scholars who edited the foundational texts are known by Westerners as neo-Confucians. A mastery of the tradition's classical texts and central doctrines was at the center of the educational system and government bureaucracy until well into the modern era (1905 in China, 1867 in Japan, 1910 in Korea). Reflecting this diversity, we use "Confucianism" without imputing to the tradition a singular creed, ritual, or institution.

Daoism can refer to both a philosophical and a religious tradition and so always needs further specification. Philosophical Daoism aims to cultivate an immediate sense of personal connection with the primal force or reality of the universe, one that its sages labeled "the *Dao,*" using a character that means "way" or "path." The sages of religious Daoism themselves are revered as humans who had realized supernatural physical powers or spiritual immortality and have become divine. Through meditation or alchemy, this strand of Daoism advocated the sages' path to immortality, and eventually monastic traditions (on the model of Buddhism, imported centuries later) were developed to sustain seekers. Many aspects of "applied" Daoism were developed to manage worldly life in East Asia: acupuncture to adjust the flow of the life force flowing in the human body, *feng shui* to help humans live their lives in harmony with the natural energy flowing in the natural and built environment, *Yi-Jing* and other forms of prognostication to determine the proper moment to perform important tasks (marriage, travel, etc.), *wu-shu* or the martial arts to focus human powers to overcome enemies.

Deity cults in traditional East Asia were universal. Springs, rivers, remarkable geographic features—particularly mountain peaks—are still thought to have extraordinary divine inhabitants whose spiritual force, or *ling,* is imminent. The same ling is evident and personified in wind, rain, the stars, and legendary figures whose souls endured and who became deities. Each sector of the earth, in fact, is thought to have a resident deity who serves as the counterpart of the government official in charge of the village, town, province, and the state itself, with a hierarchy of gods mirroring the human civil service. Across East Asia, the common popular perception is that the deities exist, and they can be contacted at temples. A person will question a god and then, through ancient divination rituals, attempt to discern an answer. In the popular conception, deities, like local officials, can be paid to provide favors; the big gods may be induced to discipline lesser gods (or demons) who cause troubles. Humans out of mutual respect are obliged to show the gods thanksgiving regularly for life, health, and prosperity.

Diffuse religion is the useful term that indicates what for most East Asians consists of a spiritual life that is centered within the family unit and immediate locality. It has its roots in the ancestor veneration and spirit worship of earliest antiquity but incorporates general and basic elements of Confucianism, Daoism, and Buddhism. The unity of a region's diffuse religion derives from the long-established practice of the state bureaucracy promulgating full expressions of the common traditions; at times, scholars were assigned to codify the myriad texts and practices to give them coherence. From medieval times until now, traditional printed almanacs have been important texts that record such teachings and orchestrate yearly practices for families. Among the major elements of the diffuse religion is belief in deities and in rituals relating to them. There is also a sense that the universe has fundamental forces and powers, requiring humans to seek harmony with them to achieve health and long life. Further, the world is believed to have certain natural hierarchies that must be acknowledged and respected, in forms prescribed by the ancient traditions. This requirement of hierarchical respect extends to one's departed kin. Finally, the strength of the diffuse religions comes from the conviction that the ways of the past should be revered and studied to discern the proper path to the future. At least since Confucius, Chinese people have accorded great respect to past traditions, resulting in a very long period in which the core elements of East Asian religion were disseminated across the entire region.

The *sectarian religions* in East Asia were institutional Buddhism and Daoism and the sects that arose periodically, often with the goal of overthrowing the state. Such separate religions were meaningful primarily for the very small elites who joined an order, adopted a singular discipline within one tradition, or sought individualistic sectarian goals. But over time, many of the sects ceased to advocate the singularity of their approach alone.

Thus it is hard to find firm boundaries separating the spiritual traditions of East Asia. The *Dao* is a concept shared by all schools, for example; indeed, the Buddhists used the term to define the Buddha's teaching (*Dharma*) in early translations. The goal of harmony is also common in each spiritual path. We are able to treat East Asia's religions under a single heading precisely because of the commonality of this "diffuse borrowing," the nexus of the diffuse religion in the home and among kin rather than in large institutions, and the attempt by elites and commoners alike to harmonize these rich traditions. In each nation, the inclusive harmonizing trait has been expressed with only slight variation: in Japan, "Shintoist in youth, Confucian as an adult, Buddhist in old age"; in Korea, "Confucian by obligation, shamanist at heart"; in China, "Confucian in the office, Daoist outside."

Yin	Yang
Dark	Bright
Earth	Heaven
Female	Male
Autumn	Spring
Valley	Mountain
West	East
Po Soul (grave)	*Hun* Soul (heaven)

The symbolism of the *Yi-Jing* was the main system for East Asians conceptualizing the incessantly changing universe, much as math equations are used to express the essential truths underlying the discoveries of modern science. The most common *yin-yang* symbol should be viewed as ever in motion, with the circles in each sector expanding until black becomes white and white black.

Earliest History: Shang (1766–1122 BCE)

In the fertile valleys of the Yellow River, urban societies formed by 2000 BCE, and their settlements reveal a distinctive complex of advanced metal technologies, writing systems, and religious practices. All three of these aspects of civilization are connected in the practice of oracle bone divination, which was discovered among the northern peoples who lived within walled cities and called their rulers "the Shang." Questions were inscribed on dried large bones of animals. A ritualist then applied a hot metal bar to the bones, and answers were discerned from the cracking patterns produced. Among the over 150,000 Shang oracle bones found and deciphered to date, "this-worldly" concerns predominate—questions regarding whether to undertake military action, hunts, journeys, or ceremonies, as well as the interpretation of omens believed to predict weather, illness, or the sex of unborn children.

Among the Shang, too, were master metal casters who made elaborately decorated bronze vessels that were used in ceremonies to worship deities and ancestors. Elaborate offerings of drink and food, including animals dispatched on altars, were arrayed at early Chinese burial sites. Inscriptions on the vessels indicate that the Shang legitimated their rule by claiming the unrivaled supernatural power of their own ancestors to act on their and the society's behalf. This Shang notion of reciprocity between dead and living—food and honor bestowed by the living in return for blessings from the dead—remains to the present day a central aspect of East Asian religions.

The cult of the dead assumed vast proportions in the case of the ruling elite, for whom large tombs were dug and around whom all the essentials for life in the "next world" were buried. Among the Shang, there was the practice of interring sacrificed human servants alongside the nobles; in the case of the later emperors, similar grand tombs were built, but terra-cotta replicas of servants and animals replaced living beings.

Another important religious belief known from earliest antiquity is that of easy access to divinities and intimacy between humans and their gods. The Shang saw gods as immanent in rain, mountains, and rivers; early Chinese attributed significance to patterns and events in nature and made offerings to them. The spirits were thought to affect all areas of life, from military battles and foreign relations to business fortunes, marriage, and illness. The presence of gods and ancestor spirits was most dramatically attested to by people who served as spirit mediums and were called *wu/xi* (women/men). Through their possession by the deities, the *wu/xi* made ready contact with the supernatural, and through them Chinese sought to solicit divine aid as well as to exorcise the demons blamed for causing personal sicknesses and disasters. Over time, this notion of spirit agency became a central characteristic of the popular religion.

There is an interesting Shang concept of a high deity called *Shang-di,* "the Lord Above," regarded as so powerful that only the Shang rulers could petition him. The name signifies the elevation of one Shang ancestor to supreme status, though *Shang-di* endured subsequently in popular imagination as the superior deity who monitors and provides cosmic sanction for human behavior. (Modern Chinese Protestants have used the term as a translation of "God.")

Thus, the diffuse religion found later in East Asia stems from beliefs prevalent in early China: the organic view of an interconnected universe, one peopled by spirits including dead ancestors, and the belief that unseen forces in heaven and on earth could be influenced by the petitions of shamans, oracle readers, and kings.

Formative Era: Zhou, Chin, and Han Dynasties (1122 BCE–220 CE)

The millennium from the Zhou dynasty (1122–221 BCE) until the fall of the Han (206 BCE–220 CE) was "formative" in the sense that during this period most of the ideas and practices inherited from the past were developed in more systematic forms and recorded for the first time in textual compilations. It is also in this era that the great sages arose whose teachings would so strongly influence not only the Chinese elite but the entire region.

The practices surrounding ancestor veneration, the worship of deities, and the important role of the spirit medium all spread as the population of China increased and dispersed into the Yangtze River basin and further southward. Some extensions of early concepts can be noted. There was the development of *yin-yang* theory and the five substances theory (*wu-xing*: water, fire, wood, metal, earth) to order observations of nature and natural signs. The cult of *Tu-di Gong*, the "earth ruler" who controls fertility, became widespread among the largely agricultural population. By Han times, reflecting the growing rationalization of state law in Chinese society, Tu-di was addressed in legalistic petitions.

At court and among commoners, Chinese polytheistic theology regarded the deities as neither good nor evil but as potentially both: they can be agents of illness and disaster as well as the bearers of blessings. Most of the notable deities by the late Zhou were viewed with both hope and fear, as with the Lord of the Yellow River, whose waters usually bring lush harvests, and yet it is well known that floods can cause widespread death

Terra-cotta warriors, unearthed from an imperial tomb outside Xi'an, China, had been placed with the emperor to serve him in the afterlife.

and destruction. The popular view of well-disposed deities pitted against chaos-disposed demons is one that contrasts strongly with views of the elite that emphasized rationalism or mysticism.

Ancestor veneration developed further in the formative era, with more elaborate concepts and practices surfacing regarding the afterlife. The tomb became the key place connecting the living and the dead. Texts found in excavated tombs mention belief in a soul that survives into an afterlife, calling it a *chao-hun* ("cloud soul"). With the notable dead were buried objects that would be useful to a revived soul, including ritual vessels for consumption (such as wine flasks).

By the Han era, texts deposited in the tombs suggest the notion that a supreme overlord, called *Tian di*, keeps records on each individual. Tomb scrolls detail personal acts that seem intended to verify celestial records and petition that the deceased be released from blame for any evil conduct. The belief that proper tombs can facilitate beneficial exchanges between living and dead grew stronger, as rulers had texts compiled to describe the proper rites, and these practices were then widely adopted across Chinese society.

The Zhou era was marked by considerable political instability and militarism. Regional states endlessly vied for control of territory and revenues, their rulers and officials showing little regard for moral order or respect for human life. Yet individuals arose who tried to formulate the principles on which a just society could be established and by which humane leaders could be guided. These ideas would become the central pillars of East Asian life. The emergence of these visionaries at roughly the same time as the Greek philosophers and Indian sages makes them part of the world's "axial age," so-called because future history turned as a result of the teachings originating then. Those who advocated individualistic retreat, learning from the natural world, and noninterference by the state as the best way to ensure humanity's flourishing were called Daoists. Those who wished to cultivate their own humanity through disciplined learning, ritual practice, humility, and active social service were called Confucians.

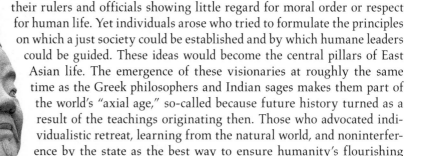

Image of Master K'ung, whose Western name, Confucius, was coined by early Jesuit missionaries.

Confucius and the Literati Tradition

Although one of the most influential figures in world history, Master K'ung (551–479 BCE) failed to realize his own goal of securing an influential position as a state minister. He was a most gifted, inspired teacher, and because his students collected and passed down his oral teachings to their own students, his ideas took hold. Confucius developed the concepts of righteousness and of *ren*, a term that has many shades of meaning, but captures the sense of "being fully human." The chief means to ren was *li*, which consisted of ethical propriety, good manners, and the cultivation of traditional ritual performances on musical instruments, in sacrifices, and in ancestor veneration.

The early Confucians imagined a male-led world, and their ideal was the *jun-zi*, a cultivated gentleman who learns from his teacher in youth and then continues to study constantly, both to develop his virtue and to serve others.

The most important aspect of the li is the individual's conduct within the family. Here the central principle is filial conduct (*xiao*). The key domain for xiao is the bond between child and parent, a relationship that implies mutual obligations on both parties within a hierarchical framework. Protection and nurturing by a superior were rendered in return for selfless service and obedience. Classical Confucianism conceived of this bond as the fundamental human connection and identified four other bonds as extensions of it. These are the ties between husband and wife, between elder and younger brother, between friend and friend, and between ruler and minister. The entire set comprised the Five Hierarchical Relationships, which, properly served, were to lead the entire society toward harmony and "human flourishing." If xiao began with serving one's parents, it was to continue with serving one's ruler, thus bringing to maturity one's own character.

In East Asia, family metaphors are likewise applied to community, state, and heaven based upon this idea. Confucius' theory was that if those who ruled and ministered both followed and encouraged the society's adherence to maintaining these ideals, all would benefit and the state's harmony would be ensured. Through the *Analects*, the compilation of the master's teachings, anecdotes, and sayings, Confucius became a model for emulation for subsequent generations. The cultured human should be at ease while always showing careful respect; he is firm but kindhearted, an advocate for the practice of moderation who finds a natural balance in all endeavors. In one passage, the *Analects* describes Confucius' own search for the ideal:

> At fifteen I set my heart on learning; at thirty, I firmly took my stand; at forty I came to be free from doubts; at fifty I understood the decree of Heaven; at sixty my ear was attuned; at seventy I follow my heart's desire without overstepping the line."[1]

Although he is described as being unsure of the reality of the spirits, Confucius was emphatic on the need for individuals to develop a deep respect for others, as well as to establish harmony in the personalities of their immediate kin by performing the rituals of funerals and ancestor veneration.

The success of Confucius' teachings was largely due to their systematic and forceful advocacy by several great disciples, notably Master Meng (or Mencius, 371–289 BCE) and Master Xun (298–238 BCE). The sayings of Mencius argue that human nature is essentially good, that humans are naturally compassionate, dutiful, courteous, and inclined toward learning. Mencius also developed the Confucian view that the well-being of society depends upon the virtue of the rulers, and that it is the state's responsibility to ensure the flourishing of its citizens. Another especially influential theory of Mencius applied Confucian theory to the destiny of a state: if a dynasty rules by virtue, then it receives the Mandate of Heaven, an authorization that can be revoked if rulers cease to be virtuous.

Master Xun, the third of the classical Confucian sages, proposed a more pessimistic, mechanistic, and hard-edged application of Master K'ung's ideas. In his view, humans are inherently antisocial and the universe turns on impersonal forces. But since people can be trained, once shown the good, they will inherently adopt practices that lead in that direction. Hence, Xun turned Confucians toward the careful study of the past, its ancient sages, language itself, and the texts that record the history of human experience.

By the end of the formative era, the two interrelated elements of the Confucian tradition were established: "inner sagehood" and "outer nobility." Dynasties recorded their histories, officials and the discontented argued about the Mandate of Heaven, scholars revered the past and sought to both safeguard and study its records, and all looked to the earliest sages to model their own lives. We must also note that the notion of Confucius as merely a human and this-worldly sage was not universal in early China. By the late Han, literature had already appeared across the empire describing him as a demigod.

Early Daoist Philosophy

The formative era saw many other teachers who proposed alternative philosophies to meet the needs of organizing society harmoniously. Yet the most important and long-enduring critique of Confucian doctrine came from those who argued that social relations would be harmonious only after humanity had synchronized itself with nature and with the *Dao*, the mystical reality underlying it. In today's English, the name of this school is rendered "Daoist."

Daoist ideas were being expressed in antiquity at roughly the same time as those of Confucius, and the first great expression of Daoism is the terse and poetic *Daodejing* (*Tao Te Ching*). This often-translated work, traditionally attributed to an anonymous "Old Sage," or Lao Zi (Lao Tzu), aims to express the nature of the Dao, while paradoxically beginning with the proviso that "the true Dao" cannot be spoken or adequately defined. Various cryptic passages suggest that the Dao that pervades all reality can be truly known only through silence and through experiences that transcend words.

In this philosophical system, Dao is the prime source of creation, from which the yin and yang forces emerge in ever-shifting harmonies. Dao determines all things and flows naturally as the mysterious and spontaneous energy (*de*) of the universe, functioning without the will or purpose of a creator god. To experience the Dao, one must let go and pursue the path of noninterference (*wu-wei*) as in Lao Zi's dictum, "Do nothing and nothing will be left undone." The best teacher is (to use the example of the *Daodejing*) water that flows freely with the natural forces and in all circumstances, yet can overcome all obstacles.

The Daoists felt that the Confucians harmed society through imposing rules and artificial practices that interfered with humanity's natural inclinations. Their political message was to return to primal simplicity, with the state interfering as little as possible with the lives of the people. The highest calling for humans, argued the Daoists, is not state service but retreat into the mountains where the reality of the Dao can be felt most clearly.

The second Daoist classic, the *Zhuang Zi,* is attributed to and named after a sage who lived several centuries later, *Zhuang Zi* (Chuang Tzu, 365–290 BCE). Through lively parables and mind-boggling paradoxes, his sayings explore the mysterious reality of the Dao in everyday human experiences. The most famous example perhaps is his meditation on waking from a dream of being a butterfly. He asks: Which is "real"? Was Zhuang Zi dreaming of being a butterfly or is the human Zhuang Zi instead merely that butterfly's dream? This text also explores death and advocates accepting the changes the mysterious Dao brings, including the naturalness of death's transforming us into other life forms. Such acceptance is the necessary step toward experiencing transcendent freedom.

Daoist mysticism provided a balance against the bounded rules and regulations of strict Confucianism, offering a rich lore of parables as well as spiritual guidance to those who retreated from government service or active social life. Daoist refuge is found in nature and the natural inspired subsequent artists, including poets and painters.

Deity from a Daoist temple, where immortals are worshiped to secure blessings.

"Religious Daoism" (Dao Jiao)

Daoism exists as a religious tradition as well as in the philosophical form we have just discussed. The tradition we refer to as religious Daoism consists of many different schools with different spiritual disciplines. All sought immortality and to emulate sages who ride the clouds like dragons and reside in paradises on islands in the eastern seas. There were two main avenues to reach this goal. The first required meditation aimed at strengthening and multiplying the life force (*qi*), typically through breathing exercises, fasting, and sexual practices. This inner alchemy (*nei-tan*) creates a subtle but undying spiritual essence that can survive the gross body's death. A second path involved the study of alchemy, the art of transforming such substances as mercury and gold into an outer elixir (*wai-tan*) that can, when ingested, give birth to an "inner child" whose body and soul are invincible to decay or death. Doubtless the Daoist mystics and alchemists, a minority of single-minded teachers who lived in secluded retreats, contributed to the development of Chinese science and medicine, as well as to the martial arts traditions, all of which applied Daoist terms and theories to specific and more worldly endeavors. Religious Daoism also focused on temples dedicated to the divine immortals who were requested to help in practical matters such as making the rain fall, helping with the harvest, or in vanquishing troublesome spirits.

Daoism Traditions: Basic Beliefs

Philosophical Daoism evolved from the *Daodejing* and through subsequent thinkers, and indeed, certain basic ideas from this elite tradition remain important across East Asia. First, there is in Daoism the "organic" notion that humanity is interconnected in a web of interacting natural forces, some visible, some unseen, all shifting and reversing direction when they reach their apex. The opposing yet complementary yin-yang forces became the means of comprehending and analyzing the universe, and its affect on human destiny. Reality is best perceived through this interconnection, for in this movement the dynamic power of the mysterious and determining Dao can be discerned from moment to moment. The classic text describing "the state of the moment" is the *Yi-Jing*, and it has helped East Asians determine the various combinations of yin and yang forces at work in a given setting. Perhaps Song era

A recluse in the mountains. Hermits like the one in this fourteenth-century Chinese painting looked to nature for inspiration and as a source of primal energy (qi).

landscape paintings influenced by Daoism best convey to outsiders this sense of human beings finding their proper place in the vast natural world: amid the great mountains and flowing waters, humans—inevitably dwarfed by the landscape—can find transcendent harmony.

The second central Daoist notion is that some individuals can attain a state of ultimate transformation, transcending mortality via alchemical, dietary, or meditative practices that impart the power to know and control unseen forces. The human condition is thus one of great positive potential; the human body is a potentially perfectible vessel, even though those who attain immortality are few. Here, Daoists join with Confucians in seeing the world as redeemable through human agency, with nature occupying the roles of humanity's home and teacher. In China, then, what many other religions refer to as secular is seen as sacred.

The third Daoist conviction is that the pursuit of simplicity is essential for spiritual development as well as for the betterment of society. Only the "natural person" who "goes with the flow" (*wu-wei*), avoiding unnatural action, can find the truth, and only a society whose citizens live in a simple manner can find true peace and justice. Daoism thus, with Buddhism, provided a counterculture to the Confucian establishment, one that served those who wished to withdraw from society or to critique the excesses of those in power, and even, at times, bolstering a rebel group's intention to overthrow the regime.

State Religion: The First Confucian Epoch (220 BCE–200 CE)

The first full unification of China—from central Asia to the eastern coast— was brought about by the first Qin emperor, who instituted a central bureaucracy and state religion. The latter served, in part, to express state unity while also seeking to harmonize the forces of nature with imperial rule. China's first emperor, though making good on many of his lofty ambitions, obsessively sought personal immortality through Daoist alchemy and ruthlessly suppressed viewpoints he considered deviant. His Mandate of Heaven lasted only fifteen years (221–206 BCE).

The next unification of China occurred under the Han, who established an imperial university and examination system (121 BCE) that was based exclusively upon Confucian teachings and texts. By the later Han (c. 175 CE) the content of the Five Confucian Classics had been officially established for the first time. Synthesizing treatises drawing upon them guided the spiritual cultivation of Chinese life thereafter. Once fixed in literary form and connected with the authority of Confucius, the Five Classics provided the literati of subsequent centuries with a multidisciplinary and holistic perspective on humanity. The canon comprises the *Yi-Jing* (*Book of Changes*), *Shu Jing* (*Book of Documents*), *Shi Jing* (*Book of Poetry*), *Li Jing* (*Book of Rites*),

Lao Zi on an ox. The sage of Daoism depicted in a Ming era painting.

With a sacred mushroom in his pocket, a Daoist immortal plays his flute in paradise.

and an historical work that records events in early Chinese states for the purpose of assessing blame and praise. The classics promoted a tradition of learning from the past to guide future governance, and they supported the view that for full development, a human must integrate historical, social, political, and metaphysical awareness.

The state religion developed in the Han placed the emperor as chief priest, advised by Confucian experts on ritual performance. The integration of Daoist thought in imperial religion is seen as well in the reliance on specialists who used Daoist techniques to interpret signs in the natural world. On behalf of the kingdom, the emperor alone could sacrifice to the spirits of the departed imperial ancestors; as the Son of Heaven, he worshiped heaven and earth as his symbolic parents and as the primary cosmic spirits. The emperor held the Confucian Mandate of Heaven as long as he acted for the well-being of the empire; earthquakes, eclipses, and unusual weather were interpreted as signs that heaven might be withdrawing its mandate.

Being Human: The Individual, the Family, and the Ancestors

The Confucian worldview fostered a sense of the self as a center for multiple relationships, with the most fundamental determined by the individual's gender, generational location in the family, and status in the empire. The notion of individualism that dominates the West and has spread across the globe through modernization is quite the opposite from this East Asian understanding. According to the norms of filial piety, the young owe obedience to parents, women to men, citizens to rulers.

The Confucian vision is that society will be in maximum harmony if individuals mute their individualistic desires to conform to the dictates of the Five Hierarchical Relationships, listed earlier. The ideal was for all the family to benefit in old age from the reciprocities that required their deference earlier in life, and to have their political obedience rewarded by heaven's blessings. To support this understanding, Daoism contributed the belief that since human beings are a combination of heaven (*yang*) and earth (*yin*), which in their exact balance determine gender, personality, and health, they must pursue harmony in their social relations and so respect these primary relations.

All persons are also seen as benefiting after death from the Confucian ordering of life, since the living descendants are expected to attend to all the necessary rites to ensure the best possible destiny in the afterlife. Indigenous beliefs going back to the Shang era (1500 BCE) later merged with Buddhist notions to create a composite (and not completely integrated) understanding of the individual's fate after death. What emerged in China (and was accepted in Korea and Japan, too) was a belief in the concept of *karma* as known from Buddhism and an understanding that after death all souls undergo processing in a netherworld. Here divine magistrates carefully calculate karma by means of rigorous bookkeeping methods, then send the soul on to its proper destiny. In this way indigenous Chinese and Buddhist ideas coexisted.

Modern Chinese family grave site in Singapore, sited and designed in accordance with the principles of feng shui. Here family members gather twice yearly to feast and make offerings to their ancestors.

Buddhist rituals for manipulating the death passage were developed throughout East Asia; in China, institutional Daoism created these rites, as well. In Japan, the great Buddhist monasteries included within their vast estates sites for family graves where the remains are kept and where ritual offerings can be made for departed kin.

In conception and in practice, then, ancestors live on in the East Asian family's presence and receive ongoing ritual attention: in the grave, in an ancestral tablet (located in the home altar or clan temple), and potentially in the underworld, especially in the first years after death. The Korean and Chinese practice of burning paper replicas of items considered useful in the underworld is thought to send relief to loved ones who are waiting out an intermediate state before reincarnation.

By the end of the Han, after centuries of state support, Confucian ethics centered on hierarchy and mutual obligation had thoroughly permeated Chinese society through proverbs, storytelling, theater, and songs. The key elements of the "diffuse religion" were widely shared and had come to include the notions of yin-yang theory, geomancy (*feng shui*), the major deities of the pantheon, and the understanding of the multiple souls. The Confucian literati were also convinced that they could unite the society around a common ritual discipline, with ancestor rites the universal and civilizing norm. The early Confucian sage, Master Xun explicitly recognized that people had different views of these rites when he wrote

Among gentlemen, rites for the dead are taken as the way of man;
Among the common people, they are taken as matters involving demons.[2]

Development of the Multiple Traditions in Post-Han China, Korea, and Japan

We now move into the fractured China of the post-Han centuries (220–617), a time when the Confucian tradition so tied to Han rule fell into disfavor, just as Buddhist missionaries moved into and secured a permanent place in China for their faith. It is in this period, as well, that Japan and Korea enter the region's religious history.

Expansion of Buddhism

The expansion and domestication of Buddhism from India into East Asia are the greatest cultural conquests in world history, matched in importance only by the conversion to Christianity of the peoples of Europe and the Americas and the conversion to Islam of the peoples of Eurasia. Buddhist monks reached China on the Silk Road through central Asia by 120 CE, and later over the sea routes. Once established in China's major urban and cultural centers, Buddhism spread to Korea by 372 and then to Japan from Korea by 552.

Mahayana Buddhism entered Asia through merchants and missionary monks but became firmly established owing to the patronage of emperors and aristocracy. Most East Asians came to believe in karma and worshiped the Buddha and celestial bodhisattvas. Many eventually accepted enlightenment as the highest spiritual goal.

Chinese literati from the beginning recognized Buddhism's deviance from Confucian values and criticized it on several grounds, including its rejection of family life and service to one's kin, and the worship of deities who originated from "barbarian" peoples outside China. The Buddhist ideal of monastic retreat for personal enlightenment was construed as an antisocial behavior. But in splintered China after the fall of the Han, the literati had no strong state backing. In Korea and Japan, the literati tradition itself was newly introduced; Buddhist monks and nuns, however, still had to win over supporters of the local deity traditions, who attributed national misfortunes and natural disasters to the acceptance of Buddhism within the nation.

The Confucian anti-Buddhist arguments would be recycled at various times, but for almost all of its first five hundred years in East Asia, Buddhism was widely and deeply incorporated into the region's religious life, finding support in the imperial courts and eventually among all segments of society, from philosophers to farmers. As time went on, Chinese, Korean, and Japanese monks would formulate their own interpretations of the many teachings, creating distinctive East Asian versions of Buddhism.

The Institutional Development of Religious Daoism

Another effect of Buddhism's rise to prominence was to motivate the hitherto disparate adherents of Daoism to systematize their texts and teachings and to create institutions modeled after Buddhist monasteries. The regularized meditative regimes and elaborate rituals that eventually developed in the Daoist monasteries gave individuals many avenues for being Daoist in their spiritual development and for propitiating local gods.

By 300, there were several branches of religious Daoism that had formalized early practices. Guo Hong (283–363) was the most prominent figure who was known for his seeking to harmonize the tradition with Confucianism. Beginning with the notion that heaven's greatest creation is life itself, he argued that pursuing longevity and immortality must be the greatest human goal. Guo prescribed a very specific path to that goal based upon moral goodness, social service, and alchemy utilizing gold (which neither corrodes nor diminishes if buried or melted) and cinnabar (a red mercury ore that keeps changing as long as it is heated). This "inner alchemy" culminated in ingesting the perfectly refined substances, reversing Lao Zi's formula of creation: through this pursuit, one turns from the myriad things to the three—essence (*jing*), life energy (*qi*), and spirit (*shen*) (each "fixed" through alchemical practices), to the two—yin and yang in perfect harmony (through taming the thought processes via meditation), to the one—a state of eternal union with the Dao.

Revived Daoism competed with Buddhism for favor at the imperial courts, and devotees among the emperors spread the reformed and newly organized tradition across China. The new monastic traditions strengthened Daoist traditions. In 471, Master Lu Xinjing (406–477) completed the first cataloging and organization of the Daoist scriptures. He found 1,226 texts for inclusion in this canon, which he called *The Three Caves*. Later commentaries expanded the tradition's literature by thousands of additional works. Organized Daoism never penetrated Korea or Japan through monasticism, but organized Buddhism did. We now turn to this important cultural export from China.

Early Korean Buddhism

For the first millennium of the Korean state, Buddhism dominated the spiritual formation of the nation. Mahayana Buddhism entered the Korean peninsula through missions by Chinese monks. A Chinese monk ordained the first Korean monks in 384, and by 554 its monks and artisans had brought Buddhism to Japan along with a wave of Korean immigrants.

From roughly 700, the Korean version of the classical Buddhist formula of "state-protection Buddhism" was in place. That is, the state protected the tradition in return for monks employing rituals by which Buddhism benefited the state. Lavish patronage enabled Buddhism to flourish; all the Chinese scholastic schools were introduced, and Koreans journeyed to China, where some became influential monks. In Korea, the scholarly assimilation of the faith led not to competition but to attempts to find common ground. As a result, under the Silla dynasty, Korean Buddhism became the most ecumenical in Asia.

Religion Under the Early Japanese Imperial State

In Japan, as elsewhere, Buddhism began among the elite, who saw in it a means to unite a fragmented land. Indeed, it was under the royal sponsorship of Prince Shotoku (d. 622) that Buddhism became the state religion. By 741, an edict called for officials to establish a Buddhist monastery and temple in every province, enroll at least twenty monks and ten nuns, and recite texts and perform rituals for the benefit of emperor and state.

But Buddhism was not the only foreign belief system to shape the development of Japan: Confucian texts and teachers from China were also influential in the early courts. A seventh-century reform established a Confucian bureaucracy modeled after that of China. Daoist ideas of natural harmony and energy flow, both in the environment and within the person, along with yin-yang analysis, were part of this broad cultural influence. Neither a Daoist priesthood nor a monastic network, however, was ever established. Moreover, the Japanese never ceased to worship their own distinct divinities, believing the islands themselves to have been established by these native deities, the *Kami*, who remain eternally present. This religious tradition is called Shinto.

The Shinto Pantheon of Japan

In many respects, the Shinto tradition in Japan shares basic assumptions and practices regarding deities found throughout East Asia. Shamanism also

Wood block print of the sun goddess Amaterasu, legendary progenitor of the Japanese people.

developed in Japan, giving access to the gods as well as to the ancestors of the devout. Pilgrimages to mountains thought to be divine abodes were common. However, as Shinto mythology developed, it was disseminated, systematized, and adapted by the early state. These accounts portrayed Japan as a unique spiritual territory filled with the distinctive deities called *kami*. The existence of an extensive set of legends focused on the kami enabled the Shinto priests to retain and relate to a unique pantheon. This helps explain why the Japanese, despite the importation of many other aspects of the country's religious life from China and Korea, were less ready to adopt Chinese deities and folk traditions.

The Shinto pantheon is headed by *Amaterasu*, the kami of the sun, credited in Japanese myth with having aided in the creation of the country and with being a progenitor of the royal family. Other kami exist in profusion. Some are associated with the natural forces of wind, thunder, lightning, and rain; some are thought to dwell in natural objects such as mountains, rivers, trees, and rocks; some are ancestral spirits; and some dwell in certain animals such as cows and foxes. Exponents of Shinto emphasize the "this-worldly" and positive perception of life, society, and nature that their indigenous faith has imparted. Shinto shrines often display mirrors as symbols of Amaterasu and for their symbolic meaning: free from dust and capable of reflecting images with natural clarity, these symbolize the Shinto ideals of purity and brilliance. For this reason, too, Shinto shrines are traditionally located in bright, sunny areas. In the modern period, the state regulated and reformed Shinto for it to become, as we shall see, a vehicle for modernization.

Amaterasu: Kami of the Sun

In Shinto mythology, a primordial couple creates the physical world and the numerous deities who inhabit it. Most important among them were the moon goddess, a male earth god, and his sister the sun goddess, Amaterasu. In the earliest myths, distressed by impertinence and rudeness from her brother, Amaterasu hid in a cave, darkening the world. Only after the other *kami* gathered offerings, put on entertainments, and attracted her with a mirror did she restore light to the world. The reformed earth god and his ally, the *kami* of Izumo prefecture, then blessed the people of the islands of Japan. A grandson of Amaterasu, having received training from the gods and blessings from the Izumo *kami*, was designated the divine ruler of the nation, and he established the chief shrine for Amaterasu on the seashore at Ise, with a mirror as her symbol. Most Shinto shrines include a mirror, where devotees can honor the sun goddess.

Classical Imperial China (645–1271 CE)

With the era of the T'ang (618–907), when China was again unified after centuries of fragmentation that followed the fall of the Han, Buddhism reached its maximum development on the continent. Early on, Buddhism in northern China appealed to non-Han conquerors and in the south succeeded through popular and charismatic monastic preachers. But in the T'ang era, there developed more unified, panregional monastic networks among seven doctrinal schools, and to interpret the confusing welter of texts from India, each school took as authoritative a different source of the Buddha's highest teachings.

T'ang China, with its capital in Chang'an (modern Xi'an), was the world's most advanced civilization of its time. Living within the high city walls were merchants from across the Asian world, distributed in communities of Nestorian Christians, Hindus, Manicheans, Zoroastrians, and Muslims. These resident aliens mixed with Buddhists and Daoists, who had their own numerous monasteries and temples. The wealth from trade, efficient taxation, and imperial patronage underwrote a golden age that found expression in all the fine arts while spreading Buddhist influences and religious practices across the empire and into both Korea and Japan. Adventurous Chinese monks, such as the renowned Xuan Zang (d. 664), even traveled to India in search of additional texts and teachers.

However, in 845, edicts by Emperor Wu-zong abruptly and destructively halted an era of religious toleration in China. The emperor was partly motivated by considerations of manpower and finances: with the success of Buddhism, more lands were being donated to the monastic community, thereby losing their taxable status; and ever more men and women were joining Buddhist orders, exempting themselves both from taxation and, in the case of the men, from military service. Wu-zong's second motivation was religious. He was an ardent Daoist and eager to advance the Daoist tradition's standing.

Within one year, Wu-zong forced 250,000 Buddhist monastics to return to lay life and confiscated all but forty-nine monasteries throughout the empire. Officials destroyed sacred texts by the tens of thousands and melted down the images for the imperial mint. Although this aggressively anti-Buddhist policy was reversed by the next emperor, the damage was quite severe: Buddhism's predominance across China's landscape was drastically reduced, never again to rise to its pre-845 pinnacle.

The later T'ang was a time marked by the resurgence of Confucianism. This tradition had continued to guide the familial life of commoners, and Confucius himself was used as a symbol of national unity. The development of Confucianism as a concern of philosophers waned, however. The literati tradition's triumph, through a selective assimilation of Buddhist and Daoist elements, lay ahead.

Song Dynasty: The Second Epoch of Confucianism (960–1279)

The so-called Second Epoch of Confucianism erected for the literati a profound philosophical edifice that rivaled that of Buddhism and Daoism while supporting the older social ideology of human relatedness based upon hierarchy, age, and gender. Thus, Confucianism again moved to the center of Chinese religious life, a development that occurred later in Korea and Japan, as well. Significantly, the Song dynasty administrators restored mastery of Confucian learning as the basis for winning a position in its burgeoning civil service. This measure, coupled with relative neglect of Buddhism by the authorities, provided a strong inducement for a return to the Confucian classics as a subject for study and further scholarship. As the best minds of the day once again were drawn into reinterpreting the indigenous tradition, private academies that instilled virtue and erudition flowered. In addition, anthologies of Confucian teachings compiled by leading Song literati were influential not only in China but across the entire East Asian region.

The tradition's great "Second Master" was Zhu Xi (also written Chu Hsi) (1130–1200). The works compiled and commented upon by him, entitled *Jinsi Lu* ("Reflections of Things at Hand"), were immensely influential. Zhu Xi gave students a curricular order in which to study the classics and powerfully expressed long-standing polemics against Buddhism and Daoism. Zhu Xi also added brilliant reinterpretations of Confucian doctrines, thus codifying the thoroughgoing system of thought that has been labeled "neo-Confucianism" in the West.

Despite its apparent criticism directed against Daoism and Buddhism, the neo-Confucians in fact were strongly influenced by both. Of equal importance in securing the success of neo-Confucianism was Zhu Xi's compilation of a ritual manual that imparted Confucian procedures and cogent rationales for all life-cycle rites, giving non-Buddhist and non-Daoist alternatives on which the Chinese people could order their lives. This ritual text, like *Jinsi Lu*, was influential across East Asia.

Neo-Confucianism's strength was that it provided both the individual and the state with a convincing framework for understanding the world. Song thinkers argued that Confucianism was built upon the interconnected unity of humanity with the natural world. They tried to understand perceived phenomena through a series of polarities that associated yin-yang forces with the trinity of heaven, earth, and humanity. The neo-Confucian philosophers emphasized that education was needed to perfect human awareness of li, and that inner meditative cultivation (a borrowing from Buddhism), which Zhu Xi called "investigating the nature of things," was needed to perfect the qi. Almost all the neo-Confucians assumed the reality of karma as one of life's causal agents.

Neo-Confucian Theories of Order, Hierarchy, and Relatedness

The established Confucian notion of the self that became reinforced in family norms and in state law is decidedly not that of the isolated individual but of the person as "a center of relatedness." It can be understood in terms of a series of concentric circles, with the assumption that to reach their highest potential, persons must act harmoniously within their families, local communities, and states, and with heaven beyond. This scheme clearly implies that engagement in culture and community is necessary for both the person and humanity overall to flourish. As the Confucian classic, the *Great Learning*, states:

> The ancients who wished to bring order to their states would first regulate their families. Those who wished to regulate their families would first cultivate their personal lives. Those who wished to cultivate their personal lives would first rectify their minds. Those who wished to rectify their minds would first make their intentions sincere.

> Those who wished to make their intentions sincere would first extend their knowledge. The extension of knowledge consists of the investigation of things. . . . Only when the personal life is cultivated, the family will be regulated; when the family is regulated, the state will be in order; and when the state is in order, there will be peace throughout the world.[3]

The elaboration of meditative practices and multidisciplinary studies by the neo-Confucian masters established a rich tradition designed to develop the individual's integral relations with each circle (see illustration):

Heaven (World (Nation (Community (Family (SELF)

Such later figures as Zhang Zai (1020–1077) went on to combine this concentric conception with the Daoist ideal of finding "full humanity" by merging with the cosmos:

> Heaven is my father and Earth is my mother, and even such a small creature as I finds an intimate place in their midst. Therefore that which fills the universe I regard as my body and that which directs the universe I consider as my nature. All people are my brothers and sisters, and all things are my companions.[4]

The popular convergence of the classical traditions in late traditional China was inspired by Zhu Xi, Zhang Zai, and other figures who sought harmony by learning from all orientations. The "diffuse religion" still extant in contemporary East Asia stems from their brilliant syntheses of ancient sources.

The Development of Buddhism, Daoism, and Confucianism in Korea and Japan

In Korea, Buddhism flourished under imperial support once the country had been united under the Silla dynasty (668–918). Ties to Chinese Buddhism were strong, and almost all of the Chinese scholastic sects had Korean counterparts. Korean monks were notable in China, and their commentaries on major texts were studied in both Japan and Tibet. Yet over time, Korean monks were most successful at finding harmony rather than division in their development of the tradition from the various schools and teachings.

Religion in the Koryo dynasty (918–1392) continued in this mode. Uniquely Korean was the dominance of the Chogye-chong branch of Son

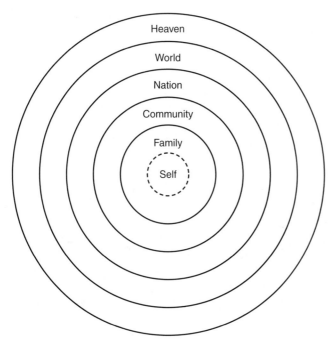

Two-dimensional representation of Confucian concentricity.

(Ch'an/Zen) Buddhism, which was to become the most influential in subsequent Korean Buddhist history. During this period the scholastic schools introduced from China were assimilated and merged into new entities that more closely reflected Korean culture.

The assimilation of Buddhism in Japan had ecumenical aspects as well. It had continued strongly with the movement of the capital to Kyoto by 800 CE, as various elements of Mahayana Buddhism and Daoist theories of yin-yang imported from China were effectively integrated with Shinto practices to meet the needs of an expanding state.

The later Kamakura era (1185–1333) ushered in almost seven hundred years of rule by military leaders who usurped the power of the emperor to establish a social system closely akin to that of European feudalism. This period was one of widespread contact with China, as trade grew and Buddhist monks were instrumental in bringing new ordination lineages from the two schools that had survived the persecutions in post-T'ang China: Pure Land and Ch'an/Zen. The notable monks of this era also brought exponents of neo-Confucian learning, literature, and the arts to Japan.

The disorder and suffering in the Kamakura also led to dramatic changes in Japanese religions, especially Buddhism. It was widely believed that the world had entered into a period of *mappo*, or decline, in which human capacity for spiritual pursuit had become degraded. This perception was used to justify new interpretations of Buddhism appropriate for this degraded age. Thus, the Kamakura religious leaders in Japan established the framework for subsequent schools that remained relatively stable until the early modern era.

The most popular Buddhist school was Pure Land, and in Chapter Seven we encountered its polemical advocate Shinran (1173–1262). Shinran and other Pure Land exponents taught that an individual's salvation was completely in the hands of the Buddha of the Pure Land, whom they called Amida, from the Sanskrit name Amitabha. They emphasized the practice of repeating Amida's name and the belief that faith alone could achieve nirvana realization in the mappo era. Shinran ended the requirement of monastic celibacy, and Pure Land remains the largest Buddhist school in Japan today.

The second new school established during the Kamakura era was Zen, and it, too, was brought from China by two Japanese monks, Eisai (1141–1215) and Dogen (1200–1253). In adopting sitting meditation, mind puzzles (koans), and unusual teaching methods, Zen masters created an innovative lineage of Buddhist practice. It also was very traditionalist, however, in rejecting the concept of mappo and resisting the other schools' radical simplification of Buddhism into mere ritual repetition and reliance upon faith. Zen teachers insisted that each individual had to win his or her own salvation on the meditation mat through persistence and self-power alone.

Another remarkable Buddhist leader of this era was Nichiren (1222–1282), a monk who opposed the Pure Land schools and in fact all the other Buddhist orders. He attributed the decline in Japanese life to the neglect of the *Lotus Sutra,* which he viewed as containing the supreme teaching. The Nichiren-shu advocated chanting the name of this text as the means for personal transformation as well as national renewal. (It is a practice continued to the present day in the Soka Gakkai, a modern Nichiren-derived school that now spans the globe.)

In the Kamakura era, ideas regarding Shinto–Buddhist accommodation were heard from both sides: Shinto exponents argued that the Buddhas and bodhisattvas were really indigenous gods, and the Buddhists built Shinto shrines in their monastic courtyards, consistent with the view that the kami were in fact protectors or bodhisattvas. This urge to harmonize the various spiritual traditions was one that Japan shared with Korea.

East Asian Religions in the Late Classical Era (1400–1800)

The four centuries preceding the modern era show few religious innovations across East Asia. It was a time when philosophies of interest to the literati were more fully commented upon, printed, and disseminated, as in the case of neo-Confucianism in Japan. For Buddhism, this era is characterized by unsteadiness in both state support and in spiritual vitality, with Korea the most prominent among those acting to reduce the political power of Buddhism.

Across East Asia, the diffuse religion remained central, as ancestor ritualism, local cults to important deities, and the role of the spirit mediums defined the religious field in cities and villages alike. For Ming era China (1368–1644), the popular text *Feng Shen Yan-yi* ("The Canonization of the Gods") was especially influential in promulgating the idea of the Chinese gods, comprising an orderly hierarchy that included Buddhas, gods, and local spirits. Throughout China, a standard organization for the state's official religion was fixed in each province. There would be a Confucian temple with major disciples, a military temple featuring the war god Guan Yu and other notable heroes, and a city god, who supervises all the village earth gods.

"The Unity of the Three Traditions": Late Ming to Early Qing Eras in China

The Chinese emphasis on harmony was also extended to "the unity of the three faiths" (*san-jiao heyi*, still a widely used phrase) meaning Confucianism, Daoism, and Buddhism. Many philosophers who were committed to one of these faiths exclusively still argued that their tradition was superior in answering the fundamental spiritual questions. But more popular were teachers such as Jiao Hong (1540–1620) who regarded all three teachings as in fact "a single teaching," stating that each merely uses separate language to articulate its truth and that all three could and should be believed. There were also other expressions of this era's delicate balance of combination and compartmentalization between these faiths:

> Use Buddhism to rule the mind, Daoism to rule the body, Confucianism to rule the world.[5]
> —*Emperor Xiaozong (1163–1189)*

> Although the Three Teachings are different, in the arguments they put forward, they are One.[6]
> —*Liu Mi (active 1324)*

> If someone is a Confucian, give him Confucius; if he is a Daoist, give him Lao Zi; if he is a Buddhist, give him Shakyamuni; if he isn't any of them, give him their unity.[7]
> —*Lin Zhao'en (1517–1598)*

Among Confucians who most powerfully conveyed this ecumenical ethos was Wang Yangming (1472–1529), whose view of the "true gentleman" was based on the assumption that everyone can know the good and that "self perfection" means knowing this goodness to the maximum. Wang argued, in language mirroring the "all beings have the Buddha nature" doctrine of Mahayana Buddhism, that all humans have the potential to achieve self-perfection, since all share a primordial awareness:

> Forming one body with Heaven, Earth, and the myriad things is not only true of the great man. Even the heart-mind of the small man is no different. . . . Therefore when he sees a child about to fall into the well, he cannot help feeling alarm and commiseration.[8]

Buddhism by the end of the Ming dynasty (1368–1644) had worked out its permanent place in Chinese civilization, as its monastic leaders taught Buddhist doctrine in ways to ensure that there would never be grounds for another imperial persecution. We thus find influential teachers such as Chu-hong (1535–1615) preaching that the essence of Buddhism was social activism as expressed through charity and moral action. He also emphasized that to be a filial child or a loyal subject was the first step in becoming a "good Buddhist." This view was expressed by many Chinese revitalizers.

The Ming dynasty also saw the beginning of regular contact with Europe, first with the Portuguese in 1514. With these traders and then with the first wave of missionaries, the Chinese found little to admire and much to resent in

Buddhism and Neo-Confucianism in a Popular Ming Tale

The *Journey to the West* (or "monkey story") written by the Confucian scholar Wu Cheng-en (1500–1582) is a prime example of the Ming era harmonization of the "three faiths." It recounts the journey of the great Buddhist monk Xuan Zang (d. 664) to search for texts in India. In this dangerous quest, he is assisted by the Monkey King, Sun Wukong, a figure from the Chinese folk pantheon. While ostensibly the account of a great Buddhist monk's journey, the incidents in the long tale (spanning four hefty volumes in English translation) are employed to teach self-discipline—a personal trait valued by both traditions—to the Monkey King and Confucian wisdom to the monk. In many episodes, the success of Xuan Zang's mission depends on the Monkey King's aid and on the monk's timely learning of the ways of the world. Translated into opera and folk ballads, the monkey story became one of China's most popular narratives, its major characters defining important personality stereotypes while conveying the pattern of accommodation under Confucian dominance accomplished by the literati elite of the Ming.

The Monkey King leads the monk Xuan Zang and other companions, illustrating a scene from the Journey to the West.

the "barbaric manners" of their guests. In this early era of small-scale contact, failure to institute good relations with the Europeans or to attempt to understand the world beyond China set up the problematic and confrontational geopolitical environment of the colonial era.

The Qing dynasty (1644–1912) brought outsiders again in control of China, this time in the form of the Manchurians, who continued most of the forms of state administration. Confucian imperial ritual remained central to the state, and mastery of the classics was the basis for the selection of the literati who ran it.

The strengthening of Confucian ideas and practices throughout all levels of Qing society occurred through the *Sheng-zhi tu* ("*Pictures of the Sage's Traces*"), captioned accounts of Confucius' life and exemplary tales of ethical practices. The stories appeared in a variety of media: on stone tablets installed in temples (Daoist as well as Buddhist), on silk paintings, and in inexpensive and widely disseminated block-printed books. Many versions on this theme appeared, offering alternative views of the great teacher. Some portrayed him as a human being living an exemplary ethical life, others described miracles and magic, while still others emphasized the sage's command to make great ritual exertions. Many of these publications were also exported to Japan, where they influenced the efflorescence of Confucian studies and related arts in the Tokugawa era (1600–1868).

Scenes from the Sheng-zhi tu, *depicting the manner of showing filial piety* (xiao).

Japan in the Time of the Shogun (Twelfth to Nineteenth Centuries)

In Japan during medieval and early modern times, there were no Daoist temples competing with institutional Buddhism or Shinto shrines, nor did the deities of "diffuse Chinese popular religion" find their way across the water. Instead, Shinto theologians presented the nation's deities in a uniquely Japanese pantheon, although the relationships between them varied by region and were not thoroughly systematized nationwide until the modern era.

Zen Buddhism, however, also exerted a strong ecumenical influence in the premodern era. The Zen school's strong relationship with China fostered studies in both the texts of Daoism and the Confucian classics. It also promoted the acceptance of the idea that Daoist concepts and Confucian morality could be combined. Zen, the vehicle for Japan's cultural elite, adopted art forms derived from China, but Japanese masters soon took them to new levels of originality in such fields as ink painting, poetry, and tea ceremony. Zen and the other Buddhist schools were closely tied to the ruling elites, who were a source of protection and patronage for their favorite sects and teachers. This relationship also led Buddhists in Japan throughout this era to vie for support among the factions at the top ranks in society, which it tended to view uncritically. The habit of overlooking discrepancies between Buddhist teachings and rulers' practices continued right into the modern period, when most monks were more concerned about accommodation with the elite than with reforming Japanese society or preventing war.

Persecution of Buddhists and Christians

Although Buddhism enjoyed official support during most of the shogunate, Nobunaga (1534–1582) waged an anti-Buddhist campaign, going so far as to burn the great center on Mount Hiei, outside Kyoto, where Japanese Buddhism was first established. It was dislike of Buddhism that probably led Nobunaga to be receptive to the first Jesuit missionaries, giving Christianity more early support than it received anywhere else in East Asia. Much to the chagrin of the European missionaries, however, most Japanese had trouble seeing in Christianity anything but an obscure form of Buddhism. Catholic rituals appeared to be similar to certain monastic rites, and the concept of a heavenly Lord whose son became incarnate to serve humanity was not unlike Mahayana Buddhism's doctrine of the cosmic Buddha whose sons, the compassionate bodhisattvas, also served humanity.

But squabbles that developed among European Franciscans, Jesuits, and later Protestants, as well as some missionary attempts to manipulate Japanese politics in the name of their home countries, convinced Iyesu, the first Tokugawa shogun, to outlaw Christianity in 1606. When in 1616 he acted to expel all missionaries, there were already an estimated 300,000 Japanese converts. The next decades saw attempts by the Japanese state to extirpate Christianity. Some officials penned vigorous attacks against Christian doctrines that pointed out how the foreign faith clashed with the region's "common-sense" spiritual understandings and its norms of secular order.

They also questioned the logic of a theology in which a reputedly omnipotent, benevolent God would allow "original sin," and they objected to biblical passages that seem to undermine loyalty to kin and ruler.

Other efforts at removing Christianity were gruesome, and many converts who would not recant their faith were tortured. A rebellion in 1637–1638 that resulted in over 37,000 deaths confirmed for its Japanese opponents the disruptive potential of Christianity. From this time onward, too, every Japanese family was required by law to be registered with a Buddhist temple, in an effort to regularize ties with Buddhism and to emphasize that in Tokugawa times being Buddhist was inherently part of being Japanese. (We will see, however, that in the post-Tokugawa era, nationalists argued the reverse, that is, that Buddhism was a "foreign religion" in Japan!)

The Regional Spread of Neo-Confucianism

Although Japan never instituted a Confucian-based civil service exam system, Confucian thought spread under the Tokugawa shoguns. Confucianism—long present among scholars, in state ritualism, and as part of Buddhist moral teachings from China—finally found its own strong supporters in a succession of prominent philosophers, many of whom were not part of the samurai elite. For some, Confucian teachings gave those of lower birth ideals to uphold against the hierarchical system instituted by Japan's hereditary nobility. Unlike in China, Confucianism flourished among both the merchant class and the samurai. Japanese intellectuals throughout the Tokugawa era studied and defended the positions of all the major neo-Confucians of the Song period and thereafter. There were even some Japanese exponents who came to reject the neo-Confucian system and urged return to the original classics. Efforts were also made to rationalize Shinto beliefs with Confucian doctrines.

Attired in white robes that symbolize purity, a Shinto priest kneels in the Meiji temple in Tokyo.

Spiritual Training for the Religious Elites

By 1600 CE, all the religious traditions of East Asia had developed institutions and courses of training for those wishing to become scholars, ritual masters, or meditative adepts. Although a small percentage of the entire populations actually were initiated into such disciplines, it is useful to understand something of the spiritual training that the region's different religious leaders (priests, monks, and nuns) had to undertake to fulfill their roles.

Confucianism Only under the guidelines set forth by the neo-Confucian masters did the literati (*rujia*) tradition acquire its own systematic regime. The first stage of training was "disciplining the body" (*shen-jiao*) by means of the zealous study of the six arts of Confucian education: ritual, music, archery, calligraphy, horsemanship, and mathematics. All were defined very broadly. For example, "ritual" means conducting religious rites as well as mastering the proper ways of eating, walking, and asking questions. The *Analects* provides many instances of seemingly trivial events associated with Confucius, but they had their use in just this context of providing the sage's life as a model for disciplined training.

Beyond foundational training, all the neo-Confucian subschools called for the "rectification of the heart-mind" and prescribed new practices: discipline manifested by outward zeal in investigating the external world, as well as the personal goal of knowing oneself. The aim was to become a perfected person, a *sheng-ren*, who has achieved fully his or her complete human nature. A common practice to realize this is called "quiet sitting," one that its proponents were adamant on distinguishing from forms of Buddhist or Daoist meditation. This neo-Confucian meditation was not based upon stopping discursive thought but upon calming the mind from the flow of events, perceiving the goodness of the in-dwelling primal human nature, and becoming aware of selfish desires.

Daoism Like the Buddhists, Daoists sought a more individualistic "ultimate transformation" through practices that originated in antiquity. For philosophers such as Zhuang Zi, only through the practice of detaching from the mind (*wai-wu*) and ceasing to distinguish separated things could one find union with the Dao. In Zhuang Zi's writings, one also finds cryptic references to a "heart-fast" (*xin-zhai*) that starved the mind of all externalities, allowing one proficient in the practice to forget his senses, ideas, feelings, and wishes and so experience only the primordial and mysterious Dao. When the spiritual adept has reached this stage, the practice of "free and easy wandering" in nature can be fully undertaken. In the traditional poetic expression, one then ascends the cloud vapors, rides the flying dragon, and travels to the infinite. Facing death involves no travail and only blissful transformation.

Shintoism Until the modern era, Shinto priests of major shrines inherited their positions and learned the rituals from their fathers; thus they were always males from aristocratic families. Over the last 150 years, priests have had to pass a state-prescribed course of training at an institution such as Kokugakuin University, founded for this purpose. The role of the *shinshoku*, as the priests are usually called, involves mastery of the daily gestures of respect offered to the kami, the annual rituals of the shrine, calligraphy, and complex forms of ritual purification. Shinto has never developed any "inner" spiritual practices. For its modern exponents, however, the artful rituals oriented to the deities throughout the seasons offer a means of achieving refined sensitivity and moral transformation.

EAST ASIAN RELIGIONS IN THE EARLY MODERN ERA

The Disruptions of Imperial Domination

Post-Enlightenment colonialism, also called imperialism, represents the first modern attempt to establish a global world order. Europeans forced Asian societies to change on European terms, abruptly imposing new ideas, technologies, and institutions that had evolved naturally over many years in Europe. European imperialism caused chaos and crises that undermined most institutions in premodern East Asia, with the organized religions especially subject to disruption and decline. Imperialism's impact in Asia can be likened to that of a strong earthquake, one that levels many structures, leaving only the strongest foundations upon which to rebuild.

Understanding the world's religions today requires an awareness of this legacy, for East Asian religions and cultures were decisively altered over the period as never before. Though the effects of colonialism were overwhelmingly destructive, the fusion of older traditions with modern changes at times led to religious innovations that were compelling and original.

By the beginning of the nineteenth century, European civilization had ascended as the supreme force on the global stage. The Renaissance had transformed Europe with powerful innovations in the intellectual, political, economic, and military spheres. The unprecedented sociopolitical dynamism and expansion of wealth accelerated further in the eighteenth century. The major states (England, Netherlands, Portugal, Germany) vied, often militarily, to exert their newfound political and economic power around the globe. Internally, of course, Europe was diverse, transformed by its own class and ethnic conflicts, and facing newly arising problems; new ideologies competed with old to provide solutions to these crises. Some of these, too, were exported to Asia.

The emerging nations of Europe were above all self-assured of their superiority in every aspect of life, from morality to intellectual understanding. For many this included belief in the primacy of the white race, and many, too, saw in the march of colonialism a confirmation that Christianity would ultimately triumph on the world stage. Thus, some European leaders felt they were the vehicles of triumphant Christianity, and their merchants were soon dedicated to making their fortunes through overseas trade, ready to pursue often risky ventures, and to do so quite ruthlessly.

Colonialism, like revolution (to paraphrase Lenin), was anything but a tea party. It forcibly changed the economic systems of East Asia, promoted trafficking in narcotics when the opium trade was profitable, challenged Asians' fundamental understandings regarding humanity and cosmos through science and Christian missions, and undermined the long-held view of Asia's ruling classes that their civilizations were the world's greatest.

The crisis of colonial presence and imperial challenge led the national elites away from their own indigenous traditions and on a forced march directed toward understanding the Western world. From about 1850, across the region, the best minds in East Asia chose to learn about the West first and about their own traditions little, with the result that the Enlightenment mentality, with its revolutionary terms of analysis, entered powerfully into the cultural heritage of the modern East Asian elite. Among a large portion of this Western-influenced elite, agnosticism or atheism replaced attachment to the indigenous spiritual traditions.

On the popular level as well, the era of colonialism has been perceived as a time of crisis. The common terms used to express the peoples' sense of inundation and powerlessness across East Asia were "humiliation" (*chi*) in Chinese, "bitterness" (*hahn*) in Korean, and "patient endurance" (*nin*) in Japanese. In sum, they give an overview of the modern era for East Asians as a time of trial, with each set of difficulties representative of the separate nations' slightly differing reactions to the experience of modernization.

It would be wrong, however, to see the history of East Asia as solely dictated by European actors and external forces. There were important internal dynamics at work in Korea, China, and Japan, and the different processes already under way in each shaped their emphatically different destinies under colonialism.

Traumatic Transitions of the Modern Era

The Decline of Confucian Ideology and Exponents

The crisis and rapid changes brought by the onslaught of imperialism ended the unchallenged influence of the Confucian elite in China, Korea, and Japan. The Confucian worldview and social ideology were subjected to scathing critiques by the native-born reformers of each nation, who took up the task of saving state sovereignty and attempting to match the wealth, knowledge, and power put on display by the Western imperialists. In addition, many young people abandoned the traditional curriculum to pursue "Western learning," honing their intellectual development by critiquing what they perceived as the disabilities imposed on society under the Confucian tradition. Finally, the fall of the Korean and Chinese states, whose political and economic resources supported Confucianism in many domains, made it certain that this tradition would lose its central place in the region's early modernization.

Confucianism was blamed for every ill visible in the region. The failure to develop modern trade was blamed on the classical ranking of social classes by occupation, which in the Confucian view of the good society placed at the top scholar-officials who administered the bureaucracy and taught in schools; below them were the farmers, followed by artisans, and finally the merchants. Confucius had no respect for merchants, whom he called "parasites," describing them as ever ready to take advantage of others, motivated by greed, and inclined to dishonesty.

The traditional Confucian educational system was also blamed for stifling the nation's technical development, inasmuch as it valued generalists over specialists and rewarded rote memorization and imitation, not independent thinking. Moreover, for the critics, the Confucian view of history as cyclical had made the elite prone to stagnation and uninclined to pursue innovation or progress.

The strongest terms of rejection were directed toward Confucian social norms and at their center, family relations. The classical formula for social harmony that East Asians had incorporated from the ancient period was framed in two triads: the three bonds (between ruler and minister, father and son, and husband and wife) and the three principles (hierarchy, age, gender). Reformers found these principles to be an obstacle to modernization in many respects. Individuals who placed loyalty to family first, for example, were unable to extend trust to others as needed in the more impersonal workings of a modern economy. Similarly, filial deference to elders made individuals dependent on the collective family, thwarting the creative thrust toward individuality and encouraging a "Confucian personality" that either (in the young) followed authority blindly or (in the elders) gave too much power to those who were merely of senior rank. All such relationships were seen as stifling innovation. On the national level, reformers saw the "three bonds" as merely serving authoritarian political control. Both East Asian reformers and Western social scientists until the 1970s agreed that Confucianism was the key obstacle to the region's modernization.

A reconsideration of the characteristics fostered by Confucian humanism reveals that these Confucian elements also played a role in the region's ultimately successful response to the challenges of the postcolonial era. These include, for example, the high emphasis on education, the practice of carefully studying problems before taking action, the expectation that state officials will act for the good of the whole, and the acceptance by the intellectual elite of responsibility for the nation's well-being. But what is certain is that the imperial system that supported the literati tradition was overthrown completely in China and Korea. By contrast, in the neighboring islands the emperor-led state endured by melding nationalism with a Japanese form of colonialism. Whatever Confucianism means exactly in the present day, a break with the past had irrevocably occurred. We must first turn to the important exception of Japan and its distinctive fusion of belief systems: melding modernization with Confucianism in the form of nationalist neo-Shintoism.

State and Civil Religion in Japan: Neo-Shintoism

By 1882, a decade and a half after the demise of the shogunate and the restoration of the Japanese monarchy in the person of the Meiji emperor, the Shinto tradition was officially adopted by the state. To bring this about, most shrines and temples were integrated into a single system under government supervision. The emperor was revered as a divinity on earth, whose presence was a blessing to the nation. This idea was expressed at the national shrines in the capital and then in rituals regularly conducted in every local

Procession bearing the local god (kami) through Kamakura, Japan, during the Spring Festival.

shrine as well; Japanese were directed to worship the emperor daily in Tokyo just as Muslims to worship Allah face Mecca. The reformed educational system also centered its curriculum on the sanctity of the emperor, and all citizens were expected to honor him by working for the good of the nation. This will turn out to be one of the Confucian elements in Japan's modernization.

A constitution adopted in 1889 limited Japanese citizens' freedom to express any opinions critical of Shinto doctrines and practices, especially the imperial ties to the indigenous deities, but it guaranteed religious freedom to followers of other religions as long as they did not undermine Shinto and were loyal to the nation. Those affected included the Buddhist schools and the Christian denominations, which were legalized again in 1863, as well as the "new religion" sects that multiplied throughout the modern era and are discussed later.

The Meiji state religion, or state-Shinto, can be labeled neo-Shintoist for it was associated with the religious tradition of ancient origins that reveres the indigenous deities of the Japanese islands. It is also fundamental to see, however, that the "civil religion" constructed around Shintoism by the Meiji elite was thoroughly Confucian in character. It emphasized loyalty to the state, the norm of filial piety, self-sacrifice, and dedication. Moreover, it heralded the contributions of individuals that would be needed to make the modernization of Japan a success. Finally, a Confucian vocabulary was used to define the emperor's and the nation's mission, with special emphasis on the emperor's Mandate of Heaven. Thus, Meiji Japan was the first political entity to successfully harness reformed Confucian values to meet the challenges of modernizing and adopting the technologies pioneered in the West.

Institutional Buddhism

As we noted in Chapter Seven, institutional Buddhism took root in Asia by way of a monastic system in which monasteries became landlords reliant upon lay believers to till the lands and on charitable donations from the faithful for other sustenance. At times of economic hardship, or when the state could not extend customary protections, Buddhism tended to decline. In general, the crises of the modern era across East Asia also deprived Buddhism of economic support, of donations, and of individuals who in other eras might have joined a monastic order and contributed to its vitality. Now the most gifted people wanted to learn about the West and to lead their countries in modernizing national industries, governments, and military establishments.

In nineteenth-century China, there were few signs of innovation and few Buddhists who rose to contribute to the national struggles. In Japan's long Tokugawa era (1600–1867), on the other hand, the military leaders supported Buddhism strongly, including the promotion of Buddhist pilgrimage as a means of having the Japanese acquire a sense of national integration. But the Meiji reformers felt it essential to reverse course, both to weaken former foes and because they believed that Buddhist influences were inimical to Japan's revitalization.

Zealous attempts in the first Meiji years to prohibit Buddhism outright were abandoned, but the Buddhist tradition sustained considerable damage: from 1871 to 1876, the number of temples throughout Japan was reduced from an estimated 465,000 to 71,000. In 1872, the government decreed that Buddhist monks were free to marry and follow nonvegetarian diets, a move that undermined discipline and popular regard for those who had been viewed as renunciants. The Buddhists successfully rallied support against further acts directed against them, but the Shinto-based nationalism and the state-encouraged challenges to institutional Buddhism forced followers to shift their emphases and rethink their doctrines in light of the changes under way in their society.

The Buddhist establishment in the Meiji period strove mightily to prove its patriotism and relevance, as a host of writers and lay organizations arose to explain why charges of disloyalty and obsolescence were unfounded. Major schools competed to implement Meiji social and national programs and they, too, fanned the rising flame of anti-Western feelings, supported the successive war efforts (in public statements and with funds), and translated into positive doctrinal terms rationales for imperial expansion.

Compared with elsewhere in Asia, early movements led by Japanese householders to reinterpret Buddhism in terms of modern philosophy were few. Instead, religious reformers were more likely to found their own sects, drawing upon doctrines as they liked, without trying to work through the Buddhist establishment.

In Korea, Confucianism was strongly supported in the nineteenth century and Buddhism was increasingly marginalized, as the government also tried to limit the economic power of monastic estates by consolidating schools and seizing lands. State decrees went so far as to prohibit Buddhist monks from setting foot in major cities. Early Western accounts of Korea describe monastic buildings falling down and the Buddhist monks as ignorant and undisciplined.

The same remarks about monastic Buddhism in the modern era apply to Daoist monasticism in China as well. The institutions carried on, but they brought little to the discussion about creating the new China in the radical intellectual climate of the early twentieth century. Daoism, too, was attacked from the standpoints of science and democracy. One reformer, Liang Qichao, described this religion as "a great humiliation whose activities have not benefited the nation at all."[9]

Scenes from missionary life in China: a missionary family resident in China c. 1898 shown in formal Chinese dress; a classroom in a Methodist boarding school for girls; a group of Chinese converts and Western missionaries with shipments of Bibles and evangelical publications.

Christian Missions in China, Japan, Korea

The Jesuits, the first Christians to proselytize in Ming China, followed a strategy of not addressing the masses, but moving to convert the elite. Unlike their counterparts in Japan, who were expelled after an era of toleration, they did succeed at winning residence. Acceptance was less for their religious teachings, however, than for their cogent introduction into China of European sciences, particularly astronomy, mathematics, and ballistics. The failure of early Catholic missionaries can be attributed to inability to explain their theology in terms of traditional Chinese language or logic. For example, they never were able to find a satisfactory way of translating "God" into Chinese. No less a drag on proselytizing efforts were the very bitter controversies that broke out between the different Christian groups, particularly on the issue of whether to tolerate Confucian morality or ancestor veneration. An imperial edict proscribed Christianity in 1724, but the censure was not as extreme or as thoroughly enforced as in Japan.

The Protestant presence grew significantly after 1800, as Americans and Europeans fanned out from Guangdong, Province, on the South China Sea. There followed missionary efforts to reach the masses, and a Chinese translation of the complete Bible appeared in 1815. As elsewhere, the missionaries were less successful at mass proselytizing than at transmitting Western medicine, schooling, and new technologies such as printing by means of movable type. By 1877, there were 347 missionary schools and an estimated 400,000 Chinese converts.

In addition to the earlier issues of Chinese receptivity, Christianity was associated with the bullying of colonialists and the horrific violence of the nineteenth-century Taiping Rebellion, which we will discuss shortly. Christianity did, however, appeal to those interested in finding a religious framework for protest against the weight of traditionalism. In addition, those needing charity or wishing to do business with Westerners often benefited by having themselves baptized.

Outlawed in 1606, its missionaries expelled in 1616, and its followers persecuted, Christianity survived underground in Japan among remarkably faithful converts. Once granted religious freedom in 1863, Japanese Christians built churches and asserted their faith in the public domain. Soon, however, like the Buddhists, the Christians began to feel the need to prove their religion's this-worldly relevance and nationalistic credentials. They joined the nationalistic chorus supporting the war efforts launched by the state and proclaimed that Christianity strengthened Japan by supporting ethics in national life, resisting radicalism, and combating communism.

Korea remained closed to Christian missionaries until the mid-nineteenth century, when representatives primarily from American Methodist and Presbyterian denominations settled and attracted converts amidst building schools and hospitals. Korean Christians, like those in Japan, emphasized their independence from Western churches. Scholars are still uncertain as to why Korea embraced Christianity so much more than other Asian countries. (Latest surveys have found that 32% of South Koreans are converts.)

The Appearance of New Religious Movements and Religions

From the imperial era until the present, "new religions" have emerged across Asia, underscoring this period as one of social dislocation, dissatisfaction, and cross-traditional synthesis. It also signals the extent to which the "established religions" of the region (Confucianism, Daoism, Buddhism) had lost their allure for some who were increasingly drawn to ideas from the West.

For the majority of peasants and artisans, the crises that resulted from foreign domination undermined many local subsistence economies with disastrous effects. Peasants continued to have faith in their own deities, shamans, and ancestors, and indeed turned to them in times of trouble. Yet given the turmoil of the modern era, it is not hard to imagine that countless rituals failed and a great many prayers went unanswered. For all these reasons, the modern era in East Asia is marked by the unprecedented flowering of "new religious movements" that did not rely on old practices or old deities. Most often, they arose from the lower classes through sects entirely independent of the traditional institutions of Daoism, Buddhism, and (premodern) Shinto.

Taiping Rebellion in China (1850–1864)

Beyond the challenges provoked by the foreigners in their midst, a rebellion led by a Chinese convert to Christianity nearly ended Manchu rule a half century before the Qing dynasty was overthrown by revolutionaries led by Sun Yat-sen. The nineteenth century rebellion began with a humble and failed village scholar, Hong Xiuquan (1814–1864).

After an illness during which he was delirious for several weeks, Hong with the help of an American Southern Baptist missionary interpreted his fevered visions as Christian revelations. Despite limited knowledge of the Bible, Hong proceeded to found his own form of Christianity, convinced that he had seen God, who had charged him with saving humanity and destroying demons, and that he had met Jesus, who was revealed to be Hong's "older brother." A charismatic preacher whose apocalyptic predictions captured the imagination of many, Hong organized his followers into a militant sect called the *Taipings*. To them he offered a prophetic, utopian vision of a future "Heavenly Kingdom of Great Peace" based upon egalitarianism, shared property, and gender equality. One of his Old Testament–inspired proclamations was that all idols be destroyed, be they Buddhist, Daoist, or even Confucian ancestor tablets. He also insisted that those joining his group adopt a puritanical moral code, abstaining from alcohol, tobacco, and opium.

Hong vilified the Manchu elite as demons standing in the way of the sect's radical transformation of China. The Qing state, in turn, persecuted the group, stepping up its efforts after 1850, by which time the Taipings had over ten thousand members. Thus provoked, Hong gathered an army whose bloody campaigns likely comprised the most destructive civil war in world history. Most of China was affected, and an estimated 20 million people perished.

China had already been humiliated and weakened by the European powers, which offered many reasons for discontent in addition to those initially proposed by Hong, and the forces of rebellion mushroomed. The Taiping army captured Nanjing in 1853 and occupied it for ten years, establishing a separate regional state ruled by Hong and his neo-Christian ministers.

Ultimately, however, the movement fell apart owing to internal divisions, refusal to cooperate with potential allies, the leadership's ruthless brutality and paranoia in governing the Taiping community, and hostility to the Confucian elements deeply embedded in China's population. Nanjing was retaken in 1864, all Taiping leaders not killed in battle were executed, and the first Asian-Christian "new religion" was utterly eradicated.

"Religion of the Heavenly Way": Ch'ondogyo in Korea

The Ch'ondogyo, which merges elements of Confucianism and Daoism, was founded by Ch'oe Suun (1824–1864) in 1860. Its original name, Tonghak ("Eastern learning"), signals its origins as an indigenous response to the challenge of newly imported Christianity (called "Western learning" in Korean). According to the sect's scriptures, Suun received a direct revelation of a new "Heavenly Way" (*Ch'ondo*) from the Heavenly Lord, who is conceived of as the totality of life or as the universe, immanent in each person and all creation. Suun attracted a large following but was martyred by the government. The Ch'ondogyo continued to grow under Suun's successors, becoming one of the major religions of the Korean peninsula. Like Korean Christians, Ch'ondogyo members were active in resisting Japanese rule. Although banned in North Korea since 1949, the group remains very popular in the south. There is an institutional center in Seoul, and in 1997 its membership, governed by an elected body, numbered over 1 million.

The collected writings of the first three leaders became the sect's chief scriptures. Ch'ondogyo's theology is simply expressed in one phrase,

"Humans bear divinity." The ethics of the sect emphasize respecting this universal divinity in others. The injunction "Treat others as divine" seems tame today but was revolutionarily democratic in the status-conscious Korea of the late nineteenth century. The group's goal is to achieve a heavenlike earthly existence marked by widespread social cooperation.

The Older "New Religions" Arising in Pre-Meiji Japan

By the end of the Tokugawa era, the medieval social order in Japan had begun to break down, and for some, the vitality of Buddhism and traditional Confucianism had waned. Of the several dozen spiritual movements that arose in this period, three were to endure to become denominations among the postmodern "new religions" of the late twentieth century.

Each of these movements began with a charismatic individual who experienced extraordinary revelations after a serious illness. Having shared their discoveries with others, these leaders began building communities of followers who felt the teachings helped them reorder their lives on new spiritual principles. Almost every "new religion" thus offered a singular path to salvation out of the maze of choices that had developed along the way of Japanese religious history: Buddhism, neo-Confucianism, elements of Daoism, Shinto. All later were harmonized with the Meiji state's neo-Shintoism, eventually becoming regarded as "Shinto sects."

Kurozumikyo Kurozumikyo ("Kurozumi's religion") was founded by Kurozumi Munetada, a charismatic teacher who in 1815 was possessed by the central Shinto deity, the sun goddess, Amaterasu, whom he identified as the single Lord of the universe. Although Kurozumi did not register his group until 1842, soon after his initial experience he began preaching and attracting disciples who spread his revelations across Japan.

Followers of Kurozumikyo believe that all humans are emanations of the kami and that individual believers may become kami, or become one with them, securing eternal life, by adopting the moral and spiritual practices of these Japanese deities. The potential for all to realize the divine state explains the Kurozumikyo emphasis on the equality of all people, a radical idea in pre-Meiji Japan, where class completely determined individual destiny. Kurozumikyo grew dramatically after winning Meiji recognition. Its leaders had a central shrine established in Okayama City, and the group numbered perhaps 700,000 by 1880; its membership had dropped to just more than 400,000 by 1980.

Tenrikyo Tenrikyo ("religion of heavenly wisdom") began with messages its founder, Nakayama Miki (1798–1887), received while in a trance. The source of these communications was a spirit Nakayama called "God the Parent" (Oyagami). Regarded by followers as the one true god of the universe, Oyagami commanded Nakayama to be his medium, to reject her role as wife and mother, and to further his mission through healing and preaching. Tenrikyo claimed that its new and universal doctrine of harmonious living would usher in a new world order, a divine kingdom in which humanity would enjoy blissful union with God the Parent. In the sect's view, the "one, true kami" in the universe had created humanity to see it find harmonious life, and then entered into creation in the form of ten other kami. Tenrikyo adherents believe that Oyagami made his new revelation to Nakayama to rectify growing human selfishness, a shortcoming that has undermined the original divine intent.

The Tenrikyo belief system accepts reincarnation until the heart is purified of the "eight dusts" (grudges, covetousness, hatred, selfish love, enmity, fury, greed, arrogance). Essential for salvation are a dance ritual, an initiation ("receiving the holy grant"), and performance of daily social service for others. Tenrikyo became a recognized Shinto sect in 1838 and rapidly spread throughout Japan. Its members carried missions to the United States in 1896, Taiwan in 1897, Korea in 1898, and China in 1901. Like the other early Shinto-related sects, after the Second World War the group made efforts to "purify" Tenrikyo of its Shinto and nationalist associations. By 1990, there were over 2.3 million members, who had established over 16,000 centers in Japan, with an additional 20,000 missions worldwide.

Nichiren-Related Sects of the Meiji Era

As the Meiji reforms opened and transformed Japanese society after 1867, and government calls to modernize Japan multiplied, the spirit of renewal found religious expression as well. In some cases, the sects arising passed beyond what the state found tolerable, and thus followers were persecuted and pressured to modify their teachings. Other groups became vehicles of resistance to the state's militarism and nationalism. Numerous laity-led groups arose because the Buddhist "establishment" gave few openings for those wishing to reinterpret the doctrines or apply them in the context of modern scientific discoveries from the West.

Many modern groups formed in association with Nichiren Buddhism, a Kamakura-era school created by the charismatic thirteenth-century monk introduced in Chapter Seven. Directly stemming from this school is the largest new religion of modern Japan, the lay organization called Soka Gakkai ("Value Creation Society"). Established in 1930 by the Nichiren disciple and educator Makiguchi Tsunesaburo (1877–1944), the Soka Gakkai aims to foster a "Third Civilization" based upon Nichiren's teachings, one in which the true faith would spread throughout the world. Its members believe that repeatedly chanting the *Nam-Myoho-renge-kyo* (the name of the great Buddhist text, the *Lotus Sutra*) is "medicine for the soul" and a means for changing the world. The Soka Gakkai also considers its mission to work for world peace and human welfare, and after 1960 it established a political party in Japan (the Komeito) to implement specific programs to achieve this goal in Japan. It has also sent missionaries to every major country of the world. By 2005, the Soka Gakkai had registered 12 million Japanese members and claimed 1.2 million international adherents.

Also originated by and for Nichiren laity, Reiyukai Kyodan ("Spiritual Friends Association") was intended to support the school's regular practices and to exert beneficial influences upon Japanese society. Founded in 1925 by Kubo Kakutaro (1890–1944) and Kotani Kimi (1901–1971), the group stressed the need for ancestor worship by the laity and attributed the upheavals of the era to ancestral distress over the ineffectiveness of the contemporary Buddhist leaders. Only when ancestors achieve peace and salvation through lay rituals utilizing the *Lotus Sutra* can the living really find spiritual grace. The Reiyukai also emphasize conservative social values and expects its members to work hard to strengthen the Confucian "three bonds" (between ruler and minister, father and son, and husband and wife). The Reiyukai are also strong supporters of imperial veneration and other conservative causes in Japanese society. One of the most active proselytizing new religions, the Reiyukai by 1990 had 3 million members and centers abroad in fourteen countries.

EAST ASIAN RELIGIONS AND POSTMODERN TRENDS IN A POSTCOLONIAL WORLD

Practitioners have pushed back at every religious barrier that the states of East Asia erected in the modern era. In Korea and Japan, this return to religious freedom opened the way for reformers of ancient traditions as well as charismatic innovators founding "new religions." The coming of the Marxist state to mainland China in 1949 and the imposition of totalitarian rule by the officially atheistic Communist party began an era of sustained religious repression. Chinese religions suffered the destruction of properties and religious institutions through concerted governmental attempts—unprecedented in world history—to exterminate any vestige of traditional religious teaching or spiritual training. In China, this lasted for almost two generations, until 1976.

But as we pointed out in Chapter One, such repression and persecution have not led to the end of religion in China. Far from it. State-sponsored substitution of modernist Marxist ideologies, utopian mythology, and the orchestration of a personality cult centered on Mao Zedong represented attempts to substitute a communist Chinese civil religion for Confucianism, Daoism, and Buddhism (see Chapter Nine). The effort failed, though it did weaken the bond between most mainland Chinese and their traditional organized religions.

Since the reform era that began soon after the death of Mao in 1976, the restoration of religion in China has been very gradual and has proceeded under the supervision of the state. A popular upsurge of practice at Daoist temples, family graves, Buddhist monasteries, Christian churches, and mosques is evident, however. Despite reverses, over the last decades, as the door has been cracked open, countless Chinese have rushed through to make pilgrimages, reopen shrines, and resume the ritual practices of their ancestors. We discuss here both the surviving traditions and new religions that have multiplied the pluralism characteristic of the postcolonial era.

Continuities and Transformations in the East Asian Religions

The Reality of Gods and Spirits in China

Chinese myths dating back to the Zhou era (700 BCE) mention deities of mountains, rivers, rain, and the earth that have remained part of the diffuse Chinese religion. Interestingly, most deities appearing later in East Asia have human origins, as heroic ancestral spirits have become gods who have won renown beyond their own kin. This is true of Guan Yu, the god of war (in life, a Han general), various deified statesmen, Confucius, and even, in recent years, Mao Zedong. Most other important deities have been Buddhist in origin.

In regional and local contexts, the East Asian pantheon has always been in flux as new heroes arise and the deities are obliged to continuously show their power (*ling*), perhaps through healing, or in dramatic shamanic displays of possessions, to prove themselves worthy of the investment of further offerings. Those manifesting strong healing powers or success in responding to popular appeals win devotees, patrons, new temples. Alternatively, other deities have lost favor and efficacy, and so have faded from popularity. Thus, the East Asian understanding of and experience with divinities has not been based so much upon faith as on dramatic experiential encounters and proven long-term efficacy.

Image of Mazu, the protective deity worshiped along the Chinese seacoast.

Who are the most common deities found on the typical altars in a Chinese community? Ubiquitous in Chinese homes and temples are icons of the *triple gods*: *Longevity* in the form of a vigorous old man, *Wealth* embodied by a Confucian official, and *Blessings* symbolized by a male god holding male progeny.

Another prominent deity, Tian Shang Sheng-mu ("Holy Mother in Heaven"), is popularly known as *Mazu* ("Grandmother"). Her origins can be traced to a girl born in the ninth century, in coastal Fujian, who saved her father and brothers at sea by exercising magical powers acquired via Daoist practice. She died young, and soon apparitions and miracles attributed to her were reported. By the mid-twelfth century, the state had recognized Tian Shang Sheng-mu and Mazu cult and temples that spread along the eastern coast of China, where the goddess remains popular today.

In every traditional Chinese and Korean home (but not in Japan) will be another deity, Zao Wangye, the "kitchen god." From the kitchen hearth, he records the household goings on and composes a yearly report right before New Year's Day. Folk belief is that Zao Wangye determines the length of every household member's life. As early as the Ming era, this popular notion was part of a more systematic articulation of the pantheon (reflecting China's urban centers and government bureaucracy), by which the kitchen gods and earth gods of each locality were viewed as reporting to the nearby city gods, who in turn informed the celestial Jade Emperor on New Year's Day. This notion of divine hierarchical officialdom was especially important in shaping the popular understanding of what happens when a person dies: the earth god of the locality reports to the city god, who then escorts the soul to the underworld to appear before ten judges who determine punishments and karmic destiny. It is to these divine "magistrates" that the family addresses prayers and sends bribes "spirit money," the latter consisting of specially purchased paper "currency" that is burned to expedite delivery.

Ritual Practices

In many respects, East Asia derives its unity as a religious and cultural area less from a common set of beliefs than from the shared ritualism within its temples and at family graves. These core rituals are simply an extension of the human custom of feasting an honored guest, in these cases an ancestral spirit or a deity. Foods offered sacrificially at temples are those humans consume, including alcoholic drinks. Offered foods are not wasted: once the deities are thought to have consumed their essence, the humans eat the material leavings. Other items presented in East Asian ritual include candles, flowers, oil lamps, and incense. In keeping with the idea that the deities are senior but essentially human is the practice of full prostration (ketou or "kowtow") before icons or tablets, an obeisance that junior kin also make before their living elders at festival times.

For most occasions in daily life, priests (be they Daoist, Buddhist, or shamans) are not needed. This is because senior householders and state officials, even at the highest level, have ritual tasks to perform according to their status.

Such tasks are particularly well defined at the time of death. In particular, Confucian filial piety is shown at a parent's death through careful carrying out of the appropriate rituals. The reward is the soul-spirit's blessings and the promise of a reunion with kin after the children's own demise.

Death is indeed a crisis, and at funerals people show their loyalty and love to the departed. In East Asia, traditionally, a long period of time is set aside to honor the dead. Further, participation in a funeral is one of the key events binding families and transmitting family values: all the relatives of the deceased remove jewelry, wear rough mourning garments, and wail ritually during specific times until actual burial. Burial will be after two days, with a longer wait in well-to-do families. The funeral itself involves the largest and most ostentatious procession that can be afforded, with musicians and mourners carrying large paper replicas of items the deceased is expected to need in the afterlife.

The traditional death rituals end in establishing the soul in two places for future worship, both in common with those who long ago expired. The cremation remains are taken out in a procession to the family grave or clan temple. Here they are left in an urn and a grave tablet with the deceased's name is fixed. The yin (earthly) soul stays with these remains. The yang (heavenly) soul is carried to the family's home placed on a sword-shaped paper brought from the graveside. It is then ritually installed on the family altar as a permanent tablet inscribed with the person's name set in place. Placed near other senior kin and the various images of the deities, this spirit receives all the offerings made to the gods. Any important event in the family is announced to the tablets as if the ancestors resided there.

Although not all families can afford family grave sites, all wish to have them, since with such a burial the family can most directly ensure the happiness of the earthbound souls. Families possessing graveyards on two occasions each year, go to clean them, make sacrifices, then eat and drink among the grave tablets. The cemeteries in East Asia are not dreaded locales but places one can go to feel close to one's deceased parents and grandparents, as well as to conform to the basic Confucian requirement of caring for them after death.

The Religious Institutions: Monasteries, Temples, Shrines

The religious institutions that sustain the three traditions in East Asia vary widely. For their surrounding householder communities, Buddhist monasteries have temples with images of compassionate bodhisattvas and include monks who specialize in healing and death rituals. The temple is considered as simply a house for human-like divinities. Temples can be modest roadside boxes where humble images or prints are kept, or they can be massive palaces with halls and side buildings, housing gilded images flanked by hosts of attending demigods.

Burning spirit money. These offerings are thought to reach the dead, easing their burden in the afterlife.

Some deities, such as the earth god (*Tudiye*) found in most agricultural settlements, can be worshiped in a simple manner outdoors on a raised mound of decorated earth. Smaller temples are merely boxes made of wood or cement, often housing a simple tablet with the name of the deity inscribed on it. Traditional Chinese towns had communities marked by a profusion of such shrines and larger temples, making it hard to understand the assertion by Westernized Chinese that "Chinese have no religion!"

The larger temples share certain characteristics. The greatest temples contain all the major deities of the pantheon, giving devotees "one-stop" access to the supernatural world. The entrance always opens to the south, an auspicious direction, and is guarded by statues of protectors in fierce poses. In larger establishments these guardians are lodged in a gatehouse through which all visitors must pass. The areas devoted to multistory pagoda temples in many cases reflect attention to geomancy calculations, complete with artificial mountains to channel positive energy to the site. In larger compounds, the main deity will be in the last hall on the same axis as the entrance, with halls containing lesser deities arrayed on the same line and separated by courtyards. Before each icon there is an altar for receiving offerings, most commonly candles or incense sticks that go into large braziers. Kneeling cushions are supplied, as well as a means of divination for the use of those posing questions to a deity: perhaps via two half-moon wooden blocks (that are thrown to derive a "yes" or "no" answer based on their resting alignment).

Chinese temple, the home of gods, featuring the ornate pillars and roof tiles of the palace style.

The aesthetic in contemporary Chinese temples can be described as highly baroque. The temples, with their curving roof lines, eaves, and finials, are full of bright colors, from roof beams to columns to the decorated vestments adorning the deities.

The larger Daoist temples are usually served by a resident priesthood and by *fa-shi*, mediums who serve in temples. The mediums specialize in exorcisms and help private clients make simple offerings. The priests, called *dao-shi*, assist in rituals such as exorcisms as well but have also mastered complex Daoist death liturgies and wear more formal attire.

Shinto Shrines: Jinja

Equipped and arrayed in keeping with norms similar to those of the Chinese temple, but in sharp decorative contrast, are the Japanese Shinto shrines, *jinja*. They are notable for their natural wood, plain roof tiles, and restrained aesthetic. Given the high emphasis upon purification in Shintoism, water sources for rinsing the face and mouth are always present at the entrance from which devotees approach the main shrine. Every jinja is also marked by a gateway called a *torii*. These distinctive features of Japan's public architecture delineate a transition from the ordinary world into sacred space.

A small Shinto shrine (jinja) dedicated to the protector of cows, the cow kami.

After purification at the entry, devotees proceed to the main and subsidiary shrines. Facing the main icon, they go before it to present their petitions. Before making a request, a visitor can pull on long thick ropes to ring a shrine bell. Ending the ritual by clapping shows respect.

The Diffuse Religion in Practice: The Major Religious Festivals

In our collective discussion of the religious practices of China, Korea, and Japan, we have pointed to the "diffuse religion" that gives the region a characteristic unity, drawing on elements of the three traditions. The festivals express this diffuse religion most clearly, since Confucian, Daoist, and Buddhist elements have clearly been woven into the yearly cycle of life. Only continued reliance on the ancient Chinese calendars in some areas of these countries has led to complications. Officially, all East Asian nations have adopted Western calendar days and selected celebrations: China from its connections with international communism, Korea and Japan through Christian influences. Yet, the Chinese system of twelve-year cycles, lunar days, and solar seasons is still used in many areas and has been intermixed with the Western calendar. Since Japan shifted many of its holidays away from the Chinese calendar and to fixed "Western" days, Japan's dates for the festivals it shares with the East Asian region are most often not on the same calendar day observed elsewhere.

National holidays have grown out of a variety of origins: mythic events or deities indigenous to the particular nation, days accentuating Confucian values, or relatively recent events that the nation's leaders wish to mark in the country's "civil religion." For example, Japan celebrates the Cherry Blossom Festival (April 1–8) to thank the kami of the forests for the renewal of life seen in the blossoming of the trees.

Every major deity in every locality is thought to have a "birthday," either a day celebrated nationally or the day a more local deity's temple was first established. On these annual occasions, which usually last for two or three days, the priests and temple supporters arrange for extravagant ritual performances, local devotees come to make their most elaborate yearly offerings (and petitions), merchants and artisans set up their wares to create a temporary fair, and in the evenings theatrical performances are staged to entertain deity and devotees alike.

Daoist New Year, celebrations in Beijing.

Most common festivals of East Asia have Chinese or Buddhist origins and can be mentioned only in passing. New Year's Day (by either calendar) is a time for gathering family and friends, settling debts, and seeking blessings and divine protection for the year ahead. The day in China and Korea is called Spring Festival, although it falls usually near the middle of winter. In traditional preholiday rites, householders send the kitchen god (Zao Wangye) off to heaven, by burning his paper icon, installing a new paper icon, and post ancient characters on doorways to invite prosperity for the year ahead. The essentials of Confucian family life are marked in sacrifices offered to ancestors at their tablets. It is customary for junior family members to kowtow to seniors, receiving gifts of money in special red envelopes in return.

Ancestor's Day or Qing-Ming ("Pure Brightness Festival") is the first of two dates over the year when families must visit the ancestral graves to maintain them, make sacrifices, and feast together there with the departed spirits, usually in early April. In Japan, this festival has been fixed as the vernal equinox (March 21) and is called Higan ("Further Shore"), with a second Higan on the autumnal equinox. In the Chinese manner, families visit family graves together. Buddhist priests are also expected to come to the home on a short visit, during which they recite sacred scriptures. The merit earned for this good deed is dedicated to the dead.

Scene from the Qing-Ming festival, the yearly family ritual for feasting and honoring the ancestors.

Japanese Buddhists mark the Buddha's birthday on April 8, when people anoint images with flowers and scented water, just as the texts describe the local deities doing at the actual birth of Siddhartha. Chinese and Korean Buddhists do the same on the eighth day of the fourth lunar month. Confucius' birthday is celebrated today only in Korea, and always on September 28. In Taiwan, on Teacher's Day, Confucius is honored with colorful rituals and elaborate sacrifices laid out before the sage's temple tablets.

All Souls Festival is a summer event when the gates of purgatory are thought to be held open. On this occasion, families integrate practices from all three traditions to connect the living members with their departed kin. Buddhist and Daoist priests perform rituals to aid families in their effort to ensure their ancestors' comfort in the afterlife.

The early fall Full Moon Festival is a time to worship the harvest moon with special sweet "moon cakes." All are urged to take sight of the "full rabbit moon," an association derived from both Buddhist and Daoist traditions: in the popular Buddhist scriptures, the Buddha was once born as a rabbit who rendered such extraordinary service to his fellow animals that the gods placed his image on the moon's surface; in the Daoist perception, a rabbit can be seen on the moon, using a pestle to pound the herbs of immortality in a mortar. Across East Asia, people view the rising moon on this night to ask for blessings that in rural communities include a good rice harvest in the month ahead.

The Return of Religion to China: Case Studies

We began the discussion of modern Hinduism with the comment that South Asia is a region of many subcultures and regional differences. The same reminder is applicable to East Asia, with a brief digression to note that China's breadth of variation is in certain respects much less pronounced now than in the past. Between 1949 and 1976, the heavy hand of the Communist party–led government succeeded in disestablishing almost every public religious institution that anchored the "three faiths." It dispersed the religious specialists (monks, nuns, and priests) and destroyed much of the formal infrastructure of the organized religions of China, demolishing Buddhist and Daoist monasteries and image shrines, as well as the nearly countless deity temples that before 1949 could be found in every community. The party also pushed the devout underground, since in the most active phase of the Cultural Revolution (1966–1969), any attempt to pray, meditate, or read religious literature was a serious offense, a sign of being "reactionary" or an "enemy of the revolution," a potentially capital crime. We now examine a few examples in pursuit of understanding the return of religion in the People's Republic of China.

Mao in the Rearview Mirror

Suppose you arrive in Beijing on your first visit to China and decide to go to the former imperial palace, the Forbidden City, the immense, walled complex from which the Yuan, Ming, and Qing emperors ruled all of China. It was at

Contemporary Mao amulet, inscribed with prayers for good fortune and safe travel, of the kind found widely in China today adorning rearview mirrors in cars.

the top of the palace's southern gateway, called the Gate of Heavenly Peace (Tian'anmen), that Mao Zedong proclaimed the establishment of the People's Republic of China in 1949. Despite all the changes that have swept China since Mao's death in 1976, you would easily see from your taxi window the immense painted portrait that hangs over that gateway. The image commemorates the "new beginning" of China then and serves as a constant reminder of Mao's heroic and determined role in leading the Communist party's triumphant success.

The style of the Tian'anmen Square portrait suggests that Mao is the ascetic servant of the people, a true communist leader whose deeds are legendary. He bravely fought the Japanese, and in the Long March of 1934 led the troops in strategic retreat halfway across China. Later he exposed the internal enemies that had kept China backward, poor, and subjugated. Inspired by Marx, Engels, and Lenin, Mao identified these enemies as the landlords who oppressed the peasant masses as well as the Western capitalist and religious ideas and institutions that kept the people from rising up and forcing China to become a just society. For Mao and so for the early Chinese Communist party leaders, religion and religious institutions were "enemies of the people." Mao was a rationalist who critiqued "superstitious" religious ideas that allegedly blocked the people's attempts to understand the world; he never ceased to highlight the classic modernist goal of setting the world free from the wrong thinking stemming from belief in supernatural "magic."

Like Marx, Engels, and Lenin, Mao believed a true communist utopia was not obtainable in a society with strong religious traditions. Although official Chinese historians have admitted that Mao's own blind faith in communist ideology led to blunders causing the death of millions (especially in the 1958–1960 famine), the massive Tian'anmen portrait still hangs as an icon of communist China. (Occasionally iconoclasts are caught defacing this portrait. Even in recent incidents, offenders have typically received multiyear prison terms.)

People who grew up during the decades of Mao's dictatorship later painfully realized how full of "superstition" they had been in their regard for the Communist party and especially in their reverence for Chairman Mao. Yet today, nearly thirty years after his death, for many Chinese, party members and nonparty members alike, Mao retains his standing as a sincere and uncorrupted champion of China's renewal who tried (however erringly) to seek justice and the common good. But regard for Mao endures in ways that even he did not anticipate.

As your taxi driver turns the corner on the great square near the stolid mausoleum where Mao's remains lie embalmed in a glass-enclosed tomb, you notice on the windshield mirror a gold-colored frame, decorated with red and yellow tassels. You immediately recognize the back-to-back portraits of Mao, a youthful one and one from middle age (similar to that overlooking Tian'anmen Square). You ask your interpreter what the object is and what it means. The answer, from the 30-something driver of a government-owned vehicle, takes a few moments to register: *"Ta shi shen"* ("He is a deity"). The driver then adds with unconcealed fervor that with so many more cars on the road, his work is quite dangerous, but this deity's amulet makes him feel safe. His income as a driver in fact has multiplied since he put it up, just as his fellow drivers in the work unit had promised. On later outings you question other drivers who display similar icons, you learn that many believe that the icon—and Mao's spirit—have helped them in business. The transformations under way in China today and the restoration of religion among the Chinese people are embedded in this fully ironic turn of fate: the most powerful man in East Asia, while alive an atheist who suppressed religion, is in death a powerful spirit.

While his transformation to a revered protective spirit and god of wealth would doubtless have dismayed Chairman Mao, it does demonstrate the global pattern of religious traditions responding to the exigencies of local life. As the state and party have moved since the early 1990s away from collectivist policies to emphasize individual and private enterprise, leaders have exhorted the Chinese people that "to get rich is glorious." At the same time, leaders have retreated from promises of guaranteed state employment, pensions, and universal medical care. So is it really surprising that an unassailable icon would be adopted as the very needed god of personal protection and wealth?

The Force of Feng Shui

Ideas about what constitutes "religion" in China not only fascinate modern scholars but have been repeatedly debated by officials of the Communist party. In the reform era, as pressure has been exerted to reintroduce almost every sort of former spiritual practice, the East Asian organized religions, with their potential for reestablishing nationwide institutional networks, have had to deal with deliberate governmental attempts aimed at controlling and regulating them. A few ancient practices, however, have been left largely unmolested. One of these is *feng shui*, the school of applied religious Daoism that seeks to maximize human flourishing in natural and man-made environments. (The name, which means literally "wind-water," refers to the principal bearers of environmental energy used in geomancy analyses.)

Feng shui consultants have proliferated across mainland China, as have books on the subject. Masters from overseas Chinese communities have returned to advise those building the myriad new hotels, residences, and factories rising so quickly across the PRC. The goal of feng shui is to determine the best sites, architectural designs, and living arrangements. Both private concerns and state ventures with party approval now take the "science" of mapping the qi, the inherent

With the allowance for religious freedom after the Cultural Revolution, traditional Daoist priests have enjoyed their restoration to temple service across China.

energy of a place, quite seriously. In mainland China today one can hear both success and disaster stories pointing to the advisability of consulting a feng shui expert before embarking on construction project.

The state's support of the return of feng shui has given credence to the classical religious worldview regarding humanity and the environment. It is based upon Daoist principles of balancing yin and yang, channeling the subterranean and atmospheric flow of their qi, and pursuing health and prosperity through expert arrangement of harmonious design features. The government's policy reflects the perennial Chinese emphasis on religion's practical, this-worldly benefits, which is visible elsewhere in society, as well. Throughout the modern and postmodern eras, for example, doctors have had unobstructed leeway to practice acupuncture, which is based on Daoist principles applied to the human body.

Nor is mainland China the only area to see the effect of this revival of the ancient worldview: as significant numbers of Chinese people have migrated overseas, real estate brokers from London to San Francisco are having to take account of feng shui analysis in marketing their properties. Feng shui's ideas about interior decorating have likewise entered into the ken of new age religion, where concern for fixing "the wealth corner" in one's house, situating decorations recognized for their "harmonious vibrations," and the plotting of energy flow from front door to back have been borrowed from this Chinese system of thought.

Ancestor Veneration and the Return of Traditional Funerals

In its zeal to end wasteful expenditures on the rituals of death and ancestor veneration, which for some traditional families meant going into nearly inescapable debt for extravagant funerals, the Communist party in 1956 issued strict regulations limiting funeral observances and—in the most radical break with the past—required secular cremation while also prohibiting rituals at ancestral graves. This attempt to break with the Confucian tradition went even further during the periods of greatest excess in the Cultural Revolution, when the young revolutionaries called Red Guards ransacked and destroyed grave sites throughout China, including parts of the great imperial tombs, some of which had been in use for several thousand years. In loosing these energetic zealots on the countryside, Mao was trying to destroy the familial tradition, which they saw as dividing "the people" and so undermining the party's quest to promote the collective good.

Beginning in the early 1990s, the practices of traditional funeral processions and burial of the dead in family graves slowly began to return, largely in villages and smaller towns and hardly at all around major cities such as Beijing. Graves are now increasingly visible, and across the rural areas, usually on sites unsuitable for agriculture, one sees burial places of elaborate design, including permanent brick structures with nameplates affixed. Also,

Sales clerk at an ancestor worship supply shop, Shanghai. Once prohibited by official regulations, government shops across China now sell the paper money, candles, and incense needed for this ancient practice.

official prohibitions on the burning of paper money or artificial gold ingots at gravesides have been dropped. Until 1996, road signs still threatened punishment for those engaging in this practice. Since 1998, however, government-owned shops have been selling the paper currency used in this exceedingly popular observance.

Nationalism and Confucianism Revived

Perhaps even more striking than the abandonment of attempts to stamp out long-favored cultural practices is the return of Confucius to an honored position in modern China. In the retreat from socialist collectivism and having tacitly recognized the failure to convert the Chinese masses to the worldview of Marxist–Maoist communism, China has been beset by problems of corruption accompanying its hastily instituted market reforms. Many Chinese writers have pointed out the crisis in faith and values that has gripped China, as the profit-seeking motive has been unleashed over the last two decades. As one of China's first rock stars, Cui Jian, sings in a popular album entitled *Eggs Under the Red Flag*, "Money is fluttering in the wind. We have no ideals."

The Communist party, in apparent recognition of this potential source of chaos, recently embarked on one of its greatest "reverse courses": it has turned back to Confucius. While the party publicly ignores its failure to make communist ideology the common foundation of postwar China, the restoration of Confucius to respectability is part of its calculated co-opting of a more primordial Chinese tradition on which to establish a permanent power base: staunch nationalism.

Regardless of whether they support the communist government, Chinese people widely share a certain pride in their civilization and its culture. Party strategists see the world economy as developing in a direction leading to eventual domination by China. Thus, in the interest of guiding the country to reach this pinnacle, they are trimming their demands that the people accept ideologies counter to millennia of Chinese tradition.

The PRC has readmitted Confucianism to the ideological stage in order to evoke nationalistic pride, another deeply ironic turn by the Communist party leadership. During the Cultural Revolution, Mao required Red Guards to denounce Confucius and his sons specifically as "villainous slave owners," tarring the master as an apologist for feudalism and exploitation, a symbol for all that the Communist party was out to replace.

Yet the hated excesses of the Cultural Revolution may have sparked renewed interest in Confucian thought in China. In 1994, to mark the 2,545th birthday of the great sage, the party launched an initiative to revive Confucian thought. An international conference was convened, the Confucian temple in Beijing was restored and reopened to the public, and Confucius' home temple in Qufu was celebrated as a place to visit. By the year 2000, China's president Jiang Zemin was frequently quoting from Confucius in his public speeches.

Qi Gong

Another area in which the spiritual has returned to mainland China in the guise of applied therapy is in the practice of *qi gong*. This healing art, like feng shui, draws upon Daoist theories of vital energy in the body and upon techniques of awakening its force in practitioners, both of which have their origins in religious Daoism's ancient paths to achieve immortality. It is now quite common in major cities for qi gong practitioners to open shops in the precincts of Buddhist or Daoist monasteries, with banners and posters unfurled outside

Women performing a qi gong ritual, with gestures designed to cultivate and concentrate the qi energy in the body.

their entranceways explaining the theory and practice. There are also testimonials from people who have been cured of various maladies. In most instances, a qi gong master uses his own body to concentrate healing energy and project it outwardly (through the hands) to affect the flow of energy in the patient. In the famous Great Goose Pagoda in Xi'an, the Buddhist committee since 1993 has rented a side assembly hall to a qi gong practitioner. This master draws a steady stream of interested people who can listen to an introductory lecture and for a modest fee take their first treatment.

In some governmental circles, there is ambivalence about such applied spirituality. Although the modern official press features an occasional article, often by a prominent scientist, that denounces "phony qi gong" as "harmful" and criticizes individual practitioners for "feudal and superstitious activities which use the flag of qi gong as a cover for swindling others," it continues to allow the practice to flourish, even in state-controlled temple precincts. Thus, while this medically oriented practice can be linked with other Chinese (and Western) therapies, qi gong now affirms in the personal experience of modern Chinese the credibility of the most elemental ideas of classical Daoism.

Shrines on Mountain Peaks, Village Squares, Shops, and Front Doors

Across mainland China since 1976, there has been the slow, hesitant, but unmistakable movement by devotees to reestablish shrines, temples, and the ritual practices destroyed or prohibited under government orders dating back to 1949. Exactly where the Communist party's line of toleration lies has varied according to the region and its succession of officials. Tensions still exist over what is "superstition" (*mixin*), so strongly discouraged by the government, and what is "religion" (*zongjiao*). Individuals have a constitutional right to practice a religion, but the state reserves the right to grant or withhold this designation from a given belief system.

Even so, the return of temples to the public domain for ritual use is in evidence almost everywhere. Daoist and Buddhist shrines are surrounded by flourishing votive markets, usually owned by or rented from the temple itself. Incense, candles, printed texts and scrolls with spiritual exhortations, souvenirs, and amulets are among the items sold. Many devotional traditions are flourishing, and in forms that were popular centuries earlier.

Accounts of village life cite the near universal attempt of rural peasants to use part of their new earnings to build (or rebuild) the public temples that house the local and regional gods. None is more telling than the practice of making offerings to the local earth gods (*tudi gong*). In pre-PRC China, the humble earth god shrines were found in every locality, possessing in fact a multiple presence according to the settlement: tudi shrines were found in homes, in neighborhoods, in villages, in government offices (where they received offerings from state officials), and even in Buddhist monasteries. All deaths, births, and troubles were reported to them, and the simple icon or tablet was taken out of the temple to "inspect" sites of severe problems. People believed that, if petitioned properly and sincerely, the earth gods would protect

*Rituals performed at a
Daoist temple in Xi'an.*

against locusts, mildew disease, and other obstacles to a rich harvest, as well as solve any other difficulties in their domain. These shrines and the cult have returned everywhere.

Even in restaurants and homes, the trend toward restoration of shrine and ritual has gone ahead. After several attempted crackdowns by the government, restaurants have succeeded in reinstalling small altars to the local gods of wealth and protection. In private homes, the Chinese New Year has been increasingly observed with the traditional pasting of calligraphic good-luck icons, including the word for good fortune (*Fu*) placed upside down to indicate the sound of good fortune's arrival.

It is in connection with the Fu symbol that we see a further example of the government's acceptance of China's diffuse religion. Here again, by being sensitive to the importance and meaning of religion, we can comprehend the profundity of changes sweeping China: as the party expands economic opportunity but ends communal social safety-net programs, people feel that to prosper, they need all the luck they can attract. Accordingly, the quest to satisfy the perceived need for good fortune is so intense that the official proponents of communist doctrine are reluctant to suppress practices many party members consider to be superstitious.

Japan: Old Traditions and New

Whereas in China the Cultural Revolution postponed the expression of religious awakening until after Mao's death in 1976, in Japan this era of innovation commenced in 1945, with the necessity of rebuilding the war-ravaged country both physically and spiritually. For seven years occupied and ruled by the Allied powers (principally the United States), Japan had to reinvent a form of government, redesign its economic system, and rebuild its major cities without reference to the emperor as their divine leader. Japan's surrender in 1945 was spoken by Emperor Hirohito in his own voice, and during the occupation he was compelled to explicitly renounce his divinity (as a Shinto kami) and underscore his purely ceremonial presence in Japan's political future. The state system of neo-Shintoism, which was integral to the modernizations that had begun in 1867, was also discredited and discarded. Shinto then survived largely in its myriad shrines dedicated to divinities in neighborhoods, villages, and regions and attended to by hereditary priests. Establishment Buddhism, like the rest of Japan's cultural institutions, also had to rebuild its physical and social presence, overcoming the stigma of having uncritically supported the fascist state. As the economic system flourished, the country's wealth eventually was used to rebuild these institutions, accelerating the traditional religion's material recovery and, in some cases, expansion.

The Claim of "Having No Religion" and the Reality of New Year's Rituals

Educated Japanese, and oftentimes their friends in intellectual Western circles, are fond of proclaiming that the Japanese are "lacking in religion," an Enlightenment attitude common among educated East Asians. Some try to project an image of Japan as a modern society comparable to Europe or North America in its scientific sophistication. While few Japanese care to learn much in depth about Shinto mythology or Buddhist doctrine, widespread indifference does not prove that Japan "lacks religion."

Beyond the unprecedented growth of the new religions, one has only to know where and when to seek a wealth of examples that dispel this widespread stereotype about a Japanese people somehow different from everyone else. While it is foolish to ignore the force of skepticism, scientific theory, and cynicism in any modern society, it is also naïve to judge "religiousness" by formal institutional measures alone. Contemporary New Year's Day observances provide an example of the strength of "diffuse popular religion" in modern Japan.

During the Meiji era, Japan had legislated a shift away from the Chinese lunar calendar determining the date of the "new year" festival and adopted the Western (or Gregorian) system that has the year begin on January 1. On this day and days around it, Japan shuts down its industrial economy. Families begin the process of renewal through a special cleaning of the house (*susuharae*, "soot and cobweb clearing"). On New Year's Eve or early New Year's morning, a visitor to any Shinto shrine—even in the most modern Tokyo urban neighborhood—will see long lines of family members coming for *hatsu-mode*, a formal visit to pay their respects to their neighborhood's kami. The people then consign to the carefully laid bonfires all the family amulets accumulated over the past year. That evening or the next day, a family member will purchase new amulets that will be carefully set up on the newly purified family altar. Many temples plan their annual festival for this period, when crowds throng to temple precincts to buy amulets and attend the priestly rituals empowering them. In nearly every shop and house are decorations dedicated to the kami residing in the neighborhood. On New Year's morning, too, families gather at their household altars to worship the Buddhas, Kannon, and local gods. Thus, in the renewal of the family shrine at the year's turning, by "being careful" with local divinities, in sacralizing family ties, and by suspending the profane activities of markets and business activities, contemporary New Year's Day traditions in Japan fit perfectly into the "religion" framework we introduced in Chapter One.

Continuing Support for Shinto Shrines

Most Japanese—housewives, salarymen, artisans—still widely believe that wherever one lives, and certainly wherever one's family still has an ancestral residence, one has loose ties to the shrine that houses the deity of that locality, the *uji-kami*. We've seen that on New Year's Day at least, paying respects to that kami remains a very popular observance. Almost equally popular in most parts of Japan is the ritual of bringing newborn babies to "meet" the kami and to pay their own respects, requesting protection. There is also a festival dedicated to the well-being of children.

When we try to understand the typical individual today visiting a Shinto shrine, it is nearly impossible to separate the spiritual from the habitual or the recreational. In a recent survey of those who visited shrines, 65 percent of men and 75 percent of women reported experiencing *aratamatta kimochi*, "a feeling of inner peace," afterward.[10] The observer at the shrine finds many

Honoring the kami at a Shinto shrine in Kyoto.

ritual activities that seem to indicate religious conviction—clapping the hands together, bowing before an image, making an offering, buying an amulet.

A modern exponent of Shinto's relevance in contemporary Japan would certainly note that, although some Shinto shrines may be neglected, there are over one hundred thousand such holy places, and none of them is in ruins.

The Zen of Daruma-san

If any single religious icon could be said to embody all the mind-boggling complexities and paradoxes of religion in Japan today, it might be *Daruma-san*. The name and identity of this figure derives from Bodhidharma, the sage renowned as the transmitter of the Buddhist meditation tradition from India (around 600 CE) that became Ch'an in China and Zen in Japan. Daruma-san became a Zen saint, and legends about him are part of the scriptural lore of this school. They celebrate his unbending commitment to meditation retreats and his terse, no-nonsense replies to students and patrons. From the Kamakura period in Japan when Zen schools were imported from China, Daruma-san became a favorite subject for painters and sculptors. Images of Daruma-san came to be popular in Japanese folk traditions as well: his visage adorns kites, toys, knock-down dolls, sake cups. Several dozen major Buddhist temples feature his icon and offer a full range of amulets.

Zen painting depicting Bodhidharma, founder of the Ch'an/Zen Buddhist school.

Today, the most widely used images of Daruma-san are limbless round papier-mâché icons called *okiagari* that are employed for making vows or wishes. The standard ritual consists of making a wish and coloring in one eye of the statue, which is then placed on the family altar. When there is success in the matter wished for, the other eye is colored in and the doll (like all other amulets) fuels the next New Year's bonfire. The Daruma-san icon is used in the same manner by businesspeople undertaking new ventures and politicians beginning election campaigns.

Thus with Daruma-san we witness the domestication into popular Japanese ritual life of the founding saint of Zen Buddhism, a fiercely ascetic meditation master who has become transmuted into an ostensibly comic figure, who none-theless commands a following of hundreds of thousands. The subtle meanings of Daruma-san stand in stark contrast to the extreme teachings of a recent Japanese cult, one that attempted to use the Buddha's Four Noble Truths to rationalize a premeditated attack with nerve gas on innocent citizens.

The Rise and Fall of the Aum Cult

In March 1995, as government investigators were about to arrest its leaders, at least ten determined disciples of the Aum Shinrikyo sect executed a terrorist attack in the centrally located Kasumigaseki Station of the Tokyo subway. Twelve people were killed, and 5,500 were injured. The terrorists were acting on the orders of the sect's guru, Shoko Asahara, a semiblind 40-year-old who claimed to be an incarnation of Jesus and a spiritual master who had distilled the final truths of tantric Buddhism, Hindu yoga, the LSD psychedelic experience, New Age astrology, and the self-proclaimed sixteenth-century seer Nostradamus. In 1989, Asahara applied for and received registration as a tax-exempt religious organization for Aum Shinrikyo ("the True Teaching of Aum"). Then he set about building his sect around a core of commune-living disciples, many of whom were highly educated, successful people who commanded considerable wealth. Devotion to Asahara himself reached cultic proportions, with Aum members buying bottles of his bathwater.

In the aftermath of the attack, the Japanese cultural elite and the media engaged in a long period of self-reflection: What does this group's success say about the moral and cultural state of the nation? What did it say about Japan's educational system that among Aum's inner circle were some of the better minds of a generation, including standouts in law and science? What manner of brainwashing could have induced cult members to accept such an unlikely collection of ideas? Why did they abandon their families and all their possessions to follow a pudgy dropout who claimed to be both Buddha and Jesus? Why did they adopt Asahara's doomsday doctrine, which led them to express murderous hatred against their fellow citizens?

Leading commentators noted that Asahara and his followers were members of the generation born after World War II. They described cult members as frustrated with the laborious old Japan of business cartels that closed off new competitors, of mindless interpersonal rituals, and of fathers who saw no avenue for success in life outside the Confucian code of work, hierarchy, and "waiting your turn."

The Aum tragedy also brought to popular attention the thousands of post–World War II "new religions" that claim the loyalty of an estimated 20 percent of modern Japanese; our survey of religion in Japan concludes with an overview and sampling of them.

The New "New Religions" in Japan

A generation of Japanese spiritual leaders have arisen to form independent groups that have met the new yearnings without bearing deadly fruit like the Aum attack. Still, the attraction of "new religions" must be kept in perspective: most Japanese today have not joined them. The majority find the older traditions, or being nonreligious, more to their liking.

Some of the new "new religions" were synthesized by charismatic founders from Japan's long-extant traditions along with aspects of modern nationalism, elements of Christianity, or scientific principles. Many of the "new religions" began in some measure as responses to the dislocations that shook Japanese society during its sudden opening to the outside world in the mid-nineteenth century and the headlong modernization and Westernization of the Meiji era. Almost every older "new religion" splintered with the passing of its founder and the struggles of interpretation and succession that followed, adding to the number of groups. But most of the popular "new religions" today are more recent in origin. They tend to draw on the extant (and themselves expanding) traditions from every world area. They also attract followers who find themselves ever-more disconnected from the melding of Shintoism and Buddhism that satisfied their ancestors.

The lives of the Japanese people are changing in many dimensions—through migration from rural homesteads to burgeoning cities, with the concomitant separation from extended families and loss of community in newly built urban enclaves, and as travel and media have engendered an awareness of every portion of the world. In this new and often frightening environment, many individuals have been drawn to the "new religions" to find original answers to life's perennial questions.

In 1999 there were no less than 182,935 sects officially registered with the Japanese government, and most of them had been formed in the nineteenth century. The great majority are exceedingly small in size, inconsequential, and for the most part inactive. Many are hard to distinguish from poetry circles, philosophy clubs, or groups formed around health practitioners. The major sects are an important part of today's spiritual landscape, however; roughly 20 percent of Japanese people surveyed as long ago as 1991 reported that their predominant religious affiliation is with one of the "new religions."[11]

While Aum's mass murder plot is almost completely atypical of the new religions, other aspects of the cult are not. Most form around a charismatic leader whose personal struggle to find the truth becomes paradigmatic for the movement. Some sort of shamanic experience or performance is the most common ritual focus. In addition, members are frequently taught to reject the diffuse eclecticism of Shintoism or Buddhism, and their gurus insist that one practice and one singular revelation are definitive. Yet many of the "new" worldviews draw upon traditions such as Buddhist karma and reincarnation doctrines, Confucian moral teachings and ancestor rites, or Shinto styles of worship. Some also import practices from the West (e.g., older psychologies like "new thought" or "the power of positive thinking") or from India (e.g., Hindu yoga). Each new religion also tends to be this-worldly in its goals (especially in an emphasis on healing) and imbued with the mission of ushering in a new divine era. The most successful sects are built around a new "sacred center," a shrine with priestly administration that both expresses the sect's mission and manages the organization. Membership in most new religions is quite open, but there is typically an initiation that requires individuals to make a personal commitment to the group, following what in other faiths would be called a conversion experience.

Japan's new religions can be conveniently arranged according to their chronological emergence. The earliest, which are "new" only in relation to Japan's long history, are those that began in the nineteenth century and were eventually aligned with Shintoism. The most popular among them, the Kurozumikyo and the Tenrikyo, discussed earlier, have survived into the present. The most prominent of the second-tier group, which arose during the Meiji era, remain among the largest new religions today: the Buddhist-derived Soka Gakkai and Reiyukai Kyodan and the Seicho no Ie, a group we have not mentioned, which teaches the unity of all religions. These now established religions have followed a standard pattern: the religions that began in prewar Japan have evolved through tumultuous times, and the survivors long ago abandoned their rebellious teachings to fit into the mainstream society. That these formerly angry sectarians have made their peace with Japanese society is demonstrated in most cases by policies allowing families to participate in once-prohibited rituals to the Shinto gods and at Buddhist temples.

Many of the most successful new religions have built schools, colleges, and hospitals; some offer residential communities and athletic facilities to sustain their members from cradle to grave. These resources are also useful for proselytizing purposes and for demonstrating the power and success of the new path itself. The Tenrikyo, for example, one of the most successful new religions, has centers in every area of Japan; its headquarters, called Tenri City (near Nara), is a center for pilgrimage comparable to Salt Lake City for Mormons.

Sociological surveys have shown that devotees of the new religions are most commonly those excluded from dominant avenues to prestige in modern Japan. That is, with certain exceptions, such as the high-achieving followers of Asahara, members do not typically have prestigious jobs in the large corporations but run small family businesses. Within the group there are characteristically hierarchies and internal ranks to which individuals can aspire. Women typically outnumber men in membership and serve as leaders; their proselytizing is notable for its distinctly maternal style.

The new religions assume a common outlook (hence social posture) in presenting themselves as experts at solving human problems. Whatever their supernatural beliefs, all hold that sickness, economic failure, and all interpersonal relations are fully under individual control. Life will improve, they assert, if devotees will only discipline themselves in realizing the core values of Japanese culture: harmony, loyalty, filial piety, selflessness, diligence, ritual service. Problems can be solved by making a concerted effort to practice these virtues, to perfect the self, and harmonize it with all levels of life (from personality integration to reconciliation with one's family, society, nature, ancestors, and the supernatural). The sects differ astoundingly in the prescriptions for accomplishing these goals, and we can give here only a sampling of representative new groups formed in the postmodern era.

Perfect Liberty Kyodan Among the most popular groups is the Perfect Liberty Kyodan (P.L. Kyodan), whose primary slogan, "religion is art," indicates its emphasis on the spiritual value of practicing the fine arts in everyday life. Its focal practice is liturgical, that is, prayers choreographed with stylized prostrations, gestures, and offerings. The theology is monotheistic and explains that troubles are actually warnings from God, although their exact message can be correctly interpreted in a ritual manner only by a P.L. priest.

Rissho Koseikai ("Society Establishing Righteousness and Harmony") Rissho Koseikai was founded by Reiyukai member Niwano Nikkyo (1906–1999), who retained the Nichiren Buddhist school's focus on the *Lotus Sutra*. After 1969, the group's focus shifted to the individual's personality development through special counseling sessions (*hoza*) led by trained lay "teachers" and the goal of world peace. The group does not forbid members to join other religious groups or to participate in their rituals. International missionary movements have brought Rissho Koseikai to Korea, Brazil, and the United States. As of 2003, the Koseikai was Japan's second largest new religion, organized uniquely according to government unit lines, and claiming over 6 million members.

Agonshu A new religion founded in 1971, Agonshu also has a Buddhist identity. The group was founded by Kiriyama Seiyu (b. 1921–), a charismatic spiritualist who declared that he had "cut off" his own karma and that through visits by Buddhas and deities, the true and original teachings of Shakyamuni Buddha were revealed to him. Kiriyama's distilled "essence of Buddhism" is that the ancestors must be properly "turned into realized Buddhas" through special rituals, a view that would be disputed by Buddhist monks and scholars almost everywhere. Agonshu teachings attribute the world's current troubles to the influence of the restless dead, who afflict the living to protest neglect. In the group's view, Kiriyama has rescued for the good of the entire world esoteric practices to pacify and enlighten the dead, particularly through fire rituals kept secret for centuries by the tantric Buddhist school in Japan called Shingon. The greatest yearly practice of this Agonshu rite, called *hoshi matsuri,* or "star festival," has become one of the most spectacular events in modern Japanese religion, attracting a half-million pilgrims to the site, while millions watch on television. Each year Agonshu priests set massive twin fires, one to benefit the ancestors, the other to promote the personal welfare of all participants, who contribute millions of small boards to fuel the fire.

The goal of world peace has also in the last decade been featured as part of the sect's mission; Kiriyama has been photographed with Pope John Paul II and with the Dalai Lama to highlight Agonshu's intention of acting on the world stage for that end. Even with its outward missionizing, like many other new religions the group does not neglect benefits for the individual. Members are urged to chant the following five verses daily, the same words used to conclude Agonshu rallies:

Let's do it!
I will certainly succeed!
I am blessed with very good luck!
I will certainly do well!
I will definitely win![12]

Sukyo Mahikari The group called Sukyo Mahikari, founded in 1963, provides an example of a more ethnocentric new religion that affirms fascist prewar values and presents a more narrow, sectarian view of salvation. It teaches that the postwar occupation unnaturally imposed democracy and materialism on the Japanese people, causing them to be possessed by evil spirits angry over the corruption of the country. Then communism was sent by the gods to warn humanity of a coming ordeal, or "baptism by fire," that will claim all but the elect, who must restore patriotic ties to the emperor and demonstrate their loyalty to other Confucian relationships (between parents and children, husbands and wives). Those who follow this vision set forth by the founder, Okada Kotama, will be the "seed people" to restart the world in its proper order, as set forth in a cosmogonic myth adapted to require, today, the leadership of Okada. This group's social programs without subtlety evoke a religious expression of prewar fascism by military-style parades during which troops of disciples honor their founder with extended arms, a replica of the Nazi salute.

A Strong Confucian Tradition Accommodates Korean Diversity

With the strong living tradition of Confucianism entrenched in family rituals, marriage arrangements, and the moral education programs in the public school curriculum, South Korea is by all accounts the "most Confucian" nation in East Asia today. Institutions dedicated to Confucian studies thrive in Korea, and exponents use the mass media to preach Confucian values. A common message is that by being true to its Confucian identity, Korea has a key role to play in achieving a harmonious "meeting of West and East."

Some among the Korean political elite (like many others in East Asia) believed Confucianism to be harmful to the nation, hindering its progress in the modern world. For those espousing this viewpoint, Westernization, agnosticism, and/or Christianity served as an antidote. However, Confucianism as the cultural center of Korea has endured even among Christian converts, most of whom openly observe their family's venerable rituals in honor of ancestors. South Korea adopted national economic goals in a Confucian framework: the central government takes responsibility for the citizenry's education and economic well-being, supports the family as the basis for social stability, accepts the intelligentsia as the conscience of the nation, and invests in education as the essential foundation for both material and cultural progress. The government has likewise supported major institutions dedicated to Confucian studies.

In the nation of North Korea, a strong if archaic emphasis on communist civil religion remains. Much as in the Maoist era, citizens are expected to renounce the culture of the past, sacrifice themselves for the common good, and participate in the "cult of personality" centered on the modern nation's ruling patriarch.

As with Japan, we highlight groups that are shaping the diverse religious environment in modern South Korea.

Confucian Revival: The T'oegyehak Movement

Since learning the lessons of history is a strong Confucian value, it is not surprising that an important South Korean group emphasizes a prominent figure in its own historical tradition. Yi T'oegye (1501–1570) was a philosopher who developed the ideas of the most famous neo-Confucian Chinese thinker Zhu Xi, whose Second Epoch leadership we have discussed. Master T'oegye was responsible for making his system of thought prominent in Korea, and to this end he wrote treatises on the works of Zhu Xi and other neo-Confucians. These texts were especially influential in the realm of state law, and they emphasized ancestor ritualism strongly.

The extraordinary industrial leader Lee Dong-choon (1919–1989) started the traditionalist T'oegyehak movement group by publishing the prolific writings of Master T'oegye. The T'oegyehak, which is a presence not only across East Asia but among East Asians living in the West, has tapped Lee's personal fortune to promote detailed studies of the Confucian values as interpreted by Chinese and Korean masters. The organization also made available across the globe low-cost copies of the Confucian classics and of the group's commissioned works.

Buddhist Revival

Despite many setbacks over the last century, the surviving Korean Buddhist institutions remain well endowed with landed income. As a result the major schools have established an important niche in Korean society through the many schools their monasteries and lay institutions have started. The Son Buddhist school, the Korean version of Zen, has sent several prominent teachers to the West, winning international support and renown.

A new school calling itself Won Buddhism arose in 1924, founded by Soe-Tae San (1891–1943), a teacher who claimed to have been enlightened from his own independent ascetic practices. He and his disciples sought to revive Buddhism by simplifying its doctrines, combining Pure Land and Zen teachings. The sole Won ritual involves the worship of a picture of a black circle in a white background, symbolizing the *dharmakaya*, the cosmic body of the Buddha. From this is derived the name of the group: "Won" is the Korean reading of the Chinese character "round."

Only after the death of San and the lifting of Japanese occupation did the group find popular acceptance across Korea. Typical of reformist "Protestant Buddhist" groups elsewhere in Asia (see Chapter Seven), Won Buddhism has been especially popular in major urban areas and emphasizes that Buddhist doctrines are compatible with modern thought. It also makes Buddhism attractive to the laity by translating classical texts into vernacular Korean and through weekly congregational worship involving chanting, simple rituals, and sermons. The group encourages women to be leaders and active participants. Won Buddhist monks, who lead the ritual services, can marry.

Another aspect of Won Buddhism that resembles reform Buddhism as practiced outside Korea is the encouragement of lay meditation and social service. For the former, members try to cultivate the "Buddha nature in all things" and bring this awareness to all work done in everyday life, an exercise known as "Zen without time or place." For Won social engagement, the Buddhist ideal of no self (anatman) is sought through service offered to the public, and these activities are also seen in classical terms as a means to address the universality of suffering. The primary form of service by Won Buddhists has been in building schools, from kindergartens to universities. Its moral emphasis is also quite Confucian, emphasizing filial relations as the proper vehicle for Buddhist ethical aspiration.

By 2005, this school claimed 430 temples and 950,000 followers; it had built a grand central headquarters in Iri in southwest Korea and a convention center in Seoul. The group has also spread to fourteen countries and the United States by way of immigrants, who have built branch temples. Won Buddhists have shown increasing interest in ecumenical relations with other faiths, both in Korea and with Japanese Buddhist groups.

Christianity in Korea

An alert observer living in North America will be aware that significant numbers of native Koreans are Christians, as signs with Korean characters dotting the landscape of many U.S. and Canadian cities announce that these congregations exist and sometimes share church sanctuaries with English-speaking Christians. As of 2000, approximately 30 percent of the South Korean population was Christian, with Protestants outnumbering Catholics by four to one.

What makes Korea a unique stronghold of Christianity in Asia? Similarities between emotional Protestant rituals and the mudang tradition have been suggested, as well as several elements unique to the recent Korean historical experience, such as the positive ties established at the turn of the century with the imperial court, the churches' prominent involvement in the struggle against Japanese occupation (1910–1945), and Korean Christians' subsequent leadership in human rights activism. With the exception of some churches tolerating shamanism and reinterpreting ancestor ritualism within a Christian framework, there has been little doctrinal innovation outside the traditional denominational frameworks.

Shamanism

Amid a rising number of Christian converts and modest revivals under way among the various Buddhist schools, old and new, one finds a steady and unmistakable reliance upon shamans, or *mudang*, in South Korea. These practitioners were discussed in Chapter Two.

Korean "New Religions"

As in Japan, the collapse of the traditional order in the nineteenth century precipitated a host of religious responses, and the one major avenue was the "new religions," formed to meet a three-part challenge: rebuilding the nation, restoring its spiritual center, and supporting individuals who were coping with rapid and often traumatic changes.

Peak times of sociopolitical turmoil—for example, the years immediately following World War II—saw an especially great upsurge in these movements. Also conforming to the pattern seen in Japan's new religions, most Korean groups have been founded around men who claim a new supernatural revelation, usually a reassemblage of traditional doctrines from Buddhism, Daoism, Confucianism, or Christianity. Korean new religions likewise focus on this-worldly problems rather than the afterlife; some also imagine their playing a leading role in establishing Korea as humanity's global leader and/or creating a utopia on earth. Most have developed their doctrinal teachings into a comprehensive worldview and have created supportive social institutions. The total number of new religion adherents was last determined in 2003 by the government to number about 1 million, or 5 percent of the South Korean population.

CONCLUSION

Our study of the religions of East Asia, past and present, has shown conclusively that contrary to assertions of many among the modern elites of China and Japan, as well as numerous Western scholars, religious belief and practices are central to the life and culture of the region. East Asians are by no means an exception to the human condition, namely, that in every known society there are religious traditions at the center of its cultural life. Moreover, only by understanding the religious dimensions of Shintoism and Confucianism can one comprehend the nationalism and economic success in Japan's recent history. Likewise, only by recognizing the religious dimensions of Maoist communism is it possible to fathom how in China the Communist party has sustained its place of power since 1949, a topic we'll return to in Chapter Nine.

Nevertheless, Confucianism and Daoism present a challenge to the Western monotheistic model of "being religious," with some scholars claiming that these belief systems are not "religions" at all. Of course, in no manner is either monotheistic. Rather, their diverse aspects, as illustrated here, suggest another way for humans to be religious: not centering the sacred on a single God above, but seeing as sacred this world "below," in which humans live together and amid nature. Respect and reverence are the central religious emotions. Confucianism and the diffuse religions of East Asia have both cultural and supernatural dimensions. They create in each society circles of reciprocal relatedness, making social relations sacred, harmonizing human existence with vital energies of nature, and respecting the creative power of the universe. In the supernatural dimension, they envision a world affected by deities and reverence the survival of ancestors as spirits with whom relations can endure forever.

Both attributes of religion outlined in Chapter One—"being bound to others" and "being careful"—are abundantly highlighted across the diverse landscape of East Asian religions. The ethos promoted by East Asian religions, old and new, can be characterized as optimistic toward human life and human potential, seeing the improvement of the individual and society as sacred goals. Respect for the multiple threads of the past serves to uphold acceptance of pluralism and the tolerance of religious diversity. The "diffuse religion" supports family cohesion as the center of a moral society, and the Confucian core of East Asia supports education for its role in cultivating character and in the acquisition of practical knowledge. This sort of "pragmatic idealism" calls for improving the world for the sake of this-worldly concerns, not as the dictate of a transcendent deity. The success in the modern global marketplace of this complex of religion and culture has given the lie to Western scholars who had argued that East Asian religions were an obstacle to development.

Continued Religious Revival in China: Problems and Possibilities

In the face of determined government efforts by the Chinese communists to extirpate religion from society, and despite three decades (1950–1980) of unchallenged propaganda in support of this goal, the reemergence of religion in China is powerful proof that Marx erred when he consigned religion to the "dustbin of history." Moreover, religion is gaining importance in the country even as modern science, technology, and nationalism advance.

If the Confucian system of family/ancestral devotion is regarded as the central pillar of Chinese tradition, then it is clear that it, too, has survived the criticisms and persecutions, and has done so strongly. What is remarkable is that this has happened largely independently of any formal institutions and simply through the family relations that continued even amid fierce totalitarian attempts to suppress Confucianism.

It is possible that the future revival of religion in China will threaten regional stability. A large state trying to hold together diverse groups and disparate regions faces certain inherent problems, and difficulties loom large in the present relationship between communist China and its principal minorities. In particular, it is around religious issues that major fault lines affecting modern China are to be found—with Muslims in Xinjiang Province and with Buddhists in the Tibetan cultural region.

Falun Gong

In general, there has been a marked lack of "new religions" in the PRC under communist rule; but barely a quarter century after Mao's death, the party leadership discovered that its relaxation of earlier repressive policies had allowed the formation of a powerful new Chinese religion called Buddhist Law Power (*Falun Gong,* or *Falun Dafa*). After Falun Gong had spread to millions across China—young and old, party members and poor migrating laborers—and built an organization across the nation, it began to attract government criticism and episodes of forceful intimidation. In late April 1999, the group staged a protest against these actions, with ten thousand members surrounding the Communist party leadership compound in central Beijing. Arriving undetected, the crowds sat in silent, nonviolent protest throughout the day and then dispersed without incident. The massive sit-in baffled and unsettled the government, provoking first an official warning against future protest actions. By summer, an all-out propaganda offensive had been capped by the arrest of Falun Gong leaders, who were charged with antigovernment subversion.

By the fall, Falun Gong had been outlawed as "pernicious superstition." Thousands of members in small groups stage protests against this persecution, fully aware that some of their number have been imprisoned and tortured and some have disappeared.

Falun Gong resembles the new religions we have described in Korea and Japan: its doctrines comprise an original recombination of Buddhist and Daoist doctrines, and its founder, a charismatic leader named Li Hongzhi, claims supernormal status, "on a level the same as Buddha and Jesus." Its principal practice of qi gong exercises promises to promote individual health and spiritual transformation through the generation of extraordinary energy, in line with Daoist traditions at least two millennia old. Claiming 100 million followers in China and thirty other countries, Master Li from his exile in the United States has written texts and used mass media (videos, audiotapes, and Internet Web sites) to maintain connections between himself and his disciples. Falun Gong is an apt example of a new East Asian religion in the age of media technology, when faiths are becoming global.

A Third Confucian Epoch?

Ascribing East Asia's economic revival mainly to its Confucian roots remains, for some, a contested position. However, there are signs of Confucian renewal in each country, as societies have modified traditions to pertain to modernity without abandoning classical roots. According to "Third Epoch" proponents, the traumas of the modern era succeeded in liberating the Confucian worldview from the trappings of power that had developed in the imperial systems of China, Korea, and Japan. The application of the highest Confucian ideals had been corrupted by abusers of the powers of governments and of organized religions, turning "mastery" of the classics into a mere exercise in memorization needed to pass imperial examinations.

Now the Confucian revival movement seeks to return to the basic teachings of the early sages (Confucius and Mencius, of the First Epoch) and do what Master Zhu Xi and other reformers did in their time (Song Dynasty, 960–1279), when they revived, reinterpreted, and adapted the tradition to the challenges of their era posed by Daoism and Buddhism (the Second Epoch of neo-Confucianism). Believers in "Third Epoch" Confucianism, working in the states on the periphery of China and loosely aware of their separate initiatives, are now addressing the challenges of economic and cultural globalization.

Such efforts to revive this spiritual tradition has made "Third Epoch" Confucians critical of the global modernizing process, especially insofar as it has caused the extreme fragmentation of society, promoted the vulgarization of social life, disregarded the public good, or overglorified wealth. The vast majority of modernist Confucians adopt this critical stance, while also being committed to empirical science, democratic politics, gender equality, and the economic development in their own countries.

Yet the global vision of "Third Epoch" exponents is to bring the Confucian tradition into the debate about how the twenty-first century's international order should be conceived. They aim to foster dialog between the Confucian worldview and the ideologies of sociopolitical modernization and consumerism prominent in the Euro-American world. One "Third Epoch" Confucian summarized this goal as follows:

> Copernicus de-centered the earth, Darwin relativized the godlike image of man, Marx exploded the ideology of social harmony, and Freud complicated our conscious life. They have redefined humanity for the modern age. Yet they have also empowered us with communal, critical self-awareness, to renew our faith in the ancient Confucian wisdom that the globe is the center of our universe and the only home for us and that we are the guardians of the good earth, the trustees of the Mandate of Heaven that enjoins us to make our bodies healthy, our hearts sensitive, our minds alert, our souls refined, and our spirits brilliant. . . . We are Heaven's partners, indeed co-creators. . . . Since we help Heaven to realize itself through our self-discovery and self-understanding in day-to-day living, the ultimate meaning of life is found in our ordinary human existence.[13]

Informed by very different notions of religious truth and by ethnocentric visions of their own central places in the cosmos, will the world's people outside East Asia be interested in such a dialog?

Discussion Questions

1 What beliefs from each of the three religious traditions of the region might explain the East Asian peoples' unique capacity for sustaining the three without choosing just one?

2 How is the cult of ancestor veneration related to the norms of Confucian family morality?

3 A Chinese novelist in the colonial period described the Chinese family as "a prison ward" that denies basic rights to the individual, exploits women, and wastes the energy of the young. How would you defend Confucian ideals against these criticisms?

4 What Daoist teachings would explain why many Chinese people over the ages have embraced Buddhism, which originated in India, despite strong teachings about the inferiority of non-Chinese people?

5 How might neo-Confucianism be seen as an attempt to harmonize Buddhism, Daoism, and early Confucianism?

6 Why, from the Daoist perspective, are disasters in the natural world taken so seriously by politicians in East Asia?

7 Why do purity and brightness sum up the ethos of Shintoism?

8 Are the twenty-first-century depictions of Daruma-san a reflection of how irrelevant Zen ideals have become in the popular imagination? Or are these an apt cultural reminder, embedded in the "diffuse popular religion," of Zen Buddhism's embrace of a spirituality that connects thetranscendent with the comic?

9 Critique the following proposition: China's religious revival was postponed by the Chinese communists who imposed a "forced conversion" of the nation to Marxism–Leninism, the "new religion" it had imported from Europe.

10 For all the nations of East Asia, the colonial era was very destructive. But certain individuals fused ideas from global culture with older beliefs, creating new and original religious understandings. Cite an example of this process in China, in Korea, and in Japan.

11 What influences from the West might have influenced elites in East Asia to claim that the Chinese (or the Japanese) are "not religious"?

Key Terms

Amaterasu	Five Classics	"new religions"	T'oegyehak
Analects	Hong Xiuquan	Nichiren	Tu-di gong
ancestor veneration	kami	qi	Unification Church
Ch'ondogyo	kitchen god	qi gong	wu-wei
city god	Lao Zi	Qing-Ming	xiao
Confucianism	li	ren	yin-yang theory
Confucius	ling	shamanism	Zhu Xi
Cultural Revolution	mappo	Shang-di	Zhuang Zi
Dao	Master K'ung	Shinto	
Daoism	Mencius	Soka Gakkai	
Daruma-san	mudang	Taiping Rebellion	
diffuse religion	neo-Confucianism	"three faiths"	
	neo-Shintoism	Tian di	

Suggested Readings

Earhart, H. Byron, *Japanese Religion: Unity and Diversity* (Belmont, CA: Wadsworth, 1983).

Kendall, Laurel, *Shamans, Housewives, and Other Restless Spirits: Women in Korean Ritual Life* (Honolulu: University of Hawaii Press, 1985).

Lancaster, Lewis R., ed., *Contemporary Korean Religion* (Berkeley, CA: Institute for East Asian Studies, 1992).

Lee, Peter H., ed., *Sources of Korean Tradition: From Early Times to the 16th Century* (New York: Columbia University Press, 1996).

Lopez, Donald S., Jr., ed., *Religions of China in Practice* (Princeton, NJ: Princeton University Press, 1996).

MacInnis, Donald E., *Religion in China Today* (New York: Orbis, 1989).

Nelson, John K., *A Year in the Life of a Shinto Shrine* (Seattle: University of Washington Press, 1996).

Picken, S. D. B., *Shinto: Japan's Spiritual Roots* (Tokyo: Kodansha International, 1980).

Reader, Ian, *Religion in Contemporary Japan* (Honolulu: University of Hawaii Press, 1991).

————— and Tanabe, George J., Jr., *Practically Religious: Worldly Benefits and the Common Religion of Japan* (Honolulu: University of Hawaii Press, 1998).

Reid, T. R., *Confucius Lives Next Door: What Living in the East Teaches Us About Living in the West* (New York: Vintage Books, 1999).

Thompson, Laurence G., *Chinese Religion: An Introduction*, 5th ed. (Belmont, CA: Wadsworth Publishing, 1996).

Welch, Holmes, *The Practice of Chinese Buddhism, 1900–1950* (Cambridge, MA: Harvard University Press, 1973).

Notes

1. In D. C. Lau, *Confucius: The Analects* (New York: Penguin, 1979), p. 63.

2. Quoted in Stephen Teiser, "Popular Religion," *Journal of Asian Studies,* 54(2), 1995, 378.

3. Quoted in Wing-tsit Chan, *A Source Book of Chinese Philosophy* (Princeton, NJ: Princeton University Press, 1973), pp. 86–87.

4. Ibid., pp. 497–498.

5. Quoted in Timothy Brook, "Rethinking Syncretism: The Unity of the Three Teachings and Their Joint Worship in Late-Imperial China," *Journal of Chinese Religions,* 21, 1993, 17.

6. Ibid., p. 18.

7. Ibid., p. 22.

8. Quoted in Wing-tsit Chan, *Instructions for Practical Living and Other Neo-Confucian Writings by Wang Yang-ming* (New York: Columbia University Press, 1962), p. 272.

9. In Donald E. MacInnis, *Religion in China Today* (New York: Orbis, 1989), p. 206.

10. S. D. B. Picken, *Shinto: Japan's Spiritual Roots* (Tokyo: Kodansha International, 1980), p. 56.

11. Ian Reader, *Religion in Contemporary Japan* (Honolulu: University of Hawaii Press, 1991), p. 100.

12. Ian Reader, "The Rise of a Japanese 'New New Religion,'" *Japanese Journal of Religious Studies,* 15(4), 1988, 244.

13. Tu Wei-ming, *Life,* December 1988, 76.

CHAPTER
NINE

Globalization
From New to New Age Religions

Overview

Marie belongs to an Episcopal parish in Minneapolis, but she has other religious interests as well. Indeed, she regularly checks her astrological chart, and tonight she and her friend Allison are going to an introductory lecture on Transcendental Meditation. Last week, Marie's friend Jack talked her into going on a weekend retreat led by a psychic medium who offered to put people in touch with their dead relatives. In addition, Marie has been reading *Dianetics,* by Scientology founder L. Ron Hubbard, and she is thinking about responding to a questionnaire entitled, "Are You Curious About Yourself?" Distributed by the local Church of Scientology, the flyer had come with the morning newspaper.

All these activities mark Marie as one of countless individuals who are on a personal quest that is typical of new age religion: they are eager to explore the mystery of the "self" and its perfection. Marie has another friend, Mark, who thinks she is too self-absorbed and needs to pay more attention to issues of social justice in a global culture that is shaped by mass media and multinational corporations and marred by racial and economic exploitation. Mark is trying to get her involved in a small interracial activist group inspired by the life and teachings of Martin Luther King Jr. All these approaches to life, and many more, as we shall see, could be grouped together under the heading of "new age religions."

In this chapter we will first explore what we mean by "new" religions and then focus primarily on "new age religions"—the distinctive forms that new religions and new ways of being religious have taken in response to globalization. New religions represent the integration of influences from multiple religions and cultures, resulting in the creation of new variations and expressions of known religious practices. In one familiar pattern, a new prophet or sage reveals new understandings of an existing tradition, given to him or her in religious experiences or revelations.

In the past the message of prophets and sages reflected primarily local situations—typically the incursion of elements imported from nearby religions and cultures. Today, however, many new religious movements reflect not just a response to local diversity—to this or that movement that has entered the environment of a relatively stable culture. Rather, they are indicative of an

awareness of global religious diversity as a whole, past and present. This awareness is fostered by mass communications and widespread access to transportation, introduced by modern science and technology.

It is in this new environment of the awareness of the diversity of human religious experience that the "new age" religions are emerging, both accommodating and integrating diverse elements of varying, often quite dissimilar, existing traditions. Some movements, however, represent the attempt to reassert particular forms of religious expression that adherents believe have been neglected but should be operative in the new age of global interdependence. Contemporary interest in shamanism and goddess worship would be examples of this. What these movements typically have in common is the belief that humanity is indeed entering a "new age" in which global harmony must be achieved, not only with other religions and cultures but also with the natural environment.

A shamanistic ritual practiced at a new age conference in Long Beach, California.

NEW RELIGIONS

Old Religions and New Religions in the History of Religions

From a historical perspective, as this book has amply indicated, no religion has ever managed to remain unchanged. Indeed, while every chapter in this book began with an "overview" description of the religious beliefs and practices of the tradition, in every case we went on to say that such a snapshot was no more than a broad generalization that did not accurately reflect the tremendous diversity found among practitioners, yesterday or today. There is not one Judaism but many, not one Buddhism but many—likewise there are many Christianities, many Islams, Hinduisms, many Daos and Confucian beliefs.

Every tradition tolerates a tremendous amount of diversity. An emerging movement that at first is treated as a form of error may finally be accepted into the fold, or at least tolerated as a distant cousin. It may, for example, by seen as a reform within the tradition to bring it back to its original purity. But then there are other movements, perhaps brought about by new religious experiences and extraordinary revelations, whose "errors" seem too great. Changes that had started out as reforms may present such a dramatic break with past beliefs and practices that they come to be perceived not as a continuation of the old tradition but as a fatal error—a deviation from the true path. The new tradition, of course, sees the error lying not in itself but in the old tradition, which had somehow lost its way.

Although before the Common Era there was more than one form of Judaism, Christianity, which began as a Jewish sect called the Nazarenes, came to be seen and, to see itself, as crossing a boundary that made it no longer a Jewish alternative but a "new religion." And while Christianity also encompasses tremendous diversity, when Islam emerged in Arabia in the seventh century it was seen by Christians as a new and heretical religion, even though Muslims recounted many of the same biblical stories and saw their faith as the continuation and culmination of God's revelations handed down through Moses and Jesus. Moreover, Islam developed two major branches, Sunni and Shiah, as well as many schools of theology and law. Later, in nineteenth-century Persia, when the Baha'i movement claimed to bring a final revelation that included all the religions, East and West, it too came to be viewed as "not true Islam," hence as a new belief system.

When we look at Asian religions we find the same pattern. Hinduism encompasses great diversity, and yet as Buddhism grew and developed, it was seen, and came to see itself, as a "new religion." Buddhism too splintered into many Buddhisms, some claiming to be more advanced than others.

Thus some movements emerged and then disappeared in every tradition. Even so, in century after century, many of "today's" new religions become tomorrow's old and established religions. We can illustrate the character of new religions with a few examples before turning to our primary concern, examples of "new age" religions that have appeared in our emerging global civilization. The relatively recent history of Christianity in North American culture presents an interesting illustration of how a new religion comes to be.

In the 1800s, Christian denominationalism began to emerge as a way of moving beyond the hostile sectarianism that had divided Christians, and by the late twentieth century there was a broad spectrum of religious diversity in America. Nevertheless, a number of very distinctive religious movements that originated in the nineteenth century tested the limits of denominationalism. As a rule, contemporary mainline Christian denominations (i.e., those representing widely established, long-accepted church traditions in America, such as the Methodists, Presbyterians, and Episcopalians) regard these unique movements as having strayed beyond the boundaries of Christianity. Mormonism provides us with a good example.

Joseph Smith Jr., receiving the sacred plates of the Book of Mormon from the Angel Moroni.

The Church of Jesus Christ of Latter-day Saints: A New American Christianity

The Church of Jesus Christ of Latter-day Saints, or Mormonism, was established on April 6, 1830, by Joseph Smith Jr. It appears to have arisen in response to the confusion created by the incredible sectarian diversity of nineteenth-century Christianity. Joseph Smith believed he had been led by angels to discover a revelation that would overcome this confusion. The new revelation, contained in the Book of Mormon, was understood by Smith and his followers as a continuation of the revelation given in the Bible. It was a revelation that had been given first to Native Americans, as descendants of the lost tribes of ancient Israel. Mormons believe that these tribes had migrated to the North American continent, where the risen Christ visited them and gave them new revelations. Eventually the book containing these pronouncements was buried by a Native American named Mormon, who was killed by tribesmen who rejected the new message and wanted to suppress it. It was these "pagan" natives who met Columbus in 1492. But the revelation could not be suppressed forever, and so Joseph Smith was guided by angels to find the Book of Mormon so that it could flourish once more.

Earlier we noted the incorporation into Christianity of traditions specific to Africa and Asia. Similarly, Mormonism links biblical religion to the history of an indigenous population—in this case producing a distinctively American Christianity, one that includes visits of the risen Christ and several of the risen apostles to a new land, to guarantee the purity of Mormon revelation and so set it apart from existing human interpretations of Christianity. The capstone of the message was the promise that at the end of the "latter days," Christ would return to establish a "New Jerusalem" in America. Mormonism, with its emphasis on family, community, and healthy, wholesome living, has flourished, with well over 10 million members worldwide.

Ahmadiyyat: A New Islamic Religion

The Ahmadiyyat is an example of a new religious movement in modern Islam. From its inception in 1899 in British India, it has been one of the most active, progressive, and controversial movements in Islam, rejected by many Muslims as heretical. Mirza Ghulam Ahmad, the founder, was born in Qadian, a village in the Punjab. He wrote prolifically, built and expanded the organization, and engaged in sometimes heated debates with many Sunni ulama and Christian missionaries.

Ghulam Ahmad described his spiritual status and mission in both messianic and prophetic terminology. His claim to be a renewer of Islam, a mujaddid, fell within the boundaries of official Islam or orthodoxy. When he assumed the titles of Mahdi and prophet, however, he was roundly condemned by the ulama and by prominent Muslim groups like the Jamaat-i-Islami. Ahmad answered criticisms by saying that unlike legislative prophets, like Jesus and Muhammad, who bring God's revelation and divine law to the people, he had a divine mandate to renew and reform the Islamic community. Thus, as a nonlegislative prophets, Ahmad could affirm the finality of the prophethood of Muhammad while maintaining that God continued to send religious reformers like himself to provide prophetic guidance to the Islamic community.

The Ahmadis are great supporters of modern education and Islamic reform. As a global missionary movement they have established a large network of mosques and centers and peacefully propagated their faith in Asia, Africa, Europe, and America.

Civil Religion in China and the United States

Civil religions represent yet another form in which religious traditions can accomplish very traditional roles in a society. In most times and most places throughout the history of civilization, religion and politics permeated all of culture and were like two sides of the same coin. It was, as we have seen, modernity that introduced secular nation-states and the idea that government should not impose on citizens the obligation to join or practice any religion. But having removed religion as a legitimizer of their own authority, these modern states faced a new problem—winning loyalty from their citizens without the traditional appeal to religion. The result has been the creation of a distinct entity we shall call "civil religion," which reintroduces religion under the disguise of "indigenous cultural history and tradition" to reinforce the authority of new and more secular political social orders.

Thus a civil religion is based on a sacred narrative of the state's founding, in which the development of the state is portrayed as a just moral enterprise, in harmony with ideals of the religious traditions shared by most citizens. Typically, the state's leaders developed a set of national rituals and yearly holidays (holy days) that celebrate and allow the regular, solemn reliving of key events the nation's history. Such civil religions come to expression in national anthems and patriotic songs, school textbooks that emphasize the righteousness of the country's founders, and war memorials honoring those who sacrificed their lives for the nation.

In many cases, the cultural pattern from one tradition (Christianity, Islam, Confucianism etc.) clearly comes to underlie the nation's civil religion, though seldom to the extent of specific endorsement. What is striking is how nearly all the great ideas in the history of religions (e.g., sacrifice, sage, prophet, martyrdom, sacred center, "chosen people," rebirth, millennialism) have been adopted across the world in the service of creating and sustaining the civil religions that support modern nations. Two examples will illustrate this: Chinese Communist civil religion and civil religion in the United States.

Chinese Communist Civil Religion   When the Red Army gained control of the mainland of China in 1949, Communist party leader Mao Zedong ascended the southern gateway to the emperor's old palace (the Forbidden City) to proclaim the creation of the People's Republic of China. This moment was later pictured on currency and in popular prints, and soon thereafter an immense portrait of Chairman Mao was mounted over the ancient gateway, where it hangs to this day. Over the next 25 years, the Communist party drew upon a variety of religious conceptions to legitimate its position in China and to wield power. The Communist millennial doctrine, imported from Russian revolutionaries but rooted in the prophetic biblical understanding, insisted that a paradise on earth was inevitable if the people changed their ways and lived in thoroughgoing cooperation. Citizens who sacrificed themselves for the common good were immortalized as "heroes of the people," their dying was said to hasten the arrival of the new age.

Early on, the government adapted ancient Confucian imperial doctrine to promote the cult of Mao himself as the sage–philosopher leader of the nation, whose words and teachings were pivotal for national salvation, whose character radiated the morality of communist truth. Statues of Mao were put up in public spaces around the nation, his portrait replaced images of family ancestors in home shrines, and during the Cultural Revolution (1966–1976) his "Little Red Book" became a sacred text to be memorized, followed, and always possessed. Officially, the Communist party disavowed religion as superstition and railed at long-dead Chinese emperors as feudal exploiters of the masses. Nevertheless, it is not hard to see how party strategists adapted powerful religious ideas from both European and Chinese traditions to create a civil religion to confirm the legitimacy of the dictatorship.

Mao Zedong, founder
of the People's Republic
of China.

American Civil Religion   American civil religion as found in the United
States develops from European colonization, justifying the history of American
ancestors claiming the land "from sea to shining sea" as being part of a divine
plan unfolding in its "manifest destiny." God is said to have given America as
a "promised land," to those who are his "chosen people" to foster the sacred
values of freedom and democracy. Thus the narrative of American civil
religion presents the United States as a "city on a hill," called by God to be a
model for all nations.

Although founded by those who consciously avoided the establishment of
any state religion, American civil religion, according to sociologist Robert
Bellah, appeals to George Washington as the "Father" of the country while
Abraham Lincoln is its "Savior" who led the nation from the sin of slavery
through the crisis of civil war, dying in the service of the sacred land and leading to its moral and spiritual renewal. National holidays such as Presidents'
Day, the Fourth of July, Memorial Day, and Thanksgiving celebrate American
civil religion. The rituals of these celebrations connect patriotism to the
sacredness of the American way of life and God's special blessings on the
United States.

As the record of the recent past makes clear, civil religion has had the effect
of assimilating individuals and diverse ethnic groups into the world's new
nations. But the rise of civil religions has also led to excesses, fueling genocidal
campaigns by states on four continents against those who are not part of their
sacred history.

NEW AGE RELIGIONS

The New Age: Modern and Postmodern

The collapse of colonialism was followed by the emergence of globalization—the development of international corporations, global mass transportation, and global mass media under the impact of science and technology. Logically enough, then, since the 1960s and 1970s new patterns of religion have appeared that reflect a global consciousness. The religions shaped by science and technology as well as by the traditional considerations, although incredibly diverse, are often grouped together under the title "new age religions." Not all new age religions are postmodern as we have defined that term. Indeed, many are content to continue the modernist pattern of privatization rather than seek a new public role for religion. But global consciousness has been a significant factor in the emergence of all new age religions. In this section and the next, we will look at examples of modernist and postmodernist new age religions.

The problem with a secular understanding of time, history, and society is that the significance and drama provided by the grand narratives of religions are missing. The resurgence of religions since the 1970s may well represent the need to fill the vacuum created by the tendency of secularization to purge events of meaning. Pluralism may have collapsed the grand metanarratives into smaller stories, but there is still a great hunger for such stories, and new age religions help people discover the meaning and significance of time and their place in it. New age religions provide a rich feast for the religious imagination as seekers attempt to penetrate the mysteries of their time and to explore the wonders it offers.

In the first chapter we cited Jean-François Lyotard's definition of postmodernism as the collapse of metanarratives, the grand stories or myths that gave each civilization a sense of meaning, purpose, and identity. The great metanarratives created a relationship of identity between religion and culture, giving us Hindu civilization, Christian civilization, Islamic civilization, and so on. Each civilization was centered in its own grand stories and the social practices that came from the vision of life the stories promoted. Modernism and its myth of scientific progress were relatively recent additions.

Postmodern culture represents the loss of a normative center in every culture that has been touched by global mass media, international corporations, and global mass transportation. Postmodern culture is pluralistic, relativistic, and eclectic—seemingly without any public norms or standards. The choice between "truths" is said to be intellectually undecidable and so is decided pragmatically, in terms of "what works for me." Truth, goodness, and beauty are in the eye of the beholder. People mix and match beliefs, practices, and aesthetic choices to their own taste in all areas of life—whether music, clothing, architecture, intellectual beliefs, or religion.

Globalization provides the social context of postmodernism. Globalization "marbelizes" all cultures so that the world's religions are accessible in everyone's hometown. Today, much more than in the past, in the same community you will find Jews, Christians, Muslims, Hindus, Buddhists, and many others. Such pluralism is a powerful social force inducing the collapse of the metanarrative, whereby a story that was once embraced by almost all people in a given culture is now simply one of many stories. In this situation religions are challenged first to relinquish their position of being identical with the culture and then to accommodate an existing cultural pluralism. In this context, almost all religious communities have had to embrace denominational identities, accepting the existence of other beliefs and practices, although fundamentalist communities strive mightily to resist such an accommodation. This, we said, was what sociologist Peter Berger meant by saying that all religions have become "Protestant." But for most new age groups their religious practices have gone a step further, moving from organizational pluralism (denominationalism) to eclecticism.

Many of the "new age" religions, like older "new religions," represent the integration of the diverse influences from different traditions. The new age religions are not based solely on the great world religions; often they incorporate elements of primal religions, exhibiting a special interest in shamanism. Moreover, today these eclectic belief systems typically reflect not only global religious diversity but the global influence of science and technology as well.

New age religious movements can be divided into modernist forms, which continue to privatize religion, and postmodernist public forms of religious practice, which seek an active role, socially and politically, in transforming society. Most modernist new age religions are highly diverse in their practices and beliefs, with minimal organizational structure. Nevertheless, there are some very important instances of highly structured new age movements; as we shall see, Scientology is one. What unites new age seekers, despite their diversity, however, is the quest for the perfection of the self. Their goal is to realize a "higher self" through intense personal experiences of transformation.

Many new age seekers are not interested in joining religious organizations. They typically integrate a variety of interests into their personal style of spiritual practice. Many read "spiritual" books and go to workshops and seminars intended to guide them to self-realization. Modernist "new agers" are interested in such shamanistic practices as channeling information from other-worldly spiritual beings, contacting the dead through mediums, spiritual healing, and the cultivation of ecstatic out-of-body experiences (sometimes referred to as astral projection). They are also interested in the mystical traditions and meditation practices of all religions, as well as the ancient divination practice of astrology. Some combine these interests with the teachings and practices of transpersonal psychologists such as Abraham Maslow (1908–1970) and Fritz Perls (1894–1970); others embrace speculative visions that combine the "new physics" with religion, believing that science itself is finally coming to discover and affirm ancient religious and metaphysical insights. The final test of each seeker's synthesis is personal experience and pragmatically evaluated usefulness.

Modernity, we learned in the chapter on Christianity, emerged out of the splitting of the medieval unity of faith and reason into *via moderna* of empirical rationality and the *devotio moderna* of personal emotional experiences of transformation (mysticism, pietism, and the experience of being "born again"). The first path became dominant in the Enlightenment and the second in the Romantic movement, as a reaction to the Enlightenment. The growth of new age religiousness is deeply rooted in this Romantic reaction to the rationalism of the Enlightenment.

The Enlightenment emphasized universal rationality (i.e., the sameness of human nature), science, and progress. Its philosophers rejected the ancient, the archaic, the traditional, the idiosyncratic, and the nonrational. The Romantic reaction did just the opposite, embracing in all their diversity the emotional, the experientially transformational, the historically unique and particular, and the "primitive" and traditional.

Like fundamentalist evangelical Christianity, modernist forms of new age religions are expressions of the human need for transformative experience, a need as old as shamanism and as recent as the Romantic reaction to Enlightenment rationalism. Both de-emphasize rationality and focus on the experiential transformation and perfection of the self through deeply emotional experiences of the kind we have called religious. And both share the conviction that all social change begins by changing the self (i.e., being born again).

The Age of Apocalypse or the Age of Aquarius?

Two new age models of religious meaning are playing a role in our emerging global civilization—the apocalyptic and the astrological. These models share a vision of the conflict and discord of the past and present giving way to a future era of global peace and harmony. Among Christian evangelicals the popularity of the belief that the end of time is near is evidenced by sales of tens of millions of books like Hal Lindsey's *The Late Great Planet Earth* and the *Left Behind* series of novels. As indicated by the popularity of biblical prophecies of the end times among evangelical Christians, there are still many heirs to the apocalyptic religious vision of the medieval monk Joachim of Fiore, who anticipated a "third age" (the age of the Spirit) as a time of global peace and harmony. However, the third age will be preceded by the biblical apocalypse, which in turn will bring the cataclysmic end of time. The belief that there will be a cataclysmic end to time followed by a new age of peace and harmony is also illustrated in such late-twentieth-century movements as the Unification Church and Aum Shinrikyo, to be reviewed shortly. But first we will turn to the alternative vision—the astrological vision of the age of Aquarius.

A gentler vision of the new age, the age of Aquarius, has been offered by some astrologers in recent decades: "We are passing out of 2,000 years of Piscean astrological influence into the influence of Aquarius, which will affect all aspects of our culture as we move from Piscean structures of hierarchical devotion to more fluid and spontaneous relationships that dance to an Aquarian rhythm."[1] Predictions of the coming of a new age by others not of the apocalyptic tradition include the writings of Jose Arguelles. In his book *The Mayan Factor,* this new age author used ancient Mayan and Aztec astrology to calculate that the age of Aquarius would begin in 1987, on August 16 or 17.[2]

In these Aquarian times, many forms of new age religion tap into a very ancient type of religious experience found in primal animistic and early urban polytheistic religious practices—that of the shaman. As we saw in Chapter Two, in his or her ecstatic or out-of-body experiences, the shaman explores the spirit world, the realm of contact with spiritual beings and dead ancestors.

Everywhere in the world, shamanism appears to be the earliest form of religious experience. And everywhere, the great world religions emerge with the discovery that the shaman's realm is really an intermediate spiritual realm between the earthly physical world and a higher unitary reality. For example, in the Vedas of Hinduism the highest realities are the many gods and goddesses of nature, but in the Upanishads the discovery is made that the gods are part of the order of this world of samsara and that there is a higher power beyond their realm, the reality of Brahman.

The emergence of monotheism out of polytheism in the Mediterranean world (in Judaism, Christianity, and Islam) provides another example. The polytheistic realm of the gods was not denied. It could not be denied because many people continued to have shamanistic-type experiences of another realm, inhabited by spiritual beings. So this realm of the deities was reassigned to a different kind of spiritual being and renamed the realm of angels and demons. Like the devas or gods of Hinduism, angels were recognized as spiritual beings, yet they were part of the cosmic order created by a higher reality, God. In China this concept of a higher unitary reality was given the impersonal name of Dao.

For all the differences between ancient urban religious cultures and religions in postmodern society, there is at least one profound similarity between them: both premodern urban society, as typified by the polytheistic culture of ancient Rome, and postmodern society, with its myriad eclectic religious practices, lack an integrating center. In both, being religious is not so much about belonging to "a religion" as it is about selecting from the chaotic variety of available beliefs and practices, a mix that will serve the pragmatic purposes of finding health, happiness, and meaning, that is, of having the unseen powers that govern your destiny on your side.

Wicca and the Resurgence of Goddess Worship

Determining how many people "practice new age religion" is next to impossible. This is because it is quite common for nominal adherents to one of these belief systems to practice several different forms in their private life, while perhaps also belonging to a traditional church or synagogue. One form this eclectic spirituality can take is sometimes called "neopaganism," which is vividly exemplified in a return to the practice of witchcraft, or attunement to the sacred powers of nature, a pattern found in all premodern societies. The most prominent such practice today is Wicca, which appears to be a self-conscious reconstruction of ancient pagan religious practices. The Wiccan movement can be traced back to England in the 1940s and the writings of Gerald Gardener,

A Wiccan ritual celebrating harmony with nature.

who claimed to be an initiate of a Wiccan coven, authorized to reveal its teachings and practices to the public. Two students of Gardener's brought the practice to America in the 1960s. By 1965 a church of Wicca was established in Mississippi, and by 1978 the handbook for U.S. military chaplains included Wicca in its list of religions.

Wiccans see the world ordered by sacred forces that can be accessed through ritual magic. These powers are personified as gods and goddesses. Wiccan rituals involve the elaborate use of chant, dance, drumming, and meditation. By following the ancient Celtic agricultural cycle of festivals for the seasons of the year, these rituals enable Wiccans to reconnect with the rhythms of nature and to experience its hidden unity. Many tend to see their ritual practice as an outward expression of the fundamental truth of the interconnectivity of all things, a view that they believe modern science also affirms. One strand of Wicca, Dianic Wicca, presents itself as a feminist religion that rejects references to gods in favor of goddess worship and has radicalized its practice by banning male membership.

The Convergence of Science, Technology, and Religion: The Path to Scientology

The precedents for Wicca and many other forms of new age religion go back to the interest in esoteric religious beliefs and practices that flourished in the nineteenth century, when historical and ethnographic researchers were just beginning to catalog the diverse practices of primal (tribal) and archaic (early urban) religions. From Europe, the teachings of Emanuel Swedenborg (1688–1772) and Franz Anton Mesmer (1734–1815) spread belief in the validity of the shamanistic experience of other worlds and in the animistic unity of all things, which made spiritual healing possible. In America, Ralph Waldo Emerson (1803–1882) and others popularized a school of thought called transcendentalism, which integrated certain Asian religious beliefs (especially Hinduism) with American philosophy, affirming the existence of a "world soul" that all beings shared. In this context the practice of spiritualism also flourished, with psychic mediums performing in private séances the ancient shamanistic rituals for contacting spirit beings and dead relatives.

Madam Helena Petrovna Blavatsky, founder of the theosophy movement.

One of the most important movements to emerge at this time was theosophy, founded in New York by Helena Petrovna Blavatsky (1831–1891) in 1875. Like the transcendentalists, theosophists found great spiritual wisdom in esoteric teachings, especially in the ancient teachings of Hinduism, with their focus on the interconnectedness of all beings through the universal Brahman. In the theosophical view, all world religions have a hidden unity of message and metaphysical reality, which could be sought through the truths of esoteric texts, as well as through the help of leaders who claimed to receive guidance from "living masters," residing in the Himalayas. As we saw in Chapter Seven, the theosophists had considerable influence among Asian reformers who were trying to modernize Buddhism. The growing interest in global religious wisdom was evident in the first Parliament of World Religions in Chicago in 1893, at which representatives of all the world's religions convened to share their views.

This historical milieu gave birth to two important nineteenth-century precursors of new age religion, both with roots in the New Thought movement: the Church of Christ, Scientist (Christian Science) and the Unity School of Christianity. Women were leaders in both movements. Mary Baker Eddy was the founder of the Christian Science movement, and Emma Curtis

Emma Curtis Hopkins, founder of the Unity School of Christianity.

Hopkins, a former disciple, broke with Eddy to form the Unity School. The two movements drew on popular forms of philosophical idealism, and the Unity School emphasized Hindu teachings, as well. These influences were integrated with an aura of "science" to affirm the higher reality of mind over matter and therefore the possibility of spiritual healing and spiritual control over the events of one's life.

As the new age religions began to appear in the twentieth century, the religious fascination with the authority of "science" broke free of its earlier linkage to Christianity in movements of the "Christian Science" type. One result was the emergence of Scientology, founded by L. Ron Hubbard (1911–1986). In 1950 Hubbard published *Dianetics: The Modern Science of Mental Healing*, in which he claimed to have discovered a cure for all human psychological and psychosomatic ills through the realization of a state of mind he called "Clear." Hubbard went on to establish the Hubbard Dianetic Research Foundation in Elizabeth, New Jersey. Later he moved the organization to Phoenix, Arizona, where the Hubbard Association of Scientologists was founded in 1952.

Mary Baker Eddy, founder of the Church of Christ, Scientist (Christian Science).

Scientology goes beyond the psychological orientation of Dianetics to develop an elaborate mythology according to which all humans were once advanced beings Hubbard called Thetans: all-powerful, eternal, and omniscient. The first Thetans relieved their boredom by playing mind games in which they used imagination to create different physical worlds. However, they soon forgot their true identity as creators and found themselves trapped in these worlds, living as mortals who died, only to be reincarnated again and again. At each reincarnation, people accumulated more psychological baggage, which Hubbard called engrams. To be liberated from this pattern and realize one's true identity, it is necessary to gain insight into one's engrams. Upon finally achieving the "Clear" state of mind, a person gains control over both mind and life. The auditing process that leads to this liberation came to involve the use of a machine that works somewhat like a lie detector. This device, the E-meter, it is believed, measures reactions of resistance to words and other symbols that reveal undissolved engrams. After achieving Clear, one can go on to higher states that involve out-of-body experiences.

In 1954 Hubbard established the first Church of Scientology in Washington, D.C., and in 1959 he started the Hubbard College of Scientology in England. Whereas many new age religious movements stress individualism and are quite loosely organized, Scientology has an elaborate global organization; bureaucratically and hierarchically, it is not unlike Roman Catholicism and Mormonism. Perhaps an even better analogy is to

L. Ron Hubbard

Scientology was founded by L. Ron Hubbard (1911–1986). Although born in Tilden, Nebraska, Ron Hubbard was exposed to Asian religion and culture as a child because his father was in the navy. As a young man with an adventurous spirit Hubbard was involved in three Central American ethnological expeditions. He received a commission in the navy during World War II, during which service he was pronounced dead twice. In one instance he apparently had something like a shamanistic out-of-body experience in which he acquired spiritual knowledge that gave him his life's mission.

In 1950 Hubbard published *Dianetics: The Modern Science of Mental Healing*, which became the foundation for Scientology. According to *Dianetics*, the mind is made up of two parts, the analytic and the reactive. Traumatic experiences in early life, or even in the womb, are said to imprint themselves on the reactive mind as "engrams," which cause psychological and psychosomatic problems if they are not dissolved. The way to dissolve these traumatic impressions is to work with a counselor called an auditor, who leads the individual into reenacting the events that caused the trauma, thus releasing or liberating the individual from the engrams' negative effects. Hubbard called this state of release "Clear", and devotees of Scientology work hard to attain it.

L. Ron Hubbard, founder of Scientology.

the modern international business corporation, with its penchant for technical language, efficient organization, and the dissemination of polished communications to interface with the world. And yet all this organization and efficiency is focused on bringing about a powerful experience of enlightenment or rebirth that perfects the self and opens it to the spiritual world that shamans have traversed throughout the ages.

Scientologists have also shown a keen interest in Buddhist teachings, and of course, the parallels of the auditing practices to depth psychology are obvious. The description of Clear by one Scientologist shows the movement's affinity with both Western experiences of being "born again" and Eastern experiences of enlightenment:

> There is no name to describe the way I feel. At last I am at cause. I am Clear—I can do anything I want to do. I feel like a child with a new life—everything is so wonderful and beautiful. Clear is Clear! It's unlike anything I could have imagined. The colors, the clarity, the brightness of everything is beyond belief. Everything is so new, I feel new born. I am filled with the wonder of everything.[3]

Scientology is, in many ways, the perfect illustration of the global eclectic integration of the elements that make up new age religions: science (especially psychology), technology (corporate and technical structure), Asian religions (reincarnation and the quest for liberation), and shamanism (out-of-body spiritual explorations). A Thetan, according to Hubbard, goes "through walls, barriers, vanishes space, appears anywhere at will and does other remarkable things."[4]

East Goes West: Transcendental Meditation

Transcendental Meditation (TM) is an example of an Asian religion moving West, yet another manifestation of the globalization process inherent in new age religion. The mantra system known by its trademarked name, Transcendental Meditation, first came to global public attention in the 1960s when its founder, Maharishi Mahesh Yogi, became the guru of the Beatles, then at the height of their popularity.

The Maharishi taught a kind of spiritual hedonism, according to which our desire to enjoy life is natural, holding that TM offers the most efficient path to this joy. One need not become an ascetic, fasting and meditating for endless hours: twenty minutes, twice a day, could suffice to bring spiritual transformation. Drawing on traditional teachings from Vedantic Hinduism, the Maharishi taught that happiness could be achieved by tapping into one's naturally serene self, a fragment of the universal Brahman self that all beings share. This is accomplished by stopping all distracting thoughts so that one's consciousness can reach its true center.

Becoming a practitioner was made fairly easy. There is an introductory lecture on the philosophy and scientific benefits of TM. Then in a second

Maharishi Mahesh Yogi

The Maharishi Mahesh Yogi, who had once studied physics in India, abandoned his academic courses to learn yoga from a master known as Guru Dev. Urged by his guru to take the teachings of yoga to the West, Maharishi journeyed to the United States, where he was able to tap the growing interest in Asian religions that was part of the cultural scene of the 1960s. He gave lectures to crowds all across America, hired a PR firm, made the TV talk shows, and drew a following among prominent actors and rock musicians. In the 1970s he founded the Maharishi International University in Fairfield, Iowa. In addition to the more conventional curriculum, the school offered a doctorate in the neuroscience of human consciousness, and all students and faculty met twice a day to practice Transcendental Meditation.

meeting, more advanced information is provided and the seeker is initiated. A short period of fasting precedes the initiation, and an offering of fruit, flowers, and money is brought to the event. Then the seeker is given a personal mantra, a secret Sanskrit phrase attuned to the individual's unique needs and temperament, that is to be chanted silently in daily meditation. This mantra must never be revealed to anyone. The initiation rites are followed by three days of supervised meditation and small-group discussions. After ten days the initiate returns for checking by his or her teacher and after that returns once a month.

Initially a countercultural protest against the commercial technobureaucracy ("the system") of modern society, TM soon adapted itself to this bureaucracy. In the 1970s the movement began to market itself to a corporate clientele, presenting workshops to upper-level personnel as a way of creating more efficient and happier professionals on and off the job. To achieve scientific legitimacy the movement attempted to accumulate hard evidence that twenty minutes of meditation twice a day improved sleep, greater oxygen consumption, and made one more creative and happier in life as a result of lower metabolism.

Like many of the new age movements, and perhaps more than most, TM offered a new "Methodism" for a new age. It provided a minimal set of required beliefs, and a simple methodical set of practices aimed at self perfection, all attuned to the needs of busy individuals in a modern scientificly and technologically oriented culture.

West Goes East: The Unification Church of Sun Myung Moon and Aum Shinrikyo

The new age religions we have looked at so far have been more Aquarian than apocalyptic. They have been rooted in the nature-oriented religions deeply attuned to the cycles of nature, like the astrological tradition that posits the Aquarian age. But other new age religions reflect the pattern of the eastward migration of biblical apocalyptic traditions, leading to some interesting integrations of West and East. The Unification Church, originating in Korea, is one such example.

Unification Church

The Unification Church reflects the impact of globalization, for it is the product of colonialism and the very successful impact of Christian missions in Korea, as noted in Chapter Four on Christianity and Chapter Eight on East Asian religions. But, even more, it is an example of the transformation of Christianity in a new cultural environment, followed by the exportation of this new form of Christianity back to the West, especially to the United States.

The founder of the Unification Church, Sun Myung Moon, established a religion of divine principle called Tong Il. Eventually, Tong Il became known in the West as the Unification Church. In its earliest form this movement drew heavily on Korean shamanism, emphasizing out-of-body travels, healing, communication with spirits, and so on. As the religion moved from East to West, these elements have been downplayed. The church's global outreach really began with the emigration of Sun Myung Moon to the United States in 1971. Like Scientology (and to a lesser degree like TM), the movement showed a penchant for organization and public relations. Just as Scientology developed a reputation for attracting famous entertainers, the Unification Church courted political and academic figures with some success.

Unification's teachings are based on Moon's book, *Divine Principle*, which is really a kind of Asian or Daoist interpretation of the Bible in terms of polarities, or opposites (divine–human, male–female, etc.), beginning with the polarity of male and female in God. As in the Confucian traditions, these polarities are arranged hierarchically. The proper fourfold foundation of social order puts God at the top, then male and female as equals, with children at the bottom. The lowest order shows deference to the next higher, and all defer to God.

According to Moon's teachings, the "original sin" was Lucifer's spiritual seduction of Eve, leading her to rebel against God, after which she seduced Adam, who had intercourse with her before the time God intended, undermining the proper order of love and deference. To restore the sacred order, says Moon, God has repeatedly sent great prophets—Abraham, Moses—Jesus— but none were able to succeed. If Jesus, for instance, had not been destroyed by his enemies, he (as the second Adam) would have married a second Eve and reinstituted the right order of family and society.

Sun Myung Moon

Sun Myung Moon, the founder of the Unification Church, was born in 1920 in northern Korea, where his family joined the Presbyterian church. Moon's experience presents striking parallels to that of Joseph Smith and the emergence of the Church of Latter-day Saints (Mormonism) in the United States. In both cases, the risen Christ visits a country far from the Middle East to establish it as the new center of salvation history.

Sun Myung Moon says that when he was 16 years old, Jesus appeared to him on Easter Sunday and told him to "complete my mission." Over time, Moon says, he also was visited by other great religious figures, including Abraham, Moses, and Buddha. For nine years he struggled against "satanic forces," and as he began to draw a small following, he was arrested, imprisoned, and tortured by the Communists—an ordeal his followers see as divinely ordained suffering that will lead to the redemption of the human race from the sin of the first parents, Adam and Eve.

Moon was liberated from his imprisonment during the Korean War and took refuge in the southern part of the penninsula. There he established a "religion of divine principle" called Tong Il. It soon became known in the West as the Holy Spirit Association for the Unification of World Christianity, or the United Family, and finally as the "Unification Church."

Moon teaches that God has sent three "Israel's" to attempt to redeem the world. First he chose the Jews, then the Gentiles. In the twentieth century he chose the Koreans as the people of salvation, and a Korean (Moon himself) is the third Adam. Just as the early Hebrews, the first Israel, suffered persecution at the hands of the Babylonians, and the second Israel, in the days of the second Temple, at the hands of the Romans, so Korea, the third Israel, suffered at the hands of the Japanese during World War II. Finally, in Korea Satan is making his last stand. For in Korea the forces of God and Satan (democracy and communism) are engaged in the final apocalyptic conflict. But God has chosen as the divine center for the salvation of the world Korea, where East and West have met. Confucianism, Buddhism, and Christianity have come together, and now God has sent Rev. and Mrs. Moon, a third Adam and Eve, to restore the human race and complete the unification mission.

Moon's followers generally believe that Moon is the new Messiah and that he and his wife are the new and true parents who are regenerating the human race. To effect this regeneration, Sun Myung Moon chooses marriage partners for his followers and then, with his wife, officiates at mass wedding

Rev. Sun Myung Moon and his wife officiate at a mass wedding of 2000 couples in Madison Square Garden in 1998.

ceremonies, which have attracted considerable media attention. For the movement, every new crop of married couples furthers the struggle against the Communists, Satan's representatives on earth, who Moon depicts as arrayed against himself as deonic agents in a lifelong cosmic battle. Though famous globally, the Unification Church claims only a modest number of adherents in Korea.

Aum Shinrikyo

An apocalyptic new age vision has also taken root in Japan, and members of one cult, Aum Shinrikyo, achieved global notoriety and terrorist status when they released deadly sarin gas into the Tokyo subway system in 1995.

The Aum Shinrikyo ("Supreme Truth") movement is the creation of Chizuo Matsumoto, who in 1986 changed his name to Shoko Asahara and registered his two-year-old group as a religion with the Japanese government. Having done this, he attracted additional followers by writing extensively in his country's new age religious publications, promising to teach seekers out-of-body shamanistic skills such as clairvoyance and teleportation. He had a charismatic personality, and his movement, which has had an extraordinary appeal to the university-educated professional class, quickly became one of the fastest growing new religions in Japan.

Through a well-developed bureaucracy with Asahara at the top, Aum Shinrikyo established monastic-like separatist communities throughout Japan, where the most devoted followers congregated, having left their families and given all their earthly belongings to the movement. Descriptions of the initiation rituals have mentioned the heavy use of hallucinogens, the drinking of vials of Asahara's blood, and a total surrender to Asahara as the spiritual master.

Shoko Asahara (Chizuo Matsumoto)

As a child in a school for the blind, Aum Shinrikyo founder Chizuo Matsumoto boasted that he would one day be prime minister of Japan. Yet the early years of the severely sight-impaired youth were not promising. After two failures to enter the Japanese university system, he joined a new religious movement called Agonshu, which mixed Buddhist, Daoist, and Hindu teachings. In 1984 he broke with Agonshu and developed a personal religious vision, integrating elements of Hindu yoga, Buddhist meditation, and Christian apocalyptic beliefs. He visited India in 1986 and had what he believed to be a powerful enlightenment experience. Convinced that he was destined to be a great spiritual master, Chizuo Matasumoto, then the leader of his own small movement, took on the name of Shoko Asahara and changed the name of his group to Aum Shinrikyo.

Shoko Asahara, founder of Aum Shinrikyo.

In the beginning Asahara taught that the world would end soon and that it was the task of his followers to save humanity through their hard work in Aum business ventures and through purification by personal spiritual practices. After Asahara and some his hand-picked leaders were decisively defeated in an attempt to win seats in Japan's parliament in 1990, Asahara's teachings took a darker turn, seeking to destroy what he believed were the demonic forces that opposed his movement.

By 1993 Aum Shinrikyo had plants producing automatic weapons, as well as chemical and biological weapons, ostensibly to protect Japan against its enemies. Believing that the United States was about to trigger an apocalyptic nuclear war, Aum scientists traveled to Russia and Africa in search of biological and nuclear weapons. Aum Shinrikyo's following in Russia by 1995 was estimated at 30,000, roughly three times its membership in Japan. The group's terrorist plans, however, were known only to a small, mostly Japanese, elite.

Asahara came under legal scrutiny for his varied activities, especially after authorities learned that the worth of Aum's assets exceeded 1 billion dollars. In 1994, convinced that the Japanese government's special police force had set out to destroy him, Asahara ordered the assassination of three judges by releasing poison gas in their neighborhoods. The judges survived, but some innocent bystanders were killed. The next year, after the Tokyo subway gassing, he was arrested.

Asahara integrated Japanese Shinto beliefs with Hinduism and Tibetan Buddhism in a way that appealed to many young Japanese professionals (including scientists) by calling into question modern materialism as well as the stress and decadence of modern life. Indeed, influenced by the science fiction of Isaac Asimov, Asahara developed a vision of the role of scientists as building an elite secret society that would save civilization from cataclysmic wars. To this he added a strong dose of Christian apocalyptic expectations (mixed with the predictions of Nostradamus) about the imminent end of the world in a battle between good and evil. He justified his murderous assaults on his fellow citizens by pronouncing that killing those who are creating bad karma was actually doing them a spiritual favor, since it stopped them before they produced even more negative karma.

To his followers, Asahara declared himself to be Jesus Christ, come to bring judgment upon the world. In preparation for the global nuclear war he believed the United States to be plotting, he bought land in Australia. There his followers could start to build a new civilization as they waited out the years of lethal radiation in a devasted Northern Hemisphere. Ultimately, Asahara was convicted for having masterminded the Tokyo sarin gas attack. He was sentenced to death in 2004, and the movement, which regrouped under the name Aleph ("the beginning") still reveres him as its spiritual leader.

Like Scientology, Aum Shinrikyo illustrates the integration of shamanism and Eastern mysticism with scientific research and technological applications organized by a highly efficient globally oriented bureaucratic organization.

The difference between them is equally important, for Asahara's eclectic religious vision adds elements of Western apocalyptic thought colored by his own paranoid vision of himself as the rejected prophet and spiritual master. The result was dangerously violent.

RELIGIOUS POSTMODERNISM AND GLOBAL ETHICS

The Challenge of Postmodern Secular Relativism

As explained in the chapter on Christianity, the difference between fundamentalists and modernists stems from an argument about the impact of science on traditional religious beliefs. Fundamentalists often seem to believe they must oppose science to reaffirm traditional religious beliefs, whereas modernists seem to embrace science, preferring to adapt religious beliefs to the changing understanding science brings.

Fundamentalists generally had no objection to the use of science to invent things like the automobile or for the creation of better medications. When science impinged on religious beliefs concerning the origins of humanity and the right way to order society, however, many drew a line. If the human self and society do not have sacred origins but are the result of biological evolution and human decisions, then the human self and society seem to be set adrift in a world without meaning, purpose, or ethical norms.

As modern science and technology—and the worldview they foster—were carried around the world by colonialism, the impact of modernity was felt in different ways in different societies and cultures. Not every religious tradition emphasizes orthodoxy ("right beliefs") the way Christianity does. For example, Hinduism, Judaism, and Islam place far more emphasis on orthopraxy ("right actions"), the maintenance of a sacred way of life. Thus the most common feature of the fundamentalist reaction to modernity across religions and cultures is the desire to preserve the premodern sacred way of life against the threat of secularization and the normless relativism it seems to engender.

The social sciences of the nineteenth century promoted a technological viewpoint according to which society itself could be redesigned, just as engineers periodically redesign cars. Thus the use of scientific and technological inventions per se was relatively uncontroversial. Many, however, rejected treating the social order in a secular and technological fashion, as if society could or should be shaped and reshaped by human choices, without regard to the sacred ways of one's ancestors. In our chapter on Christianity, we pointed to the emergence of existentialism as a watershed moment in the history of modernization, opening the door to postmodern relativism by calling into question the idea of "human nature."

For many, this seeming disappearance of human nature is terrifying, suggesting that we as human beings know neither who we are nor what we ought to do. This is the mindset Nietzsche was addressing when he said that "modern man" had murdered God and so now wandered the universe without a sense of direction. For many today, it seems that the secular "technologized" understandings of self and society can only lead to moral decadence—a decadence in which the family and the fabric of society will be destroyed. Those who believe that secularization is robbing humanity of an understanding of its sacred origins and destiny reject technologized understandings of self and society. As an antidote, they favor a return to the fundamental truths about human nature as understood in premodern times.

Modernization is often presented in terms of a story about the secularization of society, that is, the liberation of the various dimensions of cultural life from the authority of religion. Since religion in premodern societies preserves the sacred by governing every aspect of life, modernization and secularization are threats to traditional societies everywhere.

Nevertheless, sacralizing society to protect a divinely ordered way of life is not the only role religion has played in history. The great sociologist Max Weber pointed out that religion not only sacralizes and reinforces the unchanging "routine" order of society, sometimes it also "charismatically" desacralizes and transforms society. Brahmanic Hinduism sacralized caste society in ancient India, but Buddhism began as a movement to desacralize the priestly elite and see all persons in the caste system as capable of achieving spiritual deliverance. Sacralization is total and readily accommodates hierarchies (e.g., a caste system, a multitiered priesthood), whereas desacralizing breaks with caste, inviting pluralism and equality.

Because religions (even the same traditions) often manifest dramatically opposing values and orientations, the sociologist Jacques Ellul has argued that it is helpful in understanding the role of religion in society to distinguish between two terms that are typically used interchangeably: "sacred" and "holy." In his view, the experience of the sacred leads to a view of society as an order that is itself sacred and must be protected from all profane attempts to change it. The experience of the holy, on the other hand, calls into question the very idea of a sacred order. It desacralizes (or secularizes) society and seeks to introduce change in the name of a higher truth and/or justice. According to this view, the same religious tradition can express itself in opposite ways in different times and places. In the East, early Buddhism called into question the sacred order of Hindu caste society, but later Buddhist societies developed their own sacred orders. Early Daoists in China called into question the sacred hierarchical order of Confucianism but later also integrated themselves into the sacred order of Confucian society by means of a neo-Confucian synthesis.

In the West, early Christianity, sharing a common ethos with Judaism, called the sacred order of Roman civilization into question, but medieval Christianity resacralized Europe. Then later, Protestantism desacralized the medieval European social order and unleashed the dynamics of modernism. From this perspective, the struggle between fundamentalism and modernism in the modern world that we have surveyed in this textbook is an example of the conflict between the sacralizing and desacralizing (secularizing) roles of religion.

Religious fundamentalists express the desire to preserve the sacredness of human identity in a rightly ordered society against what they perceive as the chaos of today's decadent, normless secular relativism. To restore the sacred normative order, therefore, they tend to affirm the desirability of achieving the premodern ideal of one society, one religion. They remain uncomfortable with the religious diversity that thrives in a secular society.

Religious modernism as it emerged in the West rejected the fundamentalist ideal, adopted from premodern societies, of identity between religion and society. Instead of dangerous absolutism, modernists looked for an accommodation between religion and modern secular society. They argued that it is possible to desacralize one way of life and identity to create a new identity that preserves the essential values or norms of the past tradition, but in harmony with a new modern way of life. Modernists secularize society and privatize their religious practices, hoping by their encouragement of denominational forms of religion to ensure an environment that supports religious diversity.

What we are calling religious postmodernism, like religious modernism, accepts secularization and religious pluralism. But religious postmodernism, like fundamentalism, rejects the modernist solution of privatization and seeks a public role for religion. It differs from fundamentalism, however, in that it rejects the domination of society by a single religion. Religious postmodernists insist that there is a way for religious communities in all their diversity to shape the public order and so rescue society from secular relativism. The chief example of this option is the model established by Mohandas K. Gandhi. Because his disciples rejected the privatization of religion while affirming religious diversity, Gandhi's movement is a postmodern new age religious movement rather than a modern one.

Exploring Religious Diversity by "Passing Over": A Postmodern Spiritual Adventure for a New Age of Globalization

All the great world religions date back a millennium or more, and each provided a grand metanarrative for the premodern civilization in which it emerged—in the Middle East, in India, and in China. In the past these world religions were relatively isolated from one another. There were many histories in the world, each shaped by a great metanarrative, but no global history.

The perspective of religious postmodernism arises from a dramatically different situation. We are at the beginning of a new millennium, which is marked by the development of a global civilization. The diverse spiritual heritages of the human race have become the common inheritance of all. Modern changes have ended the isolation of the past, and people following one great tradition are now very likely to live in proximity to adherents of other

Leo Tolstoy, the famous Russian novelist, whose writings on Jesus' Sermon on the Mount inspired Gandhi.

faiths. New age religion has tapped this condition of globalism, but in two different ways. In its modernist forms it has privatized the religious quest as a quest for the perfection of the self. In its postmodern forms, without rejecting self-transformation, it has turned that goal outward in forms of social organization committed to bettering society, with a balance between personal and social transformation.

The time when a new world religion could be founded has passed, argues John Dunne in his book, *The Way of All the Earth*. What is required today is not the conquest of the world by any one religion or culture but a meeting and sharing of religious and cultural insight. The postmodern spiritual adventure occurs when we engage in what Dunne calls "passing over" into another's religion and culture and come to see the world through another's eyes. When we do this, we "come back" to our own religion and culture enriched with new insight not only into the other's but also our own religion and culture—insight that builds bridges of understanding, a unity in diversity between people of diverse religions and cultures. The model for this spiritual adventure is found in the lives of Leo Tolstoy (1828–1910), Mohandas K. Gandhi (1869–1948), and Martin Luther King Jr. (1929–1968).

Two of the most inspiring religious figures of the twentieth century were Mahatma Gandhi and Dr. King. They are the great champions of the fight for the dignity and rights of all human beings, from all religions and cultures. Moreover, they are models for a different kind of new age religious practice, one that absorbs the global wisdom of diverse religions, but does so without indiscriminately mixing elements to create a new religion, as is typical of the eclectic syncretism of most new age religions. Yet clearly these religious leaders initiated a new way of being religious that could occur only in an age of globalization.

Mohandas K. Gandhi, whose techniques of nonviolent civil disobedience led to the liberation of India from British colonial rule in 1947.

Martin Luther King Jr. stated repeatedly that his commitment to nonviolent resistance, or civil disobedience, as a strategy for protecting human dignity had its roots in two sources: Jesus' Sermon on the Mount and Gandhi's teachings of nonviolence derived from his interpretation of the Hindu sacred story called the *Bhagavad Gita*. Gandhi died when King was a teenager, but the American clergyman did travel to India to study the effects of Gandhi's teachings of nonviolence on Indian society. In this he showed a remarkable openness to the insights of another religion and culture. In Gandhi and his spiritual heirs, King found kindred spirits, and he came back to his own religion and culture enriched by the new insights that came to him in the process of passing over and coming back.

Martin Luther King Jr. never considered becoming a Hindu, but his Christianity was profoundly transformed by his encounter with Gandhi's Hinduism.

Just as important, however, is the spiritual passing over of Gandhi himself. As a young man, Gandhi went to England to study law. His journey led him not away from Hinduism but more deeply into it. For it was in England that Gandhi discovered the *Bhagavad Gita* and began to appreciate the spiritual and ethical power of Hinduism.

Having promised his mother that he would remain vegetarian, Gandhi took to eating his meals with British citizens who had developed similar commitments to vegetarianism through their fascination with India and its religions. It is in this context that Gandhi was brought into direct contact with the nineteenth-century theosophical roots of new age globalization. In these circles he met Madam Blavatsky and her disciple Annie Besant, both of whom had a profound influence upon him. His associates also included Christian followers of the Russian novelist Leo Tolstoy, who, after his midlife conversion, had embraced an ethic of nonviolence based on the Sermon on the Mount (Matthew 5–7).

At the invitation of his theosophist friends, Gandhi read the *Bhagavad Gita* for the first time, in an English translation by Sir Edwin Arnold, entitled *The Song Celestial*. It was only much later that he took to a serious study of the Hindu text in Sanskrit. He was also deeply impressed by Arnold's *The Light of Asia*,

Martin Luther King Jr., who led the civil rights movement for racial equality in the United States, using the techniques of nonviolent civil disobedience inspired by Gandhi.

recounting the life of the Buddha. Thus, through the eyes of Western friends, he was first moved to discover the spiritual riches of his own Hindu heritage. The seeds were planted in England, nourished by more serious study during his years in South Africa, and brought to fruition upon his return to India in 1915.

From his theosophist friends, Gandhi not only learned to appreciate his own religious tradition but came to see Christianity in a new way. For unlike the evangelical missionaries he had met in his childhood, the theosophists had a deeply allegorical way of reading the Christian scriptures. This approach to Bible study allowed people to find in the teachings of Jesus a universal path toward spiritual truth that was in harmony with the wisdom of Asia. The power of allegory lay in opening the literal stories of the scripture to reveal a deeper symbolic meaning based on what the theosophists believed was profound universal religious experience and wisdom. From the theosophists, Gandhi took an interpretive principle that has its roots in the New Testament writings of St. Paul: "the letter killeth, but the spirit giveth life"

(2 Corinthians 3:6). This insight would enable him to read the *Bhagavad Gita* in the light of his own deep religious experience and find in it the justification for nonviolent civil disobedience.

Gandhi was likewise profoundly influenced by Tolstoy's understanding of the Sermon on the Mount. The message of nonviolence—love your enemy, turn the other cheek—took hold of Gandhi. And yet Gandhi did not become a Christian. Rather, he returned to his parents' religion and culture, finding parallels to Jesus' teachings in the Hindu tradition. And so he read Hindu scriptures with new insight, interpreting the *Bhagavad Gita* allegorically, as an enjoinder to resist evil by nonviolent means that had preceded the teachings of Jesus. And just as King would later use the ideas of Gandhi in the nonviolent struggle for the dignity of blacks in America, so Gandhi was inspired by Tolstoy as he led the fight for the dignity of the lower castes and outcasts within Hindu society, and for the liberation of India from British colonial rule.

Gandhi never seriously considered becoming a Christian any more than King ever seriously considered becoming a Hindu. Nevertheless, Gandhi's Hindu faith was profoundly transformed by his encounter with the Christianity of Tolstoy, just as King's Christian faith was profoundly transformed by his encounter with Gandhi's Hinduism. In the lives of these two twentieth-century religious activists we have examples of "passing over" as a transformative postmodern spiritual adventure.

Whereas in the secular forms of postmodernism all knowledge is relative, and therefore the choice between interpretations of any claim to truth is undecidable, Gandhi and King opened up an alternate path. While agreeing that in matters of religion, truth is undecidable, they showed that acceptance of diversity does not have to lead to the kind of ethical relativism that so deeply troubles fundamentalists. For in the cases of Gandhi and King, passing over led to a sharing of wisdom among traditions that gave birth to an ethical coalition in defense of human dignity across religions and cultures—a global ethic for a new age.

By their lives, Gandhi and King demonstrated that the sharing of a common ethic and of spiritual wisdom across traditions does not require any practitioners to abandon their religious identity—another worrisome issue for fundamentalists. Instead, Gandhi and King offered the model of unity in diversity. Finally, both Gandhi and King rejected the privatization of religion, insisting that religion in all its diversity plays a decisive role in shaping the public order. And both were convinced that only a firm commitment to non-violence on the part of religious communities would allow society to avoid a return to the kind of religious wars that accompanied the Protestant Reformation and the emergence of modernity.

The spiritual adventure initiated by Gandhi and King involves passing over (through imagination, through travel and cultural exchange, through a common commitment to social action to promote social justice, etc.) into the life and stories and traditions of others, sharing in them and, in the process, coming to see one's own tradition through them. Such encounters enlarge our sense of human identity to include the other. The religious metanarratives of the world's civilizations may have become "smaller narratives" in an age of global diversity, but they have not lost their power. Indeed, in this Gandhian model, it is the sharing of the wisdom from another tradition's metanarratives that gives the stories of a seeker's own tradition their power. Each seeker remains on familiar religious and cultural ground, yet each is profoundly influenced by the other.

Tolstoy, Jesus, and "Saint Buddha": An Ancient Tale with a Thousand Faces

Although at first glance, the religious worlds of humankind seem to have grown up largely independent of one another, a closer look will reveal that hidden threads from different religions and cultures have for centuries been woven together to form a new tapestry, one that contributes to the sharing of religious insight in an age of globalization. In *Toward a World Theology*, Wilfred Cantwell Smith traces the threads of this new tapestry, and the story he tells is quite amazing.[5] Smith notes, for example, that to fully appreciate the influence on Gandhi of Tolstoy's understanding of the Sermon on the Mount, it is important to know that Tolstoy's own conversion to Christianity, which occurred in a period of midlife crisis, was deeply influenced not only by the Sermon on the Mount but also by the life of the Buddha.

Tolstoy was a member of the Russian nobility, rich and famous because of his novels, which included *War and Peace* and *Anna Karenina*. Yet in his fifties, Tolstoy went through a period of great depression that resolved itself in a powerful religious conversion experience. Although, nominally a member of the (Russian) Orthodox Church, Tolstoy had not taken his faith seriously until he came to the point of making the Sermon on the Mount a blueprint for his life. After his conversion, Tolstoy freed his serfs, gave away all his wealth, and spent the rest of his life serving the poor.

As Wilfred Cantwell Smith tells it, a second key factor in Tolstoy's conversion was his reading of a story from the lives of the saints. The story was that of Barlaam and Josaphat. It is the story of a wealthy young Indian prince by the name of Josaphat who gave up all his wealth and power, and abandoned his family, to embark on an urgent quest for an answer to the problems of old age, sickness, and death. During his search, the prince comes across a Christian monk by the name of Barlaam, who told him a story. It seems that once there was a man who fell into a very deep well and was hanging onto two vines for dear life. As he was trapped in this precarious situation, two mice, one white and one black, came along and began to chew on the vines. The man knew that in short order the vines would be severed and he would plunge to his death.

The story was a parable of the prince's spiritual situation. Barlaam points out that the two mice represent the cycle of day and night, the passing of time that brings us ever closer to death. The paradox is that like the man in the well, Josaphat cannot save his life by clinging to it. He must let go of the vines, so to speak. He can save his life only by losing it. That is, if he lets go of his life now, no longer clinging to it but surrendering himself completely to the divine will, this spiritual death will lead to a new life that transcends death. This story and its parable touched the deeply depressed writer and led him first to a spiritual surrender that brought about his rebirth. Out of this rebirth came a new Tolstoy, the author of *The Kingdom of God Is Within You,* which advocates a life of nonviolent resistance to evil based on the Sermon on the Mount.

The story of the Indian prince who abandons a life of wealth and power and responds to a parable of a man about to fall into an abyss is of course a thinly disguised version of the life story of the Buddha. Versions of the story and the parable can be found in almost all the world's great religions, recorded in a variety of languages (Greek, Latin, Czech, Polish, Italian, Spanish, French, German, Swedish, Norwegian, Arabic, Hebrew, Yiddish, Persian, Sanskrit, Chinese, Japanese, etc.). The Greek version came into Christianity from an Islamic Arabic version, which was passed on to Judaism as well. The Muslims apparently got it from members of a gnostic cult in Persia, who got it from Buddhists in India. The Latinate name *Josaphat* is a translation of the Greek *Loasaf,* which is translated from the Arabic *Yudasaf,* which comes from the Persian *Bodisaf,* which is a translation of *Bodhisattva,* a Sanskrit title for the Buddha.

The parable of the man clinging to the vine may be even older than the story of the prince (Buddha) who renounces his wealth. It may well go back to early Indic sources at the beginnings of civilization. It is one of the oldest and most universal stories in the history of religions and civilizations. Tolstoy's conversion was brought about in large part by the story of a Christian saint, Josaphat, who was, so to speak, really the Buddha in disguise.

The history of the story of a great sage's first steps toward enlightenment suggests that the process leading to globalization may have started much earlier than we had thought. Therefore the line between new religions and new age (globalized) religions may not be as sharp as previously assumed. We can see that the practice of passing over and coming back, of being open to the stories of others, and of coming to understand one's own tradition through these stories is in fact very ancient. Therefore, when Martin Luther King Jr. embraced the teachings of Gandhi, he embraced not only Gandhi but also Tolstoy, and through Tolstoy two of the greatest religious teachers of nonviolence: Jesus of Nazareth, whose committed follower King already was, and Siddhartha the Buddha. Thus from the teachings of Gandhi, King actually assimilated important teachings from at least four religious traditions—Hinduism, Buddhism, Judaism, and Christianity. This rich spiritual debt to other religions and cultures never in any way diminished Martin Luther King Jr.'s faith. On the contrary, the Baptist pastor's Christian beliefs were deeply enriched, in turn enriching the world in which we live. The same could be said about Gandhi and Hinduism.

Gandhi's transformation of the *Bhagavad Gita*—a Hindu story that literally advocates the duty of going to war and killing one's enemies—into a story of nonviolence is instructive of the transforming power of the allegorical method that he learned from his theosophist friends. The *Bhagavad Gita* is a story about a warrior named Arjuna, who argues with his chariot driver, Krishna, over whether it is right to go to war if it means having to kill one's own relatives. Krishna's answer is Yes—Arjuna must do his duty as a warrior in the cause of justice, but he is morally obliged to do it selflessly, with no thought of personal loss or gain. Gandhi, however, transformed the story of Arjuna and Krishna from a story of war as physical violence into a story of war as active but nonviolent resistance to injustice through civil disobedience.

If the message of spiritual realization in the *Gita* is that all beings share the same self (as Brahman or Purusha), how could the *Gita* be literally advocating violence? For to do violence against another would be to do violence against oneself. The self-contradiction of a literal interpretation, in Gandhi's way of thinking, forces the mind into an allegorical mode, where it can grasp the Gita's true spiritual meaning. Reading the *Gita* allegorically, Gandhi insisted that the impending battle described in the Hindu classic is really about the battle between good and evil going on within every self.

Krishna's command to Arjuna to stand up and fight is thus a "spiritual" command. But for Gandhi this does not mean, as it usually does in "modern" terms, that the struggle is purely inner (private) and personal. On the contrary, the spiritual person will see the need to practice nonviolent civil disobedience: that is, to replace "body force" (i.e., violence) with "soul force." As the *Gita* suggests, there really is injustice in the world, and therefore there really is an obligation to fight, even to go to war, to reestablish justice. One must be prepared to exert Gandhian soul force, to put one's body on the line, but in a nonviolent way. In so doing, one leaves open the opportunity to gain the respect, understanding, and perhaps transformation of one's enemy.

The lesson Gandhi derived from the *Gita* is that the encounter with the other need not lead to conquest. It can lead, instead, to mutual understanding and mutual respect. King's relationship to Gandhi and Gandhi's relationship to Tolstoy are models of a postmodern spirituality and ethics that transform postmodern relativism and eclecticism into the opportunity to follow a new spiritual and ethical path—"the way of all the earth"—the sharing of spiritual insight and ethical wisdom across religions and cultures in an age of globalization.

On this path, people of diverse religions and cultures find themselves sharing an ethical commitment to protect human dignity beyond the postmodern interest in personal transformation the modernist ideal of privatization. Gandhi and King were not engaged in a private quest to perfect the self (although neither neglected the need for personal transformation). Rather, each man embarked on a public quest to transform human communities socially and politically by invoking a global ethical commitment to protect the dignity of all persons. The religious movements associated with both men fit the pattern of the holy that affirms the secularization of society and religious pluralism. Gandhi and King recovered the premodern ideal of religion shaping the public order but now in a postmodern mode, committed to religious pluralism.

The Children of Gandhi: An Experiment in Postmodern Global Ethics

In April 1968, Martin Luther King Jr., sometimes referred to as "the American Gandhi," went to Memphis to support black municipal workers in the midst of a strike. The Baptist minister was looking forward to spending the approaching Passover with Rabbi Abraham Joshua Heschel. Heschel, who had marched with King during the voter registration drive in Selma, Alabama, three years earlier, had become a close friend and supporter. Unfortunately, King was not able to keep that engagement. On April 4, 1968, like Gandhi before him, Martin Luther King Jr., a man of nonviolence, was shot to death by an assassin.

The Buddhist monk and anti–Vietnam War activist Thich Nhat Hanh, whom King had nominated for a Nobel Peace Prize, received the news of his friend's death while at an interreligious conference in New York City. Only the previous spring, King had expressed his opposition to the Vietnam War, largely at the urging of Thich Nhat Hanh and Rabbi Heschel. King spoke out at an event sponsored by Clergy and Laymen Concerned about Vietnam, a group founded by Heschel, Protestant cleric John Bennett, and Richard Neuhaus, then a Lutheran minister. Now another champion in the struggle against hatred, violence, and war was dead. But the spiritual and ethical vision he shared with his friends, across religions and cultures, has continued to inspire followers throughout the world.

These religious activists—a Baptist minister who for his leadership in the American civil rights movement won the Noble Peace Prize, a Hasidic rabbi and scholar who narrowly escaped the death camps of the Holocaust, and a Buddhist monk who had been targeted for death in Vietnam but survived to lead the Buddhist peace delegation to the Paris peace negotiations in 1973—are the spiritual children of Gandhi. By working together to protest racial injustice and the violence of war, they demonstrated that religious and cultural pluralism do not have to end in ethical relativism and, given a commitment to nonviolence, can play a role in shaping public life in an age of globalization. The goal, Martin Luther King Jr. insisted, is not to humiliate and defeat your enemy but to win him or her over, bringing about not only justice but also reconciliation. The goal, he said, was to attack the evil in systems, not to attack persons. The goal was to love one's enemy, not in the sense of sentimental affection, nor in the reciprocal sense of friendship, but in the constructive sense of seeking the opponent's well-being.

Nonviolence, King argued, is more than just a remedy for this or that social injustice. It is, he was convinced, essential to the survival of humanity in an age of nuclear weapons. The choice, he said, was "no longer between violence and nonviolence. It is either nonviolence or nonexistence."

Truth is to be found in all religions, King said many times, and "injustice anywhere is a threat to justice everywhere. We are caught in an inescapable network of mutuality, tied in a single garment of destiny. Whatever affects one directly affects all indirectly."[6] The scandal of our age, said Abraham Joshua Heschel, is that in a world of diplomacy "only religions are not on speaking terms." But, he also said, no religion is an island, and all must realize that "holiness is not the monopoly of any particular religion or tradition."[7]

"Buddhism today," writes Thich Nhat Hanh, "is made up of non-Buddhist elements, including Jewish and Christian ones." And likewise with every tradition. "We have to allow what is good, beautiful, and meaningful in the other's tradition to transform us," the Vietnamese monk continues. The purpose of such passing over into the other's tradition is to allow each to return to his or her own place transformed. What is astonishing, says Thich Nhat Hanh, is that we will find kindred spirits in other traditions with whom we share more than we do with many in our own tradition.[8]

The Future of Religion in an Age of Globalization

Will the global future of religion and civilization be shaped by this Gandhian model of new age spiritual practice? It clearly offers an alternative to both traditional denominational modernist religions and the more privatistic modernist forms of new age religion. The Gandhian model also offers an alternative to the rejection of modernization, secularization, and the privatization of religion, which fundamentalists fear can only lead to the moral decadence of ethical relativism. But the sharing of spiritual wisdom does require seeing the religions and cultures of others as having wisdom to share, and not all will accept this presupposition. Nevertheless, the emergence of religious postmodernism means that in the future, the struggle among religions will most likely be not between fundamentalism and modernism, as a conflict between the sacred and the secular (public and private religion), but between the sacred and the holy—religious exclusivism and religious pluralism as alternative forms of public religion.

Discussion Questions

1 What is the difference between a "new religion" and a "new age religion"?

2 How do modernist new age religious belief and practice differ from post-modernist new age religious belief and practice? Give an example of each.

3 How does new age religion relate to the split between faith and reason (the *via moderna* and the *devotio moderna*) that shaped the emergence of the modern world through the Enlightenment and the Romantic reaction it provoked?

4 In what sense is "civil religion" a new way of being religious, and in what sense is it a very old way of being religious?

5 In what way is the postmodern path of religious ethics opened up by M.K. Gandhi and Martin Luther King Jr. similar to fundamentalist ideals for society, and in what way is it different?

Suggested Reading

Bruce, Steve, *Religion in the Modern World* (Oxford and New York: Oxford University Press, 1996).

Dunne, John S., *The Way of All the World* (New York: Macmillan, 1972).

Ellwood, Robert S., and Harry B. Partin, eds., *Religious and Spiritual Groups in Modern America*, 2nd ed. (Upper Saddle River, NJ: Prentice Hall, 1973, 1988).

Fasching, Darrell J., *The Coming of the Millennium* (San Jose, CA, and New York: Authors Choice Press, 1996, 2000).

———, "Stories of War and Peace: Sacred, Secular and Holy," Sarah Deets and Merry Kerry, eds., *War and Word*, (Lanham, MD: Rowman and Littlefield, 2004).

———, and Dell deChant, *Comparative Religious Ethics* (Oxford: Blackwell Publishers, 2001).

Juergensmeyer, Mark, *Terror in the Mind* (Berkeley: University of California Press, 2000).

Laderman, Gary, and Luis Leon, eds., *Religion and American Cultures*, Vol. 1 (Santa Barbara, CA: ABC Clio, 2003).

Lewis, James R., ed., *The Oxford Handbook of New Religious Movements* (Oxford and New York: Oxford University Press, 2004).

Rothstein, Mikael, ed., *New Age Religion and Globalization*, (Aarhus, Denmark: Aarhus University Press, 2001).

Reender Kronerborg., *New Religions in a Postmodern World*—, (Aarhus, Denmark: Aarhus University Press, 2003).

Notes

1. William Bloom, *The New Age: An Anthology of Essential Writings* (London: Rider/Channel 4, 1991), p. xviii. Quoted in Steve Bruce, *Religion in the Modern World* (Oxford and New York: Oxford University Press, 1996).

2. Sarah Pike, "New Age," quoted in Robert S. Ellwood and Harry B. Partin, eds., *Religious and Spiritual Groups in America*, 2nd ed. : (Upper Saddle River, NJ Prentice Hall, 1988), p. 140.

3. Quoted in Ellwood and Partin, eds.: *Religious and Spiritual Groups in America*, 2nd ed., (Upper Saddle River, NJ Prentice Hall, 1988), p. 140, citing a publication of the Church of Scientology of California dated 1970.

4. L. Ron Hubbard, *Scientology: The Fundamentals of Thought* (Edinburgh: Publications Organization Worldwide, 1968); originally published 1950. Quoted in Ellwood and Partin, eds., *Religions and Spiritual Groups in America*, 2nd ed. (Upper Saddle River, NJ, Prentice Hall, 1988), p. 147.

5. Wilfred Contrell Smith, *Toward a World Theology* (Philadelphia: Westminster Press, 1981), Chap. 1.

6. Martin Luther King Jr., "Letter from Birmingham Jail," in King, *I Have a Dream: Writings and Speeches That Changed the World*, James M. Washington, ed. (San Francisco: HarperSanFrancisco, 1992), p. 85.

7. Abraham Joshua Heschel, *Moral Grandeur and Spiritual Audacity: Essays [of] Abraham Joshua Heschel*, Susannah Herschel, ed. (New York: Farrar, Straus & Giroux, 1996), pp 241, 247.

8. Thich Nhat Hanh, *Living Buddha, Living Christ* (New York: G. P. Putnam and Sons, Riverhead Books, 1995), pp. 9, 11.

GLOSSARY

INTRODUCTION

Metanarrative: a grand cosmic and/or historical story accepted by the majority of a society as expressing its beliefs about origin, destiny, and identity

Modern: a civilization that separates its citizen's lives into public and private spheres, assigning politics to public life while restricting religion to personal and family life. A dominant scientific metanarrative provides the most certain public truths people believe they know. Society and politics are governed by secular, rational, and scientific norms rather than religion

Postmodern: a society typified by diversity in both beliefs and social practices that has no single dominant metanarrative (other than the narrative of diversity) and is skeptical of finding either certain knowledge or norms in any public form of truth, whether religious or scientific

Premodern: a civilization in which there is no separation between religion and society. A dominant religious metanarrative provides the most certain truths people believe they know. By being a member of that culture, one automatically participates in its religious vision and lives by its religious norms

via analogia: a way of knowing spiritual reality through the use of analogy, for example, "God is my shepherd"

via negativa: the mystical way of knowing the highest spiritual reality (God, Brahman, etc.) by negating all finite qualities and characteristics; Hindus, for instance, say Brahman is "neti . . . neti"—not this and not that (i.e., Brahman is not a thing, Brahman is no-thing and therefore is pure nothingness, Brahman is beyond imagination and cannot be imaged, Brahman can only be known by a mystical experience of unknowing)

PRIMAL RELIGIONS

Animism: religious tradition whose basic perception entails belief in an inner soul that gives life and ultimate identity to humans, animals, and plants and that places primary emphasis on experiential rituals in which humans interact with other souls

Cosmogony: mythological account of the creation

Numinous: the human perception of the sacred

Totem: symbol taken from the natural world that stands for a social group possessing a common origin and essence

JUDAISM

Aggadah: the stories of the *Tanak* and *Talmud* that communicate spiritual truths

amoriam: the generation of sages that created the Gemara

Ashkenazi: Jews whose traditions originated in central and Eastern Europe

bar/bat mitzvah: the rite of passage for boys (bar mitzvah) whereby they become full members of Israel who are able to read and interpret Torah; in modern times a parallel rite for girls (bat mitzvah) has been established in some forms of Judaism

circumcision: the cutting of the foreskin of the penis as a sign of the covenant of Abraham

covenant: the agreement between God and the people Israel whereby they are chosen to be God's people; God agrees to guide and protect them; the people agree to follow God's commandments (*halakhah*)

diaspora: the dispersion of a religious people outside their geographic homeland, where they must live as a minority among others

dual Torah: the scriptures of Rabbinic Judaism, composed of the written Torah (*Tanak*) and the oral Torah (*Talmud*)

Gemara: see *Talmud*

Gentile: anyone not Jewish

Halakhah: the commandments of God revealed in the *Tanak* and commented on in the *Talmud*; the word means to walk in the way of God by obeying his commands or laws

haredim: Jewish ultra-Orthodox movements that reject all modernist forms of Judaism

Hasidism: a form of Judaism emerging in the eighteenth century, focused on piety and joy, with strong roots in Jewish mysticism

Israel: either Jews as a religious people or the land and state of Israel, depending on the context

Kabbalah: Jewish mysticism; the most important Kabbalistic work is the *Zohar*; for Kabbalists, God is the *En Sof*, the limitless or infinite, who manifests himself in the world through his *Shekinah*, or "divine presence" in all things; the reunion of all with the infinite through mystical contemplation will bring about nothing less than the messianic kingdom

kosher: what is suitable or fit, used especially in reference to foods permitted by Jewish dietary laws

Marrano: the Jews of Spain who were forced to convert to Christianity during the Inquisition but secretly continued to practice their Jewish faith

Mishnah: see *Talmud*

mitzvot: the commandments of God requiring deeds of loving kindness

Rabbinic: a rabbi is a teacher; the name came to designate the Judaism of the *dual Torah* created by the Pharisees, which came to be normative in the premodern period

Sephardi: Jews whose traditions originated in Spain and Portugal

Shema: the fundamental creed of Judaism: "Hear O Israel, the Lord our God, the Lord is One"

synagogue: a community centered on the study of Torah and prayer to God; the buildings used to house these activities also came to be known as synagogues

Talmud: the oral Torah, recorded in the *Mishnah,* and the commentary on the *Mishnah* called the *Gemara.* There are two Talmuds: the Bavli (Talmud of Babylonia) and the Yerushalmi (the Jerusalem Talmud); the former is considered the more comprehensive and authoritative

Tanak: the written Torah or Hebrew Bible, made up of Torah (the first five books from Genesis to Deuteronomy), Nevi'im (the prophets and historical writings such as Jeremiah and I and II Kings), and Ketuvim (the wisdom writings, such as Proverbs, Job, etc.)

tannaim: the generation of sages, beginning with Hillel and Shammai, that created the *Mishnah*

temple: a place to worship God or the gods in diverse religions; in Judaism only one temple was allowed for the worship of God in Jerusalem, whereas each Jewish community would have a synagogue for study and prayers

Zionism: the desire to return to the land of Israel as a homeland; in modern times, the secular movement started by Theodor Herzl that led to the formation of the state of Israel

Zohar: major book of Jewish kabbalism: *The Book of Splendor*

CHRISTIANITY

Augustinian: refers to views of St. Augustine, for example, his view of the separation of church and state, in which the state is answerable to the church in religious matters while the church is answerable to the state in secular matters—yet both exist to promote the spread of the Gospel

Catholic: those churches that define their Christian authenticity through apostolic succession

Christ: from Greek translation of the Hebrew word meaning "messiah" or "anointed one," title Christians apply to Jesus of Nazareth

Constantinianism: view of the unity of church and state, in which the state exists to rule over and protect the church as the official religion of the empire

Deism: Enlightenment view that God created the world the way a watchmaker creates a clock and leaves it to run on its own without interference

evangelical: refers to pietistic Christian movements that arose in response to the Enlightenment and also dogmatic divisions within Protestantism; emphasizes the unifying power of conversion as an emotional transformation rather than a rational/dogmatic one

Fundamentalist: term first emerged to refer to evangelical Protestants who believed that certain fundamental truths of the Gospel were threatened by modern interpreters; in general, fundamentalist movements in all religions see modernity as corrupting the fundamental truths and practices as they were expressed in the premodern stage of their respective traditions

Gospel: literally, "good news"; usually refers to the four Gospels of the New Testament, which retell the words and deeds of Jesus of Nazareth; can also refer to other similar ancient writings not included in the Christian scriptures

grace: expresses the idea of unmerited divine love and assistance given to humans

heresy: comes from Greek term that means "choice"; came to be used as a negative term for choosing to believe doctrines viewed as erroneous by those who considered themselves to be "more orthodox"

homoousios/homoiousios: first term used to assert that the Word of God through which all things were created is "the same as" God; second term was used to assert that this Word was "like God"; Council of Nicaea (325 CE) affirmed the first and rejected the second

incarnation: the eternal word of God became flesh in Jesus during his earthly life

justification by faith: Protestant Reformation doctrine formulated by Martin Luther, asserting that humans are saved by faith as a gift rather than through works of obedience to the law

Kingdom of God: the kingdom occurs whenever humans live in accord with the will of God and especially at the end of time when God will be all in all

original sin: the sin of Adam and Eve, who disobeyed the command of God not to eat the fruit of the tree of knowledge of good and evil; said to have affected all human beings by corrupting their will so that they are often unable to do the good they intend

Pentecostal: refers to churches that emphasize possession by the Holy Spirit and speaking in tongues

Protestant: the churches, beginning at time of Martin Luther, that reject mediation of the church through apostolic succession as necessary for salvation in favor of a direct personal relationship with God in Christ

Protestant ethic: term coined by sociologist Max Weber, who noted that the Calvinist branch of the Reformation fostered a belief in working hard and living simply for the glory of God, and as proof that one was among those destined to be saved; such as an attitude, Weber said, contributed to the accumulation of wealth needed for investment and fueled the Industrial Revolution and the flourishing of capitalist societies

redemption: root meaning is "to be rescued or freed," especially from slavery; used in both a literal and metaphorical sense: God redeemed Israel from slavery in Egypt and exile in Babylonia; God redeems sinners from punishment and death due to sin

sacraments: ritual actions, such as baptism and Holy Communion, said to impart the grace of God to Christians, usually through the mediation of ordained clergy

Second Coming: belief that Jesus, who died on the cross, arose from the dead, and ascended into heaven will return at the end of time to raise the dead and establish a new heaven and a new earth

Son of God: title applied to Jesus of Nazareth

Trinity: God as Father, Son, and Holy Spirit; meant to suggest that the transcendent God can be immanent in the world without losing his transcendence—when God acts in the world (as Son or Spirit), God does not cease to be father and Creator of the universe; therefore God is not many gods but one God in three persons

two natures, one person: doctrine affirmed by Council of Chalcedon (451 CE); in the one person of Jesus are two natures (divine and human) said to coexist in unity but without confusion or mixture, so that Jesus is fully human in everything except sin, and yet the fullness of God is also present in him and united to him

ISLAM

Allah: God

ayatollah: literally, "sign of God"; title used by certain Shiah religious leaders who are widely reputed for their learning and piety

bida: innovation or deviation in religious belief or practice

caliph (*khalifah*): successor of Muhammad as the political and military head of the Muslim community

dar al-Islam: the house or abode of Islam, as opposed to the house of war; territory controlled and ruled by Muslims

dawah: call, missionary work, proselytization

dhimmi: literally, protected non-Muslim peoples; refers to Jews and Christians (later extended to others) who were granted "protected" status and religious freedom under Muslim rule in exchange for payment of a special tax

fana: in Sufi usage, annihilation of the ego-centered self

faqih (pl. *fuqaha*): jurist, legal scholar; one who elaborates *fiqh*

faqir: ascetic mendicant mystic ideal; Sufi *shaykh*

fatwa: legal opinion or interpretation issued upon request by legal expert (mufti) to either judges or private individuals

fiqh: understanding; science of Islamic law; jurisprudence; human interpretation and application of divine law

hadith: narrative report of Muhammad's sayings and actions

hajj: annual pilgrimage to Mecca; all Muslims should make the hajj at least once in their lifetime, but it is recognized that individual circumstances may make compliance impossible

halal: permitted, allowed; when referring to food, indicates meat that has been slaughtered in religiously prescribed manner

al-haram al-sharif: the noble sanctuary

hijab: Arabic word for veil or external covering; can consist of headscarf alone or full body covering; also known as *chador* (in Iran) or *burqa* (in Afghanistan)

hijrah: migration; Muhammad's hijrah from Mecca to Medina in 622 marks the first year of the Muslim lunar calendar

hudud: quranically prescribed crimes and punishments for consumption of alcohol, theft, fornication, adultery, and false witnessing; some countries have adopted these punishments as evidence of the "Islamic" nature of their political rule and law

ibadat: worship, ritual obligations

ijma: consensus; in Islamic law, refers to agreement of scholars on interpretation of legal questions; some have reinterpreted this principle to justify the right of a parliament to enact legislation

ijtihad: human interpretation or independent reasoning in Islamic law

imam: in Sunni Islam, the prayer leader and the one who delivers the Friday sermon; in Shiah Islam, refers to Muhammad's descendants as legitimate successors, not prophets, but divinely inspired, sinless, infallible, and the final authoritative interpreter of God's will as formulated in Islamic law

Islam: submission or surrender to God

jahiliyyah: unbelief, ignorance; used to describe the pre-Islamic era

jihad: to strive or struggle; exerting oneself to realize God's will, lead a virtuous life, fulfill the universal mission of Islam, and spread Islam through preaching and/or writing; defense of Islam and Muslim community; currently often used to refer to the struggle for educational and social reform and social justice as well as armed struggle, holy war

khatam: seal or last of the prophets; Muhammad

khutbah: sermon delivered at Friday prayer session in the mosque

Mahdi: expected or awaited one; divinely guided one who is expected to appear at the end of time to vindicate and restore the faithful Muslim community and usher in the perfect Islamic society of truth and justice

majlis al-shura: consultative assembly

masjid: mosque; Muslim place of worship and prayer

minbar: pulpit in the mosque from which the Friday sermon (*khutbah*) is preached

muamalat: social interactions

muezzin: one who issues the call to prayer from the top of the minaret

mufti: legal expert, adviser, or consultant; one who issues *fatwas* to judges and litigants

mujaddid: renewer; one who comes to restore and revitalize the Islamic community; one who purifies and restores true Islamic practice; one mujaddid is to be sent at the beginning of each century

mujtahid: expert in Islamic law; one who exercises *ijtihad,* or independent reasoning, in legal matters; one capable of interpreting Islamic law

Muslim: one who submits or surrenders himself or herself to God and his will; one who follows Islam

People of the Book (*Ahl al-Kitab*): those possessing a revelation or scripture from God; typically refers to Jews and Christians, sometimes includes Zoroastrians

purdah: seclusion of women from men who are not relatives; segregation of the sexes

qiyas: legal term for analogical reasoning

al-Quds: the holy city (i.e., Jerusalem)

Quran: revelation, recitation, message; Muslim scripture

Ramadan: month of fasting; ninth month of the Muslim calendar

salat: official prayer or worship performed five times each day

shahadah: declaration of faith, witness, testimony; refers to the declaration of Muslim faith: "There is no god but God and Muhammad is His Messenger"

shariah: Islamic law; straight path

shaykh: master, teacher, leader; head of a *Sufi* order, also known as *pir*

Shi or Shiah: follower(s), partisan(s); refers to those who followed the leadership of Ali, the nephew and son-in-law of Muhammad, as Muhammad's successor, those who believe that leadership of the Muslim community should belong to Muhammad's descendants

shirk: polytheism, idolatry, association of anyone or anything with God; the biggest sin in Islam

shura: consultation; today some have interpreted this concept as prescribing democracy

Sufi: literally "one who wears wool"; Muslim mystic or ascetic

Sufism: Islamic mysticism or asceticism

Sunnah: example; typically refers to Muhammad's example, which is believed by Muslims to be the living out of the principles of the *Quran*; "Sunni" is derived from this word

Sunni: those who accept the *sunna* and the historic succession of the Caliphs; the majority of the Muslim community

surah: chapter, particularly of the *Quran*

tajdid: revival, renewal

tariqah: path, way; used by Sufis to designate order to which they belong

tawhid: oneness, unity and uniqueness of God; absolute monotheism

ulama (sing. *alim*): religious scholars

ummah: Muslim community of believers

wali: friend or protege of God; *Sufi* term referring to saint; one reputed to have the power to bilocate, cure the sick, multiply food, and read minds

zakat: almsgiving, one of the Five Pillars of Islam: 2.5 percent tithe on one's net worth to help the poor is required of all Muslims

HINDUISM

ahimsa: nonviolence, the ideal of doing no killing, especially for its karmic effects

atman: in Hindu thought, the soul that resides in the heart, is the source of both life energy and spiritual awareness, and transmigrates after death

avatara: "incarnation" of the gods that descends to earth; avataras assume life-forms that aid creation, usually to defeat demons and overcome evil

Bhagavad Gita: Hindu scripture inserted into the great epic, the *Mahabharata*, extolling the divinity of Krishna as the ultimately real deity

bhakti: devotionalism to a divinity, a means to reach salvation from the world of rebirth

BJP (*Bharatiya Janata party*): Hindu nationalism party that rose meteorically in popularity in the 1990s and assumed national rule in 1998

Brahman: world spirit that arises at creation, which Hindus hold is either in impersonal form, *nirguna Brahman*, or human form, *saguna Brahman*

brahmin: member of the highest caste, innately possessing the highest natural purity; the men traditionally specialize in ritual performance, textual memorization and study, and theology

dharma: "duty" determined by one's caste and gender

guru: a teacher in matters spiritual and cultural, whom disciples regard as semidivine

Kali Yuga: the dark age the world has now entered, when human spiritual capacity is thought to be diminished; a view shared by some Hindus and Buddhists

karma: literally "action," but also meaning the effects of actions that, through a hidden natural causality, condition a being's future; Hindus fix karma as acting on the inborn soul, Buddhists define its effects on the consciousness and habits

moksha: "release" from *samsara*, freedom from future rebirth and redeath (i.e., salvation)

nirguna Brahman: see *Brahman*

puja: a ritual offering to a Hindu or bodhisattva deity, Buddha or bodhisattva

puranas: texts extolling the histories, theologies, and necessary rituals for expressing the *bhakti* faith for the different Hindu deities

Ramakrishna Mission: founded by Swami Vivekananda to further the teachings of his guru, Ramakrishna; an influential Hindu missionary and reform organization that today runs hospitals, schools, and temples and has centers in over a dozen countries

Ramanuja: an influential theologian (1025–1137) who argued that the ultimate reality humans could relate to was *saguna Brahman*

RSS (Rashtriya Svayamsevak Sangh): "National Union of [Hindu] Volunteers," a group that since 1923 has proposed a nativist definition of "Hinduism" as devotion to "Mother India"

saguna Brahman: see *Brahman*

samsara: "the world" of rebirth subject to the law of karma and the inevitable reality of death, a religious understanding shared by Hinduism, Buddhism, Jainism, and Sikhism

Shaivite: devotee of Shiva

Shankara: Hindu philosopher (788–820) and monastic organizer, whose monistic interpretation of the *Upanishads* became the most influential expression of *nirguna Brahman* doctrine

tantra: the esoteric tradition common to both Hinduism and Buddhism that employs practices that defy caste and gender orthopraxy to lead individuals to *moksha/nirvana* quickly

Upanishads: appendices to the Vedas that record early Hindu speculations on *Brahman, atman,* the means to realize their identity, and *moksha*

Vaishnavite: devotee of Vishnu or his incarnations

Veda: the collection of the earliest Hindu hymns directed to the pantheon of deities, including ritual directions and chanting notations for their use

yoga: a term meaning "union" that refers to the various means of realizing union with the divine; earliest use of yoga refers to ascetic practices but expands to include the path of philosophical inquiry, *bhakti,* and *tantra*

Yoga sutras: codification of yoga practices, attributed to Patanjali

BUDDHISM

anatman: "no soul," the doctrine denying the reality of a permanent, immortal soul as the spiritual center of the human being

arhat: an enlightened disciple, according to the Theravada school; an advanced disciple, according to the Mahayana

Bodh Gaya: the site of Shakyamuni Buddha's enlightenment, under a tree

bodhisattva: a Buddha to be, either in the present life or in a future life; in the Mahayana tradition, all individuals should aspire to be Buddhas, hence the bodhisattva is the highest human role; some future Buddhas can be reborn as deities, hence in Mahayana Buddhism there are also bodhisattvas who can assist humans

Buddha: literally, one who has "awakened," ended karmic bondage, and will no longer be reborn; one who will enter *nirvana*

dependent coarising/origination: a twelve-part formula explaining how individuals are bound to future rebirth until they extirpate desire and ignorance

Dharma: the Buddha's teaching, one of the three refuges; more broadly, the truth at the center of Buddhism, the basis for realizing enlightenment

Eightfold Path: the eight qualities needed to reach nirvana, concerning morality, meditation, and salvific wisdom

engaged Buddhism: a reformist movement among global Buddhists seeking to relate the teachings to contemporary suffering

Enlightenment: see *nirvana*

Four Good Deeds: a doctrinal formula guiding the laity on the uses of wealth, advising the pursuit of happiness, security, philanthropy, and ritual

Four Noble Truths: a doctrinal formula focusing on diagnosing the human condition as marked by suffering and distorted by desire, then prescribing the Eightfold Path as a solution

karuna: compassion, the quality that motivated the Buddha to preach and the principal Buddhist social virtue

koan: a Buddhist spiritual riddle desgined to foster spiritual growth, posed by monastic teacher to junior monks, such as "What is the sound of one hand clapping?" or "Does a dog have a Buddhist nature?"

Lotus Sutra: one of the earliest and most influential *Mahayana* Buddhist texts, which reveals the cosmological nature of a Buddha and the universal character of Buddhist truth

Madhyamaka: a *Mahayana* philosophical school that posits the provisional and incomplete nature of all assertions; its goal is to clear away attachment even for words, making realization possible

Mahayana: the "Great Vehicle" that was the dominant school of Buddhism in Tibet and East Asia; the Mahayana philosophical schools developed cosmological theories of Buddhahood and envisioned the universe permeated by bodhisattvas, some of whom were like deities and the focus of ritual veneration

maitri: loving-kindness, a Buddhist ethical virtue and topic of meditation

merit: (see *punya*)

nirvana: a blissful state achieved by individuals who have cut off their karma by ending desire, attachment, and ignorance; after death, they enter the final transpersonal state for eternity, free from future rebirth

Pali canon: the only complete canon among the early collection of Buddha's teachings, in this case in the Pali language derived from Sanskrit; it is divided into three divisions: *Vinaya* (monastic code), *Sutras* (sermons), and *Abhidhamma* (advanced teaching formula)

prajna: the "insight" or "wisdom" necessary for enlightenment in Buddhism, comprising the ability to "see clearly" into the nature of existence as marked by suffering, impermanence, and absence of a soul

"Protestant Buddhism": a term signifying a pattern of reform in which Buddhists protested colonial rule yet adopted perspectives and missionary techniques of Protestant Christianity

punya: merit, or the good karma that enters into the content of an individual's life earned in Buddhist doctrine by moral practices, learning, and meditation

Pure Land: in *Mahayana* Buddhism, the belief that Buddhas and advanced bodhisattvas can through their inexhaustible merit create rebirth realms where humans can easily engage in Buddhist practices conducive to enlightenment

sangha: the Buddhist monastic community of monks and nuns

shramana: wandering ascetics known at the time of the Buddha

skandha: an aggregate, used in Buddhist thought to identify each of the five components that define a human being: the physical body (*rupa*), feelings (*vedana*), perceptions (*samjna*), habitual mental dispositions (*samskaras*), and consciousness (*vijnana*)

Sthaviravadins: the traditionalists among the early Buddhist monastic schools, the only surviving school today being the Theravadins

stupa: the distinctive Buddhist shrine, a raised mound surmounted by a ceremonial pole and umbrella; contains the relics of a Buddha or enlightened saint, either the literal bodily relics or other items left behind such as words in textual form or clothing items worn

Theravada: traditionalists, the last surviving Buddhist school of elders (Sthaviravadins) that is now dominant in South and Southeast Asia

Three Marks of Existence: the Buddhist terms for analyzing human reality as marked by impermanence, suffering, and no soul

Three Refuges: see *Triratna*

Thunder Vehicle: see *Vajrayana*

Triratna: the "Three Jewels" that every Buddhist takes refuge in for all rituals: the Buddha, the Dharma, and the Sangha

Vajrayana: the Mahayana-derived Buddhist tantric "vehicle" of belief and practice that uses unorthodox means, including sexual experience, to propel individuals quickly toward enlightenment

Vipasyana (Vipassana): the widespread Buddhist meditation practice focusing on calming the mind and discerning the truly real

vihara: a Buddhist monastery

Zen: the Japanese *Mahayana* Buddhist school focused on meditation practice, as transmitted from and organized in China as the Chan

EAST ASIAN RELIGIONS

Amaterasu: the *kami* of the sun and progenitor of the Japanese imperial line

Analects: collection of sayings attributed to *Confucius*

ancestor veneration: worship, feeding, and petitioning of the souls of dead ancestors at family graves, temples, or home altars

Ch'ondogyo: Korean movement reaffirming the truth of human dignity and the vitality of *Daoism* and *Confucianism*

city god: Chinese deity with influence on spirits living within city precincts, to whom every family's *kitchen god* reported at year's end

Confucianism: culture of the literate elite (*rujia*) informed by *Confucius* and his disciples, who mastered the classics and rituals; the moral tradition upholding the "three bonds" and the "three principles" as the basis of social life; the spiritual tradition of revering ancestors as part of the family bond

Confucius: see *Master K'ung*

Cultural Revolution: period from 1966 to 1976 when China's Communist party, under leadership of Mao Zedong, attacked religious traditions and practitioners

Dao: mysterious power that moves the universe and all beings

Daoism, philosophical: Chinese tradition advocating the way to harmony for individual and society based on understanding natural forces and flowing with life naturally

Daoism, religious: Chinese tradition that cultivates individual immortality through either alchemical infusions or meditative practices

Daruma-san: Japanese name for the monk Bodhidharma, who brought a meditative-centered Buddhist tradition to China, which would be called Zen in Japan

de: mysterious and spontaneous energy of the universe

diffuse religion: spiritual tradition centered on family and locality, informed by common ideas from *Confucianism, Daoism,* and Buddhism

Five Classics: Confucian canon attributed to Master K'ung: *Book of Changes (Yi-Jhing), Book of Documents (Shu Jing), Book of Poetry (Shi Jing), Book of Rites(Li Jing),* and a historical work that uses events in the early Chinese state to show how to assess praise and blame

Guan Yu: Chinese god of war, regarded as protector of merchants

Hong Xiuquan (1814–1864): charismatic instigator of the *Taiping Rebellion,* whose trance experiences led him to believe that he was the "younger brother" of Jesus; charged with establishing a new state in China

Huang-di: "Yellow Emperor," first immortal in *religious Daoism*

jun-zi: a Confucian gentleman who has cultivated character and learning

kami: deity of Japan associated with places, certain animals, and the emperor

kitchen god (Zao Wangye): deity residing in every household, thought to observe and report on family events to his celestial superiors yearly

Lao Zi (Lao Tzu): "Old Sage," reputed author of *Daodejing* and founder of *Daoism*

li: in Confucian thought, individual performances needed for personal development, including manners, service to others, and rituals

ling: spiritual force possessed by geographic places such as rivers, mountains, caves, as well as by deities and charismatic sages

literati tradition: see *Confucianism*

mappo: Buddhist doctrine of the world in decline, especially in that humans cannot practice meditation as well as in the time of the Buddha

Master K'ung: sage (551–479 BCE) given Latin name to whom Catholic missionaries later gave the Latinate name, *Confucius*

Mencius: first major disciple of *Master K'ung,* a systematizer of Confucian ideals who lived 371–289 BCE

Mizuko cult: the newly popularized Japanese tradition of ritual apology and merit transfer to the spirits of aborted fetuses

mudang: Korean shaman

nembutsu: repetition of the name of the Buddha Amitabha, for the purpose of making merit and gaining rebirth in the Pure Land

neo-Confucianism: tradition originating in Song dynasty and developed subsequently by masters such as Zhu Xi who sought to harmonize early Confucian humanism with more cosmological theories of *Daoism* and *karma* doctrine of Buddhism, adopting meditation techniques from both

neo-Shintoism (or state Shinto): Meiji state's adoption of *Shinto* as state religion, with emperor as focal divinity, that lasted from 1868 to 1945

"new religions": sects arising in Japan from the early nineteenth century combining elements of Buddhism, *Daoism,* and *Confucianism* with ideas imported from abroad; term may be applied outside Japan

Nichiren: thirteenth-century Buddhist monk who taught that the *Lotus Sutra* was sole true Buddhist text and that chanting its title was an essential salvation practice; founded new school based on these ideas

qi: vital force of life within individuals and in nature

qi gong: discipline of cultivating the vital individual life force that can be used for worldly goals such as healing or to reach immortality

Qing-Ming festival: yearly spring festival when Chinese visit and clean family graves, then feast after making offerings to the ancestors

ren: Confucian ideal of being "fully human" in ethics, manners, cultivation

shamanism: tradition by which human mediums are possessed by spirits and communicate with the living; called in China, *wu/xi or fa-shih;* in Korea, *mudang*

Shang-di: Heavenly Lord, thought to preside over early Chinese pantheon; term Christians used to translate "God"

shen: usual term in Chinese for a kindly god or goddess

Shinto: indigenous religion of Japan that reveres the deities of the islands including the emperor

Soka Gakkai: *Nichiren* Buddhist offshoot, now global religion seeking world peace through Mahayana Buddhist teachings

Taiping Rebellion: nineteenth-century revolt in China led by converts to Christianity, who established a separate state in city of Nanjing; resulting civil war was bloodiest in world history

Three Faiths: Chinese grouping of the three great traditions: *Confucianism, Daoism,* and Buddhism

t'i: affection for siblings, in Confucianism a marker of character

Tian: "heaven" understood as impersonal yet responsive to human actions

T'oegyehak: modern Korean Confucian group based on teachings of master Yi T'oegye (1501–1570)

Tu-di (or Tu Chu): "Earth Ruler," local god who controls earth's fertility

Unification Church: Korean *"new religion"* founded by Rev. Sun Myung Moon, who claims to be completing the work of Jesus as a messiah by establishing a global community

wu-wei: "noninterference" or "non-[forced] action," an ideal in *Daoism*

xiao: Confucian ideal of children honoring their parents, attitude that extends to the ruler

yin-yang **theory:** twin forces by which the Dao is known, each complementing the other (female–male, valley–mountain, etc.)

Zhu Xi: great Chinese master of neo-Confucian thought who integrated into *Confucianism* elements of Buddhism and *Daoism* and established core rituals of subsequent tradition

Zhuang Zi: second great s

ART CREDITS

Hartung; page 287 (bottom), © Frank Ossen, www.frankossen.com; page 288, Todd Lewis; page 291, Todd Lewis; page 292, Bridgeman-Giraudon/Art Resource, New York; page 293, Todd Lewis; page 294, Todd Lewis; page 296, Sally Rose Dolak, www.myyantras.com. Used with kind permission from the artist; page 300, the Golden Temple/ Amritsar, Punjab, India, Dinodia/Bridgeman Art Library; page 306, Snark/Art Resource, New York; page 310, Todd Lewis; page 311, © Rameshwar Das; page 312, Todd Lewis; page 313, Todd Lewis; page 314, Todd Lewis; page 319, Todd Lewis; page 321, © Frank Ossen, www.frankossen.com; page 322, © Frank Ossen, www.frankossen.com; page 323, photo by Jean-Philippe Soulé/www.jpsviewfinder.com courtesy of www.nativeplanet.org; page 324, Todd Lewis; page 325, Todd Lewis; page 326, Dash Avatar, India Book House; page 334, India Abroad; page 346, photo by Keystone/Getty Images; page 349, Todd Lewis; page 350, Todd Lewis; page 351, Todd Lewis; page 352, Todd Lewis; page 358, Todd Lewis; page 360, Todd Lewis; page 369, Todd Lewis; page 370, Todd Lewis; page 372 (top), Christie's Images Inc., 2006; page 372 (bottom), Todd Lewis; page 373, Todd Lewis; page 377, Todd Lewis; page 378, Todd Lewis; page 379, Todd Lewis; page 380, Nichiren Confuses His Enemies, 1830 (woodcut), Utagawa, Kuniyoshi (1798–1861)/private collection, Ancient Art and Architecture Collection Ltd/Bridgeman Art Library; page 381, Todd Lewis–page 384, World Religions Photo Library/Alamy; page 385, Todd Lewis; page 386, Todd Lewis; page 388, Todd Lewis; page 398, Todd Lewis; page 402, Todd Lewis; page 410, AFP PHOTO/Sena VIDANAGAMA/Getty Images; page 413, John Kaplan; page 417, FREDERIC J. BROWN/AFP/Getty Images; page 429, GOH CHAI HIN/AFP/ Getty Images; page 430, Todd Lewis; page 433, Todd Lewis; page 434, the Avery Brundage Collection, B60D74+ and B60D73+. © Asian Art Museum of San Francisco. Used by permission; page 435, Lao-tzu (c. 604–531 BC) Riding His Ox, Chinese, Ming dynasty (1368–1644) (ink and water color on silk)/National Palace Museum, Taipei, Taiwan/ Bridgeman Art Library; page 436, Werner Forman/Art Resource, New York; page 437, Todd Lewis; page 440, Todd Lewis; page 448, Todd Lewis; page 449, Todd Lewis; page 451, LifeFile Photos Ltd/Alamy; page 456, LMR Group/ Alamy; page 458 (top), Special Collections, Yale Divinity School Library; page 458 (middle), Special Collections, Yale Divinity School Library; page 464, David Hartung; page 466, Todd Lewis; page 467, Todd Lewis; page 468, Todd Lewis; page 469, World Religions Photo Library/Alamy; page 470, © 30 March 2003 Choo Jen-Sin, Singapore, All Rights Reserved; page 472, Todd Lewis; page 473, Douglas Kanter Photography; page 475, Todd Lewis; page 476, Pat Behnke/Alamy; page 478, Todd Lewis; page 480, Todd Lewis; page 481, Todd Lewis; page 498, David McNew/Getty Images; page 500, Library of Congress LC-USZ62-3657; page 503, Zhou Zhenbiao/Library of Congress LC-USZC4-3345; page 508, Hilary Athame; page 509 (top), the Theosophical Society in America; page 509 (bottom), Library of Congress LC-USZ61-215; page 510, International New Thought Alliance; page 511, Express Newspapers/Getty Images; page 516, Jeff Christensen/Getty Images; page 517, Time & Life Pictures/Getty Images; page 522 (top), F.W. Taylor/Library of Congress LC-USZ62-67518; page 522 (bottom), Popperfoto/Alamy; page 523, Black Star/Alamy.

COLOR INSERT 1

color fig. 1-1, Gordon Wiltsie/National Geographic Image Collection; color fig. 1-2, World Religions Photo Library/ Alamy; color fig. 1-3, Wieste Michiels/Alamy; color fig. 1-4, Alinari/Art Resource, New York; color fig. 1-5, Israel Images/Alamy; color fig. 1-6, MENAHEM KAHANA/AFP/Getty Images; color fig. 1-7, 2005 Artists Rights Society (ARS), New York/ADAGP, Paris/Bridgeman-Giraudon/Art Resource, New York; color fig. 1-8, Worldwide Picture Agency/Alamy; color fig. 1-9, Photo by Marco Di Lauro/Getty Images; color fig. 1-10, Borromeo/Art Resource, New York; color fig. 1-11, AP/Wide World Photos.

COLOR INSERT 2

color fig. 2-1, © Frank Ossen, www.frankossen.com; color fig. 2-2, Erwin Voogt; color fig. 2-3, Todd Lewis; color fig. 2-4, John Kaplan; color fig. 2-5, Todd Lewis; color fig. 2-6, Thierry Falise/OnAsia.com; color fig. 2-7, the Avery Brundage Collection, B62D28. © Asian Art Museum of San Francisco. Used by permission; color fig. 2-8, Cedar Blomberg; color fig. 2-9, © Paul Saltzman (Contact Press Images); color fig. 2-10, AP/Wide World Photos.

INDEX

Abbasid Dynasty, 215, 217, 218, 228, 229, 232
Ablutions, 220
Abortion, 191, 403
Abraham, 22, 60, 74, 75, 76, 79, 119, 149, 198, 206, 209, 210, 222, 244, 514, 515
Abu Bakr, 214–15
Acts of the Apostles, 141, 148
Acupuncture, 426, 474
Adam, 22, 66, 75, 100, 106, 134–35, 158, 514, 515
Adi Granth, 299, 300
Advaita Vedanta, 295, 374
Affirmative action, 277
Afghanistan, 241, 242, 245, 247, 249, 250, 251, 263, 264, 357
Africa, 518
   Christianity in, 182, 184–85, 186, 188
   colonialism in, 182, 184–85
   Islam in, 184, 198, 201, 203, 212, 229, 230, 234, 235, 251, 254, 255, 256
   Judaism in, 65
African Americans, 256–59. See also Civil rights movement
Afterlife. See also Heaven; Hell
   in Confucianism, 437
   in Hinduism, 280–81
   in primal religions, 42–45, 49
Age of Aquarius, 506–7
Age of reason, 173
Agni, 280, 281
Agnosticism, 454
Agonshu, 485, 517
Agriculture, 41
Agudat Yisrael, 70, 71
Ahimsa, 307
Ahmad, Mirza Ghulam, 501
Ahmad, Muhammad, 234–35
Ahmadiyyat, 501
Ainu, 52–53, 56
Aisha, 215
Ajima, 294
Akal Takht, 332
Akbar, Emperor, 299
Alaska, 53
Alberuni, 274
Albigensians, 163
Alchemu, 433, 439
Alchemy, 433, 439
Aleph, 518
Alexander the Great, 79, 80, 358
Alexandria, 152
Alexius I, Emperor, 232
Algeria, 195, 196, 203, 241, 246, 264

Ali, 215, 216
Ali, Muhammad (boxer), 258
Ali, Muhammad (Egyptian ruler), 235
Allah, 204, 205, 206, 207, 208, 210, 257, 456
All-Buddhist Network Television, 401–2
All-India Action Committee, 393
All Souls Festival, 471
Almanacs, 427
Almsgiving, 220–21
Alpert, Richard, 311
Altered state of consciousness. See Trance states
Altneuland (Herzl), 112
Amar Citra Katha comic book series, 325
Amarnath Cave, 321f
Amaterasu, 441, 461
Amazon rain forest, 53–54, 56, 59
Ambedkar, Bhimrao, 286, 406
Ambika, 293
American Muslim Mission, 259
American Revolution, 173
Amida, 371, 446
Amir, Yigal, 73
Amish, 169
Amitâbha Buddha, 371, 378, 383, 446
Amitofo, 371
Amoraim, 85, 86
Amos, 77, 84, 206
Amritsar, 299, 304, 332
Amulets, 402, 472–73, 479–80, 481
Anabaptist religion, 169–70, 171
Analects, 431, 452
Anatman, 363, 366, 382, 487
Anatolia, 212, 231
Ancestor's Day, 470
Ancestor veneration, 60, 420, 427, 429, 458, 463
   in Confucianism, 430, 431, 437, 487
   festivals for, 470
   in Hinduism, 280–81
   in primal religions, 43
   return to, 474–75
Andalusia, 231, 233
Angels, 160, 507
Anglicanism, 169, 170, 186
Animal sacrifice, 52–53, 271, 319
Animism, 35, 42–45, 60, 507, 509
Anitya, 382. See also Impermanence
Anna Karenina (Tolstoy), 525
Ansar, 234
Antioch, 147, 152
Antiochus Epiphanes IV, 79
Anti-Semitism, 109, 110, 111, 149, 180, 259
Apocalyptic religions, 22, 80–81, 147, 506–7, 514–19

al-Aqsa mosque, 244
Aquinas, Thomas, 153, 164, 165, 171
Arabia, 205, 206, 208, 209, 212, 226, 234
Arabian Gulf, 201
Arabic language, 211, 259
Arada Kalama, 350
Arafat, Yasir, 127
Aratamatta kimochi, 480
Archaeology, 37, 41, 279, 391, 393, 406
Archbishop of Canterbury, 170
Arguelles, Jose, 507
Aristotle, 164, 165, 214
Arjan, 299
Arjuna, 527
Ark of the Covenant, 77
Armed Islamic Group, 216, 264
Army of God, 203, 216
Arnold, Sir Edwin, 523
Aryans (Nazi), 116
Aryans (premodern), 279, 280, 281, 288, 289, 349
Arya Samaj, 303–4, 325
Artha, 288
Articles of Religion, 170
Arunachal Pradesh, 396
Asahara, Shoko, 481–82, 484
Asana, 282
Asanga, 369
Asceticism, 226, 271, 281, 295, 300, 350, 357, 399
Ashaka, 360
Ashara, Shoko, 516–19
Ashkenazi Judaism, 109
Ashoka, 357, 380, 391, 408
Ashrams, 186, 310, 322
Ashura, 209
Asia. See also Central Asia; East Asia; South Asia; Southeast Asia
   Buddhism in, 344, 346, 347, 348, 359–62, 406
   Christianity in, 182, 185–88
   colonialism in, 182, 185–88
   immigrants from, 189
   Islam in, 198
   Japanese imperialism in, 392
   Judaism in, 65
   shamanism in, 58–59
Asimov, Isaac, 518
Assimilation, 55, 103, 109, 112, 114, 235, 255
Assyrians, 78
Astral projection. See Out-of-body experiences
Astrology, 312, 316, 366, 505, 506–7. See also Horoscopes

Ataturk (Mustafa Kemal), 242
Athavale, Pandurang Shastri, 332
Atheism, 274, 391, 454
Atman, 20, 281, 282, 295, 308, 363
Atomic bomb, 30–31, 181, 187, 330
Atzut, 101
Auditing, 510, 511, 512
Augustine of Hippo, Saint, 98, 117, 148, 152, 153–55, 161
Augustinianism, 168, 175, 182, 185, 188, 192
AUM, 284
Aum Shinrikyo, 481–82, 483, 506, 516–19
Aung San Suu Kyi, 397
Auschwitz concentration camp, 116, 119, 120
Australia, 185, 518
Australian Aborigines, 44–45
Avalokiteshvara, 370, 376, 377f, 400, 403
Avataras, 292–93
Averroes (Ibn Rushd), 164
Avicenna (Ibn Sina), 214
Axial age, 430
Axis mundi, 35, 48, 60
Ayahuasca, 55
Ayodhya, 278, 331
al-Azhar University, 235, 250
Aztec culture, 507

Ba'al Shem Tov, 100–102, 106
Babar, 278
Babel, tower of, 75
Babri Mosque, 278
Babylonian exile, 78, 82, 146, 515
Babylonian Talmud, 98
Badge of shame, 93
Badr, 208–9, 212
Badrinath, 295
Baghdad, 212, 215, 228
Baghdad University, 236
Bahai movement, 499
Bahrain, 243, 246
Balfour, Lord James, 113
Balfour Declaration, 113, 121
Bangladesh, 198, 243, 276, 393
al-Banna, Hassan, 237–38, 240, 241
Baptism, 81, 157, 158, 169, 171
Baptist religion, 170
Bar Kokhba, Simon, 81
Barlaam, 525–26
Bar mitzvah, 88, 90, 107
Baronsia, 145
Barrett, James, 191
Bat mitzvah, 88, 107
Bear sacrifice, 52–53
Beat Generation, 404

Beatles, 512
Begging rounds, 365, 382
Begin, Menachem, 126
Beijing, 474, 476, 490
Belgium, 203
Bellah, Robert, 503
Benares, 331
Benedictines, 156–57, 161, 168
Benedict of Nursia, 156–57
Ben Eliezer, Israel, 100–102
Ben Isaac, Solomon. *See* Rashi
Ben Maimon, Moses. *See* Maimonides
Bennett, John, 528
Ben Zakkai, Johanan, 84
Berger, Peter, 32, 505
Beruriah, 106
Besant, Annie, 523
Beshr, 100–102
Bet Hillel, 84
Bhagavad Gita, 289, 290, 331, 332, 522,
    523, 524, 526–27
Bhaktas, 290, 317
Bhakti, 289, 290, 291, 296
Bhaktipheri, 332
Bharati, Uma, 333
Bharatiya Janata party (BJP) (India),
    277–78, 304, 308, 330
Bhikkhunis, 352, 412
Bhovctiredanta, 276
Bhutan, 393, 395, 396, 406, 409
Bhutto, Benazir, 263f
Bhutto, Zulfikar Ali, 203
Bible
    Chinese translation of, 458
    Christianity and, 136, 137, 171
    Gandhi influenced by, 523–24
    Judaism and, 74–79, 81–82, 113, 115,
        146
    Latin version of, 171
    layers of historical materials in, 81–82
    Mormonism and, 500
    Nietzsche on, 179, 180
Biblical criticism, 137
Bida, 252
Bihar, 393
Billy Graham Crusade, 132
Bin Laden, Osama, 197, 223, 247,
    249–50, 251, 266
Birth rates, 182, 203
Birth rituals, 315
Bishop of Rome, 152
Bishops, 157, 159, 161, 187
Black Death, 94, 98
Black Muslims. *See* Nation of Islam
Blavatsky, Helena Petrovna, 509, 523
Blessings, god of, 465
Bodh Gaya, 375, 393, 412
Bodhi, 382
Bodhidharma, 372, 481
Bodhiraksa, Phra, 399
Bodhisattvas, 12, 370, 371, 372, 375–76,
    378, 450, 526
Bodhi tree, 351–52, 381, 393
Boke Fuji ("Senility") Kannon, 402, 403
Bombay, 303, 333, 334
Bone divination, 428
Book of Changes. See Yi-Ching
Book of Documents, 435
Book of Mormon, 500
Book of Poetry, 435
Book of Rites, 435
Boonsong, Phra, 398, 399
Born-again experience, 136, 167, 183,
    506, 512. *See also* Twice-born
    individuals
Borobudor, 377
Bosnia, 247, 249

Brahma, 284, 292, 294
Brahma Kumari, 328–29
Brahman, 12, 14, 16, 20, 281, 282, 295,
    296, 507, 509, 512, 527
Brahmins, 280, 286, 293, 300, 316, 330
    Buddhism and, 349, 357
    colonialism and, 303
    in postcolonial era, 323
    rank in caste system, 285
Brahmo Samaj, 303
Bray, Michael, 191
Brazil, 485
Breath, in meditation, 382
Bris/Brit Milah, 88
Britton, John, 191
Brunei, 201
Bryan, William Jennings, 138
Buddha, 9, 60, 295, 349–53, 354, 363,
    367, 373, 397, 515, 523. *See also*
        Amitâbha Buddha; Shakyamuni
        Buddha; Siddhartha
    birthday celebration for, 471
    context of life, 349
    death of, 353, 370
    early life of, 349–53
    enlightenment of, 351–52, 393
    as Hindu deity, 285
    life work of, 352–53
    organizational genius of, 356–57
    root meaning of term, 348, 351
    Tolstoy influenced by, 525
    Western view of, 391
Buddhadasa, 347
Buddhaghosa, 356
Buddha nature, 16
Buddha Nature school of Mahayana, 369
Buddhism, 6, 16, 185, 189, 282, 294,
    333, 341–415, 417, 420, 427, 428,
    439–40, 442, 444–46, 447–48,
    459, 461, 463, 466, 469, 470–71,
    479, 509, 520
    Buddha Nature school of, 369
    Ch'an. *See* Ch'an Buddhism
    Chogye-chong, 444–45
    civilization of, 367
    colonialism and, 387–91, 394, 407
    Consciousness Only school of, 368,
        369
    core doctrines of, 362–66
    decline of, 374–75, 387–88
    economic development and, 406–7
    engaged, 346–48, 352, 408, 413
    expansion of, 357–62, 373–80, 438
    Gelugna, 380, 395
    graded teaching in, 383
    institutional, 456–58
    Lotus Sutra schools of, 370, 378–79,
        446, 462, 463, 484
    Madhyamaka, 368, 369
    Mahayana. *See* Mahayana Buddhism
    modernity and, 346–48, 380–92
    modernization and, 406–7
    myths of liberation and, 20–21
    as a new religion, 499
    new religions based on, 461, 483, 485
    Nichiren, 378–79, 405, 446, 462–63,
        484
    Northern, 344
    passing over and, 526, 529
    persecution of followers, 450–51
    postmodern/postcolonial, 392–409
    premodern, 349–80
    Protestant, 394–95, 404, 487
    Pure Land. *See* Pure Land Buddhism
    relationship with Confucianism, 375,
        376, 435, 437, 438, 443, 448
    relationship with Daoism, 375, 376,
        401, 439

    relationship with Hinduism, 284–85,
        295, 347, 363, 374, 393, 406, 499
    relationship with Islam, 298, 375
    relationship with neo-Confucianism,
        448
    relationship with Shintoism, 456
    Rinzai, 378
    Scientology and, 512
    Shingon, 485
    size of, 344
    Son, 444–45, 487
    Soto, 377–78
    Southern, 344
    state, 377, 407–9, 439
    tantric, 296, 372–73, 383
    Theravada. *See* Theravada Buddhism
    Tibetan, 375, 376, 379–80, 395–96,
        404, 407, 413, 490, 518
    timeline, 342–43
    via negativa in, 14
    Won, 487–88
    Zen. *See* Zen Buddhism
Buddhist Catechism, 394
Buddhist Council, Fifth, 381
Buddhist Law Power. *See* Falun Gong
Buddhist Publication Society, 407
Buddhist socialism, 397
Bukkyo Denko Kyokai, 407
Bullroarers, 45
Bund, 111, 112, 113
Burial practices
    in Buddhism, 437
    in China, 428, 430, 474–75
    in East Asian religions, 466
    in Judaism, 89
    in primal religions, 40, 41, 42, 43
Burma, 185, 276, 368, 374, 375, 381,
    387, 392, 394, 396, 409. *See also*
        Myanmar
Bush, George Walker, 250
Byzantine Empire, 152, 204, 212, 225,
    226, 231

Cairo, 212
Cairo University, 236
Caityas, 386
Cakras, 297
Cakravartin, 360
Calcutta, 301, 303
Calendars, 207, 469, 479
Caliphate, 215, 228, 229
Caliphs, 212, 214–15, 216, 217, 218, 230
Calvin, John, 153, 166, 168–69, 174
Calvinism, 168–69, 175
Cambodia, 185, 344, 375, 400
Canaan, 74, 75
Cannibalism, 44
Canon, 168
Capitalism, 28, 30, 169, 183, 238, 244
Caribbean, 276
Caritas, 154
Carolingian era, 93, 162
Carter, Jimmy, 126
Caste system, 274, 277, 289, 330, 331,
    524
    Buddhism and, 347, 349, 358, 359,
        406, 520
    Sikhism and, 299
    structure and rules of, 285–86
Cathari, 163
Cathedral of St. Peter, 131, 167
Catherine of Aragon, 170
Catherine of Sienna, Saint, 162
Catholicism, 131, 136, 140, 153, 157,
    176, 232–33, 400
    in China, 186, 187, 458
    colonialism and, 182, 183
    Counter-Reformation in, 171, 267

    the Holocaust and, 181
    in Japan, 450, 458
    in Korea, 187, 488
    modernity and, 138–39
    Protestant Reformation and, 167–68,
        169, 170
    relationship with Buddhism, 388
    relationship with Hinduism, 301
    relationship with Judaism, 94, 98
    Scientology compared with, 510
    size of, 135
    in the United States, 189
Causality, 355, 363, 366
Cave paintings, 41, 46
Cave rituals, 41
Celestial bodhisattvas, 370, 371, 372,
    375–76, 378
Celibacy, 329, 371, 378, 446
Cemeteries, 466. *See also* Burial practices;
    Death rituals
Center for Nonviolent Social Change, 72
Center of the world. *See* Axis mundi
Central Asia, 203, 230, 247, 251, 358,
    361
Ceylon, 185, 357, 361, 373, 374, 375,
    377, 380, 393, 396, 407. *See also*
        Sri Lanka
    colonialism in, 387, 388, 389–90
    Protestant Buddhism in, 394–95
Chaitanya, 298
Ch'an Buddhism, 369, 371–72, 376, 377,
    382, 445, 481. *See also* Zen
        Buddhism
Chandalas, 285
Chandogya Upanishad, 282
Chang-an, 376, 442
Change Your Mind Day, 405
Chao-hun, 430
Chariot festivals, 277
Charlemagne, Emperor, 153, 161
Chati, 315
Chechnya, 247, 249
Chenrizi, 370
Chi, 454
Chidester, David, 59
Children of Abraham, 259, 261
China, 12, 22, 28, 336–37, 373, 417,
    425–39, 441, 450, 454–55, 467–
    68, 469, 470, 489, 507, 520, 521
    Buddhism in, 344, 346, 360, 361,
        369, 370, 371, 372, 375–76, 397,
        400–401, 408–9, 411, 412, 428,
        437, 438, 442, 445, 446, 447–48,
        457, 463, 471, 481
    Christianity in, 186–87, 188, 458,
        459–60, 463
    civil religion in, 502
    colonialism in, 186–87, 387–88
    continued religious revival in, 490
    as core of East Asia, 421–24
    earliest history of, 428–29
    imperial, 442–44
    Islam in, 251, 442, 490
    Japanese invasion of, 187, 389, 392
    Judaism in, 65
    myths of harmony in, 20, 74
    new religions in, 490–91
    population of, 420
    reality of gods and spirits in, 464–65
    return of religion to, 463, 471–78
    shamanism in, 59
    Taiping Rebellion in, 458, 459–60
    Tenrikyo in, 462
    Tibet and, 393, 395, 396, 408, 421
    tribal-urban transition in, 15, 16
    unifications of, 435, 442
    unity of three faiths in, 447–49, 471
Ching Dynasty, 389

Chin River, 399
Chogye-chong branch of Son Buddhism, 444–45
Ch'ondogyo, 460–61
Chosen deity, 290–91, 294, 315
Chosen people
  Americans as, 503
  Buddhists as, 395
  Hindus as, 286
  Jews as, 75, 87
Christian existentialism, 179, 519
Christianity, 10, 14, 131–93, 463, 488, 507, 520
  colonialism and, 23, 161, 182–88
  the Holocaust and, 180–81
  imperialism and, 453
  modernity and, 136–40, 164–81
  myths of history and, 22, 165, 185
  new forms of, 500
  as a new religion, 499
  passing over and, 522–24
  persecution of followers, 450–51
  postmodern/postcolonial, 182–89
  premodern, 140–64
  relationship with Buddhism, 389, 390, 407
  relationship with East Asian religions, 458–59
  relationship with Hinduism, 186, 301, 309, 330, 331, 335
  relationship with Islam, 94, 162–64, 206, 207–8, 209, 210, 212, 230, 231–33, 235, 259
  relationship with Judaism, 66, 84–85, 91–95, 98, 116–18, 146, 147, 149, 151, 162–64, 499
  relationship with Shintoism, 456
  size of, 135
  Taiping Rebellion and, 458, 459–60
  timeline, 132–33
  Tolstoy's conversion to, 525–26
  Unification Church and, 514
Christian missionaries, 147, 175, 182, 450, 458–59, 514
  in Africa, 184
  in Buddhist countries, 389, 407
  in China, 186–87, 458
  in Hindu countries, 301, 302
  in India, 186
  in Islamic countries, 235
  in Japan, 187, 458, 459
  in Korea, 187, 459
  in Latin America, 183
  primal religions and, 55
  Sikhs and, 304
Christian Science, 176, 509–10
Christmas, 160, 201
Chuang Tzu, 433
Chuhong, 448
Chu Hsi. See Zhu Xi
Church of England. See Anglicanism
Church of Ethiopia, 184
Church of Jesus Christ of Latter-day Saints. See Mormonism
Church of South India, 186
Cicero, 154
Cinnabar, 439
Circumcision, 9, 81, 88, 90, 146, 147
Cittamatra, 369
City gods, 465
City of God, The (Augustine), 153, 154–55
Civil disobedience, 189, 190, 522, 524, 527
Civil religion, 60, 469, 486, 501–3
  communism as, 486, 502
  Shintoism as, 455–56
Civil Rights Act of 1964, 190

Civil rights movement, 72, 185, 189, 258. See also King, Martin Luther, Jr.
Clans, 205
Classical era, 24
  Buddhism in, 361–73
  China in, 443–44
  Christianity in, 155–64
  East Asian religions in, 446–52
  Hinduism in, 284–94
  Islam in, 217–35
  Judaism in, 89–102
Clear, 510, 511, 512
Clement VII, Pope, 98, 170
Clergy and Laymen Concerned about Vietnam, 72, 528
Clinton, Bill, 127
Cloud soul, 430
Cluny reforms, 161
Cold war, 31, 201
Collective identity, 15, 16, 36–37
Colonialism, 23, 26, 175–76, 504, 514, 519. See also Imperialism
  Buddhism and, 387–91, 394, 407
  Christianity and, 23, 161, 182–88
  Hinduism and, 301–5
  Islam and, 201–4, 231, 233, 235–36, 238, 254
  modern, 28–31
  primal religions and, 55–56
Columbus, Christopher, 500
Comic books, 288, 325, 326f
Coming of age rituals, 315–16
Commandments, in Judaism, 67, 77, 119
Communion (Holy Eucharist), 10, 157, 158, 171
Communism, 28
  Buddhism and, 389, 396–97, 400, 401
  in China, 187, 389, 397, 401, 463, 471, 472, 473, 474, 475–76, 477, 478, 489, 490, 502
  as a civil religion, 486, 502
  Islam and, 239
  in North Korea, 188, 421, 486
  Unification Church and, 515, 516
Companions of the Prophet, 214, 215, 234
Comte, Auguste, 165
Conditioned origination, 363–64
Confession (sacrament), 157, 159
Confessions, The (Augustine), 153–54
Confirmation, 157, 158
Confucianism, 20, 58, 185, 400, 420, 427, 435–37, 447, 449, 469, 489, 490, 514
  basic principles of, 430–32
  bourgeois vs. high, 424
  Ch'ondogyo based on, 460
  communism and, 502
  decline of, 454–55
  defined, 426
  First Epoch of, 435–36, 491
  in Japan, 6, 426, 440, 443, 449, 450, 451, 456, 491
  in Korea, 426, 443, 455, 457, 486–87, 491
  modernity and, 424–25
  new religions based on, 483
  postcolonial challenge of, 424–25
  on relationships, 436–37
  relationship with Buddhism, 375, 376, 435, 437, 438, 443, 448
  relationship with Christianity, 458
  relationship with Daoism, 432, 433, 435, 439, 443, 444, 520
  relationship with Shintoism, 451, 456
  revival of, 475–76, 486–87
  Second Epoch of, 442–43, 486, 491

spiritual training in, 452
  Third Epoch of, 491–92
Confucius, 420, 425, 426, 430–32, 442, 449, 452, 454, 464, 471, 476, 491
Congregationalism, 170, 176
Congress party (India), 277
Consciousness Only school of Mahayana, 368, 369
Conservative Islam, 251, 252
Conservative Judaism, 68, 69, 70, 107–8
Constantine, Emperor, 151, 153
Constantinianism, 151–52, 155, 168, 169, 188, 192
Constantinople, 150, 152, 163, 232, 233
Constitution of Medina, 209
Copernicus, 139–40
Coptic Church, 184
Corporate charters, 164
Cosmic Buddhahood, 370, 450
Cosmic eras, 289
Cosmogony, 36
Council of Chalcedon, 150
Council of Constantinople, 150
Council of Jerusalem, 147
Council of Nicaea, 150
Council of Trent, 171
Covenant
  in Christianity, 231
  in Judaism, 67, 69, 77, 78, 79, 82, 83, 87, 88, 90, 105, 119, 120, 181
Craft guilds, 164
Creation stories, 18, 75, 88, 106, 289
Cremation, 316, 466, 474
Cromwell, Oliver, 170
Crucifixion, 144–45
Crusades, 94, 98, 161, 162–64, 175, 200, 231–33
Cui Jian, 475
Cult of personality, 486
Cult of Reason, 178
Cult of the dead, 428
Cult of the Supreme Being, 178
Cultural relativism. See Relativism
Cultural Revolution, 187, 395, 397, 401, 408, 447, 474, 476, 478, 502
Cultural Survival, 57
Cupiditas, 154
Cyprus, 112
Cyrus, King, 79

Dalai Lama, 380, 395, 396, 405, 485
Damascus, 215, 226
Damascus University, 236
Dana, 383–84, 385, 387
Dance of Shiva, 292
Dangki, 58
Dani, 43
Danka, 403
Dao, 12, 16, 20, 426, 427, 432–33, 452, 507
Daodejing, 432, 434
Daoism, 185, 400, 420, 427, 430, 432–35, 436, 437, 442, 447, 459, 468, 469, 471, 489
  basic beliefs in, 434–35
  Ch'ondogyo based on, 460
  decreasing relevance of, 457
  defined, 426
  early philosophy, 432–33
  feng shui and, 426, 473, 474, 476
  institutional development of, 438
  in Japan, 6, 440, 445, 450, 461
  new religions based on, 461
  qi gong and, 476, 491
  relationship with Buddhism, 375, 376, 401, 439

relationship with Confucianism, 432, 433, 435, 439, 443, 444, 520
  religious, 433
  spiritual training in, 452
  upsurge of practice in, 463
Dao jiao, 433
Dao-shi, 468
Dar al-Islam, 229
Darrow, Clarence, 138
Darshan/darshana, 294, 320
Daruma-san, 481
Darwin, Charles, 137, 139–40, 179, 180
Dashara, 319
Datura, 55
David, King, 76–77, 78, 81, 82, 112, 114, 210, 231, 244
Dayananda, Lahore, 303–4
Days of Awe, 91
De, 432
Death. See also Afterlife; Mortality
  Buddhism and, 383
  Hinduism and, 280–81
  myths of history on, 21–22
Death rituals
  in Buddhism, 387, 403, 437
  in East Asian religions, 465, 466
  in Hinduism, 316–17
  in Judaism, 89
Deborah, 106
Declaration of faith, 219
Declaration of Principles, 127
Declaration on the Relationship of the Church to Non-Christian Religions, 139
Defender of the Faith (title), 170
Deism, 174, 178, 309
Deities/gods, 425
  birthday celebrations for, 469
  in Chinese religions, 429–30, 464–65
  chosen, 290–91, 294, 315
  Hindu, 280, 281, 284, 290–94, 295, 309, 317
  Shinto, 440–41, 450
  tribal, 205
Deity cults, 420, 426
Delhi, 333, 375
Delhi sultanate, 297–98
Democracy, 239, 246, 253, 277, 329, 330, 515
Demons, 430, 507
Denmark, 181
Denominationalism, 171–73, 189, 500, 505
Deprivatization of religion, 68
Desacralization, 520
Desert fathers, 156
Deuteronomic (D) biblical materials, 81
Deuteronomy, 78, 84, 90
Dev, Guru, 513
Devas, 507
Devekut, 100, 101
Devi, 293–94, 318, 319, 327
Devil, 160
Devotio moderna, 164, 165–66, 176, 177, 506
  Protestant Reformation and, 167–68, 169, 174
  Romanticism and, 178, 179
Devotion, 37
Dhahran, 247
Dhammakaya, 398–99
Dharamsala, 396
Dharana, 282
Dharani, 367
Dharma, 281, 289, 293, 296, 315
  in Buddhism, 352, 353, 357, 361, 362, 367, 370, 377, 392, 395, 411, 427

caste and, 286, 288
Dharma-deshana, 383
Dharmakaya, 487
Dharmapala, Anagarika, 394–95, 409
Dharmashastras, 285, 286, 287, 288, 289, 315
Dharma yudha, 299
Dhimmi, 212, 230
Dhutanga, 359
Dhyna, 367
Dianetics: The Modern Science of Mental Healing (Hubbard), 497, 510, 511
Dianic Wicca, 508
Diaspora
    Buddhist, 344, 391, 404–6
    Christian model of, 184, 185, 186, 188, 189, 192
    Jewish, 80, 85, 93, 124, 125
Dietary laws and customs, 9–10, 87, 104, 201, 314
Diffuse religion, 420, 426–27, 429, 437, 444, 447, 450, 469, 479, 489
Diplomas of protection, 93
Disaster, the, 202
Diversity, 26, 499
    of Buddhism, 344, 410
    of Christianity, 134, 135, 171–73, 188, 189, 500
    of Hinduism, 274
    historical change and, 22–24
    of Islam, 214–16, 256, 261
    of Judaism, 70, 74, 80–81, 120, 125
    in Korea, 486–89
    passing over and, 521–25
    unity in, 524
Divination, 58, 428, 467, 505
Divine
    gestures of respect for, 313–14
    presence of, 308–9
Divine Principle (Moon), 514
Divine rejection, 149
Divorce, 225, 226, 287
Diwali, 317
Dogen, 378, 446
Dogma, 174
Dome of the Rock, 244
Dominicans, 186, 301
Dong-choon, Lee, 487
Doordarshan, 325, 326
Dowry, 223, 225, 316
Dravidian languages, 279
Dreamtime, 44, 45
Dreyfus affair, 112, 113
Dukkha, 348, 382
Dunne, John, 522
Durga, 290, 294, 314, 319
Durga Puja, 319
Durkheim, Émile, 45
Dutch. *See* Holland/Netherlands
Dvaraka, 295
Dvija, 285. *See also* Twice-born individuals

Early childhood rituals, 315
Earth goddesses, 293–94
Earth gods, 465, 467, 477–78
East Asia, 60, 387, 417–95
    Buddhism in, 361, 367–73, 375, 382, 400–403
    Chinese core and periphery of, 421–24
    defining religious terms, 426–27
    imperialism and, 453–54
    important religious sites in, 422–23f
    modernity and, 424–25, 453–63
    postmodern/postcolonial, 463–89
    premodern, 425–52

religious continuity and transformation in, 464–71
    religious institutions of, 466–68
    religious orientations in, 420–21
    shamanism in, 58–59
    spiritual training for elites in, 451–52
    time line of religions in, 418–19
    traumatic transitions in, 454–59
Easter, 160
Eastern Europe, 70, 94, 95, 100–101, 106, 109, 111, 118, 121
Eastern Roman Empire. *See* Byzantine Empire
East India Company, 301
Ebene, 54
Eckhart, Meister, 162
Eclecticism, 505, 527
Eddy, Mary Baker, 176, 509–10
Edict of Toleration/Milan, 151
Education, 136–37, 164, 235–36, 455, 456
Eggs Under the Red Flag (album), 475
Egypt, 152, 279
    Christianity in, 184
    Gulf War and, 219
    Islam in, 195, 196, 202, 203, 212, 235, 237, 240, 241, 242, 245, 246, 247, 251, 265
    Israelite bondage in, 74, 75, 92, 93
    Israel *vs.*, 123, 126, 208–9, 243
    tribal-urban transition in, 15
Eight dusts, 462
Eightfold Path, 352, 355–56, 367
Eight great relic caityas, 386
Eight moral precepts, 365
Eisai, 378, 446
Elder traditionalists, 354
Eliade, Mircea, 37
Ellis, Marc, 120
Ellul, Jacques, 520
Emerson, Ralph Waldo, 509
Emperor worship, 455–56
Engaged Buddhism, 346–48, 352, 408, 413
Engels, Friedrich, 472
England, 28, 182, 453, 508, 523. *See also* Great Britain
    Christianity in, 161
    Islam in, 199
    religious reform in, 170
    religious tolerance in, 174
    Renaissance in, 166
    slavery abolished in, 175
Engrams, 510, 511
Enlightened theism, 174
Enlightenment (era), 21, 165, 176, 189, 454
    Buddhism and, 388–89, 407
    Christianity and, 173–74, 189
    Hinduism and, 276, 278, 302
    Jewish, 91, 102–3, 104, 106, 108–9, 110, 115
    Romanticism vs., 178–79, 506
    Zionism and, 111
Enlightenment (experience)
    in Buddhism, 20, 351–52, 362, 368, 370, 371, 372, 382, 393, 438
    in Hinduism, 283
    in Scientology, 512
    of Tolstoy, 526
En Sof, 99, 100
Environmentalism, 399
Epic of Gilgamesh, 16
Epics, 288–89, 325–26
Equal Rights for Women law (Israel), 107
Equatorial Africa, 201
Erbakan, Ecmettin, 246–47
Essenes, 80, 146, 149

Ethics, 11
    global, 519–29
    in Judaism, 83
Ethnic cleansing, 409. *See also* Genocide
Ethnic conflicts, 407–9
Ethnic (Yiddish) Judaism, 105, 110, 111
Eurasia, 37, 40, 41, 55
Europe, 509. *See also* Colonialism; Eastern Europe; Western Europe
    Christianity in, 162–64, 171–73, 182
    Hinduism in, 276
    Islam in, 199, 200, 203, 212, 214, 251
    Judaism in, 65, 70, 94–95, 96–97f, 100–101, 103, 106, 109, 111, 118, 121
    modernity and, 164
Evangel, 210
Evangelical Protestantism, 136–38, 140, 174–76, 182, 183–84, 185, 506
Eve, 22, 66, 75, 106, 134–35, 158, 514, 515
Evenk, 47
Everlasting Gospel (Joachim of Fiore), 164
Evolutionary theory, 137, 138, 139–40, 179
Exile and return stories, 79, 81, 110, 114, 121
Exodus, 8, 75, 76f, 81–82, 84, 90, 92
Exorcism, 468
Extreme unction, 157, 159
Ezekiel, 78, 84
Ezra, 79, 82

Fackenheim, Emil, 119
Fa-Hsien, 357
Faith, 148, 165–66, 167, 168, 169, 173, 178–79, 228, 236, 506. *See also* Via moderna
Falun Gong, 401, 490–91
Falwell, Jerry, 250
Fard, Wallace D., 257
Farrakhan, Louis, 257, 259
Fa-shi, 468
Fasting, 48. *See also* Ramadan
Fatima, 215
Fatwas, 219, 260
Feast of Booths, 90
Feast of Sacrifice, 222, 256f
Feast of the Breaking of the Fast, 221
Feast of Weeks, 90
Feminism, 177, 265, 508. *See also* Women
Feng Shen Yan-yi, 447
Feng shui, 426, 437, 473–74, 476
Fertility, 40–41, 60, 429
Festivals, 8, 10
    of Buddhism, 386
    of Christianity, 160
    of East Asian religions, 469–71
    of Hinduism, 317–19
    of Judaism, 90
    of Sikhism, 300
Feudalism, 155
Fiji, 276
Fiqh, 252
Fire sacrifices, 280
Five Confucian Classics, 435–36
Five Hierarchical Relationships, 431, 436
Five moral precepts, 365
Five Pillars of Islam, 208, 218–22, 223, 257, 259
Five substances theory, 429
Forbidden city, 502
Forest dwellers (life stage), 287
Forest monasteries, 359
Forest monks, 382, 399
Formative era, 24
    Buddhism in, 349–61

China in, 429–30
Christianity in, 140–55
Hinduism in, 279–84
Islam in, 204–17
Judaism in, 74–88
Four aims of life, 288
Four Conditions, 366
Four Good Deeds, 366
Four Noble Truths, 352, 354–55, 366, 383, 481
Four passing sights, 350
Four stages of life, 287
France, 28, 301, 387, 388, 400
    Christianity in, 161, 163
    the Holocaust and, 181
    in Indochina, 185
    in Islamic countries, 201, 235, 242
    Islam in, 199, 203, 255
    Judaism in, 94
    Renaissance in, 166
    Zionism and, 113
Franciscans, 450
French Revolution, 102, 109, 173, 178
Freud, Sigmund, 140
Fu (symbol), 478
Fulani, 233
Full Moon Festival, 471
Funan region, 368
Fundamentalism, 23, 24, 26, 524
    Christian, 136–40, 177, 180, 189, 506
    Islamic, 202, 237–39
    modernity vs., 136–40, 519–21, 529
    ultra-Orthodox Judaism as, 71–74
Fundamentalist-nationalist movements, 278–79
Fundamentals, The, 137
Funerals. *See* Burial practices; Death rituals

Gabriel (angel), 206, 222
Gadhafi, Muammar, 203, 245
Gamaa Islamiyya, 247
Gandhara, 358
Gandhi, Indira, 333
Gandhi, Mohandas K., 33, 183, 190, 277, 331, 332, 521, 528, 529
    life and work of, 306–8
    passing over of religion by, 522–25, 526–27
Ganesh, 291, 324–25, 334
Ganges River, 298, 320, 336
Gardener, Gerald, 508
Gate of Heavenly Peace, 472
Gautama Buddha, 351
Gaya, 350, 373–74, 393
Gaza, 202, 241, 243
Gelugna school of Buddhism, 380, 395
Gemara, 85, 86, 98
Genesis, Book of, 75, 78, 84, 86, 106
Genocide, 55, 56, 503. *See also* Ethnic cleansing; Holocaust
Gentiles, 70, 146, 147, 148, 149, 515
Geomancy, 437, 467, 473
Geonim, 85
Germany, 116, 117, 137, 180, 453.
    See also Nazism
    Christianity in, 181
    Islam in, 199, 203
    Judaism in, 109, 162
    religious wars in, 171
    Renaissance in, 166
Ghat, 316
al-Ghazali, Muhammad, 226, 228, 234
Ghettos, Jewish, 94, 95, 163
Ghost Dance, 56
Ghuride armies, 298
Ginsberg, Allen, 405

Globalization, 3, 497–531
  of Buddhism, 412–13
  ethical issues and, 519–29
  future of religion in, 529
  of Hinduism, 334
  of jihad, 248–50
  new age religions and, 497, 498, 500, 504–19
  new religions and, 497–503
  of Sikhism, 331–33
Gnosticism, 99, 102, 176
God
  in Buddhism, 364
  in Christianity, 134, 135, 150
  death of, 179–80, 520
  in Islam. *See* Allah
  in Judaism, 66–67, 74–79, 81, 83–84, 86–87, 88, 90–91
  in Sikhism, 300
  in the Unification Church, 514, 515
Goddesses
  earth, 293–94
  Hindu, 293–94, 329
  mother, 40
  tribal, 205
  washing the hair of, 53, 54
  in Wiccan religions, 508
God hypothesis, 173
Gods. *See* Deities/gods
Golan Heights, 123, 126, 202
Gold, Daniel, 278–79
Golden Temple, 299, 300f, 332
Goldstein, Baruch, 73
Goliath, 76
Golwalkara, Guru, 278
Gopis, 293
Gospels, 141–42, 144, 145, 183. *See also* New Testament
Grace, 157, 167
Graham, Franklin, 250
Grand Mosque, 222, 245, 251
Great Britain, 188, 391, 394, 396, 397. *See also* England
  in China, 387–88
  in Hindu countries, 274
  in India, 183, 185, 201, 276, 277, 279, 301–5, 306–8, 327, 330, 331, 387, 393, 524
  in Islamic countries, 235, 242
  Islam in, 203, 255
  in Palestine, 121, 201
  Zionism and, 112–13
Great Enlightenment temple, 393
Great Goose Pagoda, 477
Great Learning, 444
Great persecutions, 376
Great Plains, 56
Great Vehicle, 354, 362, 367, 369, 370, 371, 373. *See also* Mahayana Buddhism
Greeks, ancient, 140–41
Greenberg, Irving, 119–20
Gregory I, Pope, 153, 156
Gregory VII, Pope, 161
Guangdong Province, 458
Guanyin, 370, 376, 400–401
Guan Yu, 447, 464
Guide of the Perplexed (Maimonides), 99
Gunas, 295
Guo Hong, 439
Gupta Dynasty, 285, 373
Guru Busters, 325
Gupta Dynasty, 285, 373
Guru Busters, 325
Guru Granth Sahito, 299
Guru Purnima, 310
Gurus, 10
  Hindu, 272, 278, 281, 296, 310–11, 316, 323, 327–29

Sikh, 299
Ten, 299, 300
Gush Emunim, 70–71, 73, 126
Gyatso, Tenzin, 395
Gyawali, Dipak, 337

Hadith, 11, 218, 262
Hagar, 198
Hahn, 454
Hajj, 222, 258. *See also* Pilgrimages, in Islam
Halakhah, 67, 69, 70, 87, 88, 91, 99, 100, 105
HAMAS, 249
Han era, 420, 429, 430, 432, 435–36, 437, 438, 442
Hanifs, 206
Hanuman, 290, 293
Hardwar, 273
Haredim, 70, 106
Hare Krishna movement (ISKON), 276
Harmony. *See* Myths, of harmony
Haroset, 92
Harris, Marvin, 318
Hasidism, 91, 100–102, 106
Haskalah, 103, 108. *See also* Jewish Enlightenment
Hatsu-mode, 479
Healing, 46, 49–51, 505, 509, 510
Heaven, 157, 218, 313, 383–84. *See also* Afterlife
Heavenly Lord, 460
Hebrew, 104, 105, 115
Hebrew Union College, 107
Hegel, Georg, 165
Hell, 157, 218
Hellenism, 228
Hellenistic Judaism, 80, 146, 147, 148
Hellenization, 79
Henotheism, 78
Henry VIII, King, 170
Heresy, 32–33, 150, 163
Heretical imperative, 32, 335
Hermits, 156
Herod, 142
Herzl, Theodor, 112
Heschel, Abraham Joshua, 72, 528, 529
Heterodoxy, 282, 294, 300, 333
Hezbollah, 203, 246, 249
Hidden Christians, 187
Higan, 470
Hijab, 255, 264
Hijra, 207
Hill, Paul, 191
Hillel, 84, 85, 86
Himachel Pradesh, 396
Himalayan Mountains, 59, 291, 320, 322f, 375, 509
Himalayan region, 379–80, 395–96
Hinayana, 368
Hinduism, 10, 14, 16, 183, 185, 189, 271–339, 377, 442, 507, 519, 520
  Aum Shinrikyo and, 518
  colonialism and, 301–5
  contemporary practices in, 310–17
  four aims of life in, 288
  four stages of life in, 287
  geography and demography of, 274–76
  modernity and, 276–79, 301–8
  myths of liberation and, 20–21
  new religions based on, 483
  passing over and, 522–24, 526
  persistence of traditional understandings in, 308–10
  postcolonial, 308–17, 323–29
  postmodern, 308–17
  in practice, 317–34

premodern, 279–301
Protestant, 302
  relationship with Buddhism, 284–85, 295, 347, 363, 374, 393, 406, 499
  relationship with Christianity, 186, 301, 309, 330, 331, 335
  relationship with Sikhism, 300
  religious institutions of, 321–23
  religious language of, 12
  schools of thought in, 294–97
  sectarianism in, 309–10
  size of, 274
  tantric, 294, 296–97
  timeline, 272–73
  transcendentalism and, 509
  Transcendental Meditation and, 512
  Unity School and, 510
Hinduism Today, 335
Hindu-ness, 277, 278
Hindu rashtra, 277
Hindutva. *See* Hindu-ness
Hirohito, Emperor, 479
Hiroshima, 181
Hirsch, Samson Raphael, 106
Hisjab, 201
Historiography, 140
History
  Enlightenment view of, 173
  Islam and, 210, 217
  Marx's view of, 30
  as progress, 164–65, 179–81
Hitlahavut, 101
Hitler, Adolf, 116, 117, 119, 120, 180, 181
Hokkaido Island, 52
Holi, 319
Holidays, national, 469, 502, 503
Holiness, 520, 529
Holland/Netherlands, 201, 203, 301, 387, 388, 453
Holocaust, 31, 65, 69, 91, 95, 116–21, 125, 180–81, 528
  devastation of, 116–18
  Jewish faith challenged by, 118–20
  Zionism and, 112, 115
Holy days, 8
Holy Land, 162, 163
Holy orders, 157, 159
Holy Spirit, 145, 160, 164, 165
Holy Week, 160
Homa, 280
Homeless wanderers. See Sadhus
Homoousios, 150
Homo religiousus, 37
Homo sapiens, 35, 39
Hong Kong, 185
Hong Xiuquan, 459–60
Hopkins, Emma Curtis, 176, 509–10
Horoscopes, 315, 316. *See also* Astrology
Hortensius (Cicero), 153–54
Hosea, 77, 84
Hoshi matsuri, 485
House churches, 187, 188
Householders
  Buddhist, 352, 356–57, 359, 362, 366, 367, 371, 376, 378, 383, 384, 385
  Hindu, 287, 288, 316, 329
  Sikh, 300
Hoza, 484
Hubbard, L. Ron, 497, 510, 511, 512
Hudaybiyah, 209
Hudud, 263, 264
Huldah, 106
Humanism, 168
Human nature, 519–20
Human rights, 173, 174, 413, 522
Human sacrifice, 428
Hunger strikes, 307

Hunter-gatherer societies, 15, 18, 35, 36, 37, 39–41, 52, 60
Hunting rituals, 41
Huppah, 89
Husayn, 216
Hutterites, 169

Ibadat, 218–19, 223
Ibn Abd al-Wahhab, Muhammad, 234, 250
Ibn Saud, Muhammad, 234
Ibrahim. *See* Abraham
Icons, 292, 314–15, 322, 334, 401, 402, 465, 472–73, 478, 481
Id al-Adha, 222
Id al-Fitr, 221
Ideology of merit, 365
Idolatry, 134, 205, 207, 234
Ijma, 218, 253
Ijtihad, 201, 233, 236
Ikhtilaf, 219
Ikhwan al-Muslimi. *See* Muslim Brotherhood
Imams, 217, 220, 251, 259, 260
Iman, 208
Immigration, 189, 254, 255–56, 412–13
Imperialism. *See also* Colonialism
  East Asian religions and, 453–54
  Japanese, 387, 389, 391–92, 455
Impermanence, 363–64, 366, 382
Inau, 52
Incarnate lineages, 380
Incarnation. *See also* Avataras; Reincarnation
  of Jesus, 135, 150
  in shamanism, 52
India, 22, 392, 442, 521, 522, 523, 524
  Ahmadiyyat in, 501
  Buddhism in, 347, 349, 352, 357, 358, 360, 368, 371, 372, 373–75, 376, 382, 393, 396, 406, 408, 438
  Christianity in, 132, 186, 188
  colonialism in, 183, 185, 186, 387
  Hinduism in, 271, 272–73, 274–79, 281–82, 285, 301–5, 306–8, 309, 315–37, 393, 483, 520
  independence of, 277, 302, 308
  Islam in, 93, 198, 201, 237, 298, 377
  Judaism in, 65
  major ancient and holy places of, 275f
  myths of liberation in, 20–21, 74
  nationalism in, 306–8, 329–33
  partition of, 308
  Sikhism in, 298–301
  tribal-urban transition in, 15, 16
Indian National Congress, 306, 307
Indigenous spiritual communities, 176
Individualism, 37, 164, 166, 168, 302, 314, 436
Individuation of identity, 15, 16
Indochina, 185, 387, 392, 400
Indo-Europeans, 41, 279
Indonesia, 197, 198, 201, 203, 233, 242, 276, 344, 387, 400
Indra, 280, 281, 293
Indra's jeweled net, 369
Indulgences, 94, 167, 171
Indus River, 274, 298, 358
Industrial Revolution, 28, 175
Indus Valley, 279
Infallibility
  of the imam, 217
  papal, 138
Infidels, 216
Inheritance rights, 223, 224, 225, 226
Initiation rites, 50–51
Inner alchemy, 439
Inner Mongolia, 408

Inner sagehood, 432
Innocent III, Pope, 161
Inquisitions, 95, 161, 163, 175, 200
Interdependence, 363–64, 366, 368, 370
International Network of Engaged Buddhists, 347, 413
Inuit, 53, 54
Iqbal, Muhammad, 248
Iran, 202, 221, 229, 235, 241, 242, 263, 264
Iranian revolution, 200, 202, 217, 243, 245, 246
Iraq, 123, 201, 202, 212, 219, 242, 243, 247
Isaac, 76, 79, 198, 222
Isaiah, 78, 115, 147
Islah, 233, 234
Islam, 6, 14, 184, 189, 195–269, 300, 377, 400, 442, 456, 490, 507, 519, 526
    activist worldview of, 245
    Ahmadiyyat, 501
    calendars in, 207
    challenges facing, 260–67
    colonialism and, 201–4, 231, 233, 235–36, 238, 254
    conservative, 251, 252
    Crusades and, 94
    division and dissent in, 214–16
    Enlightenment and, 103
    forced dress codes and, 163
    Golden Age of, 212–14
    issues of authority and interpretation, 251–54
    in mainstream politics and society, 246–47
    meaning of term, 198
    modernity and, 201–4, 235–41, 243–44
    in modern state and society, 242–43
    morality in, 11
    myths of history and, 22
    Nation of, 256–59
    neofundamentalist, 251, 252
    neomodernist (reformist), 251, 252–53
    as a new religion, 499
    postcolonial, 241–60
    postmodern, 241–67
    premodern, 204–35
    radical, 240–41
    relationship with Buddhism, 298, 375
    relationship with Christianity, 94, 162–64, 206, 207–8, 209, 210, 212, 230, 231–33, 235, 259
    relationship with Hinduism, 274, 277–78, 297–98, 302–3, 308, 309, 330, 331, 332, 333
    relationship with Judaism, 66, 93, 95, 206, 207–8, 209, 210, 212, 230, 231, 259
    relationship with Sikhism, 298–99
    resurgence of, 241–42
    Shiah, 216–17, 243, 246, 258, 499
    social justice and, 207, 208
    Sufi. See Sufism
    Sunni. See Sunni Islam
    timeline, 196–97
    Wahhabi, 233, 234, 247, 250–51
Islamic alternative, 238
Islamic Group, 247
Islamic Jihad, 216, 247
Islamic Jihad Palestine, 249
Islamic law (sharia), 208, 234, 237, 252, 262–63
    family, 223–26
    revivalism and, 239

sources and development of, 212, 217–19
    Sufism and, 227–28
Islamic Order, 198
Islamic Research Council, 250
Islamic Salvation Front (FIS) (Algeria), 246
Islamic Society (Jamaat-i-Islami), 202, 237–39, 501
Islamic world, 198
Islamists (neofundamentalists), 251, 252
Islamization, 253, 262–63
Islamophobia, 254
Ismail, 198, 222
Israel, 73, 74, 113, 120–27, 196, 200, 202, 239, 240, 243–44, 246, 249, 250. See also Zionism
    changing of Jacob's name to, 86, 127–28
    conflict over public life in, 69–71
    Declaration of Independence of, 107
    holy and secular in, 121
    Islam in, 195
    lost tribes of, 500
    in premodern Judaism, 75–79, 82, 90–91, 93
    Reform Judaism and, 104, 105
    statehood established, 121
    tribes of, 75
    in Unification Church, 515
Ista deva, 290. See also Chosen deity
Istanbul, 233
Italy, 98, 113, 166, 230
Iyesu, 450

Jacob, 76, 79, 86, 127–28
Jade Emperor, 465
Jahiliyya, 205, 234
Jahwist and Elohist (J&E), 81, 82
Jainism, 282, 294, 333
Jal, 314
Jamaat-i-Islami. See Islamic Society
Jammu, 334
Janai, 317
Japan, 30, 181, 381, 417, 424, 427, 437, 442, 450–51, 454, 468–69, 489
    Aum Shinrikyo in, 481–82, 483, 516–19
    Buddhism in, 344, 347, 359, 360, 369, 370, 371, 372, 377–79, 391–92, 400, 402–3, 404, 405, 406, 411, 438, 439–40, 444, 445–46, 450–51, 456, 457, 461, 470–71, 479
    Christianity in, 187, 188, 450–51, 456, 458, 459
    colonialism and, 28
    Confucianism in, 6, 426, 440, 443, 449, 450, 456, 461, 491
    Daoism in, 6, 440, 445, 450, 461
    imperial, 439–41
    imperialism of, 387, 389, 391–92, 455
    Korea occupied by, 392, 460, 488, 515
    nationalism in, 392, 457
    neo-Confucianism in, 445, 446, 451, 461
    new religions in, 461–63, 482–86, 488
    "no religion" claim for, 479–80
    old and new traditions in, 478–86
    population of, 421
    religious freedom in, 463
    shamanism in, 52, 56, 59, 440–41
    state and civil religion in, 455–56
Jatakas, 353
Jati, 285
Jatra, 317

Java, 373, 377, 400
Jebus, 77
Jeremiah, 78, 84, 206
Jerusalem, 112, 115, 152
    Council of, 147
    Crusades and, 94, 162–63, 231–32
    Islam and, 209, 243–44
    Israeli takeover of, 123, 202, 243–44
    naming of, 77
    New (in Mormonism), 501
    temples of. See Temples, of Jerusalem
Jesuits, 187, 301, 450, 458
Jesus Christ, 60, 80, 117, 134, 135, 140, 141, 153, 154, 157, 160, 164, 169, 176, 179, 191, 204, 244, 304
    in Aum Shinrikyo, 482, 518
    Gandhi influenced by, 523–24, 526
    Hong Xiuquan and, 460
    in Islam, 210, 499
    King (Martin Luther) influenced by, 522, 526
    in Mormonism, 500, 501
    Nazareth movement and, 184
    Paul's encounter with, 148
    search for historical, 390
    as the son of God, 149–50
    stories of, 142–46
    in the Unification Church, 514, 515
Jewish Defense League (JDL), 73
Jewish Enlightenment, 91, 102–3, 104, 106, 108–9, 110, 115
Jewish Peace Fellowship, 72
Jewish problem, 93, 98, 109
Jewish socialism, 105, 110–11, 114–15
Jewish State, The (Herzl), 112
Jiang Zemin, 476
Jiao Hong, 447
Jihad, 200, 217, 230, 240, 299
    globalization and hijacking of, 248–50
    philosophy of, 223
Jihad (organization), 203, 216
Jihadi, 251
Jimson, 55
Jing, 439
Jinja, 468–69
Jinsi Lu, 443
Jizo, 403
Jnana yoga, 295
Joachim of Fiore, 164–65, 169, 176, 177, 506
Jodo Shinshu, 378
John XXIII, Pope, 139, 149
John of the Cross, 162
John Paul II, Pope, 485
John the Baptist, 142
Jordan, 123, 195, 202, 203, 241, 242, 243, 246, 265
Jordan River, 123
Josaphat, 525–26
Joseph (foster father of Jesus), 142
Joseph (Old Testament figure), 75
Joshua, 75
Josiah, King, 78, 81
Journey to the West (Wu), 448
Judah, 77, 78
Judaism, 6, 8, 14, 65–129, 181, 189, 203, 507, 519, 520
    anti-Semitism and, 109, 110, 111, 149, 180, 259
    Ashkenazi, 109
    biblical roots of, 74–79
    Conservative, 68, 69, 70, 107–8
    ethnic (Yiddish), 105, 110, 111
    forced dress codes and, 93, 94, 163
    Hasidic, 91, 100–102, 106

of Holocaust and Redemption, 110, 115, 116–21, 125. See also Holocaust
    modernity and, 68–74, 102–15
    myths of history and, 21–22, 74, 110
    oral tradition in, 84, 85
    Orthodox. See Orthodox Judaism
    passing over and, 526
    postmodern/postcolonial, 116–25
    premodern, 74–102
    Rabbinic. See Rabbinic Judaism
    racial definitions of, 109
    Reform. See Reform Judaism
    relationship with Christianity, 66, 84–85, 91–95, 98, 116–18, 146, 147, 149, 151, 162–64, 499
    relationship with Islam, 66, 93, 95, 206, 207–8, 209, 210, 212, 230, 231, 259
    Sephardic, 109
    size of, 65
    timeline, 66–67
    ultra-Orthodox. See Ultra-Orthodox Judaism
    Unification Church and, 515
Judges, Israelite, 75
Julian of Norwich, Saint, 162
Jund Allah. See Army of God
Junzi, 431
Justification by faith, 148, 167
Justinian, Emperor, 93

Kaaba, 205, 208, 222
Kabbalah, 91, 99–100, 101, 102
Kabir, 298
Kach party (Israel), 73
Kahane, Meir, 73
Kahane Chai, 73
Kaivalya, 282
Kakutaro, Kubo, 463
Kali, 271, 294, 304
Kali Yuga, 289, 290, 293, 296
Kalki, 293
Kama, 288
Kama Sutra, 288
Kamakura era, 445–46, 462, 481
Kami, 440, 441, 446, 452, 461, 462, 479, 480
Kamui, 52–53
Kannon, 370, 400, 402, 403, 480
Kant, Immanuel, 178
Kanwar, Roop, 327
Kanzo, Uchimura, 187
Kaplan, Mordecai, 108
Karachi, 329
Karajites, 215, 216, 223
Karbala, 216
Karma, 3
    in Aum Shinrikyo, 518
    in Buddhism, 349, 353, 354, 363, 365, 366, 369, 371, 377, 382, 383, 384, 387, 437, 438, 483
    caste and, 285–86
    death rituals and, 387
    deities' power to alter, 290
    in Hinduism, 281–84, 285–86, 288, 290, 312–13, 330
    living with, 312–13
    in neo-Confucianism, 443
    punya and, 383, 384
    in Sikhism, 300
Karmabhumi, 283
Karuna, 355, 365, 384
Karunamaya, 370
Kashmir, 247, 249
Kashmir Valley, 358
Kasumigaseki Station, 481
Kathmandu, 395–96

Kathmandu Valley, 359
Kaur (surname), 299
Kavanah, 100, 101
Kennedy, John F., 72
Kenya, 196, 247
Ketubah, 89
Ketuvim, 84
Khadija, 206, 215
Khalifah, 215. *See also* Caliphs
Khalistan, 332
Khalsa, 299
Khartoum, 235
Khartoum conference, 124
Khmer Empire, 368, 375, 377
Khmer Rouge, 400
Khomeini, Ayatolla Ruhallah, 219, 245
Khutba, 220
Kia, 50. *See also* Trance states
Kierkegaard, Søren, 179, 180
Kimi, Kotani, 463
King, Martin Luther, Jr., 33, 72, 185, 497, 528–29
  assassination of, 528
  passing over of religion by, 522–23, 524, 526, 527
  religious vision of, 190
King Abdul-Aziz University, 249
Kingdom of God, 135, 137, 145
Kingdom of God Is Within You, The (Tolstoy), 526
King's Jews, 93
Kitchen gods, 465, 470
Kleshas, 354
Knesset, 69, 73
Koans, 372, 446
Kokugakuin University, 452
Komeito, 462
Kook, Zvi Yehuda, 126
Korea, 417, 424, 427, 437, 441, 442, 454, 469, 470. *See also* North Korea; South Korea
  Buddhism in, 407, 411, 420, 438, 439, 444–45, 446, 471, 487–88
  Ch'ondogyo in, 460–61
  Christianity in, 187–88, 459, 488
  Confucianism in, 426, 443, 455, 457, 486–87, 491
  culture of, 420–21
  diversity in, 486–89
  Japanese occupation of, 392, 460, 488, 515
  kitchen gods in, 465
  new religions in, 488–89
  religious freedom in, 463
  Rissho Koseikai in, 485
  shamanism in, 59, 420–21, 488, 514
  Tenrikyo in, 462
  Unification Church in, 514, 515, 516
Korean War, 515
Koryo Dynasty, 444
Kosher dietary laws, 87, 104, 201
Kosovo, 247, 249
Kotama, Okada, 486
Kowtow/ketou, 465, 470
Krishna, 9, 12, 290, 294, 304, 326, 527
  attributes of, 293
  festival honoring, 319
Krita Yuga, 289
Kshatriyas, 285, 298
Kuala Lumpur, 243
Kuei, 58
Kufa, 215, 216
Kumara, 291
Kumbha Mela, 320–21
Kunda lini, 297
K'ung, Master. *See* Confucius
!Kung San, 39, 46, 49–51, 52, 56
Kurozumikyo, 461, 483

Kushinagar, 353
Kut, 59
Kuwait, 195, 202, 219, 241, 243, 246
Kyoto, 445

Labor party (Israel), 71, 126
Ladakh, 395, 396
Lakota Sioux, 52
Lakshmi, 317
Lame Deer, 52
Language
  in early humans, 39, 40
  religious, 12–14
Laos, 185, 344, 375, 400
Lao Zi, 432, 439
Laplace, Pierre, 173
Last Judgment, 226, 227
Late Great Planet Earth, The (Lindsey), 506
Lateran Council, Fourth, 94, 163
Latin (language), 171, 211
Latin America, 65, 182, 183–84, 185, 186, 188
Latin (Western) Christianity, 152, 156, 182
Laws of Manu, The, 285, 286
League of Nations, 121
Lebanon, 123, 196, 201, 203, 241, 242, 243, 246
Lebensraum, 116
Le Chambon sur Lignon, 181
Lee, Ann, 176
Left Behind series, 506
Lekhraj, 329
Lenin, Vladimir, 453, 472
Lent, 160
Leo X, Pope, 167, 170
Lesser Vehicle, 368
Lessing, Gotthold, 103, 165, 173
Levant, 201
Leviticus, 84
Li, 20, 430–31, 443
Liang Qichao, 457
Liberal evangelicalism, 137, 140
Liberation
  myths of, 18, 19f, 20–21, 22, 23, 74
  quest for, 281–82
Liberation theology, 176, 183, 184–85, 188, 189
Libya, 202, 203, 233, 245
Life-cycle rites
  Christian sacraments in, 158–59
  in Hinduism, 315–17
  in Judaism, 88
Light of Asia, The (Arnold), 523
Li Hongzhi, 491
Li Jing, 435
Likud party (Israel), 71, 126
Lila, 319
Lincoln, Abraham, 503
Lindsey, Hal, 506
Ling, 426, 464
Linga, 291f, 318, 393
Lin Zhao'en, 447
Literacy, 10, 360
Literati tradition, 426, 430–32, 437, 438, 442, 443, 452, 455
Littell, Franklin, 181
"Little Red Book" (Mao), 502
Liu Mi, 447
Long March of 1934, 472
Lost Horizon (film), 395
Lotus Sutra schools of Buddhism, 370, 378–79, 446, 462, 463, 484
Louis I, Emperor (Louis the Pious), 93
Louis XVI, King, 178
Lucifer, 514
Lucius III, Pope, 163

Luther, Martin, 95, 148, 153, 166, 167–68, 169, 170
Lu Xinjing, 439
Lyotard, Jean-François, 25, 504

Maccabaeus, Judas, 79
Maccabean revolt, 79, 114
Madhyamaka school of Buddhism, 368, 369
Madras, 334
Mahabharata (epic), 288–89, 326, 393
Mahabodhi, 393
Mahabodhi Society, 395
Mahant, 322
Maha Pasana cave, 397
Maharashtra, 393, 406
Mahar caste, 393, 406
Maharaj-ji, 311
Maharishi Mahesh Yogi, 512, 513
Maha Sangha, 409
Mahayana Buddhism, 365, 375–76, 382, 383, 384, 398, 439, 445, 447, 450
  death rituals of, 387
  decline of, 377
  expansion of, 438
  origins of, 354
  philosophies and schools of, 367–73
  religious language of, 12
  resurgence of, 379
  rituals of, 385
  size of, 344
  Theravada Buddhism compared with, 362, 368
  in Vietnam, 400
  in the West, 391
  women and, 412
Mahdi, 233, 234–35, 501
Mahdiyya, 234–35
Mahisha, 319
Maimonides, 98–99, 104, 164
Maitreya, 378
Maitri, 355
Majlis al-shura, 253
Malaya, 201
Malaysia, 185, 400
  Buddhism in, 344
  Hinduism in, 276
  Islam in, 195, 201, 202, 203, 241, 242, 246, 265, 266
Malcolm X, 257–58
Manchu Dynasty, 459, 460
Manchuria, 389, 392
Manchurians, 449
Mandalay, 381
Mandarin dialect, 420
Mandarin Dynasty, 424
Mandate of Heaven, 431, 432, 435, 436, 456
Manicheans, 442
Manifest destiny, 503
Manjushri, 369f, 375–76
Manliness, 205
Mantras, 284, 316, 367, 383, 385, 512, 513
Mao Zedong, 187, 401, 463, 464, 471–73, 476, 478, 490, 502, 503f
Mappo, 378, 445–46
Mara, 350–51, 352
Marie Antoinette, Queen, 178
Marriage
  in Christianity, 157, 159
  in Hinduism, 287, 309, 312, 316
  in Islam, 224–25, 226
  in Judaism, 69, 89
  in the Unification Church, 515–16
Martel, Charles, 162
Marx, Karl, 28, 30, 110, 165, 472, 490
Marxism, 30, 183, 189, 238, 244, 463

Mary (mother of Jesus), 142, 210
Masada, 114
Mashiah, 76. *See also* Messiah
Maslow, Abraham, 505
Materialism, 261–62
Mathas, 272, 295, 322, 336
Mathura, 331
Matriarchal period, 40–41
Matsumoto, Chizuo. *See* Ashara, Shoko
Matzah, 92
Mauryan Empire, 284, 357, 358
Mawdudi, Mawlana Abul Ala, 237–38, 239, 241
Maya, 281, 295
Mayan culture, 507
Mayan Factor, The (Arguelles), 507
May Day, 11
May 4th movement, 389
Mazu, 464f, 465
Meaning, 15–16, 22, 37
Mecca, 205, 206, 207, 208–9, 238, 243, 245, 456
  facing during prayer, 220
  Nanak's journey to, 299
  pilgrimages to, 208, 209, 222, 258–59
  surahs of, 261
Media, 259, 277, 278, 491, 504
Medina, 208, 209, 214, 215, 229, 243
  naming of, 207
  surahs of, 261
Meditation, 21
  in Buddhism, 356, 367, 369, 371–72, 382–83, 389, 390, 391, 394, 398, 404
  in Confucianism, 443
  in Daoism, 433
  in Hinduism, 284, 287
  mindfulness, 372, 382
  in neo-Confucianism, 452
  practices, 382–83
  in Protestantism, 394
  in the West, 391
Meditation halls, 381
Meiji era, 402, 424, 455–56, 457, 461, 462–63, 479, 483
Meir, Rabbi, 106
Memorial Day, 503
Mencius, 431, 491
Mendelsohn, Moses, 103
Meng, Master. *See* Mencius
Mennonites, 169
Menstruation, rituals surrounding, 315
Merit account sheet, 374
Merit-making rituals, 381
Merit transfer, 384
Mesmer, Franz Anton, 509
Mesopotamia, 15, 279
Messiah
  Christianity and, 141, 144, 149
  Judaism and, 70, 73, 76, 79, 81, 104, 105, 112
  Moon as, 188, 515
Metanarratives, 25–26, 504, 505, 521, 525
Metaphors, 12, 13, 21
Methodism, 138, 174–75, 186, 459
Mexico, 57
Micronesia, 392
Middle Ages
  Christianity in, 155–64
  Judaism in, 91–100
Middle East, 521
  immigrants from, 189
  Islam in, 202, 229, 230, 235, 237, 255, 256
  Judaism in, 65
  myths of history in, 21–22

tribal-urban transition in, 16
Middle Way, 350
Miki, Nakayama, 461
Milarepa, 372f
Milk miracle, Ganesh's, 324–25
Millennialism, 164–65, 176–77, 502
Million Man March, 259
Minbar, 220
Mindanao, 229
Mindfulness meditation, 372, 382
Mindon, King, 381
Ming Dynasty, 376, 447–49, 458, 465
Minjung theology, 188
Mirabai, 298
Miracles, 144, 227, 324–25
Miriam, 106
Mishnah, 84, 85, 86
Mishneh Torah, 99
Missionaries
    Buddhist, 361–62, 385, 404, 438
    Christian. *See* Christian missionaries
    Hindu, 305, 329, 331
    Muslim, 228, 298
Mission churches, 188
Mitnaggedim, 102
Mitzvot, 67, 83
Mixin, 477
Mizrahi party (Israel), 71
Mizuko, 403
Modernity, 5, 23–24
    Buddhism and, 346–48, 380–92
    Christianity and, 136–40, 164–81
    Confucianism and, 424–25
    East Asian religions and, 424–25,
        453–63
    end of, 28–31
    fundamentalism vs., 136–40, 519–21,
        529
    in global perspective, 25–27
    Hinduism and, 276–79, 301–8
    Islam and, 201–4, 235–41, 243–44
    Judaism and, 68–74, 102–15
    myth of, 30
    new age religions and, 504–6
Modernization, 166, 406–7
Moksha, 281, 282, 284, 287, 288, 290,
    295, 296, 297, 310, 313
Monasteries and monasticism
    Buddhist, 358–61, 367, 374, 375,
        376, 377, 380, 381–87, 401, 456,
        466. *See also* Sangha
    Christian, 155, 156–57, 161, 175, 176
    Hindu, 285, 295, 322, 374
    women and, 176
Monastic landlordism, 361, 456
Mongol Empire, 376, 380
Mongolia, 57, 346, 375, 379, 408, 409
Monism, 295, 296
Monkey King, 290, 448
Monks, Buddhist, 356, 357, 358, 359,
    360, 361, 362, 365, 367, 379, 385,
    393, 398, 439, 444, 445
    in China, 389, 401
    communism and, 396–97, 401
    criticism of, 376
    forest, 382, 399
    number of, 344
    political action by, 409
    relationship with nuns, 352, 412
    relationship with the state, 380, 381
    relaxation of strictures on, 457
    self-immolation by, 346f, 347, 393
    village, 382
    Won school, 487
Monogamy, 224–25
Monotheism, 5, 6, 13–14, 302, 489
    of Christianity, 66, 150, 507
    of Hinduism, 273, 304

of Islam, 66, 198, 206, 207, 208, 219,
    507
of Judaism, 66, 78, 507
mysticism in, 99
Montanist movements, 176
Montgomery, Alabama bus boycott, 190
Moon, Sun Myung, 188, 514–16
Moon cakes, 471
Moral community, 344
Morality, 11, 22
    Buddhist, 356, 365, 367, 383
    Islamic, 11
    tribal-urban transition and, 15–16
Moral precepts, 365
Moravianism, 174
Mormon (Native American), 500
Mormonism, 500–501, 512, 515
Morocco, 197
Mortality, 15–16, 22. *See also* Death
Moses, 60, 74, 75, 78, 80, 84, 101, 114,
    204, 206, 210, 499, 514, 515
Mosques, 219, 220, 259–60, 265, 278,
    330, 331
Mother goddess, 40
Mount Abu, 329
Mount Hiei, 450
Mount Hira, 206
Mount Sinai, 66, 77, 87, 105, 206
Muamalat, 219, 223
Muawiya, 215, 216
Mudang, 59, 488
Mudras, 372
Muezzin, 219
Muftis, 219, 260
Mughal Empire, 229, 298–301, 304
Muhammad, Elijah, 256–57, 258, 259
Muhammad, Wallace D., 257, 258–59
Muhammad ibn Abdullah, 11, 60,
    204–9, 210, 212, 215, 216, 217,
    219, 222, 227, 229, 230, 231, 234,
    235, 250, 251, 261, 262, 297, 304
    in Ahmadiyyat, 501
    contemporary views of, 236, 238,
        239, 245
    death of, 214
    early life of, 204–7
    message of, 207–8
    Nation of Islam view of, 257
    Night Journey of, 9, 244
    significance of, 205
Muhammad Speaks (newspaper), 258
Muhammad's Youth, 216
Mujaddid, 234, 501
Mujahideen, 245, 249
Munetada, Kurozumi, 461
Mushrooms, psychoactive, 48
Muslim Brotherhood, 202, 203, 216,
    246, 252
    founding and philosophy of, 237–39
    increasing radicalism of, 240–41
Mutiny, the, 305
Myanmar, 185, 276, 344, 397, 406, 408,
    411. *See also* Burma
Mystery religions, 158
Mysticism, 13, 22, 506
    Christian, 152, 162, 165, 169
    of identity, 99, 162
    Islamic. *See* Sufism
    Jewish, 99–100, 101
    of love and union, 99, 162
Myths, 7–10, 16–22, 26
    of harmony, 18, 19f, 20, 21, 22, 23,
        74
    of history, 18, 19f, 21–22, 23, 30, 74,
        110, 165, 185
    of liberation, 18, 19f, 20–21, 22, 23,
        74
    of modernity, 30

morality and, 11
of nature, 18, 19f, 21, 22, 23
of progress, 31, 504
of the three ages, 176

Nagarjuna, 368, 369
Nagas, 293, 352
Nagasaki, 187
Nahda (Renaissance) party (Tunisia),
    246
Nalanda, 373
Namaskara/namaste, 271, 313
Namkaran, 315
Nanak, 298–99, 300
Nanjing, 460
Naraka, 313
Nasser, Gamal Abdel, 240
Nataraja, 292
Nationalism, 28
    in China, 475–76
    Hinduism and, 277, 278–79, 306–8,
        329–33
    Shinto-based, 392, 457
National Union of Hindu Volunteers.
    See Rashtriya Svayamsevak Sangh
Nation of Islam, 256–59
Native Americans, 44, 56–57
Nature
    ancients' relationship with, 6
    Enlightenment view of, 173
    Islam and, 210
    Judaism and, 74
    myths of, 18, 19f, 21, 22, 23
    primal religions and, 36
    Wiccan religions and, 508
Nazarenes, 80, 146, 147, 148, 499
Nazareth movement, 184
Nazism, 31, 93, 116, 121, 180–81
Neanderthals, 39
Negation. *See* Via negativa
Negative witness theory, 98, 117
Nehemiah, 79, 82
Nehru, Jawaharlal, 277
Nei-tan, 433
Nembutsa, 378
Neo-Brahminism, 330
Neo-Confucianism, 426, 491, 520
    Buddhism and, 448
    in Japan, 445, 446, 451, 461
    order, heirarchy, and relatedness in,
        443–44
    spiritual training in, 452
Neofundamentalist Islam, 251, 252
Neolithic period, 10
Neomodernist (reformist) Islam, 251,
    252–53
Neopaganism, 508
Neoplatonism, 99, 102, 228
Neo-shamanism, 59
Neo-Shintoism, 455–56, 479
Neotraditionalism, 327–29
Nepal, 276, 285, 344, 370, 373, 379,
    393, 395–96, 411
Nestorian Christianity, 442
Neturei Karta, 70–71
Neuhaus, Richard, 528
Neusner, Jacob, 82
Neviim, 84
New age religions, 18, 497, 498, 500, 522
    examples of, 504–19
    modern and postmodern, 504–6
New religions, 456, 459–63, 488–89,
    490–91, 497–503
    in historical context, 499–501
    new, 482–86

older, 461–63
New Testament, 84–85, 141–46, 149,
    210, 231
    Gandhi influenced by, 523–24
    Protestant Reformation and, 166, 168
    Puritanism and, 170
    stories of, 142–46
New Thought movement, 509
New Year's rituals, 90, 91, 465, 470, 476,
    479–80
Nichiren, 378–79, 446, 462
Nichiren Buddhism, 378–79, 405, 446,
    462–63, 484
Nietzsche, Friedrich, 179–80, 181, 520
Nigeria, 198, 233
Night Journey, of Muhammad, 9, 244
Night of Power and Excellence, 206
Nikkyo, Niwano, 484
al-Nimeiri, Jaafar, 203, 245
Nin, 454
Nine Nights, 319
*Ninety-five Theses Against the Sale of
    Indulgences*, 167
Nirguna Brahman, 295, 300
Nirvana, 12, 20, 22, 344, 349, 352, 366,
    368, 370, 378, 382, 390, 446
    Buddha Nature school on, 369
    explanation of doctrine, 362
    meditation and, 372
    path to, 353–56
    root meaning of, 354
Nishapur, 212
Noah, 75
Nobel Peace Prize, 396, 397, 528
Nobunaga, 450
Nominalism, 165
Nonchurch movement, 187
Nonconformism, 170
Noninterference. *See* Wu-wei
Non-self doctrine. *See* Anatman
Nonviolence, 190, 191, 271, 284–85, 307,
    522–24, 526–27
North Africa, 201, 203, 212, 235, 255
Northern Buddhism, 344
North India, 276, 279, 285, 298, 329,
    330, 349, 373–75
North Korea, 401, 420, 421, 460
    Buddhism in, 346
    Christianity in, 188
    civil religion in, 486
Nostradamus, 482, 518
Nuclear weapons, 181
Numata, Yenan, 407
Numbers, Book of, 84
N/um kxausi, 49
Nuns, Buddhist, 356, 357, 358, 359, 361,
    362, 365, 367, 379, 382
    in China, 389, 401
    criticism of, 376
    number of, 344
    relationship with monks, 352, 412

Obeyesekere, Gananath, 394
Oil embargo, 202
Okayama City, 461
Okiagari, 481
Olcott, Henry Steele, 394
Old Testament, 80, 84, 141, 198
OM, 284
Om-kara, 300
On the Origin of Species (Darwin), 139
Operation Badr, 208–9
Opium trade, 453
Oracles, 10
Ordination, 157, 159, 176
Original sin, 66, 134–35, 152, 158, 174,
    451, 514

Orthodox Christianity, 135, 152, 156, 163, 182, 519
Orthodox Judaism, 65, 68, 69, 70, 112
    beliefs and background of, 105–7
    Conservative Judaism compared with, 107–8
Orthodoxy, 9, 108, 519
    Hindu, 282, 294
    Islamic, 228
Orthopraxy, 9, 108, 519
Otto, Rudolf, 6
Ottoman Empire, 229, 233, 234–35
Oudil, 106
Outer Mongolia, 408
Outer nobility, 432
Out-of-body experiences, 505, 507, 510, 511, 512, 514, 517
Oyagami, 461–62

Padri, 233
Pagan (Myanmar), 379f
Paganism, 149–50, 151, 508
Pakistan, 195, 198, 202, 203, 221, 241, 242, 245, 250, 251, 263, 264, 266, 276, 278, 298
    Buddhism in, 393
    civil war in, 243, 308
    creation of, 308, 332
Palermo, 212
Palestine, 80, 81, 83, 91, 112–13, 239, 250. See also Zionism
    Crusades and, 162
    Islam in, 201
    mandate system in, 121
    terrorist attacks in, 196
    at the time of Jesus, 143f
Palestinian Liberation Organization (PLO), 124, 127
Pali Canon, 381
Pali Text Society, 407
Panchen Lama, 380
Pandits, 317
Pap, 366
Papacy, 98, 138, 139, 152, 157, 161, 171
Parampara, 310
Parinirvana, 362, 381
Paritta, 367
Parks, Rosa, 190
Parliament of World Religions, 394, 509
Parousia, 160
Parvati, 291, 294, 319, 324
Passing over, 521–25, 526–27, 529
Passover, 8, 90, 91, 92
Patanjali, 282
Paternalism, 28, 182
Patriarchal societies, 41, 176, 200, 224
Paul of Tarsus, 140, 141, 147, 148, 149, 153, 167, 176, 524
Pax Islamica, 230
Peace of Augsburg, 171
Peace of Westphalia, 171
Pearl Harbor, 392
Pentacostal Christianity, 131, 183
Pentagon, attack on, 196
Pentateuch, 84, 87
Pentecost, 160
People of the Book, 209, 230
Perfection of Wisdom, 368
Perfect Liberty Kyodan, 484
Perls, Fritz, 505
Persia, 78–79, 204, 212, 225, 226, 499, 526
Persian Gulf states, 242, 243
Persian Gulf War (1991), 219
Pesach. See Passover
Peter, 157
Peyote, 54
Pharisees, 80, 82–84, 113, 144, 146, 147

Philippines, 188, 197, 249
Philistines, 77
Phranon Wat, 399
Phylacteries, 90
Pietism, 173, 174–77, 179, 189, 506
Pilgrimages
    in Buddhism, 373, 403, 457
    in Hinduism, 273, 287, 320–21
    in Islam, 208, 209, 222
Pilgrims (New World), 170
Pinda puja, 316
Pir, 227
Pitri, 280–81
Pitrilika, 281
Pius IV, Pope, 171
Pius IX, Pope, 138, 161
Pius XI, Pope, 181
Plain of Arafat, 222
Plenary indulgences, 94
Pluralism, 26–27, 520, 521, 527, 528
    Buddhism and, 354, 357
    in East Asia, 420
    Hinduism and, 309–10
    Judaism and, 69, 120
    new age religions and, 504, 505
    shamanism and, 58
Pogroms, 95, 100, 101, 109
Poland, 100, 111, 112
Pol Pot, 400
Polygyny, 224–25, 226
Polytheism, 205, 207, 208, 274, 290, 304, 429
    myths of nature and, 18
    new age religions and, 507
Portugal, 182, 183, 387, 388, 448, 453
Postclassical era, 294–301
Postcolonial era, 23, 24, 26
    Buddhism in, 392–409
    Christianity in, 182–89
    Confucianism in, 424–25
    East Asian religions in, 463–89
    Hinduism in, 308–17, 323–29
    Islam in, 241–60
    Judaism in, 116–25
    trends in, 31–33
Postmodernism, 5, 23, 24, 69
    Buddhism in, 392–409
    Christianity in, 182–89
    defined, 504
    East Asian religions in, 463–89
    global ethics and, 519–29
    in global perspective, 25–27
    Hinduism in, 308–17
    Islam in, 241–67
    Judaism in, 116–25
    new age religions in, 504–6, 507
    trends in, 31–33
    universal heresy in, 32–33
Potala, 381f
Pradakshina, 314
Prajna, 351, 355, 356, 366, 367, 373, 382
    explanation of doctrine, 362
    meditation and, 372
Prajnaparamita, 368
Prakriti, 294–95
Pranam, 313
Pranayama, 282
Prasad, 314
Pratityasamutpada, 355, 363–64
Prayag, 320
Pregnancy, rituals during, 315
Pre-Meiji era, 461
Premodernism, 5, 24, 27, 31, 507. See also
    Classical era; Formative era;
    Postclassical era
    Buddhism and, 349–80
    Christianity and, 140–64
    East Asian religions and, 425–52

in global perspective, 25
Hinduism and, 279–301
Islam and, 204–35
Judaism and, 74–102
metanarratives and, 26
retaining religious ideals of, 519, 520, 521, 527
Presbyterianism, 170, 459
Preta, 316, 387
Priestly (P) biblical materials, 81–82
Priests, 176, 465–66, 468
Primal, defined, 36
Primal religions, 35–63, 509
    the afterlife in, 42–45, 49
    animism in, 35, 42–45, 60
    colonialism and, 55–56
    current status of, 56–59
    new age religions and, 505
    origins of, 39–41
Primitive, defined, 36
Principalities and powers, 140
Printing press, 166
Privatization of religion, 26, 27, 28, 171, 173, 504, 505, 521, 522, 524, 527, 529
Progress, 173, 176–77, 504
    God of, 180
    history as, 164–65, 179–81
    myths of, 31, 504
Prophets, 77–79, 206, 234
Protected people. See Dhimmi
Protestant Buddhism, 394–95, 404, 487
Protestant Church of North India, 186
Protestant Church of Pakistan, 186
Protestant Hinduism, 302
Protestantism, 166, 400, 450, 520
    in China, 186, 187, 458
    colonialism and, 182
    evangelical, 136–38, 140, 174–76, 182, 183–84, 185, 506
    the Holocaust and, 181
    in Korea, 187, 488
    modernity and, 136–39
    relationship with Buddhism, 389, 390, 394–95
    relationship with Hinduism, 302
    size of, 135
    in the United States, 189
Protestant Reformation, 95, 137, 139, 153, 155, 158, 166, 167–71, 173, 182, 183, 211, 267, 524
    devotio moderna and, 167–68, 169, 174
    grassroots movements in, 169
    impact on women, 176
Protestant work ethic, 168–69
Psychoactive substances, 48, 54–55, 280
Ptolemies, 79
Puja, 10, 291, 313, 314–15, 317, 318, 322
Punjab, 299, 304, 331–33, 501
Punya, 366, 371, 383–84, 387
Puranas, 290, 291, 312
Purdah, 225–26, 266
Pure Brightness Festival, 470
Pure Land Buddhism, 354, 376, 378, 382–83, 404, 405, 445, 446
    beliefs and practices of, 371
    Won Buddhism based on, 487
Puri, 295
Purim, 90
Puritanism, 170
Purusha, 12, 14, 294–95, 527

Qadian, 501
Qadosh, 75
al-Qaeda, 197, 216, 247–48, 249, 266
Qi, 439, 443, 474
Qi gong, 476–77, 491

Qin Dynasty, 435
Qing Dynasty, 425, 449, 459, 460
Qing-Ming, 470
Qiyas, 218
Quaker religion, 132, 174
Qualified monism, 296
Qufu, 476
Qui, 433
Quran, 11, 198, 200, 204, 206, 208, 212, 216, 217, 218, 220, 222, 226, 230, 233, 234, 245, 251, 252
    on Jews, 209
    meaning of word, 207
    message of, 210–11
    postmodern applications of, 261, 262
    revivalism and, 239
    on women, 223, 224–25
Quraysh, 206, 207, 209
Qutb, Sayyid, 237, 240–41

Rabbinic Judaism, 65, 68, 70, 71, 80, 104, 112, 147
    Conservative Judaism and, 108
    Hasidism and, 101, 102
    Orthodox Judaism and, 105
    Pharisaic roots of, 82–84
    women in, 106
    world of, 89–91
    Zionism and, 113–14
Rabbis, 10, 83, 84–88, 101, 102, 107
Rabin, Yitzhak, 73, 123, 127
Radha, 290, 294
Rahman, Fazlur, 267
Rajas, 295
Rajasthan, 327
Raja Yoga centers, 328–29
Rama, 278, 289, 290, 294, 304, 326
    attributes of, 293
    festival honoring, 319
Ramadan, 206, 221, 222
Ramakrishna, 304–5
Ramakrishna Mission, 305, 322, 324, 335, 336
Rama Navami, 319
Ramanuja, 296
Ramayana (epic), 289, 293, 325–26
Ram Dass, 311
Rangoon, 397
Rania, Queen, 262f
Rashi, 86, 98
Rashtriya Svayamsevak Sangh (RSS), 277, 278, 330
Rationalism, 173–74, 176, 228, 506. See also Reason
Ravana, 289, 293, 319
Ravidas, 298
Reason, 167, 168, 173, 178, 236. See also Via moderna
Receiving the holy grant, 462
Reconstructionism, 108
Reconstruction of Religious Thought in Islam (Iqbal), 248
Reconstruction theology, 191
Red Sea, 75
Reformation Lutheran Church, 191
Reformism
    in Buddhism, 377, 389–90, 397–98, 399, 408, 410–12
    in Hinduism, 303, 327, 329
    in Islam, 233–35, 251, 252–53, 266–67
    in Sikhism, 304
Reform Judaism, 68, 69, 70, 107, 110, 112, 113, 114
    beliefs and background of, 102–5
    Conservative Judaism compared with, 108

Orthodox Judaism compared with, 105–6
Reign of Terror, 178
Reincarnation, 163
in Buddhism, 349, 363, 483
in Hinduism, 281, 285, 312–13
in Scientology, 510
in Tenrikyo, 462
Reiyukai Kyodan, 462–63, 483
Relativism, 31–32, 519–21, 524, 527, 528
existentialist response to, 179
Judaism and, 69, 125
Relics, 171, 367, 373, 376, 377, 386–87, 397
Religion of the Heavenly Way, 460–61
Religious freedom, 188, 463
Religious language, 12–14
Religious tolerance, 93, 174
Ren, 430
Renaissance, 98, 166, 168
Renewere, 234
Renunciants, 352, 356, 357, 367, 376.
See also Monks, Buddhist; Nuns, Buddhist
Repairing the world, 53–55
Responsa, 85
Resurgence
of Islam, 241–42
of Sikhism, 304
Resurrection, 22, 134, 146
of Jesus, 145, 150, 178–79
in Judaism, 83
Revelation, Book of, 141, 151, 165
Revivalist movements
in Buddhism, 347, 390–91, 396, 400, 401–2, 487–88
in China, 490
in Confucianism, 475–76, 486–87
in Hinduism, 277
in Islam, 233–35, 237–39, 243–44
Revivification of the Religious Sciences (al-Ghazali), 228
Richard the Lion Hearted, 232
Rightly Guided Caliphs, 212, 215
Rig Veda, 280
Rig Vedic Gayatri, 316
Rinzai Zen school of Buddhism, 378
Rissho Koseikai, 484–85
Rita, 281
Rituals, 7–10
of Buddhism, 385
of East Asian religions, 465–66
of Hinduism, 308–9, 312
of Judaism, 88
morality and, 11
myths of nature and, 18
of primal religions, 37
of tribal societies, 15
Riyadh, 247
Robertson, Pat, 250
Roman Empire, 515
Christianity and, 116–17, 144, 151–52, 153, 155, 156, 161
collapse of, 155
Judaism and, 70, 79, 80, 81, 82, 83, 91–93, 116–17, 147
Romanticism, 178–79, 506
Romulus Augustulus, Emperor, 155
Rosh Hashanah, 90, 91
Roy, Rammohan, 303, 304
RSS. See Rashtriya Svayamesevak Sangh
Rubenstein, Richard, 119
Rujia, 426, 452
Rushdie, Salman, 219
Russia, 28, 111, 518
Russian Revolution, 111

Sabbath, 65, 69, 90
Sacralization, 520–21
Sacraments, 157–59, 171
Sacred centers, 483
Sacred cows, 318
Sacredness, 6, 8, 11, 519–21, 529
Sacred space, 37
Sacred thread, 316
Sacred traces, 373
Sadat, Anwar, 126, 203, 209, 245
Sadducees, 80, 81, 144, 146, 147
Sadhana, 372, 383
Sadhus, 271, 287, 288
Safavid Empire, 229
Sages, 429
Saguna Brahman, 295, 296
Sai Baba, Sathya, 328, 335
Saikoku route, 403
Saints, 160, 171, 227, 234, 298
Salah al-Din (Saladin), 232
Salat, 220
Samadhi, 282, 382
Samaritans, 80, 146
Sambodhi, 20, 349
Samsara, 20, 286, 290, 291, 292, 312, 354, 368, 507
Buddha Nature school on, 369
defined, 281–82
nirvana and, 372
Samsarai, 370
Samskaras, 315–17, 363
Samurai, 392, 451
San, Soe-Tae, 487
Sanchi stupa, 353f
Sangha, 352, 354, 355, 367, 371, 377, 378, 394. See also Monasteries and monasticism, Buddhist
adaptive reformism and, 410–12
in China, 389
colonialism and, 388
development of, 356–57
importance to Buddhist expansion, 358–61
in Japan, 403
purifying, 361
relationship with the state, 380–81
Santi Asoke and, 399
Sangharaja, 380
San-jiao heyi, 447
Sankhya, 294–95
Sanskrit, 279, 280, 281, 370, 379, 523
Santi Asoke, 398, 399
Sanusi, 233
Sarah, 198
Saraswati, 294, 318
Saraswati River, 320
Sarnath, 352
Sarvodaya Shramadana, 347
Sassanid Empire, 204. See also Persia
Satan, 515, 516
Satanic Verses, The (Rushdie), 219
Sat Guru, 300
Sati, 293, 303, 327
Sattva, 295
Satyagraha, 307
Saudi Arabia, 123, 209, 219, 233, 234, 242, 243, 245, 246, 247, 250, 251, 263
Saul, 76–77
Savitri, 327
Sayyid Qutb, 216
Scheduled caste members, 277
Schleiermacher, Friedrich, 178–79
Science and technology, 5, 25, 27, 28, 179, 519–20
Buddhism and, 388, 389, 407
Christianity and, 136–37, 139–40, 165, 173

destructive potential of, 30–31
the Holocaust and, 181
Islam and, 239
new age religions and, 504–5, 506, 509–12, 513, 518
Scientific socialism, 28, 30, 110
Scientific theory of race, 109
Scientology, 497, 505, 510–12, 514, 518
Scopes, John (trial of), 138
Scotland, 170
Séances, 54, 59, 509
Second Coming, 145, 160
Sectarianism, 309–10
Sectarian religions, 427
Secularism, 25, 27, 32, 519–21, 527, 529
Christianity and, 136, 164, 165, 166, 173, 182, 183
Hinduism and, 276–79, 329–33
Islam and, 200, 202, 236, 239, 242, 245, 251–52, 261–62
Judaism and, 65, 68, 69, 71, 73, 102, 103–5, 108–15, 121, 125, 126
new age religions and, 504
Seder (Passover meal), 8, 92
Seders (oral tradition categories), 85
Seed people, 486
Seed sound, 284
Sefiroth, 99
Seich no Ie, 483
Seiyu, Kiriyama, 485
Seleucids, 79
Self-perfection, 447, 505, 527
Self power, 371
Seljuq army, 232
Selma, Alabama voter registration drive, 528
Semites, 212
Seoul, 460, 488
Separate nondifference, 296
Separatism, 170, 331–33
Sephardic Judaism, 109
September 11 terrorist attacks, 196, 197, 200, 247–48, 250–51
Serfs, 155
Sermon on the Mount, 142, 144, 169, 190, 191, 522, 523, 524, 525, 526
Service Corps, 328
Shahadah, 219
Shaivites, 291, 293
Shakers, 176
Shakta, 293, 294
Shakti, 293, 294
Shakyaditya, 412
Shakyamuni Buddha, 351, 352, 353, 354, 357, 359, 361, 363, 370, 371, 378
Agonshu based on teachings of, 485
festivals honoring, 381, 386
Shammai, 84, 85, 86
Shang-di, 428
Shang era, 425, 428–29, 437
Shangri-la myth, 395–96
Shankara, 295, 296, 374
Shan-tao, 371
Sharia. See Islamic law
Shaykh, 10, 227
Shaykh al-Islam, 230
Shekinah, 99–100
Shema, 78
Shembe, Isaiah, 184

Shen, 439
Sheng-ren, 452
Sheng-zhi tu, 449
Shen-jiao, 452
Shiah Islam, 216–17, 243, 246, 258, 499
Shi Jing, 435
Shila, 356, 367, 383. See also Morality
Shingon, 485
Shinran, 378, 446
Shinshoku, 452
Shintoism, 6, 187, 392, 417, 427, 445, 446, 450, 459, 461, 468–69, 479, 489
Aum Shinrikyo and, 518
continuing support for, 480–81
neo-, 455–56, 479
new religions based on, 483
pantheon of, 440–41
relationship with Confucianism, 451, 456
spiritual training in, 452
as state and civil religion, 455–56
Shinto sects, 461, 462
Shir Islam. See Shiah Islam
Shiromani Gurudwara Pradandhak Committee, 332
Shitala, 294
Shiva, 12, 284, 290, 294, 314, 319, 324, 326, 328, 329, 393
attributes of, 291
Dance of, 292
festival dedicated to, 318
Shiva Ratri, 318
Shiva Sena, 333
Shogun era, 450, 455
Shotoku, Prince, 439
Shraddha, 281, 317
Shramanas, 349, 357
Shrines, 467
Buddhist, 360, 367, 374, 386–87.
See also Stupas
in contemporary China, 477–78
Hindu, 309
Kurozumikyo, 461
of new religions, 483
Shinto, 468–69, 480–81
Shringeri, 295
Shrivijaya Empire, 377
Shudras, 285
Shu Jing, 435
Shunya, 383
Shunyata, 368
Shura, 253
Siam, 375, 390. See also Thailand
Siberia, 47, 57, 59
Sicily, 212, 231
Siddha, 296–97
Siddhartha, 349–53, 471, 526
Signposts (Qutb), 240
Sikhism, 282, 298–301, 303
development of, 299
reform and resurgence in, 304
rise of, 298–99
separatism and globalization of, 331–33
theology and spiritual practices of, 300–301
Sikkim, 395, 396
Silk Road, 376, 438
Silk routes, 361, 375
Silla Dynasty, 439, 444
Simhah, 101
Sin, 22
in Christianity, 134–35, 150, 152, 158
in Islam, 216
in Judaism, 66

original, 66, 134–35, 152, 158, 174, 451, 514
  in Unification Church, 514
Sinai peninsula, 126, 202, 243
Sindus, 274
Singapore, 185, 201, 344, 400, 424
Singh (surname), 299
Singh, Gobind, 299
Singh, Mal, 327
Singh Sabha (Lion Society), 304
Sioux vision quests, 52
Sisters in Islam, 266
Sita, 293, 294, 304, 319, 327
Sivaraksa, Sulak, 347, 348, 413
Six-Day War (1967), 123–24, 125, 202, 243–44
Sixtus IV, Pope, 98
Skanda Purana, 320
Skandhas, 363, 364
Slavery, 175, 255, 256, 503
SLORC, 397
Smallpox goddess, 294
Smith, Joseph, Jr., 500, 515
Smith, Wilfred Cantwell, 525
Social Gospel theology, 137
Socialism, 28–30, 396, 397
  Buddhist, 397
  Jewish, 105, 110–11, 114–15
  scientific, 28, 30, 110
Social justice and reform
  Hinduism and, 335–37
  Islam and, 207, 208
Social sciences, 140, 519
Society Establishing Righteousness and Harmony, 484–85
Sociology, 165
Sodom, 119
Soka Gakkai, 347, 404, 405, 446, 462, 483
Soldiers of God, 216
Solomon, 76, 77, 78, 81, 82, 210, 231, 244
Soma, 280, 281
Son Buddhism, 444–45, 487
Song Celestial, The, 523
Song Dynasty, 434–35, 442–43, 491
Son of Heaven, 436
Soto Zen school of Buddhism, 377–78
Soul, 363, 466. *See also* Atman
Soul journeys, 48, 51, 53
South Africa, 184, 307, 523
South Asia, 295
  Buddhism in, 361, 365, 367, 373–80, 386, 393–96
  Hinduism in, 274–77, 284–85, 289, 308–9, 322
  Islam in, 202, 229, 230, 235, 237, 254, 255, 256, 297–98
  Sikhism in, 298
  terrorism in, 247
Southeast Asia
  Buddhism in, 361, 365, 373, 375, 377, 396–97
  Hinduism in, 289
  Islam in, 201, 203, 229, 230, 235, 251, 256
  terrorism in, 247
Southern Buddhism, 344
Southern Christian Leadership Conference, 190
South India, 276, 279
South Korea, 420, 424
  Buddhism in, 344, 401–2
  Ch'ondogyo in, 460
  Christianity in, 188, 459
  diversity in, 486–89
  shamanism in, 59
Soviet Union, 11, 31, 57, 181, 201, 242

Afghanistan invaded by, 245, 247, 249
  Israel and, 121, 127
Spain, 162
  Christianity in, 182, 183
  Islam in, 93, 95, 212, 230, 231
  Judaism in, 95
  terrorist attacks in, 197
Spirit flights. *See* Soul journeys
Spirit mediums, 10, 43, 52, 53–55, 58–59, 428, 429, 468, 505, 509
Spirits, 464–65
Spiritualism, 509
Spring Festival, 470
Sri Lanka, 185, 276, 285, 344, 347, 357, 359, 375, 395, 406, 408, 409.
  See also Ceylon
Sri Panchami, 318
Srivijaya kingdom, 373
Star festival, 485
State Buddhism, 377, 407–9, 439
State-religion relationship, 25
  in Buddhism, 377, 380–81, 406, 407–9, 439
  in Christianity, 152, 154–55, 168, 173, 182
  in Confucianism, 435–36
  in Islam, 199, 229–31, 236, 239, 252
  in Shintoism, 455–56
Sthaviravadins, 354, 367, 375
Stories. *See also* Myths
  of Jesus, 142–46
  of Judaism, 89–91, 113, 114, 115
  of supersession, 146, 149
Strasbourg, 94
Students (life stage), 287
Stupas, 353, 357, 373, 377, 381, 386–87.
  See also Shrines, Buddhist
Subsistence societies, 36, 39, 55
Sudan, 202, 203, 221, 233, 234–35, 241, 245, 263, 264
Suez Canal, 123
Suffering. *See* Dukkha
Sufism, 10, 216, 217, 234–35, 298
  beliefs and practices of, 226–29
  Mahayana Buddhism compared with, 368
  origin of term, 226
Suicide bombings, 247. *See also*
  September 11 terrorist attacks
Sukhavati, 371, 382–83
Sukyo Mahikari, 485–86
Sultanates, 229, 230
Sumatra, 373, 377, 400
Sung Dynasty, 376
Sunnah, 212, 216, 233, 251, 252, 261, 262
  revivalism and, 239
  source of, 218
Sunni Islam, 230–31, 243, 245, 258, 499
  relationship with Ahmadiyyat, 501
  Shiah split with, 216–17
  in the United States, 258
Sun Wukong, 448
Sun Yat-sen, 459
Supersession, story of, 146, 149
Supreme Truth. *See* Aum Shinrikyo
Surahs, 210, 261
Susuharae, 479
Suun, Ch'oe, 460
Suzuki, D. T., 391
Svarga, 313, 383
Swadhyaya, 332
Swedagon stupa, 398f
Swedenborg, Emanuel, 509
Symbolism, 13
Synagogues, 80
Syncretism, 184, 186, 522

Syria, 123, 126, 152, 201, 202, 203, 212, 215, 242, 243

Taboos, 44
Taiping Rebellion, 458, 459–60
Taiwan, 58–59, 412, 421, 424, 462, 471
Tajdid, 233, 234
Taj Mahal, 229f, 298
Takanakapsaluk, 53, 54
Takfir wal Hijra, 216
Taliban, 263, 264
Talmud, 83, 89
  Babylonian, 98
  central role in Judaism, 85
  formation of, 84–88
  Hasidism and, 101, 102
  Jewish socialism and, 110
  Orthodox Judaism and, 105
  Reform Judaism and, 104
  uniqueness of, 86
Talmudic Judaism. *See* Rabbinic Judaism
Talmud Torah, 66
Tamas, 295
Tamil revolt, 409
Tanak, 80, 84, 85, 86
T'ang Dynasty, 376, 401, 442, 445
Tannaim, 85, 86
Tanner castes, 318
Tantric Buddhism, 296, 372–73, 383.
  See also Thunderbolt Vehicle
Tantric Hinduism, 294, 296–97
Tanzania, 196, 247
Tao. *See* Dao
Tao Te Ching. See Daodejing
Tara, 370f
Tathagatagarbha, 369, 372, 382
Tawhid, 207, 219
Tefillin, 90
Television, 325–26, 341, 401–2
Temple Mount, 126
Temples
  Buddhist, 393, 457, 466
  Confucian, 476
  Daoist, 468
  of East Asian religions, 466–68
  Hindu, 314–15, 322
  of Jerusalem, 77, 78, 79, 82, 83, 118, 123, 141, 147, 244, 515
  Sikh, 299, 300f, 332
Temples of Reason, 178
Templeton Prize, 332
Ten Gurus, 299, 300
Ten moral precepts, 365
Tenri City, 484
Tenrikyo, 461–62, 483, 484
Terrorism, 196–97, 241, 259, 266, 330
  by Aum Shinrikyo, 481–82, 483, 516, 518
  September 11 attacks, 196, 197, 200, 247–48, 250–51
Teshuvah, 69
Thailand. *See also* Siam
  Buddhism in, 344, 347, 381, 397–99, 406, 407, 408, 411
  Islam in, 195
Thanksgiving, 503
Theism, 12, 174
Theodosius, Emperor, 93, 151, 152, 153
Theosis, 84
Theosophical Society, 307, 390
Theosophy, 509, 523, 527
Thepmuni, Phra Monghon, 398
Theravada Buddhism, 14, 365, 366, 367, 375, 377, 382, 383, 398
  current status of, 396–97
  death rituals in, 387
  in the diaspora, 404
  Mahayana Buddhism compared with, 362, 368

origins of, 354
  relationship with the state, 380–81
  religious language of, 12
  rituals of, 385
  size of, 344
  in Vietnam, 400
  women and, 412
Theresa of Avila, Saint, 162
Theresa of Lisieux, Saint, 162
Thetans, 510, 512
Thich Nhat Hanh, 72, 347, 348, 408, 528, 529
Third age, 506
Third Civilization, 462
Thirteen Articles of Faith, 99
Thirty Years War, 171
Thomas (apostle), 186
Thousand-petaled lotus, 297
Three Caves, 439
Three faiths, unity of, 447–49, 471
Threefold goals, 344
Three Marks of Existence, 362, 363
Three principles, 455
Three Refuges, 341, 354, 361, 367
Thunderbolt Vehicle, 368, 372–73.
  See also Vajrayana
Tian'anmen Square, 472
Tian di, 430
Tian Shang Sheng-mu. *See* Mazu
Tibet, 299, 359, 370, 373, 381, 387, 393, 395–96, 408, 421, 444
Tibetan Buddhism, 375, 376, 379–80, 395–96, 404, 407, 413, 490, 518
T'ien (Lord of Heaven), 12
Tij, 319
Tilak, 314
Timbuktu, 229
Time
  in Hinduism, 289
  in Judaism, 74
  in myths of history, 22
  in myths of nature, 18
  in primal religions, 36
Time to Kill, A (Bray), 191
Tirthas, 320
Tisha B'Av, 82, 90, 118
T'oegye, Yi, 486–87
T'oegyehak movement, 486–87
Tokugawa era, 403, 449, 450, 451, 457, 461
Tokyo, 456
Tolstoy, Leo, 522, 523, 524, 525–26, 527
Tonghak. *See* Ch'ondogyo
Tong II, 514, 515. *See also* Unification Church
Tooth relic, 397
Torah, 69, 70, 74, 84–88, 104, 119, 206
  central role in Judaism, 89–91
  continuous development of, 85
  dual, 67, 71, 80, 83, 84, 90, 105, 113
  Hasidism and, 100, 101, 102
  Islam on, 210
  Jewish socialism and, 110
  Mishneh, 99
  multiple meanings of term, 87–88
  Orthodox Judaism and, 105
  Rashi's teaching of, 98
  works included in, 84
  wrestling with, 86–87
Torii, 468
Tosafot, 86
Totemism, 10, 44–45
Tours, 162
Toward a World Theology (Smith), 525
Trade, 360, 361, 375, 442, 445
Trailokya Bauddha Mahasangha Gana, 347

Trance states
    in Buddhism, 382
    in Hinduism, 281, 282
    in shamanism, 48, 49, 50, 54–55, 58
Transcendentalism, 509
Transcendental Meditation (TM), 497,
    512–13, 514
Transjordan, 201
Treatises on Dharma. See Dharmashastras
Tribal, defined, 36
Tribes
    defined, 205
    of Israel, 75
    transition to urban life from, 14–16,
    18
Tricycle magazine, 405
Trinity, doctrine of, 150, 164
Triple gods, 465
Trishna, 355
Truth Seekers, 332
Tsunami, 347
Tsunesaburo, Matiguchi, 462
Tu Chu, 429
Tu-di Gong, 429, 477–78
Tudiye, 467
Tulkus, 379–80
Tunisia, 242, 246
Turkey, 195, 203, 227, 241, 242, 246–47
Tutelary spirits, 48, 51, 56
Tutu, Desmond, 184
"12 Precepts of the Order of Inter-being"
    (Thich Nhat Hanh), 408
Twice-born individuals, 285, 287, 316
Tylor, E. B., 42, 43
Tzaddik, 101
Tzitzit, 90

Udraka Ramaputra, 350
Uganda, 112
Uji-kami, 480
Ulama, 217, 218, 225, 226, 236, 237,
    238, 243, 245, 252, 253, 254, 262,
    368
    Ahmadiyyat and, 501
    reform hindered by, 266
    role of, 230
    Sufism and, 227–28
    on women, 263
Ultimate Reality, 293
Ultra-Orthodox Judaism, 65, 106, 112,
    120, 125–27
    challenge of, 68–74
    as fundamentalism, 71–74
Uma, 294
Umar ibn al-Khattab, 215
Umayyad Dynasty, 215–16, 217, 218,
    226, 229
Ummah, 198, 207, 226, 238
Unification Church, 188, 506, 514–16
Unitarianism, 174, 176
United Nations (U.N.), 113, 121, 329
United States, 31, 181, 400, 491, 508
    attacks on embassies of, 247
    Aum Shinrikyo and, 518
    Buddhism in, 189, 488
    Christianity in, 132, 136, 188–89
    civil religion in, 502, 503
    civil war of, 503
    cold war and, 201
    Hinduism in, 189, 276, 332, 334
    Islam in, 189, 200–201, 203, 251,
    255–60, 265
    Israel and, 121, 127, 240, 247
    Japan occupied by, 479
    Judaism in, 65, 109, 111, 189
    Rissho Koseikai in, 485
    Tenrikyo in, 462

terrorist attacks in. *See* September 11
    terrorist attacks
Unification Church in, 514
Zionism and, 113
Unity
    of Buddhism, 361
    of Christianity, 174
    in diversity, 524
    of Hinduism, 274
    of Islam, 261
    of three faiths, 447–49, 471
Unity School of Christianity, 176,
    509–10
Universalism, 174, 176
Universities, 164, 235–36
University of Malaya, 236
Untouchables, 286, 307, 318, 331, 393
Uopsatha, 385
Upanishads, 281, 282, 284, 296, 310,
    363, 507
Upaya, 373
Urban II, Pope, 94, 163, 232
Urban life, transition from tribal life to,
    14–16, 18
Urban religions, 507, 509
U.S.S. *Cole*, 247
Uthman ibn Affan, 215
Utsavas, 317

Vaishnavites, 292–93
Vaishyas, 285
Vaitulika, 368
Vajrayana, 372–73, 376, 379, 383. *See
    also* Thunderbolt Vehicle
Varanasi, 273, 323f, 352
Varnas, 285
Varnashrama Dharma, 287
Varuna, 280, 281
Vassals, 155
Vasubandhu, 369
Vatican I, 138, 139, 140, 161
Vatican II, 139, 140, 149, 181, 267
Vedas, 279–81, 282, 287, 289, 290, 304,
    316, 323, 507
    contemporary interpretations of, 324
    description of, 280
    Sikh rejection of, 300
    women excluded from learning, 315
Vedic era/religion, 279–81, 305, 512
Vegetarianism, 271, 282, 284–85, 295,
    329, 382, 523
Venus figurines, 40
Vernacular, 104, 105
Via analogia, 13–14
Via antiqua, 165
Via moderna, 164, 165–66, 169, 176,
    177, 178, 506
Via negativa, 13–14
Victory Tenth Day, 319
Vietnam, 346, 347, 400, 408, 411, 428
Vietnam Buddhist Church, 400
Vietnamese Buddhist Peace Movement,
    72
Vietnam War, 72, 258, 400, 528
Viharas, 359, 361, 381
Vikramashila, 373
Village monks, 382
Vinayas, 356, 357, 361, 362, 367, 385,
    394, 412
Vindhya Mountains, 279
Vipashyana, 382
Vipassana, 382, 404
Vishishta Advaita, 296
Vishnu, 278, 284, 289, 290, 296, 314
    attributes and avataras of, 292–93
    website for shrine, 334
Vishnuto Lakshmi, 294

Vishva Hindu Parishad (VHP), 330–31,
    333, 336
Vision quests, 52
Visualization, 382–83
Vivekananda, 305

Wahhabi Islam, 233, 234, 247, 250–51
Wai-tan, 433
Wai-wu, 452
Wali, 227
Wangchuck family, 396
Wang Yangming, 447
War and Peace (Tolstoy), 525
Way of All the Earth, The (Dunne), 522
Weber, Max, 169, 406–7, 520
Web sites, 57, 273, 324, 334, 404, 491
Welfare (Refah) party (Turkey), 246–47
Wesley, John, 138, 174–75
West
    Buddhism in, 390–91, 404–5
    Eastern influences in, 512–13
    Hinduism in, 334
    influence on Eastern religions,
    514–19
    Islam in, 254–60
West Africa, 201
West Bank, 202, 241, 243
Western Christianity. *See* Latin
    Christianity
Western Europe, 165
    Islam in, 254–55
    Judaism in, 70, 94–95, 103, 106, 109
Westernization
    Confucianism and, 424–25
    Islam and, 202, 235–36, 238–39,
    242, 245
Western Wall of the Second Temple, 123
White Clouds Daoist temple, 417
White man's burden, 235
Wicca, 508, 509
Wiesel, Elie, 119, 120
William of Ockham, 165
Will to power, 180
Wittenberg Castle, 167
Women
    in Buddhism, 352, 412, 487
    in Christianity, 176–77
    in Christian Science, 509–10
    in Hinduism, 287, 315, 319, 328, 329
    in Islam, 195, 200, 223–26, 263–66
    in Judaism, 69, 106–7
    in Methodism, 175
    in Nation of Islam, 259
    in new religions, 484
    ordination of, 176
    in primal religions, 39, 40–41
    in shamanism, 59
    in Unity School, 509–10
    in Wiccan religions, 508
Women Living Under Muslim Laws, 266
Won Buddhism, 487–88
World Community of al-Islam in the
    West (WCIW), 258–59
World Islamic Front for Jihad Against
    Jews and Crusaders, 247
Worldly blessings, 344
World soul, 509
World Trade Center, attacks on, 196, 247
World War I, 30, 31, 116, 242
World War II, 5, 30–31, 109, 116, 121,
    180–81, 188, 242, 346, 392, 403,
    515
World Zionist Organization, 112, 113
Wounded Knee, South Dakota, 56
Wu Cheng-en, 448
Wu-shu, 426
Wu Tai Shan, 375–76
Wu-wei, 20, 432, 435

Wu/xi, 428
Wu-xing, 429
Wu-zong, Emperor, 442

Xavier, Francis, 187, 301
Xi'an, 376, 442, 477
Xiao, 431
Xiaozong, Emperor, 447
Xinjiang Province, 490
Xin-zhai, 452
Xuan Zang, 442, 448
Xun, Master, 431, 432, 437

Yajna, 280
Yaksha, 387
Yamuna River, 320
Yangtze River, 429
Yanomami, 53–54
Yathrib, 207
Yavneh, 83, 84
Yazid, 216
Yemen, 195, 241
Yiddish, 111
Yi Dynasty, 420
Yi-Jing, 426, 427, 434, 435
Yin-yang theory, 20, 74, 427, 429, 432,
    434, 436, 437, 439, 440, 443,
    466, 474
Yoga, 483
    in Buddhism, 349
    in Hinduism, 272, 278, 282–84, 287,
    290, 329
Yogacara (Yoga Practice) school, 369
Yoga Journal, 334
Yoga Sutras, 282
Yogins, 282
Yom Ha'atzmaut, 121
Yom Hashoah, 121
Yom Kippur, 90, 91
Yom Kippur War (1973), 126
Yuan Dynasty, 376
Yugas, 289

Zakat, 220–21
Zao Wangye, 465, 470
Zealots, 80, 81, 83, 91, 113, 114, 144,
    146, 147, 149
Zen Buddhism, 354, 369, 372, 382, 392,
    445, 446, 450. *See also* Ch'an
    Buddhism
    Daruma-san in, 481
    Rinzai school, 378
    Soto school, 377–78
    in the West, 391, 404
    Won Buddhism based on, 487
Zenshoji temple, 403
Zhang Zai, 444
Zhou era, 429, 430, 464
Zhuang Zi, 433, 452
Zhu Xi, 443, 444, 486–87, 491
Zia ul-Haq, Muhammad, 203, 245, 264
Zionism, 69, 91, 105, 110, 111–15, 121,
    126
    coining of term, 112
    Islam relationship with, 238
    messianic, 73
    origins of, 111–12
    religious, 70–71
Zionist Congress, First, 112
Zohar, 99
Zola, Émile, 113
Zongjiao, 477
Zoroastrians, 442